STUDENT'S SOLUTIONS MANUAL

Charles T. Horngren
Stanford University

George Foster
Stanford University

Srikant M. Datar
Stanford University

Howard D. Teall
Wilfrid Laurier University

David G. Gowing
P. Eng., MScA. (Finance), C.F.P.

Jeff Power
Ph.D., F.C.M.A.
St. Mary's University

COST ACCOUNTING
A Managerial Emphasis

Fourth Canadian Edition

Charles T. Horngren
Stanford University

George Foster
Stanford University

Srikant M. Datar
Stanford University

Howard D. Teall
Wilfrid Laurier University

Maureen P. Gowing
University of Windsor

PEARSON
Prentice Hall

Toronto

ISBN-10: 0-13-197224-3
ISBN-13: 978-0-13-197224-7

Executive Acquisitions Editor: Samantha Scully
Senior Developmental Editor: Madhu Ranadive
Production Editor: Jennifer Handel
Production Coordinator: Andrea Falkenberg

10 11 12 DPC 10 09 08

Printed and bound in Canada.

Contents

CHAPTER 1
THE ACCOUNTANT'S ROLE IN THE ORGANIZATION

1-2 Financial accounting is constrained by generally accepted accounting principles. Management accounting is not restricted to these principles. The result is that:

- management accounting can include assets or liabilities (such as "brand names" developed internally) not recognized under GAAP, and
- management accounting can use asset or liability measurement rules (such as present values or resale prices) not permitted under GAAP.

1-4 The business functions in the value chain are:

- **Research and development**—the generation of, and experimentation with, ideas related to new products, services, or processes.
- **Design of products, services, and processes**—the detailed planning and engineering of products, services, or processes.
- **Production**—the coordination and assembly of resources to produce a product or deliver a service.
- **Marketing**—the process of promoting and selling products or services to customers or prospective customers.
- **Distribution**—the mechanism by which products or services are delivered to the customer.
- **Customer service**—the support activities provided to customers.

1-6 A successful management accountant requires general business skills (such as understanding the strategy of an organization) and people skills (such as motivating other team members) as well as technical skills (such as using computer software). Accountants also analyze costs throughout the value chain and co-ordinate cost reductions to assure no impairment to the product that customers demand.

1-8 Planning decisions are made in choosing goals. Control decisions are made when implementing the planning decision(s) and evaluating personnel and operations with respect to the goal(s).

1-10 The three guidelines are:

(a) the cost/benefit approach that assures the improvement in quality of the data provides a benefit to the managers that exceeds the cost of improvement.

(b) Sensitivity to the balance of information that not only supports decisions to improve profits and motivates honest effort to achieve those profits but also is understandable.

(c) There are different costs to achieve different purposes.

1-12 The new controller could reply in one or more of several ways:

(a) Demonstrate to the plant manager how he or she could make better decisions if the plant controller was viewed as a resource rather than a dead weight. In a related way, the plant controller could show how the plant manager's time and resources could be saved by viewing the new plant controller as a team member.

(b) Demonstrate to the plant manager a good knowledge of technical aspects at the plant. This approach may involve doing background reading. It certainly will involve spending much time on the plant floor speaking to plant personnel.

(c) Show the plant manager examples of the new plant controller's past successes in working with line managers in other plants. Examples could include:
  • assistance in preparing the budget,
  • assistance in analyzing problem situations, and
  • assistance in submitting capital budget requests.

(d) Seek assistance from the corporate controller to highlight to the plant manager the importance of many tasks undertaken by the new plant controller. This approach is a last resort but may be necessary in some cases.

1-14 The SMAC sets standards of ethical conduct for management accountants. The four areas in which standards of ethical conduct exist for management accounts are:

1) Mastery of specific intellectual skill acquired by education and training
2) Acceptance of duties to society (i.e., protection of the public) as a whole in addition to duties to the employer or client
3) An outlook that is essentially objective
4) A high standard in the conduct and performance of personal service

1-16 (10 min.) **Value Chain and customer relationship management.**

1. Line managers are the primary customers of the management accounting function. Line managers in each of the six business function areas (R&D, design, production, marketing, distribution, and customer service) use management accounting information in their decisions.

2. Line managers require both relevant and timely information. The task and responsibility of management accounting systems is to fulfill this need. Cost

accounting methods that improve accuracy and relevance, as well as accountants able to teach line managers to understand how the methods were applied, will improve the management accounting system.

1-18 (15 min.) Value chain and classification of costs, pharmaceutical company.

Cost Item	Value Chain Business Function
a.	Design
b.	Marketing
c.	Customer service
d.	Research and development
e.	Marketing
f.	Production
g.	Marketing
h.	Distribution

1-20 (15 min.) Problem solving, scorekeeping, and attention directing.

Because the accountant's duties are often not sharply defined, some of these answers might be challenged.

a. Scorekeeping
b. Attention directing
c. Scorekeeping
d. Problem solving
e. Attention directing
f. Attention directing
g. Problem solving
h. Scorekeeping, depending on the extent of the report
i. This question is intentionally vague. The give-and-take of the budgetary process usually encompasses all three functions, but it emphasizes scorekeeping the least. The main function is attention directing, but problem solving is also involved.
j. Problem solving

1-22 (10 min.) Problem solving, scorekeeping, and attention directing.

Report Statement	Purpose
a	Problem solving
b	Scorekeeping
c	Attention directing and scorekeeping
d	Scorekeeping
e	Scorekeeping

1-24 (15 min.) Major purposes of accounting systems.

The plan or budget communicates the financial goals the organization will achieve while control arises from feedback on how well the plan has been achieved and reasons why the plan has not been achieved.

1. Annual financial statements communicate what was achieved. The annual report is a standardized control report on financial performance. It is feedback on what the organization accomplished.
2. Internal periodic reports of financial performance are control reports.
3. Studies of new business development opportunities communicate planned costs and revenue.
4. Weekly reports of the total quantity of particular books sold are feedback. They are control reports internally because a comparison can be made with the plan to determine if the plan was achieved and if not, why not.
5. The report of losses suffered from a storm is a financial report that is a control report. Externally the insurer will use the report to estimate the amounts it will reimburse Indigo according to the insurance contract. Internally the managers will use the report to modify their plan and generate the most appropriate response to an unanticipated event.

   The actual event will also initiate review of the adequacy of the insurance coverage relative to its cost. This new data will be used in subsequent plans for future insurance coverage and its cost.

1-26 (15 min.) Planning and control decisions; Internet company.

1. **Planning decisions**
   a. Decision to raise monthly subscription fee
   c. Decision to upgrade content of online services
   e. Decision to decrease monthly subscription fee

Control decisions

    b.   Decision to inform existing subscribers about the rate of increase—an implementation part of control decisions

    d.   Dismissed the VP of Marketing—performance evaluation and feedback aspect of control decisions

2.   Planning decisions at WebNews.com focus on organizational goals, predicting results under various alternative ways of achieving those goals, and then deciding how to attain the desired goal, for example:

    (a)   WebNews.com could have the objective of revenue growth to gain critical mass.

    (b)   it could have the objective of increasing operating income.

Many Internet companies in their formative years make revenue growth (and subscriber growth) their primary goal.

Control focuses on deciding on, and taking actions that implement, the planning decision, and deciding on performance evaluation and the related feedback that will help future decision making. For example, WebNews.com will

    (a)   communicate the new rates to advertisers

    (b)   communicate the new price to marketing representatives

1-28 (15 min.) Management accounting guidelines.

1.   Cost-benefit approach
2.   Behavioural and technical considerations
3.   Different costs for different purposes
4.   Cost-benefit approach
5.   Behavioural and technical considerations
6.   Cost-benefit approach
7.   Behavioural and technical considerations
8.   Different costs for different purposes
9.   Behavioural and technical considerations

1-30 (15 min.) The chief financial officer and the controller.

1.   As a controller, Rodriguez was primarily responsible for management accounting and financial accounting functions. Typical functions of a controller include:

- Financial planning and budgeting
- Operations administration

- Profitability reporting
- Inventory accounting
- General ledger
- Accounts payable
- Accounts receivable

2. The chief financial officer's responsibilities include:

- Controllership
- Treasury
- Risk management
- Taxes
- Internal audit
- Information systems (in some organizations)
- Investor relations
- Financial planning

1-32 (30-40 min.) Professional ethics and end-of-year games.

1. The possible motivations for the snack foods division president wanting to play end-of-year games include:

   (a) Management incentives. National Foods may have a division bonus scheme based on one-year reported division earnings. Efforts to front-end revenue into the current year or transfer costs into the next year can increase this bonus.

   (b) Promotion opportunities and job security. Top management of National Foods likely will view those division managers that deliver high reported earnings growth rates as being the best prospects for promotion. Division managers who deliver "unwelcome surprises" may be viewed as less capable.

   (c) Retain division autonomy. If top management of National Foods adopts a "management by exception" approach, divisions that report sharp reductions in their earnings growth rates may attract a sizable increase in top management oversight.

2. Several of the "end-of-year games" clearly are in conflict with these requirements and should be viewed as unacceptable by Taylor:

   (b) The fiscal year-end should be closed on midnight of December 31. "Extending" the close falsely reports next year's sales as this year's sales.

   (c) Altering shipping dates is falsification of the accounting reports.

(f)   Advertisements run in December should be charged to the current year. The advertising agency is facilitating falsification of the accounting records of National Foods as well as falsifying its own records.

The other "end-of-year games" occur in many organizations and may fall into the "grey" to "acceptable" area. However, much depends on the circumstances surrounding each one:

(a)   If the independent contractor does not do maintenance work in December, there is no transaction regarding maintenance to record. The responsibility for ensuring packaging equipment is well maintained is that of the plant manager's. The division controller probably can do little more than observe the absence of a December maintenance charge.

(d)   In many organizations sales are heavily concentrated in the final weeks of the fiscal year-end. If the double-bonus is approved by the division marketing manager, the division controller can do little more than observe the extra bonus paid in December.

(e)   If T.V. spots are reduced in December, the advertising cost in December will be reduced. There is no record falsification here.

(g)   Much depends on the means of "persuading" carriers to accept the merchandise. For example, if an under-the-table payment is involved, it is clearly unethical. If, however, the carrier receives no extra consideration and willingly agrees to accept the assignment, the transaction appears ethical.

Each of the (a), (d), (e) and (g) "end-of-year games" may well disadvantage National Foods in the long-run. The divisional controller is well advised to raise this issue in meetings with the division president. However, if National Foods has a rigid set of line/staff distinctions, the division president is the one who bears primary responsibility for justifying division actions to senior corporate officers.

3.   If Taylor believes that Ryan wants her to engage in unethical behaviour, she should first directly raise her concerns with Ryan. If Ryan is unwilling to change his request, Taylor should discuss her concerns with the Corporate Controller of National Foods. Taylor also may well ask for a transfer from the snack foods division if she perceives Ryan is unwilling to listen to pressure brought by the Corporate Controller, CFO, or even President of National Foods. In the extreme, she may want to resign if the corporate culture of National Foods is to reward division managers who play "end-of-year games" that Taylor views as unethical and possibly illegal.

1-34 (40 min.) Global company, ethical challenges with bribery.

1. The following decision tree is a useful way to structure the class discussion:

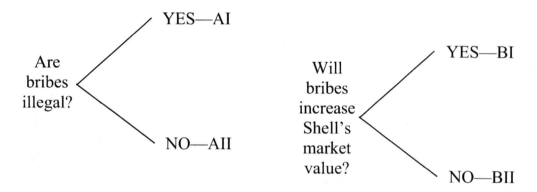

The comment by Shell's Chairman addresses the AI branch, which assumes that bribes are illegal. One difficult issue here is when certain kinds of payments are illegal in one country but not illegal in other countries.

Even if "bribes" are not illegal, students should debate two questions:

(a) Should Shell engage in activities many regard as unethical even if they are not illegal? Similar questions arise with tobacco companies.

(b) Do the "bribes" increase the market value of Shell?

Both (a) and (b) raise issues that are not black or white. Some students will argue on (a) that as long as the government does not prohibit an activity, it is commercially acceptable to undertake it. They will assert that as long as shareholders are aware of that activity (such as a company selling tobacco), those opposed to it can always not invest in the company. This is not as strong an argument for supporting bribes as it is unlikely that companies will admit to bribes being paid.

Even if bribes are not illegal, they do not always increase shareholder wealth. Bribery can become a very large cost in some areas. They may not generate revenues sufficient to offset the cost of bribes.

2. The investigation could be made at several levels:

(a) Ask Shell employees at the subsidiary to explain why payments are being made to the local law firm and to the Swiss-based humanitarian fund. What is the deliverable that each organization provides to Shell?

(b) Question the local law firm on what they are billing Shell for and whether they are making related payments to a third party.

(c) Question those who it is alleged are being paid by the local law firm.

The billing rates and the services provided by the law firm could be examined to see how much other firms are charging for comparable work.

The Shell Chairman has outlined an outright prohibition policy on bribes. If this is company policy, then requesting a resignation may be the only viable course. The difficult issues here include:

(a) What is and is not a bribe is sometimes not black or white, and

(b) Even in the "grey" or "black" area, a company may be reluctant to request a resignation, especially for a highly valued employee. This person could feel he or she was doing what "many other competitors were doing" and had no option if the business was to be secured for Shell.

3. The Board presentation needs to promote a full and thorough debate on investment in the dictator's country. Even if the discovery was of lower financial value, the political and economic risks of investing in a country under questionable terms can be very high. Issues to consider are:

(a) Are the requests "official" ones? The dictator's key advisor may not represent the government or indeed the dictator's son. It may be a "trial balloon" to see what was possible for one individual to obtain. Other companies may have agreed to make payments due to their not calling the advisor's bluff.

(b) How will the proposed transaction be recorded? Some countries require a 10% (or more) equity in successful ventures. However, the request implies the 10% goes to a private individual. A good working requirement is that each board member should be able to publicly explain the payments made as being both economically justified and in accordance with Shell's ethical position.

(c) What is the "world opinion" on the dictator's government? Does the dictator have a reputation for suppressing human rights, private wealth diversion, cronyism, and so on? Shell has to avoid being portrayed as a financial backer of a repressive regime. In some cases, there can be a backlash against companies that supported a prior regime when a dictator is replaced by another regime. Putting the son of a dictator on a board can be a visible signal (and symbol) of an association that over time Shell may wish to avoid.

(d) What can be learned from the experience of other companies who have conducted business in the country? Are there allegations of them making facilitating payments? Are questions being raised in the press about those companies acting illegally or unethically?

CHAPTER 2
AN INTRODUCTION TO COST TERMS AND PURPOSES

2-2   **Cost assignment** is a general term that encompasses both (1) tracing accumulated costs to a cost object, and (2) allocating accumulated costs to a cost object. **Cost tracing** is the assigning of direct costs to a chosen cost object. **Cost allocation** is the assigning of indirect costs to a chosen cost object.

The relationship between these terms is as follows:

2-4   Managers believe that costs that are traced to a particular cost object are more accurately assigned to that cost object than are allocated costs. Managers prefer to use more accurate costs in their decisions.

2-6   Cost reduction efforts frequently focus on:

1.   doing only value-added activities, and
2.   efficiently managing the use of the cost drivers in those value-added activities.

2-8   A **variable cost** is a cost that changes in total in proportion to changes in the quantity of a cost driver.

A **fixed cost** is a cost that does not change in total despite changes in the quantity of a cost driver.

Suppose the cost object is a Ford motor vehicle. A dashboard is a variable cost of the motor vehicle. The annual lease of the plant in which the vehicle is assembled illustrates a fixed cost for that year.

2-10   A unit cost is computed by dividing some total cost (the numerator) by some number of units (the denominator). In many cases the numerator will include a fixed cost that will not change despite changes in the number of units to be assembled. It is erroneous in those cases to multiply the unit cost by volume changes to predict changes in total costs at different volume levels.

2-12   No. Service sector companies have no inventories and, hence, no inventoriable costs.

2-14   **Direct materials costs:** The acquisition costs of all materials that eventually become part of the cost object (say, units finished or in process) and that can be traced to that cost object in an economically feasible way. Acquisition costs of direct materials include freight-in (inward delivery) charges, sales taxes, and custom duties.

Direct manufacturing labour costs: The compensation of all manufacturing labour that is specifically identified with the cost object (say, units finished or in process) and that can be traced to the cost object in an economically feasible way. Examples include wages and fringe benefits paid to machine operators and assembly-line workers.

Indirect manufacturing costs: All manufacturing costs considered to be part of the cost object (say, units finished or in process) but that cannot be individually traced to that cost object in an economically feasible way. Examples include power, supplies, indirect materials, indirect manufacturing labour, plant rent, plant insurance, property taxes on plants, plant amortization, and the compensation of plant managers.

Prime costs: All direct manufacturing costs. In the two-part classification of manufacturing costs, prime costs would comprise direct materials costs. In the three-part classification, prime costs would comprise direct materials costs and direct manufacturing labour costs.

Conversion costs: All manufacturing costs other than direct materials costs.

2-16 (10 min.) Total costs and unit costs.

1. Total cost, $4,800. Unit cost per person, $4,800 ÷ 500 = $9.60

2. Total cost, $4,800. Unit cost per person, $4,800 ÷ 2,000 = $2.40

3. The main lesson of this problem is to alert the student early in the course to the desirability of thinking in terms of total costs rather than unit costs wherever feasible. Changes in the number of cost driver units will affect total variable costs but not total fixed costs. In our example, it would be perilous to use either the $9.60 or the $2.40 unit cost to predict the total cost because the total costs are not affected by the attendance. Instead, the student association should use the $4,800 total cost. Obviously, if the musical group agreed to work for, say $4.80 per person, such a unit variable cost could be used to predict the total cost.

2-18 (15 min.) Computing and interpreting unit manufacturing costs.

1.

	Supreme	Deluxe	Regular
Direct materials costs	$100.80	$ 64.80	$ 74.40
Direct manuf. labour costs	16.80	33.60	9.60
Indirect manuf. costs	50.40	100.80	28.80
Total manuf. costs	$168.00	$199.20	$112.80
Kilograms produced	80	120	100
Cost per kilogram	$2.100	$1.660	$1.128

2. Given the unit volume changes for August 2007, the use of unit costs from the past month at a different unit volume level (both in aggregate and at the individual product level) will yield incorrect estimates of total costs in August 2007.

2-20 (15 min.) Cost drivers and the value chain.

1.

Business Function Area	Representative Cost Driver
A. Research and development	– Number of patents filed with government agency
B. Design of products/processes	– Hours spent designing tamper-proof bottles
C. Production	– Hours Tylenol packing line in operation
D. Marketing	– Minutes of television advertising time
E. Distribution	– Number of packages shipped
F. Customer service	– Number of calls to toll-free customer phone line

2.

Business Function Area	Representative Cost Driver
A. Research and development	– Hours of laboratory work – Number of new drugs in development
B. Design of products/processes	– Number of focus groups on alternative package designs – Hours of process engineering work
C. Production	– Number of units packaged – Number of tablets manufactured
D. Marketing	– Number of promotion packages mailed – Number of sales personnel
E. Distribution	– Weight of packages shipped – Number of supermarkets on delivery route
F. Customer service	– Number of units of a product recalled – Number of personnel on toll-free customer phone lines

2-22 (15-20 min.) Variable costs and fixed costs.

1. Variable cost per tonne of beach sand mined:

Subcontractor	$96 per tonne
Government tax	60 per tonne
Total	$156 per tonne

Fixed costs per month:

0 to 100 tonnes of capacity per day	=	$180,000
101 to 200 tonnes of capacity per day	=	$360,000
201 to 300 tonnes of capacity per day	=	$540,000

2.

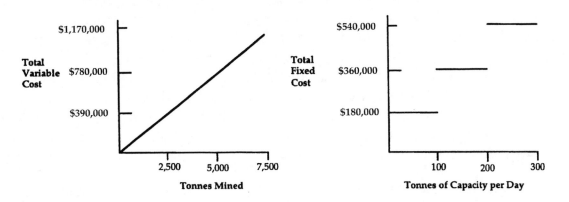

The concept of relevant range is potentially relevant for both graphs. However, the question does not place restrictions on the unit variable costs. The relevant range for the total fixed costs is from 0 to 100 tonnes; 101 to 200 tonnes; 201 to 300 tonnes, and so on. Within these ranges, the total fixed costs do not change in total.

3.

Tonnes Mined per Day	Tonnes Mined per Month	Fixed Unit Cost per Tonne	Variable Unit Cost per Tonne	Total Unit Cost per Tonne
(1)	(2) = (1) × 25	(3) = FC ÷ (2)	(4)	(5) = (3) + (4)
(a) 180	4,500	$360,000 ÷ 4,500 = $80.00	$156	$236.00
(b) 220	5,500	$540,000 ÷ 5,500 = $98.18	$156	$254.18

The unit cost for 220 tonnes mined per day is $254.18, while for 180 tonnes it is only $236.00. This difference is caused by the fixed cost increment from 101 to 200 tonnes being spread over an increment of 80 tonnes, while the fixed cost increment from 201 to 300 tonnes is spread only over an increment of 20 tonnes.

2-24 (20-30 min.)   Inventoriable costs vs. period costs.

1.   *Manufacturing-sector companies* purchase materials and components and convert them into different finished goods.

Merchandising-sector companies purchase and then sell tangible products without changing their basic form.

Service-sector companies provide services or intangible products to their customers—for example, legal advice or audits.

Only manufacturing and merchandising companies have inventories of goods for sale.

2.   *Inventoriable costs* are all costs of a product that are regarded as an asset when they are incurred and then become cost of goods sold when the product is sold. These costs for a manufacturing company are included in work-in-process and finished goods inventory (they are "inventoried") to build up the costs of creating these assets.

Period costs are all costs in the income statement other than cost of goods sold. These costs are treated as expenses of the period in which they are incurred because they are presumed not to benefit future periods (or because there is not sufficient evidence to conclude that such benefit exists). Expensing these costs immediately best matches expenses to revenues.

3.   (a) Mineral water purchased for resale by Loblaw—inventoriable cost of a merchandising company. It becomes part of cost of goods sold when the mineral water is sold.

(b) Electricity used at a GE assembly plant—inventoriable cost of a manufacturing company. It is part of the manufacturing overhead that is included in the manufacturing cost of a refrigerator finished good.

(c) Amortization on Excite's computer equipment—period cost of a service company. Excite has no inventory of goods for sale and, hence, no inventoriable cost.

(d) Electricity for Loblaw's store aisles—period cost of a merchandising company. It is a cost that benefits the current period and is not traceable to goods purchased for resale.

(e) Amortization on GE's assembly testing equipment—inventoriable cost of a manufacturing company. It is part of the manufacturing overhead that is included in the manufacturing cost of a refrigerator finished good.

(f) Salaries of Loblaw's marketing personnel—period cost of a merchandising company. It is a cost that is not traceable to goods purchased for resale. It is presumed not to benefit future periods (or at least not to have sufficiently reliable evidence to estimate such future benefits).

(g) Water consumed by Excite's engineers—period cost of a service company. Excite has no inventory of goods for sale and, hence, no inventoriable cost.

(h) Salaries of Excite's marketing personnel—period cost of a service company. Excite has no inventory of goods for sale and, hence, no inventoriable cost.

2-26 (15-20 min.) Classification of costs, merchandising sector.

Cost object: Video section of store

Cost variability: With respect to changes in the number of videos sold

There may be some debate over classifications of individual items. Debate is more likely as regards cost variability.

Cost Item	D or I	V or F
A	D	F
B	I	V
C	D	V
D	D	F
E	I	F
F	I	V
G	I	F
H	D	V

2-28 (20 min.) **Computing cost of goods purchased and cost of goods sold.**

(a)

Marvin Department Store
Schedule of Cost of Goods Purchased
for the Year Ended December 31, 2007
(in thousands)

Purchases		$186,000
Add transportation-in		8,400
		194,400
Deduct:		
Purchase return and allowances	$4,800	
Purchase discounts	7,200	12,000
Cost of goods purchased		$182,400

(b)

Marvin Department Store
Schedule of Cost of Goods Sold
for the Year Ended December 31, 2007
(in thousands)

Beginning merchandise inventory 1/1/2007	$ 32,400
Cost of goods purchased (above)	182,400
Cost of goods available for sale	214,800
Ending merchandise inventory 12/31/2007	40,800
Cost of goods sold	$174,000

2-30 (25-30 min.) Income statement and schedule of cost of goods manufactured.

Howell Corporation
Income Statement for the Year Ended December 31, 2007
(in millions)

Revenues		$1,140
Cost of goods sold:		
Beginning finished goods, Jan. 1, 2007	$ 84	
Cost of goods manufactured (below)	774	
Cost of goods available for sale	858	
Ending finished goods, Dec. 31, 2007	66	792
Gross margin		348
Marketing, distribution, and customer-service costs		288
Operating income		$ 60

Howell Corporation
Schedule of Cost of Goods Manufactured
for the Year Ended December 31, 2007
(in millions)

Direct materials costs:		
Beginning inventory, Jan. 1, 2007	$ 18	
Purchases of direct materials	390	
Cost of direct materials available for use	408	
Ending inventory, Dec. 31, 2007	24	
Direct materials used		$384
Direct manufacturing labour costs		120
Indirect manufacturing costs:		
Indirect manufacturing labour	72	
Plant supplies used	12	
Plant utilities	36	
Amortization—plant, building, and equipment	96	
Plant supervisory salaries	6	
Miscellaneous plant overhead	42	264
Manufacturing costs incurred during 2007		768
Add beginning work in process inventory, Jan. 1, 2007		12
Total manufacturing costs to account for		780
Deduct ending work in process, Dec. 31, 2007		6
Cost of goods manufactured		$774

2-32 (25-30 min.) Income statement and schedule of cost of goods manufactured.

Chan Corporation
Income Statement
for the Year Ended December 31, 2007
(in millions)

Revenues		$420.00
Cost of goods sold:		
Beginning finished goods, Jan. 1, 2007	$ 48.00	
Cost of goods manufactured (below)	244.80	
Cost of goods available for sale	292.80	
Ending finished goods, Dec. 31, 2007	14.40	278.40
Gross margin		141.60
Marketing, distribution, and customer service costs		108.00
Operating income		$ 33.60

Chan Corporation
Schedule of Cost of Goods Manufactured
for the Year Ended December 31, 2007
(in millions)

Direct material costs:		
Beginning inventory, Jan. 1, 2007	$ 36.00	
Direct materials purchased	96.00	
Cost of direct materials available for use	132.00	
Ending inventory, Dec. 31, 2007	6.00	
Direct materials used		$126.00
Direct manufacturing labour costs		48.00
Indirect manufacturing costs:		
Plant supplies used	7.20	
Property taxes on plant	1.20	
Plant utilities	6.00	
Indirect manufacturing labour costs	24.00	
Amortization—plant, building, and equipment	10.80	
Miscellaneous manufacturing overhead costs	12.00	61.20
Manufacturing costs incurred during 2007		235.20
Add beginning work in process inventory, Jan. 1, 2007		12.00
Total manufacturing costs to account for		247.20
Deduct ending work in process inventory, Dec. 31, 2007		2.40
Cost of goods manufactured (to income statement)		$244.80

2-34 (20-30 min.) Overtime premium, defining accounting terms.

1.

	Westec	La Electricidad	BBC
Revenues	$504	$984	$576
Direct materials	300	492	324
Direct manuf. labour	48	120	72
Indirect manufacturing	96	240	144
Total manuf. costs	444	852	540
Gross margin	$ 60	$132	$ 36
Gross margin percentage	11.9%	13.4%	6.2%

2. The BBC job is the only one with overtime charges. The charge is $24 (2 hours × $12 per hour overtime rate). The exclusion of this $24 from direct manufacturing labour costs will also affect indirect manufacturing labour costs allocated (at the 200% rate) to the BBC job. The revised gross margin is:

	BBC
Revenues	$ 576
Direct materials	324
Direct manuf, labour	48
Indirect manufacturing	96
Total manuf, costs	468
Gross margin	$ 108
Gross margin percentage	18.7%

The sizable increase in gross margin for BBC is due to $72 of costs being excluded—the $24 of overtime premium plus the $48 of indirect manufacturing costs allocated using the 200% rate.

3. The main pro of charging BBC the $36 per hour labour rate is that this is the actual labour cost. The BBC job was, in fact, done in overtime hours.

The main con is that it penalizes the BBC job for a factor unrelated to its manufacture. The job was brought in one week ago, and there was much flexibility when it could be scheduled. It was done in overtime due to the Westec job being a rushed one.

A preferable approach is to assign all jobs with no special "rush" requirements the same labour cost per hour. This means that differences in job scheduling will not affect job profitability. Jobs that have a "rush" requirement ("hot-hot") are given an extra expediting cost to reflect any additional costs the expedition requires.

4.   The incentive payments would be:

	5% of Revenues	Incentive
Westec	0.05 × $504	$ 25.20
La Electricidad	0.05 × 984	49.20
BBC	0.05 × 576	28.80
		$103.20

	20% of Gross Margin	Incentive
Westec	0.20 × $ 60	$12.00
La Electricidad	0.20 × 132	26.40
BBC	0.20 × 108	21.60
		$60.00

EMI prefers jobs that produce high gross margins rather than high gross revenues. The 20% incentive better aligns the sales representative's incentive with that of EMI.

EMI should define how revenues and costs are to be measured so that ambiguities are reduced. The revenue and cost rules should be known in advance. If a rushed job is requested by a customer, the salesperson should know the rush-job charge so that he or she knows the consequences of accepting the request.

A fairer incentive for the salespeople would be 5% of revenues, minus a penalty for any discounts given to the customer in order to gain or win the contract. Too large a percentage of the Gross Margin is attributed in measurement to the performance of the manufacturing and purchasing groups. The salespeople should not be penalized for deficiency in the other groups.

2-36 (30-40 min.)   Fire loss, computing inventory costs.

1. = $60,000	2. = $33,600	3. = $74,400

This problem is not as easy as it first appears. These answers are obtained by working from the known figures to the unknowns in the schedule below. The basic relationships between categories of costs are:

Prime costs (given) = $352,800

Direct materials used = $352,800 − Direct manufacturing labour costs
= $352,800 − $216,000 = $136,800

Conversion costs = Direct manufacturing labour costs ÷ 0.6
= $216,000 ÷ 0.6 = $360,000

Indirect manuf. costs = $360,000 − $216,000 = $144,000
(or 0.40 × $360,000)

Schedule of Computations

Direct materials, Jan. 1, 2007			$ 19,200
Direct materials purchased			192,000
Direct materials available for use			211,200
Direct materials, Feb. 26, 2007	3.	=	74,400
Direct materials used ($352,800 − $216,000)			136,800
Direct manufacturing labour costs			216,000
Prime costs			352,800
Indirect manufacturing costs			144,000
Manufacturing costs incurred during the current period			496,800
Add work in process, Jan. 1, 2007			40,800
Manufacturing costs to account for			537,600
Deduct work in process, Feb. 26, 2007	2.	=	33,600
Cost of goods manufactured			504,000
Add finished goods, Jan. 1, 2007			36,000
Cost of goods available for sale (given)			540,000
Deduct finished goods, Feb. 26, 2007	1.	=	60,000
Cost of goods sold (80% of $600,000)			$480,000

Some instructors may wish to place the key amounts in a Work in Process T-account. This problem can be used to *introduce* students to the flow of costs through the general ledger (amounts in thousands):

Work in Process				Finished Goods			Cost of Goods Sold	
BI	40.8			BI	36			
DM used	136.8	COGM 504.0			→ 504	COGS 480	→ 480	
DL	216.0							
OH	144.0			Available				
To account for	537.6			for sale	540			
EI	33.6			EI	60			

2-38 (30 min.) Budgeted income statement.

1. | | |
    |---|---|
    | Target ending finished goods, Dec. 31, 2008 | 12,000 units |
    | Forecasted sales for 2008 | 122,000 units |
    | Total finished goods required in 2008 | 134,000 units |
    | Beginning finished goods, Jan. 1, 2008 | 9,000 units |
    | Finished goods production required in 2008 | 125,000 units |

2. | | | |
    |---|---|---|
    | Revenues (122,000 units sold × $5.76) | | $702,720 |
    | Cost of units sold: | | |
    | Beginning finished goods, Jan. 1, 2008 | $ 25,164 | |
    | Cost of goods manufactured | 337,500a | |
    | Cost of goods available for sale | 362,664 | |
    | Ending finished goods, Dec. 31, 2008 | 32,400c | 330,264 |
    | Gross margin | | 372,456 |
    | Operating costs: | | |
    | Marketing, distn., and customer-service costs | 245,640 | |
    | Administrative costs | 60,000 | 305,640d |
    | Operating income | | $ 66,816 |

Supporting Computations

a.

	Manufacturing Costs for 125,000 Units		
	Variable	Fixed	Total
Direct materials costs	$210,000b	$ –	$210,000
Direct manufacturing labour costs	45,000	–	45,000
Plant energy costs	7,500	–	7,500
Indirect manufacturing labour costs	15,000	19,200	34,200
Other indirect manufacturing costs	12,000	28,800	40,800
Cost of goods manufactured	$289,500	$48,000	$337,500

b. Direct materials costs = 250,000 kg × $0.84 per kg = $210,000.

c. The average unit manufacturing costs in 2005 is $337,500 ÷ 125,000 units = $2.70.
    Finished goods, December 31, 2008 = 12,000 × $2.70 = $32,400.

d. Variable mktg., distn., and customer-service costs, 122,000 × $1.62 $197,640
    Fixed marketing, distn., and customer-service costs   48,000
    Fixed administrative costs   60,000
         $305,640

2-40 (30 min.) Missing data.

		(in millions)
1.	Direct materials inventory, Aug. 1, 2008	$ 108
	Direct materials purchased	432
	Direct materials available	540
	Deduct direct materials used	450
	Direct materials inventory, Aug. 31, 2008	$ 90
2.	Total manufacturing overhead costs	$ 576
	Variable manufacturing overhead costs	300
	Fixed manufacturing overhead costs	$ 276
3.	Total manufacturing costs	$1,920
	Deduct:	
	Direct materials used $450	
	Manufacturing overhead 576	1,026
	Direct manufacturing labour costs	$ 894
4.	Work-in-Process inventory, Aug. 1, 2008	$ 240
	Total manufacturing costs	1,920
		2,160
	Deduct cost of goods manufactured	1,980
	Work-in-Process inventory Aug. 31, 2008	$ 180
5.	Finished goods inventory Aug. 1, 2008	$ 150
	Cost of goods manufactured	1,980
	Goods available for sale	$2,130
6.	Goods available for sale	$2,130
	Deduct cost of goods sold	2,040
	Finished goods inventory, Aug. 31, 2008	$ 90

2-42 (40 min.) Movie profit sharing, defining terms.

a. The G.V. Distribution Statement has multiple weaknesses for an author:

(i)   It is based on the bottom line, which means the author lines up last in the distribution. The best approach is to have a percentage of the top line (gross receipts), other things being equal.

(ii) The definition of revenues is "overly narrow." Only North American theatre and television revenues are given 100% of their amounts. Non-North American revenues get only 50% recognition while only 20% of home video revenues are included. The aim should be to have all "revenues" given 100% recognition. Items excluded include many potentially large amounts—e.g., cross-promotions for clothes, toys, licensing of characters in theme parks, and restaurants. Also excluded are revenues from airline screenings and revenues from use of film clips in other movies, advertisements, executive presentations, and so on.

(iii) The deductions made by other parties (from Golden Ventures as well as gross participation fees) appear extremely large. An author will likely have no ability to audit the magnitude of these deductions.

(iv) Many key terms appear to be ambiguous, giving Golden Venture much discretion to allocate an excessive amount of costs to the movie. For example, "negative cost is the cost of producing everything that is seen on screen, from film, sets, and up front fees paid to the cast and crew." There appears to be no limit to what could be included here. For example, some screen stars have outlandish parties and fly in friends to a movie set. Should these costs be included in "negative costs"? Without well-defined guidelines on admissible costs, "negative costs" could include costs related to other films, as well as costs arising from film studio inefficiencies.

b. Key guidelines can be developed, but it is questionable whether any film studios would be willing to be restricted by them:

(i)   Define revenues to be "all-encompassing," both domestically and internationally.

(ii) Base the compensation on numbers as close to the gross-revenue line as possible. The more cost items included as deductions, the higher the likelihood of a loss being reported.

(iii) Define all terms so that revenue and cost inclusions and exclusions are relatively unambiguous and auditable.

(iv) Transfer to other parties the risks associated with management inefficiencies, e.g., cost overruns. This could be done via allowable cost items having upper limits (say, film star non-salary expenses being no more than 2% of revenues).

(v)   Ensure that your percentage take is similar to that of participants with large amounts of bargaining power. If Fittler agrees to take 5% of the amount paid to the "major talent," the agents of these participants will be bargaining for his interests at the time they are crafting the participants' agreements for major talent.

Note: This Collaborative Learning Problem generates much interest from students. Useful background is in B. Daniels, D. Leedy, and S. Sills, *Movie Money* (Silman-James Press, Los Angeles, 1998).

CHAPTER 3
COST-VOLUME-PROFIT ANALYSIS

3-2 The assumptions underlying the CVP analysis outlined in Chapter 3 are:

1. Changes in the level of revenues and costs arise only because of changes in the number of product (or service) units produced or sold.
2. Total costs can be divided into a fixed component and a component that is variable with respect to the level of output.
3. The behaviour of total revenues and total costs is linear (straight-line) in relation to output units within the relevant range.
4. The unit selling price, unit variable costs, and fixed costs are known.
5. The analysis either covers a single product or assumes that a given revenue mix of products will remain constant as the level of total units sold changes.
6. All revenues and costs can be added and compared without taking into account the time value of money.

3-4 Contribution margin is computed as revenues minus all costs that vary with respect to the output level.

Gross margin is computed as revenues minus cost of goods sold.

Contribution-margin percentage is the total contribution margin divided by revenues.

Variable-cost percentage is the total variable costs (with respect to units of output) divided by revenues.

Margin of safety is the excess of budgeted revenues over breakeven revenues.

3-6 Breakeven analysis denotes the study of the breakeven point, which is often only an incidental part of the relationship between cost, volume, and profit. Cost-volume-profit analysis is a more comprehensive term than breakeven analysis.

3-8 An increase in the income tax rate does not affect the breakeven point. Operating income at the breakeven point is zero and thus no income taxes will be paid at this point.

3-10 Examples include:
Manufacturing—substituting a robotic machine for hourly wage workers.
Marketing—changing a sales force compensation plan from a percentage of sales dollars to a fixed salary.
Customer service—hiring a subcontractor to do customer repair visits on an annual retainer basis rather than a per visit basis.

3-12   Operating leverage describes the effects that fixed costs have on changes in operating income as changes occur in units sold and hence in contribution margin. Knowing the degree of operating leverage at a given level of sales helps managers calculate the effect of fluctuations in sales on operating incomes.

3-14   A company with multiple products can compute a breakeven point by assuming there is a constant mix of products at different levels of total revenue.

3-16 (10 min.) CVP analysis computations.

Case	Revenues	Variable Contribution Costs	Fixed Costs	Total Costs	Operating Income	Contribution Margin	Margin %
a.	$2,400	$ 600	$360	$ 960	$1,440	$1,800	75.0%
b.	2,400	1,800	360	2,160	240	600	25.0%
c.	1,200	840	360	1,200	0	360	30.0%
d.	1,800	1,080	360	1,440	360	720	40.0%

3-18 (15-20 min.)   CVP analysis, changing revenues and costs.

1. USP   =   8% × $1,200 = $96
    UVC   = $42 ($20.40 + $21.60)
    UCM   = $54
    FC   = $26,400 a month

(a) $Q = \dfrac{FC}{UCM} = \dfrac{\$26,400}{\$54}$

   =   489 tickets (rounded up)

(b) $Q = \dfrac{FC + TOI}{UCM} = \dfrac{\$26,400 + \$12,000}{\$54}$

   $= \dfrac{\$38,400}{\$54}$

   =   712 tickets (rounded up)

2. USP   = $96
    UVC   = $34.80 ($20.40 + $14.40)
    UCM   = $61.20
    FC   = $26,400 a month

(a) $\quad Q \quad = \quad \dfrac{FC}{UCM} \quad = \quad \dfrac{\$26,400}{\$61.20}$

$\quad = \quad$ 432 tickets (rounded up)

(b) $\quad Q \quad = \quad \dfrac{FC + TOI}{UCM} \quad = \quad \dfrac{\$26,400 + \$12,000}{\$61.20}$

$\quad = \quad \dfrac{\$38,400}{\$61.20}$

$\quad = \quad$ 628 tickets (rounded up)

This scenario allows for fewer tickets sold (628 vs. 712) to reach the breakeven (432 vs. 489) and target income of $12,000.

3-20 (20 min.) CVP exercises.

	Revenues	Variable Costs	Contribution Margin	Fixed Costs	Budgeted Operating Income
Orig.	$12,000,000^G	$9,840,000^G	$2,160,000	$2,040,000^G	$120,000
1.	12,000,000	9,624,000	2,376,000	2,040,000	336,000
2.	12,000,000	10,056,000	1,944,000	2,040,000	(96,000)
3.	12,000,000	9,840,000	2,160,000	2,142,000	18,000
4.	12,000,000	9,840,000	2,160,000	1,938,000	222,000
5.	12,960,000	10,627,200	2,332,800	2,040,000	292,800
6.	11,040,000	9,052,800	1,987,200	2,040,000	(52,800)
7.	13,200,000	10,824,000	2,376,000	2,244,000	132,000
8.	12,000,000	9,348,000	2,652,000	2,142,000	510,000

^{G} stands for given.

3-22 (10-15 min.) CVP, income taxes.

1. Operating income = Net income ÷ (1 − tax rate)
   $\quad$ = $100,800 ÷ (1 − 0.40) = $168,000

2. Contribution margin − Fixed costs = Operating income
   Contribution margin − $360,000 = $168,000
   Contribution margin = $528,000

3. Revenues − 0.80 Revenues = Contribution margin
   $\quad$ 0.20 Revenues = $528,000
   $\quad$ Revenues = $2,640,000

4. Breakeven point = Fixed costs ÷ Contribution margin percentage
    Breakeven point = $360,000 ÷ 0.20
                    = $1,800,000

3-24 (10 min.) CVP, margin of safety.

1. $$\text{Breakeven point} = \frac{\text{Fixed costs}}{\text{Contribution margin percentage}}$$

        $$\text{Contribution margin percentage} = \frac{\$480,000}{\$1,200,000} = 0.40$$

2. $$\text{Contribution margin percentage} = \frac{\text{Selling price} - \text{Variable cost per unit}}{\text{Selling price}}$$

        $$0.40 = \frac{\text{USP} - \$14.40}{\text{USP}}$$

        $$0.40\ \text{USP} = \text{USP} - 14.40$$
        $$0.60\ \text{USP} = \$14.40$$
        $$\text{USP} = \$24$$

3. | | |
    |---|---:|
    | Revenues, 80,000 units × $24 | $1,920,000 |
    | Breakeven revenues | 1,200,000 |
    | Margin of safety | $ 720,000 |

3-26 (15 min.) Gross margin and contribution margin, making decisions.

Salaries and wages of $180,000 could be variable costs and fixed costs. The answer assumes they are all fixed costs.

1.
Revenues		$600,000
Deduct variable costs:		
Cost of goods sold	$240,000	
Sales commissions	60,000	
Other operating costs	57,600	357,600
Contribution margin		$242,400

2. $$\text{Contribution margin percentage} = \frac{\$242,400}{\$600,000} = 40.4\%$$

3. Incremental revenue (20% × $600,000) = $120,000

Incremental contribution margin	
(42% × $120,000)	$50,400
Incremental fixed costs (advertising)	12,000
Incremental operating income	$38,400

If Mr. Schmidt spends $12,000 more on advertising, the operating income will increase by $38,400 converting an operating loss of $12,000 to an operating income of $26,400.

Proof (Optional):

Revenues (120% × $600,000)		$720,000
Cost of goods sold (40% of sales)		288,000
Gross margin		432,000
Operating costs:		
Salaries and wages	$180,000	
Sales commissions (10% of sales)	72,000	
Amortization of equipment and fixtures	14,400	
Store rent	57,600	
Advertising	12,000	
Other operating costs:		
Variable $\left(\dfrac{\$48,000}{\$600,000} \times \$720,000 \right)$	57,600	
Fixed	12,000	405,600
Operating income		$ 26,400

3-28 (30 min.) CVP, sensitivity analysis.

1. USP = $36.00 × (1 − 0.30 margin to bookstore)
         = $36.00 × 0.70 = $25.20

    UVC = $4.80 variable production and marketing cost
          3.78 variable author royalty cost (0.15 × $36.00 × 0.70)
          $8.58

    UCM = $25.20 − $8.58 = $16.62

    FC = $ 600,000   fixed production and marketing cost
          3,600,000   up-front payment to Washington
         $4,200,000

Exhibit 3-28A shows the PV graph.

EXHIBIT 3-28A
PV Graph for Media Publishers

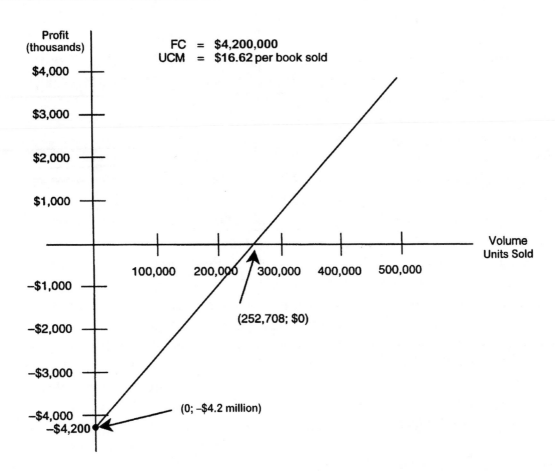

2.   (a)   Breakeven number of units $=$

$$= \frac{FC}{UCM}$$

$$= \frac{\$4,200,000}{\$16.62}$$

$$= 252,708 \text{ copies sold (rounded)}$$

    (b)   Target OI

$$= \frac{FC + OI}{UCM}$$

$$= \frac{\$4,200,000 + \$2,400,000}{\$16.62}$$

$$= \frac{\$6,600,000}{\$16.62}$$

$$= 397,112 \text{ copies sold (rounded)}$$

3. (a) Decreasing the normal bookstore margin to 20% of the listed bookstore price of $36 has the following effects:

USP $=$ $36.00 $\times$ $(1 - 0.20)$
$=$ $36.00 $\times$ 0.80 = $28.80

UVC $=$ $ 4.80 variable production and marketing cost
$=$ + 4.32 variable author royalty cost $(0.15 \times \$36.00 \times 0.80)$
$ 9.12

UCM $=$ $28.80 − $9.12 = $19.68

$$\text{Breakeven number of units} = \frac{FC}{UCM}$$
$$= \frac{\$4,200,000}{\$19.68}$$
$$= 213,415 \text{ copies sold (rounded)}$$

The breakeven point decreases from 252,708 copies in requirement 2 to 213,415 copies.

(b) Increasing the listed bookstore price to $48 while keeping the bookstore margin at 30% has the following effects:

USP $=$ $48.00 $\times$ $(1 - 0.30)$
$=$ $48.00 $\times$ 0.70 = $33.60

UVC $=$ $4.80 variable production and marketing cost
$=$ +5.04 variable author royalty cost $(0.15 \times \$40.00 \times 0.70)$
$9.84

UCM $=$ $33.60 − $9.84 = $23.76

$$= \frac{\$4,200,000}{\$23.76}$$
$$= 176,768 \text{ copies sold (rounded)}$$

The breakeven point decreases from 252,708 copies in requirement 2 to 176,768 copies.

3-30 (30 min.) Revenue mix, new and upgrade customers.

1.

	New Customers	Upgrade Customers
USP	$252	$144
UVC	108	48
UCM	144	96

Let S = Number of upgrade customers

$1.5S$ = Number of new customers

Revenues – Variable costs – Fixed costs = Operating income

$[\$252 (1.5S) + \$144S] - [\$108 (1.5S) + \$48S] - \$16,800,000 = OI$

$\$522S - \$210S - \$16,800,000 = OI$

$\$312S$	=	$\$16,800,000$
S	=	53,846 (rounded)
1.5S	=	80,770
		134,616

Breakeven point is 134,616 units when OI = 0

Check

Revenues ($252 × 80,770; $144 × 53,846)	$28,107,864
Variable costs ($108 × 80,770; $48 × 53,846)	11,307,768
Contribution margin	16,800,096
Fixed costs	16,800,000
Operating income	$ 96 rounding error

2. When 200,000 units are sold, mix is:

New customers	120,000
Upgrade customers	80,000

Revenues ($252 × 120,000; $144 × 80,000)	$41,760,000
Variable costs ($108 × 120,000; $48 × 80,000)	16,800,000
Contribution margin	24,960,000
Fixed costs	16,800,000
Operating income	$ 8,160,000

3. (a) $[\$252S + \$144S] - [\$108S + \$48S] - \$16,800,000 = OI$

$$
\begin{aligned}
396S - 156S &= \$16,800,000 \\
240S &= \$16,800,000 \\
S &= 70,000 \\
S &= \underline{70,000} \\
&\underline{140,000} \text{ units}
\end{aligned}
$$

As S = number of upgrade customers and S = number of new customers

Check

Revenues ($252 × 70,000; $144 × 70,000)	$27,720,000
Variable costs ($108 × 70,000; $48 × 70,000)	10,920,000
Contribution margin	16,800,000
Fixed costs	16,800,000
Operating income	$ 0

(b) $[\$252 (9S) + \$144S] - [\$108 (9S) + \$48S] - \$16,800,000 = OI$

$$
\begin{aligned}
2,412S - 1,020S &= \$16,800,000 \\
1,392S &= \$16,800,000 \\
S &= 12,069 \qquad \text{(rounded)} \\
9S &= \underline{108,621} \\
&\underline{120,690} \qquad \text{units}
\end{aligned}
$$

Check

Revenues ($252 × 108,621; $144 × 12,069)	$29,110,428
Variable costs ($108 × 108,621; $48 × 12,069)	12,310,380
Contribution margin	16,800,048
Fixed costs	16,800,000
Operating income	$ 48 rounded

As Zapo increases its percentage of new customers, which have a higher contribution margin than upgrade customers, the number of units required to break even decreases:

	New Customers	Upgrade Customers	Breakeven Point
Requirement 3(a)	50%	50%	140,000
Requirement 1	60%	40%	134,616
Requirement 3(b)	90%	10%	120,690

3-32 (20 min.) Gross margin and contribution margin.

1.
Cost of Goods Sold	$1,920,000
Fixed Manufacturing Costs	600,000
Variable Manufacturing Costs	$1,320,000

Variable manufacturing costs per unit = $1,320,000 ÷ 200,000 = $6.60 per unit

2.
Total marketing and distribution costs	$1,380,000
Variable marketing and distribution (200,000 × $6)	1,200,000
Fixed marketing and distribution costs	$ 180,000

3. Selling price = $3,120,000 ÷ 200,000 units = $15.60 per unit

$$\text{Contribution margin per unit} = \begin{matrix}\text{Selling} \\ \text{price}\end{matrix} - \begin{matrix}\text{Variable} \\ \text{manufacturing} \\ \text{costs per unit}\end{matrix} - \begin{matrix}\text{Variable marketing} \\ \text{and distribution} \\ \text{costs per unit}\end{matrix}$$

$$= \$15.60 - \$6.60 - \$6.00 = \$3.00$$

Operating income =

$$\left(\begin{matrix}\text{Contribution margin} \\ \text{per unit}\end{matrix} \times \begin{matrix}\text{Sales} \\ \text{quantity}\end{matrix}\right) - \begin{matrix}\text{Fixed manufacturing} \\ \text{costs}\end{matrix} - \begin{matrix}\text{Fixed marketing} \\ \text{and distribution} \\ \text{costs}\end{matrix}$$

$$= (\$3.00 \times 230,000) - \$600,000 - \$180,000$$
$$= -\$90,000$$

Foreman has confused gross margin with contribution margin. He has interpreted gross margin as if it were all variable, and interpreted marketing and distribution costs as all fixed. In fact, the manufacturing costs, subtracted from sales to calculate gross margin, and marketing and distribution costs contain both fixed and variable components.

4. Breakeven point in units =

$$\frac{\text{Fixed manufacturing, marketing and distribution costs}}{\text{Contribution margin per unit}}$$

$$= \frac{\$780,000}{\$3.00} = 260,000 \text{ units}$$

Breakeven point in revenues = 260,000 × $15.60 = $4,056,000

3-34 (15-20 min.) Appendix, uncertainty, CVP.

1. King pays Foreman $2.4 million plus $4.80 (25% of $19.20) for every home purchasing the pay-per-view. The expected value of the variable component is:

Demand (1)	Payment (2) = (1) × $4.80	Probability (3)	Expected payment (4) = (2) × (3)
100,000	$ 480,000	0.05	$ 24,000
200,000	960,000	0.10	96,000
300,000	1,440,000	0.30	432,000
400,000	1,920,000	0.35	672,000
500,000	2,400,000	0.15	360,000
1,000,000	4,800,000	0.05	240,000
			$1,824,000

The expected value of King's payment is $4,224,000 ($2,400,000 fixed fee + $1,824,000).

2.
USP	=	$19.20
UVC	=	$7.20 ($4.80 payment to Foreman + $2.40 variable cost)
UCM	=	$12
FC	=	$2,400,000 + $1,200,000 = $3,600,000

$$Q = \frac{FC}{UCM}$$
$$= \frac{\$3,600,000}{\$12}$$
$$= 300,000$$

If 300,000 homes purchase the pay-per-view, King will break even.

3-36 (15-20 min.) CVP analysis, service firm.

1.
Revenue per package	$4,800
Variable cost per package	4,320
Contribution margin per package	$ 480

Breakeven (units) = Fixed costs ÷ Contribution margin per package
$$= \frac{\$576,000}{\$480 \text{ per package}} = 1,200 \text{ tour packages}$$

2. Contribution margin ratio $= \dfrac{\text{Contribution margin per package}}{\text{Selling price}} = \dfrac{\$480}{\$4,800} = 10\%$

Revenue to achieve target income = (Fixed costs + target OI) ÷ Contribution margin ratio

$$= \frac{\$576,000 + \$120,000}{0.10} = \$6,960,000, \text{ or}$$

Number of tour packages to earn \$120,000 operating income:

$$\frac{\$576,000 + \$120,000}{\$480} = 1,450 \text{ tour packages}$$

Revenues to earn \$120,000 OI = 1,450 tour packages × \$4,800 = \$6,960,000.

3. Fixed costs = \$576,000 + \$28,800 = \$604,800

$$\text{Breakeven (units)} = \frac{\text{Fixed costs}}{\text{Contribution margin per unit}}$$

$$\text{Contribution margin per unit} = \frac{\text{Fixed costs}}{\text{Breakeven (units)}}$$

$$= \frac{\$604,800}{1,200 \text{ tour packages}} = \$504 \text{ per tour package}$$

Desired variable cost per tour package = \$4,800 − \$504 = \$4,296

Because the current variable cost per unit is \$4,320, the unit variable cost will need to be reduced by \$24 to achieve the breakeven point calculated in requirement 1.

Alternate Method: If fixed cost increases by \$28,800, then total variable costs must be reduced by \$28,800 to keep the breakeven point of 1,200 tour packages.

Therefore the variable cost per unit reduction = \$28,800 ÷ 1,200 = \$24 per tour package.

3-38 (20-25 min.) CVP analysis (CMA adapted).

1. Selling price $19.20
    Variable costs per unit:
      Purchase price $12.00
      Shipping and handling   2.40   14.40
    Contribution margin per unit (CMU) $ 4.80

$$\text{Breakeven point in units} = \frac{\text{Fixed costs}}{\text{Contr. margin per unit}} = \frac{\$720,000}{\$4.80} = 150,000 \text{ units}$$

2. Since Galaxy is operating above the breakeven point, any incremental contribution margin will increase operating income dollar for dollar.

    Increase in units sales = 10% × 200,000 = 20,000
    Incremental contribution margin = $4.80 × 20,000 = $96,000

    Therefore, the increase in operating income will be equal to $96,000.
    Galaxy's operating income in 2008 would be $240,000 + $96,000 = $336,000.

3. Selling price $19.20
    Variable costs:
      Purchase price $12 × 130% $15.60
      Shipping and handling   2.40   18.00
    Contribution margin per unit $ 1.20

$$\text{Target sales in units} = \frac{\text{FC + TOI}}{\text{CMU}} = \frac{\$720,000 + \$240,000}{\$1.20} = 800,000 \text{ units}$$

Target sales in dollars = $19.20 × 800,000 = $15,360,000

3-40 (20-25 min.) CVP, shoe stores (continuation of 3-39).

1. Because the unit sales level at the point of indifference would be the same for each plan, the revenue would be equal. Therefore, the unit sales level sought would be that which produces the same total costs for each plan.

$$
\begin{aligned}
\text{Let Q} &= \text{unit sales level} \\
\$23.40Q + \$432,000 + \$97,200 &= \$25.20Q + \$432,000 \\
\$97,200 &= \$1.80Q \\
Q &= 54,000 \text{ units}
\end{aligned}
$$

2.

	Commission Plan		Salary Plan	
Sales in units	50,000	60,000	50,000	60,000
Revenues @ $36.00	$1,800,000	$2,160,000	$1,800,000	$2,160,000
Variable costs				
@ $25.20 and @ $23.40	1,260,000	1,512,000	1,170,000	1,404,000
Contribution margin	540,000	648,000	630,000	756,000
Fixed costs	432,000	432,000	529,200	529,200
Operating income	$ 108,000	$ 216,000	$ 100,800	$ 226,800

The decision regarding the plans will heavily depend on the unit sales level that is generated by the fixed salary plan. For example, as part (1) shows, at identical unit sales levels in excess of 54,000 units, the fixed salary plan will always provide a more profitable final result than the commission plan.

3. Let TQ = Target number of units

a.
$$\$36.00TQ - \$23.40TQ - \$529,200 = \$201,600$$
$$\$12.60TQ = \$730,800$$
$$TQ = \$730,800 \div \$12.60$$
$$TQ = 58,000 \text{ units}$$

b.
$$\$36.00TQ - \$25.20TQ - \$432,000 = \$201,600$$
$$\$10.80TQ = \$633,600$$
$$TQ = \$633,600 \div \$10.80$$
$$TQ = 58,667 \text{ units (rounded)}$$

The decision regarding the salary plan heavily depends on predictions of demand. For instance, the salary plan offers the same operating income at 58,000 units as the commission plan offers at 58,667 units.

3-42 (30 min.) CVP analysis, income taxes, sensitivity.

1. a. In order to break even, Almo Company must sell 500 units. This amount represents the point where revenues equal total costs.

Let Q denote the quantity of canopies sold.

$$\text{Revenue} = \text{Variable costs} + \text{Fixed costs}$$
$$\$480Q = \$240Q + \$120,000$$
$$\$240Q = \$120,000$$
$$Q = 500 \text{ units}$$

The calculation can also be expressed as

$$
\begin{aligned}
\text{Breakeven} &= \text{Fixed Costs} \div \text{Contribution margin per unit} \\
&= \$120{,}000 \div \$240 \\
&= 500 \text{ units}
\end{aligned}
$$

1. b. In order to achieve its net income objective, Almo Company must sell 2,500 units. This amount represents the point where revenues equal total costs plus the corresponding operating income objective to achieve *net* income of $288,000.

$$
\begin{aligned}
\text{Revenue} &= \text{Variable costs} + \text{Fixed costs} + \text{Operating income} \\
\$480Q &= \$240Q + \$120{,}000 + [\$288{,}000 \div (1 - 0.4)] \\
\$480Q &= \$240Q + \$120{,}000 + \$480{,}000 \\
Q &= 2{,}500 \text{ units}
\end{aligned}
$$

2. To achieve its net income objective, Almo Company should select the first alternative where the sales price is reduced by $48, and 2,700 units are sold during the remainder of the year. This alternative results in the highest net income and is the only alternative that equals or exceeds the company's net income objective. Calculations for the three alternatives are shown below.

Alternative 1

$$
\begin{aligned}
\text{Revenues} &= (\$480 \times 350) + (\$432 \times 2{,}700) = \$1{,}334{,}400 \\
\text{Variable costs} &= \$240 \times 3{,}050 = \$732{,}000 \\
\text{Operating income} &= \$1{,}334{,}400 - \$732{,}000 - \$120{,}000 = \$482{,}400 \\
\text{Net income} &= \$482{,}400 \times (1 - 0.4) = \$289{,}440
\end{aligned}
$$

Alternative 2

$$
\begin{aligned}
\text{Revenues} &= (\$480 \times 350) + (\$444 \times 2{,}200) = \$1{,}144{,}800 \\
\text{Variable costs} &= (\$240 \times 350) + (\$228 \times 2{,}200) = \$585{,}600 \\
\text{Operating income} &= \$1{,}144{,}800 - \$585{,}600 - \$120{,}000 = \$439{,}200 \\
\text{Net income} &= \$439{,}200 \times (1 - 0.4) = \$263{,}520
\end{aligned}
$$

Alternative 3

$$
\begin{aligned}
\text{Revenues} &= (\$480 \times 350) + (\$456 \times 2{,}000) = \$1{,}080{,}000 \\
\text{Variable costs} &= \$240 \times 2{,}350 = \$564{,}000 \\
\text{Operating income} &= \$1{,}080{,}000 - \$564{,}000 - \$108{,}000 = \$408{,}000 \\
\text{Net income} &= \$408{,}000 \times (1 - 0.4) = \$244{,}800
\end{aligned}
$$

3-44 (20 min.) CVP, cost structure differences, movie production (continuation of 3-43).

1. Contract A

    Fixed costs for Contract A:

Production costs	$25,200,000
Fixed salary	18,000,000
Total fixed costs	$43,200,000

    Unit variable cost = $0.25 per $1 revenue marketing fee
    Unit contribution margin = $0.75 per $1 revenue

    (a) Breakeven point in revenues $= \dfrac{\text{Fixed costs}}{\text{Unit contribution margin per \$1 revenue}}$

    $$= \frac{\$43,200,000}{\$0.75}$$

    $$= \$57,600,000$$

    Box-office receipts of $92,160,000 translate to $57,600,000 in revenues to Royal Rumble.

    Contract B

    Fixed costs for Contract B:

Production costs	$25,200,000
Fixed salary	3,600,000
Total fixed costs	$28,800,000

    Unit variable cost $=$ $0.25 per $1 revenue fee to Media Productions
    $0.15 per $1 revenue residual to directors/actors
    $0.40 per $1 revenue

    Unit contribution margin = $0.60 per $1 revenue

    Breakeven point in revenues $= \dfrac{\$28,800,000}{\$0.60} = \$48,000,000$

    Box-office receipts of $76,800,000 translate to $48,000,000 in revenues to Royal Rumble.

    ### Difference in Breakeven Points

    Contract A has a higher fixed cost and a lower variable cost per sales dollar. In contrast, Contract B has a lower fixed cost and a higher variable cost per sales dollar. In Contract B, there is risk-sharing between Royal Rumble and Savage, Michaels, and Martel that lowers the breakeven point, but results in Royal Rumble's receiving less operating income if *Feature Creatures 2* is a mega-success.

2. Revenues, $0.625 \times \$360,000,000$ $225,000,000

    Variable costs, $0.40 \times \$225,000,000$ 90,000,000

    Contribution margin   135,000,000

    Fixed costs   28,800,000

    Operating income $106,200,000

Revenues, $0.625 \times \$360,000,000$	\$225,000,000
Variable costs, $0.40 \times \$225,000,000$	90,000,000
Contribution margin	135,000,000
Fixed costs	28,800,000
Operating income	\$106,200,000

Feature Creatures 2 has a higher breakeven point than *Feature Creatures* because FC2 has a higher level of fixed costs and a lower unit contribution margin. This means after breakeven is reached, under Contract A, $0.75 of every additional revenue dollar will contribute to OI, but under Contract B only $0.60 of every additional revenue dollar will contribute to OI. All other things being equal, for the same total revenue after breakeven, Contract A will result in the higher OI because the deduction for unit variable costs is lower per dollar than under Contract B.

3-46 (20-25 min.)   Revenue mix, two products.

1. Let Q = Number of units of Deluxe product to break even

       3Q = Number of units of Standard product to break even

Revenues – Variable costs – Fixed costs = Zero operating income

$$\$24(3Q) + \$36Q - \$16.80(3Q) - \$21.60Q - \$1,440,000 \;=\; 0$$

$$\$36Q \;=\; \$1,440,000$$

$$Q \;=\; 40,000 \text{ units of Deluxe}$$

$$3Q \;=\; 120,000 \text{ units of Standard}$$

The breakeven point is 120,000 Standard units plus 40,000 Deluxe carriers, a total of 160,000 units.

2. Unit contribution margins are: Standard: $24 – $16.80 = $7.20; Deluxe: $36 – $21.60 = $14.40

    (a) If only Standard carriers were sold, the breakeven point would be: $1,440,000 ÷ $7.20 = 200,000 units

    (b) If only Deluxe carriers were sold, the breakeven point would be: $1,440,000 ÷ $14.40 = 100,000 units

3. Operating income = 180,000($7.20) + 20,000($14.40) − $1,440,000
   = $1,296,000 + $288,000 − $1,440,000
   = $144,000

Let Q = Number of units of Deluxe product to break even
   9Q = Number of units of Standard product to break even

$24(9Q) + $36Q − $16.80(9Q) − $21.60Q − $1,440,000 = 0
                                          $79.20Q = $1,440,000
                                                Q = 18,182 units of
                                                    Deluxe (rounded)
                                               9Q = 163,638 units of
                                                    Standard

The breakeven point is 163,638 Standard + 18,182 Deluxe, a total of 181,820 units.

The major lesson of this problem is that changes in sales mix change breakeven points and operating incomes. In this example, the budgeted and actual total sales in number of units were identical, but the proportion of the product having the higher contribution margin declined. Operating income suffered, falling from $360,000 to $144,000. Moreover, the breakeven point rose from 160,000 to 181,820 units.

3-48 (15-25 min.) Revenue mix, three products.

1. Let A = Number of units of A to break even
      5A = Number of units of B to break even
      4A = Number of units of C to break even

Contribution margin − Fixed costs = Zero operating income

$3.60A + $2.40(5A) + $1.20(4A) − $306,000 = 0
                                 $20.40A = $306,000

                                       A = 15,000 units of A
                                      5A = 75,000 units of B
                                      4A = 60,000 units of C
                                   Total = 150,000 units

2. Contribution margin:

A: 20,000 × $3.60	$ 72,000	
B: 100,000 × $2.40	240,000	
C: 80,000 × $1.20	96,000	
Contribution margin		$408,000
Fixed costs		306,000
Operating income		$102,000

3. Contribution margin

A: 20,000 × $3.60	$ 72,000	
B: 80,000 × $2.40	192,000	
C: 100,000 × $1.20	120,000	
Contribution margin		$384,000
Fixed costs		306,000
Operating income		$ 78,000

Let A = Number of units of A to break even
  4A = Number of units of B to break even
  5A = Number of units of C to break even

Contribution margin – Fixed costs = Breakeven point

$$\$3.60A + \$2.40(4A) + \$1.20(5A) - \$306{,}000 = 0$$
$$\$19.2A = \$306{,}000$$

A =	15,938	units of A (rounded)
4A =	63,752	units of B
5A =	79,690	units of C
Total =	159,380	units

3-50 (30 min.) CVP, nonprofit event planning.

1. Computation of fixed costs.

	Golf Club	Town Hall
Rental cost of venue	$2,400	$ 7,920
Chamber administration/marketing	4,200	4,200
Band	3,000	3,000
	$9,600	$15,120

Computation of contribution margin per person:

	Golf Club	Town Hall
Selling (ticket) price per person	$144	$144
Catering cost per person	96	72
Contribution margin per person	$ 48	$ 72

$$\text{Breakeven point} = \frac{\text{Fixed costs}}{\text{Unit contribution margin}}$$

$$\text{Breakeven point for Golf Club venue} = \frac{\$9,600}{\$48} = 200 \text{ tickets}$$

$$\text{Breakeven point for Town Hall venue} = \frac{\$15,120}{\$72} = 210 \text{ tickets}$$

2. Operating income = Revenues – Variable costs – Fixed costs

$$\text{Let } Q = \text{Number of tickets sold}$$
$$OI = \text{Operating income}$$

Golf Club Venue

$$OI = \$144Q - \$96Q - \$9,600$$
$$\text{When } Q = 150: OI = (\$144 \times 150) - (\$96 \times 150) - \$9,600$$
$$= -\$2,400$$
$$\text{When } Q = 300: OI = (\$144 \times 300) - (\$96 \times 300) - \$9,600$$
$$= \$4,800$$

Town Hall Venue

$$OI = \$144Q - \$72Q - \$15,120$$
$$\text{When } Q = 150: OI = (\$144 \times 150) - (\$72 \times 150) - \$15,120$$
$$= -\$4,320$$
$$\text{When } Q = 300: OI = (\$144 \times 300) - (\$72 \times 300) - \$15,120$$
$$= \$6,480$$

The Golf Club venue has higher variable costs per person and lower fixed costs. In contrast, the Town Hall venue has lower variable costs per person and higher fixed costs.

3. Requirement 2 gives the operating income equation for each venue. Setting these two equations equal and solving for Q, gives 230 as the level of ticket sales at which the operating incomes for the two venues are equal:

$$
\begin{aligned}
\$144Q - \$96Q - \$9{,}600 &= \$144Q - \$72Q - \$15{,}120 \\
\$48Q - \$72Q &= \$9{,}600 - \$15{,}120 \\
\$24Q &= \$5{,}520 \\
Q &= 230
\end{aligned}
$$

Above 230, the Town Hall venue will yield higher operating income than the Golf Club venue.

3-52 (30-40 min.)   CVP, income taxes. (CMA)

1. $\text{Revenues} - \text{Variable costs} - \text{Fixed costs} = \dfrac{\text{Target net income}}{1 - \text{Tax rate}}$

    Let X = Net income for 2008

$$
\begin{aligned}
20{,}000(\$30.00) - 20{,}000(\$16.50) - \$162{,}000 &= \frac{X}{1 - 0.40} \\
\$600{,}000 - \$330{,}000 - \$162{,}000 &= \frac{X}{0.60} \\
(0.6)(\$108{,}000) &= X \\
X &= \$64{,}800
\end{aligned}
$$

2. Let Q = Number of units to break even
    $\$30.00Q - \$16.50Q - \$162{,}000 = 0$
    $Q = \$162{,}000 \div \$13.50 = 12{,}000$ units

3. Let X = Net income for 2009

$$
\begin{aligned}
22{,}000(\$30.00) - 22{,}000(\$16.50) - (\$162{,}000 + \$13{,}500) &= \frac{X}{1 - 0.40} \\
\$297{,}000 - \$175{,}500 &= \frac{X}{0.60} \\
\$121{,}500 &= \frac{X}{0.60} \\
X &= \$72{,}900
\end{aligned}
$$

4. Let Q = Number of units to break even with new fixed costs of $175,500

$$
\begin{aligned}
\$30.00Q - \$16.50Q - \$175{,}500 &= 0 \\
Q = \$175{,}500 \div \$13.50 &= 13{,}000 \text{ units} \\
\text{Revenues} = 13{,}000(\$30.00) &= \$390{,}000
\end{aligned}
$$

Alternatively, the computation could be $175,500 divided by the contribution margin percentage of 45% to obtain $390,000.

5. Let S = Required sales units to equal 2008 net income

$$\$30.00S - \$16.50S - \$175,500 = \frac{\$64,800}{0.6}$$

$$\$13.50S = \$283,500$$

$$S = 21,000 \text{ units}$$

$$\text{Revenues} = 21,000 \text{ units} \times \$30.00 = \$630,000$$

6. Let A = Amount spent for advertising in 2009

$$\$660,000 - \$363,000 - (\$162,000 + A) = \frac{\$72,000}{0.6}$$

$$\$297,000 - \$162,000 - A = \$120,000$$

$$A = \$15,000$$

3-54 (20-30 min.) Appendix, CVP under uncertainty.

1. (a) At a selling price of $120, the unit contribution margin is ($120 – $60) = $60, and it will require the sale of ($240,000 ÷ $60) = 4,000 units to break even. The sales in dollars are $480,000 and there is a 2/3 probability of equalling or exceeding this sales level—that is, that 2/3 of the area under the graph exists between $480,000 and $720,000.

    (b) At a selling price of $84, the unit contribution margin is ($84 – $60) = $24, and it will require the sale of ($240,000 ÷ $24) = 10,000 units to break even. At the lower price, the sales in dollars are $840,000 and there is a 2/3 probability of equalling or exceeding this sales volume.

    Therefore, if you seek to maximize the probability of showing an operating income, you are indifferent between the two strategies.

2. $$\begin{array}{l}\text{Expected} \\ \text{operating} \\ \text{income}\end{array} = \left[\left(\begin{array}{l}\text{Selling} \\ \text{price per unit}\end{array} - \begin{array}{l}\text{Variable} \\ \text{cost per unit}\end{array} \right) \times \left(\begin{array}{l}\text{Expected} \\ \text{sales} \\ \text{level}\end{array} \right) \right] - \left(\begin{array}{l}\text{Fixed} \\ \text{costs}\end{array} \right)$$

    At a selling price of $120:

    Expected revenues   = $540,000 ($120 × 4,500)
    Expected operating income   = [($120 – $60) × 4,500] – $240,000
                                     = $30,000

At a selling price of $84:

Expected revenues	=	$900,000 ($84 × 10,715)
Expected operating income	=	[($84 − $60) × 10,715] − $240,000
	=	$17,160

A selling price of $120 will maximize the expected operating income.

3-56 (20-25 min.) Ethics, CVP, cost analysis.

1. (a) USP = $66
        UVC = $26.40 ($16.80 + $9.60)
        UCM = $39.60
        FC   = $24,000,000

$$Q = \frac{FC}{UCM} = \frac{\$24,000,000}{\$39.60}$$

        = 606,061 monthly treatments (rounded up)

    (b) USP = $66
        UVC = $16.80
        UCM = $49.20
        FC   = $24,000,000

$$Q = \frac{FC}{UCM} = \frac{\$24,000,000}{\$49.20}$$

        = 487,805 monthly treatments (rounded up)

2. Diba believes that $9.60 per monthly visit should be included in the variable costs per visit. His argument is that a product like "Vital Hair" has a positive probability of attracting product litigation. By excluding any allowance for the possible event, the assumption is that it will be zero.

    Diba faces an integrity issue. His report to the Executive Committee will understate his expected cost estimates when he takes Kelly's advice. His report likely will be seen by those not attending the Executive Committee meeting. Moreover, even those attending the meeting may not remember any verbal comments Diba makes at the meeting.

    One possibility Diba should have explored is reporting the $16.80 per treatment variable cost in the breakeven computations as well as including qualifications in the report about possible product litigation costs.

3. Diba likely has been placed in a compromised situation. He may feel Kelly deliberately set him up to avoid the $9.60 amount being reported to the Executive Committee. At a minimum, he should directly confront Kelly with his concerns. If she is unresponsive, he faces a very tough dilemma. His options are:

(a) Stay in his current position and be more determined next time to have his concerns registered.

(b) Report his concerns to Kelly's immediate superior.

(c) Resign.

If he selects (a), it would be useful to show Kelly the <u>Code of Professional Ethics</u> and stress how her behaviour has put him in a difficult ethical situation.

3-58 (35 min.) Deciding where to produce.

1. The annual breakeven point in units at the Peoria plant is 73,500 units and at the Moline plant is 47,200 units, calculated as follows.

Unit contribution calculation:

	Peoria	**Moline**
Selling price	$180.00	$180.00
Less variable costs:		
Manufacturing	86.40	105.60
Commissions	9.00	9.00
Marketing and distribution	7.80	7.80
Contribution margin per unit	$ 76.80	$ 57.60

Fixed costs calculation:

Total fixed costs = (Fixed manufacturing costs per unit + Fixed marketing and distribution costs per unit) × Production rate per day × Normal working days

Peoria = ($36.00 + $22.80) × 400 × 240 = $5,644,800

Moline = ($18.00 + $17.40) × 320 × 240 = $2,718,720

Breakeven calculation:

Breakeven units = Fixed costs ÷ Contribution margin per unit

Peoria = $5,644,800 ÷ $76.80 = 73,500 units

Moline = $2,718,720 ÷ $57.60 = 47,200 units

2. The operating income that would result from the division production manager's plan to produce 96,000 units at each plant is $4,354,560. The normal capacity at the Peoria plant is 96,000 units (400 × 240); however, the normal capacity at the Moline plant is 76,800 units (320 × 240). Therefore, 19,200 units (96,000 − 76,800) will be manufactured at Moline at a reduced contribution of $48.00 per unit ($57.60 − $9.60).

Contribution margin per plant:

Peoria, 96,000 × $76.80	$ 7,372,800
Moline, 76,800[1] × $57.60	4,423,680
Moline, 19,200[2] × $48.00	921,600
Total contribution margin	12,718,080
Less total fixed costs, $5,644,800 + $2,718,720	8,363,520
Operating income	$ 4,354,560

3. The optimal production plan is to produce 120,000 units at the Peoria plant and 72,000 units at the Moline plant. The full capacity of the Peoria plant, 120,000 units (400 units × 300 days), should be utilized as the contribution from these units is higher at all levels of production than the contribution from units produced at the Moline plant.

Contribution margin per plant:

Peoria, 96,000 × $76.80	$ 7,372,800
Peoria, 24,000[3] × $73.20[4]	1,756,800
Moline, 72,000 × $57.60	4,147,200
Total contribution margin	13,276,800
Less total fixed costs	8,363,520
Operating income	$ 4,913,280

[1] $\dfrac{240}{300}$ × 96,000 units = 76,800 units

[2] $\dfrac{60}{300}$ × 96,000 units = 19,200 units

[3] $\dfrac{60 \text{ days}}{300 \text{ days}}$ × 120,000 units = 24,000 units at lower CM. (120,000 − 24,000 = 96,000 units at higher CM).

[4] Peoria VC go up $3.60 per unit, for >240 working days. Therefore CM goes down 3.60 = (76.80 − 3.60 = 73.20).

CHAPTER 4
JOB COSTING

4-2 In a *job-costing system* costs are assigned to a distinct unit, batch, or a lot of. a product or service. In a *process-costing system*, the cost of a product or service is obtained by using broad averages to assign costs to masses of similar units.

4-4 The seven steps in job costing are (1) identify the chosen cost object or job, (2) identify the direct costs of the job, (3) select the cost-allocation base(s) to use for allocating indirect costs to the job, (4) identify the indirect costs associated with each cost-allocation base, (5) compute the rate per unit of each cost-allocation base used to allocate indirect costs to the job, (6) compute the indirect costs allocated to the job, and (7) compute the total cost of the job by adding all direct and indirect costs assigned to it.

4-6 Three major source documents used in job-costing systems are (1) job cost record or job cost sheet, a document that records and accumulates all costs assigned to a specific job, (2) materials requisition record, a document used to charge job cost records and departments for the cost of direct materials used on a specific job, and (3) labour-time record, a document used to charge job cost records and departments for labour time used on a specific job.

4-8 Two reasons for using six-month or annual budget periods are:
  a. The numerator reason—the longer the time period, the lesser the influence of seasonal patterns, and
  b. The denominator reason—the longer the time period, the lesser the effect of variations in output levels on the allocation of fixed costs.

4-10 An accounting firm can use job cost information (a) to determine the profitability of individual jobs, (b) to assist on bidding on future jobs, and (c) to evaluate professionals who are in charge of managing individual jobs.

4-12 Debit entries to Work-in-Process Control represent increases in work in process. Example of debit entries are: (a) direct materials used (credit to Materials Control), (b) direct manufacturing labour billed to job (credit to Wages Payable Control), and (c) manufacturing overhead allocated to job (credit Manufacturing Overhead Allocated).

4-14 A service company might use budgeted costs rather than actual costs to compute direct labour rates because it may be difficult to trace some costs to jobs as they are completed.

4-16 (20 min.) Actual costing, normal costing, manufacturing overhead.

1. $$\text{Budgeted manufacturing overhead rate} = \frac{\text{Budgeted manufacturing overhead costs}}{\text{Budgeted direct manufacturing labour costs}}$$

$$= \frac{\$2,100,000}{\$1,200,000} = 1.75 \text{ or } 175\%$$

$$\text{Actual manufacturing overhead rate} = \frac{\text{Actual manufacturing overhead costs}}{\text{Actual direct manufacturing labour costs}}$$

$$= \frac{\$2,234,400}{\$1,176,000} = 1.9 \text{ or } 190\%$$

2. Costs of Job 626 under actual and normal costing follow:

	a. **Actual Costing**	b. **Normal Costing**
Direct materials	$ 48,000	$ 48,000
Direct manufacturing labour costs	36,000	36,000
Manufacturing overhead costs		
$36,000 × 1.75; 1.90	68,400	63,000
Total manufacturing costs of Job 626	$152,400	$147,000

3. $$\text{Total manufacturing overhead allocated under normal costing} = \text{Actual manufacturing labour costs} \times \text{Budgeted overhead rate}$$

$$= \$1,176,000 \times 1.75 = \$2,058,000$$

$$\text{Underallocated manufacturing overhead} = \text{Actual manufacturing overhead costs} - \text{Manufacturing overhead allocated}$$

$$= \$2,234,400 - \$2,058,000 = \$176,400^a$$

[a] $176,400 ÷ (1.9% − 1.75%) = $1,176,000: direct manufacturing labour costs

There is no under- or overallocated overhead under actual costing because overhead is allocated under actual costing by multiplying actual manufacturing labour costs and the actual manufacturing overhead rate. This, of course, equals the actual manufacturing overhead costs. All actual overhead costs are allocated to products. Hence, there is no under- or overallocated overhead.

4. Actual costing reflects the actual results incurred, while normal costing reflects expectations of the amount the overhead should be. Normal costing can be done in advance and thus can be used in pricing, planning, and cost management decisions.

4-18 (20-30 min.) Job costing, accounting for manufacturing overhead, budgeted rates.

1. An overview of the product costing system is:

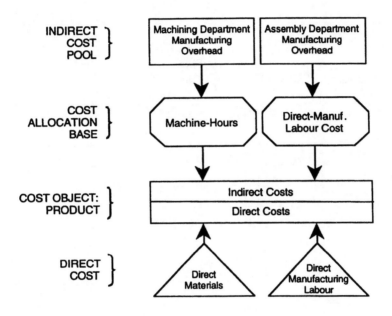

Budgeted manufacturing overhead divided by allocation base:

Machining overhead: $\dfrac{\$2,160,000}{60,000}$ = $36 per machine-hour

Assembly overhead: $\dfrac{\$4,320,000}{2,400,000}$ = 180% of direct manuf. labour costs

2.

Machining overhead, 2,400 hours × $36	$86,400
Assembly overhead, 180% of $18,000	32,400
Total manufacturing overhead allocated to Job 494	$118,800

3.

	Machining	Assembly
Actual manufacturing overhead	$2,520,000	$4,440,000
Manufacturing overhead allocated,		
66,000 × $36	2,376,000	
180% of $2,640,000		4,752,000
Underallocated (Overallocated)	$ 144,000	$(312,000)

4-20 (20-30 min.) Computing indirect-cost rates, job costing.

1. a.

	Budgeted Fixed Indirect Costs	Budgeted Professional Labour Hours	Budgeted Fixed Indirect Cost Rate per Hour	Budgeted Variable Indirect Cost Rate per Hour	Budgeted Total Indirect Cost Rate per Hour
Jan.-March	$ 60,000	24,000	$ 2.50	$12	$14.50
April-June	60,000	12,000	5.00	12	17.00
July-Sept.	60,000	4,800	12.50	12	24.50
Oct.-Dec.	60,000	7,200	8.33	12	20.33
b.	$240,000	48,000	$ 5.00	$12	$17.00

2. a. All four jobs use 10 hours of professional labour time. The only difference in job costing is the indirect cost rate. The quarterly-based indirect job cost rates are:

Hansen:	(10 × $14.50)			=	$145.00
Kai:	(6 × $14.50)	+ (4 × $17.00)		=	$155.00
Patera:	(4 × $17.00)	+ (6 × $24.50)		=	$215.00
Stevens:	(5 × $14.50)	+ (2 × $24.50) + (3 × $20.33)		=	$182.49

	Hansen	Kai	Patera	Stevens
Revenues, $78 × 10	$780	$780	$780	$780.00
Direct costs, $36 × 10	360	360	360	360.00
Indirect costs	145	155	215	182.49
Total costs	505	515	575	542.49
Operating income	$275	$265	$205	$237.51

b. Using annual-based indirect job cost rates, all four customers will have the same operating income:

Revenues, $78 × 10	$780
Direct costs, $36 × 10	360
Indirect costs, $17 × 10	170
Total costs	530
Operating income	$250

3. All four jobs use 10 hours of professional labour time. Using the quarterly-based indirect cost rates, there are four different operating incomes as the work done on them is completed in different quarters. In contrast, using the annual indirect cost rate, all four jobs have the same operating income. All these different operating income figures for jobs with the same number of professional labour-hours are due to the allocation of fixed indirect costs.

An overview of the Tax Assist job costing system is:

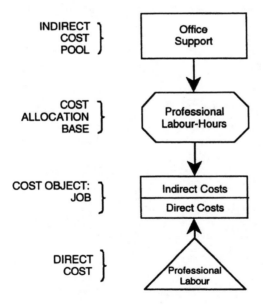

4-22 (20 min.) Job costing, journal entries, and source documents (continuation of 4-21).

The analysis of source documents and subsidiary ledgers follows:

1. a. Approved invoice
   b. dr. Materials record, "received" column

2. a. Materials requisition record
   b. dr. Job cost records
      cr. Materials record, "issued" column

3. a. Materials requisition record
   b. dr. Department overhead cost records, appropriate column
      cr. Materials record, "issued" column

4. a. Summary of time records or daily time analysis. This summary is sometimes called a *labour cost distribution summary*.
   b. dr. Job cost records
      dr. Department overhead cost records, appropriate columns for various classes of indirect labour

5. a. Special authorization from the responsible accounting officer
   b. dr. Department overhead cost records, appropriate columns

6. a. Various approved invoices and special authorizations
   b. dr. Department overhead cost records, appropriate columns

7. a. Use of an authorized budgeted manufacturing overhead rate
   b. dr. Job cost record

8. a. Completed job cost records
   b. dr. Finished goods records
      cr. Job cost record

9. a. Approved sales invoice
   b. dr. Customers' accounts (or Cash)
      cr. Sales ledger, if any

10. a. Costed sales invoice
    b. cr. Finished goods records

11. a. Special authorization from the responsible accounting officer
    b. Subsidiary records are generally not used for these entries

4-24 (10-15 min.) Accounting for manufacturing overhead.

1. Budgeted manufacturing overhead rate $= \dfrac{\$8,400,000}{200,000}$

   $= \$42$ per machine-hour

2. Work-in-Process Control   8,190,000
       Manufacturing Overhead Allocated   8,190,000
       (195,000 machine-hours $\times$ \$42 = \$8,190,000)

3. $\$8,190,000 - \$8,160,000 = \$30,000$ overallocated, an insignificant amount.

   Manufacturing Overhead Allocated   8,190,000
       Manufacturing Overhead Control   8,160,000
       Cost of Goods Sold   30,000

4-26 (10 min.) Job order costing, process costing.

a. Job costing
b. Process costing
c. Job costing
d. Process costing
e. Job costing
f. Process costing
g. Job costing
h. Job costing (but some process costing)
i. Process costing
j. Process costing
k. Job costing
l. Job costing
m. Process costing
n. Job costing
o. Job costing
p. Job costing
q. Job costing
r. Process costing
s. Job costing
t. Process costing
u. Job costing

4-28 (20-30 min.) Job costing, unit cost, ending work in process.

1. Cost of Job M1:
   Direct materials   \$ 90,000
   Direct manufacturing labour   324,000
   Manufacturing overhead allocated   216,000*
   Total cost $\underline{\$630,000}$

   *Budgeted rate \$36 $\times$ 6,000 direct manufacturing labour-hours = \$216,000

2. Per-unit cost $= \dfrac{\text{Total cost of the job}}{\text{Number of units in the job}}$

$= \dfrac{\$630,000}{15,000 \text{ units}} = \$42 \text{ per unit}$

3. Finished Goods Control   630,000
       Work in Process Control   630,000

4. The work in process consists of Job M2 only:

Direct materials	$ 60,000
Direct manufacturing labour	252,000
Manufacturing overhead allocated	180,000†
Work in process May 31	$492,000

†Budgeted rate of $36 × 5,000 direct manufacturing labour-hours = $180,000

4-30 (20-30 min.) Job costing; actual, normal, and variation of normal costing.

1.

Actual direct cost rate $= \$132$ per professional labour-hour

Actual indirect cost rate $= \dfrac{\$2,923,200}{42,000 \text{ hours}} = \$69.60$ per professional labour-hour

Budgeted direct cost rate $= \dfrac{\$4,800,000}{40,000 \text{ hours}} = \$120$ per professional labour-hour

Budgeted indirect cost rate $= \dfrac{\$3,120,000}{40,000 \text{ hours}} = \$78$ per professional labour-hour

	(a) Actual Costing	(b) Normal Costing	(c) Variation of Normal Costing
Direct Cost Rate	$132 (Actual rate)	$132 (Actual rate)	$120 (Budgeted rate)
Indirect Cost Rate	$69.60 (Actual rate)	$78 (Budgeted rate)	$78 (Budgeted rate)

2.

	(a) Actual Costing	(b) Normal Costing	(c) Variation of Normal Costing
Direct Costs Indirect Costs Total Job Costs	$132 × 1,720 = $227,040 69.60 × 1,720= 119,712 $346,752	$132 × 1,720 = $227,040 78 × 1,720 = 134,160 $361,200	$120 × 1,720 = $206,400 78 × 1,720 = 134,160 $340,560

The differences in job costs arise from the different uses of actual versus budgeted rates. The actual costing figure of $346,752 is less than the normal costing figure of $361,200 because the actual indirect cost rate ($69.60) is less than the budgeted indirect cost rate ($78). The normal costing figure of $361,200 exceeds the variation of normal costing figure of $340,560 because the actual direct cost rate ($132) exceeds the budgeted direct cost rate ($120).

All three job-costing systems use the actual professional labour-hours of 1,720. The budgeted 1,500 hours is not used in the job-costing system. However, it may have been used by Vista Group in budgeting on the Carefree Years job. If Vista quoted a fixed price, it may well have lost money on this job.

An overview of the Vista Group job costing system is:

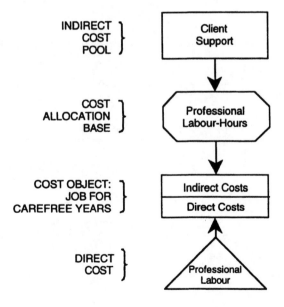

4-32 (15-20 min.) **Job costing, law firm.**

1.

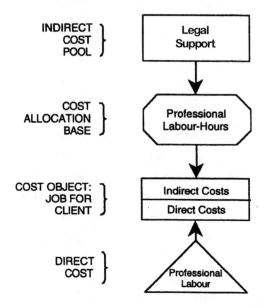

2.

$$\text{Budgeted professional labour-hour direct-cost rate} = \frac{\text{Budgeted total direct labour compensation}}{\text{Budgeted total direct labour-hours}}$$

$$= \frac{\$124{,}800}{1{,}600 \text{ hours}}$$

$$= \$78 \text{ per professional labour-hour}$$

3.

$$\text{Budgeted indirect-cost rate} = \frac{\text{Budgeted total costs in the indirect-cost pool}}{\text{Budgeted total professional labour-hours}}$$

$$= \frac{\$2{,}640{,}000}{1{,}600 \text{ hours} \times 25}$$

$$= \frac{\$2{,}640{,}000}{40{,}000 \text{ hours}}$$

$$= \$66 \text{ per professional labour-hour}$$

4.

	Richardson	Punch
Direct costs:		
Professional labour, $78 × 100; 150	$7,800	$11,700
Indirect costs:		
Legal support, $66 × 100; 150	6,600	9,900
	$14,400	$21,600

4-34 (20 min.) Normal costing, overhead allocation, working backwards.

1.

$$\text{Manufacturing overhead allocated} = \$4,320,000$$

Manufacturing overhead is allocated at 200% of direct manufacturing labour costs.

$$\text{Manufacturing overhead allocated} = 200\% \times \text{Direct manufacturing labour costs}$$

$$\text{That is, } \$4,320,000 = 2 \times \text{Direct manufacturing labour costs}$$

$$\text{Hence, Direct manufacturing labour costs} = \frac{\$4,320,000}{2} = \$2,160,000$$

2.

$$\text{Total manufacturing costs} = \text{Direct materials costs} + \text{Direct manufacturing labour costs} + \text{Manufacturing overhead allocated}$$

$$\text{That is, } \$9,600,000 = \text{Direct materials costs} + \$2,160,000 + \$4,320,000$$

Hence, Direct materials costs = \$3,120,000

3.   Note the structure of entries made to the Work-in-Process T-account

Work in Process			
Beginning balance, 1-1-2007	xxx	Costs of goods manufactured	
Manufacturing costs	xxx	(transferred to finished goods)	xxx
Ending balance, 12-31-2007	xxx		

It follows that

$$\text{Work in Process on 1-1-2007} + \text{Total manufacturing costs} = \text{Cost of goods manufactured} + \text{Work in Process on 12-31-2007}$$

Hence,

$$\text{Work in Process on 12-31-2007} = \text{Work in Process on 1-1-2007} + \text{Total manufacturing costs} - \text{Cost of goods manufactured}$$

$$= \$384,000 + \$9,600,000 - \$9,504,000$$

$$= \$480,000$$

4-36 (40 min.) Disposition of overhead over/underallocation, two indirect-cost pools.

1.

$$\text{Budgeted manufacturing overhead cost rate for the Machining Department} = \frac{\text{Budgeted manufacturing overhead costs in the Machining Department}}{\text{Budgeted machine-hours in the Machining Department}}$$

$$= \frac{\$7,200,000}{100,000} = \$72 \text{ per machine-hour}$$

$$\text{Budgeted manufacturing overhead cost rate for the Assembly Department} = \frac{\text{Budgeted manufacturing overhead costs in the Assembly Department}}{\text{Budgeted direct manufacturing labour-hours in the Assembly Department}}$$

$$= \frac{\$6,000,000}{125,000} = \$48 \text{ per direct manufacturing labour-hour}$$

2. **Machining Department**

Total actual machine-hours	=	67,500 + 4,500 + 18,000 = 90,000 machine-hours
Manufacturing overhead allocated	=	90,000 × $72 = $6,480,000
Underallocated manufacturing overhead costs	=	Actual manufacturing overhead costs − Manufacturing overhead allocated
	=	$7,440,000 − $6,480,000 = $960,000

Assembly Department

Total actual direct manufacturing labour-hours	=	90,000 + 4,800 + 25,200 = 120,000 direct manufacturing labour-hours
Manufacturing overhead allocated	=	120,000 × $48 = $5,760,000
Overallocated manufacturing overhead costs	=	Manufacturing overhead allocated − Actual manufacturing overhead costs
	=	$5,760,000 − $5,640,000 = $120,000

2. a. Write-off to Cost of Goods Sold leads to

   (i) higher Cost of Goods Sold of $960,000 as a result of underallocation of manufacturing overhead in the Machining Department

   (ii) lower Cost of Goods Sold of $120,000 as a result of overallocation of manufacturing overhead in the Assembly Department. Hence,

Cost of Goods Sold = $19,200,000 + $960,000 – $120,000 = $20,040,000

b. Proration based on ending balances (before proration) in Work in Process, Finished Goods, and Cost of Goods Sold.

Account balances in each account after proration follows:

Account (1)	Account Balance (2)		Proration of $960,000 Underallocated Overhead in Machining Dept. (3)	Proration of $(120,000) Overallocated Overhead in Assembly Dept. (4)	Account Balance (after Proration) (5)=(2)+(3)+(4)
Work in Process	$3,900,000	(16.25%)	0.1625 × $960,000 = $156,000	0.1625 × ($120,000) = ($ 19,500)	$ 4,036,500
Finished Goods	900,000	(3.75%)	0.0375 × $960,000 = 36,000	0.0375 × ($120,000) = ($4,500)	931,500
Cost of Goods Sold	19,200,000	(80.00%)	0.80 × $960,000 = 768,000	0.80 × ($120,000) = ($ 96,000)	19,872,000
	$24,000,000	(100.00%)	$960,000	$(120,000)	$24,840,000

c. Proration based on the overhead allocated (before proration) in the ending balances of Cost of Goods Sold, Finished Goods, and Work in Process for each Department follows.

Machining Department

Account (1)	Overhead Costs Allocated to Each Account in Machining Department Using Budgeted Machine-Hour Rate × Actual Machine-Hours (2)			Proration of $960,000 Underallocated Overhead (3)	
Work in process	$72 × 18,000 =	$1,296,000	(20%)	0.20 × $960,000 =	$192,000
Finished goods	$72 × 4,500 =	324,000	(5%)	0.05 × $960,000 =	48,000
Cost of goods sold	$72 × 67,500 =	4,860,000	(75%)	0.75 × $960,000 =	720,000
		$6,480,000	(100%)		$960,000

Assembly Department

Account (1)	Overhead Costs Allocated to Each Account in Assembly Department Using Budgeted Direct Manuf. Labour-Hour Rate × Actual Direct Manuf. Labour-Hours (2)			Proration of ($120,000) Overallocated Assembly Overhead (3)	
Work in process	$48 × 25,200 =	$1,209,600	(21%)	0.21 × ($120,000) =	$ (25,200)
Finished goods	$48 × 4,800 =	230,400	(4%)	0.04 × ($120,000) =	(4,800)
Cost of goods sold	$48 × 90,000 =	4,320,000	(75%)	0.75 × ($120,000) =	(90,000)

$5,760,000 (100%) $(120,000)

Account balances in each account after proration of underallocated Machining Department costs and overallocated Assembly Department costs follow.

Account (1)	Account Balance (before) Proration) (2)	Prorated $960,000 of Underallocated Machining Department Overhead (calculated earlier) (3)	Prorated ($120,000) of Overallocated Assembly Department Overhead (calculated earlier) (4)	Account Balance (after Proration) (5)=(2)+(3)+(4)
Work in process	$3,900,000	$192,000	$ (25,200)	$ 4,066,800
Finished goods	900,000	48,000	(4,800)	943,200
Cost of goods sold	19,200,000	720,000	(90,000)	19,830,000
	$24,000,000	$960,000	$(120,000)	$24,840,000

3. If the purpose is to report the most accurate inventory and cost of goods sold figures, the preferred method is to prorate based on the manufacturing overhead allocated amount in the inventory and cost of goods sold accounts (as in requirement 2c). Note, however, that prorating based on ending balances in Work in Process, Finished Goods, and Cost of Goods Sold (as in requirement 2b) yields a close approximation to the more accurate proration in requirement 2c. Also note that the write-off to Cost of Goods Sold method (as in requirement 2a) results in account balances in Work in Process, Finished Goods, and Cost of Goods Sold that are not very different from the most accurate method. Furthermore, the Write Off to Cost of Goods Sold method is simpler than the other methods. Depending on the objectives of the disposal of over/underallocation, a manager may prefer any one of the methods over the other two.

4-38 (20 min.) Job costing, contracting, ethics.

1. Direct manufacturing costs:

Direct materials	$30,000	
Direct manufacturing labour	7,200	$37,200
Indirect manufacturing costs,		
150% × $7,200		10,800
Total manufacturing costs		$48,000

Aerospace bills the Armed Forces $62,400 ($48,000 × 130%) for 100 X7 seats or $624 ($62,400 ÷ 100) per X7 seat.

2. Direct manufacturing costs:

Direct materials	$30,000	
Direct manufacturing labour[a]	6,000	$36,000
Indirect manufacturing costs,		
150% × $6,000		9,000
Total manufacturing costs		$45,000

[a]$7,200 − $480 ($30 × 16) setup − $720 ($60 × 12) design

Aerospace should have billed the Armed Forces $58,500 ($45,000 × 130%) for 100 X7 seats or $585 ($58,500 ÷ 100) per X7 seat.

3. The problems the letter highlights (assuming it is correct) include:

a. Costs included that should be excluded (design costs),
b. Costs double-counted (setup included both as a direct cost and in an indirect cost pool), and
c. Possible conflict of interest in Aerospace Comfort purchasing materials from a family-related company.

Steps the Armed Forces could undertake include:

(i) Use only contractors with a reputation for ethical behaviour as well as quality products or services.
(ii) Issue guidelines detailing acceptable and unacceptable billing practices by contractors. For example, prohibit the use of double-counting cost allocation methods by contractors.
(iii) Issue guidelines detailing acceptable and unacceptable procurement practices by contractors. For example, if a contractor purchases from a family-related company, require that the contractor obtain quotes from at least two other bidders.
(iv) Employ auditors who aggressively monitor the bills submitted by contractors.

4-40 (35 min.) **General ledger relationships, under- and overallocation.**

A summary of the T-accounts for Needham Company before adjusting for under- or overallocation of overhead follows.

Direct Materials Control			
1-1-2007	36,000	Material used	
Purchases	480,000	for manufac-	
		turing	456,000
12-31-2007	60,000		

Work-in-Process Control			
1-1-2007	24,000	Transferred to	
Direct materials	456,000	finished goods	1,128,000
Direct manuf. labour	432,000		
Manuf. overhead allocated	576,000		
12-31-2007	360,000		

Finished Goods Control			
1-1-2007	12,000	Cost of goods sold	1,080,000
Transferred in from WIP	1,128,000		
12-31-2007	60,000		

Cost of Goods Sold		
Finished goods sold	1,080,000	

Manufacturing Overhead Control	
Manufacturing overhead costs	648,000

Manufacturing Overhead Allocated	
Manufacturing overhead allocated to work in process	576,000

1. From the credit entry to Direct Materials T-account,
   Direct materials issued to manufacturing = $456,000.

2. Direct manufacturing labour-hours $= \dfrac{\text{Direct manufacturing labour costs}}{\text{Direct manufacturing wage rate per hour}}$

$= \dfrac{\$432{,}000}{\$18 \text{ per hour}} = 24{,}000 \text{ hours}$

$$\text{Manufacturing overhead allocated} = \text{Direct manufacturing labour-hours} \times \text{Manufacturing overhead rate}$$

$$= 24{,}000 \text{ hours} \times \$24 = \$576{,}000$$

3. From the debit entry to Finished Goods T-account,
    Cost of jobs completed and transferred from WIP = $1,128,000

4. From Work-in-Process T-account,

    $$\text{Work-in-process inventory on 12/31/2007} = \$24{,}000 + \$456{,}000 + \$432{,}000 + \$576{,}000 - \$1{,}128{,}000$$

    $$= \$360{,}000$$

5. From the credit entry to Finished Goods Control T-account,

    Cost of goods sold (before proration) = $1,080,000

6. $$\text{Manufacturing overhead underallocated} = \text{Debits to Manufacturing Overhead Control} - \text{Credit to Manufacturing Overhead Allocated}$$

    $$= \$648{,}000 - \$576{,}000$$
    $$= \$72{,}000 \text{ underallocated}$$

7. a. Write-off to Cost of Goods Sold will increase (debit) Cost of Goods Sold by $72,000. Hence, Cost of Goods Sold = $1,080,000 + $72,000 = $1,152,000.

    b. Proration based on ending balances (before proration) in Work in Process, Finished Goods, and Cost of Goods Sold.

Account balances in each account after proration follows.

Account (1)	Account Balance (2)	Proration of $72,000 Underallocated Manufacturing Overhead (3)	Account Balance (after Proration (4)=(2)+(3)
Work in Process	$360,000 (24%)	0.24 × $72,000 = $17,280	$ 377,280
Finished Goods	60,000 (4%)	0.04 × $72,000 = 2,880	62,880
Cost of Goods Sold	1,080,000 (72%)	0.72 × $72,000 = 51,840	1,131,840
Total	$1,500,000 (100%)	$72,000	$1,572,000

8. Needham's operating income under the write-off to Cost of Goods Sold and Proration based on ending balances (before proration) follows:

	Write-off to Cost of Goods Sold	Proration Based on Ending Balances
Revenues	$1,308,000	$1,308,000
Cost of goods sold	1,152,000	1,131,840
Gross margin	156,000	176,160
Marketing and distribution costs	168,000	168,000
Operating income/(loss)	$ (12,000)	$ 8,160

9. If the purpose is to report the most accurate inventory and cost of goods sold figures, the preferred method is to prorate based on the manufacturing overhead allocated component in the Work in Process, Finished Goods, and Cost of Goods Sold accounts. Proration based on the balances in Work in Process, Finished Goods, and Cost of Goods Sold will equal the proration based on the manufacturing overhead allocated component if the proportions of direct costs to manufacturing overhead costs are constant in the Work in Process, Finished Goods, and Cost of Goods Sold accounts. Even if this is not the case, the proration based on Work in Process, Finished Goods, and Cost of Goods Sold balances will better approximate the results if actual cost rates had been used than the write-off to Cost of Goods Sold method.

Another consideration in Needham's decision about how to dispose of underallocated manufacturing overhead is the effects on operating income. The write-off to Cost of Goods Sold will lead to an operating loss. Proration based on the balances in Work in Process, Finished Goods, and Cost of Goods Sold will help Needham avoid the loss and show an operating income.

The main merit of the write-off to cost of goods sold method is its simplicity. However, accuracy and the effect on operating income favour the preferred and recommended proration approach.

CHAPTER 5
ACTIVITY-BASED COSTING AND ACTIVITY-BASED MANAGEMENT

5-2 Overcosting may result in competitors entering a market and taking market share for products that a company erroneously believes are low-margin or even unprofitable.

Undercosting may result in companies selling products on which they are in fact losing money, when they erroneously believe them to be profitable.

5-4 An activity-based approach focuses on activities as the fundamental cost objects. It uses the cost of these activities as the basis for assigning costs to other cost objects such as products, services, or customers.

5-6 No. The purpose for computing a product cost is to determine whether unit costs should be based on total manufacturing costs in all or only some levels of the cost hierarchy. Inventory valuation for financial reporting requires *total* or only some manufacturing costs (all levels of the hierarchy) to be expressed on a per output-unit basis. In contrast, for cost management purposes, the cost hierarchy need not be unitized, as units of output are not the cost driver at each level in the hierarchy.

5-8 Four decisions for which ABC information is useful are:

(1) pricing and product mix decisions,
(2) cost reduction and process improvement decisions,
(3) design decisions, and
(4) planning and managing activities

5-10 "Tell-tale" signs that indicate when ABC systems are likely to provide the most benefits are:

1. Significant amounts of indirect costs are allocated using only one or two cost pools.
2. All or most indirect costs are identified as output-unit-level costs (i.e., few indirect costs are described as batch-level, product-sustaining, or facility-sustaining costs).
3. Products make diverse demands on resources because of differences in volume, process steps, batch size, or complexity.
4. Products that a company is well suited to make and sell show small profits, whereas products that a company is less suited to produce and sell show large profits.
5. Complex products appear to be very profitable, and simple products appear to be losing money.
6. Operations staff have significant disagreements with the accounting staff about the costs of manufacturing and marketing products and services.

5-12 No. ABC systems apply equally well to service companies such as banks, railroads, hospitals, and accounting firms, and to merchandising companies such as retailers and distributors.

5-14 Increasing the number of indirect-cost pools does NOT guarantee increased accuracy of product, service, or customer costs. If the existing cost pool is already homogeneous, increasing the number of cost pools will not increase accuracy. If the existing cost pool is not homogeneous, accuracy will increase only if the increased cost pools themselves increase in homogeneity vis-a-vis the single cost pool.

5-16 (30 min.) Cost smoothing or peanut butter costing, cross-subsidization.

1. Cost smoothing or peanut butter costing is a costing approach that uniformly assigns the cost of resources to customers when the individual customers use those resources in a nonuniform way. The reunion dinner averages the costs across all five people. These five people differ sizably in what they consume.

2.

Diner	Entree	Dessert	Drinks	Total
Armstrong	$32	$10	$29	$71
Gonzales	29	4	0	33
King	25	7	16	48
Poffo	37	7	14	58
Young	18	5	7	30
Total	$141	$33	$66	$240
Average	$28.20	$6.60	$13.20	$48

The average-cost pricing will result in each person paying $48.

	Amount Over- or Undercosted
Accurately costed person	
• King, $48 – $48	$ 0
Undercosted people	
• Armstrong, $48 – $71	$(23)
• Poffo, $48 – $58	$(10)
Overcosted people	
• Gonzales, $48 – $33	$ 15
• Young, $48 – $30	$ 18

Yes, Young's complaint is justified. He is "overcharged" $18. He could point out likely negative behaviours with this approach to costing. These include:

a. It can lead some people to order the most expensive items because others will "subsidize" their extravagance.

b. It can lead to friction when those who dine economically are forced to subsidize those who dine extravagantly. At the limit, some people may decide not to attend the reunion dinners.

Likely benefits of this approach are:
a. it is simple, and
b. it (purportedly) promotes a group atmosphere at the dinner.

3. Each one of the costs in the data is directly traceable to an individual diner. This makes it straightforward to compute the individual cost per diner. Examples where this is not possible include:
- A plate of hors d'oeuvres is shared by two or more diners
- A loaf of garlic bread is shared by two or more diners
- A bottle of mineral water or wine is shared by two or more diners

Each of these items cannot be directly traced to only one diner.

Some possible behaviours if each person pays for his or her own bill are:
a. Some people may reduce their ordering of more expensive items because they will not be subsidized by other diners.
b. May encourage some potential diners to attend who otherwise would have stayed away.
c. May encourage a person "trying to impress others with his or her success" to order the most expensive items.

5-18 (25 min.) Cost hierarchy, ABC, distribution.

1. Total distribution costs (given), $2,556,000

$$\text{Distribution cost per case under existing system} = \frac{\text{Total distribution costs}}{\text{Total cases of specialty and regular wine shipped}} = \frac{\$2,556,000}{200,000} = \$12.78 \text{ per case}$$

	Regular		Specialty	
	Total	Per Case (2) =	Total	Per Case (4) =
	(1)	(1) ÷ 120,000	(3)	(3) ÷ 80,000
Distribution costs $12.78 × 120,000; 40,000	$1,533,600	$12.78	$1,022,400	$12.78

2. a. Promotional activity—distributor-level costs because these costs do not depend on the number of cases shipped or the number of batches in which the cases are shipped. An amount of $9,600 is incurred for each of Niagara's distributors.

Order-handling costs—batch-level costs because these costs are incurred each time a customer places an order regardless of the number of cases ordered. These costs total $360 per order.

Freight distribution costs—Unit-level costs because a cost of $10 is incurred on freight for each case shipped.

b.

	Regular		Specialty	
	Total (1)	Per Case (2) = (1) ÷ 120,000	Total (3)	Per Case (4) = (3) ÷ 80,000
Distribution costs of freight				
$10 × 120,000 cases	$1,200,000	$10.00		
$10 × 80,000 cases			$800,000	$10.00
Ordering costs				
$360 × 10 orders/year × 10 distr.	36,000	0.30		
$360 × 20 orders/year × 30 distr.			216,000	2.70
Promotion costs				
$9,600 × 10 distributors	96,000	0.80		
$9,600 × 30 distributors			288,000	3.60
Total costs	$1,332,000	$11.10	$1,304,000	$16.30

3. The existing costing system uses cases shipped, a unit-level cost driver, as the only cost allocation base for distribution costs. As a result, the distribution cost per case is the same for specialty and regular wines ($12.78). In fact, specialty wines use distribution resources more intensively than regular wines: (a) Niagara spends $9,600 on promotional activity at each distributor independent of cases sold. Specialty wine distributors sell fewer cases a year than regular wine distributors. As a result the promotional cost per case of wine sold is higher for specialty wines than for regular wines. (b) Niagara's cost per order is $360 regardless of the number of cases sold in each order. Because specialty wine distributors order fewer cases per order, the ordering costs per case are higher for specialty wines than for regular wines.

The existing costing system undercosts distribution costs per case for specialty wines and overcosts distribution costs per case for regular wines.

Niagara's management can use the information from the ABC system to make better pricing and product mix decisions, to reduce costs by eliminating processes and activities that do not add value, to identify and evaluate new designs that reduce the activities demanded by various products, to reduce the costs of doing various activities, and to plan and manage activities.

5-20 (15 min.) Alternative allocation bases for a professional services firm.

1.

	Direct Professional Time			Support Services		Amount Billed to Client
Client (1)	Rate per Hour (2)	Number of Hours (3)	Total (4)=(2)×(3)	Rate per hour (5)	Total (6)=(4)×(5)	(7)=(4)+(6)
Winnipeg Dominion						
Wolfson	$600	15	$9,000	30%	$2,700	$ 11,700
Ku	144	3	432	30%	130	562
Anderson	96	22	2,112	30%	634	2,746
						$15,008
Tokyo Enterprises						
Wolfson	$600	2	$1,200	30%	$360	$1,560
Ku	144	8	1,152	30%	346	1,498
Anderson	96	30	2,880	30%	864	3,744
						$6,802

2.

	Direct Professional Time			Support Services		Amount Billed to Client
Client (1)	Rate per Hour (2)	Number of Hours (3)	Total (4)=(2)×(3)	Rate per hour (5)	Total (6)=(3)×(5)	(7)=(4)+(6)
Winnipeg Dominion						
Wolfson	$600	15	$9,000	$60	$900	$ 9,900
Ku	144	3	432	60	180	612
Anderson	96	22	2,112	60	1,320	3,432
						$13,944
Tokyo Enterprises						
Wolfson	$600	2	$1,200	$60	$120	$1,320
Ku	144	8	1,152	60	480	1,632
Anderson	96	30	2,880	60	1,800	4,680
						$7,632

	Requirement 1	Requirement 2
Winnipeg Dominion	$15,008	$13,944
Tokyo Enterprises	6,802	7,632
	$21,810	$21,576

Both clients use 40 hours of professional labour time. However, Winnipeg Dominion uses a higher proportion of Wolfson's time (15 hours), which is more costly. This attracts the highest support-services charge when allocated on the basis of direct professional labour costs.

3. Assume that the Wolfson Group uses a cause-and-effect criterion when choosing the allocation base for support services. You could use several pieces of evidence to determine whether professional labour costs or hours is the driver of support-service costs:

   a. *Interviews with personnel.* For example, staff in the major cost categories in support services could be interviewed to determine whether Wolfson requires more support per hour than, say, Anderson. The professional labour costs allocation base implies that an hour of Wolfson's time requires 6.25 ($600 ÷ $96) times more support-service dollars than does an hour of Anderson's time.

   b. *Analysis of tasks undertaken for selected clients.* For example, if computer-related costs are a sizable part of support costs, you could determine if there was a systematic relationship between the percentage involvement of professionals with high billing rates on cases and the computer resources consumed for those cases.

5-22 (30 min.) Department indirect-cost rates as activity rates (continuation of 5-21).

1.

	2007 Variable MOH Costs	Total Driver Units	Rate
Design-CAD	$ 46,800	390	$120 per design-hour
Engineering	35,520	370	$ 96 per engineering-hour
Production	288,000	4,000	$ 72 per machine hour

2.

	United Motors	Holden Motors	Leland Vehicle
Design			
$120 × 110; 200; 80	$13,200	$ 24,000	$ 9,600
Engineering			
$96 × 70; 60; 240	6,720	5,760	23,040
Production			
$72 × 120; 2,800; 1,080	8,640	201,600	77,760
Total	$28,560	$231,360	$110,400

3.

	United Motors	Holden Motors	Leland Vehicle
a. Department rate (Exercise 5-22)	$28,560	$231,360	$110,400
b. Plantwide rate (Exercise 5-21)	11,110	259,224	99,986
Ratio of (a) ÷ (b)	2.57	0.89	1.10

The three contracts differ sizably in the way they use the resources of the three departments. The percentage of total driver units in each department is:

	United Motors	Holden Motors	Leland Vehicle
Design	28%	51%	21%
Engineering	19	16	65
Production	3	70	27

The United Motors contract uses only 3% of total machine-hours in 2007, yet uses 28% of CAD design-hours and 19% of engineering hours. The result is that the plantwide rate, based on machine-hours, will greatly underestimate the cost of resources used on the United Motors contract. Hence, the 157% increase in indirect costs assigned to the United Motors contract when department rates are used.

In contrast, the Holden Motors contract uses less of design (51%) and engineering (16%) than of machine-hours (70%). Hence, department rates will report lower indirect costs than does a plantwide rate.

5-24 (15-20 min.) ABC, wholesale, customer profitability.

	Chain			
	1	2	3	4
Gross sales	$60,000	$36,000	$120,000	$84,000
Sale returns	12,000	6,000	8,400	7,200
Net sales	48,000	30,000	111,600	76,800
Cost of goods sold (80%)	38,400	24,000	89,280	61,440
Gross margin	9,600	6,000	22,320	15,360
Customer-related costs:				
Regular orders $24 × 40; 150; 50; 70	960	3,600	1,200	1,680
Rush orders $120 × 10; 50; 10; 30	1,200	6,000	1,200	3,600
Returned items $12 × 100; 26; 60; 40	1,200	312	720	480
Catalogues and customer support	1,200	1,200	1,200	1,200
Customer-related costs	4,560	11,112	4,320	6,960
Contribution (loss) margin	$ 5,040	$ (5,112)	$ 18,000	$ 8,400
Contribution (loss) margin as percentage of gross sales	8.4%	(14.2%)	15.0%	10.0%

The analysis indicates that customers' profitability (loss) contribution varies widely from (14.2%) to 15.0%. Immediate attention to Chain 2 is required since it is currently showing a loss contribution. The chain has a disproportionate number of both regular orders and rush orders. Villeagas should work with the management of Chain 2 to find ways to reduce the number of orders, while maintaining or increasing the sales volume. If this is not possible, Villeagas should consider dropping Chain 2, if it can save the customer-related costs.

Chain 1 has a disproportionate number of the items returned as well as total value of sale returns. The causes of these should be investigated so that the profitability contribution of Chain 1 can be improved.

5-26 (30 min.) ABC, product costing at banks, cross-subsidization.

1.

	Robinson	Skerrett	Farrel	Total
Revenues				
Spread revenue on annual basis				
(3% ×; $1,320, $960, $30,000)	$ 39.60	$ 28.80	$900.00	$ 968.40
Monthly fee charges				
($24 ×; 0, 12, 0)	0.00	288.00	0.00	288.00
Total revenues	39.60	316.80	900.00	1,256.40
Costs				
Deposit/withdrawal with teller				
$3.00 × 40; 50; 5	120.00	150.00	15.00	285.00
Deposit/withdrawal with ATM				
$0.96 × 10; 20; 16	9.60	19.20	15.36	44.16
Deposit/withdrawal prearranged monthly:				
$0.60 × 0; 12; 60	0	7.20	36.00	43.20
Bank cheques written				
$9.60 × 9; 3; 2	86.40	28.80	19.20	134.40
Foreign currency drafts				
$14.40 × 4; 1; 6	57.60	14.40	86.40	158.40
Inquiries				
$1.80 × 10; 18; 9	18.00	32.40	16.20	66.60
Total costs	291.60	252.00	188.16	731.76
Operating income	$(252.00)	$ 64.80	$711.84	$ 524.64

The assumption that the Robinson and Farrel accounts exceed $1,200 every month and the Skerrett account is less than $1,200 each month means the monthly charges apply only to Skerrett.

One student with a banking background noted that in this solution 100% of the spread is attributed to the "borrowing side of the bank." He noted that often the spread is divided between the "borrowing side" and the "lending side" of the bank.

2.   Cross-subsidization across individual Premier Accounts occurs when profits made on some accounts are offset by losses on other accounts. The aggregate profitability on the three customers is $524.64. The Farrel account is highly profitable ($711.84), while the Robinson account is sizably unprofitable.

FIB should be very concerned about the cross-subsidization. Competition likely would "understand" that high-balance low-activity type accounts (such as Farrel) are highly profitable. Offering free services to these customers is not likely to retain these accounts if other banks offer higher interest rates. Competition likely will reduce the interest rate spread FIB can earn on the high-balance low-activity accounts they are able to retain.

3.   Possible changes FIB could make are:

a.   Offer higher interest rates on high-balance accounts to increase FIB's competitiveness in attracting and retaining these accounts.

b.   Introduce charges for individual services. The ABC study reports the cost of each service. FIB has to decide if it wants to price each service at cost, below cost, or above cost. If it prices above cost, it may use advertising and other means to encourage additional use of those services by customers.

5-28 (20-30 min.) Activity-based job-costing system.

1.   Solution Exhibit 5-28 presents costing overviews of the previous job costing system and the refined activity-based job-costing system.

SOLUTION EXHIBIT 5-28
Job-Costing Systems for Calgary Company

2. Direct manufacturing costs:
    Direct materials $3,600.00
    Indirect manufacturing costs:
    Materials handling, $9.60 × 50 .... $ 480.00
    Machining, $81.60 × 12 .... 979.20
    Assembly, $90.00 × 15 .... 1,350.00
    Inspection, $124.80 × 4 .... 499.20   3,308.40
    Total manufacturing costs $6,908.40
    Total manufacturing costs = $6,908.40 × 50 = $345,420

3. A direct cost is a cost that is related to the particular cost object and that can be traced to it in an economically feasible way. Calgary may differ from its competitor in several ways.

    (a) Calgary uses a more automated production approach with the result that manufacturing labour provides support to the machines.
    (b) Calgary uses a less sophisticated information tracking system for manufacturing labour than its competitors.

    Manufacturing labour costs are included in the individual indirect manufacturing (overhead) cost pools.

4. The refined activity-based costing system can provide information to:

    (a) Product designers—The indirect cost rates in each of the four indirect cost areas can guide decisions about how much (say) machine-hours to use versus assembly-line-hours when designing packaging machines.
    (b) Manufacturing personnel—Decisions about productivity and cost management can focus on ways to reduce the indirect cost rates (such as decisions on how to make more efficient use of machines).
    (c) Marketing personnel—The ABC approach can help guide pricing decisions and negotiations with potential customers on ways to manufacture a lower-cost packaging machine.

5-30 (15-20 min.) Job costing with single direct-cost category, single indirect-cost pool, law firm.

1. Pricing decisions at Wigan Partners are heavily influenced by reported cost numbers. Suppose Wigan is bidding against Hull & Kingston for a client with a job similar to that of Widnes Coal. If the costing system overstates the costs of these jobs, Wigan may bid too high and fail to land the client. If the costing system understates the costs of these jobs, Wigan may bid low, land the client, and then lose money in handling the case.

2. Panel A of Solution Exhibit 5-30/5-31/5-32 presents an overview of the single direct/single indirect (SD/SI) costing approach.

SOLUTION EXHIBIT 5-30/5-31/5-32
Alternative Job (Case)-Costing Approaches for Wigan Partners

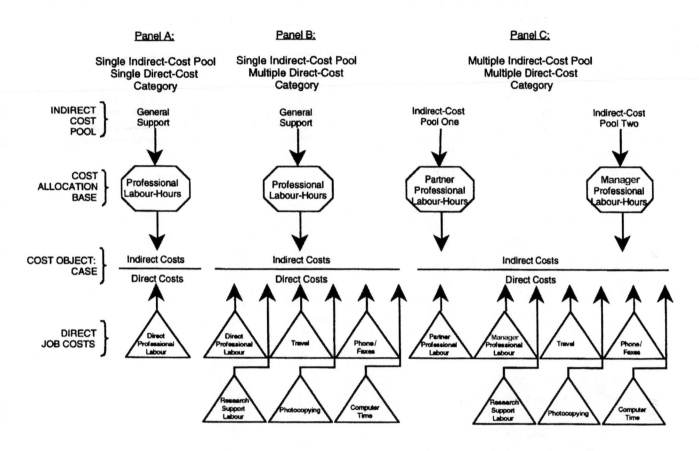

3.

	Widnes Coal	St. Helen's Glass	Total
Direct professional labour, $84 × 104; 96	$ 8,736	$ 8,064	$16,800
Indirect costs allocated, $126 × 104; 96	13,104	12,096	25,200
Total costs to be billed	$21,840	$20,160	$42,000

5-32 (30 min.) **Job costing with multiple direct-cost categories, multiple indirect-cost pools, law firm (continuation of 5-30 and 5-31).**

1. Panel C of the Solution Exhibit to 5/30/5-31/5-32 presents the costing overview for the multiple direct/multiple indirect (MD/MI) approach.

2.

	Widnes Coal	St. Helen's Glass	Total
Direct costs:			
Partner professional labour, $120 × 24; 56	$ 2,880	$ 6,720	$ 9,600
Manager professional labour, $60 × 80; 40	4,800	2,400	7,200
Research support labour	1,920	4,080	6,000
Computer time	600	1,560	2,160
Travel and allowances	720	5,280	6,000
Telephone/faxes	240	1,200	1,440
Photocopying	300	900	1,200
Total direct costs	$11,460	$22,140	$33,600
Indirect costs allocated:			
Indirect costs for partners, $69 × 24; 56	$ 1,656	$ 3,864	$ 5,520
Indirect costs for managers, $24 × 80; 40	1,920	960	2,880
Total indirect costs	3,576	4,824	8,400
Total costs to be billed	$15,036	$26,964	$42,000

	Widnes Coal	St. Helen's Glass	Total
Summary of data:			
SD/SI Approach			
Single direct cost/			
Single indirect cost pool	$21,840	$20,160	$42,000
MD/SI Approach			
Multiple direct costs/			
Single indirect cost pool	$16,884	$25,116	$42,000
MD/MI Approach			
Multiple direct costs/			
Multiple indirect cost pools	$15,036	$26,964	$42,000

The MD/MI approach has a higher percentage of direct costs to total costs than do the MD/SI and the SD/SI approaches:

	Direct Costs / Total Costs	Indirect Costs / Total Costs
SD/SI	40.0%	60.0%
MD/SI and MD/MI	80.0%	20.0%

The higher the percentage of costs directly traced to each case, the more accurate will be the product cost of each individual case.

The Widnes and St. Helen's cases differ in how they use "resource areas" of Wigan Partners:

	Widnes Coal	St. Helen's Glass
Partner professional labour	30.0%	70.0%
Manager professional labour	66.7	33.3
Research support labour	32.0	68.0
Computer time	27.8	72.2
Travel and allowances	12.0	88.0
Telephones/faxes	16.7	83.3
Photocopying	25.0	75.0

The Widnes Coal case makes relatively low use of the higher-cost partners but relatively higher use of the lower-cost managers than does St. Helen's Glass. The Widnes Coal case also makes relatively lower use of the support labour, computer time, travel, phone/faxes, and photocopying resource areas than does the St. Helen's Glass case.

The SD/SI approach imposes an averaging of the resources used in several (or all) of the seven "resource areas" recognized in MD/MI. The assumed use of resources in each of the seven "resource areas" by the SD/SI and MD/MI approaches are:

	SD/SI		MD/MI	
Helen's	Widnes	St. Helen's	Widnes	St.
Partners prof. labour	52.0%	48.0%	30.0%	70.0%
Associate prof. labour	52.0	48.0	66.7	33.3
Research support labour	52.0	48.0	32.0	68.0
Computer time	52.0	48.0	27.8	72.2
Travel and allowances	52.0	48.0	12.0	88.0
Telephones/faxes	52.0	48.0	16.7	83.3
Photocopying	52.0	48.0	25.0	75.0

3. The specific areas where the MD/MI approach can provide better information for decisions at Wigan Associates include:

a. *Pricing and product (case) mix decisions.* In a bidding situation using SD/SI data, Wigan may win legal cases on which it will subsequently lose money. It may also not win legal cases on which it would make money with a lower-priced bid. MD/MI signals to senior managers those legal cases that are the most profitable; these signals can be used in decisions where Wigan should increase its business development efforts.

From a strategic viewpoint, SD/SI exposes Wigan Partners to cherry-picking by competitors. Other law firms may focus exclusively on Widnes Coal-type cases and take sizable amounts of "profitable" business from Wigan Partners. MD/MI reduces the likelihood of Wigan Partners losing cases on which it would have made money.

b. *Client relationships.* MD/MI provides a better "road map" for clients to understand how costs are accumulated at Wigan Partners. Wigan can use this road map when meeting with clients to plan the work to be done on a case *before* it commences. Clients can negotiate ways to get a lower-cost case from Wigan, given the information in MD/MI—for example, (a) use a higher proportion of manager labour time and a lower proportion of partner time, and (b) use fax machines more and air travel less. If clients are informed in advance how costs will be accumulated, there is less likelihood of disputes about bills submitted to them *after* the work is done.

c. *Cost control. The* MD/MI approach better highlights the individual cost areas at Wigan Partners than does the SD/SI approach:

	MD/MI	SD/SI
Number of direct cost categories	7	1
Number of indirect cost categories	2	1
Total	9	2

MD/MI is more likely to promote better cost-control practices than SD/SI (as the nine cost categories in MD/MI may differ in terms of how to effectively manage costs).

5-34 (15 min.) Activity-based job costing.

1.   An overview of the product-costing system is:

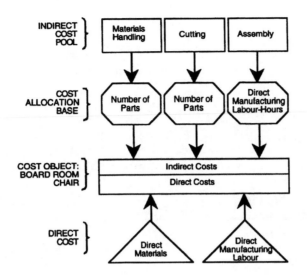

	Executive Chair	Chairperson Chair
Direct manufacturing costs:		
Direct materials	$720,000	$30,000
Direct manufacturing labour,		
$24 × 7,500; 500	180,000	12,000
Direct manufacturing costs	900,000	42,000
Indirect manufacturing costs:		
Materials handling,		
$0.30 × 100,000; 3,500	30,000	1,050
Cutting,		
$3.00 × 100,000; 3,500	300,000	10,500
Assembly,		
$30.00 × 7,500; 500	225,000	15,000
Indirect manufacturing costs	555,000	26,550
Total manufacturing costs	$1,455,000	$68,550

Unit Costs
   Executive chair: $1,455,000 ÷ 5,000 = $291.00
   Chairperson chair: $68,550 ÷ 100 = $685.50

2.

	Executive Chair	Chairperson Chair
Upstream costs	$ 72.00	$175.20
Manufacturing costs	291.00	685.50
Downstream costs	132.00	283.20
Total costs	$495.00	$1,143.90

5-36 (40 min.) ABC, health care.

1. a.

$$\text{Medical supplies indirect cost rate} = \frac{\text{Medical supplies cost}}{\text{Number of physicians (or physician years)}} = \frac{\$360,000}{6} = \$60,000 \text{ per physician}$$

$$\text{General overhead rate} = \frac{\text{General overhead rate}}{\text{Total physician, psychologist, and nurse labour cost}} = \frac{\$1,530,000}{\$2,550,000} = 60\%$$

b. The cost of each job (program) follows.

	Alcoholic Rehabilitation	Drug Rehabilitation	Children's Clinical	After-Care
Direct labour:				
Physicians at $120,000	—	$240,000	$ 480,000	—
Psychologists at $60,000	$360,000	240,000	—	$540,000
Nurses at $30,000	120,000	180,000	120,000	270,000
Total direct labour	480,000	660,000	600,000	810,000
Medical supplies:				
at $60,000 per physician year	—	120,000	240,000	—
General overhead:				
at 60% of direct labour	288,000	396,000	360,000	486,000
Total costs	$768,000	$1,176,000	$1,200,000	$1,296,000

The total cost of all programs is $4,440,000. The costs per patient-year for the alcoholic and drug programs are:

	Alcohol	Drug
Total costs	$768,000	$1,176,000
Divided by patient-years of service	40	50
Cost per patient-year	$19,200	$23,520

c. Drug rehabilitation is 22.5% higher ($4,320* ÷ $19,200) than alcohol rehabilitation. Therefore, Clayton should apply additional funds to alcohol rehabilitation.

*23,520 – 19,200

2. a. The activity-based approach would allocate costs to Alcohol and Drug Programs using the appropriate cost drivers and cost-driver rates.

$$\frac{\text{Medical supplies}}{\text{rate}} = \frac{\text{Medical supplies cost}}{\text{Total number of patient-years}} = \frac{\$360,000}{200} = \$1,800/\text{patient-year}$$

$$\frac{\text{Rent and clinic}}{\text{maintenance rate}} = \frac{\text{Rent and clinic mtce. costs}}{\text{Total amount of square metres of space}} = \frac{\$240,000}{40,000} = \$6 \text{ per square metre}$$

$$\frac{\text{Admin. cost rate for patient charts, food, and laundry}} = \frac{\text{Admin. costs to manage patient charts, food, laundry}}{\text{Total number of patient-years}} = \frac{\$960,000}{200} = \$4,800 \text{ per patient-year}$$

$$\text{Laboratory service rate} = \frac{\text{Laboratory services costs}}{\text{Total number of laboratory tests}} = \frac{\$330,000}{\$5,500} = \$60 \text{ per test}$$

These cost drivers are chosen as the ones that best match the descriptions of why the costs arise. Other answers are acceptable, provided clear explanations are given.

b. Activity-based costs for each program and cost per patient-year of the alcohol and drug program follow:

	Alcohol	Drugs	Children	After-Care
Direct labour				
Physicians at $120,000 × 0; 2; 4; 0	—	$240,000	$480,000	—
Psychologists at $60,000 × 6; 4; 0; 9	$360,000	240,000	—	$540,000
Nurses at $30,000 × 4; 6; 4; 9	120,000	180,000	120,000	270,000
Direct labour costs	480,000	660,000	600,000	810,000
Medical supplies[1] $1,800 × 40; 50; 50; 60	72,000	90,000	90,000	108,000
Rent and clinic maintenance[2] $6 × 9,000; 9,000; 10,000; 12,000	54,000	54,000	60,000	72,000
Administrative costs to manage patient charts, food, and laundry[3] $4,800 × 40; 50; 50; 60	192,000	240,000	240,000	288,000
Laboratory services[4] $60 × 400; 1,400; 3,000; 700	24,000	84,000	180,000	42,000
Total costs	$822,000	$1,128,000	$1,170,000	$1,320,000
Divided by number of patient-years	÷ 40	÷ 50	÷ 50	÷ 60
Cost per patient-year	$20,550	$22,560	$23,400	$22,000

[1] Allocated using patient-years
[2] Allocated using square metres of space
[3] Allocated using patient-years
[4] Allocated using number of laboratory tests

c.   The refining of the cost system (more direct tracing, more cost pools, and better cost drivers) results in the cost per drug patient per year being lower ($22,560) and the cost per alcohol patient per year being higher ($20,550). Using these numbers, the cost per drug patient per year would be only 9.8% ($2,010* ÷ $20,550) higher than alcohol rehabilitation. In these circumstances, the board's staff would have preferred to use the additional funds for drug rehabilitation (rather than alcohol rehabilitation as we concluded in requirement 1). The choice of cost system will have real effects on the allocation of Uppervale Health Centre's resources.

*22,560 – 20,550

3.   The ABC system more accurately allocates greater costs to the alcohol rehabilitation program because it identifies better cost drivers. For example, the ABC system allocates $72,000[a] of medical supplies costs to alcohol rehabilitation, whereas the existing system allocates $0. The existing system allocates medical supplies costs based on physician labour-hours and physicians spent 0 hours in alcohol rehabilitation. Nevertheless, patients in the alcohol program required medical supplies. The ABC system allocates medical supplies costs based on patient-years, a more plausible cost driver. Similarly, the ABC system chooses cost drivers for the other overhead costs to have a better cause-and-effect relationship between the cost drivers and the costs. Of course, Clayton should continue to evaluate if better cost drivers can be found than the ones they have identified so far.

[a]$1,800/patient-year) × 40 patient years = $72,000

        By implementing the ABC system, Clayton can gain a more detailed understanding of costs and cost drivers. This is valuable information from a cost management perspective. The system can yield insight into the efficiencies with which various activities are performed. Clayton can then examine if redundant activities can be eliminated or their efficiencies improved. For example, by tracking food and laundry costs per patient-day, Clayton can study trends and work toward improving the efficiency of these services.

4.   The concern with using costs per patient per year as the rule to allocate resources between drug and alcohol programs is that it emphasizes "input" to the exclusion of "outputs" or effectiveness of the programs. After all, Clayton's goal is to cure patients while controlling costs, not minimize costs per patient-year. The problem, of course, is measuring outputs in nonprofit organizations.

        Unlike in many manufacturing companies, where the outputs are obvious because they are tangible and measurable, the outputs of nonprofit organizations are more difficult to measure. Examples are "cured" mental patients as distinguished from "processed" or "discharged" mental patients, "educated" as distinguished from "partially educated" students, and so on.

        Also, an argument could be made to allocate funds where the need is more critical, drug or alcohol.

5-38 (30 min.) **Plantwide, department, and activity-cost rates.**

1. Budgeted manufacturing overhead rates:

    i. Plantwide rate:

    $$\frac{\$408,000}{20,000} = \$20.40 \text{ per direct manufacturing labour-hour}$$

    ii. Departmental rates:

Department 1:	$288,000 ÷ 10,000 = $28.80/hour
Department 2:	$120,000 ÷ 10,000 = $12.00/hour

Manufacturing overhead portion of ending inventories:

    i. Using plantwide overhead rate:

    800 units × 5 hours × $20.40 $81,600

    ii. Using department overhead rates:

Product A: 200 × [(4 × $28.80) + (1 × $12.00)] =	$25,440
Product B: 600 × [(1 × $28.80) + (4 × $12.00)] =	46,080
	$71,520

The difference in inventory costs due to the different methods of allocating manufacturing overhead is $10,080 ($81,600 – $71,520).

2. *Product A*

	Plantwide Overhead Rate	Department Overhead Rates
Direct materials	$144.00	$144.00
Direct manufacturing labour	96.00	96.00
Manufacturing overhead:		
$20.40 × 5	102.00	—
($28.80 × 4) + ($12 × 1)	—	127.20
Total manufacturing costs	342.00	367.20
Markup		
($342 × 120%; $367.20 × 120%)	410.40	440.64
Selling price	$752.40	$807.84

Product B

	Plantwide Overhead Rate	Department Overhead Rate
Direct materials	$180.00	$180.00
Direct manufacturing labour	96.00	96.00
Manufacturing overhead:		
$20.40 × 5	102.00	—
($28.80 × 1) + ($12 × 4)	—	76.80
Total manufacturing costs	378.00	352.80
Markup		
($378.00 × 120%; $352.80 × 120%)	453.60	423.36
Selling price	$831.60	$776.16

3. Sayther Company should use budgeted department manufacturing overhead rates because:

    a. The two manufacturing departments differ sizably in their overhead cost structures, despite having the same budgeted direct manufacturing labour-hours. Department 1 has $288,000 budgeted overhead, and Department 2 has $120,000 budgeted overhead.

    b. The two products use resources in the two manufacturing departments quite differently. The direct manufacturing labour-hours used in each department are:

Department	Product A	Product B
1	4	1
2	1	4

Differences a. and b. mean that more refined product costs will be calculated with budgeted department manufacturing overhead rates.

4. Sayther should further subdivide the department cost pools into activity-cost pools if (a) significant costs are incurred on *different* activities within the department, (b) the different activities have different cost-allocation bases, and (c) different products use the different activities in different proportions.

5-40 (50 min.) ABC, implementation, ethics.

1. Applewood Electronics should not emphasize the Regal model and phase out the Monarch model. Under activity-based costing, the Regal model has an operating income percentage of less than 3%, while the Monarch model has an operating income percentage of nearly 43%.

Cost driver rates for the various activities identified in the activity-based costing (ABC) system are as follows:

Soldering	$1,130,400	÷	1,570,000	=	$0.72 per solder point
Shipments	1,032,000	÷	20,000	=	$51.60 per shipment
Quality control	1,488,000	÷	77,500	=	$19.20 per inspection
Purchase orders	1,140,480	÷	190,080	=	$6.00 per order
Machine power	69,120	÷	192,000	=	$0.36 per machine-hour
Machine setups	900,000	÷	30,000	=	$30.00 per setup

Applewood Electronics
Calculation of Costs of Each Model
under Activity-Based Costing

	Monarch	Regal
Direct costs		
Direct materials ($249.60 × 22,000; $700.80 × 4,000)	$5,491,200	$2,803,200
Direct manufacturing labour ($21.60 × 22,000; $50.40 × 4,000)	475,200	201,600
Machine costs ($172.80 × 22,000; $86.40 × 4,000)	3,801,600	345,600
Total direct costs	9,768,000	3,350,400
Indirect costs		
Soldering ($0.72 × 1,185,000; 385,000)	853,200	277,200
Shipments ($51.60 × 16,200; 3,800)	835,920	196,080
Quality control ($19.20 × 56,200; 21,300)	1,079,040	408,960
Purchase orders ($6.00 × 80,100; 109,980)	480,600	659,880
Machine power ($0.36 × 176,000; 16,000)	63,360	5,760
Machine setups ($30 × 16,000; 14,000)	480,000	420,000
Total indirect costs	3,792,120	1,967,880
Total costs	$13,560,120	$5,318,280

Profitability analysis

	Monarch	Regal	Total
Revenues	$23,760,000	$5,472,000	$29,232,000
Cost of goods sold	13,560,120	5,318,280	18,878,400
Gross margin	$10,199,880	$ 153,720	$10,353,600
Per-unit calculations:			
Units sold	22,000	4,000	
Selling price	$1,080.00	$1,368.00	
Cost of goods sold ($13,560,120 ÷ 22,000; $5,318,280 ÷ 4,000)	616.37	1,329.57	
Gross margin	$463.63	$ 38.43	
Gross margin percentage	42.9%	2.8%	

2. Applewood's existing costing system allocates all manufacturing overhead other than machine costs on the basis of machine-hours, an output unit-level cost driver. Consequently, the more machine-hours per unit that a product needs, the greater is the manufacturing overhead allocated to it. Because Monarch uses twice the number of machine-hours per unit compared with Regal, a large amount of manufacturing overhead is allocated to Monarch.

   The ABC analysis recognizes several batch-level cost drivers such as purchase orders, shipments, and setups. Regal uses these resources much more intensively than Monarch. The ABC system recognizes Regal's use of these overhead resources. Consider, for example, purchase order costs. The existing system allocates these costs on the basis of machine-hours. As a result, each unit of Monarch is allocated twice the purchase order costs of each unit of Regal. The ABC system allocates \$480,600 of purchase order costs to Monarch [equal to \$21.85 (\$480,600 ÷ 22,000) per unit] and \$659,880 of purchase order costs to Regal [equal to \$164.97 (\$659,880 ÷ 4,000) per unit]. Each unit of Regal uses 7.55 (\$164.97 ÷ \$21.85) times the purchase order costs of each unit of Monarch.

   Recognizing Regal's more intense use of manufacturing overhead results in Regal showing a much lower profitability under the ABC system. By the same token, the ABC analysis shows that Monarch is quite profitable. The existing costing system overcosted Monarch, and so made it appear less profitable.

3. Figueira's comments about ABC implementation are valid. When designing and implementing ABC systems, managers and management accountants need to trade off the costs of the system against its benefits. Adding more activities makes the system harder to understand and more costly to implement but would probably improve the accuracy of cost information, which, in turn, would help Applewood make better decisions. Similarly, using inspection-hours and setup-hours as allocation bases would also probably lead to more accurate cost information but would increase measurement costs.

4. Activity-based management (ABM) is the use of information from activity-based costing to make improvements in a firm. For example, a firm could revise product prices on the basis of revised cost information. For the long term, activity-based costing can assist management in making decisions regarding the viability of product lines, distribution channels, marketing strategies, etc. ABM highlights possible improvements, including reduction or elimination of non-value-added activities, selecting lower cost activities, sharing activities with other products, and eliminating waste. ABM is an integrated approach that focuses management's attention on activities with the ultimate aim of continuous improvement. As a whole-company philosophy, ABM focuses on strategic, as well as tactical and operational activities of the company.

5. Incorrect reporting of ABC costs with the goal of retaining both the Monarch and Regal product lines is unethical. In assessing the situation, the management accountant could consider the following:

Competence

Clear reports using relevant and reliable information should be prepared. Preparing reports on the basis of incorrect costs in order to retain product lines violates competence standards. It is unethical for Benzo to change the ABC system with the specific goal of reporting different product cost numbers that Figueira favours.

Integrity

The management accountant has a responsibility to avoid actual or apparent conflicts of interest and advise all appropriate parties of any potential conflict. Benzo may be tempted to change the product cost numbers to please Figueira, the Division President. This action, however, would violate the responsibility for integrity.

Objectivity

The management accountant should require that information should be fairly and objectively communicated and that all relevant information should be disclosed. From a management accountant's standpoint, adjusting the product cost numbers to make both the Monarch and Regal lines look profitable would violate the standard of objectivity.

Benzo should indicate to Figueira that the product cost calculations are, indeed, appropriate. If Figueira still insists on modifying the product cost numbers, Benzo should raise the matter with one of Figueira's superiors. If, after taking all these steps, there is continued pressure to modify product cost numbers, Benzo should consider resigning from the company, rather than engage in unethical behaviour.

CHAPTER 6
MASTER BUDGET AND RESPONSIBILITY ACCOUNTING

6-2   The budgeting cycle includes the following elements:

a.   Planning the performance of the organization as a whole as well as of its subunits. The entire management team agrees as to what is expected.

b.   Providing a frame of reference, a set of specific expectations against which the actual results can be compared.

c.   Investigating variations from the plans. If necessary, corrective action follows investigation.

d.   Planning again, considering feedback and changed conditions.

6-4   Yes, budgeted performance is better than past performance for judging managers. Why? Mainly because inefficiencies included in past results can be detected and eliminated in budgeting. Also, new opportunities in the future, which did not exist in the past, may be ignored if past performance is used.

6-6   A company that shares its own internal budget information with other companies can gain multiple benefits. One benefit is better coordination with suppliers, which can reduce the likelihood of supply shortages. Better coordination with customers can result in increased sales as demand by customers is less likely to exceed supply. Better coordination across the whole supply chain can also help a company reduce inventories and thus reduce the costs of holding inventories. Suppliers and customers become "partners in profit." Here satisfied customers sell the final product to new customers.

6-8   *A rolling budget* is a budget or plan that is always available for a specified future period by adding a month, quarter, or year in the future as the month, quarter or year just ended is dropped. For example, a 12-month rolling budget for the March 2006 to February 2007 period becomes a 12-month rolling budget for the April 2006 to March 2007 period the next month, and so on.

6-10   The revenue budget is typically the cornerstone for budgeting because production (and hence costs) and inventory levels generally depend on the forecasted level of demand and revenue.

6-12   Factors reducing the effectiveness of budgeting of companies include:

1.   Lack of a well-defined strategy,
2.   Lack of a clear linkage of strategy to operational plans,
3.   Lack of individual accountability for results, and
4.   Lack of meaningful performance measures.

6-14 Non-output-based cost drivers can be incorporated into budgeting by the use of activity-based budgeting (ABB). ABB focuses on the budgeted cost of activities necessary to produce and sell products and services. Non-output-based cost drivers, such as the number of part numbers, number of batches, and number of new products, can be used with ABB.

6-16 (15 min.) Production budget (in units), fill in the missing numbers.

	Model 101	Model 201	Model 301
Budgeted sales	216[G]	233[c]	1,040[G]
Add target ending FGI	17[a]	7[G]	40[G]
Total requirements	233[G]	240[G]	1,080[e]
Deduct beginning FGI	13[G]	10[G]	54[f]
Units to be produced	220[b]	230[d]	1,026[G]

[a]233 – 216 = 17   [d]240 – 10 = 230   G = given
[b]233 – 13 = 220   [e]1,040 + 40 = 1,080
[c]240 – 7 = 233   [f]1,080 – 1,026 = 54

6-18 (5 min.) Direct materials budget.

Direct materials to be used in production (bottles)	1,800,000
Add target ending direct materials inventory (bottles)	60,000
Total requirements (bottles)	1,860,000
Deduct beginning direct materials inventory (bottles)	24,000
Direct materials to be purchased (bottles)	1,836,000

6-20 (30 min.) Sales and production budget.

1.

	Selling Price	Units Sold	Total Revenues
l-litre bottles	$0.30	5,760,000[a]	$1,728,000
16-litre units	1.80	1,440,000[b]	2,592,000
			$4,320,000

[a]480,000 × 12 months = 5,760,000
[b]120,000 × 12 months = 1,440,000

2.

Budgeted unit sales (1-litre bottles)	5,760,000
Add target ending finished goods inventory	720,000
Total requirements	6,480,000
Deduct beginning finished goods inventory	1,080,000
Units to be produced	5,400,000

3.
$$\underset{\text{inventory}}{\text{Beginning}} = \underset{\text{sales}}{\text{Budgeted}} + \underset{\text{ending inventory}}{\text{Target}} - \underset{\text{production}}{\text{Budgeted}}$$

$$= \quad 1,440,000 + 240,000 - 1,560,000$$

$$= \quad 120,000 \text{ 16-litre units}$$

6-22 (15-20 min.) Revenue, production, and purchases budget.

1. 960,000 motorcycles × 480,000 yen = 460,800,000,000 yen

2.
Budgeted sales (units)	960,000
Add target ending finished goods inventory	120,000
Total requirements	1,080,000
Deduct beginning finished goods inventory	144,000
Units to be produced	936,000

3.
Direct materials to be used in production, 936,000 × 2	1,872,000
Add target ending direct materials inventory	36,000
Total requirements	1,908,000
Deduct beginning direct materials inventory	24,000
Direct materials to be purchased	1,884,000
Cost per wheel in yen	19,200
Direct materials purchase cost in yen	36,172,800,000

Note the relatively small inventory of wheels. In Japan, suppliers tend to be located very close to the major manufacturer. Inventories are controlled by just-in-time (JIT) and similar systems. Indeed, some direct materials inventories are almost nonexistent.

6-24 (20-30 min.) Activity-based budgeting.

1.

	Soft Drinks	Fresh Produce	Packaged Food	Total
Ordering				
$108 × 14; 24; 14	$1,512	$2,592	$1,512	$5,616
Delivery				
$98 × 12; 62; 19	1,176	6,076	1,862	9,114
Shelf-stocking				
$25 × 16; 172; 94	400	4,300	2,350	7,050
Customer-support				
$0.22 × 4,600; 34,200; 10,750	1,012	7,524	2,365	10,901
	$4,100	$20,492	$8,089	$32,681

2. An ABB approach recognizes how different products require different mixes of support activities. The relative percentage of how each product area uses the cost driver in each activity area is:

Activity Area	Soft Drinks	Fresh Produce	Packaged Food	Total
Ordering	26.9	46.2	26.9	100.0%
Delivery	12.9	66.7	20.4	100.0
Shelf-stocking	5.7	61.0	33.3	100.0
Customer-support	9.3	69.0	21.7	100.0

By recognizing these differences, FS managers are better able to budget for different unit sales levels and different mixes of individual product-line items sold. Using a single cost driver (such as COGS) assumes homogeneity across product lines which does not occur at FS.

Other benefits cited by managers include: (1) better identification of resource needs, (2) clearer linking of costs with staff responsibilities, and (3) identification of budgetary slack.

6-26 (20 min.) Budgeting and behaviour.

1. (a) Gain additional insight into the strategy of an organization. Exhibit 6-1 shows arrows pointing both ways between strategy analysis and long-term planning and short-term planning. Detailed analysis for budgeting can sometimes highlight strategy assumptions (such as cost levels and demand levels) that are not likely to hold.

   (b) Anticipate resource demands in a timely way. Budgeting can highlight working capital shortages, cash shortages, personnel shortages, and so on. Early warning signals can enable a company to take action to avoid having small problems become large problems.

   (c) Improve the communication level in an organization. The budgeting process itself can assist in having diverse groups gain a better understanding of how other groups affect their performance. Sharing budgets across organizations in a supply chain can help a company better meet end-point customer demand. Communication with suppliers can reduce parts shortages.

2. Factors to consider when preparing sales forecasts include:

   (a) Any constraining variables on sales. For example, if demand outstrips available productive capacity or a key component is in short supply, the sales forecast should be based on the maximum units that can be produced.

(b) Information from customers about their new product developments and advertising plans. Proactive not reactive.

(c) Feedback from customers about satisfaction with a company's products vis-à-vis satisfaction levels for the products of competitors. This is customer conformance feedback telling managers how well the actual output conformed to the customer's expectations.

(d) Likely new product releases by competitors or new entrants into a market. Again proactive not reactive.

6-28 (30 min.) Appendix: Cash flow analysis

1. The cash that TabComp Inc. can expect to collect during April 2008 is calculated below:

April cash receipts:	
April cash sales ($480,000 × .25)	$120,000
April credit card sales ($480,000 × .30 × .96)	138,240
Collections on account:	
March ($576,000 × .45 × .70)	181,440
February ($600,000 × .45 × .28)	75,600
January (uncollectible not relevant)	0
Total collections	$515,280

2. (a) The projected number of the MZB-33 computer hardware units that TabComp Inc. will order on January 25, 2008, is calculated as follows.

	MZB-33 Units
March sales	110
Plus: Ending inventory[a]	27
Total needed	137
Less: Beginning inventory[b]	33
Projected purchases in units	104

[a].30 × 90 unit sales in April
[b].30 × 110 unit sales in March

(b) Purchase price =

$3,600 selling price per unit[c]	
× 60%	$ 2,160
× Projected unit purchases	104
Total MZB-33 purchases	$224,640

[c]Selling price = $2,430,000 ÷ 675 units
= $3,600 per unit

(c)   In April 2008: n/45 from time units are delivered to TabComp.

3.   Monthly cash budgets are prepared by companies such as TabComp Inc. in order to plan for their cash needs. This means identifying when both excess cash and cash shortages may occur. A company needs to know when cash shortages will occur so that prior arrangements can be made with lending institutions in order to have cash available for borrowing when the company needs it. At the same time, a company should be aware of when there will be excess cash available for investment or for repaying loans.

6-30 (20 min.) Continuous improvement, budgeting (continuation of 6-29).

Areas where continuous improvement might be incorporated into the budgeting process:

(a)   Direct materials. An improvement in either usage or price could be budgeted. For example, the budgeted usage amounts could reflect a 1% reduction per month, up to a maximum improvement of 0.1 square metre for either desk.

Thus, a 1% reduction target in the first month would be:

- Executive: 1.5 m^2 × 0.99 = 1.485 m^2
- Chairperson: 2.3 m^2 × 0.99 = 2.277 m^2

Some students suggested the monthly 1% deduction always be applied to the original 1.5 m^2 and 2.3 m^2 amounts. This is incorrect since, after several improvement cycles, the budgeted amount would be less than the minimum desk requirements (1.365 m^2 and 2.16 m^2 respectively).

Note that even when applied to the decreasing amount, the 1% reduction will eventually hit results below the minimum desk requirements.

(b)   Direct manufacturing labour. The budgeted usage of 3 hours/5 hours could be continuously revised on a monthly basis. Similarly, the manufacturing labour cost per hour of $36 could be continuously revised down. The former appears more feasible than the latter. Improvements here are usually technology-driven, as labour rates seldom go down. More efficient equipment equals less time per unit.

(c) Variable manufacturing overhead. By budgeting more efficient use of the allocation base, a signal is given for continuous improvement. A second approach is to budget continuous improvement in the budgeted variable overhead cost per unit of the allocation base.

(d) Fixed manufacturing overhead. The approach here is to budget for reductions in the year-to-year amounts of fixed overhead. If these costs are appropriately classified as fixed, then they are more difficult to adjust down on a monthly basis. For example, more efficient heat exchangers will reduce overall energy requirements.

6-32 (30-40 min.) Revenue and production budgets.

This is a routine budgeting problem. The key to its solution is to compute the correct <u>quantities</u> of finished goods and direct materials. Use the following general formula:

$$\begin{pmatrix} \text{Budgeted} \\ \text{production} \\ \text{or purchases} \end{pmatrix} = \begin{pmatrix} \text{Target} \\ \text{ending} \\ \text{inventory} \end{pmatrix} + \begin{pmatrix} \text{Budgeted} \\ \text{sales or} \\ \text{materials used} \end{pmatrix} - \begin{pmatrix} \text{Beginning} \\ \text{inventory} \end{pmatrix}$$

1.

Scarborough Corporation
Revenue Budget
For 2008

	Units	Price	Total
Thingone	60,000	$198	$ 11,880,000
Thingtwo	40,000	300	12,000,000
Projected sales			$23,880,000

2.

Scarborough Corporation
Production Budget (in units)
For 2008

	Thingone	Thingtwo
Budgeted sales in units	60,000	40,000
Add target finished goods inventories, December 31, 2008	27,000	11,000
Total requirements	87,000	51,000
Deduct finished goods inventories, January 1, 2008	22,000	10,000
Units to be produced	65,000	41,000

3.

Scarborough Corporation
Direct Materials Purchases Budget (in quantities) for 2008

	Direct Materials		
	A	B	C
Direct materials to be used in production			
• Thingone (budgeted production of 65,000 units times 4 kg of A, 2 kg of B)	260,000	130,000	—
• Thingtwo (budgeted production of 41,000 units times 5 kg of A, 3 kg of B, 1 unit of C)	205,000	123,000	41,000
Total	465,000	253,000	41,000
Add target ending inventories, December 31, 2008	36,000	32,000	7,000
Total requirements in quantities	501,000	285,000	48,000
Deduct beginning inventories, January 1, 2008	32,000	29,000	6,000
Direct materials to be purchased (quantities)	469,000	256,000	42,000

4.

Scarborough Corporation
Direct Materials Purchases Budget (in dollars) for 2008

	Budgeted Purchases (Quantities)	Expected Purchase Price per Unit	Total
Direct material A	469,000	$14	$6,566,000
Direct material B	256,000	7	1,792,000
Direct material C	42,000	5	210,000
Budgeted purchases			$8,568,000

5.

Scarborough Corporation
Direct Manufacturing Labour Budget for 2008

	Budgeted Production (Units)	Direct Manufacturing Labour-Hours per Unit	Total Hours	Rate per Hour	Total
Thingone	65,000	2	130,000	$15	$1,950,000
Thingtwo	41,000	3	123,000	19	2,337,000
Total					$4,287,000

6.   Scarborough Corporation
                       Budgeted Finished Goods Inventory
                           At December 31, 2008

Thingone:
    Direct materials costs:
        A, 4 kilograms at $14 $56
        B, 2 kilograms at $7   14 $70
    Direct manufacturing labour costs,
        2 hours at $15   30
    Manufacturing overhead costs at $24 per direct
        manufacturing labour-hour (2 hours)   48
    Budgeted manufacturing costs per unit $148

    Finished goods inventory of Thingone
        $148 × 27,000 units $3,996,000

Thingtwo:
    Direct materials costs:
        A, 5 kilograms at $14 $70
        B, 3 kilograms at $7   21
        C, 1 each at $5   5 $96
    Direct manufacturing labour costs,
        3 hours at $19   57
    Manufacturing overhead costs at $24 per direct
        manufacturing labour-hour (3 hours)   72
    Budgeted manufacturing costs per unit $225

    Finished goods inventory of Thingtwo
        $225 × 11,000 units   2,475,000
Budgeted finished goods inventory, December 31, 2008 $6,471,000

6-34 (60 min.) Operating budget.

1. **Schedule 1: Revenue Budget**
   for the Year Ended December 31, 2008

	Units	Selling Price	Total Revenues
Snowboards	1,200	$540	$648,000

2. **Schedule 2: Production Budget (in Units)**
for the Year Ended December 31, 2008

	Snowboards
Budgeted unit sales (Schedule 1)	1,200
Add target ending finished goods inventory	200
Total requirements	1,400
Deduct beginning finished goods inventory	100
Units to be produced	1,300

3. **Schedule 3A: Direct Materials Usage Budget**
For the Year Ended December 31, 2008

	Wood	Fibreglass	Total
Physical Budget			
To be used in production	6,500		
(Wood: 1,300 × 5.00 b.f.			
Fibreglass: 1,300 × 6.00 yards)		7,800	
	6,500	7,800	
Cost Budget (uses FIFO)			
Available from beginning inventory			
(Wood: 2,000 b.f. × $34.00	68,000		
Fibreglass: 1,000 yards × 5.80)		5,800	
To be used from purchases this period			
(Wood: (6,500 – 2,000) × $36.00	$162,000		
Fibreglass: (7,800 – 1,000) × $6.00)		$40,800	
Total cost of direct materials to be used	$230,000	$46,600	$276,600

Schedule 3B: Direct Materials Purchases Budget
For the Year Ended December 31, 2008

	Wood	Fibreglass	Total
Physical Budget			
Production usage (from Schedule 3A)	6,500	7,800	
Add target ending inventory	1,500	2,000	
Total requirements	8,000	9,800	
Deduct beginning inventory	2,000	1,000	
Purchases	6,000	8,800	
Cost Budget			
(Wood: 6,000 × $36.00	$216,000		
Fibreglass: 8,800 × $6.00)		$52,800	
	$216,000	$52,800	$268,800

Note: All units of measurement are standard in this industry.

4. **Schedule 4: Direct Manufacturing Labour Budget**
   for the Year Ended December 31, 2008

Labour Category	Cost Driver Units	DML Hours per Driver Unit	Total Hours	Wage Rate	Total
Manufacturing Labour	1,300	5.00	6,500	$25.00	$162,500

5. **Schedule 5: Manufacturing Overhead Budget**
   for the Year Ended December 31, 2008

	At Budgeted Level of 6,500 Direct Manufacturing Labour-Hours
Variable manufacturing overhead costs	
($8.40 × 6,500)	$ 54,600
Fixed manufacturing overhead costs	78,000
Total manufacturing overhead costs	$132,600

6. Budgeted manufacturing overhead rate: $\frac{\$132,600}{6,500}$ = $20.40 per DML hour

7. Budgeted manufacturing overhead cost per output unit: $\frac{\$132,600}{1,300} = \$102.00$ per output unit

8. **Schedule 6A: Computation of Unit Costs of Finished Goods Inventory at End of 2008**

	Cost per Unit of Input[a]	Inputs[b]	Total
Direct materials			
Wood	$36.00	5.00	$180.00
Fibreglass	6.00	6.00	36.00
Direct manufacturing labour	25.00	5.00	125.00
Total manufacturing overhead			102.00
Total cost per unit			$443.00

[a]Cost is per board-foot, yard, or hour.
[b]Inputs is the amount of input per board.

9. **Schedule 6B: Ending Inventory Budget**
December 31, 2008

	Units	Cost per Unit	Total
Direct materials			
Wood	1,500	$36.00	$ 54,000
Fibreglass	2,000	6.00	12,000
Finished goods			
Snowboards	200	443.00	88,600
Total Ending Inventory			$154,600

10. **Schedule 7: Cost-of-Goods-Sold Budget**
    for the Year Ended December 31, 2008

	From Schedule		Total
Beginning finished goods inventory January 1, 2008	Given		$ 44,976
Direct materials used	3A	$276,600	
Direct manufacturing labour	4	162,500	
Manufacturing overhead	5	132,600	
Cost of goods manufactured			571,700
Cost of goods available for sale			616,676
Deduct ending finished goods inventory, December 31, 2008	6B		88,600
Cost of goods sold			$528,076

11. **Budgeted Income Statement for Slopes, Inc.**
    for the Year Ended December 31, 2008

Revenues	Schedule 1		$648,000
Costs			
Cost of goods sold	Schedule 7		528,076
Gross margin			119,924
Operating costs			
Marketing costs ($300 × 36)		$ 10,800	
Other costs*		36,000	46,800
Operating income			$ 73,124

*Fixed nonmanufacturing costs

6-36 (15 min.) **Responsibility of purchasing agent.**

The time lost in the plant should be charged to the purchasing department. Certainly, the plant manager could not be asked to underwrite a loss which is due to failure of delivery over which he had no supervision. Although the purchasing agent may feel that he has done everything he possibly could, he must realize that, in the whole organization, he is *the one* who is in the best position to evaluate the situation. He receives an assignment. He may accept it or reject it. But if he accepts, he must perform. If he fails, the damage is evaluated. Everybody makes mistakes. The important point is to avoid making too many mistakes and also to understand fully that the extensive control reflected in "responsibility accounting" is the necessary balance to the great freedom of action that individual executives are given.

Discussions of this problem have again and again revealed a tendency among students (and among accountants and managers) to "fix the blame"—as if the variances arising from a responsibility accounting system should pinpoint misbehaviour and provide answers. The point is that no accounting system or variances can provide answers. However, variances can lead to questions. In this case, in deciding where the penalty should be assigned, the student might inquire *who should be asked—not who should be blamed.*

Classroom discussions have also raised the following diverse points:

(a) Is the railway company liable? Yes, and they have liability insurance.

(b) Costs of idle time are usually routinely charged to the production department. Should the information system be fine-tuned to reallocate such costs to the purchasing department? Both purchasing and the plant manager answer to either a business manager or an operations manager. The buck stops here. Some companies have the purchasing department answer directly to the plant manager, which would be a probable result of the above mistake. Give accountability to the plant manager as his/her authority warrants it.

(c) How will the purchasing managers behave in the future regarding willingness to take risks?

The text emphasizes the following: Beware of overemphasis on controllability. For example, a time-honoured theme of management is that responsibility should not be given without accompanying authority. Such a guide is a useful first step, but responsibility accounting is more far-reaching. The basic focus should be on *information* or *knowledge*, not on control. The key question is: "Who is the best informed?" Put another way, "Who is the person who can tell us the most about the specific item, regardless of ability to exert personal control?"

6-38 (20 min.) **Traditional budgeting and its critics.**

1. Budgets can be a powerful means of coordination and communication in organizations. They help turn managers' perspectives forward. The extract is from the CEO of General Electric (John Welch).

   Exhibit 6-6 presents six criticisms of traditional budgeting. These criticisms echo some of the concerns raised by Welch. The proposals for change in Exhibit 6-6 indicate that the solution to problems with traditional budgeting is *not* to dispense with budgeting. This is "throwing the baby out with the bath water." Rather the solution is to revamp budgeting to incorporate stretch goals. Six months after the quoted interview with Welch, another General Electric executive noted how they "get more from people."

   a. By definition, stretch goals are very difficult to meet. Don't punish people for not hitting them.

   b.   Don't set goals that stretch your employees crazily.

   c.   Understand that stretch targets can unexpectedly affect other parts of the organization.

   d.   Don't give tough stretch goals to those people already pushing themselves to the limit.

   e.   Share the wealth generated by reaching stretch goals. This is very important; employees who perform above the "call of duty" must be rewarded in a timely fashion. Waiting for the end-of-year merit increases demotivates this behaviour, as the odds are a cycle downturn may negate increases. This does not always have to be money, perhaps an extra vacation, time with family and friends, etc.

Budgets are one mechanism by which some of these approaches can be implemented. For example, budgets highlight connections across parts of organizations.

2.   Dispensing with "the annual budget ritual" is not the same as dispensing with budgeting. The CEO should ask the marketing manager to identify those aspects of the annual budget that are ritualistic and to suggest alternatives. Marketing managers often like to have unlimited budgets for advertising and counter-moves against competitions. However, organizations are increasingly requiring marketing to accept the same budgeting discipline as other functional areas. This discipline is not the same as "an exercise in minimization." Rather it should focus on budgeting expenditures to enhance the economic value of the organization.

   Here the CEO delegates downward to his/her marketing manager, as he/she asks for alternatives to any rituals the marketing manager identifies. Never let a subordinate delegate upward. You cannot do your job efficiently and the subordinate's job also.

6-40 (40 min.) Appendix, cash budgeting for distributor.

1. The pro forma cash budget for Alpha-Tech for the second quarter of 2008 is presented below. Supporting calculations are presented on the next page.

Alpha-Tech Cash Budget
For the Second Quarter 2008

	April	May	June
Beginning balance	$ 600,000	$ 600,000	$ 1,476,000
Collections[1]			
February sales	4,800,000		
March sales	6,480,000	4,320,000	
April sales		8,280,000	5,520,000
May sales			9,000,000
Total receipts	11,280,000	12,600,000	14,520,000
Total cash available	11,880,000	13,200,000	15,996,000
Disbursements			
Accounts payable[5]	4,986,000	5,682,000	6,342,000
Hourly wages[2]	4,140,000	4,500,000	5,040,000
General & administrative[3]	1,080,000	1,080,000	1,080,000
Property taxes			408,000
Income taxes[4]	1,536,000		
Total disbursements	11,742,000	11,262,000	12,870,000
Cash balance	138,000	1,938,000	3,126,000
Cash borrowed	462,000		
Cash repaid		(462,000)	
Ending balance	$ 600,000	$1,476,000	$ 3,126,000

[1]60% of sales in first month; 40% of sales in second month
[2]30% of current month sales
[3](Total less property taxes and amortization) ÷ 12
[4] 40% × $3,840,000
[5] See schedule on next page.

Supporting Calculations

Accounts payable——parts received:

Month	40% of Revenues	Timing	February	March	April	May	June
February	$4,800,000	.30	$1,440,000				
March	4,320,000	.70	3,024,000				
March	4,320,000	.30		$1,296,000			
April	5,520,000	.70		3,864,000			
April	5,520,000	.30			$1,656,000		
May	6,000,000	.70			4,200,000		
May	6,000,000	.30				$1,800,000	
June	6,720,000	.70				4,704,000	
			$4,464,000	$5,160,000	$5,856,000	$6,504,000	

Payment							
February	$4,464,000	.25			$1,116,000		
March	5,160,000	.75			3,870,000		
March	5,160,000	.25				$1,290,000	
April	5,856,000	.75				4,392,000	
April	5,856,000	.25					$1,464,000
May	6,504,000	.75					4,878,000
			$ 0	$ 0	$4,986,000	$5,682,000	$6,342,000

2. Cash budgeting is important for Alpha-Tech because as sales grow so will expenditures for input factors. Since these expenditures generally precede cash receipts, the company must plan for possible financing to cover the gap between payments and receipts. The cash budget shows the probable cash position at certain points in time, allowing the company to plan for borrowing, as Alpha-Tech must do in April.

   Cash budgeting also facilitates the control of excess cash. The company may be losing investment opportunities, if excess cash is left idle in a chequing account. The cash budget alerts management to periods when there will be excess cash available for investment, thus facilitating financial planning and cash control.

6-42 (30 min.) Activity-based budgeting.

a. Machining
    Indirect materials [$0 + ($12/hour × 10,000 hours)] $120,000
    Indirect labour [$24,000 + ($18/hour × 10,000 hours)]   204,000
    Utilities [$0 + ($6/hour × 10,000 hours)]   60,000
                                                                 $384,000

b. Setups and quality assurance

Indirect materials [$0 + $1,200/run × 40 runs]	48,000
Indirect labour [$0 + $1,440/run × 40 runs)]	57,600
Inspection [$96,000 + ($2,400/run × 40 runs)]	192,000
	$297,600

c. Procurement

Indirect materials [$0 + ($4.80/order × 15,000 orders)]	$ 72,000
Indirect labour [$54,000 + $0]	54,000
	$126,000

d. Design

Engineering hours [$90,000 + ($60/hour × 100 hours)]	$96,000

e. Material handling

Indirect materials [$0 + ($2.40/m² × 100,000 m²)]	$240,000
Indirect labour ($36,000 + $0)	36,000
	$276,000

6-44 (15 min.) Budgetary slack and ethics.

The use of budgetary slack, particularly if it has a detrimental effect on the company, may be unethical. In assessing the situation, the management accountant should consider the following:

Competence
Clear reports using relevant and reliable information should be prepared. Reports prepared on the basis of incorrect revenue or cost projections would violate the management accountant's responsibility for competence. Ford's and Granger's performances would appear to look better than they actually are because their performances are being compared with understated (revenues in the case of Ford) or overstated (costs in the case of Granger) and unreliable budgets.

Integrity
Any activity that subverts the legitimate goals of the company should be avoided. Incorrect reporting of revenue and cost budgets could be viewed as violating the responsibility for integrity. The management accountant should communicate unfavourable as well as favourable information. Atkins will probably regard Ford's and Granger's behaviour as unethical because it is attempting to project their results in a favourable light.

Objectivity

The management accountant should require that information be fairly and objectively communicated and that all relevant information be disclosed. From a management accountant's standpoint, Ford and Granger are clearly violating both these precepts. For the various reasons cited above, Atkins should take the position that the behaviour described by Ford and Granger is unethical.

CHAPTER 7
FLEXIBLE BUDGETS, VARIANCES, AND MANAGEMENT CONTROL: I

7-2   Sources of information about budgeted amounts include (a) past amounts, and (b) detailed engineering studies.

7-4   The key difference is the output level used to set the budget. A *static budget* is based on the level of output planned at the *start of the budget period. A flexible budget* is developed using budgeted revenues or cost amounts based on the level of output actually achieved in the budget period. The actual level of output is not known until the *end of the budget period.* Flexible budgets give managers more insight into the causes of variance than static budgets.

7-6   The steps in developing a flexible budget are:

Step 1:   Determine the budgeted selling price per unit, the budgeted variable costs per unit, and the budgeted fixed costs.

Step 2:   Determine the actual quantity of the revenue driver.

Step 3:   Determine the flexible budget for revenue based on the budgeted unit revenue and the actual quantity of the revenue driver.

Step 4:   Determine the actual quantity of the cost driver(s).

Step 5:   Determine the flexible budget for costs based on the budgeted unit variable costs and fixed costs and the actual quantity of the cost driver(s).

7-8   A manager should decompose the flexible-budget variance for direct materials into a price variance and an efficiency variance. The individual causes of these variances can then be investigated, recognizing possible interdependencies across these individual causes.

7-10   Direct materials price variances are often computed at the time of purchase while direct materials efficiency variances are often computed at the time of usage. Purchasing managers are typically responsible for price variances, while production managers are typically responsible for usage variances.

7-12   An individual business function, such as production, is interdependent with other business functions. Factors outside of production can explain why variances arise in the production area. For example:

- purchasing of lower quality materials that creates excess waste
- poor design of products or processes can lead to a sizable number of defects, and
- marketing personnel making promises for delivery times that require a large number of rush orders that create production-scheduling difficulties.

7-14 Variances can be calculated at the activity level as well as at the company level. For example, a price variance and an efficiency variance can be computed for an activity area.

7-16 (20-30 min.) Flexible budget.

1.

	Actual Results (1)	Flexible-Budget Variances (2)=(1)–(3)	Flexible Budget (3)	Sales-Volume Variances (4)=(3)–(5)	Static Budget (5)
Units sold	2,800[G]		2,800	200 U	3,000[G]
Revenues	$375,200[a]	5,600 F	$369,600[b]	$26,400 U	$396,000[c]
Variable costs	275,520[d]	29,120 U	246,400[e]	17,600 F	264,000[f]
Contribution margin	99,680	23,520 U	123,200	8,800 U	132,000
Fixed costs	60,000[G]	4,800 F	64,800[G]	0	64,800[G]
Operating income	$ 39,680	$18,720 U	$ 58,400	$ 8,800 U	$ 67,200
		$18,720 U		$ 8,800 U	
		Total flexible-budget variance		Total sales-volume variance	

$27,520 U

Total static-budget variance

[a]$134 × 2,800 = $375,200
[b]$132 × 2,800 = $369,600
[c]$132 × 3,000 = $396,000
[d]Given. Unit variable cost = $275,520 ÷ 2,800 = $98.40 per tire
[e]$88 × 2,800 = $246,400
[f]$88 × 3,000 = $264,000
[G]Given

2. The key information items are:

	Actual	Budgeted
Units	2,800	3,000
Unit selling price	$ 134	$ 132
Unit variable cost	$ 98.40	$ 88
Fixed costs	$60,000	$64,800

The total static-budget variance in operating income is $27,520 U. There is both an unfavourable flexible-budget variance ($18,720) and an unfavourable sales-volume variance ($8,800).

The unfavourable sales-volume variance arises solely because actual units manufactured and sold were 200 fewer than the budgeted 3,000 units. The unfavourable flexible-budget variance of $18,720 in operating income is due primarily to the $10.40 increase in unit variable costs. This increase in unit variable costs is only partially offset by the $2 increase in unit selling price and the $4,800 decrease in fixed costs.

7-18 (10 min.) Flexible budget.

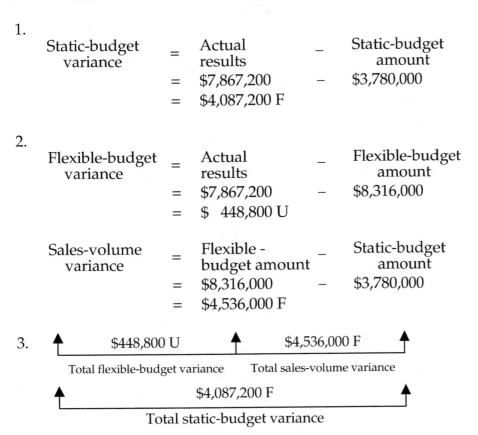

1.

Static-budget variance	=	Actual results	−	Static-budget amount
	=	$7,867,200	−	$3,780,000
	=	$4,087,200 F		

2.

Flexible-budget variance	=	Actual results	−	Flexible-budget amount
	=	$7,867,200	−	$8,316,000
	=	$ 448,800 U		

Sales-volume variance	=	Flexible-budget amount	−	Static-budget amount
	=	$8,316,000	−	$3,780,000
	=	$4,536,000 F		

3.

$448,800 U — Total flexible-budget variance | $4,536,000 F — Total sales-volume variance

$4,087,200 F — Total static-budget variance

The total flexible-budget variance is $448,800 unfavourable. This arises because for the actual output level: (a) selling prices were lower than budgeted, or (b) variable costs were higher than budgeted, or (c) fixed costs were higher than budgeted, or (d) some combination of (a), (b), and (c) existed.

7-20 (15 min.) **Materials and manufacturing-labour variances.**

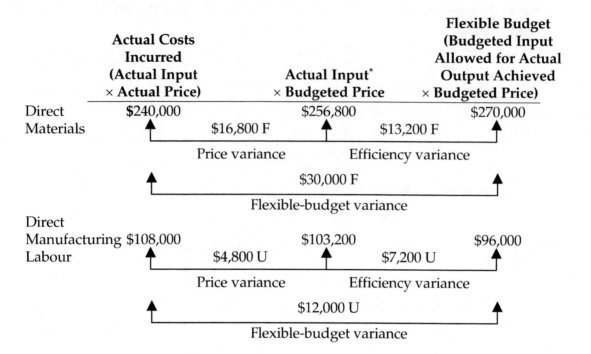

*Assume amount of direct materials purchased and used is the same (no inventory effect).

7-22 (30-40 min.) Comprehensive variance analysis.

1.

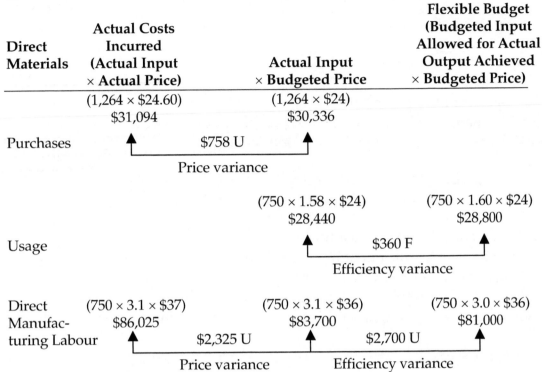

2. **Direct Materials Price Variance** ($758 U, due to actual price of $24.60 exceeding budgeted price of $24)

- Escalation clauses with supplier realized (i.e., raw material costs at supplier increased and were passed on)
- Standard wrongly (unrealistically) set
- Poor price negotiation
- Purchase of higher quality wood
- Materials price unexpectedly increased due to external shocks (e.g., a natural disaster in major forest areas)
- Purchased in smaller lot sizes than budgeted and did not get quantity discounts
- Change in supplier when lower-priced supplier went out of business

Direct Materials Efficiency Variance ($360 F, due to actual usage of 1.58 square metres per desk, compared to budgeted 1.6 square metres)

- Standard wrongly (unrealistically) set
- Increased skills of workers
- Use of more automated machinery (e.g., laser cutting)

- Workers did more extensive planning and scheduling for materials usage
- Economies of scale in production

Direct Manufacturing Labour Price Variance ($2,325 U, due to actual rate of $37.00 compared to budgeted $36.00)

- Standard wrongly (unrealistically) set
- Use of higher skill mix than budgeted
- Poor negotiations with labour
- Overtime may have been necessary to produce the extra 50 desks
- Unexpected labour shortage due to external factors

Direct Manufacturing Labour Efficiency Variance ($2,700 U, due to actual time being 3.1 hours compared to budgeted 3.0 hours per desk)

- Standard wrongly (unrealistically) set
- Labour may be less efficient at higher output levels due to tiredness
- Scheduler assigned less skilled workers to desk production
- Machine breakdowns required more use of labour
- Lower quality wood purchased requiring more labour input to finish desks

7-24 (25-30 min.) Flexible budget preparation and analysis.

1. Variance Analysis for Bank Management Printers for September 2007

Level 1 Analysis

	Actual Results (1)	Static-Budget Variances (2)=(1)–(3)	Static Budget (3)
Units sold	12,000	3,000 U	15,000
Revenues	$302,400a	$57,600 U	$360,000c
Variable costs	100,800d	43,200 F	144,000f
Contribution margin	201,600	14,400 U	216,000
Fixed costs	180,000	6,000 U	174,000
Operating income	$ 21,600	$ 20,400 U	$ 42,000

$20,400 U

Total static-budget variance

2. Level 2 Analysis

	Actual Results (1)	Flexible-Budget Variances (2)=(1)–(3)	Flexible Budget (3)	Sales-Volume Variances (4)=(3)–(5)	Static Budget (5)
Units sold	12,000	0	12,000	3,000 U	15,000
Revenues	$302,400[a]	$14,400 F	$288,000[b]	$72,000 U	$360,000[c]
Variable costs	100,800[d]	14,400 F	115,200[e]	28,800 F	144,000[f]
Contribution margin	201,600	28,800 F	172,800	43,200 U	216,000
Fixed costs	180,000	6,000 U	174,000	0	174,000
Operating income	$ 21,600	$22,800 F	$ (1,200)	$43,200 U	$ 42,000
		$22,800 F		$43,200 U	

Total flexible-budget variance   Total sales-volume variance

$20,400 U

Total static-budget variance

[a] $12,000 \times \$25.20 = \$302,400$ [d] $12,000 \times \$8.40 = \$100,800$

[b] $12,000 \times \$24 = \$288,000$ [e] $12,000 \times \$9.60 = \$115,200$

[c] $15,000 \times \$24 = \$360,000$ [f] $15,000 \times \$9.60 = \$144,000$

3. Level 2 analysis provides a breakdown of the static-budget variance into a flexible-budget variance and a sales-volume variance. The primary reason for the static-budget variance being unfavourable ($20,400 U) is the reduction in unit volume from the budgeted 15,000 to an actual 12,000. One explanation for this reduction is the increase in selling price from a budgeted $24.00 to an actual $25.20. Operating management was able to reduce variable costs by $14,400 relative to the flexible budget. This reduction could be a sign of efficient management. Alternatively, it could be due to using lower-quality materials (which in turn might have adversely affected unit volume).

7-26 (45-50 min.) Activity-based costing, flexible-budget variances for finance function activities.

1. *Receivables*

   Receivables is an output unit level activity. Its flexible-budget variance can be calculated as follows:

$$\text{Flexible-volume variance} = \text{Actual costs} - \text{Flexible-budget costs}$$
$$= (\$0.90 \times 948,000) - (\$0.767 \times 948,000)$$
$$= \$853,200 - \$727,116$$
$$= \$126,084 \text{ U}$$

Payables

Payables is a batch level activity.

		Static-budget Amounts	Actual Amounts
a.	Number of deliveries	1,000,000	948,000
b.	Batch size (units per batch)	5	4.46801
c.	Number of batches (a ÷ b)	200,000	212,175
d.	Cost per batch	$3.48	$3.36
e.	Total payables activity cost (c × d)	$696,000	$712,908

Step 1: The number of batches in which payables should have been processed = 948,000 actual units ÷ 5 budgeted units per batch = 189,600 batches

Step 2: The flexible-budget amount for payables
= 189,600 batches × $3.48 budgeted cost per batch
= $659,808

The flexible-budget variance can be computed as follows:

$$\text{Flexible-budget variance} = \text{Actual costs} - \text{Flexible-budget costs}$$
$$= (212,175 \times \$3.36) - (189,600 \times \$3.48)$$
$$= \$712,908 - \$659,808 = \$53,100 \text{ U}$$

Travel expenses

Travel expenses is a batch level activity.

		Static-Budget Amounts	Actual Amounts
a.	Number of deliveries	1,000,000	948,000
b.	Batch size (units per batch)	500	501.587
c.	Number of batches (a ÷ b)	2,000	1,890
d.	Cost per batch	$9.12	$8.88
e.	Total travel expenses activity cost (c × d)	$18,240	$16,783

Step 1: The number of batches in which the travel expense should have been processed = 948,000 actual units ÷ 500 budgeted units per batch = 1,896 batches

Step 2: The flexible-budget amount for travel expenses
= 1,896 batches × $9.12 budgeted cost per batch
= $17,292

The flexible budget variance can be calculated as follows:

$$
\begin{aligned}
\text{Flexible-budget variance} \ &= \ \text{Actual costs} - \text{Flexible-budget costs} \\
&= \ (1,890 \times \$8.88) - (1,896 \times \$9.12) \\
&= \ \$16,783 - \$17,292 = \$509 \text{ F}
\end{aligned}
$$

2. The flexible budget variances can be subdivided into price and efficiency variances.

$$
\text{Price variance} = \left[\begin{array}{c} \text{Actual price} \\ \text{of input} \end{array} - \begin{array}{c} \text{Budgeted price} \\ \text{of input} \end{array} \right] \times \begin{array}{c} \text{Actual quantity} \\ \text{of input purchased} \end{array}
$$

$$
\text{Efficiency variance} = \left[\begin{array}{c} \text{Actual quantity} \\ \text{of input used} \end{array} - \begin{array}{c} \text{Budgeted quantity of} \\ \text{input allowed for} \\ \text{actual output} \end{array} \right] \times \begin{array}{c} \text{Budgeted price} \\ \text{of input} \end{array}
$$

Receivables

Price variance	=	($0.90 − $0.767) × 948,000
	=	$126,084 U
Efficiency variance	=	(948,000 − 948,000) × $0.767
	=	$0

Payables

Price variance	=	($3.36 − $3.48) × 212,175
	=	$25,461 F
Efficiency variance	=	(212,175 − 189,600) × $3.48
	=	$78,561 U

Travel expenses

Price variance	=	($8.88 − $9.12) × 1,890[a]
	=	$454 F
Efficiency variance	=	(1,890 − 1,896) × $9.12
	=	$55 F

[a] 948,000 ÷ 501.587 = 1,890

7-28 (30 min.) Flexible budget, direct materials and direct manufacturing labour variances.

1.

	Actual Results (1)	Flexible-Budget Variances (2)=(1)–(3)	Flexible Budget (3)	Sales-Volume Variances (4)=(3)–(5)	Static Budget (5)
Units sold	6,000[a]	0	6,000	1,000 F	5,000[a]
Direct materials	$792,000[f]	$72,000 U	$ 720,000[b]	$120,000 U	$600,000[c]
Direct manufacturing labour	1,125,000[a]	27,000 F	1,152,000[d]	192,000 U	960,000[e]
Fixed costs	1,206,000[a]	6,000 U	1,200,000[a]	0	1,200,000[a]
Total costs	$3,123,000	$51,000 U	$3,072,000	$312,000 U	$2,760,000

$51,000 U $312,000 U

Flexible-budget variance   Sales-volume variance

$363,000 U

Static-budget variance

[a]Given
[b]$120 × 6,000 = $720,000
[c]$120 × 5,000 = $600,000
[d]$192 × 6,000 = $1,152,000
[e]$192 × 5,000 = $960,000
[f]60,000 kg × $13.20/kilogram = $792,000

2.

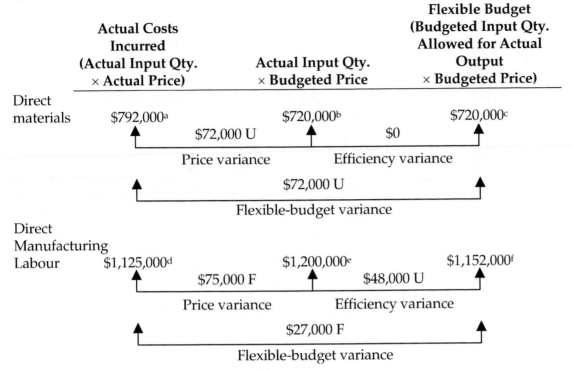

	Actual Costs Incurred (Actual Input Qty. × Actual Price)		Actual Input Qty. × Budgeted Price		Flexible Budget (Budgeted Input Qty. Allowed for Actual Output × Budgeted Price)

Direct materials $792,000[a] — $72,000 U — $720,000[b] — $0 — $720,000[c]

Price variance   Efficiency variance

$72,000 U

Flexible-budget variance

Direct Manufacturing Labour $1,125,000[d] — $75,000 F — $1,200,000[e] — $48,000 U — $1,152,000[f]

Price variance   Efficiency variance

$27,000 F

Flexible-budget variance

[a]60,000 kilograms × $13.20/kilogram = $792,000
[b]60,000 kilograms × $12.00/kilogram = $720,000
[c]6,000 statues × 10 kilograms/statue × $12/kilogram = 60,000 kilograms × $12/kilogram = $720,000
[d]25,000 labour-hours × $45/hour = $1,125,000
[e]25,000 labour-hours × $48/hour = $1,200,000
[f]6,000 statues × 4 hours/statue × $48/hour = 24,000 hours × $48/hour = $1,152,000

7-30 (20 min.) Continuous improvement (continuation of 7-29).

1. Standard quantity input amounts per output unit are:

Direct Materials: March = Feb. × 0.997 = Jan. × 0.997 × 0.997
$$= 10 \text{ kg} \times 0.997 \times 0.997 = 9.94 \text{ kg}$$
Direct Manufacturing Labour: March = 0.5 hrs. × 0.997 × 0.997 = 0.497 hrs.

2. The answer to requirement 1 of Question 7-29 is identical except for the flexible-budget amount.

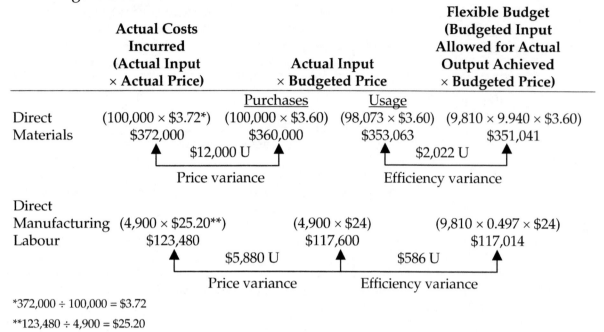

	Actual Costs Incurred (Actual Input × Actual Price)		**Actual Input × Budgeted Price**	**Flexible Budget (Budgeted Input Allowed for Actual Output Achieved × Budgeted Price)**
		Purchases	Usage	
Direct Materials	(100,000 × $3.72*) $372,000	(100,000 × $3.60) $360,000	(98,073 × $3.60) $353,063	(9,810 × 9.940 × $3.60) $351,041
	↑ $12,000 U ↑		↑ $2,022 U ↑	
	Price variance		Efficiency variance	
Direct Manufacturing Labour	(4,900 × $25.20**) $123,480		(4,900 × $24) $117,600	(9,810 × 0.497 × $24) $117,014
	↑ $5,880 U ↑		↑ $586 U ↑	
	Price variance		Efficiency variance	

*372,000 ÷ 100,000 = $3.72

**123,480 ÷ 4,900 = $25.20

Using continuous improvement standards sets a tougher benchmark. The efficiency variances for March (from Exercise 7-29) and the revised ones that represent a continuous improvement approach (from Exercise 7-30) are:

	March	**March (with continuous improvement)**
Direct materials	$97 F	$2,022 U
Direct manufacturing labour	$120 F	$586 U

Note that the question assumes the continuous improvement applies only to quantity inputs. An alternative approach is to have continuous improvement apply to budgeted input cost per output unit ($36 for direct materials and $12 for direct manufacturing labour originally). This approach is more difficult to incorporate in a Level 2 variance analysis as Level 2 requires separate amounts for quantity inputs and the cost per input.

7-32 (15-25 min.) Journal entries and T-accounts (continuation of 7-31).

The following journal entries relate to the measurement of variances when materials and manufacturing labour are used.

(a) Work in Process Control $480,000
    Direct Materials Price Variance   8,880
        Direct Materials Efficiency Variance $ 36,000
        Materials Control   452,880
    To record direct materials used

(b) Work in Process Control $240,000
        Direct Manufacturing Labour Price Variance $ 4,320
        Direct Manufacturing Labour Efficiency Variance   24,000
        Wages Payable Control   211,680
    To record liability and allocation of direct labour costs

Materials Control		Direct Materials Price Variance		Direct Materials Efficiency Variance	
	(a) $452,880	(a) 8,800			(a) 36,000

Work in Process Control		Direct Manufacturing Labour Price Variance		Direct Manufacturing Labour Efficiency Variance	
(a) 480,000			(b) 4,320		(b) 24,000
(b) 240,000					

Wages Payable Control	
	(b) 211,680

The following journal entries pertain to the measurement of price variances when materials are purchased:

(c) Materials Control $720,000
    Direct Materials Price Variance   14,400
        Accounts Payable Control $734,400
    To record direct materials purchased

(d) Work in Process Control $480,000
         Materials Control $444,000
         Direct Materials Efficiency Variance   36,000
      To record direct materials used

Materials Control		Direct Materials Price Variance	
(c) 720,000	(d) 444,000	(c) 14,400	

Accounts Payable Control		Work in Process Control	
	(c) 734,400	(d) 480,000	

Direct Materials Efficiency Variance	
	(d) 36,000 F

The difference between standard costing and normal costing for direct cost items is:

	Standard Costs	Normal Costs
Direct Costs	Standard price(s) × Standard input allowed for actual outputs achieved	Actual price(s) × Actual input

These journal entries differ from the <u>normal costing</u> entries because Work in Process Control is no longer carried at "actual" costs. Furthermore, Materials Control can also be carried at standard unit prices rather than actual unit prices. Finally, variances appear for direct materials and direct manufacturing labour under <u>standard costing</u> but not under <u>normal costing</u>.

7-34 (30 min.) Flexible budget preparation, service sector.

1. • Budgeted selling price (revenue per loan application)
       1/2% × budgeted average loan amount = 1/2% × $240,000 = $1,200
    • Budgeted variable costs per output unit are:
         Professional labour (6 × $48) $288
         Loan filing fees   120
         Credit worthiness checks   144
         Courier mailings   60
         Budgeted variable costs $612
    • Budgeted fixed costs = $37,200 per month.

The static budget for the 90 loan applicant level (and the flexible budget for the 120 loan application level in Requirement 2) are:

	Requirement 1 90 Loan Applications	Requirement 2 120 Loan Applications
Budgeted revenue (90, 120 × $1,200)	$108,000	$144,000
Budgeted variable costs (90, 120 × $612)	55,080	73,440
Contribution margin	52,920	70,560
Fixed costs	37,200	37,200
Operating income	$ 15,720	$ 33,360

2. The actual results are:

Revenue (120 × 1/2% × $268,800)		$161,280
Variable costs:		
Professional labour (120 × 7.2 × $50.40)	$ 43,546	
Loan filing fees (120 × $120)	14,400	
Credit worthiness checks (120 × $150)	18,000	
Courier mailings (120 × $64.80)	7,776	83,722
Contribution margin		77,558
Fixed costs		40,200
Operating income		$ 37,358

These actual results can be analyzed in a Level 2 variance analysis.

Level 2 Analysis

	Actual Results (1)	Flexible- Budget Variances (2)=(1)–(3)	Flexible Budget (3)	Sales- Volume Variances (4)=(3)–(5)	Static Budget (5)
Units sold	120	0	120	30 F	90
Revenue	$161,280	$17,280 F	$144,000	$36,000 F	$108,000
Variable costs	83,722	10,282 U	73,440	18,360 U	55,080
Contribution margin	77,558	6,998 F	70,560	17,640 F	52,920
Fixed costs	40,200	3,000 U	37,200	0	37,200
Total costs	$ 37,358	$ 3,998 F	$ 33,360	$17,640 F	$15,720

$3,998 F — Total flexible-budget variance

$17,640 F — Total sales-volume variance

$21,638 F — Total static-budget variance

125

Note that the $21,638 favourable static-budget variance is largely the result of an increase in loan applications from a budgeted 90 to an actual 120. In addition, the average size of a loan increased from a budgeted $240,000 to $268,800 which explains the flexible-budget variance of $17,280 F for revenues (0.5% × $28,800 × 120 = $17,280).

One possible explanation is a rapid decrease in interest rates leading to an increase in demand for loan refinancing.

7-36 (30-40 min.) Direct materials variances, long-term agreement with supplier.

1.

Month (1)	Total Actual Direct Materials Usage in Dollars (2)	Average Actual Direct Materials Purchase Price per Kilogram of Metal (3)	Total Actual Quantity of Direct Materials in Kilograms (4) = (2) ÷ (3)	Number of Machining Systems Produced (5)	Actual Direct Materials Input in Kilograms per Machining System (6) = (4) ÷ (5)
January	$290,880	$144	2,020	10	202
February	343,872	144	2,388	12	199
March	530,712	151.2	3,510	18	195
April	474,317	153.6	3,088	16	193
May	304,128	144	2,112	11	192

Materials Price Variance

Month (1)	Actual Costs Incurred: Actual Input × Actual Price (2)	Actual Input (3)	Budgeted Price per Unit of Input (4)	Actual Input × Budgeted Price (5) = (3) × (4)	Direct Materials Price Variance (6) = (2) − (5)
January	$290,880	2,020	$144	$290,880	$ 0
February	343,872	2,388	144	343,872	0
March	530,712	3,510	144	505,440	25,272 U
April	474,317	3,088	144	444,672	29,645 U
May	304,128	2,112	144	304,128	0

Materials Efficiency Variance

Month (1)	Actual Input × Budgeted Price (2)	Budgeted Input per Unit of Output (3)	Actual Output Achieved (4)	Budgeted Price per Unit of Input (5)	Flexible Budget (Budgeted Input Allowed for Actual Output Achieved × Budgeted Price) (6) = (3) × (4) × (5)	Direct Materials Efficiency Variance (7) = (2) − (6)
January	$290,880	198	10	$144	$285,120	$ 5,760 U
February	343,872	198	12	144	342,144	1,728 U
March	505,440	198	18	144	513,216	7,776 F
April	444,672	198	16	144	456,192	11,520 F
May	304,128	198	11	144	313,632	9,504 F

2. The unfavourable materials price variances in March and April imply that Mazak paid more than $144 per kilogram above the 2,400 kilogram contract amount.

Month (1)	Total Actual Costs Incurred (2)	Contract Amount for 2,400 kg: 2,400 × $144 (3)	Cost for Purchases Above 2,400 kg (4) = (2) − (3)	Quantity of Purchases Above 2,400 kg (5)	Actual Price per Kilogram of Purchases Above 2,400 kg (6) = (4) ÷ (5)
March	$530,712	$345,600	$185,112	1,110	$166.77
April	474,317	345,600	128,717	688	187.09

The percentage price increases for the additional purchases above 2,400 kilograms are:

	Actual Price	Standard Price	% Increase
March	$166.77	$144	15.8
April	187.09	144	29.9

With a long-term agreement that has a fixed purchase-price clause for a set minimum quantity, no price variance will arise when the purchase amount is below the minimum quantity (assuming the budgeted price per unit is the contract price per unit). A price variance will occur only when the purchased amount exceeds the set minimum quantity. A price variance signals that the purchased amount exceeds this set minimum quantity (2,400 kilograms per month).

It is likely that the supplier will charge a higher price (above $144) for purchases above the 2,400 base. If a lower price were charged, the purchaser might apply pressure to renegotiate the contract purchase price for the base amount. If the purchasing officer is able to negotiate only a small price increase for additional purchases above the base amount, the purchasing performance may well be "favourable" despite the materials price variance being labelled "unfavourable."

Mazak may see the advantage of a long-term contract in factors other than purchase price (for example, a higher quality of materials, a lower required level of inventories because of more frequent deliveries, and a guaranteed availability of materials). In general, the existence of a long-term agreement reduces the importance of materials price variances when evaluating the month-to-month performance of a purchasing officer.

7-38 (20-30 min.) **Direct materials and manufacturing labour variances, solving unknowns.**

All given items are designated by an asterisk.

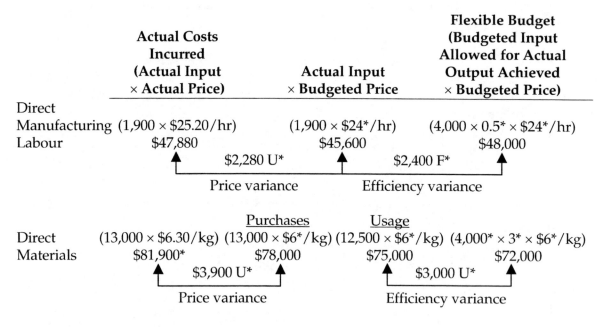

1. $4,000 \times 0.5 = 2,000$ hours
2. $1,900$ hours [($48,000 - 2,400) \div \$24/hr = 1,900$ hours]
3. $\$25.20$ [($48,000 - 2,400 + 2,280) \div 1,900 = \$25.20/hr$]
4. $4,000 \times 3 = 12,000$ kilograms
5. $12,500$ kilograms [($72,000 + 3,000) \div \$6/kg = 12,500$ kg]
6. $13,000$ kilograms [($81,900 - 3,900) \div \$6/kg = 13,000$ kg]
7. $\$6.30/kg$ [$81,900 \div 13,000$ kg = $\$6.30/kg$]

7-40 (30 min.) Activity-based costing, variance analysis.

			Static-Budget Amounts	Actual Amounts
1.	a.	Units of cakes produced and sold	240,000	330,000
	b.	Average batch size (cakes per batch)	6,000	10,000
	c.	Number of batches (a ÷ b)	40	33
	d.	Changeover labour-hours per batch	20	24
	e.	Total changeover labour-hours (c × d)	800	792
	f.	Cost per changeover labour-hours	$24	$25
	g.	Total changeover labour cost (e × f)	$19,200	$19,800

Step 1: The number of batches in which the actual output units should have been produced:
330,000 actual units of output ÷ 6,000 budgeted batch size = 55 batches

Step 2: The number of changeover labour-hours that should have been used:
20 budgeted changeover-hours × 55 batches = 1,100 changeover-hours.

Step 3: The flexible-budget amount for changeover hours:
1,100 changeover-hours × $24 budgeted cost per changeover-hour = $26,400.

Flexible-budget variance = Actual costs – Flexible-budget costs
= (792 × $25) – (1,100 × $24)
= $19,800 – $26,400 = $6,600 F

2. Price variance = $\left[\begin{array}{c} \text{Actual price} \\ \text{of input} \end{array} - \begin{array}{c} \text{Budgeted price} \\ \text{of input} \end{array} \right] \times \begin{array}{c} \text{Budgeted price} \\ \text{of input} \end{array}$

= ($25 – $24) × 792 = $1 × 792 = $792 U

Efficiency variance = $\left[\begin{array}{c} \text{Actual quantity} \\ \text{of input used} \end{array} - \begin{array}{c} \text{Budgeted quantity} \\ \text{of input allowed} \\ \text{for actual output} \end{array} \right] \times \begin{array}{c} \text{Budgeted price} \\ \text{of input} \end{array}$

= (792 – 1,100) × $24 = 308 × $24 = $7,392 F

The favourable flexible-budget variance of $6,600 comprises two offsetting amounts:

- Price variance of $792 U due to actual changeover labour cost of $25 per hour exceeding the $24 budgeted rate.
- Efficiency variance of $7,392 F due to the actual batch size of 10,000 being *sizably* above the budgeted batch size of 6,000. Efficiency variance is favourable because less batches were required to produce 330,000 cakes even

though actual changeover labour-hours of 24 per batch were higher than the budgeted changeover-hours per batch of 20 hours.

3. Explanations for the price variance of $792 U include:

- More highly trained workers hired to make changeovers.
- Change in labour market required unexpected increase in labour rates to retain workers.
- Budgeted amounts were set without adequate analysis.

Explanations for the efficiency variance of $7,392 F include:

- More highly trained workers were able to produce larger batch sizes.
- More automated machinery was acquired.
- Budgeted amounts were set without adequate analysis.

7-42 (30 min.) Comprehensive variance analysis.

1. (a) Aunt Molly's Old Fashioned Cookies unit selling prices and unit costs of inputs:

Actual selling price = $4,266,000 ÷ 450,000 kg
= $9.48

Budgeting selling price = $3,840,000 ÷ 400,000 kg
= $9.60

$$\text{Selling-price variance} = \left(\begin{array}{c}\text{Actual} \\ \text{selling price}\end{array} - \begin{array}{c}\text{Budgeted} \\ \text{selling price}\end{array}\right) \times \begin{array}{c}\text{Actual} \\ \text{units sold}\end{array}$$

= ($9.48 − $9.60) × 450,000 kg
= $54,000 U

(b) to (e)

The actual and budgeted unit costs are:

	Actual	Budgeted
Direct materials		
Cookie mix	$0.384	$0.384
Milk chocolate	$3.84	$2.88
Almonds	$9.60	$9.60
Direct labour		
Mixing	$17.28	$17.28
Baking	$21.60	$21.60

The actual output achieved is 450,000 kilograms of chocolate nut supreme.

The direct cost price and efficiency variances are:

	Actual Costs Incurred (Actual Input × Actual Price) (1)	Price Variance (2)=(1)–(3)	Actual Input × Budgeted Prices (3)	Efficiency Variance (4)=(3)–(5)	Flex. Budget (Budgeted Input Allowed for Actual Output Achieved × Budgeted Price) (5)
Direct materials					
Cookie mix	$ 111,360	$ 0	$111,360[a]	$ 3,360 U	$108,000[h]
Milk chocolate	$ 621,005	155,251 U	465,754[b]	60,754 U	405,000[i]
Almonds	$ 285,000	0	285,000[c]	15,000 U	270,000[j]
	$1,017,365	$155,251 U	$862,114	$79,114 U	$783,000
Direct labour costs					
Mixing	$129,600	$ 0	$129,600[d]	$ 0	$129,600[k]
Baking	$288,000	0	288,000[e]	36,000 F	324,000[l]
	$417,600	$ 0	$417,600	$36,000 F	$453,600

[a]$0.384 × 290,000 kg = $111,360
[b]$2.88 × 161,720 kg = $465,754
[c]$9.60 × 29,688 kg = $285,000
[d]$17.28 × (450,000 ÷ 60) = $129,600
[e]$21.60 × (800,000 ÷ 60) = $288,000

[h]$0.384/kg × 281,250* kg = $108,000
[i]$2.88/kg × 140,625* kg = $405,000
[j]$9.60/kg × 28,125* kg = $270,000
[k]$17.28 × (1/60) × 450,000 = $129,600
[l]$21.60 × (2/60) × 450,000 = $324,000

*Cookie mix: $0.625 \left(\dfrac{\text{kg mix}}{\text{kg total}} \right) \times 450{,}000 \text{ kg total} = 281{,}250 \text{ kg}$

Milk chocolate: $0.3125 \left(\dfrac{\text{kg choc.}}{\text{kg total}} \right) \times 450{,}000 \text{ kg total} = 140{,}625 \text{ kg}$

Almonds: $0.0625 \left(\dfrac{\text{kg almonds}}{\text{kg total}} \right) \times 450{,}000 \text{ kg total} = 28{,}125 \text{ kg}$

2. (a) Selling price variance. This may arise from a proactive decision to reduce price to expand market share or from a reaction to a price reduction by a competitor. It could also arise from unplanned price discounting by salespeople.

   (b) Material price variance. The $0.96 increase in the price per kilogram of milk chocolate could arise from uncontrollable market factors or from poor contract negotiations by Aunt Molly's.

   (c) Material efficiency variance. For all three material inputs, usage is greater than budgeted. Possible reasons include lower quality inputs, use of lower quality workers, and the mixing and baking equipment not being maintained in a fully operational mode.

   (d) Labour price variance. The zero variance is consistent with workers being on long-term contracts that are not renegotiated on a month-by-month basis.

   (e) Labour efficiency variance. The favourable efficiency variance for baking could be due to workers eliminating non-valued-added steps in production.

7-44 (60 min.) Continuous improvement (continuation of 7-43).

1. Monthly Standards

	Dec. 2006	Jan. 2007	Feb. 2007
Frames	3.00 grams	2.985	2.970075
		(3.00×0.995)	(2.985×0.995)
Lenses	6.00 grams	5.97	5.94015
		(6.00×0.995)	(5.97×0.995)

These are expressed in physical terms. Assuming a constant standard price ($2.64 for frames and $3.72 for lenses; see Problem 7-43 solution 1b), we can express these in dollars:

	Dec. 2006	Jan. 2007	Feb. 2007
Frames	$7.92[1]	$7.881	$7.841
Lenses	$22.32[2]	22.208	22.097

2. Pros: Puts in a culture of continuous improvement.

   Can be flexible by allowing for different percentages to apply to different materials and to different stages in life cycle.

   Cons: Difficult to have 0.995 forever—you can't ever get down to zero material.

Far too incremental in perspective. A competitor may do a major redesign or use a new material that drops costs dramatically.

[1] $2.64 \times 3.00 = \$7.92$
[2] $3.72 \times 6.00 = \$22.32$

7-46 (30-40 min.) Procurement costs, variance analysis, ethics.

1. Purchase price variances can be computed for each country.

$$\begin{array}{c} \text{Purchase price} \\ \text{variance} \end{array} = \left(\begin{array}{c} \text{Actual price} \\ \text{of input} \end{array} - \begin{array}{c} \text{Budgeted price} \\ \text{of input} \end{array} \right) \times \begin{array}{c} \text{Actual quantity} \\ \text{of input} \end{array}$$

Hergovia

$$= (\$15.60^* - \$14.00) \times 250,000$$
$$= \$400,000 \text{ U}$$

*$3,900,000 \div 250,000 = \$15.60$

On a per-unit basis, there is a $12.43[1] payment to the shoe manufacturer and a $3.17[2] payment for "other costs."

(1) $3,108,000 \div 250,000 = \$12.43$
(2) $792,000 \div 250,000 = \$3.17$

Tanistan

$$= (\$13.67^* - \$14.00) \times 900,000$$
$$= \$297,000 \text{ F}$$

*$12,300,000 \div 900,000 = \$13.67$

On a per-unit basis, there is an $11.26[3] payment to the shoe manufacturer and a $2.40[4] payment for "other costs."

(3) $10,136,000 \div 900,000 = \$11.26$
(4) $2,164,000[5] \div 900,000 = \$2.40$
(5) $12,300,000 - 10,136,000 = \$2,164,000$

2.   The organization structure is:

Daley and Mullins face many ethical issues:

(a)   Reliability of cost information to be presented to the board of directors. There are minimal or questionable receipts for $792,000 in Hergovia and $2,164,000 in Tanistan.

(b)   Potential existence of kickback payments in both Hergovia and Tanistan.

(c)   Employment of young children (many of them under 15 years).

Should Daley and Mullins be forthright and present all their concerns on (a), (b) and (c)?

Both Daley and Mullins face the dilemma that any discussion of (a), (b) or (c) will raise questions about their own behaviour at the time the acquisitions were made. Board members may ask "when did they first know about (a), (b) and (c)?," and "if it is only recently, why did they not undertake examination of these issues at the time they supported the acquisitions?"

3.   Mullins has very high standards of ethical conduct to meet—see Exhibit 1-5 of the text. She should not make presentations to the Board based on information she has strong doubts about. If she decides to make the presentation, all her concerns and caveats should be presented.

She should require detailed documentation for all payments. No future payments should be made without adequate documentation.

Investigation of kickback allegations should be made, however difficult that may be. Mullins should be able to show she made a good-faith effort to ensure kickback payments are not an ongoing practice in Hergovia or Tanistan.

7-48 (30 min.) Price and efficiency variances, problems in standard-setting, benchmarking.

1. Budgeted materials input per shirt = 0.10 roll of cloth (400 rolls ÷ 4,000 shirts)
   Budgeted manufacturing labour hours per shirt = 0.25 hours (1,000 hrs. ÷ 4,000 shirts)
   Budgeted materials cost = $60 per roll ($24,000 ÷ 400 rolls)
   Budgeted manufacturing labour cost = $21.60 per hour ($21,600 ÷ 1,000 hrs.)
   Actual output achieved = 4,488 shirts

2. Actions employees may have taken include:

   (a) Adding steps in working on a shirt that are not necessary.
   (b) Taking more time on each step than is necessary.
   (c) Creating problem situations so that the budgeted amount of average downtime will be overstated.
   (d) Creating defects in shirts so that the budgeted amount of average rework will be overstated.

   Employees may take these actions for several possible reasons.
   (a) They do not share in profits above the survival threshold.
   (b) They may be paid on a piece-rate basis with incentives for above budgeted production.
   (c) They may want to create a relaxed work atmosphere, and less demanding standards can reduce stress.
   (d) They may have a "them versus us" mentality rather than a partnership perspective.

   This behaviour is unethical if it is deliberately designed to undermine the credibility of the standards used at Winston Fabrics.

3. NorthWest could use Benchmarking Clearing House information in several ways:

    (a) For pricing and product emphasis purposes. NorthWest should avoid getting into a pricing war with a competitor who has a sizably lower cost structure.
    (b) As indicators of areas where NorthWest is either highly cost-competitive or highly cost non-competitive.
    (c) As performance targets for motivating and evaluating managers

4. Main pros of Benchmarking Clearing House information:

    (a) Highlights to NorthWest in a direct way how it may or may not be cost competitive.
    (b) Provides a "reality check" to many internal positions about efficiency or effectiveness.

    Main cons are:

    (a) NorthWest may not be comparable to companies in the database.
    (b) Data about other company's costs may not be reliable.
    (c) Cost of Benchmarking Clearing House reports.

CHAPTER 8
FLEXIBLE BUDGETS, VARIANCES, AND MANAGEMENT CONTROL: II

8-2 At the start of an accounting period, a larger percentage of fixed overhead costs are locked-in than is the case with variable overhead costs.

8-4 Steps in developing a budgeted variable-overhead cost rate are:

1. Choose the period to be used for the budget,
2. Select the cost allocation base(s),
3. Identify the costs to include in the variable-overhead cost pool(s), and
4. Estimate the budgeted variable-overhead rate(s).

8-6 Reasons for a $25,000 favourable variable-overhead efficiency variance are:

- workers more skillful in using machines than budgeted
- production scheduler was able to schedule jobs better than budgeted, resulting in lower-than-budgeted machine-hours
- machines operated with fewer slowdowns than budgeted
- machine time standards set with padding built in by machine-workers.

8-8 Steps in developing a budgeted fixed-overhead rate are:

Step 1: Choose the time period used to compute the budget,
Step 2: Select the cost allocation base,
Step 3: Identify the costs in the fixed-overhead cost pool(s),
Step 4: Estimate the budgeted quantity of the allocation base(s), and
Step 5: Compute the budgeted fixed-overhead rate(s).

8-10 A four-variance analysis relies on

(a) a breakdown of overhead into its variable and fixed components, and
(b) a breakdown for each type of overhead into three components—spending, efficiency, and production volume.

A three-variance analysis relies only on the breakdown of variances into the three components in (b).

A two-variance analysis breaks down variances into only two components (flexible-budget and production-volume).

A one-variance analysis reports only one total variance where there is no breakdown of the (a) or (b) categories noted above.

8-12 Fixed manufacturing costs represent resources sacrificed in acquiring capacity that cannot be decreased if the resources needed are less than the resources acquired. A lump-sum amount of fixed costs will be unaffected by the degree of operating efficiency in a given budget period.

8-14 For planning and control purposes, fixed overhead costs are a lump sum amount that is not controlled on a per-unit basis. In contrast, for inventory costing purposes fixed overhead costs are allocated to products on a per-unit basis. See Exhibit 8-4 (page 301) in the text.

8-16 (20 min.) Variable manufacturing overhead, variance analysis.

1.

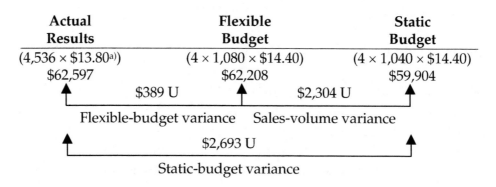

Actual Results		Flexible Budget		Static Budget
(4,536 × $13.80ª))		(4 × 1,080 × $14.40)		(4 × 1,040 × $14.40)
$62,597		$62,208		$59,904
	$389 U		$2,304 U	
	Flexible-budget variance		Sales-volume variance	
		$2,693 U		
		Static-budget variance		

a) $62,597 ÷ 4,536 hrs. = $13.80 per hr.

2. Esquire manufactured 40 suits more than the 1,040 budgeted. This accounts for the unfavourable sales-volume variance of $2,304 for variable manufacturing overhead.

   The actual variable manufacturing overhead of $62,597 exceeds the flexible budget amount of $62,208 for 1,080 suits by $389—hence the flexible budget variance is $389 U.

NOT REQUIRED

Further insight into the flexible-budget variance of $389 U for variable MOH is provided by the spending and efficiency variances:

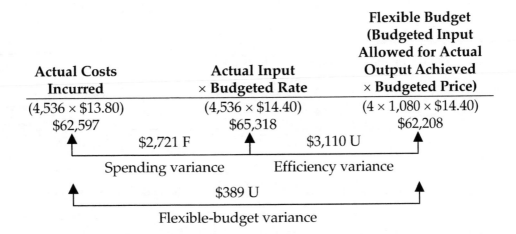

Esquire had a favourable spending variance of $2,721, (the actual variable overhead rate was $13.80 per direct manufacturing labour-hour versus the $14.40 budgeted). It had an unfavourable efficiency variance of $3,110 U (each suit averaged 4.2 labour-hours versus 4.00 budgeted).

8-18 (30 min.) **Variable manufacturing overhead variance analysis.**

1. Denominator level =
    (3,200,000 ÷ 100 × 2 hours) =
    (3,200,000 × 0.02 hours) = 64,000 hours

2.

		Actual Results	Flexible Budget Amount
1.	Output units (baguettes)	2,800,000	2,800,000
2.	Direct labour-hours	50,400	56,000[a]
3.	Labour-hours per output unit (2 ÷ 1)	0.018	0.020
4.	Variable MOH costs	$816,480	$672,000[b]
5.	Variable MOH per labour-hour (4 ÷ 2)	$16.20	$12.00
6.	Variable MOH per output unit (4 ÷ 1)	$0.292	$0.240

[a] 2,800,000 × 0.020 = 56,000 hours

[b] $\frac{\$12.00}{hr.}$ × 56,000 hrs. = $672,000

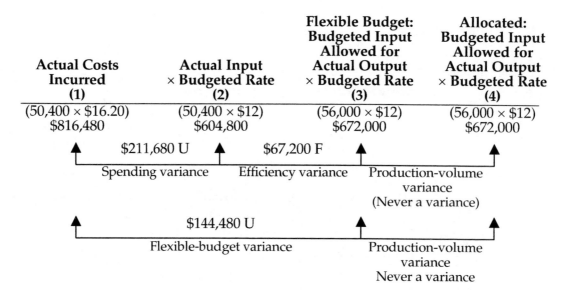

	Actual Costs Incurred (1)	Actual Input × Budgeted Rate (2)	Flexible Budget: Budgeted Input Allowed for Actual Output × Budgeted Rate (3)	Allocated: Budgeted Input Allowed for Actual Output × Budgeted Rate (4)
	(50,400 × $16.20) $816,480	(50,400 × $12) $604,800	(56,000 × $12) $672,000	(56,000 × $12) $672,000

$211,680 U ← Spending variance → $67,200 F ← Efficiency variance → Production-volume variance (Never a variance)

$144,480 U ← Flexible-budget variance → Production-volume variance Never a variance

3. Spending variance of $211,680 U. It is unfavourable because variable manufacturing overhead was 35% higher than planned. A possible explanation could be an increase in energy rates relative to the rate per standard labour-hour assumed in the flexible budget.

Efficiency variance of $67,200 F. It is favourable because the actual number of direct manufacturing labour-hours required was lower than the number of hours budgeted. Labour was more efficient in producing the baguettes than management had anticipated in the budget. This could occur because of improved morale in the company, which could result from an increase in wages or an improvement in the compensation scheme.

Flexible-budget variance of $144,480 U. It is unfavourable because the favourable efficiency variance was not large enough to compensate for the large unfavourable spending variance.

8-20 (30-40 min.) Manufacturing overhead, variance analysis.

1. The summary analysis is:

	Spending Variance	Efficiency Variance	Production-Volume Variance
Variable Manufacturing Overhead	$48,840 F	$71,040 U	Never a variance
Fixed-Manufacturing Overhead	$28,104 U	Never a variance	$43,200 U

Variable Manufacturing Overhead

	Actual Costs Incurred	Actual Input × Budgeted Price	Flexible Budget (Budgeted Input Allowed for Actual Output Achieved × Budgeted Price)
		(16,280 × $48)	(7,400 × 2 × $48)
	$732,600	$781,440	$710,400

$48,840 F → Spending variance

$71,040 U → Efficiency variance

$22,200 U → Flexible-budget variance

Fixed Manufacturing Overhead

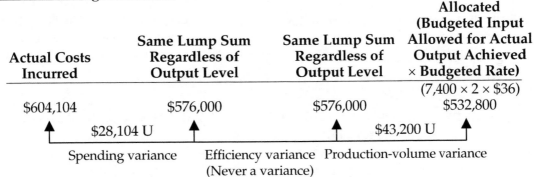

Actual Costs Incurred	Same Lump Sum Regardless of Output Level	Same Lump Sum Regardless of Output Level	Allocated (Budgeted Input Allowed for Actual Output Achieved × Budgeted Rate)
			(7,400 × 2 × $36)
$604,104	$576,000	$576,000	$532,800

$28,104 U → Spending variance

Efficiency variance (Never a variance)

$43,200 U → Production-volume variance

Summary information is:

	Actual	Flexible Budget	Static Budget
Output units	7,400	7,400	8,000
Allocation base (hours)	16,280	14,800[a]	16,000[b]
Allocation base per output unit	2.20	2.00	2.00
Variable MOH	$732,600	$710,400[c]	—
Variable MOH per hour	$45.00[d]	$48.00	—
Fixed MOH	$604,104	$576,000	$576,000
Fixed MOH per hour	$39.32[e]	—	$36.00[f]

[a]7,400 × 2.00 = 14,800 [b]8,000 × 2.00 = 16,000
[c]7,400 × 2 × $48 = $710,400 [d]$732,600 ÷ 16,280 hours = $45.00 per hour
[e]$640,104 ÷ 16,280 hours = $39.32 per hour [f]$576,000 ÷ 16,000 hours = $36 per hour

2. Zyton produced 600 fewer CardioX units than were budgeted. The variable manufacturing overhead cost efficiency variance of $71,040 U arises because more assembly time hours per output unit (16,280 ÷ 7,400 = 2.2 hours) were used than the budgeted 2.0 hours per unit. The variable manufacturing overhead cost spending variance of $48,840 F indicates one or more of the following probably

occurred—(i) actual prices of individual items included in variable overhead differ from their budgeted prices, or (ii) actual usage of individual items included in variable overhead differs from their budgeted usage.

The fixed manufacturing overhead cost spending variance of $28,104 U means fixed overhead was above that budgeted. For example, it could be due to an unexpected increase in plant leasing costs. The unfavourable production-volume variance of $43,200 arises because actual output of 7,400 units is below the 8,000 units used in determining the $36.00 per assembly-hour budgeted rate.

3. Planning and control of *variable* manufacturing overhead costs has both a long-run and a short-run focus. It involves Zyton planning to undertake only value-added overhead activities (a long-run view) and then managing the cost drivers of those activities in the most efficient way (a short-run view). Planning and control of *fixed* manufacturing overhead costs at Zyton has primarily a long-run focus. It involves undertaking only value-added fixed-overhead activities for a budgeted level of output. Zyton makes most of the key decisions that determine the level of fixed-overhead costs at the start of the accounting period.

8-22 (20-25 min.) Spending and efficiency overhead variances, distribution.

1. Budgeted variable overhead rate = $2.40 per hour of delivery time

Budgeted fixed overhead rate $= \dfrac{\$144,000}{100,000 \times 0.25} = \dfrac{\$144,000}{25,000}$

= $5.76 per hour of delivery time

A detailed comparison of actual and flexible budgeted amounts is:

	Actual	Flexible Budget	Static Budget
Output units (deliveries)	96,000	96,000	100,000
Allocation base (hours)	28,800	24,000[a]	25,000[b]
Allocation base per output unit	0.30[c]	0.25	0.25
Variable MOH	$72,000	$57,600[d]	—
Variable MOH per hour	$2.50[e]	$2.40	$2.40
Fixed MOH	$154,080	$144,000	$144,000
Fixed MOH per hour	$5.35[f]	—	$5.76[g]

[a]$96,000 \times 0.25 = 24,000$
[b]$100,000 \times 0.25 = 25,000$
[c]$28,800 \div 96,000 = 0.30$
[d]$96,000 \times 0.25 \times \$2.40 = \$57,600$
[e]$\$72,000 \div 28,800 = \$2.50$
[f]$\$154,080 \div 28,800 = \$5.35$
[g]$\$144,000 \div 25,000 = \$5.76$

The required variances are:

	Spending Variance	Efficiency Variance
Variable overhead	$2,880 U	$11,520 U
Fixed overhead	$10,080 U	—

These variances are computed as follows:

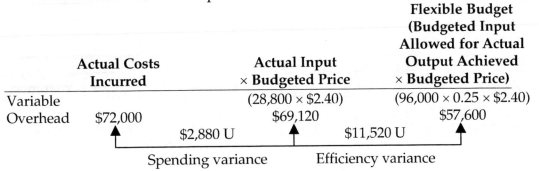

	Actual Costs Incurred	Actual Input × Budgeted Price	Flexible Budget (Budgeted Input Allowed for Actual Output Achieved × Budgeted Price)
Variable Overhead	$72,000	(28,800 × $2.40) $69,120	(96,000 × 0.25 × $2.40) $57,600

$2,880 U ← Spending variance

$11,520 U ← Efficiency variance

	Actual Costs Incurred	Same Lump Sum Regardless of Output Level	Same Lump Sum Regardless of Output Level	Allocated (Budgeted Input Allowed for Actual Output Achieved × Budgeted Rate)
Fixed Overhead	$154,080	$144,000	$144,000	(96,000 × 0.25 × $5.76) $138,240

$10,080 U ← Spending variance | Efficiency variance (Never a variance) | $5,760 U ← Production-volume variance

The spending variances for variable and fixed overhead are both unfavourable. This means that PPS had increases in either or both the cost of individual items (such as gasoline and truck maintenance) or higher-than-budgeted usage of these individual items per unit of the allocation base (delivery time). The unfavourable efficiency variance for variable overhead results from less efficient use of the cost allocation base—each delivery takes 0.30 hours versus a budgeted 0.25 hours.

2. The single direct cost category is delivery driver payments. The major problem in managing these costs is to restrain the rate of increase in the rate paid to drivers per delivery. PPS faces the challenge of having a low-cost delivery infrastructure. For example, purchasing delivery trucks with low fuel consumption will help reduce variable overhead costs. Purchasing vehicles with low annual maintenance will help reduce fixed overhead costs. Variable overhead costs are controlled by

both cost planning, well prior to their incurrence, and day-to-day decisions. In contrast, most fixed overhead cost items are controlled by planning decisions made prior to the start of the year.

8-24 (20-30 min.) Straightforward four-variance overhead analysis.

The budget for fixed manufacturing overhead is $4,000 \times 6 \times \$18 = \$432,000$.

1.

Four-Variance Analysis	Spending Variance	Efficiency Variance	Production-Volume Variance
Variable Manufacturing Overhead	$20,020 U	$21,120 U	Never a variance
Fixed Manufacturing Overhead	$15,590 U	Never a variance	$43,200 F

Solution Exhibit 8-24 has details of these variances.

A detailed comparison of actual and flexible budgeted amounts is:

	Actual	Flexible Budget	Static Budget
Output units (auto parts)	4,400	4,400	4,000
Allocation base (machine hours)	28,600	26,400[a]	24,000[b]
Allocation base per output unit	6.50[c]	6.00	6.00
Variable MOH	$294,580	$253,440[d]	—
Variable MOH per hour	$10.30[e]	$9.60	$9.60
Fixed MOH	$447,590	$432,000[f]	$432,000[f]
Fixed MOH per hour	$15.65[g]	—	$18.00[h]

[a]$4,400 \times 6.00 = 26,400$ hours
[b]$4,000 \times 6.00 = 24,000$ hours
[c]$28,600 \div 4,400 = 6.50$
[d]$4,400 \times 6.00 \times \$9.60 = \$253,440$
[e]$\$294,580 \div 28,600 = \$10.30$
[f]$4,000 \times 6.00 \times \$18 = \$432,000$
[g]$\$447,590 \div 28,600 = \$15.65$
[h]$\$432,000 \div 24,000 = \$18.00$

SOLUTION EXHIBIT 8-24

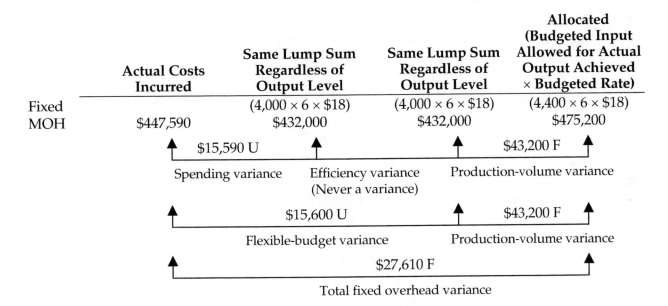

2. Variable Manufacturing Overhead Control $294,580

      Accounts Payable Control and other accounts $294,580

Work in Process Control $253,440

      Variable Manufacturing Overhead Allocated $253,440

Fixed Manufacturing Overhead Control $447,590

      Wages Payable Control, Accumulated Amortization

         Control, etc. $447,590

Work in Process Control $475,200

      Fixed Manufacturing Overhead Allocated $475,200

3. The control of variable manufacturing overhead requires the identification of the cost drivers for such items as energy, supplies, and repairs. Control often entails monitoring nonfinancial measures that affect each cost item, one by one. Examples are kilowatts used, quantities of lubricants used, and repair parts and hours used. The most convincing way to discover why overhead performance did not agree with a budget is to investigate possible causes, line item by line item.

Individual fixed manufacturing overhead items are not usually affected very much by day-to-day control. Instead, they are controlled periodically through planning decisions and budgeting procedures that may sometimes have horizons covering six months or a year (for example, management salaries) and sometimes covering many years (for example, long-term leases and amortization on plant and equipment).

8-26 (35-50 min.) **Total overhead, three-variance analysis.**

1. This problem has two major purposes: (a) to give experience with data allocated on a total overhead basis instead of on separate variable and fixed bases, and (b) to reinforce distinctions between actual hours of input, budgeted (standard) hours allowed for actual output, and denominator level.

An analysis of direct manufacturing labour will provide the data for actual hours of input and standard hours allowed. One approach is to plug the known figures (designated by asterisks) into the analytical framework and solve for the unknowns. The direct manufacturing labour efficiency variance of $5,760 can be computed by subtracting $11,568 from $17,328. The complete picture is:

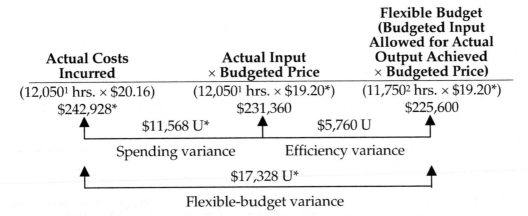

1) $242,928* - $11,568* = $231,360; $231,360 ÷ $19.20* = 12,050^1$ hrs.
2) $231,360 - $5,760 = $225,600; $225,600 ÷ $19.20* = 11,750^2$ hrs.

Manufacturing Overhead

Variable overhead rate = $76,800* ÷ 8,000* hrs. = $9.60 per standard labour-hour
Budgeted fixed overhead costs = $237,120* - 10,000*($9.60) = $141,120

If total manufacturing overhead is allocated at 120% of direct standard manufacturing labour cost, the single overhead rate must be 120% of $19.20, or $23.04 per hour. Therefore, the fixed overhead component of the rate must be $23.04 - $9.60, or $13.44 per direct standard manufacturing labour-hour.

Let D = denominator level in input units

$$\text{Budgeted fixed overhead rate per input unit} = \frac{\text{Budgeted fixed overhead costs}}{\text{Denominator level in input units}}$$

$$\$13.44 = \frac{\$141,120}{D}$$

$$D = 10,500 \text{ standard direct manufacturing labour-hours}$$

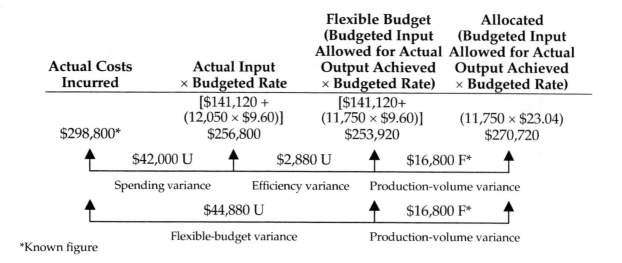

	Actual Costs Incurred	Actual Input × Budgeted Rate	Flexible Budget (Budgeted Input Allowed for Actual Output Achieved × Budgeted Rate)	Allocated (Budgeted Input Allowed for Actual Output Achieved × Budgeted Rate)
		[$141,120 + (12,050 × $9.60)] $256,800	[$141,120 + (11,750 × $9.60)] $253,920	(11,750 × $23.04) $270,720
	$298,800*			

$42,000 U → Spending variance
$2,880 U → Efficiency variance
$16,800 F* → Production-volume variance

$44,880 U → Flexible-budget variance
$16,800 F* → Production-volume variance

*Known figure

An overview of the three-variance analysis using the block format in the text is:

Three-Variance Analysis	Spending Variance	Efficiency Variance	Production-Volume Variance
Total Manufacturing Overhead	$42,000 U	$2,880 U	$16,800 F*

2. The control of variable manufacturing overhead requires the identification of the cost drivers for such items as energy, supplies, equipment, and maintenance. Control often entails monitoring nonfinancial measures that affect each cost item, one by one. Examples are kilowatts used, quantities of lubricants used, and equipment parts and hours used. The most convincing way to discover why overhead performance did not agree with a budget is to investigate possible causes, line item by line item.

    Individual fixed manufacturing overhead items are not usually affected very much by day-to-day control. Instead, they are controlled periodically through planning decisions and budgeting that may sometimes have horizons covering six months or a year (for example, management salaries) and sometimes covering many years (for example, long-term leases and amortization on plant and equipment).

8-28 (30 min.) Overhead variances, missing information.

1. Variable overhead

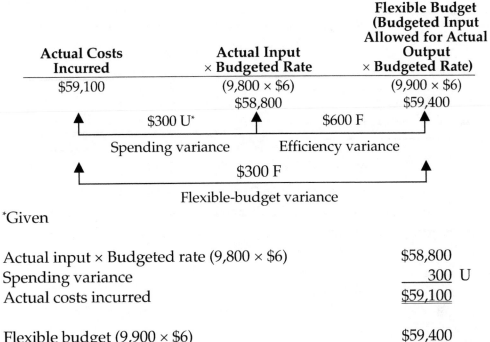

Actual Costs Incurred		Actual Input × Budgeted Rate		Flexible Budget (Budgeted Input Allowed for Actual Output × Budgeted Rate)
$59,100		(9,800 × $6) $58,800		(9,900 × $6) $59,400
	$300 U*		$600 F	
	Spending variance		Efficiency variance	
		$300 F		
		Flexible-budget variance		

*Given

Actual input × Budgeted rate (9,800 × $6)	$58,800
Spending variance	300 U
Actual costs incurred	$59,100
Flexible budget (9,900 × $6)	$59,400
Actual input × Budgeted rate (9,800 × $6)	58,800
Efficiency variance	$ 600 F
Flexible budget variance (300 U + 600 F)	$ 300 F

Variable overhead is overallocated in the amount of $300 (the same amount as favourable flexible-budget variance).

2. Fixed overhead

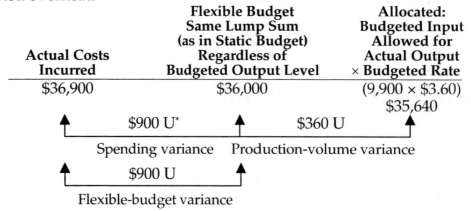

Actual Costs Incurred		Flexible Budget Same Lump Sum (as in Static Budget) Regardless of Budgeted Output Level		Allocated: Budgeted Input Allowed for Actual Output × Budgeted Rate
$36,900		$36,000		(9,900 × $3.60) $35,640

↑ $900 U*   ↑ $360 U   ↑

Spending variance   Production-volume variance

↑ $900 U   ↑

Flexible-budget variance

*Given

Actual total overhead costs incurred	$96,000	
Actual variable overhead costs incurred	59,100	
Actual fixed overhead costs incurred	$36,900	
Spending variance (fixed overhead)	900	U
Flexible budget	$36,000	
Flexible budget	$36,000	
Divide by denominator volume in machine-hours	÷10,000	
Budgeted rate per machine-hour	$ 3.60	
Allocated ($3.60 × 9,900 machine-hours)	$35,640	
Flexible budget	36,000	
Production-volume variance	360	U
Flexible-budget variance = spending variance	$ 900	U
Underallocated amount ($360 U + $900 U)	$ 1,260	U

8-30 (15 min.) Comprehensive review of Chapters 7 and 8, static budget.

1.

	Actual Results (1)	Static-Budget Amounts (2)	Variances (3)
Revenues			
Circulation	$184,800	$168,000	$16,800 F
Advertising	473,520	432,000	41,520 F
	658,320	600,000	58,320 F
Costs			
Direct materials	269,568	216,000	53,568 U
Direct labour costs	60,134	54,000	6,134 U
Variable indirect costs	76,723	72,000	4,723 U
Fixed indirect costs	116,400	108,000	8,400 U
	522,825	450,000	72,825 U
Operating income	$135,495	$150,000	$14,505 U

2. The *Monthly Herald* had an increase in total revenues of $58,320 above that budgeted. This arose from both a favourable circulation variance ($16,800 increase or 28,000 extra copies sold at $0.60 per copy) and a favourable advertising revenue variance of $41,520.

The actual costs are $72,825 above budget. The largest source of this increase is direct materials. The sources of this increase include (a) 20,000 extra copies printed, and (b) quality problems leading to many pages being unusable. The budgeted print pages for 320,000 copies of 50 pages each was 16,000,000 pages; an extra 1,280,000 pages were used above this budgeted amount.

8-32 (30-40 min.) **Graphs and overhead variances.**

Variable Manufacturing Overhead

1.

Fixed Manufacturing Overhead

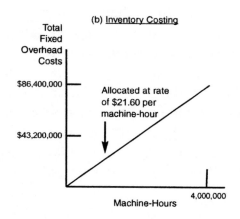

*Budgeted fixed-manufacturing-overhead rate per hour $=$ $\dfrac{\text{Budgeted fixed-manufacturing overhead}}{\text{Denominator level}}$

$$= \frac{\$86,400,000}{4,000,000 \text{ hours}} = \$21.60 \text{ per machine-hour}$$

2.

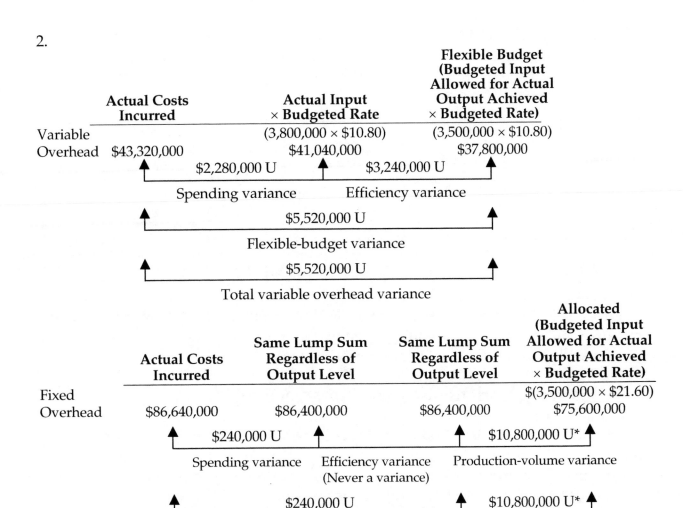

*Alternative computation:
4,000,000 denominator hours − 3,500,000 budgeted hours allowed = 500,000 hours
500,000 × $21.60 = $10,800,000 U

3.   The underallocated manufacturing overheads were: variable, $5,520,000, and fixed, $11,040,000. The flexible-budget variance and underallocated overhead are always the same amount for variable overhead because the flexible-budget amount and the allocated amounts coincide. In contrast, the only time the budget and allocated amounts coincide for fixed overhead is when the budgeted input of the allocation base for the actual output level achieved exactly equals the denominator level.

4. The choice of the denominator level will affect inventory costs. The new fixed overhead rate would be $86,400,000 ÷ 3,000,000 = $28.80. In turn, the allocated amount of fixed overhead and the production-volume variance would change. No other variances would be influenced:

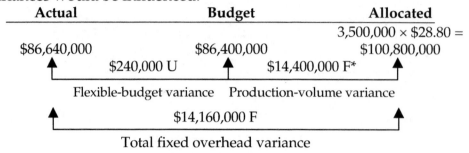

Actual	Budget	Allocated
		3,500,000 × $28.80 =
$86,640,000	$86,400,000	$100,800,000

$240,000 U $14,400,000 F*

Flexible-budget variance   Production-volume variance

$14,160,000 F

Total fixed overhead variance

*Alternative computation: (3,000,000 – 3,500,000) × $28.80 = $14,400,000 F

The major point of this requirement is that inventory costs (and hence income determination) can be heavily affected by the choice of the denominator level used for setting the fixed manufacturing overhead rate.

8-34 (60 min.) Variance analysis for an activity area.

The flexible budget is flexed on the number of technical-support hours, which has the budgeted relationship with output units of one hour of technical support for every 5,000 minutes of airtime sold (or every minute of airtime sold has a budgeted 0.0002 minutes of technical service). Key data items for August 31, 2002, are:

		Actual Results	Flexible Budget Amount	Static Budget Amount
1.	Output units (minutes)	7,350,000	7,350,000	6,850,000
2.	Technical support hours	1,500	1,470	1,370**
3.	Technical support hours per minute	0.000204	0.0002	0.0002
4.	Variable technical service activity area costs	$37,800*	$42,336	$39,456*
5.	Variable technical service activity area costs per technical service hour (4/2)	$25.20[a]	$28.80	$28.80[a]
6.	Variable technical service activity area costs per minute (4/1)	$0.00514	$0.00576	$0.00576
7.	Fixed technical service activity area costs	$81,000	$83,844	$83,844
8.	Fixed technical service activity area costs per technical support hour (7/2)	$54.00	$57.04	$61.20

9. Fixed technical service activity
    area costs per minute (7/1) $0.0110 $0.0114 $0.0122

[a]Variable technical service activity area costs per technical support hour is calculated by dividing the total variable technical service activity area costs by the number of technical support hours.

Actual: $37,800/1,500 = $25.20
Budgeted: $39,456/1,370 = $28.80

**The budgeted denominator of 1,370 is calculated as budgeted airtime sold (6,850,000) divided by 5,000.
*Given

2. Allocated fixed technical service activity area overhead is calculated by multiplying the budgeted input allowed for actual output achieved (given as 1,470 technical service hours) by the budgeted rate for fixed overhead. The budgeted rate for fixed overhead is calculated by dividing the budgeted amount for fixed technical service activity area costs (given as $83,844) by the budgeted number of technical service hours (1,370):

$$83,844/1,370 = \$61.20$$

Allocated fixed technical service activity area overhead is therefore:

$$1,470 \times \$61.20 = \$89,964$$

3. Variable overhead analysis:

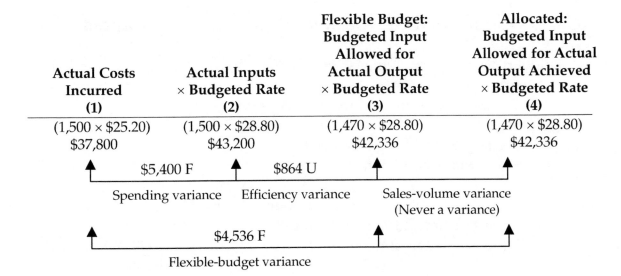

155

The favourable spending variance of $5,400 can be attributed to the lower variable costs incurred in the technical service activity area ($25.20 versus $28.80). The unfavourable efficiency variance ($864) is due to the larger number of technical service hours utilized compared with the number of hours that would have been allowed per plan for the actual number of minutes sold. Since the favourable spending variance is greater than the unfavourable efficiency variance, the flexible-budget variance, in the amount of $4,536, is favourable.

4. Fixed overhead analysis:

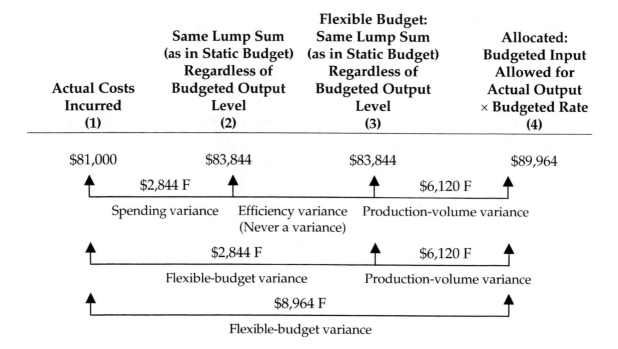

CellOne management overallocated fixed overhead by $8,964.

8-36 (30-40 min.) Working backward from given variances.

1. Solution Exhibit 8-36 outlines the Chapter 7 and 8 framework underlying this solution:

(a) $211,200 ÷ $1.32   = 160,000 kilograms

(b) $82,800 ÷ $13.80   = 6,000 kilograms

(c) $12,420 – $21,600   = $9,180 F

(d) Standard direct manufacturing labour rate

   = $960,000 ÷ 40,000 hours

   = $24 per hour

Actual direct manufacturing labour rate   = $24 + $0.60 = $24.60

Actual direct manufacturing labour hours   = $627,300 ÷ $24.60

                   = 25,500 hours

(e)	Standard variable manufacturing overhead rate	=	$576,000 ÷ 40,000
		=	$14.40 per direct manufacturing labour-hour

Variable manufacturing overhead efficiency variance

of $21,600 ÷ $14.40	=	1,500 excess hours
Actual hours – Excess hours	=	Standard hours allowed
25,500 – 1,500	=	24,000 hours

(f)	Budgeted fixed manufacturing overhead rate	=	$768,000 ÷ 40,000 hours
		=	$19.20 per direct manufacturing labour-hour
	Fixed manufacturing overhead allocated	=	$19.20 × 24,000 hours
		=	$460,800
	Production-volume variance	=	$768,000 – $460,800
		=	$307,200 U

2. The control of variable manufacturing overhead requires the identification of the cost drivers for such items as energy, supplies, and repairs. Control often entails monitoring nonfinancial measures that affect each cost item, one by one. Examples are kilowatts used, quantities of lubricants used, and repair parts and hours used. The most convincing way to discover why overhead performance did not agree with a budget is to investigate possible causes, line item by line item.

Individual fixed overhead items are not usually affected very much by day-to-day control. Instead, they are controlled periodically through planning decisions and budgeting procedures that may sometimes have planning horizons covering six months or a year (for example, management salaries) and sometimes covering many years (for example, long-term leases and amortization on plant and equipment).

Components of the Flexible Budget Variances

	Actual	Flexible	Flexible Budget Var	Static	Components of the Flexible Budget Variances
DM purchased	**160,000**	154,000	6,000 U	-	
DM used		90,000			
Output volume	30,000	30,000		3	
DM kg./output	3	3		3	
DM $/kg	$ 12.48	$ 13.80	$ (1.32) F	$ 13.80	**DM**
					$ (1.32) price/kg 160,000 = $211,200 ÷ $1.32/kg
Total DM purchased	$ 1,996,800	$2,125,200			F $ (211,200) Price ($12.48/kg - $13.80/kg) x 160,000
Total DM used	$ -	$ -	$ (128,400) F		F $ 82,800 Efficiency (160,000 kg - 154,000 kg) x $13.80/kg
					U $ (128,400) **6000** 82,800÷$13.80/kg =excess kg used
					DL
DLH	**25,500**	24,000		40,000	$ 0.60 per DLH variance U
$/DLH	$ 24.60	$ 24.00		$ 24.00	U $ 15,300 Price ($24.60/DLH - $24/DLH) x 25,500 DLH
Total DL costs	$ 627,300	$ 576,000	51,300 U	$ 960,000	U $ 36,000 Efficiency (25,500 DLH - 24,000 DLH) x $24/DLH
					U $ 51,300 $24/DLH = $960,000 ÷ 40,000 DLH
					VMO/H
VMO/H	$ 566,820		12,420 U	$ 576,000	F $ (9,180) spending $12,420 U - $21,600 U = ($9,180) F
VMO/H rate $/DLH	$ 22.23			$ 14.40	U $ 21,600 Efficiency given
					U $ 12,420 given **1,500** $21,600 ÷ $14.40/DLH $14.40 = $576,000 ÷ 40,000 DLH
					FMO/H
FMO/H	$ 716,952	$ 768,000		$ 768,000	F $ (51,048) Spending Both actual and budget are given
FMO/H rate $/DLH		$ 460,800		$ 19.20	U $ (307,200) PVV
PVV		$ (307,200)	U		U $ (256,152) $19.20 = $768,000 ÷ 40,000 DLH

8-38 (30 min.) Overhead analysis.

1. Variable overhead analysis.

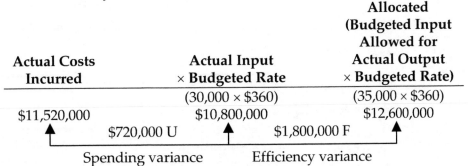

Actual Costs Incurred		Actual Input × Budgeted Rate		Allocated (Budgeted Input Allowed for Actual Output × Budgeted Rate)
		(30,000 × $360)		(35,000 × $360)
$11,520,000		$10,800,000		$12,600,000
	$720,000 U		$1,800,000 F	
	Spending variance		Efficiency variance	

2.

$$\text{Budgeted fixed overhead cost rate} = \frac{\text{Budgeted total costs in fixed overhead cost pool}}{\text{Budgeted total quantity of machine-hours}}$$

$$= \frac{5,940,000}{33,000}$$

$$= \$180 \text{ per machine-hour}$$

Fixed overhead analysis:

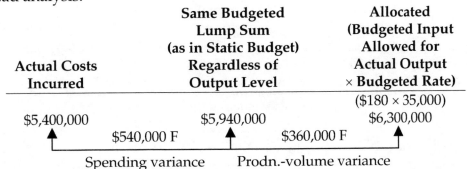

Actual Costs Incurred		Same Budgeted Lump Sum (as in Static Budget) Regardless of Output Level		Allocated (Budgeted Input Allowed for Actual Output × Budgeted Rate)
				($180 × 35,000)
$5,400,000		$5,940,000		$6,300,000
	$540,000 F		$360,000 F	
	Spending variance		Prodn.-volume variance	

8-40 (40 min.) Activity-based costing, variance analysis.

1.

		Static-Budget Amounts	Actual Amounts
a.	Units of SFA produced and sold	21,000	22,000
b.	Batch size	500	550
c.	Number of batches (a ÷ b)	42	40
d.	Testing-hours per batch	5.5	5.4
e.	Total testing-hours (c × d)	231	216
f.	Variable overhead cost per testing-hour	$48	$50.40
g.	Variable testing overhead costs (e × f)	$11,088	$10,886
h.	Total fixed testing overhead costs	$34,650	$32,659
i.	Fixed overhead cost per testing hour (h ÷ e)	$150	$151

The flexible budget is based on the budgeted number of testing-hours for the actual output achieved, 22,000 units ÷ 500 units per batch = 44 batches.

Computation of variable testing overhead cost variances follows:

The unfavourable spending variance is due to the actual variable overhead cost per testing-hour increasing from the budgeted $48 per hour to the actual rate of $50.40 per hour. The favourable efficiency variance is due to the actual output of 22,000 units (1) requiring fewer batches, 40, than the budgeted amount of 42 and (2) each batch taking less time, 5.4 hours, than the budgeted time of 5.5 hours.

2. Computation of the fixed testing overhead cost variances follows:

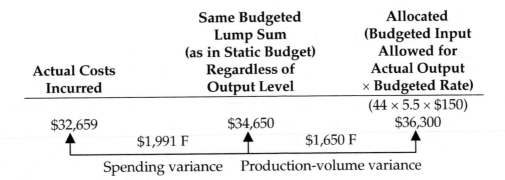

Actual Costs Incurred	Same Budgeted Lump Sum (as in Static Budget) Regardless of Output Level	Allocated (Budgeted Input Allowed for Actual Output × Budgeted Rate)
		(44 × 5.5 × $150)
$32,659	$34,650	$36,300
	$1,991 F	$1,650 F
	Spending variance	Production-volume variance

The fixed testing overhead cost spending variance is $1,991 F because the amount of actual costs was lower than the budgeted amount of $34,650. The production-volume variance is $1,650 F because the actual number of SFA produced and sold required less costs than budgeted.

8-42 (60 min.) Journal entries (continuation of 8-41).

Key information underlying the computation of variances is:

		Actual Results	Flexible Budget Amount	Static-Budget Amount
1.	Output units (panels)	19,200	19,200	17,760
2.	Machine-hours	36,480	38,400	35,520
3.	Machine-hours per panel	1.90	2.00	2.00
4.	Variable MOH costs	$1,838,592	$1,843,200	$1,704,960
5.	Variable MOH costs per machine-hour (4/2)	$50.40	$48.00	$48.00
6.	Variable MOH costs per unit (4/1)	$95.76	$96.00	$96.00
7.	Fixed MOH costs	$8,404,992	$8,354,304	$8,354,304
8.	Fixed MOH costs per machine-hour (7/2)	$230.40	$217.56	$235.20
9.	Fixed MOH costs per unit (7/1)	$437.76	$435.12	$470.40

Solution Exhibit 8-42 has the computation of the variances.

SOLUTION EXHIBIT 8-42

Variable MOH

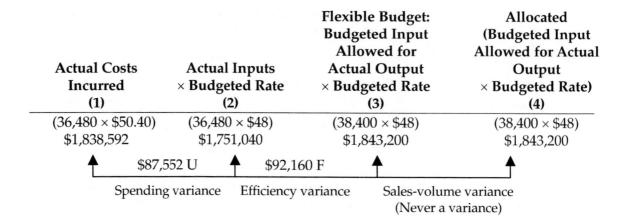

Actual Costs Incurred (1)	Actual Inputs × Budgeted Rate (2)	Flexible Budget: Budgeted Input Allowed for Actual Output × Budgeted Rate (3)	Allocated (Budgeted Input Allowed for Actual Output × Budgeted Rate) (4)
(36,480 × $50.40) $1,838,592	(36,480 × $48) $1,751,040	(38,400 × $48) $1,843,200	(38,400 × $48) $1,843,200

$87,552 U → Spending variance
$92,160 F → Efficiency variance
Sales-volume variance (Never a variance)

Fixed MOH

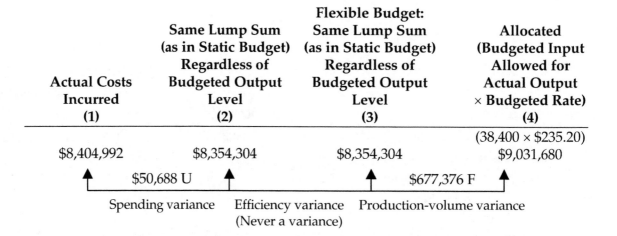

Actual Costs Incurred (1)	Same Lump Sum (as in Static Budget) Regardless of Budgeted Output Level (2)	Flexible Budget: Same Lump Sum (as in Static Budget) Regardless of Budgeted Output Level (3)	Allocated (Budgeted Input Allowed for Actual Output × Budgeted Rate) (4)
$8,404,992	$8,354,304	$8,354,304	(38,400 × $235.20) $9,031,680

$50,688 U → Spending variance
Efficiency variance (Never a variance)
$677,376 F → Production-volume variance

1. Journal entries for variable MOH, year ended December 31, 2007:

Variable MOH Control	1,838,592	
Accounts Payable Control and Other Accounts		1,838,592
Work-in-Process Control	1,843,200	
Variable MOH Allocated		1,843,200
Variable MOH Allocated	1,843,200	
Variable MOH Spending Variance (U)	87,552	
Variable MOH Control		1,838,592
Variable MOH Efficiency Variance (F)		92,160

Journal Entries for fixed MOH, year ended December 31, 2007:

Fixed MOH Control	8,404,992	
Wages Payable, Accumulated Amortization, etc.		8,404,992
Work-in-Process Control	9,031,680	
Fixed MOH Allocated		9,031,680
Fixed MOH Allocated	9,031,680	
Fixed MOH Spending Variance (U)	50,668	
Fixed MOH Control		8,404,992
Fixed MOH Production-Volume Variance		677,376

2. **Adjustment of COGS**

Cost of Goods Sold		631,296[1]
Variable MOH Efficiency Variance (F)	92,160	
Fixed MOH Production-Volume Variance (F)	677,376	
Variable MOH Spending Variance (U)		87,552
Fixed MOH Spending Variance (U)		50,688

1) 677,376 + 92,160 − [87,552 + 50,688] = 631,296

8-44 (20-30 min.) **Variance analysis for ABC.**

1. ABC Variance Analysis——Calculation of Key Information

		Actual Results	Flexible Budget Amount	Static Budget Amount
1.	Output units (launches)	265	265	250
2.	Launch-hours	5,300	5,300	5,500
3.	Launch-hours per launch (2/1)	20	20	22
4.	Variable launch activity area costs	$445,200,000	$432,480,000[1]	$448,800,000
5.	Variable launch activity area costs per launch-hour (4/2)	$84,000	$81,600	$81,600
6.	Variable launch activity area costs per launch (4/1)	$1,680,000	$1,632,000	$1,795,200
7.	Fixed launch activity area costs	$1,971,600,000	$2,032,800,000	$2,032,800,000
8.	Fixed launch activity area costs per launch-hour (7/2)	$372,000	$383,547	$369,600
9.	Fixed launch activity area costs per launch (7/1)	$7,440,000	$7,670,943	$8,131,200

2,3. Starport engaged in 15 (265 – 250) more launches than planned. Each launch took 2 (20 – 22) hours less than budgeted. The cost of each launch hour was $2,400 ($84,000 – $81,600) more than budgeted, and each launch was $48,000 ($1,680,000 – $1,632,000) more than budgeted. The fixed costs incurred totalled $61,200,000 ($1,971,600,000 – $2,032,800,000) less than budget.

Variable Costs: actual = 5,300 × $84,000 = $445,200,000
budget = 5,500 × $81,600 = $448,800,000

1) flexible budget = 5,300 × 81,600 = 432,480,000

8-46 (20 min.) Standard setting, benchmarking, ethics (continuation of 8-45)

1. Padding of standard costs and standard amounts for billing operations can arise from:

   (a) Deliberately taking longer time to process the bills when standards are being set.

   (b) Deliberately not taking advantage of information technology in the standard-setting period and then exploiting that technology later on.

   (c) Creating problems in billing for which solutions have already been worked out and using those solutions only in the non-standard-setting period.

   (d) Not purchasing items in the most economic way during the standard-setting period.

   Reasons for padding include:

   (a) Individual performance evaluation—individuals who wish to look "good" for bonuses, promotion, etc., purposes.

   (b) Department performance evaluation—departments wish to retain autonomy which is more likely with favourable variances.

   (c) Defying authority and control systems—some individuals have an inherent opposition to "standards" and "controls."

2. Stone can operate at several levels:

   (a) Best practice observation—MEG's report should be a catalyst to Sharon's examining what other hospitals in the survey are doing and then using this best practice internally. MEG may be hired to facilitate field visits to other more efficient hospitals.

   (b) Operations—make flowcharts of how billing occurs at Sharon and eliminate all unnecessary steps.

   (c) Incentive systems—provide economic and other incentives to Sharon employees to implement efficiency and effectiveness improvements. The emphasis here should be on accuracy and timeliness of billing as well as the cost of billing.

   (d) Corporate culture—Sharon should emphasize that "padding" and the deliberate misrepresentation it entails are unacceptable. This could be done via in-house programs on ethics and culture or by making "examples" of those found deliberately undermining a culture of honesty and teamwork for Sharon.

CHAPTER 9
INCOME EFFECTS OF ALTERNATIVE
INVENTORY COSTING METHODS

9-2   The term **direct costing** is a misnomer for variable costing for two reasons:

a.   Variable costing does not include all direct costs as inventoriable costs. Only variable direct manufacturing costs are included. Any fixed direct manufacturing costs and any direct nonmanufacturing costs (either variable or fixed) are excluded from inventoriable costs.
b.   Variable costing includes as inventoriable costs not only direct manufacturing costs but also some indirect costs (variable indirect manufacturing costs).

9-4   The main issue between variable costing and absorption costing is the proper timing of the release of fixed manufacturing costs as costs of the period:

a.   at the time of incurrence, or
b.   at the time the finished units to which the fixed overhead relates are sold. Variable costing uses (a) and absorption costing uses (b).

9-6   Variable costing does not view fixed costs as unimportant or irrelevant, but it maintains that the distinction between behaviours of different costs is crucial for certain decisions. The planning and management of fixed costs is critical, irrespective of what inventory costing method is used.

9-8   The factors that affect the breakeven point under variable costing are:

1.   Fixed costs
2.   Unit contribution margin
3.   Sales level in units

9-10   Examples of dysfunctional decisions managers may make to increase reported operating income are:

a.   Plant managers may switch production to those orders that absorb the highest amount of manufacturing overhead, irrespective of the demand by customers.
b.   Plant managers may accept a particular order to increase production even though another plant in the same company is better suited to handle that order.
c.   Plant managers may defer maintenance beyond the current period to free up more time for production.

9-12 The *downward demand spiral* is the continuing reduction in demand for a company's product that occurs when the prices of competitors' products are not met and (as demand drops further), higher and higher unit costs result in more and more reluctance to meet competitors' prices. Pricing decisions need to consider competitors and customers as well as costs.

9-14 The *theoretical capacity* and *practical capacity* denominator-level concepts emphasize what a plant can supply. The *normal capacity utilization* and *master-budget capacity utilization* concepts emphasize what customers demand in products produced by a plant.

9-16 (30 min.) Variable and absorption costing, explaining operating income differences.

1. Key inputs for income statement computations are:

	April	May
Beginning inventory	0	150
Production	500	400
Goods available for sale	500	550
Units sold	350	520
Ending inventory	150	30

The unit fixed and total manufacturing costs per unit under absorption costing are:

		April	May
(a)	Fixed manufacturing costs	$2,000,000	$2,000,000
(b)	Units produced	500	400
(c)=(a)÷(b)	Unit fixed manufacturing costs	$4,000	$5,000
(d)	Unit variable manufacturing costs	$12,000	$12,000
(e)=(c)+(d)	Unit total manufacturing costs	$16,000	$17,000

(a) Variable costing

	April 2005		May 2005	
Revenues[a]		$10,080,000		$14,976,000
Variable costs				
Beginning inventory	$ 0		$1,800,000	
Variable cost of goods manufactured[b]	6,000,000		4,800,000	
Cost of goods available for sale	6,000,000		6,600,000	
Ending inventory[c]	1,800,000		360,000	
Variable manufacturing cost of goods sold	4,200,000		6,240,000	
Variable marketing costs[d]	1,050,000		1,560,000	
Total variable costs		5,250,000		7,800,000
Contribution margin		4,830,000		7,176,000
Fixed costs				
Fixed manufacturing costs	2,000,000		2,000,000	
Fixed marketing costs	600,000		600,000	
Total fixed costs		2,600,000		2,600,000
Operating income		$2,230,000		$ 4,576,000

[a]$28,800 × 350; 520
[b]$12,000 × 500; 400
[c]$12,000 × 150; 30
[d]$3,000 × 350; 520

(b) Absorption costing

	April 2007			May 2007		
Revenues[a]			$10,080,000			$14,976,000
Cost of goods sold						
Beginning inventory	$		0	$2,400,000		
Variable manufacturing costs[b]		6,000,000		4,800,000		
Fixed manufacturing costs[c]		2,000,000		2,000,000		
Cost of goods available for sale		8,000,000		9,200,000		
Ending inventory[d]		2,400,000		510,000		
Cost of goods sold			5,600,000			8,690,000
Gross margin			4,480,000			6,286,000
Marketing costs						
Variable marketing costs[e]		1,050,000		1,560,000		
Fixed marketing costs		600,000		600,000		
Total marketing costs			1,650,000			2,160,000
Operating income			$2,830,000			$ 4,126,000

[a]$28,800 × 350; 520
[b]$12,000 × 500; 400
[c]($4,000 × 500); ($5,000 × 400)
[d]($16,000 × 150; $17,000 × 30); April's Production – Sales = Ending inventory: May's beginning inventory (150);
May's beginning inventory plus production minus sales = May's ending inventory (30)

[e]($3,000 × 350; $3,000 × 520)

2.

$$\begin{pmatrix} \text{Absorption-costing} \\ \text{operating income} \end{pmatrix} - \begin{pmatrix} \text{Variable-costing} \\ \text{operating income} \end{pmatrix} = \begin{pmatrix} \text{Fixed manufacturing} \\ \text{costs in} \\ \text{ending inventory} \end{pmatrix} - \begin{pmatrix} \text{Fixed manufacturing} \\ \text{costs in} \\ \text{beginning inventory} \end{pmatrix}$$

April:

$$\$2,830,000 - \$2,230,000 \;=\; (\$4,000 \times 150) - (\$0)$$
$$\$600,000 \;=\; \$600,000$$

May:

$$\$4,126,000 - \$4,576,000 \;=\; (\$5,000 \times 30) - (\$4,000 \times 150)$$
$$-\$450,000 \;=\; \$150,000 - \$600,000$$
$$-\$450,000 \;=\; -\$450,000$$

The difference between absorption and variable costing is due solely to moving fixed manufacturing costs into inventories as inventories increase (as in April) and out of inventories as they decrease (as in May).

Therefore:

when inventories ↑: absorption costing > variable costing

and when inventories ↓: absorption costing < variable costing

9-18 (40 min.) Variable and absorption costing, explaining operating income differences.

1. Key inputs for income statement computations are:

	January	February	March
Beginning inventory	0	300	300
Production	1,000	800	1,250
Goods available for sale	1,000	1,100	1,550
Units sold	700	800	1,500
Ending inventory	300	300	50

The unit fixed and total manufacturing costs per unit under absorption costing are:

		January	February	March
(a)	Fixed manufacturing costs	$400,000	$400,000	$400,000
(b)	Units produced	1,000	800	1,250
(c)=(a÷b)	Unit fixed manufacturing costs	$ 400	$ 500	$ 320
(d)	Unit variable manufacturing costs	$ 1,080	$ 1,080	$ 1,080
(e)=(c+d)	Unit total manufacturing costs	$ 1,480	$ 1,580	$ 1,400

(a) Variable Costing

	January 2007	February 2007	March 2007
Revenues[a]	$2,100,000	$2,400,000	$4,500,000
Variable costs			
Beginning inventory[b]	$ 0	$324,000	$ 324,000
Variable cost of goods manufactured[c]	1,080,000	864,000	1,350,000
Cost of goods available for sale	1,080,000	1,188,000	1,674,000
Ending inventory[d]	324,000	324,000	54,000
Variable manufacturing cost of goods sold	756,000	864,000	1,620,000
Variable marketing costs[e]	420,000	480,000	900,000
Total variable costs	1,176,000	1,344,000	2,520,000
Contribution margin	924,000	1,056,000	1,980,000
Fixed costs			
Fixed manufacturing costs	400,000	400,000	400,000
Fixed marketing costs	140,000	140,000	140,000
Total fixed costs	540,000	540,000	540,000
Operating income	$ 384,000	$ 516,000	$1,440,000

[a]$3,000 × 700; 800; 1,500
[b]0; $1,080 × 300; 300
[c]$1,080 × 1,000; 800; 1,250
[d]$1,080 × 300; 300; 50
[e]$600 × 700; 800; 1,500

(b) Absorption Costing

	January 2007		February 2007		March 2007	
Revenues[a]		$2,100,000		$2,400,000		$4,500,000
Cost of goods sold						
Beginning inventory[b]	$ 0		$ 444,000		$ 474,000	
Variable manufacturing costs[c]	1,080,000		864,000		1,350,000	
Fixed manufacturing costs[d]	400,000		400,000*		400,000*	
Cost of goods available for sale	1,480,000		1,708,000		2,224,000	
Ending inventory[e]	444,000		474,000		70,000	
Cost of goods sold		1,036,000		1,234,000		2,154,000
Gross margin		1,064,000		1,166,000		2,346,000
Marketing costs						
Variable marketing costs[f]	420,000		480,000		900,000	
Fixed marketing costs	140,000		140,000		140,000	
Total marketing costs		560,000		620,000		1,040,000
Operating income		$ 504,000		$ 546,000		$1,306,000

[a]$3,000 × 700; 800; 1,500
[b](0; $1,480[1) × 300; $1,580[2) × 300)
[c]$1,080 × 1,000, 800, 1,250
[d]($400 × 1,000); ($500 × 800); ($320 × 1,250)
[e]($1,480[1) × 300); ($1,580[2) × 300); ($1,400[3) × 50)
[f]$600 × 700; 800; 1,500

[1) 1,480 = 1,080 + (400,000 ÷ 1,000 production) = 1,080 + 400 = 1,480
[2) 1,580 = 1,080 + (400,000 ÷ 800 production) = 1,080 + 500 = 1,580
[3) 1,400 = 1,080 + (400,000 ÷ 1,250 production) = 1,080 + 320 = 1,400

2.

$$\begin{pmatrix} \text{Absorption-costing} \\ \text{operating income} \end{pmatrix} - \begin{pmatrix} \text{Variable-costing} \\ \text{operating income} \end{pmatrix} = \begin{pmatrix} \text{Fixed manufacturing} \\ \text{costs in} \\ \text{ending inventory} \end{pmatrix} - \begin{pmatrix} \text{Fixed manufacturing} \\ \text{costs in} \\ \text{beginning inventory} \end{pmatrix}$$

January:	$504,000 – $384,000	=	$120,000[1) – $0
	$120,000	=	$120,000
February:	$546,000 – $516,000	=	$150,000 – $120,000
	$30,000	=	$30,000
March:	$1,306,000 – $1,440,000	=	$16,000 – $150,000
	–$134,000	=	–$134,000

The difference between absorption and variable costing is due solely to moving fixed manufacturing costs into inventories as inventories increase (as in January) and out of inventories as they decrease (as in March).

Therefore:

1) The difference between the value of "ending inventory" re absorption costing and the value of "ending inventory" re variable costing = fixed manufacturing costs in ending inventory for January 2007: $444,000 – $324,000 = $120,000

$$\begin{matrix} \text{Fixed Manufacturing Costs} \\ \text{in Ending Inventory} \end{matrix} = \begin{matrix} \text{Absorption Costing} \\ \text{Inventory} \end{matrix} - \begin{matrix} \text{Variable Costing} \\ \text{Inventory} \end{matrix}$$

9-20 (10 min.) Absorption and variable costing.

The answers are l(a), $920,000, and 2(c), $680,000. Computations follow:

1. **Absorption Costing:**

Revenues[a]		$5,760,000
Cost of goods sold:		
Variable manufacturing costs[b]	$2,880,000	
Fixed manufacturing costs[c]	360,000	3,240,000
Gross margin		2,520,000
Marketing and administrative costs:		
Variable marketing and administrative[d]	1,200,000	
Fixed marketing and administrative	400,000	1,600,000
Operating income		$ 920,000

[a]$48 × 120,000
[b]$24 × 120,000
[c]Fixed manufacturing rate = $600,000 ÷ 200,000
                = $3 per output unit
$3 × 120,000
[d]$10 × 120,000

2. **Variable Costing:**

Revenues[a]		$5,760,000
Variable costs:		
Variable manufacturing costs of goods sold[b]	$2,880,000	
Variable marketing and administrative costs[c]	1,200,000	4,080,000
Contribution margin		1,680,000
Fixed costs:		
Fixed manufacturing costs	600,000	
Fixed marketing and administrative costs	400,000	1,000,000
Operating income		$ 680,000

[a]$48 × 120,000
[b]$24 × 120,000
[c]$10 × 120,000

Comparison re two methods:

FMOH in Absorption Costing Inventory:
    $3 × 80,000 units = $240,000

Absorption costing operating income – Variable costing operating income = FMOH in absorption costing inventory:
    $920,000 – $680,000 = $240,000

9-22 (30-40 min.) **Income statements.**

1.

The Mass Company

Income Statements for the Year 2007

(in thousands)

(a) **Variable Costing:**

Revenues (25,000 × $48)		$1,200.00
Variable costs:		
Beginning inventory (1,000 × $26.10)	$ 26.10	
Variable cost of goods manufactured (29,000[1] × $26.10)	756.90	
Cost of goods available for sale	783.00	
Ending inventory (5,000 × $26.10)	130.50	
Variable manufacturing cost of goods sold	652.50	
Variable marketing and administrative costs		
(25,000 × $1.20)	30.00	
Variable costs		$ 682.50
Contribution margin		$ 517.50
Fixed costs:		
Fixed manufacturing overhead costs	120.00	
Fixed marketing and admin. costs	190.00	
Fixed costs		310.00
Operating income		$ 207.50

[1] Production = Sales – Beginning inventory + Ending inventory
    = 25,000 – 1,000 + 5,000 = 29,000

b) **Absorption Costing:**

Revenues (25,000 × $48)		$1,200.00
Cost of goods sold:		
Beginning inventory (1,000 × $30.90[2])	$ 30.90	
Variable manufacturing costs (29,000 × $26.10)	756.90	
Fixed manufacturing costs (given)	120.00	
Cost of goods available for sale	907.80	
Ending inventory (5,000 × $30.24)[3]	151.20	
Cost of goods sold		756.60
Gross margin		443.40
Marketing and administrative costs:		
Variable marketing and admin. costs (25,000×$1.20)	30.00	
Fixed marketing and admin. costs	190.00	
Marketing and admin. costs		220.00
Operating income		$ 223.40

[2] Production 2006 = Sales − Beginning inventory + Ending inventory
        = 25,000 − 1,000 + 1,000 = 25,000
∴ Fixed Manufacturing O/H per unit = $120,000 ÷ 25,000 = $4.80
∴ Standard Variable cost per unit plus fixed manufacturing O/H per unit = $26.10 + 4.80 = $30.90

[3] Production 2007 = 29,000 units
∴ Fixed Manufacturing O/H per unit = $120,000 ÷ 29,000 = $4.14
∴ Standard Variable cost per unit plus fixed manufacturing O/H per unit = $26.10 + 4.14 = $30.24

2.

$$\begin{pmatrix} \text{Absorption} \\ \text{costing} \\ \text{operating} \\ \text{income} \end{pmatrix} - \begin{pmatrix} \text{Variable} \\ \text{costing} \\ \text{operating} \\ \text{income} \end{pmatrix} = \begin{pmatrix} \text{Fixed} \\ \text{manuf. costs} \\ \text{in ending} \\ \text{inventory} \end{pmatrix} - \begin{pmatrix} \text{Fixed} \\ \text{manuf. costs} \\ \text{in beginning} \\ \text{inventory} \end{pmatrix}$$

$223,400 − $207,500	=	[(5,000 × $4.14) − (1,000 × $4.80)]
$15,900	=	$20,700 − $4,800
$15,900	=	$15,900

The operating income figures differ because the amount of fixed manufacturing costs in the ending inventory differs from that in the beginning inventory.

3.   Advantages:

(a)   The fixed costs are reported as period costs (and not allocated to inventory), thus increasing the likelihood of better control of these costs.
(b)   Operating income is directly influenced by changes in unit sales (and not influenced by build-up of inventory).
(c)   The impact of fixed costs on operating income is emphasized.
(d)   The income statements are in the same form as used for cost-volume-profit analysis.
(e)   Product line, territory, etc., contribution margins are emphasized and more readily ascertainable.

Disadvantages:

(a)   Total costs may be overlooked when considering operating problems.
(b)   Distinction between fixed and variable costs is arbitrary for many costs.
(c)   Emphasis on variable costs may cause some managers to ignore fixed costs.
(d)   A new variable-costing system may be too costly to install unless top managers think that operating decisions will be improved collectively.

9-24 (10-20 min.) Breakeven under variable and absorption costing (continuation of 9-23).

1.   The unit contribution margin is $6.00 − $3.60 − $1.00 = $1.40. Total fixed costs ($540,000) divided by the unit contribution margin ($1.40) equals 385,714 units. Therefore, under variable costing, 385,714 units must be <u>sold</u> to break even.

2.   If there are no changes in inventory levels, the breakeven point can be the same, 385,714 units, under both variable costing and absorption costing. However, as the preceding problem demonstrates, under absorption costing the breakeven point is not unique; operating income is a function of both sales and production. Some fixed overhead is "held back" when inventories rise (10,000 units × $0.70 = $7,000), so operating income is positive even though sales are at the breakeven level as commonly conceived.

$$\text{Breakeven sales in units} = \frac{\left(\begin{array}{c}\text{Total fixed}\\\text{costs}\end{array}\right) + \left(\begin{array}{c}\text{Fixed manuf.}\\\text{overhead}\\\text{rate}\end{array}\right) \times \left(\begin{array}{c}\text{Breakeven}\\\text{sales in}\\\text{units}\end{array} - \begin{array}{c}\text{Units}\\\text{produced}\end{array}\right)}{\text{Unit contribution margin}}$$

$$\text{Let N} = \text{Breakeven sales in units}$$

$$N = \frac{\$540,000 + \$0.70(N - 550,000)}{\$1.40}$$

$$N = \frac{\$540,000 + \$0.70N - \$385,000}{\$1.40}$$

$$\$0.7N = \$155,000$$

$$N = 221,429 \text{ units (rounded)}$$

Therefore, under absorption costing when 550,000 units are produced, 221,429 units must be sold for the income statement to report zero operating income.

Proof of 2007 breakeven point:

Gross margin, 221,429 units × ($6.00 − $4.30)		$376,429
Output level MOH variance, as before	$ 35,000	
Marketing and administrative costs:		
Variable, 221,429 units × $1.00	221,429	
Fixed	120,000	376,429
Operating income		$ 0

3. If no units are sold, variable costing will show an operating loss equal to the fixed manufacturing costs, $420,000 in this instance. In contrast, the company would break even under absorption costing, although nothing was sold to customers. This is an extreme example of what has been called "selling fixed manufacturing overhead to inventory."

A final note: We find it helpful to place the following comparisons on the board, keyed to the three parts of this problem:

1. Breakeven = f (sales)
2. Breakeven = f (sales and production)
3. Breakeven = f (0 units sold and 385,714 units produced), an extreme case

9-26 (40 min.) Absorption vs. variable costing.

1. The number of Mimic™ pills sold in 2007 is:
   44,800 × 365 × 3 = 49,056,000 pills

   Ending inventory on December 31, 2007, is 5,694,000 pills:
   Unit data

Beginning inventory	0
Production	54,750,000
Sales	49,056,000
Ending inventory	5,694,000

   Variable cost data
   Manufacturing costs per pill produced

Direct materials	$0.06
Direct manufacturing labour	0.04
Manufacturing overhead	0.11
Total variable manufacturing costs	$0.21

   Fixed cost data

Manufacturing costs	$7,358,400
R&D	4,905,600
Marketing	19,622,400

Wholesale selling price per pill	$1.44

Fixed manufacturing costs allocation rate per pill	$0.15 (allocated—given)
($7,358,400 ÷ 54,750,000 = $0.1344 actual)	

2. **Variable costing:**

Revenues: $1.44 × 49,056,000		$70,640,640
Variable costs		
Beginning inventory	$ 0	
Variable manuf. cost: $0.21 × 54,750,000	11,497,500	
Cost of goods available for sale	11,497,500	
Deduct ending inventory: $0.21 × 5,694,000	1,195,740	
Variable cost of goods sold	10,301,760	
Variable marketing costs: $0.07 × 49,056,000	3,433,920	
Adjust for variable-cost variance	0	
Total variable costs		13,735,680
Contribution margin		56,904,960
Fixed costs		
Fixed manufacturing costs	7,358,400	
Fixed R&D	4,905,600	
Fixed marketing	19,622,400	
Total fixed costs		31,886,400
Operating income		$25,018,560

Absorption costing:

Revenues: $1.44 × 49,056,000		$70,640,640
Costs of goods sold		
Beginning inventory	$ 0	
Variable manuf. cost: $0.21 × 54,750,000	11,497,500	
Fixed manuf. costs: $0.15 × 54,750,000	8,212,500	
Cost of goods available for sale	19,710,000	
Deduct ending inventory: $0.36 × 5,694,000	(2,049,840)	
Adjust for manuf. variances[a]	(854,100)	
Cost of goods sold		16,806,060
Gross margin		53,834,580
Operating costs		
Variable marketing costs: $0.07 × 49,056,000	3,433,920	
Fixed R&D	4,905,600	
Fixed marketing	19,622,400	
Adjustment for operating cost variances	0	
Total operating costs		27,961,920
Operating income		$25,872,660

[a]Production-Volume variance = (0.15 × 54,750,000 units) − $7,358,400 = $854,100F

3. The difference of $854,100 is due to:

$$
\begin{aligned}
&= \left(\begin{array}{c} \text{Fixed manufacturing} \\ \text{costs in ending inventory} \\ \text{under absorption costing} \end{array} \right) - \left(\begin{array}{c} \text{Fixed manufacturing} \\ \text{costs in beginning inventory} \\ \text{under absorption costing} \end{array} \right) \\
&= (\$0.15 \times 5,694,000) \quad - \quad \$0 \\
&= \$854,100
\end{aligned}
$$

9-28 (10 min.) Capacity management, denominator-level capacity concepts.

1. d
2. c, d
3. d
4. a
5. c
6. a, b
7. a
8. b
9. c, d
10. b
11. a, b

9-30 (25-30 min.) Alternative denominator-level concepts.

1.

Denominator-Level Capacity	Budgeted Fixed Manufacturing Overhead per Period	Budgeted Denominator Level	Budgeted Fixed Manufacturing Overhead Cost Rate
Theoretical capacity	$50,000,000	5,256,000	$ 9.51
Practical capacity	50,000,000	3,500,000	14.29
Normal capacity utilization	50,000,000	2,800,000	17.86
Master-budget capacity utilization			
(a) Jan.–June 2007	25,000,000	1,120,000	22.32
(b) July–Dec. 2007	25,000,000	1,680,000	14.88

The differences arise for several reasons:

a. The theoretical and practical capacity concepts emphasize supply factors, while normal capacity utilization and master-budget capacity utilization emphasize demand factors.

b. The two separate six-month rates for the master-budget capacity utilization concept differ because of seasonal differences in budgeted production.

2. Theoretical capacity—based on the production of output at maximum efficiency for 100% of the time.

   Practical capacity—reduces theoretical capacity for unavoidable operating interruptions such as scheduled maintenance time, shutdowns for holidays and other days, and so on.

   For each of the three determinants of capacity in Lucky Lager's plant, practical capacity is less than theoretical capacity:

	Barrels per Hour	Working Hours per Day	Working Days per Year	Capacity
Theoretical capacity	600	× 24	× 365	= 5,256,000
Practical capacity	500	× 20	× 350	= 3,500,000

3. The smaller the denominator, the higher will be the amount of overhead costs capitalized for inventory units. Thus, if the plant manager wishes to be able to "adjust" plant operating income by building inventory, master-budget capacity utilization or possibly normal capacity utilization would be preferred.

9-32 (60 min.) Standard absorption, variable, and throughput costing.

1.

$$\text{Unit fixed manufacturing overhead cost} = \frac{\$10,000}{2,000}$$

$$= \$5 \text{ per unit produced}$$

Unit manufacturing costs

(a) **Absorption costing:**

	2006	2007
Variable direct manuf. costs per unit	$48.70	$48.70
Variable indirect manuf. costs per unit	15.00	15.00
Fixed manuf. costs per unit	5.00	5.00
Total manuf. cost per unit	$68.70	$68.70

b) **Variable costing:**

	2006	2007
Variable direct manuf. costs per unit	$48.70	$48.70
Variable indirect manuf. costs per unit	15.00	15.00
Total variable manuf. cost per unit	$63.70	$63.70

c) **Throughput costing:**

	2006	2007
Variable direct materials per unit	$28.00	28.00

Unit data for 2006 and 2007 are:

	2006	2007
Beginning inventory	900	1,400
Production	2,000	400
Goods available for sale	2,900	1,800
Sales	1,500	1,700
Ending inventory	1,400	100

(a) **Absorption costing**

	2006	2007
Revenues[a]	$180,000	$204,000
Cost of goods sold		
Beginning inventory[b]	61,830	96,180
Variable manuf. costs[c]	127,400	25,480
Fixed manuf. costs[d]	10,000	2,000
Cost of goods available for sale	199,230	123,660
Ending inventory[e]	96,180	6,870
Cost of goods sold (at std. cost)	103,050	116,790
Adjustment for variances—variable	1,000 U	1,000 U
Adjustment for variances—fixed[f]	0	8,000 U
Total cost of goods sold	104,050	125,790
Gross margin	75,950	78,210
Variable marketing costs[g]	1,500	1,700
Fixed marketing costs	3,000	3,000
Total marketing costs	4,500	4,700
Operating income	$ 71,450	$ 73,510

[a]$120 × 1,500; $120 × 1,700
[b]$68.70 × 900; $68.70 × 1,400
[c]$63.70 × 2,000; $63.70 × 400
[d]$5 × 2,000; $5 × 400
[e]$68.70 × 1,400; $68.70 × 100
[f]Production-volume variance = 2006: (2,000 – 2,000) × 5; 2007: (2,000 – 400) × $5
[g]$1 × 1,500; $1 × 1,700

(b) Variable costing

	2006	2007
Revenues[a]	$180,000	$204,000
Variable costs		
Beginning inventory[b]	57,330	89,180
Variable cost of goods manufactured[c]	127,400	25,480
Cost of goods available for sale	184,730	114,660
Ending inventory[d]	89,180	6,370
Variable manuf. COGSs	95,550	108,290
Variable marketing costs[e]	1,500	1,700
Variable costs (at standard costs)	97,050	109,990
Adjustment for variances	1,000 U	1,000 U
Total variable costs	98,050	110,990
Contribution margin	81,950	93,010
Fixed costs		
Fixed manufacturing overhead costs	10,000	10,000
Fixed marketing costs	3,000	3,000
Fixed costs (at standard costs)	13,000	13,000
Adjustment for variances	0	0
Total fixed costs	13,000	13,000
Operating income	$ 68,950	$ 80,010

[a]$120 × 1,500; $120 × 1,700
[b]$63.70 × 900; $63.70 × 1,400
[c]$63.70 × 2,000; $63.70 × 400
[d]$63.70 × 1,400; $63.70 × 100
[e]$1 × 1,500; $1 × 1,700

(c) Throughput costing

	2006	2007
Revenues[a]	$180,000	$204,000
Variable direct materials costs		
Beginning inventory[b]	25,200	39,200
Direct materials in goods manuf.[c]	56,000	11,200
Cost of goods available for sale	81,200	50,400
Ending inventory[d]	39,200	2,800
Direct materials costs (at std.)	42,000	47,600
Adjustment for direct materials variances	0	0
Total variable direct materials costs	42,000	47,600
Throughput contribution	138,000	156,400
Other costs		
Manufacturing	81,400[e]	24,280[f]
Marketing	4,500[g]	4,700[h]
Adjustment for variances	1,000 U	1,000 U
Total other costs	86,900	29,980
Operating income	$ 51,100	$126,420

[a]$120 × 1,500; $120 × 1,700
[b]$28 × 900; $28 × 1,400
[c]$28 × 2,000; $28 × 400
[d]$28 × 1,400; $28 × 100

[e][($20.70[1)]+$15) × 2,000] + $10,000 = $81,400
[f][($20.70[1)]+$15) × 400] + $10,000 = $24,280
[g][($1 × 1,500) +$3,000] = $4,500
[h][($1 × 1,700) + $3,000] = $4,700

[1)] $48.70 − $28.00 = $20.70

2. Absorption costing makes operating income a function of both sales levels and production levels. This can create an incentive for managers to manipulate production levels to increase their operating income in a period when this is not in Byrd Company's best interest. It is not always the case that managers will manipulate production to increase inventory levels. They would also consider differences across periods in the fixed manufacturing overhead rates.

Variable costing highlights the effect of changes in units sold on operating income. It thus reduces the incentives for using production variations to "manage" operating income for manager performance evaluation purposes.

3. *Pros of Throughput Costing*

(a) Extreme form of variable costing. There is even less incentive to build for inventory than under variable costing. Indeed, managers who produce but do not sell the output in the same period, will see operating income decline because of variable costs other than direct materials being expensed to that period. Hence there is a disincentive for inventory buildup.

(b) Very simple to operate.

(c) Avoids disputes between absorption costing and variable costing over, say, whether a manufacturing cost item is variable indirect or fixed indirect. Throughput costing reduces incentives of managers to play games with respect to cost classifications.

Cons of Throughput Costing

(a) Procuring for inventory is not universally a negative. In industries where there is high uncertainty about demand and huge economies of scale in production, having some inventory may be economically appropriate. Throughput costing does not reinforce the economics of such situations.

(b) Can lead to large swings over time in operating income that managers may not feel represent their underlying performance.

(c) Some managers have maintained that when inventory is reported at only direct materials costs there is an incentive to reduce selling prices at the end of the year to get large increases in reported operating income for that period. This may not be in the company's best interest. This effect is marked for industries with a low direct materials cost to total manufacturing cost ratio.

(d) Can create need to run "dual" systems because of throughput costing being unacceptable for financial reporting or taxation.

9-34 (30 min.) The Semi-Fixed Company.

1. a. Variable-Costing Income Statements (in thousands):

		2006	2007	Together
Revenues ($36 × 10,000)		$360	$360	$720
Variable cost of sales ($8.40 × 10,000)		84	84	168
Contribution margin		276	276	552
Fixed manufacturing costs	$140			
Fixed marketing and admin, costs	40	180	180	360
Operating income		$ 96	$ 96	$192

b. Absorption-Costing Income Statements (in thousands):

	Alternative 1			Alternative 2		
	2006	**2007**	**Together**	**2006**	**2007**	**Together**
Revenues	$360	$360	$720	$360	$360	$720
Beginning inventory	—	154[1]	—	—	224[2]	—
Manufacturing costs	308	—	308	448	—	448
Available for sales	308	154	308	448	224	448
Ending inventory	154[1]	—	—	224[2]	—	—
Cost of goods sold	154	154	308	224	224	448
Underallocated overhead	—	140	140	—	140	—
Overallocated overhead	—	—	—	(140)	—	—
Marketing & administrative costs	40	40	80	40	40	80
Total costs	194	334	528	124	404	528
Operating income (loss)	$166	$ 26	$192	$236	$ (44)	$192

Alternative 1: Rate for fixed manufacturing overhead allocation based on 20,000 units: $140,000 ÷ 20,000 = $7.00 per tonne.

Alternative 2: Rate for fixed manufacturing overhead allocation based on 10,000 units: $140,000 ÷ 10,000 = $14.00 per tonne.

[1] Alternative 1: Variable manufacturing cost + Fixed manufacturing costs = $8.4 + $7.0 = $15.4 per tonne
[2] Alternative 2: Variable manufacturing cost + Fixed manufacturing costs = $8.4 + $14.00 = $22.4 per tonne

Note: The problem states that the denominator level is 20,000 tonnes per year. Therefore, alternative 2 is not required.

2. The Semi-Fixed Company has a positive operating income because some of its costs were variable. They could be avoided when the plant shut down for the second year. Variable costs can be "stored" as measures of assets, while fixed costs cannot. When the Semi-Fixed Co. paid $84,000 for direct materials, direct manufacturing labour, and variable manufacturing overhead to produce 10,000 additional tonnes of fertilizer during the first year for sale in the second year, it saved that amount of cost in the second year. Of course Semi-Fixed had double the variable costs in its first year. We are looking at timing of expenses rather than any cash savings over the two-year period. This emphasizes the importance of establishing an appropriate time horizon for any decisions that is consistent with the total cash effect of the decision. What appears to be a sensible justification for a one-year horizon is not sensible over two years.

3.

	Variable Costing	Absorption Costing	
		20,000 Unit Base*	10,000 Unit Base
Inventory, end of 2006	$84,000	$154,000	$224,000
Inventory, end of 2007	0	0	0

*Fixed manufacturing overhead rate is $7.00 when denominator level is 20,000 units and is $14.00 when denominator level is 10,000 units.

4. Reported operating income is affected by both production *and* sales under absorption costing. Hence, most managers would prefer absorption costing because their performance in any given reporting period, at least in the short run, is influenced by how much production is scheduled near the end of a reporting period.

9-36 (20-30 min.) Inventory costing and management planning.

Note that under variable costing the production schedule will not affect the bonus because all fixed manufacturing overhead is an expense in any event. Therefore, the production decision can be influenced by marketing needs, and unaffected by how costs are being charged to inventory or income.

1. Under absorption costing, the greater the production, the greater the operating income. The division manager would want to maximize production, given the constraints of storage space and practical capacity.

Target ending inventory	200
December expected sales	70
Total needs	270
November 30 inventory	150
Production to be scheduled	120 units

2. Operating income would be lower under variable costing because inventories are increasing. Specifically, inventory increased by 110 (150 + 80 – 70 – 50) units at a fixed manufacturing overhead rate of $720; so standard absorption-costing operating income would be $79,200 higher than variable costing income.

3. The division manager should set the minimum production schedule of 40 units, because the outlook for ending inventory is far in excess of reasonable sales demands.

4. 40 units. This amount of production will maximize the unfavourable production volume variance and will minimize income taxes for 2007. In other words, the deductions that are taken now rather than later are extremely valuable because their impact on tax savings is greater now than in 2008.

5. If 70 units fewer are scheduled in 2007, 70 units more must be scheduled in 2008. Therefore, operating income will be lower in 2007 and higher in 2008 by $50,400.

> Impact on operating income:
>> Schedule 50 units
>> Production-volume variance,
>>> (100 – 50) units × $720 $36,000 U
>> Schedule 120 units
>> Production-volume variance,
>>> (100 – 120) units × $720   14,400 F
>
> Impact on operating income $50,400 lower

The 2008 income must be higher because the total production level will be 70 units higher, resulting in a favourable effect on the production volume variance of 70 units × $720 = $50,400.

9-38 (20-35 min.) Effects of denominator-level concept choice.

1. Normal capacity utilization. Givens are denoted by *

Actual Costs Incurred	Same Lump Sum Regardless of Output Level	Same Lump Sum Regardless of Output Level	Allocated (Budgeted Input Allowed for Actual Output Achieved × Budgeted Rate)
			70,000 hrs.* × $2.40[a] = $168,000
$156,000	$144,000*	$144,000*	

    $12,000 U* $24,000 F*

Spending variance   Efficiency variance   Production-volume variance
                   (Never a variance)

$$\text{Production-volume variance} = \left(\begin{array}{c} \text{Budgeted} \\ \text{fixed} \\ \text{overhead} \end{array} - \begin{array}{c} \text{Fixed overhead allocated} \\ \text{using budgeted input allowed for} \\ \text{actual output achieved} \end{array} \right)$$

$$X - \$24,000^{b} = (\$144,000 - X)$$
$$X = \$168,000$$

[a] Budgeted fixed manufacturing $= \dfrac{\$168,000}{70,000 \text{ machine-hours}}$
overhead rate per unit

$$= \$2.40 \text{ per machine-hour}$$

Denominator level $= \dfrac{\$144,000}{\$2.40}$

$$= 60,000 \text{ machine-hours}$$

[b] Production-volume variance is negative, as it is favourable (therefore less than allocated fixed O/H).

2. Practical capacity. Givens denoted*

Actual Costs Incurred	Same Lump Sum Regardless of Output Level	Same Lump Sum Regardless of Output Level	Allocated (Budgeted Input Allowed for Actual Output Achieved × Budgeted Rate)
			70,000 hrs.* × $1.44[a] = $100,800
$156,000	$144,000*	$144,000*	

$12,000 U* — Spending variance

Efficiency variance (Never a variance)

$43,200 F* — Production-volume variance

$$\text{Production-volume variance} = \left(\begin{array}{c} \text{Budgeted} \\ \text{fixed} \\ \text{overhead} \end{array} \begin{array}{c} \text{Fixed overhead allocated} \\ - \text{using budgeted input allowed for} \\ \text{actual output achieved} \end{array} \right)$$

$$\$43,200 = (\$144,000 - X)$$
$$X = \$100,800$$

$$\text{[a] Budgeted fixed manufacturing overhead rate per unit} = \frac{\$100,800}{70,000 \text{ machine-hours}}$$

$$= \$1.44 \text{ per machine-hour}$$

$$\text{Denominator level} = \frac{\$144,000}{\$1.44}$$

$$= 100,000 \text{ machine-hours}$$

3. To maximize operating income, the executive vice-president would favour using normal capacity utilization rather than practical capacity. Why? Because normal capacity utilization is a smaller base than practical capacity, resulting in any year-end inventory having a higher unit cost. Thus, less fixed manufacturing overhead would become a 2007 expense if normal capacity utilization were used as the denominator level.

9-40 (20 min.) Cost allocation, downward demand spiral.

1.

$$\text{Budgeted fixed costs per meal} = \frac{\text{Budgeted fixed costs}}{\text{Budgeted denominator level}}$$

$$= \frac{\$5,256,000}{\text{Budgeted denominator level}}$$

Budgeted denominator level = 2,920,000 meals

WHM is using budgeted usage as its denominator level for calculating the budgeted fixed costs per meal in 2007.

2. Alternative denominator levels include:

a. Capacity available. The data in the problem note that the facility can serve 3,650,000 meals a year. With this denominator level, there will be budgeted unused capacity, which could be recorded as a separate line in the cost report for the Santa Monica facility.

b. Budgeted usage of capacity. With the 2007 budgeted usage of 2,920,000 meals, the fixed costs charge is $1.80 per meal. The marketplace is signalling that WHM's own central food-catering facility is not providing value for the costs charged. If Cheung decides to raise prices to recover fixed costs from a declining demand base, he will likely encounter the downward demand spiral:

Budgeted Denominator (1)	Variable Cost per Meal (2)	Fixed Cost per Meal $5,256,000 ÷ (1) (3)	Total Cost per Meal (4)
3,650,000	$4.56	$1.44	$6.00
2,920,000	4.56	1.80	6.36
2,550,000	4.56	2.06	6.62
2,000,000	4.56	2.63	7.19

Cheung might adopt a contribution margin approach, which means viewing the $4.56 variable cost as the only per-unit cost and the $5,256,000 as a fixed cost. Alternatively, Cheung could use practical capacity to cost the meals and work to reduce costs of unused capacity.

3. Three factors managers should consider in pricing decisions:

   a. Customers. Cheung is facing customers who are dissatisfied with both the cost and the quality of the meal service. Three of the 10 hospitals have already elected to use an outside canteen service.

   b. Competitors. For the three hospitals terminating use of the Santa Monica facility, at least one competitor is more cost-effective. The seven remaining hospitals likely will be very interested in how this competitor performs at the three hospitals.

   c. Costs. Jenkins should consider ways to reduce both the variable costs per meal and the fixed costs.

9-42 (15 min.) ABC and capacity usage.

Activity	Rate per Unit of Cost Driver
Power	$240,000 activity costs ÷ 50,000 kilowatt hours = $4.80 per kilowatt hour
Quality inspection	$360,000 activity costs ÷ 10,000 inspections = $36 per inspection

Cost Allocation:

Power
Tulsa (10,000 kilowatt hours × $4.80)	$ 48,000
Okla (35,000 kilowatt hours × $4.80)	168,000
Total power costs allocation	$216,000

Quality inspection
Tulsa (5,000 inspections × $36)	$180,000
Okla (4,000 inspections × $36)	144,000
Total quality inspection costs allocation	$324,000

2. Cost of unused capacity:

Power ($240,000 – $216,000)	$ 24,000
Quality inspection ($360,000 – $324,000)	36,000
Total cost of unused capacity	$ 60,000

9-44 (20 min.) Downward demand spiral.

1.		
	Budgeted variable manufacturing costs per unit	$240
	Allocated fixed manufacturing overhead costs per unit	120[a]
	Budgeted total manufacturing costs per unit	360
	Markup (100% × $360)	360
	Budgeted selling price	$720

[a]$1,200,000 ÷ 10,000 units = $120 per unit

2.		
	Budgeted variable manufacturing costs per unit	$240
	Allocated fixed manufacturing overhead costs per unit	150[b]
	Budgeted total manufacturing costs per unit	390
	Markup (100% × $390)	390
	Revised budgeted selling price	$780

[b]$1,200,000 + 8,000 units = $150 per unit

3. Considering that the market is highly competitive, raising the selling price, in an attempt to recover fixed manufacturing overhead costs, will make Pismo Company less competitive. Pismo's higher selling price would likely make it lose its customers to the competitors. This is the classic syndrome of the start of a downward demand spiral. Pismo Company should use its practical capacity to allocate fixed manufacturing overhead costs. If an upturn is expected, Pismo should keep its excess capacity. Otherwise, it should either lease or get rid of the excess capacity in order to bring down its fixed manufacturing overhead costs to the demand level.

9-46 (30 min.) Variable and absorption costing and breakeven points.

1. Production = Sales + Ending Inventory – Beginning Inventory
= 242,400 + 24,800 – 32,600
= 234,600

2. Breakeven point in cases:

   a.   Variable Costing:

   $$QT = \frac{\text{Total Fixed Costs + Target Operating Income}}{\text{Contribution Margin per Unit}}$$

   $$QT = \frac{(\$4,504,320 + \$7,882,560) + \$0}{\$112.80 - (\$19.20 + \$12.00 + \$7.20 + \$16.80 + \$2.40)}$$

   $$QT = \frac{\$12,386,880}{\$55.20}$$

   $$QT = 224,400 \text{ cases}$$

   b.   Absorption costing:

   $$QT = \frac{\begin{array}{l}\text{Total Fixed} \\ \text{Cost}\end{array} + \begin{array}{l}\text{Target} \\ \text{OI}\end{array} + \left[\begin{array}{l}\text{Fixed Manuf.} \\ \text{Cost Rate}\end{array} \times \left(\begin{array}{l}\text{Breakeven} \\ \text{Sales in Units}\end{array} - \begin{array}{l}\text{Units} \\ \text{Produced}\end{array}\right)\right]}{\text{Contribution Margin per Unit}}$$

   $$QT = \frac{\$12,386,880 + \left[\$19.20^{1)}(QT - 234,600)\right]}{\$55.20}$$

   $$QT = \frac{\$12,386,880 + \$19.20\,QT - 4,504,320}{\$55.20}$$

   $$QT = \frac{\$7,882,560 + 19.20\,QT}{\$55.20}$$

   $$55.20QT - 19.20QT = \$7,882,560$$

   $$36QT \qquad\qquad = \$7,882,560$$

   $$QT \qquad\qquad = 218,960 \text{ cases}$$

1) $\$4,504,320 \div 234,600 \text{ cases} = \$19.20$

3. If grape prices increase by 25%, the cost of grapes per case will increase from $19.20 in 2007 to $24 in 2008. This will decrease the unit contribution margin from $55.20 in 2007 to $50.40 in 2008.

   a.   Variable Costing:

   $$QT = \frac{\$12,386,880}{\$50.40}$$

   $$= 245,771 \text{ cases (rounded off)}$$

b.   Absorption Costing:

$$QT = \frac{\$7,882,560 + \$19.20\,QT}{\$50.40}$$

$$\$50.4\,QT = \$7,882,560 + \$19.20\,QT$$

$$\$31.20\,QT = \$7,882,560$$

$$QT = 252,646 \text{ cases (round off)}$$

4.   a. OI 2007 $= (242,400 - 224,400) \times CM$

$= (18,000) \times (\text{Revenue} - \text{Variable Costs})$

$= (18,000) \times \$55.20 = \$993,600$

$\therefore$ Variable costing: $\$993,600 \times 110\%\uparrow = \$1,092,960$ OI

$\therefore$ Variable costing: Required OI $= \$1,092,960$ in 2008

$\therefore$ Breakeven $= 245,771$ cases (from question 3a.)

1) OI $= \$1,092,960$

2) CM $= \$50.40$

Required Sales $= BE + 1) \div 2)$

$= 245,771 + (1,092,960 \div 50.40)$

$= 245,771 + 21,686 = 267,457$ cases (rounded off)

b. Absorption costing: $QT = \dfrac{\$12,386,880 + \$1,092,960 + \$19.20\,(QT - 234,600)}{\$50.40}$

$$31.20\,QT = 8,975,520$$
$$QT = 287,677 \text{ rounded}$$

9-48   (20 min.)   **Absorption costing, management ethics (continuation of 9-47).**

1.   Behaviours that might suggest problems for IEC with the existing bonus plan and accounting system include:

a.   Plant managers switching production orders at year-end to those orders that absorb the highest amount of manufacturing overhead, irrespective of the demand by customers of IEC.

b.   Plant managers at one division of IEC accepting orders that they know another plant of IEC is better suited to handle.

c.   Plant managers deferring maintenance beyond the normal maintenance period.

2. Possible changes include:

    a. Change the incentive scheme so that there are not the major discontinuities at 15% and 10%.
    b. Change the operating income measure to variable costing rather than absorption costing.
    c. Add other performance measures (such as inventory turnover) that explicitly penalize "building for inventory."
    d. Emphasize the importance of managers considering IEC total benefits and costs of their decisions. This could be done via persuasion or by an incentive system based on IEC operating income rather than 100% of each division's operating income.

CHAPTER 10
DETERMINING HOW COSTS BEHAVE

10-2 Three alternative linear cost functions are:
1. Variable cost function—a cost function in which total costs change in proportion to the cost driver in the relevant range.
2. Fixed cost function—a cost function in which total costs do not change with changes in the cost driver in the relevant range.
3. Mixed cost function—a cost function that has both variable and fixed elements. Total costs change but not in proportion to the changes in the cost driver in the relevant range.

10-4 No. High correlation merely indicates that the two variables move together in the data examined. It is essential to consider also economic plausibility before making inferences about cause and effect. Without any economic plausibility for a relationship, it is less likely that a high level of correlation observed in one set of data will be similarly found in other sets of data.

10-6 The conference method develops cost estimates on the basis of analysis and opinions gathered from various departments of an organization (purchasing, process engineering, manufacturing, employee relations, etc.). Advantages of the conference method include:
1. The speed with which cost estimates can be developed.
2. The pooling of knowledge from experts across functional areas.
3. The improved credibility of the cost function to all personnel.

10-8 The six steps are:
1. Choose the dependent variable (the variable to be predicted, which is some type of cost).
2. Identify the cost driver(s) (independent variables).
3. Collect data on the dependent variable and the cost driver(s).
4. Plot the data.
5. Estimate the cost function.
6. Evaluate the estimated cost function.
Step 3 typically is the most difficult for a cost analyst.

10-10 Criteria important when choosing among alternative cost functions are:
1. Economic plausibility.
2. Goodness of fit.
3. Slope of the regression line.

10-12 Frequently encountered problems when collecting cost data on variables included in a cost function are:

1. The time period used to measure the dependent variable is not properly matched with the period used to measure the cost driver(s).
2. Fixed costs are allocated as if they are variable.
3. Data either are not available for all observations or are not uniformly reliable.
4. Extreme values of observations occur from errors in recording costs.
5. A homogeneous relationship between the individual cost items in the dependent variable and the cost driver(s) does not exist.
6. The relationship between cost and the cost driver is not stationary.
7. Inflation has occurred in a dependent variable, a cost driver, or both.

10-14 No. A cost driver is any factor whose change causes a change in the total cost of a related cost object. A cause-and-effect relationship underlies selection of a cost driver. Some users of regression analysis include numerous independent variables in a regression model in an attempt to maximize goodness of fit, irrespective of the economic plausibility of the independent variables included. Some of the independent variables included may not be cost drivers.

10-16 (10 min.) Estimating a cost function.

1. Slope coefficient $= \dfrac{\text{Difference in costs}}{\text{Difference in machine-hours}}$

$\qquad\qquad\qquad = \dfrac{\$4,680 - \$3,600}{7,000 - 4,000}$

$\qquad\qquad\qquad = \dfrac{\$1,080}{3,000} = \$0.36$ per machine-hour

Add $y = a + bx$
Thus: $a = y - bx$
Constant $\quad=\;$ Total cost − (Slope coefficient × Quantity of cost driver)
$\qquad\qquad=\;$ $\$4,680 - (\$0.36 \times 7,000) = \$2,160$
$\qquad\qquad=\;$ $\$3,600 - (\$0.36 \times 4,000) = \$2,160$

The cost function based on the two observations is:

Maintenance costs = \$2,160 + \$0.36 (machine-hours)

2. The cost function in requirement 1 is an estimate of how costs behave within the relevant range, not at cost levels outside the relevant range. If there are no months with zero machine-hours represented in the maintenance account, data in that account cannot be used to estimate the fixed costs at the zero machine-hours

level. Rather, the constant component of the cost function provides the best available starting point for a straight line that approximates how a cost behaves within the relevant range.

10-18 (20 min.) **Various cost-behaviour patterns.**

1. K
2. B
3. G
4. J   Note that A is incorrect because, although the cost per kilogram eventually equals a constant at $9.20, the total dollars of cost increases linearly from that point onward.
5. I   The total costs will be the same regardless of the volume level.
6. L
7. F   This is a classic step-function cost.
8. K
9. C

10-20 (20 min.) **Account analysis method.**

1.

Variable costs:	
Car wash labour	$288,000
Soap, cloth, and supplies	38,400
Water	33,600
Power to move conveyor belt	86,400
Total variable costs	$446,400

Fixed costs:	
Amortization	$ 76,800
Supervision	36,000
Cashier	19,200
Total fixed costs	$132,000

2. Variable costs per car $= \dfrac{\$446,400}{80,000} = \$5.58$ per car

Total costs estimated for 90,000 cars = $132,000 + ($5.58 × 90,000) = $634,200

$y = a + bx$, where $x = 90,000$

$b = 5.58$

$a = 132,000$

3. Average cost in 2007 $= \dfrac{\$446,400 + \$132,000}{80,000} = \dfrac{\$578,400}{80,000} = \$7.23$

Average cost in 2008 $= \dfrac{\$634,200}{90,000} = \$7.05^{\text{i)}}$

Some students may assume that power costs of running the continuously moving conveyor belt is a fixed cost. In this case the variable costs in 2007 will be $360,000 and the fixed costs $218,400.

The variable costs per car in 2007 = $360,000 ÷ 80,000 cars = $4.50 per car

Total costs for 90,000 cars in 2008 = $218,400 + ($4.50 × 90,000) = $623,400

The average cost of washing a car in 2008 = $623,400 ÷ 90,000 = $6.93.

i) Note the average costs per car washed in 2008 are lower than the average costs in 2007. This is because the fixed costs remained constant. This is relevant over a limited range, as eventually fixed costs would also increase with the increase in the total number of cars washed.

10-22 (20 min.) Estimating a cost function, high-low method.

1. See Solution Exhibit 10-22. There is a positive relationship between the number of service reports (a cost driver) and the customer service department costs. This relationship is economically plausible.

2.

	Number of Service Reports	Customer Service Department Costs
Highest observation of cost driver	436	$ 26,268
Lowest observation of cost driver	122	15,530
Difference	314	$ 10,738

Customer service department costs = a + b (number of service reports)

$y = a + bx$

Slope[1] coefficient $(b) = \dfrac{\$10,738}{314} = \$34.197$ per service report

Constant $(a) = \$26,268 - \$34.197 (436) = \$11,358$
$= \$15,530 - \$34.197 (122) = \$11,358$

Customer service department costs $= \$11,358 + \$34.197$ (number of service reports)

3.   Other possible cost drivers of customer service department costs are:

   (a) Number of products replaced with a new product (and the dollar value of the new products charged to the customer service department).
   (b) Number of products repaired and the time and cost of repairs.

(1) slope b = $\dfrac{\Delta y}{\Delta x}$, where y = Customer service dept. costs

and x = Number of service reports

Using the upper (high) or the lowest (low) point to determine the fixed costs renders the same response. Fixed costs remain the same for different levels of activity within the relevant range.

SOLUTION EXHIBIT 10-22
Plot of Number of Service Reports Versus
Customer Service Costs for Capitol Products

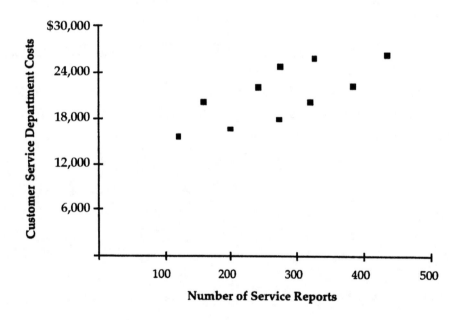

10-24   (20 min.) Cost-volume-profit and regression analysis.

1.   a.   Average cost of manufacturing = $\dfrac{\text{Total manufacturing costs}}{\text{Number of bicycle frames}}$

   = $\dfrac{\$1,080,000}{30,000}$ = $36 per frame

This cost is greater than the $34.20 per frame that Ryan has quoted.

b. Oxbow cannot take the average manufacturing cost in 2007 of $36 per frame and multiply it by 36,000 bicycle frames to determine the total cost of manufacturing 36,000 bicycle frames. The reason is that some of the $1,080,000 (or equivalently the $36 cost per frame) are fixed costs and some are variable costs. Without distinguishing fixed from variable costs, Oxbow cannot determine the cost of manufacturing 36,000 frames. For example, if all costs are fixed, the manufacturing costs of 36,000 frames will continue to be $1,080,000. If, however, all costs are variable, the cost of manufacturing 36,000 frames would be $36 × 36,000 = $1,296,000. If some costs are fixed and some are variable, the cost of manufacturing 36,000 frames will be somewhere between $1,080,000 and $1,296,000.

Some students could argue that another reason for not being able to determine the cost of manufacturing 36,000 bicycle frames is that not all costs are output unit-level costs. If some costs are, for example, batch-level costs, more information would be needed on the number of batches in which the 36,000 bicycle frames would be produced, in order to determine the cost of manufacturing 36,000 bicycle frames.

2. Expected cost to make 36,000 bicycle frames

$$= \$518,400 + (\$18 \times 36,000)$$

$$= \$518,400 + \$648,000 = \$1,166,400$$

Purchasing bicycle frames from Ryan will cost $34.20 × 36,000 = $1,231,200. Hence it will cost Oxbow $1,231,200 − $1,166,400 = $64,800 more to purchase the frames from Oxbow rather than manufacture them in-house.

3. Oxbow would need to consider several factors before being confident that the equation in requirement 2 accurately predicts the cost of manufacturing bicycle frames.

a. Is the relationship between total manufacturing costs and quantity of bicycle frames economically plausible? For example, is the quantity of bicycles made the only cost driver or are there other cost-drivers (for example, batch-level costs of setups, production-orders, or material handling) that affect manufacturing costs?

b. How good is the goodness of fit? That is, how well does the estimated line fit the data?

c. Is the relationship between the number of bicycle frames produced and total manufacturing costs linear?

d. Does the slope of the regression line indicate that a strong relationship exists between manufacturing costs and the number of bicycle frames produced?

e. Are there any data problems such as, for example, errors in measuring costs, trends in prices of materials, labour or overheads that might affect variable or fixed costs over time, extreme values of observations, or a nonstationary relationship over time between total manufacturing costs and the quantity of bicycles produced?

10-26 (30-40 min.) **Regression analysis, activity-based costing, choosing cost drivers.**

1. a. Solution Exhibit 10-26A presents the plots and regression line of number of packaged units moved on distribution costs.

SOLUTION EXHIBIT 10-26A

Plots and Regression Line of Number of Packaged Units Moved on Distribution Costs

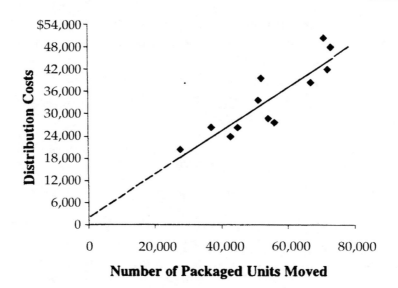

b. Solution Exhibit 10-26B presents the plots and regression line of number of shipments made on distribution costs.

SOLUTION EXHIBIT 10-26B

Plots and Regression Line of Number of Shipments Made on Distribution Costs

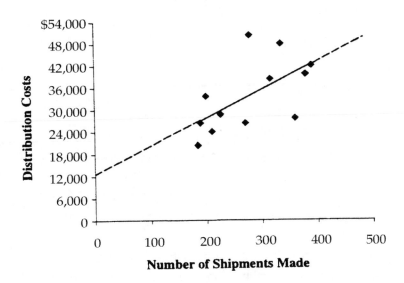

Number of packaged units moved appears to be a better cost driver of distribution costs for the following reasons:

(i) *Economic plausibility.* Both number of packaged units moved and number of shipments are economically plausible cost drivers. Because the product is heavy, however, costs of freight are likely to be a sizable component of distribution costs. Thus, number of packaged units moved will affect distribution costs significantly because freight costs are largely a function of the number of units transported.

(ii) *Goodness of fit.* Compare Solution Exhibits 10-26A and 10-26B. Number of packaged units moved has a better goodness of fit with distribution costs than do number of shipments made. That is, the vertical differences between actual and predicted values are smaller for the number of packaged units moved regression than for the number of shipments made regression.

(iii) *Slope of regression line.* Again, compare Solution Exhibits 10-26A and 10-26B. The number of packaged units moved regression line has a relatively steep slope indicating a strong relationship between number of packaged units moved and distribution costs. On average, distribution costs increase with the number of packaged units moved. The number of shipments made regression line is flatter and has a wider scatter of observations about the line, indicating a weak relationship between number of shipments made and distribution costs. On average, the number of shipments made has a smaller effect on distribution costs.

2. Using the preferred cost function,
Distribution costs = $1,618.45 + ($0.595 × Number of packaged units moved), Goldstein would budget distribution costs of
$1,618.45 + ($0.595 × 40,000) = $1,618.45 + 23,800 = $25,418.45

3. Using the "other" cost function
Distribution costs = $12,500.57 + ($76.52 × Number of shipments made), Goldstein would budget distribution costs of
$12,500.57 + ($76.52 × 220) = $12,500.57 + $16,834.40 = $29,334.97

The actual costs are likely to be lower than the prediction of $29,335 made using the number of shipments as the cost driver. The reason is that budgeted distribution costs are likely to be closer to the $25,418.45 predicted by the regression equation with number of packaged units moved as the cost driver. This regression equation provides a better explanation of the factors that affect distribution costs.

Choosing the "wrong" cost driver and estimating the incorrect cost function can have repercussions for pricing, cost management, and cost control. To the extent that Goldstein uses predicted costs of $29,335 for making pricing decisions, she may overprice the 40,000 packages she expects to move and could potentially lose business.

Question 10 - 26
X1

Regression Statistics	
Multiple R	0.88671984
R Square	0.78627207
Adjusted R Square	0.76489928
Standard Error	4732.36378
Observations	12

Here the R squared value is poor at 0.76. This means that only 76% of the variation in 'distribution costs' is explained by variation in the X1 variable, '# of packaged units moved'.
The model fit is good however with a Significance F of 0.00012.
The intercept coefficient is poor with a 0.77 p-value. This means that the intercept value is only significant at 33% confidence level or a level of significance of 77 %.
The coefficient for the X1 variable '# of packaged units moved' is highly significant with p-value of 0.00012 or a confidence level of > 99.99%.
X1 or the # of packaged units moved is a much better cost driver than the # of shipments made (X2 ..next pg) as the R sq. value is far superior ie a better correlation between variances.

ANOVA

	df	SS	MS	F	Significance F	
Regression	1	823887330.2	823887330.2	36.788458	**0.000121119**	0.999878881
Residual	10	223952669.8	22395266.98			
Total	11	1047840000				

	Coefficients	Standard Error	t Stat	P-value	Lower 95%	Upper 95%	
Intercept	1618.45074	5478.852297	0.295399593	**0.7737311**	-10589.19288	13826.0944	0.226268873
X1; packaged units	0.59503635	0.098104224	6.065348927	**0.0001211**	0.376446518	0.81362618	0.999878881

Distribution Costs = 1618.451 + 0.595036*(# of packaged units moved)

RESIDUAL OUTPUT

Observation	Predicted Y	Residuals	month	Y 2004 distibution costs	X1 # of packaged units moved
1	31965.3046	1634.695412	January	33600	51000
2	27205.0138	-3205.013788	February	24000	43000
3	18279.4685	2120.531462	March	20400	28000
4	41485.8862	-3085.886187	April	38400	67000
5	45056.1043	2943.895713	May	48000	73000
6	33750.4136	-4950.413638	June	28800	54000
7	23634.7957	2765.204312	July	26400	37000
8	44461.0679	-2461.067937	August	42000	72000
9	43866.0316	6533.968413	september	50400	71000
10	34940.4863	-7340.486337	October	27600	56000
11	32560.3409	7039.659062	November	39600	52000
12	28395.0865	-1995.086488	December	26400	45000
			sum	405600	649000

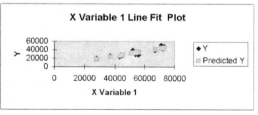

X Variable 1 Line Fit Plot

Question 10 - 26

X2

Regression Statistics	
Multiple R	0.59930534
R Square	0.3591669
Adjusted R Square	**0.29508359**
Standard Error	8194.45276
Observations	12

Here we have a model fit or Significance F at 96% confidence level (4% level of significance); howeverthe **R square value of 0.295 is very poor**, meaning only 29.5% of the variation in Y (distribution costs) dependent variable is explained by the variation in the independent variable X2 (# of shipments made).
The intercept coefficient has a level of significant of 20.8 % (or at a 79.2% level of confidence).
The coefficient for the X2 independent variable has a level of significance of 3.9% or a confidence level of > 96%.
Here X2 or the # of shipments made is a much poorer cost driver with respect to distribution costs than the # of packaged units moved (X1); as X2's R sq. value is much lower than X1's R sq. value and has a C.L. of 96% whereas X1 has a C.L. of 99.9%.

ANOVA

	df	SS	MS	F	Significance F	
Regression	1	376349439.8	376349439.8	5.604687	**0.039450435**	0.960549565
Residual	10	671490560.2	67149056.02			
Total	11	1047840000				

	Coefficients	Standard Error	t Stat	P-value	Lower 95%	Upper 95%	
Intercept	12500.5705	9302.673759	1.343761037	**0.20872**	-8227.078202	33228.219	0.791279945
X2 shipments	**76.5248963**	32.32414665	2.367422011	**0.03945**	4.502209565	148.54758	0.960549565

Distribution Costs = 12500.5705 + 76.5248963*(# of shipments)

RESIDUAL OUTPUT

				Y	X2
				2004 distibution	# of shipments
Observation	Predicted Y	Residuals	month	costs	made
1	27805.5498	5794.450207	January	33600	200
2	28570.7988	-4570.798755	February	24000	210
3	26657.6763	-6257.676349	March	20400	185
4	36605.9129	1794.087137	April	38400	315
5	38136.4108	9863.589212	May	48000	335
6	29718.6722	-918.6721992	June	28800	225
7	27040.3008	-640.3008299	July	26400	190
8	42345.2801	-345.280083	August	42000	390
9	33927.5415	16472.45851	september	50400	280
10	40049.5332	-12449.5332	October	27600	360
11	41580.0311	-1980.03112	November	39600	380
12	33162.2925	-6762.292531	December	26400	270
				405600	3340

Data for Q 10 - 26

2004 month	distribution costs	# of packaged units moved	# of shipments made		**2002**
January	33600	51000	200		28000
February	24000	43000	210		20000
March	20400	28000	185		17000
April	38400	67000	315		32000
May	48000	73000	335		40000
June	28800	54000	225		24000
July	26400	37000	190		22000
August	42000	72000	390		35000
september	50400	71000	280		42000
October	27600	56000	360		23000
November	39600	52000	380		33000
December	26400	45000	270		22000
	405600	649000	3340 sums		338000
	Y	**X1**	**X2**		

To see the problems in cost management, suppose Waterloo Corporation moves 40,000 units in 220 shipments in the next month while incurring actual costs of $28,200. Compared with the budget of $29,335, management would consider this a good performance and seek ways to replicate it. In fact, on the basis of the preferred cost driver, the number of packaged units moved, actual distribution costs of $28,200 are higher than what they should be ($25,418)—a performance that management should seek to correct and improve rather than replicate.

10-28 (20 min.) Learning curve, incremental unit time learning curve

1. The direct manufacturing labour-hours (DMLH) required to produce the first 2, 3, and 4 units given the assumption of an incremental unit-time learning curve of 90% is as follows:

Cumulative Number of Units (1)	Individual Unit Time for Xth Unit (2)	Cumulative Total Time (3)
1	3,000	3,000
2	2,700 (3,000 × 0.90)	5,700
3	2,539	8,239
4	2,430 (2,700 × 0.90)	10,669

Values in column 2 are calculated using the formula $y = aX^b$

where $a = 3{,}000$, $X = 2, 3,$ or 4 and $b = -0.1520$, which gives

$$\text{when } X = 2, y = 3{,}000 \times 2^{-0.1520} \quad = 2{,}700$$
$$\text{when } X = 3, y = 3{,}000 \times 3^{-0.1520} \quad = 2{,}539$$
$$\text{when } X = 4, y = 3{,}000 \times 4^{-0.1520} \quad = 2{,}430$$

	Variable Costs of Producing		
	2 Units	3 Units	4 Units
Direct materials $96,000 × 2; 3; 4	$192,000	$288,000	$384,000
Direct manufacturing labour $30 × 5,700; 8,239; 10,669	171,000	247,170	320,070
Variable manufacturing overhead $18 × 5,700; 8,239; 10,669	102,600	148,302	192,042
Total variable costs	$465,600	$683,472	$896,112

2.

	Variable Costs of Producing	
	2 Units	**4 Units**
Incremental unit time learning curve (from requirement 1)	$465,600	$896,112
Cumulative average time learning curve (from Exercise 10-27)	451,200	850,560
Difference	$ 14,400	$ 45,552

Total variable costs for manufacturing 2 and 4 units are lower under the cumulative average time learning curve than under the incremental unit time learning curve. Direct manufacturing labour-hours required to make additional units decline more slowly in the incremental unit-time learning curve than in the cumulative average-time learning curve assuming the same 90% factor is used for both curves. The reason is that, in the incremental unit time learning curve, as the number of units doubles, only the last unit produced has a cost of 90% of the initial cost. In the cumulative average time model, doubling the number of units causes the average cost of *all* the additional units produced (not just the last unit) to be 90% of the initial cost.

10-30 (30-40 min.) High-low versus regression method.

1. Solution Exhibit 10-30 presents the plots of advertising costs on revenues.

SOLUTION EXHIBIT 10-30
Plot and Regression Line of Advertising Costs on Revenues

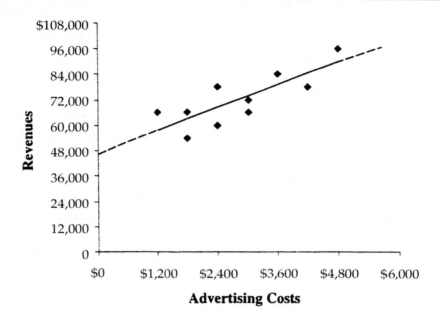

2. Solution Exhibit 10-30 also shows the regression line of advertising costs on revenues. We evaluate the estimated regression equation using the criteria of economic plausibility, goodness of fit, and slope of the regression line.

    Economic plausibility. Advertising costs appears to be a plausible cost driver of revenues. Restaurants frequently use newspaper advertising to promote their restaurants and increase their patronage.

    Goodness of fit. The vertical differences between actual and predicted revenues appears to be reasonably small. This indicates that advertising costs are related to restaurant revenues.

    Slope of regression line. The slope of the regression line appears to be relatively steep. This indicates that, on average, restaurant revenues increase with newspaper advertising.

3. The high-low method would estimate the cost function as follows:

	X	Y
	Advertising Costs	**Revenues**
Highest observation of cost driver	$4,800	$96,000
Lowest observation of cost driver	1,200	66,000
Difference	$3,600	$30,000

$$y = a + bx$$
$$\text{Revenues} = a + (b \times \text{advertising costs})$$
$$\text{Slope coefficient } (b) = \frac{\$30,000}{\$3,600} = 8.333$$
$$\text{Constant } (a) = \$96,000 - (\$4,800 \times 8.333)$$
$$= \$96,000 - \$40,000 = \$56,000$$
$$\textit{or} \quad \text{Constant } (a) = \$66,000 - (\$1,200 \times 8.333)$$
$$= \$66,000 - \$10,000 = \$56,000$$

$$\text{Revenues} = \$56,000 + (8.333 \times \text{Advertising costs})$$

4. The increase in revenues for each $1,000 spent on advertising within the relevant range is
   a. Using the regression equation, 8.723 × $1,000 = $8,723
   b. Using the high-low equation, 8.333 × $1,000 = $8,333

5. The high-low equation does fairly well in estimating the relationship between advertising costs and revenues. However, Martinez and Brown should use the regression equation. The reason is that the regression equation uses information from all observations, whereas the high-low method relies only on the observations that have the highest and lowest values of the cost driver. These observations are generally not representative of all the data.

Q 10 - 30

Regression Statistics	
Multiple R	0.801703384
R Square	0.642728316
Adjusted R Square	**0.598069356**
Standard Error	7816.230418
Observations	10

The model fit re Significance F is not bad with a confidence level > 99%.
However the R squared value of 0.598, means only 60% of the variation in the dependent variable Revenue (Y) is explained by variation in the independent variable Advertising Expense or X.
the level of significance is good for both the intercept coefficient and the coefficient for Advertising Expense (< 0.0001 or < 0.01% and < 0.01 or < 1%...this corresponds to confidence levels of > 99.99 % and > 99% respectively)

ANOVA

	df	SS	MS	F	Significance F
Regression	1	879252336.4	879252336.4	14.39192	**0.005284118**
Residual	8	488747663.6	61093457.94		
Total	9	1368000000			

	Coefficients	Standard Error	t Stat	P-value	Lower 95%	Upper 95%	ower 95.0%	Jpper 95.0%
Intercept	**47401.86916**	6939.131186	6.831095693	**0.000134**	31400.20396	63403.53	31400.2	63403.53
Advertising Expen:	**8.722741433**	2.299289135	3.793668792	**0.005284**	3.420571185	14.02491	3.420571	14.02491

$$Y = 47,401.869 + 8.7227 \cdot X$$

RESIDUAL OUTPUT

Observation	Predicted Revenue	Residuals
1	68336.4486	-8336.448598
2	78803.73832	5196.261682
3	63102.80374	2897.196262
4	84037.38318	-6037.383178
5	57869.15888	8130.841121
6	68336.4486	9663.551402
7	63102.80374	-9102.803738
8	89271.02804	6728.971963
9	73570.09346	-7570.093458
10	73570.09346	-1570.093458

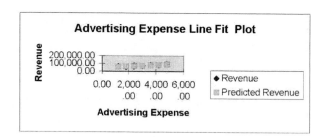

Advertising Expense Line Fit Plot

Data for Q 10 - 30

Month	Y **Revenue**	X **Advertising Expense**
March	60,000.00	2,400.00
April	84,000.00	3,600.00
May	66,000.00	1,800.00
June	78,000.00	4,200.00
July	66,000.00	1,200.00
August	78,000.00	2,400.00
September	54,000.00	1,800.00
October	96,000.00	4,800.00
November	66,000.00	3,000.00
December	72,000.00	3,000.00
sums	720,000.00	28,200.00

10-32 (30-40 min.) Cost estimation, cumulative average time learning curve.

1. Cost to produce the second through the eighth search and rescue boats:

Direct materials, 7 × $120,000	$ 840,000
Direct manufacturing labour, 39,130* × $36	1,408,680
Variable manufacturing overhead, 39,130 × $24	939,120
Other manufacturing overhead, 25% of $1,408,680	352,170
Total costs	$3,539,970

*The direct manufacturing labour-hours to produce the second to eighth boats can be calculated in several ways, given the assumption of a cumulative average-time learning curve of 85%:

(a) Use of table format:

Cumulative Number of Units	Cumulative Average Time per Unit	Cumulative Total Time
1	10,000.00	10,000
2	8,500.00 (10,000 × 0.85)	17,000
4	7,225.00 (8,500 × 0.85)	28,900
8	6,141.25 (7,225 × 0.85)	49,130

The direct labour-hours required to produce the second through the eighth boats is 49,130 − 10,000 = 39,130 hours.

(b) Use of formula:

$$y = aX^b$$

where $a = 10,000$, $X = 8$, and $b = -0.2345$.

$$y = 10,000 \times 8^{-0.2345} = 6,141 \text{ hours (rounded)}$$

The total direct labour-hours for 8 units is 6,141 × 8 = 49,128 hours

The direct labour-hours required to produce the second through the eighth boats is 49,128 − 10,000 = 39,128 hours. (By taking the b factor to 6 decimal digits, an estimate of 49,130 hours would result.)

Note: Some students will debate the exclusion of the tooling cost. The question specifies that the tooling cost was assigned to the first boat. Although Nautilus may well seek to ensure that its total revenue covers the $870,000 cost of the first boat, the concern in this question is only with the cost of producing seven more PT109s.

2.   Cost to produce the second through the eighth boats assuming linear function for direct labour-hours and units produced:

Direct materials, 7 × $120,000	$ 840,000
Direct manufacturing labour, 7 × 10,000 hours × $36	2,520,000
Variable manufacturing overhead, 7 × 10,000 hours × $24	1,680,000
Other manufacturing overhead, 25% of $2,520,000	630,000
Total costs	$5,670,000

The difference in predicted costs is:

• Predicted cost in requirement 2 (based on linear cost function)	$5,670,000
• Predicted cost in requirement 1 (based on an 85% learning curve)	3,539,970
Difference	$2,130,030

10-34   (30 min.)   Appendix: Promotion of a new product, simple and multiple regression analysis.

At 95% confidence level on 5% level of significance:

1.   The *t*-values (value of the coefficient ÷ standard error of the coefficient) of the coefficients in each of the regressions follow. A *t*-value greater than 2 indicates that the coefficient is significantly different from zero, providing d.f. ≥ 60, i.e. sample size is ≥ 61.[a]

> a) If the sample size (# of data pairs (x + y) = 12, the degrees of freedom = 11 and the *t*-value must be ≥ 2.20 to be statistically significant at 95% confidence level.
>
> [d.f. = degrees of freedom] There is only one independent variable.

Regression 1: *t*-value of coefficient of X_1 = $4.78 ÷ $2.08 = 2.30, indicating that there is a relation between dollars incurred on discount coupons and estimated sales. Providing d.f. ≥ 9, i.e. sample size n ≥ 9. If n < 9, this *t*-value is not statistically significant.

Regression 2: t-value of coefficient of X2 = $5.08 ÷ $2.23 = 2.28, indicating that there is a relation between dollars spent on TV advertising and estimated sales providing d.f. ≥ 9.

Regression 3: t-value of coefficient of X_1 = \$1.04 ÷ \$0.95 = 1.09, indicating that there is no relation between dollars incurred on discount coupons and estimated sales given dollars spent on TV advertising; t-value of coefficient of X_2 = \$1.09 ÷ \$1.19 = 0.92, indicating that there is no relation between dollars spent on TV advertising and estimated sales given dollars incurred on discount coupons.

2. The t-value indicates that the coefficients in the simple regressions are statistically significant, but that the coefficients of the same variables are insignificant in a multiple regression. The likely reason is multicollinearity. Because the two independent variables are correlated, the standard errors of the coefficients increase and make the variables appear insignificant and difficult to interpret.

3. Omitting a correlated variable (as the first two regressions do) causes the estimated coefficient of the independent variable to be biased away from its true value. Including both variables induces multicollinearity, which makes interpreting the significance of the coefficients difficult. To make predictions about estimated sales, it is probably best to use both dollars incurred on discount coupons and dollars spent on TV advertising despite the multicollinearity problems.

To understand the separate effects of dollars incurred on discount coupons and dollars spent on TV advertising on estimated sales, Rick would need to find months of data where either dollars incurred on discount coupons or dollars spent on TV advertising were high, but not both. Such new data will not suffer from the problems of multicollinearity and will allow Rick to estimate the relationship between each cost driver and estimated sales.

10-36 (30 min.) Appendix: Evaluating multiple regression models, not-for-profit (continuation of problem 10-35).

1. It is economically plausible that the correct form of the model of overhead costs includes both number of academic programs and number of enrolled students as cost drivers. The findings in Problem 10-35 indicate that each of the independent variables affects overhead costs. (Each regression has a significant r^2 and t-value on the independent variable.) Hanks could choose to divide overhead costs into two cost pools, (i) those overhead costs that are more closely related to number of academic programs and (ii) those overhead costs more closely related to number of enrolled students, and rerun the simple regression analysis on each overhead cost pool. Alternatively, Hanks could run a multiple regression analysis with total overhead costs as the dependent variable and the number of academic programs and number of enrolled students as the two independent variables.

2. Solution Exhibit 10-36A evaluates the multiple regression model using the format of Exhibit 10-21. Hanks should use the multiple regression model rather than the two simple regression models of Problem 10-35. The multiple regression model

appears economically plausible and the regression model performs very well when estimating overhead costs. It has an excellent goodness of fit, significant t-values on both independent variables, and meets all the specification assumptions for ordinary least squares regression. The adjusted R^2 value = 0.766 is higher than the 10-35 simple linear regression models R^2 values.

There is some correlation between the two independent variables, but multicollinearity does not appear to be a problem here. The significance of both independent variables (despite some correlation between them) suggests that each variable is a driver of overhead cost. Of course, as the chapter describes, even if the independent variables exhibited multicollinearity, Hanks should still prefer to use the multiple regression model over the simple regression models of Problem 10-35. Omitting any one of the variables will cause the estimated coefficient of the independent variable included in the model to be biased away from its true value.

3. The Durbin-Watson statistic = 1.91, so serial correlation in the residuals is not apparent. Caution: The sample size of 12 is small. Possible uses for the multiple regression results include:

    a. *Planning and budgeting at Eastern University.* The regression analysis indicates the variables (number of academic programs and number of enrolled students) that help predict changes in overhead costs.

    b. *Cost control and performance evaluation.* Hanks could compare actual performance with budgeted or expected numbers and seek ways to improve the efficiency of the university operations, and evaluate the performance of managers responsible for controlling overhead costs.

    c. *Cost management.* If cost pressures increase, the University could save costs by closing down academic programs that have few students enrolled.

SOLUTION EXHIBIT 10-36A

Evaluation of Cost Function for Overhead Costs Estimated with Multiple Regression for Eastern University

Criterion	Number of Academic Programs and Number of Enrolled Students as Independent Variables
1. Economic Plausibility	A positive relationship between overhead costs and number of academic programs and number of enrolled students is economically plausible at Eastern University.
2. Goodness of Fit	$r^2 = 0.81$, Adjusted $R^2 = 0.766$ Excellent goodness of fit
3. Significance of Independent Variable(s)	t-values of 3.46 on number of academic programs and 2.02 on number of enrolled students are both significant, at 99% and 90% C.L.s respectively. MLR d.f. = $n - k = 12 - 2 = 10$ degrees of freedom At 95% C.L. t-critical = 2.23 Therefore t-stat of 2.02 for # of students enrolled is only statistically significant at 90% C.L. t-critical re 90% C.L. = 1.81 with 10 d.f.
4. Specification Analysis of Estimation Assumptions	The assumptions of linearity, constant variance, and normality of residuals hold, but inferences drawn from only 12 observations are not reliable; the Durbin-Watson statistic = 1.91 indicates that independence of residuals holds.

Q 10 - 36 MLR

Regression Statistics	
Multiple R	0.899067723
R Square	0.80832277
Adjusted R Square	**0.76572783**
Standard Error	3964.95982
Observations	12

ANOVA

	df	SS	MS	F	Significance F	
Regression	2	596670242.7	298335121	18.97697	0.000590973	0.999409
Residual	9	141488157.3	15720906.4			
Total	11	738158400				0.992849
						0.926431

	Coefficients	Standard Error	t Stat	P-value	Lower 95%	Upper 95%
Intercept	3335.542702	4344.058977	0.76784011	0.462251	-6491.401409	13162.4868
#of programs X1	214.0410628	61.84644956	3.46084641	**0.007151**	74.13467419	353.947451
# of students X2	2.244306026	1.10849703	2.02463874	**0.073569**	-0.263288465	4.75190052

costs = 3335.54 + 214.04*X1 + 2.24*X2
Durbin Watson = 1.91

RESIDUAL OUTPUT

						academic	
Observation	Predicted #of costs	Residuals	year	#of costs	#of programs		# of students
1	17173.37401	-973.3740111	1	16200	29		3400
2	22262.55109	777.4489075	2	23040	36		5000
3	19658.75045	501.2495546	3	20160	49		2600
4	25227.95735	-1107.957352	4	24120	53		4700
5	23646.55359	-246.5535934	5	23400	54		3900
6	26747.02387	972.9761293	6	27720	58		4900
7	34963.70057	-6523.700575	7	28440	88		5700
8	27499.29272	-3379.292723	8	24120	72		3900
9	28956.022	-1596.022003	9	27360	83		3500
10	27264.47258	8375.527419	10	35640	73		3700
11	37521.80379	-81.80378793	11	37440	101		5600
12	42438.49797	3281.502034	12	45720	103		7600
			sums	333360			

Q 10 - 36

The adjusted R squared value = 0.766, meaning that 76% of the variation in the costs, Y is explained by variation in the X1 and X2 variables.

The model fit or Significance F is excellent at 99.9% C.L.

The Durbin Watson statistic = 1.91 indicating no 1st order serial correlation in the residuals. However due to small sample size (n = 12, d.f = 10) caution is warranted.

A check on correlation between the independent variables = 0.597, which is < 0.70 therefore correlation should not be a problem.

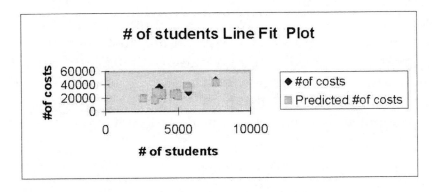

10-38 (30-40 min.) **Appendix: Purchasing department cost drivers, multiple regression analysis (continuation of 10-37).**

The problem reports the exact t-values from the computer runs of the data. Because the coefficients and standard errors given in the problem are rounded to three decimal places, dividing the coefficient by the standard error may yield slightly different t-values.

1. Regression 4 is a well-specified regression model:

    Economic plausibility: Both independent variables are plausible and are supported by the findings of the Couture Fabrics study.

    Goodness of fit: The r^2 of 0.63 indicates an excellent goodness of fit. The adjusted R^2 = 0.529.

    Significance of independent variables: The t-value on # of POs is 2.14, while the t-value on # of Ss is 2.00. These t-values are not significant at a 95% C.L. with only 8 degrees of freedom. To be statistically significant the t-stats must be ≥ 2.30. They are both statistically significant at 90% C.L., here t-critical = 1.86.

    Specification analysis: Results are available to examine the independence of residuals assumption. The Durbin-Watson statistic of 2.098 indicates that the assumption of independence is not rejected.

    Regression 4 is consistent with the findings in Problem 10-37 that both the number of purchase orders and the number of suppliers are drivers of purchasing department costs. Regressions 2, 3, and 4 all satisfy the four criteria outlined in the text. regression 4 has the best goodness of fit (0.63 for regression 4 compared with 0.42 and 0.39 for regressions 2 and 3, respectively). Most importantly, it is economically plausible that both the number of purchase orders and the number of suppliers drive purchasing department costs. We would recommend that Lee use regression 4 over regressions 2 and 3.

2. Regression 5 adds an additional independent variable (MP$) to the two independent variables in regression 4. This additional variable (MP$) has a t-value of -0.07, implying that its slope coefficient is insignificantly different from zero. The r^2 in regression 5 (0.63) is the same as that in regression 4 (0.63), implying that the addition of this third independent variable adds close to zero explanatory power. However, the adjusted R^2 value of 0.45 for regression 5 is less than the adjusted R^2 value of 0.529 for regression 4. The adjusted R^2 values are adjusted for degrees of freedom. Regression 5 = 7 d.f. Regression 4 = 8 d.f. Therefore, regression 4 is statistically superior to #5. In summary, regression 5 adds nothing to regression 4. We would highly recommend that Lee use regression 4 over regression 5.

3. Budgeted purchasing department costs for the Saskatoon store next year are:

    $$\$582,460 + (\$147.86 \times 3,900) + (\$3,542.80 \times 110) = \$1,548,822$$

4. Multicollinearity is a frequently encountered problem in cost accounting; it does not arise in simple regression because there is only one independent variable in a simple regression. One consequence of multicollinearity is an increase in the standard errors of the coefficients of the individual variables. This frequently shows up in reduced t-values in the multiple regression relative to the t-values in the simple regression:

Variables	t-value in Multiple Regression	t-value from Simple Regressions in Problem 10-37
Regression 4:		
# of POs	2.14	2.43
# of Ss	2.00	2.28
Regression 5:		
# of POs	1.95	2.43
# of Ss	1.80	2.28
MP$	–0.07	0.84

The declines in the t-values in the multiple regressions are consistent with some (but not very high) collinearity among the independent variables. Pairwise correlations between the independent variables are

	Correlation
# of POs / # of Ss	0.29
# of POs/MP $	0.27
# of Ss / MP	0.34

These correlation values are well below the threshold of 0.70 and will not cause difficulty in the model.

5. Decisions in which the regression results in Problems 10-37 and 10-38 could be used are:

    Cost management decisions: Fashion Flair could restructure relationships with the suppliers so that fewer separate purchase orders are made. Alternatively, it may aggressively reduce the number of existing suppliers.

    Purchasing policy decisions: Fashion Flair could set up an internal charge system for individual retail departments within each store. Separate charges to each department could be made for each purchase order and each new supplier added to the existing ones. These internal changes would signal to each department ways in which their own decisions affect the total costs of Fashion Flair.

<u>Accounting system design decisions:</u> Fashion Flair may want to discontinue allocating purchasing department costs on the basis of the dollar value of merchandise purchased. Allocation bases better capturing cause-and-effect relations at Fashion Flair are the number of purchase orders and the number of suppliers.

Q 10 - 38

Regression 4

Regression Statistics	
Multiple R	0.795854815
R Square	**0.633384887**
Adjusted R Square	**0.528637712**
Standard Error	410426.0399
Observations	10

This MLR model with two cost drivers as independent variables (# of purchase orders and # of supliers is the best fit. The Singificance F = 0.0298 or has a 97% C.L.
the adjusted R square value is 0.528, meaning 52.86% of the variation in costs are explained by the variation in these cost drivers or independent variables.
The Durbin Watson statistic = 2.098 ...no 1st order serial correlation in the residuals.

ANOVA

	df	SS	MS	F	Significance F
Regression	2	2.03716E+12	1.01858E+12	6.046797	**0.029835703**
Residual	7	1.17915E+12	1.6845E+11		
Total	9	3.21631E+12			

	Coefficients	Standard Error	t Stat	P-value	Lower 95%	Upper 95%
Intercept	582460.8886	308972.1637	1.885156519	0.101395	-148142.1825	1313064
# P.O.s	147.8621452	69.23105649	2.135777681	**0.07007**	-15.84328984	311.56758
# suppliers	3542.799749	1771.744279	1.999611225	**0.085668**	-646.7097399	7732.3092

Costs = 582,460.88 + 147.86*(#P.O.'s) + 3542*(# of suppliers)

RESIDUAL OUTPUT   Durbin Watson statistic = 2.098

Observation	Predicted PDC	Residuals
1	1694345.822	133254.1776
2	1746010.903	-426010.9033
3	833318.14	-176918.14
4	2134485.432	324314.5677
5	1076924.255	190275.7455
6	895586.3471	-260786.3471
7	2072594.296	-226994.2964
8	1538871.438	565928.5619
9	1571763.918	362636.0816
10	1994099.447	-485699.4474

part 3 =   1,548,831.23

Q 10 - 38
Regression 5

Regression Statistics	
Multiple R	0.796029932
R Square	**0.633663653**
Adjusted R Square	**0.45049548**
Standard Error	443142.216
Observations	10

The correlation matricies show no correlation between dependent variables (i.e. correl > 0.69)
The adjusted R squared = 0.45
The model fit = 0.091 ...good at 90% C.L.
The cost driver MP (value of purchase orders) is statistically insignificant (hugely so).
The other two independent variable (cost drivers) are statistically significant. So use the previous MLR (multiple linear regression) with 'the # of purchase orders' and "the # of suppliers" as the only two independent variable. This MLR has a better fit and higher R sq. value; as well the independent variables are statistically significant at a higher C.L.

ANOVA

	df	SS	MS	F	Significance F
Regression	3	2.03806E+12	6.794E+11	3.4594637	**0.091480637**
Residual	6	1.17825E+12	1.964E+11		
Total	9	3.21631E+12			

	Coefficients	Standard Error	t Stat	P-value	Lower 95%	Upper 95%
Intercept	593620.6314	372245.5736	1.5947017	0.1618894	-317231.4725	1504472.735
# P.O.s	148.8577446	76.1879879	-1.9538217	**0.0985355**	-37.56754558	335.2830347
# suppliers	3580.871354	1994.2252	1.7956204	**0.1226943**	-1298.821912	8460.56462
MP$	-0.000198541	0.002938285	-0.0675703	**0.9483232**	-0.007388265	0.006991183

costs = 593620 + 148.85*(#P.O.'s) + 3580.87*(#suppliers) - 0.0002* (MP$)

RESIDUAL OUTPUT

Durbin Watson statistic = 2.093

Observation	Predicted PDC	Residuals
1	1698592.872	129007.1284
2	1760190.466	-440190.4663
3	817457.1312	-161057.1312
4	2130310.158	328489.8421
5	1083757.825	183442.1753
6	902210.9313	-267410.9313
7	2070756.25	-225156.2499
8	1548948.748	555851.2523
9	1559351.116	375048.8836
10	1986424.503	-478024.503

Correlation Matrix Dependent Variables

	MP$	# P.O.s
MP$	1	
# P.O.s	0.27334398	1
# suppliers	0.339848275	0.292534941

Total Correlation Matrix: all variables

	PDC	MP$	# P.O.s
PDC	1		
MP$	0.286945209	1	
# P.O.s	0.651131304	0.27334398	1
# suppliers	0.628076701	0.339848275	0.2925349

part 3 =   1,568,043.82

10-40 (20 min.) Data analysis and ethics.

1. (a) Average annual labour costs over the last ten years $1,440,000
        Expected annual labour costs if robots introduced   660,000
        Expected annual savings $ 780,000

    (b) Average annual labour costs over the last three years $ 960,000
        Expected annual labour costs if robots introduced   660,000
        Expected annual savings $ 300,000

    Yes, it makes a difference in terms of justifying the robot investment. Using a 10-year average, the expected annual savings exceed the desired amount of $400,000 per year. Using average annual labour costs over the last three years, expected annual savings in labour costs falls short of the $480,000 target needed to justify the robot investment.

2. One explanation for average labour costs over the most recent three-year period being less than the average labour costs over the past ten years is learning curve effects. Learning-by-doing has caused workers to become more efficient. Alternatively, Comdex may have changed the VCR design to simplify manufacturing and reduce costs. Comdex may also have introduced new equipment that reduced labour costs.

3. The behaviour of both Helen Gibbs and Joan Mistry to deliberately overestimate the savings in labour costs to justify investments in robots is unethical. In assessing the situation, and considering the "Code of Professional Ethics" described in Exhibit 1-5, the issues that Joan Mistry, the management accountant, should consider are listed below.

    (a) Clear reports using relevant and reliable information should be prepared. Reports prepared on the basis of overestimating savings in direct and indirect manufacturing labour (by considering older costs that are much higher than current costs) violate the management accountant's responsibility for competence. It is unethical for Gibbs to suggest that Mistry overestimate the cost savings that were computed for the robot investment and for Hansen to change the numbers to justify the investment in robots.
    (b) Management accountants should communicate favourable as well as unfavourable information. In this regard, both Gibbs's and Mistry's behaviour of inflating manufacturing labour cost savings to justify the investment in robots could be viewed as unethical.

(c) Management accountants should communicate information fairly and objectively and all relevant information should be disclosed. From a management accountant's standpoint, overestimating manufacturing labour cost savings to justify the robot investment violates objectivity. For the various reasons cited above, we should take the position that the behaviour of Gibbs and Mistry is unethical.

4. Mistry should indicate to Gibbs that the savings in manufacturing labour costs alone are not large enough to justify the robot investment. She should also indicate to Gibbs her concern about inflating cost savings to justify the robot investment, quite independent of how important she thinks it is for the company to invest in the robots. She may wish to point out that part of the problem is the excessive focus on cost savings alone to justify the robot investment. An important benefit of the robot investment is the ability to generate higher revenues by producing superior products. If Gibbs still insists on inflating costs to justify the investment, Mistry should raise the matter with Gibbs's superior. If, after taking all these steps, there is continued pressure to overstate cost savings, Mistry should consider resigning from the company, rather than engage in unethical behaviour.

CHAPTER 11
DECISION MAKING AND RELEVANT INFORMATION

11-2 *Relevant costs* are those expected future costs that differ among alternative courses of action. Historical costs are irrelevant because they are past costs and therefore cannot differ among alternative future courses of action.

11-4 *Quantitative factors* are outcomes that are measured in numerical terms. Some quantitative factors are financial—that is, they can be easily expressed in financial terms. Direct materials is an example of a quantitative financial factor. *Qualitative factors* are factors that are not measured in numerical terms. An example is employee morale.

11-6 No. Some variable costs may not differ among the alternatives under consideration and hence will be irrelevant. Some fixed costs may differ among the alternatives and hence will be relevant.

11-8 *Opportunity cost* is the contribution to income that is forgone (rejected) by not using a limited resource in its next-best alternative use.

11-10 No. Managers should aim to get the highest contribution margin per unit of the constraining (that is, scarce, limiting, or critical) factor. The constraining factor is what restricts or limits the production or sale of a given product (for example, availability of machine-hours).

11-12 No. Cost written off as amortization is irrelevant when it pertains to a past cost. But the purchase cost of new equipment to be acquired in the future that will then be written off as amortization is often relevant.

11-14 The three steps in solving a linear programming problem are:
(a) Determine the objective.
(b) Specify the constraints.
(c) Compute the optimal solution.

11-16 (20 min.) **Disposal of assets.**

1. This is an unfortunate situation, yet the $88,000 costs are irrelevant regarding the decision to remachine or scrap. The only relevant factors are the future revenues and future costs. By ignoring the accumulated costs and deciding on the basis of expected future costs, operating income will be maximized (or losses minimized). The difference in favour of remachining is $3,300:

	(a) Remachine	**(b)** Scrap
Future revenues	$38,500	$2,200
Deduct future costs	33,000	—
Operating income	$ 5,500	$2,200

Difference in favour of remachining ⬆ $3,300 ⬆

2. This too is an unfortunate situation. But the $110,000 original cost is irrelevant to this decision. The difference in favour of rebuilding is $7,700:

	(a) Replace	**(b)** Rebuild
New truck	$112,200	—
Deduct current disposal price of existing truck	11,000	—
Rebuild existing truck	—	$93,500
	$101,200	$93,500

Difference in favour of rebuilding ⬆ $7,700 ⬆

Note here that the current disposal price of $11,000 is relevant, but the original cost (or book value, if the truck were not brand new) is irrelevant.

11-18 (15 min.) Multiple choice.

1. (b)

Special order price per unit	$6.60
Variable manufacturing costs per unit	4.95
Contribution margin per unit	$1.65

Effect on operating income = $1.65 × 20,000 units
= $33,000 increase

2. (b) Costs of purchases, 20,000 units × $66 $1,320,000

Total relevant costs of making:

Variable manufacturing costs, $70.40 – $17.60	$52.80	
Fixed costs eliminated	9.90	
Costs saved by not making	$62.70	
Multiply by 20,000 units, so total		
costs saved are $62.70 × 20,000		1,254,000

Extra costs of purchasing outside	66,000
Minimum savings necessary for Part No. 575	27,500
Necessary relevant costs that would have	
to be saved in manufacturing Part No. 575	$ 93,500

11-20 (30 min.) Make versus buy, activity-based costing.

1.   The expected manufacturing cost per unit of CMCBs in 2007 is as follows:

	Total Manufacturing Costs of CMCB (1)	Manufacturing Cost per Unit (2) = (1) ÷ 10,000
Direct materials $187 × 10,000	$1,870,000	$187.00
Direct manufacturing labour $49.50 × 10,000	495,000	49.50
Variable batch manufacturing costs $1,650 × 80	132,000	13.20
Fixed manufacturing costs		
Avoidable fixed manufacturing costs	352,000	35.20
Unavoidable fixed manufacturing costs	880,000	88.00
Total manufacturing costs	$3,729,000	$372.90

2. The following table identifies the incremental costs in 2007 if Svenson (a) made CMCBs and (b) purchased CMCBs from Minton.

Incremental Items	Total Incremental Costs Make	Total Incremental Costs Buy	Per-Unit Incremental Costs Make	Per-Unit Incremental Costs Buy
Cost of purchasing CMCBs from Minton $330 × 10,000				$330
Direct materials	$1,870,000	$3,300,000	$187.00	
Direct manufacturing labour	495,000		49.50	
Variable batch manufacturing costs	132,000		13.20	
Avoidable fixed manufacturing costs	352,000		35.20	
Total incremental costs	$2,849,000	$3,300,000	$284.90	$330
Difference in favour of making	▲ $451,000 ▲		▲ $45.10 ▲	

Note that the opportunity cost of using capacity to make CMCBs is zero since Svenson would keep this capacity idle if it purchases CMCBs from Minton.

Svenson should continue to manufacture the CMCBs internally, since the incremental costs to manufacture are $284.90 per unit compared with the $330 per unit that Minton has quoted. Note that the unavoidable fixed manufacturing costs of $880,000 ($88 per unit) will continue to be incurred whether Svenson makes or buys CMCBs. These are not incremental costs under either the make or the buy alternative and are hence irrelevant.

3. Svenson should continue to make CMCBs. The simplest way to solve this problem is to recognize that Svenson would prefer to keep any excess capacity idle rather than use it to make CB3s. Why? Because expected incremental future revenues from CB3s ($2,200,000) are <u>less</u> than expected incremental future costs ($2,365,000). If Svenson keeps its capacity idle, we know from requirement 2 that it should make CMCBs rather than buy them.

An important point to note is that, because Svenson forgoes no contribution by not being able to make and sell CB3s, the opportunity cost of using its facilities to make CMCBs is zero. It is therefore not forgoing any profits by using the capacity to manufacture CMCBs. If it does not manufacture CMCBs, rather than lose money on CB3s, Svenson will keep the capacity idle.

A longer and more detailed approach is to use the total alternatives or opportunity cost analyses shown in the chapter.

TOTAL-ALTERNATIVES APPROACH TO MAKE-OR-BUY DECISIONS

	Choices for Svenson		
Relevant Items	Make CMCBs and Do Not Make CB3s	Buy CMCBs and Do Not Make CB3s	Buy CMCBs and Make CB3s
Total incremental costs of making/buying CMCBs (from requirement 2)	$2,849,000	$3,300,000	$3,300,000
Excess of future costs over future revenues from CB3s	0	0	165,000
Total relevant costs	$2,849,000	$3,300,000	$3,465,000

Svenson will minimize manufacturing costs by making CMCBs.

OPPORTUNITY COST APPROACH TO MAKE-OR-BUY DECISIONS

	Choices for Svenson	
Incremental Items	Make CMCB	Buy CMCB
Total incremental costs of making/buying CMCBs (from requirement 2)	$2,849,000	$3,300,000
Opportunity cost: profit contribution forgone because capacity cannot be used to make CB3s	0*	0
Total relevant costs	$2,849,000	$3,300,000
Difference in favour of making CMCBs	▲ $451,000 ▲	

*Opportunity cost is 0 because Svenson does not give up anything by manufacturing CMCBs. Had it not manufactured CMCBs, it would be best off leaving the capacity idle (rather than manufacturing and selling CB3s).

11-22 (10 min.) Inventory decision, opportunity cost.

1. Unit cost, orders of 20,000 $8.80
   Unit cost, order of 240,000 (0.95 × $8.80) $8.36

   Alternatives under consideration:
   (a) Buy 240,000 units at start of year.
   (b) Buy 20,000 units at start of each month.

   Average investment in inventory:
   (a) (240,000 × $8.36) ÷ 2 $1,003,200
   (b) (20,000 × $8.80) ÷ 2   88,000
   Difference in average investment $915,200

   Opportunity cost of interest forgone from 240,000-unit purchase at start of year
   = $915,200 × 0.08 = $73,216

2. No. The $73,216 is an opportunity cost rather than an incremental or outlay cost. No actual transaction records the $73,216 as an entry in the accounting system.

3. The following table presents the two alternatives:

	Alternative A: Purchase 240,000 Spark Plugs at Beginning of Year (1)	Alternative B: Purchase 20,000 Spark Plugs at Beginning of Each Month (2)	Difference (3)=(1)−(2)
Annual purchase (incremental) costs (240,000 × $8.36; 240,000 × $8.80)	$2,006,400	$2,112,000	$(105,600)
Ordering cost	220	2,640	$ (2,420)
Annual interest income that could be earned if investment in inventory were invested (opportunity cost) (8% × $1,003,200; 8% × $88,000)	80,256	7,040	73,216
Relevant costs	$2,086,876	$2,121,680	$ (34,804)

Column (3) indicates that purchasing 240,000 spark plugs at the beginning of the year is preferred relative to purchasing 20,000 spark plugs at the beginning of each month because the lower purchase cost exceeds the opportunity cost of holding larger inventory. If other incremental benefits of holding lower inventory such as lower insurance, materials handling, storage, obsolescence, and breakage costs had been considered, the costs under Alternative A would have been higher, and Alternative B might have been preferred.

11-24   (10 min.)   Selection of most profitable product.

Only Model 14 should be produced. The key to this problem is the relationship of manufacturing overhead to product. Note that it takes twice as long to produce Model 9; machine-hours for Model 9 are twice that for Model 14. Management should choose the product mix that maximizes operating income for a given production capacity (the scarce resource in this situation). In this case, Model 14 will yield a $20.90 contribution to fixed costs per unit of machine time, and Model 9 will yield $19.80:

	Model 9	Model 14
Selling price per unit	$110.00	$77.00
Variable costs per unit	90.20	66.55
Contribution margin per unit	$ 19.80	$ 10.45
Relative output (units of product) per machine-hour	× 1	× 2
Contribution margin per unit of machine time	$ 19.80	$20.90

11-26   (20-25 min.)   Customer profitability, choosing customers.

1. Broadway should not drop the Kelly Corporation business as the following analysis shows.

Loss in revenues from dropping Kelly	$(88,000)
Savings in costs:	
Variable costs	52,800
Fixed costs 20% × $110,000	22,000
Total savings in costs	74,800
Effect on operating income	$(13,200)

Broadway Printers would be worse off by $13,200 if it drops the Kelly Corporation business.

2. If Broadway accepts the additional business from Kelly, it would take an additional 500 hours of machine time. If Broadway accepts all of Kelly's and Taylor's business for February, it would require 2,500 hours of machine time (1,500 hours for Taylor and 1,000 hours for Kelly). Broadway only has 2,000 hours of machine capacity. It must therefore choose how much of the Taylor and Kelly business to accept. If Broadway accepts any additional business from Kelly, it must forgo some of Taylor's business.

To maximize operating income, Broadway should maximize contribution margin per unit of the constrained resource. (Fixed costs will remain unchanged at $110,000, whatever business Broadway chooses to accept in February, and is therefore irrelevant.) The contribution margin per unit of the constrained resource for each customer in January is:

	Taylor Corporation	Kelly Corporation
Revenues	$132,000	$88,000
Variable costs	46,200	52,800
Contribution margin	$ 85,800	$35,200
Contribution margin per machine-hour	$\frac{\$85,800}{1,500}=\$57.20$	$\frac{\$35,200}{500}=\$70.40$

Since the $88,000 of additional Kelly business in February is identical to jobs done in January, it will also have a contribution margin of $70.40 per machine-hour, which is greater than the contribution margin of $57.20 per machine-hour from Taylor. To maximize operating income, Broadway should first allocate all the capacity needed to take the Kelly Corporation business (1,000 machine-hours) and then allocate the remaining 1,000 (2,000 − 1,000) machine-hours to Taylor. Broadway's operating income in February would then be $17,600 as shown below, greater than the $11,000 operating income in January.

	Taylor Corporation	Kelly Corporation	Total
Contribution margin per machine-hour	$ 57.20	$ 70.40	
Machine hours to be worked	1,000	1,000	
Contribution margin	$57,200	$70,400	$127,600
Fixed costs			110,000
Operating income			$ 17,600

Alternatively, we could present Broadway's operating income by taking 2/3 (1,000 ÷ 1,500 machine-hours) of Taylor's January revenues and variable costs, and doubling (1,000 ÷ 500 machine-hours) Kelly's January revenues and variable costs.

	Taylor Corporation	Kelly Corporation	Total
Revenues	$88,000	$176,000	$264,000
Variable costs	30,800	105,600	136,400
Contribution margin	$57,200	$ 70,400	127,600
Fixed costs			110,000
Operating income			$ 17,600

The problem indicated that Broadway could choose to accept as much of the Taylor and Kelly business for February as it wants. However, some students may raise the question that Broadway should think more strategically before deciding what to do. For example, how would Taylor react to Broadway's inability to satisfy its needs? Will Kelly continue to give Broadway $176,000 of business each month or is the additional $88,000 of business in February a special order? For example, if Kelly's additional work in February is only a special order and Broadway wants to maintain a long-term relationship with Taylor, it may in fact prefer to turn down the additional Kelly business. It may feel that the additional $6,600 in operating income in February is not worth jeopardizing Taylor's long-term relationship. Other students may raise the possibility of Broadway accepting all the Taylor and Kelly business for February if it can subcontract some of it to another reliable, high-quality printer.

11-28 (30 min.) Equipment upgrade versus replacement.

1. Solution Exhibit 11-28 presents a cost comparison of the upgrade and replacement alternatives for the three years taken together. It indicates that Pacifica Corporation should replace the production line because it is better off by $198,000 by replacing rather than upgrading.

2. (a) Suppose the capital expenditure to replace the production line is $X. Using data from Solution Exhibit 11-28, the cost of replacing the production line is equal to $1,782,000 – $99,000 + $X. Using data from Solution Exhibit 11-28, the cost of upgrading the production line is equal to $2,376,000 + $330,000 = $2,706,000. We want to find $X such that

$$\$1,782,000 - \$99,000 + \$X = \$2,706,000$$
that is, $\$1,683,000 + \$X = \$2,706,000$
that is, $\$X = \$2,706,000 - \$1,683,000$
or $\$X = \$1,023,000$

Pacifica would prefer replacing rather than upgrading the existing line if the replacement cost of the new line does not exceed $1,023,000.

(b) Suppose the units produced and sold each year equals y. Using data from Solution Exhibit 11-28, the cost of replacing the production line is $9.90y - \$99,000 + \$825,000$, while the cost of upgrading is $13.20y + \$330,000$. We solve for the y at which the two costs are the same:

$$
\begin{aligned}
\$9.90y - \$99,000 + \$825,000 &= \$13.20y + \$330,000 \\
\$9.90y + \$726,000 &= \$13.20y + \$330,000 \\
\$3.30y &= \$396,000 \\
y &= 120,000 \text{ units}
\end{aligned}
$$

For expected production and sales of less than 120,000 units over 3 years (40,000 units per year), the upgrade alternative is cheaper. When production and sales are low the higher operating costs of upgrading are more than offset by the significant savings in capital costs when upgrading relative to replacing. For expected production and sales exceeding 120,000 units over 3 years, the replace alternative is cheaper. For high output the benefits of the lower operating costs of replacing relative to upgrading exceed the higher capital costs.

SOLUTION EXHIBIT 11-28
Comparing Upgrade and Replace Alternatives

	Three Years Together		
	Upgrade (1)	Replace (2)	Difference (3)=(1)–(2)
Cash-operating costs $13.20; $9.90 × 180,000	$2,376,000	$1,782,000	$594,000
Current disposal price		(99,000)	99,000
One-time capital costs, written off periodically as amortization	330,000	825,000	(495,000)
Total relevant costs	$2,706,000	$2,508,000	$198,000

Note that sales and book value of the existing machine are the same under both alternatives and hence irrelevant.

3. Operating income for the first year under the upgrade and replace alternatives are as follows:

	Upgrade	Replace
Sales $27.5 × 60,000	$1,650,000	$1,650,000
Cash-operating costs $13.20; $9.90 × 60,000	792,000	594,000
Amortization	242,000[a]	275,000[b]
Loss on disposal of old production line	—	297,000[c]
Total costs	1,034,000	1,166,000
Operating income	$ 616,000	$ 484,000

[a]($396,000 + $330,000) ÷ 3 = $242,000
[b]$825,000 ÷ 3 = $275,000
[c]Book value – current disposal price = $396,000 – $99,000 = $297,000

First-year operating income is higher by $132,000 under the upgrade alternative. If first year's operating income is an important component of Azinger's bonus, he would prefer the upgrade over the replace alternative even though the decision model in requirement 1 prefers the replace to the upgrade alternative. This exercise illustrates the conflict between the decision model and the performance-evaluation model (requirement 3).

11-30 (15 min.) Make or buy (continuation of 11-29).

The maximum price Class Company should be willing to pay is $4.33583 per unit.

Expected unit production and sales of the new product must be half of the old product (1/2 × 240,000 = 120,000) because the fixed manufacturing overhead rate for the new product is twice that of the fixed manufacturing overhead rate for the old product.

	Present	Proposed Make New Product	Proposed Old Product	Total
Sales	$1,584,000	$1,188,000	$1,584,000	$2,772,000
Variable (or purchase) costs:				
Manufacturing	792,000	660,000	1,040,600*	1,700,600
Marketing and other	396,000	264,000	316,800	580,800
Total variable costs	1,188,000	924,000	1,357,400	2,281,400
Contribution margin	396,000	264,000	226,600	490,600
Fixed costs:				
Manufacturing	132,000	132,000	—	132,000
Marketing and other	237,600	66,000	237,600	303,600
Total fixed costs	369,600	198,000	237,600	435,600
Operating Income	$ 26,400	$ 66,000	$ –11,000	$ 55,000

*This is an example of opportunity costs, whereby subcontracting at a price well above the $3.85 current manufacturing (absorption) cost is still desirable because the old product will be displaced in manufacturing by a new product that is more profitable.

Because the new product promises an operating income of $66,000 (ignoring the irrelevant problems of how fixed marketing costs may be newly reallocated between products), the old product can sustain up to a $11,000 loss and still help accomplish management's overall objectives. Maximum costs that can be incurred on the old product are $1,584,000 plus the $11,000 loss, or $1,595,000. Maximum purchase cost: $1,595,000 – ($316,800 + $237,600) = $1,040,600. Maximum purchase cost per unit: $1,040,600 ÷ 240,000 units = $4.33583 per unit.

Alternative Computation

Operating income is $9.90 – $9.35 = $0.55 per unit		
for 120,000 new units	$66,000	
Target operating income	55,000	
Maximum loss allowed on old product	$11,000	
Maximum loss per unit allowed on old product,		
$11,000 ÷ 240,000 =		$0.04583
Sales price of old product		$6.60000
Allowance for loss		0.04583
Total costs allowed per unit		6.64583
Continuing costs for old product other than purchase cost:		
Fixed manufacturing costs—all transferred to		
new product	$ —	
Variable marketing costs ($1.65 × 80%)	1.32	
Fixed marketing costs	0.99	2.31000
Maximum purchase cost per unit		$4.33583

11-32 (30-40 min.) Product mix, relevant costs.

	R3	HP6
Selling price	$120	$180
Variable manufacturing costs per unit	72	120
Variable marketing costs per unit	18	42
Total variable costs per unit	90	162
Contribution margin per unit	$ 30	$ 18
Contribution margin per hour of the constrained resource (the regular machine)	$\frac{\$30}{1} = \$30$	$\frac{\$18}{0.5} = \$36$
Total contribution margin from selling Only R3 or only HP6 R3: $30 × 50,000; HP6: $36 × 50,000	$1,500,000	$1,800,000
Less: Lease costs of high-precision machine to produce HP6	—	360,000
Net relevant benefit	$1,500,000	$1,440,000

Even though HP6 has the higher contribution margin per unit of the constrained resource, the fact that Pendleton must incur additional costs of $360,000 to achieve this higher contribution margin means that Pendleton is better off using its entire 50,000-hour capacity on the regular machine to produce and sell 50,000 units (50,000 hours ÷ 1 hour per unit) of R3. The additional contribution from selling HP6 rather than R3 is $300,000 ($1,800,000 – $1,500,000), which is not enough to cover the additional costs of leasing the high-precision machine. Note that, because all other overhead costs are fixed and cannot be changed, they are irrelevant for the decision.

2. If capacity of the regular machine is increased by 15,000 machine-hours to 65,000 machine-hours (50,000 originally + 15,000 new), the net relevant benefit from producing R3 and HP6 is as follows:

	R3	HP6
Total contribution margin from selling only R3 or only HP6 R3: $30 × 65,000; HP6: $36 × 65,000	$1,950,000	$2,340,000
Less: Lease costs of high-precision machine that would be incurred if HP6 is produced	—	360,000
Less: Cost of increasing capacity by 15,000 hours on regular machine	180,000	180,000
Net relevant benefit	$1,770,000	$1,800,000

Investing in the additional capacity increases Pendleton's operating income by $300,000 ($1,800,000 calculated in requirement 2 *minus* $1,500,000 calculated in requirement 1), so Pendleton should add 15,000 hours to the regular machine. With the extra capacity available to it, Pendleton should use its entire capacity to produce HP6. Using all 65,000 hours of capacity to produce HP6 rather than to produce R3 generates additional contribution margin of $390,000 ($2,340,000 – $1,950,000) which is more than the additional cost of $360,000 to lease the high-precision machine. Pendleton should therefore produce and sell 130,000 units of HP6 (65,000 hours ÷ 0.5 hours per unit of HP6) and zero units of R3.

3.

	R3	HP6	S3
Selling price per unit	$120	$180	$144
Variable manufacturing costs per unit	72	120	84
Variable marketing costs per unit	18	42	18
Total variable costs per unit	90	162	102
Contribution margin per unit	$ 30	$ 18	$ 42
Contribution margin per hour of the constrained resource (the regular machine)	$\frac{$30}{1} = 30	$\frac{$18}{0.5} = 36	$\frac{$42}{1} = 42

The first step is to compare the operating profits that Pendleton could earn if it accepted the Carter Corporation offer for 20,000 units with the operating profits Pendleton is currently earning. S3 has the highest contribution margin per hour on the regular machine and requires no additional investment such as leasing a high-precision machine. To produce the 20,000 units of S3 requested

by Carter Corporation, Pendleton would require 20,000 hours on the regular machine, resulting in a contribution margin of $42 × 20,000 = $840,000.
Pendleton now has 45,000 hours available on the regular machine to produce R3 or HP6.

	R3	HP6
Total contribution margin from selling only R3 or only HP6		
R3: $30 × 45,000; HP6: $36 × 45,000	$1,350,000	$1,620,000
Less: Lease costs of high-precision machine to produce and sell HP6	—	360,000
Net relevant benefit	$1,350,000	$1,260,000

Pendleton should use all the 45,000 hours of available capacity to produce 45,000 units of R3. Thus, the product mix that maximizes operating income is 20,000 units of S3, 45,000 units of R3, and zero units of HP6. This optimal mix results in a contribution margin of $2,190,000 ($840,000 from S3 and $1,350,000 from R3). Relative to requirement 2, operating income increases by $390,000 ($2,190,000 minus $1,800,000 calculated in requirement 2). Hence, Pendleton should accept the Carter Corporation business and supply 20,000 units of S3.

11-34 (20 min.) Opportunity cost.

1. The opportunity cost to Wolverine of producing the 2,000 units of Orangebo is the contribution margin lost on the 2,000 units of Rosebo that would have to be forgone, as computed below:

Revenue per unit		$22.00
Variable costs per unit:		
Direct materials	$2.20	
Direct manufacturing labour	3.30	
Variable manufacturing overhead	2.20	
Variable nonmanufacturing costs	4.40	12.10
Contribution margin per unit		$ 9.90
Contribution margin for 2,000 units @ $9.90		$19,800

The opportunity cost is $19,800. Opportunity cost is the maximum contribution to operating income that is forgone (rejected) by not using a limited resource in its next-best alternative use.

2. Contribution margin from manufacturing 2,000 units of Orangebo and purchasing 2,000 units of Rosebo from Buckeye is $17,600 as follows:

	Manufacture Orangebo	Purchase Rosebo	Total
Revenue per unit	$16.50	$22.00	
Variable costs per unit:			
Purchase costs	—	15.40	
Direct materials	2.20	—	
Direct manufacturing labour	3.30	—	
Variable manufacturing overhead	2.20	—	
Variable nonmanufacturing overhead	2.20	4.40	
Variable costs per unit	9.90	19.80	
Contribution margin per unit	$ 6.60	$ 2.20	
Contribution margin from selling 2,000 units of Orangebo and 2,000 units of Rosebo	$13,200	$4,400	$17,600

As calculated in requirement 1, Wolverine's contribution margin from continuing to manufacture 2,000 units of Rosebo is $19,800. Accepting the Windsor Company order and the Buckeye offer will cost Wolverine $2,200 ($17,600 – $19,800). Hence Wolverine should refuse the Windsor Company order and Buckeye Corporation's offer.

3. The minimum price would be $9.90, the sum of the incremental costs as computed in requirement 2. This follows because if Wolverine has surplus capacity, the opportunity cost = $0. For the short-run decision of whether to accept Orangebo's offer, fixed costs of Wolverine are irrelevant. Only the incremental costs need to be covered for it to be worthwhile for Wolverine to accept the Orangebo offer.

11-36 (30-40 min.) **Considering three alternatives.**

1. The 5% surcharge is irrelevant.

	Sell to Kaytell as Special Order	Convert to Standard Model	Sell as Special Order As Is
Selling price	$75,240.00	$68,750.00	$57,200
Deduct cash discount	—	1,375.00	—
Net selling price	75,240.00	67,375.00	57,200
Additional manufacturing costs:			
Direct materials	6,820.00	3,135.00	—
Direct manufacturing labour	4,620.00	3,630.00	—
Variable manufacturing overhead	2,310.00	1,815.00	—
Total additional manufacturing costs	13,750.00	8,580.00	—
Commissions	2,257.20	1,347.50	1,716
Total costs	16,007.20	9,927.50	1,716
Contribution to operating income	$59,232.80	$57,447.50	$55,484

2.

Kaytell contribution	$59,232.80
Next-best alternative:	
Standard model contribution	57,447.50
Change in contribution to operating income	$ 1,785.30

$$\text{Change in net sales price} = \frac{\text{Change in contribution}}{1 - \text{Commission \%}}$$

$$= \frac{\$1,785.30}{1-0.03} = \frac{\$1,785.30}{0.97}$$

$$= \$1,841 \text{ (rounded)}$$

Original Kaytell price	$75,240
Reduction in contribution permissible before Auer switches to the next-best alternative	1,841
Minimum price Auer should accept from Kaytell and be indifferent between standard model and Kaytell offer	$73,399

3. Fixed manufacturing overhead should have no influence on the selling price quoted by Auer Company for (one-time-only) special orders:

(a) Auer Company should accept special orders whenever the company is operating substantially below capacity, including below the breakeven point, if incremental revenue from an order exceeds incremental cost. Normally, this approach would mean that the order should be accepted as long as the selling price of the order exceeds the variable manufacturing costs. The special order will result in a positive contribution toward fixed costs. The fixed manufacturing overhead is not considered in the pricing because it will be incurred whether the order is accepted or not.

(b) If Auer Company is operating above its breakeven point and if a special order will allow the company to utilize unused capacity efficiently, the special order should be accepted as long as incremental revenue exceeds incremental cost, or, in most cases, the selling price exceeds the variable manufacturing costs. If the selling price exceeds the variable manufacturing costs, the order will yield a positive contribution toward the company's fixed costs. Fixed manufacturing overhead is not considered because it will be incurred whether the order is accepted or not. The only time the fixed manufacturing overhead would be relevant would be if Auer were near capacity and additional fixed costs would have to be incurred to complete the order. If this situation occurred, Auer's incremental costs would be higher, and they would have to be covered by the selling price.

11-38 (30-40 min.) Make or buy, unknown level of volume.

1. Let $X = 1$ starter assembly. The variable costs required to manufacture $165,000X$ are:

Direct materials	$220,000
Direct manufacturing labour	165,000
Variable manufacturing overhead (25% of O/H)	110,000
Total variable costs	$495,000

The total variable costs per unit is $495,000 ÷ 165,000 = $3.00 per unit.

The data can be presented in both "all data" and "relevant data" formats:

	All Data		Relevant Data	
	Alternative 1: Make	Alternative 2: Buy	Alternative 1: Make	Alternative 2: Buy
Variable manufacturing costs	$ 3X	—	$ 3X	—
Fixed general manufacturing overhead	165,000	$165,000	—	—
Fixed overhead—avoidable	110,000	—	110,000	—
Division 2 manager's salary	44,000	55,000	44,000	$55,000
Division 3 manager's salary	55,000	—	55,000	—
Purchase cost—if bought from Tidnish Electronics	—	4X	—	4X
Total	$374,000 + $3X	$220,000 +$4X	$209,000 +$3X	$55,000 +$4X

The number of units at which the costs of make and buy are equivalent is:

All data analysis:

$$\$374{,}000 + \$3X = \$220{,}000 + \$4X$$
$$X = 154{,}000$$

or

Relevant data analysis:

$$\$209{,}000 + \$3X = \$55{,}000 + \$4X$$
$$X = 154{,}000$$

Assuming cost minimization is the objective, then:
- If production is expected to be less than 154,000 units, it is preferable to buy units from Tidnish.
- If production is expected to exceed 154,000 units, it is preferable to manufacture internally (make) the units.
- If production is expected to be 154,000 units, this is the indifference point between buying units from Tidnish and internally manufacturing (making) the units.

2. The information on the storage cost, which is avoidable if self-manufacture is discontinued, is relevant; these storage charges represent current outlays that are avoidable if self-manufacture is discontinued. Assume these $55,000 charges are represented as an opportunity cost of the make alternative. The costs of internal manufacture that incorporate this $55,000 opportunity cost become:

All data analysis:	$429,000 + $3X
Relevant data analysis:	$264,000 + $3X

The number of units at which the costs of make and buy are equivalent are:

All data analysis:

$$\$429{,}000 + \$3X = \$220{,}000 + \$4X$$
$$X = 209{,}000$$

Relevant data analysis:

$$\$264{,}000 + \$3X = \$55{,}000 + \$4X$$
$$X = 209{,}000$$

If production is expected to be less than 209,000, it is preferable to buy units from Tidnish. If production is expected to exceed 209,000, it is preferable to manufacture the units internally.

11-40 (30-40 min.) **Relevant cost of materials.**

1. Hernandez Corporation has already purchased the 10,000 kilograms of the special cement that it needs, so it will incur no incremental costs. Alternatively stated, the costs of materials are past (sunk) costs.

    If Hernandez obtained Contract No. 2 a month from now, it would cost $25,000 in substitute material (10,000 kilograms × $2.50 per kilogram). There is, therefore, a cost (lost benefit) of $25,000 by using the special cement on Contract No. 1 now. Alternatively, Hernandez could sell the special cement immediately for $16,000. The opportunity cost that Hernandez should use is the benefit it would get in the next-best alternative should it not use the cement in Contract No. 1. The greater of these two benefits is using the cement in Contract No. 2. The opportunity cost is $25,000. The relevant cost that Gomez should use when bidding on Contract No. 1 is:

Incremental cost	$ 0
Plus opportunity cost	25,000
Relevant cost	$25,000

2. As in Question 1, the incremental costs of acquiring the special cement for use on Contract No. 1 are zero because Hernandez has already purchased the material. If Hernandez does not land Contract No. 2, the opportunity cost of using the special cement for Contract No. 1 is $15,000 (10,000 kilograms × $1.50 per kilogram), the amount Hernandez would get if it sold the special cement one month from now.

    Gomez assesses a probability of 0.7 that the special cement will be used on Contract No. 2 and a probability of 0.3 that the special cement will be sold.

The expected benefit of holding the special cement and not using it on Contract No. 1 is:

$$= \quad (0.7 \times \$25{,}000^*) + (0.3 \times \$15{,}000^{**})$$
$$= \quad \$17{,}500 + \$4{,}500$$
$$= \quad \$22{,}000$$

* relevant cost if special cement is used in Contract No. 2 (see requirement 1)
** relevant cost if special cement is sold one month from now

Alternatively, the special cement can be sold right away and fetch $16,000. The opportunity cost is the greater of these two benefits and hence equals $22,000. When bidding on the Contract, Gomez should use:

Incremental cost	$ 0
Plus opportunity cost	22,000
Relevant cost	$22,000

3.   In this case, the benefit of selling the cement now is $23,000, while the benefit of using the cement in Contract No. 2 is $25,000. The opportunity cost of using the cement in Contract No. 1 is the lesser of these two numbers, $23,000.

Incremental cost	$ 0
Plus opportunity cost	23,000
Relevant cost	$23,000

11-42   (30 min.)   Appendix: Optimal production plan, computer manufacturer.

1.   Let X = Units of printers
and Y = Units of desktop computers

Objective: Maximize total contribution margin of $240X + $120Y
Constraints:

For production line 1:	$7.2X + 4.8Y \leq 28.8$	equation 1)
For production line 2:	$12X \leq 24$	equation 2)
Sales of X and Y:	$X - Y \leq 0$	equation 3)
Negative production impossible:	$X \geq 0$	equation 4)
	$Y \geq 0$	equation 5)

2. Solution Exhibit 11-42 presents a graphical summary of the relationships. The sales-mix constraint here is somewhat unusual. The X − Y = 0 line is the one going upward at a 45' angle from the origin. Using the trial-and-error method:

Using equations 1) and 2):
$$7.2X + 4.8Y = 28.8$$
$$12X = 24$$
$$X = 2$$

$$(7.2 \times 2) + 4.8Y = 28.8$$
$$4.8Y = 14.4$$
$$Y = 3$$

Using equations 3) and 2):
$$X - Y = 0$$
$$12X = 24$$
$$X = 2$$
$$2 - Y = 0$$
$$Y = 2$$

Using equations 1) and 4):
$$7.2X + 4.8Y = 28.8$$
$$X = 0$$
$$0 + 4.8Y = 28.8$$
$$Y = 6$$

Using equations 1) and 5):
$$7.2X + 4.8Y = 28.8$$
$$Y = 0$$
$$7.2X + 0 = 28.8$$
$$X = 4$$

Using equations 4) and 5):
$$X = 0$$
$$Y = 0$$

The 4 corners of the area of feasible solutions are:
(0,0), (2,2), (2,3), and (0,6)

Trial	Corner (X,Y)	Total Contribution Margin
1	(0; 0)	$240(0) + $120(0) = $ 0
2	(2; 2)	240(2) + 120(2) = 720
3	(2; 3)*	240(2) + 120(3) = 840
4	(0; 6)	240(0) + 120(6) = 720

*The optimal solution that maximizes operating income is 2 printers and 3 computers.

SOLUTION EXHIBIT 11-42
Graphic Solution to Find Optimal Mix, Information Technology, Inc.

11-44 (30 min.) **Make versus buy, ethics.**

1. An analysis of relevant costs that shows whether or not Paibec Corporation should make MTR-85 or purchase it from Marley Company for 2008 follows:

	Total Costs for 32,000 Units
Cost to purchase MTR-85 from Marley	
Bid price from Marley, $19.03 × 32,000	$608,960
Equipment lease penalty	6,600
Total incremental cost to purchase	615,560
Cost for Paibec to make MTR-85 in 2008	
Direct materials ($214,500 × 1.08) × $\frac{32,000}{30,000}$	247,104
Direct labour ($132,000 × 1.05) × $\frac{32,000}{30,000}$	147,840
Plant space rental	92,400
Equipment leasing costs	39,600
Variable manufacturing overhead ($247,500 × 40%) × $\frac{32,000}{30,000}$	105,600
Fixed manufacturing overhead (not relevant)	—
Total incremental cost to make MTR-85	632,544
Savings if purchased from Marley	$ 16,984

2. Based solely on the financial results, the 32,000 units of MTR-85 for 2008 should be purchased from Marley. The total cost to purchase from Marley would be $615,560 or $16,984 less than if the units were made by Paibec.

    At least three other factors that Paibec Corporation should consider before agreeing to purchase MTR-85 from Marley Company are the following:

    - The quality of the Marley component should be equal to, or better than, the quality of the internally made component, or else the quality of the final product might be compromised and Paibec's reputation affected.
    - Marley's reliability as an on-time supplier is important, since late deliveries could hamper Paibec's production schedule and delivery dates for the final product.
    - Layoffs may result if the component is outsourced to Marley. This could impact Paibec's other employees and cause labour problems or affect the company's position in the community. In addition, there may be termination costs which have not been factored into the analysis.

3. Lynn Hardt would consider the request of John Porter to be unethical for the following reasons, based on the CMA Code of Ethics standard:

    •   Prepare complete and clear reports and recommendations after appropriate analysis of relevant and reliable information. Adjusting cost is unethical.

    •   Refrain from either actively or passively subverting the attainment of the organization's legitimate and ethical objectives. Paibec has a legitimate objective of trying to obtain the component at the lowest cost possible, regardless of whether it is manufactured by Paibec or outsourced to Marley.

    •   Communicate unfavourable as well as favourable information and professional judgments or opinions. Hardt needs to communicate the proper and accurate results of the analysis, regardless of whether or not it is favourable to Paibec.

    •   Refrain from engaging in or supporting any activity that would discredit the profession. Falsifying the analysis would discredit Hardt and the profession.

    •   Communicate information fairly and objectively. Hardt needs to perform an objective make/buy analysis and communicate the results fairly.

    •   Disclose fully all relevant information that could reasonably be expected to influence an intended user's understanding of the reports, comments, and recommendations presented. Hardt needs to disclose fully the analysis and the expected cost increases.

Hardt should indicate to Porter that the costs derived under the make alternative are correct. If Porter still insists on making the changes to lower the costs of making MTR-2000 internally, Hardt should raise the matter with Porter's superior, after informing Porter of her plans. If, after taking all these steps, there is continued pressure to understate the costs, Hardt should consider resigning from the company, rather than engage in unethical conduct.

11-46   (40 min.) Optimal product mix.

In order to maximize OmniSport's profitability, OmniSport should manufacture 12,000 snowboard bindings, manufacture 1,000 pairs of skates, and purchase 6,000 pairs of skates from Colcott Inc. This combination of manufactured and purchased goods maximizes the contribution per available machine-hour, which is the limiting resource, as shown below.

Because snowboards have a higher contribution per machine-hour than skates, OmniSport should manufacture the maximum number of snowboards. Because the contribution per manufactured pair of skates is higher than the contribution from a purchased pair of skates, total contribution will be maximized by using the remaining manufacturing capacity to produce skates and then purchasing the remaining required skates. This optimal combination is calculated as presented.

	Purchased Skates 6,000 pairs		Manufactured Skates 1,000 pairs		Manufactured Snowboard Bindings 12,000		Total
	Per Unit	Total	Per Unit	Total	Per Unit	Total	Total
Selling price	$117.60	$705,600	$117.60	$117,600	$72.00	$864,000	$1,687,200
Variable costs							
Direct & other materials	90.00	540,000	24.00	24,000	24.00	288,000	852,000
Machine operating costs	—	—	28.80	28,800	9.60	115,200	144,000
Manufacturing overhead costs[1]	—	—	14.40	14,400	4.80	57,600	72,000
Selling & administrative costs	4.80[2]	28,800	10.80[3]	10,800	9.60[4]	115,200	154,800
Variable costs	94.80	568,800	78.00	78,000	48.00	576,000	1,222,800
Contribution margin	$ 22.80	$136,800	$39.60	$39,600	$24.00	$288,000	464,400
Fixed costs							
Manufacturing overhead							36,000
Marketing & administrative costs							72,000[5]
Fixed costs							108,000
Operating income							$ 356,400
Machine-hours per unit	—		1.5		0.5		
Contribution per machine-hour ($39.60 ÷ 1.5; $24 ÷ 0.5)	—		$26.40		$48.00		

[1]*Supporting calculations:*

Manufacturing overhead:

Manufactured skates
Machine-hours	=	$28.80 per pair/$19.20 per hour = 1.5 hours per pair
Manufacturing capacity	=	5,000 pairs × 1.5 hours per pair = 7,500 hours
Overhead per machine-hour	=	$21.60 per pair/1.5 hours per pair = $14.40 per hour
Total overhead	=	7,500 hours × $14.40 per hour = $108,000
Total variable overhead	=	$108,000 (total) – $36,000 (fixed) = $72,000 (variable)
Variable overhead per machine-hour	=	$72,000/7,500 hours = $9.60 per hour
Fixed overhead per machine-hour	=	$36,000 fixed overhead/7,500 hours = $4.80 per hour
Variable overhead per pair of skates	=	1.5 hours × $9.60 per hour = $14.40 per pair
Fixed overhead per pair of skates	=	1.5 hours × $4.80 per hour = $7.20 per pair

Snowboard bindings
Machine-hours	=	$9.60 per board/$19.20 per hour = 0.5 hour per board
Variable overhead per snowboard	=	$9.60 per hour × 0.5 hour per board = $4.80 per board
Fixed overhead per snowboard	=	$4.80 per hour × 0.5 hour per board = $2.40 per board

[2] $12.00 – $7.20 = $4.80
[3] $18.00 – $7.20 = $10.80
[4] $16.80 – $7.20 = $9.60
[5] $12.00 × 6,000 = $72,000

The task is to maximize contribution margin per machine hour, not per unit of product, given that the constraint is machine hours of capacity.

The cost for manufacturing a pair of skates = $36.90

The contribution margin per hour = $39.60 ÷ 1.5 hours per pair = $26.40/hour = A

The cost to manufacture for snowboards = $24

The contribution margin per snowboard = $24 ÷ 0.5 hours per board = 48.00 = B

The cost to purchase a pair of skates (no machining required) = $22.80/pair

Let the contribution margin per purchased pair of skates = C

Maximize subject to the machine capacity constraint of 7,500 hours:

1.5A + 0.5B = 7,500   (1)

A ≤ 8,000   (2)

B ≤ 12,000   (3)

To solve, substitute (2) into (1): 1.5(8,000) + 0.5B = 7,500

0.5B = 7,500 – 12,000

B = (4,500) ÷ 0.5 ∴ B = (9,000), an impossible solution (extraneous root).

Now substitute (3) into (1): 1.5A + 0.5(12,000) = 7,500

1.5A + 6,000 = 7,500

1.5A = 7,500 – 6,000 = 1,500 ∴ A = 1,000 a possible solution (good root)

Substitute this solution into (1)

1.5 × 1,000 + 0.5B = 7,500

0.5B = 7,500 – 1,500 = 6,000

B = 6,000 ÷ 0.5 ∴ B = 12,000

To maximize the contribution margin manufacture 12,000 snowboards and purchase 6,000 pairs of skates from Colcott. Notice that purchasing a pair of skates consumes none of the constrained resource (machine hours).

OmniSport Contribution Analysis

	Quantity (1)	Machine-Hours per Unit (2)	Total Machine-Hours Used (3)= (1)×(2)	Machine-Hour Balance (4)	Unit Contribution (5)	Total Product Contribution (6)= (1)×(5)
Machine-hours available				7,500		
Snowboard bindings	12,000	0.5	6,000	1,500	$24.00	$288,000
Skates (pairs)—manufacture	1,000	1.5	1,500	—	39.60	39,600
Skates (pairs)—purchase	6,000	—	—	—	22.80	136,800
Total contribution						464,400
Less original contribution (5,000 pairs of skates × $39.60 per pair)						(198,000)
Improvement in contribution						$266,400

CHAPTER 12
PRICING DECISIONS, PRODUCT PROFITABILITY DECISIONS, AND COST MANAGEMENT

12-2 Not necessarily. For a one-time-only special order the relevant costs are only those costs that will change as a result of accepting the order. In this case, full product costs will rarely be relevant. It is more likely that full product costs will be relevant costs for long-run pricing decisions.

12-4 Activity-based costing helps managers in pricing decisions in two ways.
(a) It gives managers more accurate product-cost information for making pricing decisions.
(b) It helps managers to manage costs during value engineering by identifying the cost impact of eliminating, reducing or changing various activities.

12-6 A target cost per unit is the estimated long-run cost per unit of a product (or service) that, when sold at the target price, enables the company to achieve the targeted operating income per unit.

12-8 A value-added cost is a cost that customers perceive as adding value, or utility, to a product or service. Examples are costs of materials, direct labour, tools, and machinery. Examples of nonvalue-added costs are costs of rework, scrap, expediting, and breakdown maintenance.

12-10 Cost-plus pricing is a pricing approach in which managers add a markup to cost in order to determine price.

12-12 Two examples where the difference in the incremental or outlay costs of two products or services is much smaller than the differences in their prices follow:
1. The difference in prices charged for a telephone call, hotel room, or car rental during busy versus slack periods is often much greater than the difference in costs to provide these services.
2. The difference in incremental or outlay costs for an airplane seat sold to a passenger travelling on business or a passenger travelling for pleasure is roughly the same. However, airline companies routinely charge business travellers—those who are likely to start and complete their travel during the same week excluding the weekend—a much higher price than pleasure travellers, who generally stay at their destinations over at least one weekend.

12-14 Three benefits of using a product life-cycle reporting format are:
1. The full set of revenues and costs associated with each product becomes more visible.

2. Differences among products in the percentage of total costs committed at early stages in the life cycle are highlighted.
3. Interrelationships among business function cost categories are highlighted.

12-16 (20-30 min.) Relevant-cost approach to pricing decisions, special order.

1. Relevant revenues, $4.56 × 1,000 $4,560
    Relevant costs
    Direct materials, $1.80 × 1,000 $1,800
    Direct manufacturing labour, $0.96 × 1,000   960
    Variable manufacturing overhead, $0.84 × 1,000   840
    Variable selling costs, 0.05 × 4,560   228
       Total   3,828
       Increase in operating income $ 732

This calculation assumes that:

(a) The monthly fixed manufacturing overhead of $180,000 and $65,000 of monthly fixed marketing costs will be unchanged by acceptance of the 1,000 unit order.
(b) The price charged and the volumes sold to other customers are not affected by the special order.

Chapter 12 uses the phrase "one-time-only special order" to describe this special case.

2. The president's reasoning is defective on at least two counts:

(a) The inclusion of irrelevant costs—assuming the monthly fixed manufacturing overhead of $180,000 will be unchanged; it is irrelevant to the decision.
(b) The exclusion of relevant costs—variable selling costs (5% of the selling price) are excluded.

3. Key issues are:

(a) Will the existing customer base demand price reductions? If this 1,000-tape order is not independent of other sales, cutting the price from $6.00 to $4.56 can have a large negative effect on total revenues.
(b) Is the 1,000-tape order a one-time-only order, or is there the possibility of sales in subsequent months? The fact that the customer is not in Dill

Company's "normal marketing channels" does not necessarily mean it is a one-time-only order. Indeed, the sale could well open a new marketing channel. Dill Company should be reluctant to consider only short-run variable costs for pricing long-run business.

12-18 (25 min.) Short-run pricing, capacity constraints.

1. With no constraints on availability of Pyrone or on plant capacity, Boutique would want to charge a minimum price for Seltium that would cover its incremental costs to manufacture Seltium. (Because there is excess capacity, there is no opportunity cost.) In this case, the incremental costs are the variable costs to manufacture a kilogram of Seltium:

Pyrone (2 kilograms × $480 per kilogram)	$ 9.60
Direct manufacturing labour	4.80
Variable manufacturing overhead costs	3.60
Total variable manufacturing costs	$18.00

Hence, the minimum price that Boutique should charge to manufacture Seltium is $18 per kilogram. For 3,000 kilograms of Seltium it should charge a minimum of $54,000 ($18 × 3,000).

2. Now Pyrone is in short supply. Using it to make Seltium reduces the Bolzene that Boutique can make and sell. There is therefore an opportunity cost of manufacturing Seltium, the lost contribution from using the Pyrone to manufacture Bolzene. To make 3,000 kilograms of Seltium requires 6,000 (2 × 3,000) kilograms of Pyrone.

    The 6,000 kilograms of Pyrone can be used to manufacture 4,000 (6,000 ÷ 1.5) kilograms of Bolzene, since each kilogram of Bolzene requires 1.5 kilograms of Pyrone.

    The contribution margin from 4,000 kilograms of Bolzene is $28,800 ($7.20 per kilogram × 4,000 kilograms). This is the opportunity cost of using Pyrone to manufacture Seltium. The minimum price that Boutique should charge to manufacture Seltium should cover not only the incremental (variable) costs of manufacturing Seltium but also the opportunity cost:

| | Costs of Manufacturing Seltium | |
	Total for 3,000 Kilogram (1)	**Per Kilogram (2) = (1) ÷ 3,000**
Incremental (variable) costs of manufacturing Seltium	$54,000	$18.00
Opportunity cost of forgoing manufacture and sale of Bolzene	28,800	9.60
Minimum cost of order	$82,800	$27.60

The minimum price that Boutique should charge for Seltium is $27.60 per kilogram. For 3,000 kilograms of Seltium, Boutique should charge a minimum of $82,800 ($27.60 × 3,000 kgs).

12-20 (25-30 min.) Target operating income, value-added costs, service company.

1. The classification of total costs in 2007 into value-added, non-value added, or in the grey area in between follows.

	Value-Added (1)	**Grey Area (2)**	**Non-Value-Added (3)**	**Total (4) = (1)+(2)+(3)**
Doing calculations and preparing drawings 75% × $480,000	$360,000			$360,000
Checking calculations and drawings 4% × $480,000		$19,200		19,200
Correcting errors found in drawings 7% × $480,000			$ 33,600	33,600
Making changes in response to client requests 6% × $480,000	28,800			28,800
Correcting errors to meet government building code, 8% × $480,000			38,400	38,400
Total professional labour costs	388,800	19,200	72,000	480,000
Administration and support costs at 40% ($192,000 – $480,000) of professional labour costs	155,520	7,680	28,800	192,000
Travel	21,600		—	21,600
Total	$565,920	$26,880	$100,800	$693,600

Doing calculations and responding to client requests for changes are value-added costs because customers perceive these costs as necessary for the service of preparing architectural drawings. Costs incurred in correcting errors in drawings and making changes because they were inconsistent with building codes are non-value-added costs. Customers do not perceive these costs as necessary and would be unwilling to pay for them. Carasco should seek to eliminate these costs. Checking calculations and drawings is in the grey area (some, but not all, checking may be needed). There is room for disagreement on these classifications. For example, checking calculations may be regarded as value added, and making changes to conform to the building code might be regarded as in the grey area.

Carasco's staff can reduce non-value-added costs by checking government building code requirements before drawing up the plans and taking more care when doing the actual work. To reduce value-added costs, Carasco's staff must work faster and more efficiently while at the same time maintaining quality. To achieve these goals, Carasco may want to consider investing in computer-aided drawing programs and training its professional staff to work with these tools.

2.   Reduction in professional labour-hours by

(a)	Correcting errors in drawings (7% × 8,000)	560	hours
(b)	Correcting errors to conform to building code (8% × 8,000)	640	hours
	Total	1,200	hours
	Cost savings in professional labour costs (1,200 hours × $60)	$ 72,000	
	Cost savings in variable administration and support costs (40% x $72,000)	28,800	
	Total cost savings	$100,800	
	Current operating income in 2007	$122,400	
	Add: Cost savings from eliminating errors	100,800	
	Operating income in 2007 if errors are eliminated	$223,200	

3.   Currently 85% × 8,000 hours = 6,800 hours are billed to clients generating revenues of $816,000. The remaining 15% of professional labour-hours (15% × 8,000 = 1,200 hours) is lost in making corrections. Carasco bills clients at the rate of $\frac{\$816,000}{6,800}$ = $120 per professional labour-hour. If the 1,200 professional labour-hours currently not being billed to clients were billed to clients, Carasco's revenues would increase by 1,200 hours × $120 = $144,000 from $816,000 to $960,000.

Costs remaining unchanged

Professional labour costs	$480,000
Administration and support (40% × $480,000)	192,000
Travel	21,600
Total costs	$693,600

Carasco's operating income would be

Revenues	$960,000
Total costs	693,600
Operating income	$266,400

12-22 (20 min.) Cost-plus target return on investment pricing.

1. Target operating income = target return on investment × invested capital

Target operating income, 25% of $1,152,000	$288,000
Total fixed costs	422,400
Target contribution margin	$710,400

Target contribution per room-night, ($710,400 ÷ 16,000)	$44.40
Add variable costs per room-night	3.60
Price to be charged per room-night	$48.00

Proof

Total room revenues ($48 × 16,000 room-nights)		$768,000
Total costs:		
Variable costs ($3.60 × 16,000)	$ 57,600	
Fixed costs	422,400	
Total costs		480,000
Operating income		$288,000

The full cost of a room-night = variable cost per room-night + fixed cost per room-night
The full cost of a room-night = $3.60 + ($422,400 ÷ 16,000) = $3.60 + $26.40 = $30

Markup per room-night = Rental price per room-night – Full cost of a room-night
= $48 – $30 = $18
Markup percentage as a fraction of full cost = $18 ÷ $30 = 60%

2. If price is reduced by 10%, the number of room-nights Beck could rent would increase by 10%.

The new price per room-night would be 90% of $48 = $43.20

The number of room-night Beck expects to rent is 110% of 16,000 = 17,600

The contribution margin per room-night would be $43.20 – $3.60 = $39.60

Contribution margin = $39.60 × 17,600 = $696,960

Since the contribution margin at the reduced price of $43.20 is less than the contribution margin at a price of $48, Beck should not reduce the price of the room-nights. Note that the fixed costs of $422,400 will be the same under the $48 and the $43.20 price alternatives and are hence irrelevant to the analysis.

12-24 (25 min.) Target costs, effect of product-design changes on product costs.

1. & 2. Indirect cost-allocation rates for 2007 and 2008 are as follows:

	2007			2008		
Indirect Cost Category	Total Costs (1)	Quantity of Cost-Allocation Base (2)	Cost Allocation Rate (3) = (1) ÷ (2)	Total Costs (4)	Quantity of Cost-Allocation Base (5)	Cost Allocation Rate (6) = (4) ÷ (5)
Batch-level costs	$8,640,000	900	$9,600	$9,000,000	1,000	$9,000
Manuf. operations costs	14,520,000	220,000	66	15,000,000	250,000	60
Engineering change costs	3,168,000	220	14,400	2,400,000	200	12,000

Manufacturing costs of HJ6 in 2007 and 2008 are as follows:

	2007		2008	
	Total (1)	Per Unit (2) = (1) ÷ 3,500	Total (3)	Per Unit (4) = (3) ÷ 4,000
Direct materials, $1,440 × 3,500; $1,320 × 4,000	$5,040,000	$1,440	$5,280,000	$1,320
Batch-level costs, $9,600 × 70; $9,000 × 80	672,000	192	720,000	180
Manuf. operations costs, $66 × 21,000; $60 × 22,000	1,386,000	396	1,320,000	330
Engineering change costs, $14,400 × 15; $12,000 × 10	216,000	62	120,000	30
Total	$7,314,000	$2,090	$7,440,000	$1,860

3.
$$\begin{array}{cc} \text{Target manufacturing cost} \\ \text{per unit of HJ6 in 2008} \end{array} = \begin{array}{c} \text{Manufacturing cost} \\ \text{per unit in 2007} \end{array} \times 88\%$$

$$= \quad \$2,090 \times 0.88 = \$1,839.20$$

Budgeted manufacturing cost per unit of HJ6 in 2008 is \$1,860. Hence, Medical Instruments has not achieved its target manufacturing cost per unit of \$1,839.20.

4. To reduce the manufacturing cost per unit in 2008, Medical Instruments reduced the cost per unit in each of the four cost categories—direct materials costs, batch-level costs, manufacturing operations costs, and engineering change costs. It achieved this by reducing setup, production order, and materials handling costs per batch, the cost per machine hour, and cost per engineering change, perhaps by becoming more efficient in performing these activities. Efficiency improvements also helped Medical Instruments reduce the quantities of the cost allocation bases used to manufacture HJ6. For example, although production of HJ6 increased by 14.3% [(4,000 – 3,500) ÷ 3,500] between 2007 and 2008, machine-hours worked increased by only 4.8% [(22,000 ÷ 21,000) ÷ 21,000]. Medical Instruments achieved these gains through value engineering activities that retained only those product features that customers wanted while eliminating non-value-added activities and costs.

12-26 (30-40 min.) Life-cycle product costing, product emphasis.

1. A life-cycle income statement traces revenue and costs of each individual software package from its initial research and development to its final customer servicing and support in the marketplace. The two main differences from a fiscal-year-based income statement are:
   (a) Costs incurred in different fiscal periods are included in the same statement.
   (b) Costs and revenue of each package are reported separately rather than aggregated into company-wide categories.

   The benefits of using a product life-cycle report are:
   (a) The full set of revenues and costs associated with each product becomes visible.
   (b) Differences among products in the percentage of total costs committed at early stages in the life cycle are highlighted.
   (c) Interrelationships among business function cost categories are highlighted. What is the effect, for example, of cutting back on R&D and product-design cost categories on customer-service costs in subsequent years?

2.

	EE-46		ME-83		IE-17	
Revenue ($000s)	$3,000		$1,800		$1,920.00	
Costs ($000s)						
Research and development	$840		$540		$288.00	
Design	240		144		115.20	
Production	360		252		249.60	
Marketing	600		324		537.60	
Distribution	90		72		115.20	
Customer service	450	2,580	180	1,512	729.60	2,035.20
Operating income ($000s)		$ 420		$ 288		$ (115.20)

As emphasized in this chapter, the time value of money is not taken into account when summing life-cycle revenue or life-cycle costs. Chapters 21 and 22 discuss this topic in detail.

Rankings of the three packages on profitability (and relative profitability) are:

	Operating Income				**Operating Income Revenues**	
1.	ME-83:	$288,000		1.	ME-83:	16.0%
2.	EE-46:	$420,000		2.	EE-46:	14.0%
3.	IE-17:	$(115,200)		3.	IE-17:	(6.0%)

The EE-46 and ME-83 packages should be emphasized, and the IE-17 package should be de-emphasized. It is interesting that IE-17 had the lowest R&D costs but was the least profitable. But its customer service costs were 405% of the ME-83 and 162% of the EE-46.

3. The cost structures of the three software packages are:

	EE-46	ME-83	IE-17
Research and development	32.5%	35.7%	14.1%
Design	9.3	9.5	5.7
Production	14.0	16.7	12.3
Marketing	23.3	21.4	26.4
Distribution	3.5	4.8	5.7
Customer service	17.4	11.9	35.8
	100.0%	100.0%	100.0%

The major differences are:
(a) EE-46 and ME-83 have over 40% of their costs in the R&D/product design categories compared to less than 20% (19.8%) for IE-17.
(b) IE-17 has 35.8% of its costs in the customer-service category compared to 17.4% for EE-46 and 11.9% for ME-83.

There are several explanations for these differences:

(a) EE-46 and ME-83 differ sizably from IE-17 in their R&D/product design intensity. For example, EE-46 and ME-83 may require considerably (a) more interaction with users, and (b) more experimentation with software algorithms than does IE-17.

(b) The software division should have invested more in the R&D/product design categories for IE-17. The high percentage for customer service could reflect the correcting of problems that should have been corrected prior to manufacture. Life-cycle reports highlight possible causal relationships among cost categories. It is stated in the problem that major efforts were made to cut down R&D for the IE-17 product. This is most probably reflected in a lower quality product that requires more customer support.

12-28 (30 min.) Relevant-cost approach to pricing decisions.

1.

Revenues (1,000 crates at $120 per crate)		$120,000
Variable costs:		
Manufacturing	$48,000	
Marketing	16,800	
Total variable costs		64,800
Contribution margin		55,200
Fixed costs:		
Manufacturing	$24,000	
Marketing	19,200	
Total fixed costs		43,200
Operating income		$ 12,000

Normal markup percentage: $55,200 ÷ $64,800 = 85.19% of total variable costs.

2. Only the manufacturing-cost category is relevant to considering this special order; no additional marketing costs will be incurred. The relevant manufacturing costs for the 200-crate special order are:

Variable manufacturing cost per unit $48* × 200 crates	$ 9,600
Special packaging	2,400
	$12,000

*$48,000/1,000 crates = $48 per crate

Any price above $60 per crate ($12,000 ÷ 200) will make a positive contribution to operating income.

The reasoning based on a comparison of $66 per-crate price with the $72 per-crate absorption cost ignores monthly cost-volume-profit relationships. The $72 per-crate absorption cost includes a $24 per-crate cost component that is irrelevant to the special order. The relevant range for the fixed manufacturing costs is from 500 to 1,500 crates per month; the special order will increase production from 1,000 to 1,200 crates per month. Furthermore, the special order requires no incremental marketing costs.

3. If the new customer is likely to remain in business, Stardom should consider whether a strictly short-run focus is appropriate. For example, what is the likelihood of demand from other customers increasing over time? If Stardom accepts the 200-crate special order for more than one month, it may preclude accepting other customers at prices exceeding $66 per crate. Moreover, the existing customers may learn about Stardom's willingness to set a price based on variable cost plus a small contribution margin. The longer time frame over which Stardom keeps selling 200 crates of canned peaches at $66 a crate, the more likely that the existing customers will approach Stardom for their own special price reductions.

12-30 (50-60 min.) Target cost, activity-based costing systems (continuation of 12-29).

1. A target cost per unit is the estimated long-run cost per unit of a product (or service) that, when sold at the target price, enables the company to achieve the target operating income per unit. A target cost per unit is the estimated unit long-run cost of a product that will enable a company to enter or to remain in the market and compete profitably against its competitors.

2. The following table presents the manufacturing cost per unit for different cost categories for P-41REV and P-63 REV.

Cost Categories	P-41 REV	P-63 REV
Direct manufacturing product costs:		
Direct materials	$457.44	$315.72
Indirect manufacturing product costs:		
Materials handling (71 × $1.44; 39 × $1.44)	102.24	56.16
Assembly management (2.1 × $48; 1.6 × $48)	100.80	76.80
Machine-insertion of parts (59 × $0.84; 29 × $0.84)	49.56	24.36
Manual insertion of parts (12 × $2.52; 10 × $2.52)	30.24	25.20
Quality testing (1.2 × $30; 0.9 × $30)	36.00	27.00
Total indirect manufacturing costs	318.84	209.52
Total manufacturing costs	$776.28	$525.24
Target cost	$816.00	$468.00

P-41 REV is \$39.72 below its target cost. However, P-63 REV is \$57.24 above its target cost. It appears that Executive Power will have major problems competing with the foreign printer costing \$468.

3.

		P-41				P-63	
P-41	=	\$938.88		P-63	=	\$604.80	
P-41 REV	=	776.28		P-63 REV	=	525.24	
Difference	=	\$162.60		Difference	=	\$ 79.56	

The sources of the cost reductions in the redesigned products are:

	P-41	P-63
(a) Reduction in direct materials costs	\$31.56	\$34.80
(b) Changes in design:		
Reduced materials handling costs because of fewer parts		
$(85 - 71); (46 - 39) \times \$1.44$	20.16	10.08
Reduced assembly time		
$(3.2 - 2.1); (1.9 - 1.6) \times \$48$	52.80	14.40
Reduced insertion of parts[1]		
P-41: $(49 - 59) \times \$0.84 + (36 - 12) \times \$2.52$	52.08	
P-63: $(31 - 29) \times \$0.84 + (15 - 10) \times \$2.52$		14.28
Reduced quality testing		
$(1.4 - 1.2); (1.1 - 0.9) \times \$30$	6.00	6.00
	\$162.60	\$79.56

[1]Note that the reduced costs for insertion of parts comes from two sources: (a) a reduction in total number of parts to be inserted, and (b) an increase in the percentage of parts inserted by the lower-cost machine method.

4. The \$14.40 reduction in cost per hour of assembly time (from \$48 to \$33.60) reduces product costs as follows:

P-41 REV: \$14.40 × 2.1 hours = \$30.24. The new total manufacturing product cost is \$746.04 (\$776.28 – \$30.24)

P-63 REV: \$14.40 × 1.6 hours = \$23.04. The new total manufacturing product cost is \$502.20 (\$525.24 – \$23.04)

The reduction in the assembly management activity rate further reduces the cost of P-41 REV below the target cost. It also makes it more likely that P-63 REV will achieve its target cost.

12-32 (25 min.) Cost-plus and market-based pricing.

1. Construction Temps' full cost per hour of supplying contract labour is:

Variable costs	$14.40
Fixed costs ($288,000 ÷ 80,000 hours)	3.60
Full cost per hour	$18.00

Price per hour at full cost plus 20% = $18 × 1.20 = $21.60 per hour.

2. Contribution margins for different prices and demand realizations are as follows:

Price per Hour (1)	Variable Cost per Hour (2)	Contribution Margin per Hour (3)=(1)-(2)	Demand in Hours (4)	Total Contribution (5)=(3)x(4)
$19.20	$14.40	$4.80	120,000	$576,000
20.40	14.40	6.00	100,000	600,000
21.60	14.40	7.20	80,000	576,000
22.80	14.40	8.40	70,000	588,000
24.00	14.40	9.60	60,000	576,000

Fixed costs will remain the same regardless of the demand realizations. Fixed costs are therefore irrelevant since they do not differ among the alternatives.

The table above indicates that Construction Temps can maximize contribution margin and hence operating income by charging a price of $20.40 per hour.

3. The cost-plus approach to pricing in requirement 1 does not explicitly consider the effect of prices on demand. The approach in requirement 2 models the interaction between price and demand and determines the optimal level of profitability using concepts of relevant costs. The two different approaches lead to two different prices in requirements 1 and 2. As the chapter describes, pricing decisions should consider both demand or market considerations and supply or cost factors. The approach in requirement 2 is the more balanced approach. In most cases, of course, managers use the cost-plus method of requirement 1 as only a starting point. They then modify the cost-plus price on the basis of market considerations—anticipated customer reaction to alternative price levels and the prices charged by competitors for similar products.

12-34 (35-40 min.) Life-cycle product costing, activity-based costing.

1. The budgeted life-cycle operating income for the new watch MX3 is $2,223,000 as shown below.

	Year 1 (1)	Year 2 (2)	Year 3 (3)	Life-Cycle (4)=(1)+(2)+(3)
Revenues $54 × 50,000; $48 × 200,000; $42 × 150,000	$2,700,000	$9,600.000	$6,300,000	$18,600,000
R&D and design costs	1,080,000	120,000	0	1,200,000
Manufacturing costs:				
Variable $19.20 × 50,000; $18 × 200,000; $18 × 150,000	960,000	3,600,000	2,700,000	7,260,000
Batch $840 × 125[1]; $720 × 400[2]; $720 × 300[3]	105,000	288,000	216,000	609,000
Fixed	720,000	720,000	720,000	2,160,000
Marketing costs:				
Variable $4.32 × 50,000; $3.84 × 200,000; $3.36 × 150,000	216,000	768,000	504,000	1,488,000
Fixed	480,000	360,000	360,000	1,200,000
Distribution costs:				
Variable $1.20 × 50,000; $1.20 × 200,000; $1.20 × 150,000	60,000	240,000	180,000	480,000
Batch $144 × 250[4]; $144 × 1,250[5]; $120 × 1,250[6]	36,000	180,000	150,000	366,000
Fixed	288,000	288,000	288,000	864,000
Customer service costs:				
Variable $2.40 × 50,000; $1.80 × 200,000; $1.80 × 150,000	120,000	360,000	270,000	750,000
Total costs	4,065,000	6,924,000	5,388,000	16,377,000
Operating income	$(1,365,000)	$2,676,000	$ 912,000	$ 2,223,000

[1] 50,000 ÷ 400 = 125   [2] 200,000 ÷ 500 = 400   [3] 150,000 ÷ 500 = 300
[4] 50,000 ÷ 200=250   [5] 200,000 ÷ 160 = 1,250   [6] 150,000 ÷ 120 = 1,250

2. Budgeted product life-cycle costs for R&D and design $1,200,000
Total budgeted product life-cycle costs $16,377,000

$$\text{Percentage of budgeted product life-cycle costs incurred till the R\&D and design stages} = \frac{1,200,000}{16,377,000} = 7.33\%$$

3. An analysis reveals that 80% of the total product life-cycle costs of the new watch will be locked in at the end of the R&D and design stages when only 7.33% of the costs have been incurred (requirement 2). The implication is that it will be difficult to alter or reduce the costs of MX3 once Destin finalizes the design of MX3. To reduce and manage total costs, Destin must act to modify the design before costs get locked in.

4. The budgeted life-cycle operating income for MX3 if Destin reduces its price by $3.60 is $1,501,200 as shown below. This is less than the operating income of $2,223,000 calculated in requirement 1. Therefore, Destin should not reduce MX3's price by $3.60.

	Year 1 (1)	Year 2 (2)	Year 3 (3)	Life-Cycle (4)=(1)+(2)+(3)
Revenues $50.40 × 55,000; $44.40 × 220,000;				
$38.40 × 165,000 [a],[b]	$2,772,000	$9,768,000	$6,336,000	$18,876,000
R&D and design costs	1,080,000	120,000	0	1,200,000
Manufacturing costs:				
Variable $19.20 × 55,000; $18 × 220,000;				
$18 × 165,000	1,056,000	3,960,000	2,970,000	7,986,000
Batch $840 × 125[1]; $720 × 400[2];				
$720 × 300[3]	105,000	288,000	216,000	609,000
Fixed	720,000	720,000	720,000	2,160,000
Marketing costs:				
Variable $4.32 × 55,000; $3.84 × 220,000;				
$3.36 × 165,000	237,600	844,800	554,400	1,636,800
Fixed	480,000	360,000	360,000	1,200,000
Distribution costs:				
Variable $1.20 × 55,000; $1.20 × 220,000;				
$1.20 × 165,000	66,000	264,000	198,000	528,000
Batch $144 × 250[4]; $144 × 1,250[5];				
$120 × 1,250[6]	36,000	180,000	150,000	366,000
Fixed	288,000	288,000	288,000	864,000
Customer service costs:				
Variable $2.40 × 55,000; $1.80 × 220,000;				
$1.80 × 165,000	132,000	396,000	297,000	825,000
Total costs	4,200,600	7,420,800	5,753,400	17,374,800
Operating income	$(1,428,600)	$2,347,200	$ 582,600	$ 1,501,200

[1] 55,000 ÷ 440 = 125 [2] 220,000 ÷ 550 = 400 [3] 165,000 ÷ 550 = 300
[4] 55,000 ÷ 220 = 250 [5] 220,000 ÷ 176 = 1,250 [6] 165,000 ÷ 132 = 1,250

a) Reduce selling price by 3.60 each year:
   Year 1 $54 – $3.60 = $50.40
   Year 2 $48 – $3.60 = $44.40
   Year 3 $42 – $3.60 = $38.40

b) Increase sales of units 10% each year:
   Year 1 50,000 × 1.1 = 55,000
   Year 2 200,000 × 1.1 = 220,000
   Year 3 150,000 × 1.1 = 165,000

12-36 (30 min.) **Airline pricing, considerations other than cost in pricing.**

1. If the fare is $2,400,
    (a) Air North would expect to have 190 business and 20 pleasure travellers.
    (b) Variable costs per passenger would be: food and beverages, $48; and ticket commissions of 8% × 2,400 = $192.
    (c) Contribution margin per passenger = $2,400 – $48 – $192 = $2,160.

    If the fare is $600,
    (a) Air North would expect to have 200 business and 100 pleasure travellers.
    (b) Variable costs per passenger would be: food and beverages, $48; and ticket commissions of 8% × $600 = $48.
    (c) Contribution margin per passenger = $600 – $48 – $48 = $504

    Contribution margin from business travellers at prices of $600 and $2,400 respectively follow:

At a price of $600: $504 × 200 passengers	= $100,800
At a price of $2,400: $2,160 × 190 passengers	= $410,400

    Air North would maximize contribution margin and operating income by charging business travellers a fare of $2,400. The reason is that the demand for business travel drops only slightly (from 200 passengers per flight to 190 passengers per flight) despite the large increase in fare. Also note that in deciding between the alternative prices all other costs such as fuel costs, allocated annual lease costs, allocated ground services costs, and allocated flight crew salaries are irrelevant. Why? Because these costs will not change, whatever price Air North chooses to charge.

    Contribution margin from pleasure travellers at prices of $600 and $2,400 respectively follow:

At a price of $600: $504 × 100 passengers	= $50,400
At a price of $2,400: $2,160 × 20 passengers	= $43,200

    Air North would maximize contribution margin and operating income by charging pleasure travellers a fare of $600. The reason is that the demand for pleasure travel drops significantly (from 100 passengers per flight to 20 passengers per flight) as a result of increasing the fare. Once again, in deciding between the alternative prices to charge pleasure travellers, all other costs such as fuel costs, allocated annual lease costs, allocated ground services costs, and allocated flight crew salaries are irrelevant.

Air North would maximize contribution margin and operating income by a price differentiation strategy, where business travellers are charged $2,400 and pleasure travellers $600.

2. The elasticity of demand of the two classes of passengers drives the different demands of the travellers. Business travellers are relatively price insensitive because they must get to their destinations during the week (exclusive of weekends) and their fares are paid by their companies. A 300% increase in fares from $600 to $2,400 will deter only 5% of the business passengers from flying with Air North.

    In contrast, a similar fare increase will lead to an 80% drop in pleasure travellers who are paying for their own travel costs, unlike business travellers, and who may have alternative vacation plans they could pursue instead.

3. Since business travellers often want to return within the same week, while pleasure travellers often stay over weekends, a requirement that a Saturday night stay is needed to qualify for the $600 discount fare would discriminate between the passenger categories. This price discrimination is legal because airlines are service companies rather than manufacturing companies and because these practices do not, nor are they intended to, destroy competition.

12-38 (40-50 min.) Target prices, target costs, value engineering.

1. Activity-based allocation of overhead costs:

	Tvez		Premia	
	Units of Cost Drivers (1)	Cost Allocation (2) = (1) × Rate/Hour	Units of Cost Drivers (3)	Cost Allocation (4) = (3) × Rate/Hour
Machine setup costs:				
$30 per setup hour	$100^a \times 12 = 1,200$ hrs.	$ 36,000	$125^b \times 18 = 2,250$ hrs.	$ 67,500
Testing costs:				
$2.40 per testing hour	$50,000 \times 2.5 = 125,000$ hrs.	300,000	$25,000 \times 4.75 = 118,750$ hrs.	285,000
Engineering costs		204,000		336,000
Total ABC overhead allocation		$540,000		$688,500

[a]100 setups = 50,000 units ÷ 500 units per setup   [b]125 setups = 25,000 units ÷ 200 units per setup

Activity-based full-product costs of Tvez and Premia are as follows:

	Tvez	Premia
Direct materials costs	$1,020,000	$ 720,000
Direct manufacturing labour costs	360,000	240,000
Direct machine costs	180,000	120,000
Machine setup costs	36,000	67,500
Testing costs	300,000	285,000
Engineering costs	204,000	336,000
Total manufacturing and full product costs	$2,100,000	$1,768,500
Number of units	50,000	25,000
Full product cost per unit	$42.00	$70.74

2. Markup on full product cost per unit of Tvez $= \dfrac{\text{Selling price} - \text{Full product cost}}{\text{Full product cost}}$

$$= \frac{\$48.72 - \$42}{\$42} = \frac{\$6.72}{\$42} = 16\%$$

3. The target price for New Tvez is $41.76.

Suppose the target cost per unit of New Tvez is $X.

Then $X(1.16) = $41.76

That is, $X $= \dfrac{\$41.76}{1.16} = \$36$

4. Activity-based costs of New Tvez are as follows:

Direct materials ($20.40 − $2.40) × 50,000 units	$ 900,000
Direct manufacturing labour ($7.20 − $0.60) × 50,000 units	330,000
Direct machining* (fixed)	180,000
Machine setup costs	
(7 hours × 100 setups × $30 per setup hour)	21,000
Testing costs (2.5 hours − 0.5 hours) × 50,000 × $2.40	240,000
Engineering costs (same as for Tvez)	204,000
Manufacturing and full product costs	$1,875,000
Number of units	50,000
Manufacturing and full product costs per unit	$ 37.50

*Machining costs are long-run fixed costs and so will not change even though it requires 20 fewer minutes to make each unit of New Tvez.

The New Tvez design will reduce the manufacturing costs per unit by $4.50 ($42 – $37.50), not the $6 ($42 – $36) necessary to reduce the cost of New Tvez to $36. Hence New Tvez will not achieve the targeted cost reductions.

5. Price of New Tvez using a 16% markup on full product costs of $37.50 = $37.50 × 1.16 = $43.50.

6. Avery should charge the target price of $41.76 to maintain its market of 50,000 units. If it uses the cost-plus price of $43.50, Avery risks losing some of its market share for New Tvez. Avery should strive to further reduce costs and achieve its target cost, either by changing the design to reduce cost drivers more, or by reducing the costs per unit of the cost driver.

CHAPTER 13
STRATEGY, BALANCED SCORECARD, AND STRATEGIC PROFITABILITY ANALYSIS

13-2 The five key forces to consider in industry analysis are: (a) competitors, (b) potential entrants into the market, (c) equivalent products, (d) bargaining power of customers, and (e) bargaining power of input suppliers.

13-4 The four key perspectives in the balanced scorecard are: (1) Financial perspective—this perspective evaluates the profitability of the strategy, (2) Customer perspective—this perspective identifies the targeted market segments and measures the company's success in these segments, (3) Internal business process perspective—this perspective focuses on internal operations that further both the customer perspective by creating value for customers and the financial perspective by increasing shareholder wealth, and (4) Learning and growth perspective—this perspective identifies the capabilities in which the organization must excel in order to achieve superior internal processes that create value for customers and shareholders.

13-6 A good balanced scorecard design has several features:
1. It tells the story of a company's strategy by articulating a sequence of cause-and-effect relationships.
2. It helps to communicate the strategy to all members of the organization by translating the strategy into a coherent and linked set of understandable and measurable operational targets.
3. It places strong emphasis on financial objectives and measures in for-profit companies. Nonfinancial measures are regarded as part of a program to achieve future financial performance.
4. It limits the number of measures to only those that are critical to the implementation of strategy.
5. It highlights suboptimal tradeoffs that managers may make when they fail to consider operational and financial measures together.

13-8 Three key components in doing a strategic analysis of operating income are:
1. The growth component which measures the change in operating income attributable solely to an increase in the quantity of output sold from one year to the next.
2. The price-recovery component which measures the change in operating income attributable solely to changes in the prices of inputs and outputs from one year to the next.
3. The productivity component which measures the change in costs attributable to a change in the quantity of inputs used in the current year relative to the quantity

of inputs that would have been used in the previous year to produce current year output.

13-10 Engineered costs result from a cause-and-effect relationship between the cost driver, output, and the (direct or indirect) resources used to produce that output. Discretionary costs arise from periodic (usually) annual decisions regarding the maximum amount to be incurred. There is no measurable cause-and-effect relationship between output and resources used.

13-12 Downsizing (also called rightsizing) is an integrated approach configuring processes, products, and people in order to match costs to the activities that need to be performed for operating effectively and efficiently in the present and future.

13-14 Total factor productivity is the quantity of output produced divided by the costs of all inputs used, where the inputs are costed on the basis of current period prices.

13-16   (15 min.)   Balanced scorecard.

1. La Quinta's 2007 strategy is a cost leadership strategy. La Quinta plans to grow by producing high-quality boxes at a low cost delivered to customers in a timely manner. La Quinta's boxes are not differentiated, and there are many other manufacturers who produce similar boxes. To succeed, La Quinta must achieve lower costs relative to competitors through productivity and efficiency improvements.

2. Measures that we would expect to see on La Quinta's balanced scorecard for 2007 are

    Financial Perspective
    (1) Operating income from productivity gain, (2) operating income from growth, (3) cost reductions in key areas.
    These measures evaluate whether La Quinta has successfully reduced costs and generated growth through cost leadership.

    Customer Perspective
    (1) Market share, (2) new customers, (3) customer satisfaction index, (4) customer retention, (5) time taken to fulfill customer orders.
    The logic is that improvements in these customer measures are leading indicators of superior financial performance.

Internal Business Process Perspective
(1) Yield, (2) productivity, (3) order delivery time, (4) on-time delivery.

Improvements in these measures are expected to lead to more satisfied customers and in turn to superior financial performance.

Learning and Growth Perspective
(1) Percentage of employees trained in process and quality management, (2) employee satisfaction, (3) number of major process improvements.

Improvements in these measures have a cause-and-effect relationship with improvements in internal business processes, which in turn lead to customer satisfaction and financial performance.

13-18 (15 min.) Strategy, balanced scorecard.

1. Meredith Corporation follows a product differentiation strategy in 2007. Meredith's D4H machine is distinct from its competitors and generally regarded as superior to competitors' products. To succeed, Meredith must continue to differentiate its product and charge a premium price.

2. Balanced Scorecard measures for 2007 follow:

Financial Perspective
(1) Increase in operating income from charging higher prices, (2) Price premium earned on products.

These measures indicate whether Meredith has been able to charge premium prices and achieve operating income increases through product differentiation.

Customer Perspective
(1) Market share in high-end special-purpose textile machines, (2) customer satisfaction, (3) new customers.

Improvements in these customer measures are leading indicators of superior financial performance.

Internal Business Process Perspective
(1) Manufacturing quality, (2) new product features added, (3) order delivery time.

Improvements in these measures are expected to result in more satisfied customers and in turn superior financial performance.

Learning and Growth Perspective

(1) Development time for designing new machines, (2) improvements in manufacturing processes, (3) employee education and skill levels, (4) employee satisfaction.

Improvements in these measures have a cause-and-effect relationship with improvements in internal business processes, which in turn lead to customer satisfaction and financial performance.

13-20 (20 min.) Analysis of growth, price-recovery, and productivity components (continuation of 13-19).

Effect of the industry-market-size factor
If the 10-unit increase in sales from 200 to 210 units, 3% or 6 (3% × 200) units is due to growth in market size, and 4 (10 – 6) units is due to an increase in market share. The change in Meredith's operating income from the industry-market-size factor rather than from specific strategic actions is:

\$336,000 F (the growth component in Exercise 13-19) $\times \dfrac{6}{10}$	\$201,600 F

Effect of product differentiation
The change in operating income due to:

Increase in the selling price of D4H (revenue effect of price recovery)	\$504,000 F
Increase in price of inputs (cost effect of price recovery)	221,400 U

Growth in market share due to product differentiation

\$336,000 (the growth component in Exercise 13-19) $\times \dfrac{4}{10}$	134,400 F
Change in operating income due to product differentiation	\$417,000 F

Effect of cost leadership
The change in operating income from cost leadership is:

Productivity component	\$110,400F

The change in operating income between 2006 and 2007 can be summarized as follows:

Change due to industry-market-size	\$201,600 F
Change due to product differentiation	417,000 F
Change due to cost leadership	110,400 F
Change in operating income	\$729,000 F

Meredith has been successful in implementing its product differentiation strategy. Over 57.2% ($417,000 ÷ $729,000) of the increase in operating income during 2007 was due to product differentiation. Meredith's operating income increase in 2007 was also helped by a growth in the overall market and some productivity improvements.

13-22 (15 min.) Strategy, balanced scorecard, service company.

1. Snyder Corporation's strategy in 2007 is cost leadership. Snyder's consulting services for implementing sales management software are not distinct from its competitors. The market for these services is very competitive. To succeed, Snyder must deliver quality service at low cost. Improving productivity while maintaining quality is key.

2. Balanced Scorecard measures for 2007 follow:

Financial Perspective
(1) Increase operating income from productivity gains and growth, (2) revenues per employee, (3) cost reductions in key areas, for example, software implementation and overhead costs.

   These measures indicate whether Snyder has been able to reduce costs and achieve operating income increases through cost leadership.

Customer Perspective
(1) Market share, (2) new customers, (3) customer responsiveness, (4) customer satisfaction.

   Improvements in these customer measures are regarded as leading indicators of superior financial performance.

Internal Business Process Perspective
(1) Time to complete customer jobs, (2) time lost due to errors, (3) quality of job (Is system running smoothly after job is completed?). (4) Customer conformance exceeded.

   Improvements in these measures are expected to lead to more satisfied customers, lower costs, and superior financial performance.

Learning and Growth Perspective
(1) Time required to analyze and design implementation steps, (2) time taken to perform key steps implementing the software, (3) skill levels of employees, (4) hours of employee training, (5) employee satisfaction and motivation.

Improvements in these measures have a cause-and-effect relationship with improvements in internal business processes, customer satisfaction, and financial performance.

13-24 (25 min.) Analysis of growth, price-recovery and productivity components (continuation of 13-23).

Effect of industry-market-size factors
Of the 10-unit increase in sales from 60 to 70 units, 5% or 3 units (5% x 60) is due to growth in market size, and 7 (10 – 3) units is due to an increase in market share. The change in Snyder's operating income from the industry market-size factor rather than from specific strategic actions is:

$$\$240,000 \text{ (the growth component in Exercise 13-23)} \times \frac{3}{10} \qquad \$72,000 \text{ F}$$

Effect of product differentiation
Of the $2,400 decrease in selling price, 1% or $600 (1% × $60,000) is due to a general decline in prices, and the remaining decrease of $1,800 ($2,400 – $600) is due to a strategic decision by Snyder's management to implement its cost leadership strategy of lowering prices to stimulate demand.

The change in operating income due to a decline in selling price (other than the strategic reduction in price included in the cost leadership component) $600 × 70 units	$ 42,000 U
Increase in prices of inputs (cost effect of price recovery)	154,800 U
Change in operating income due to product differentiation	$196,800 U

Effect of cost leadership

Productivity component	$226,800 F
Effect of strategic decision to reduce selling price, $1,800 × 70	126,000 U

Growth in market share due to productivity improvement and strategic decision to reduce selling price

$$\$240,000 \text{ (the growth component in Exercise 13-23)} \times \frac{7}{10} \qquad 168,000 \text{ F}$$

Change in operating income due to cost leadership	$268,800 F

The change in operating income between 2006 and 2007 can then be summarized as

Change due to industry-market-size	$72,000 F
Change due to product differentiation	196,800 U
Change due to cost leadership	268,800 F
Change in operating income	$144,000 F

Snyder has been very successful in implementing its cost leadership strategy. Due to a lack of product differentiation, Snyder was unable to pass along increases in labour costs by increasing the selling price—in fact selling price declined by $2,400 per work unit. However, Snyder was able to take advantage of its productivity gains to reduce price, gain market share, and increase operating income.

13-26 (20-30 min.) **Balanced scorecard.**

Perspectives	Strategic Objectives	Performance Measures
• Financial	• Increase shareholder value	• Earnings per share • Net income • Return on assets • Return on sales • Return on equity • Product cost per unit
	• Increase profit generated by each salesperson	• Customer cost per unit • Profit per salesperson
• Customer	• Acquire new customers • Retain customers • Develop profitable customers	• Number of new customers • Percentage of customers retained • Customer profitability
• Internal Business Process	• Improve manufacturing quality • Introduce new products • Minimize invoice error rate • On-time delivery by suppliers • Increase proprietary products	• Percentage of defective product units • Percentage of error-free invoices • Percentage of on-time deliveries by suppliers • Number of patents
• Learning and Growth	• Increase information system capabilities • Enhance employee skills	• Percentage of processes with real-time feedback • Employee turnover rate • Average job-related training hours per employee

13-28 (20 min.) **Balanced scorecard.**

1. Caltex's strategy is to focus on "service-oriented customers" who are willing to pay a higher price for services. Even though its product is largely a commodity product, gasoline, Caltex wants to differentiate itself through the service it provides at its retailing stations.

    Does the scorecard represent Caltex's strategy? By and large it does. The focus of the scorecard is on measures of process improvement, quality, market share, and financial success from product differentiation. There are some deficiencies that the subsequent assignment questions raise but, abstracting from these concerns for the moment, the scorecard does focus on implementing a product differentiation strategy.

    Having concluded that the scorecard has been reasonably well designed, how has Caltex performed relative to its strategy in 2007? It appears from the scorecard that Caltex was successful in implementing its strategy in 2007. It achieved all targets in the financial, internal business, and learning and growth perspectives. The only target it missed was the market share target in the customer perspective. At this stage, students may raise some questions about whether this is a good scorecard measure. Requirement 3 gets at this issue in more detail. The bottom line is that measuring "market share in the overall gasoline market" rather than in the "service-oriented customer market segment" is not a good scorecard measure, so not achieving this target may not be as big an issue as it may seem at first.

2. Yes, Caltex should include some measure of employee satisfaction and employee training in the learning and growth perspective. Caltex's differentiation strategy and ability to charge a premium price is based on customer service. The key to good, fast, and friendly customer service is well-trained and satisfied employees. Untrained and dissatisfied employees will have poor interactions with customers and cause the strategy to fail. Hence, training and employee satisfaction are very important to Caltex for implementing its strategy. These measures are leading indicators of whether Caltex will be able to successfully implement its strategy and, hence, should be measured on the balanced scorecard.

3. Caltex's strategy is to focus on the 60% of gasoline consumers who are service-oriented not on the 40% price-shopper segment. To evaluate if it has been successful in implementing its strategy, Caltex needs to measure its market share in its targeted market segment, "service-oriented customer," not its market share in the overall market. Given Caltex's strategy, it should not be concerned if its market share in the price-shopper segment declines. In fact, charging premium prices will probably cause its market share in this segment to decline. Caltex should replace "market share in overall gasoline market" with "market share in the service-oriented customer segment" in its balanced scorecard customer measure. Caltex may also want to consider putting a customer satisfaction measure on the scorecard. This measure should capture an overall evaluation of

customer reactions to the facility, the convenience store, employee interactions, and quick turnaround. The customer satisfaction measure would serve as a leading indicator of market share in the service-oriented customer segment.

4. Although there is a cause-and-effect link between internal business process measures and customer measures on the current scorecard, Caltex should add more measures to tighten this linkage. In particular, the current scorecard measures focus exclusively on refinery operations and not on gas station operations. Caltex should add measures of gas station performance such as cleanliness of the facility, turnaround time at the gas pumps, the shopping experience at the convenience store, and the service provided by employees. Many companies do random audits of their facilities to evaluate how well their branches and retail outlets are performing. These measures would serve as leading indicators of customer satisfaction and market share in Caltex's targeted segments.

5. Caltex is correct in not measuring changes in operating income from productivity improvements on its scorecard under the financial perspective. Caltex's strategy is to grow by charging premium prices for customer service. The scorecard measures focus on Caltex's success in implementing this strategy. Productivity gains per se are not critical to Caltex's strategy and, hence, should not be measured on the scorecard.

13-30 (35 min.) Analysis of growth, price-recovery, and productivity improvements.

1. Halsey is following a product differentiation strategy. Halsey offers a wide selection of clothes and excellent customer service. Halsey's strategy is to distinguish itself from its competitors and to charge a premium price.

2. Operating income for each year is as follows:

	2006	2007
Revenues ($72 × 40,000; $70.80 × 40,000)	$2,880,000	$2,832,000
Costs		
Materials costs ($48 × 40,000; $49.20 × 40,000)	1,920,000	1,968,000
Selling & customer service costs		
($8.40 × 51,000); $8.28 × 43,000)	428,400	356,040
Purchasing & admin. costs ($300 × 980; $288 × 850)	294,000	244,800
Total costs	2,642,400	2,568,840
Operating income	$ 237,600	$ 263,160
Change in operating income	$25,560 F	

3. **The Growth Component**

$$
\begin{pmatrix} \text{Revenue effect} \\ \text{of growth} \\ \text{component} \end{pmatrix} = \begin{pmatrix} \text{Actual units of} & & \text{Actual units of} \\ \text{output sold} & - & \text{output sold} \\ \text{in 2007} & & \text{in 2006} \end{pmatrix} \times \begin{matrix} \text{Output} \\ \text{price} \\ \text{in 2006} \end{matrix}
$$

$$
= (40{,}000 - 40{,}000) \times \$72 = \$0
$$

$$
\begin{pmatrix} \text{Cost effect of} \\ \text{price-recovery} \\ \text{component} \end{pmatrix} = \begin{pmatrix} \text{Actual units of input or} \\ \text{capacity that would} \\ \text{have been used to produce} & - & \begin{matrix} \text{Actual units of} \\ \text{inputs or capacity} \\ \text{used to produce} \\ \text{2006 output} \end{matrix} \\ \text{year 2007 output assuming} \\ \text{the same input-output} \\ \text{relationship that existed in 2006} \end{pmatrix} \times \begin{matrix} \text{Input} \\ \text{prices} \\ \text{in 2006} \end{matrix}
$$

Materials costs that would be required in 2007 would be the same as that required in 2006 because output is the same between 2006 and 2007. Manufacturing conversion costs and selling and customer-service costs will not change since adequate capacity exists in 2006 to support year 2007 output and customers.

The cost effects of growth component are:

Materials costs	$(40{,}000 - 40{,}000)$	$\times$	$\$72$	$=$	$\$0$
Selling & cust.-serv. costs	$(51{,}000 - 51{,}000)$	$\times$	$\$8.40$	$=$	0
Purch. & admin. costs	$(980 - 980)$	$\times$	$\$300$	$=$	$\underline{0}$
Cost effect of growth component				$=$	$\underline{\underline{\$0}}$

In summary, the net effect on operating income as a result of the growth component equals:

Revenue effect of growth component	$\$0$
Cost effect of growth component	$\underline{0}$
Change in operating income due to growth component	$\underline{\underline{\$0}}$

The Price-Recovery Component

$$\begin{matrix} \text{Revenue effect of} \\ \text{price-recovery} \\ \text{component} \end{matrix} = \begin{pmatrix} \text{Output price} \\ \text{in 2007} \end{pmatrix} - \begin{matrix} \text{Output price} \\ \text{in 2006} \end{matrix} \times \begin{matrix} \text{Actual units} \\ \text{of output} \\ \text{sold in 2007} \end{matrix}$$

$$= (\$70.80 - \$72) \times 40,000 = \$48,000 \text{ U}$$

$$\begin{matrix} \text{Cost effect of} \\ \text{price-recovery} = \\ \text{component} \end{matrix} \begin{pmatrix} \text{Input} \\ \text{prices in} \\ \text{year} \\ 2007 \end{pmatrix} - \begin{matrix} \text{Input} \\ \text{prices in} \\ \text{year} \\ 2006 \end{matrix} \times \begin{matrix} \text{Actual units of inputs or capacity} \\ \text{that would have been used} \\ \text{to produce year 2007 output} \\ \text{assuming the same input-output} \\ \text{relationship that} \\ \text{existed in 2006} \end{matrix}$$

Materials costs	($49.20 – $48)	×	40,000	= $48,000 U
Selling & cust.-serv. costs	($8.28 – $8.40)	×	51,000	= 6,120 F
Purch. & admin. costs	($288 – $300)	×	980	= $11,760 F
Total cost effect of price-recovery component				$30,120 U

In summary, the net decrease in operating income as a result of the price-recovery component equals:

Revenue effect of price-recovery component	$48,000 U
Cost effect of price-recovery component	30,120 U
Change in operating income due to price-recovery component	$78,120 U

The Productivity Component

$$\begin{matrix} \text{Productivity} \\ \text{component} \end{matrix} = \begin{pmatrix} \text{Actual units of} \\ \text{inputs or capacity} \\ \text{used to produce} \\ \text{year 2007 output} \end{pmatrix} - \begin{matrix} \text{Actual units of inputs or} \\ \text{capacity that would} \\ \text{have been used to produce} \\ \text{year 2007 output assuming} \\ \text{the same input-output} \\ \text{relationship that existed in 2006} \end{matrix} \times \begin{matrix} \text{Input} \\ \text{prices} \\ \text{in 2007} \end{matrix}$$

The productivity component of cost changes are:

Materials costs (40,000 – 40,000)	× $49.20	=	0
Selling & cust.-serv. costs (43,000 – 51,000)	× $8.28	=	$66,240 F
Purchasing & admin. costs (850 – 980)	× $288	=	37,440 F
Change in operating income due to productivity component			$103,680 F

The change in operating income between 2006 and 2007 can be analyzed as follows:

	Income Statement Amounts in 2006 (1)	Revenue and Cost Effects of Growth Component in 2007 (2)	Revenue and Cost Effects of Price-Recovery Component in 2007 (3)	Cost Effect of Productivity Component in 2007 (4)	Income Statement Amounts in 2007 (5) = (1)+(2)+(3)+(4)
Revenues	$2,880,000	$0	$48,000 U	—	$2,832,000
Costs	2,642,400	0	30,120 U	$103,680 F	2,568,840
Operating income	$ 237,600	$0	$78,120 U	$103,680 F	$ 263,160

$25,560 F

Change in operating income

4. The analysis of operating income indicates that a significant amount of the increase in operating income resulted from productivity gains rather than product differentiation. The company was unable to charge a premium price for its clothes. Thus, the strategic analysis of operating income indicates that Halsey has not been successful at implementing its premium price and product differentiation strategy, despite the fact that operating income increased by more than 10% between 2006 and 2007. Halsey could not pass on increases in purchase costs to its customers via higher prices. Halsey must either reconsider its strategy or focus managers on increasing margins and growing market share by offering better product variety and superb customer service.

13-32 (20 min.) Engineered and discretionary overhead costs, unused capacity, repairs and maintenance.

1. Rowland's repair and maintenance costs are indirect, engineered costs. The amount of repair and maintenance costs each year may not correlate directly to the quantity of gears produced. Over time, however, there is a clear cause-and-effect relationship between the output (quantity of gears produced) and repair and maintenance costs—the more gears that are produced, the greater the number of hours the machines will be run, and the greater the repairs and maintenance the machines will need.

2. (1) Available repair and maintenance capacity
       8 hours per day x 250 days × 4 workers   8,000 hours
   (2) Repair and maintenance work actually done   6,000 hours
   (3) = (1) – (2) Hours of unused repair and maintenance capacity   2,000 hours
   (4) Repair and maintenance cost per hour, $48,000 ÷ 2,000 $24 per hour
   (5) = (3) × (4) Cost of unused repair and maintenance capacity $48,000

Reasons why Rowland might want to downsize its repair and maintenance capacity are:

    a.   to reduce costs of carrying unused capacity

    b.   to create a culture of streamlining processes and operating efficiently

Reasons why Rowland might not want to downsize its repair and maintenance capacity are:

    a.   it projects greater demand for repairs and maintenance activity in the near future

    b.   it would negatively affect employee morale

    c.   it may want to use the expertise of the repairs and maintenance staff in other areas such as process improvements

    d.   it does not regard the unused capacity as particularly excessive

3.   If repair and maintenance costs are discretionary costs, calculating unused capacity is much more difficult. Repair and maintenance costs would be discretionary if repair and maintenance are mostly of a preventive type that management can choose when to do. In this case, the lack of a cause-and-effect relationship between output and repair and maintenance activity means that Rowland cannot determine the repair and maintenance resources used and, hence, the amount of unused capacity.

13-34 (20 min.) Partial productivity measurement.

1.   Berkshire Corporation's partial productivity ratios in 2007 are as follows:

$$\frac{\text{Direct materials}}{\text{partial productivity}} = \frac{\text{Quantity of output produced in 2007}}{\text{Kilograms of direct materials used in 2007}} = \frac{525,000}{610,000} = 0.86 \text{ units per kg}$$

$$\frac{\text{Direct manuf. labour}}{\text{partial productivity}} = \frac{\text{Quantity of output produced in 2007}}{\text{Direct manuf. labour-hours used in 2007}} = \frac{525,000}{9,500} = 55.26 \text{ units per labour-hour}$$

$$\frac{\text{Manufacturing overhead}}{\text{partial productivity}} = \frac{\text{Quantity of output produced in 2007}}{\text{Units of manuf. capacity in 2007}} = \frac{525,000}{582,000} = 0.9 \text{ units per unit of capacity}$$

To compare partial productivities in 2007 with partial productivities in 2006, we first calculate the inputs that would have been used in 2006 to produce year 2007's 525,000 units of output assuming the year 2006 relationship between inputs and outputs.

$$\text{Direct materials} \quad = \quad 450{,}000 \text{ kg (2006)} \times \frac{525{,}000 \text{ output units in 2007}}{375{,}000 \text{ output units in 2006}}$$

$$= \quad 450{,}000 \times 1.4 = 630{,}000 \text{ kg}$$

$$\text{Direct manuf. labour} \quad = \quad 7{,}500 \text{ hours (2006)} \times \frac{525{,}000 \text{ output units in 2007}}{375{,}000 \text{ output units in 2006}}$$

$$= \quad 7{,}500 \times 1.4 = 10{,}500 \text{ labour-hours}$$

Manufacturing capacity = 600,000 units of capacity, because manufacturing capacity is fixed, and adequate capacity existed in 2006 to produce year 2007 output.

Partial productivity calculations for 2006 based on year 2007 output (to make the partial productivities comparable across the two years)

$$\frac{\text{Direct materials}}{\text{partial productivity}} = \frac{\text{Quantity of output produced in 2007}}{\substack{\text{Kilograms of direct materials that would} \\ \text{have been used in 2006 to produce} \\ \text{year 2007 output}}} = \frac{525{,}000}{630{,}000} = 0.83 \text{ units per kg}$$

$$\frac{\text{Direct manuf. labour}}{\text{partial productivity}} = \frac{\text{Quantity of output produced in 2007}}{\substack{\text{Direct manuf. labour-hours that would} \\ \text{have been used in 2006 to produce} \\ \text{year 2007 output}}} = \frac{525{,}000}{10{,}500} = \substack{50 \text{ units} \\ \text{per} \\ \text{labour-hour}}$$

$$\frac{\text{Manufacturing overhead}}{\text{partial productivity}} = \frac{\text{Quantity of output produced in 2007}}{\substack{\text{Units of manuf. capacity that would} \\ \text{have been used in 2006 to produce} \\ \text{year 2007 output}}} = \frac{525{,}000}{600{,}000} = \substack{0.875 \text{ units} \\ \text{per unit of} \\ \text{capacity}}$$

The calculations indicate that Berkshire improved the partial productivity of all its inputs between 2006 and 2007 via improvements in efficiency of direct materials and direct manufacturing labour and by reducing unused manufacturing capacity.

2. All partial productivity ratios increase from 2006 to 2007. We can therefore conclude that total factor productivity definitely increased from 2006 to 2007. Partial productivities cannot, however, tell us how much total factor productivity changed, because partial productivity measures cannot be aggregated over different inputs.

3. Berkshire Corporation management can use the partial productivity measures to set targets for the next year. Partial productivity measures can easily be compared over multiple periods. For example, they may specify bonus payments if partial

productivity of direct manufacturing labour increases to 60 units of output per direct manufacturing labour-hour and if partial productivity of direct materials improves to 0.90 units of output per kilogram of direct materials. A major advantage of partial productivity measures is that they focus on a single input; hence, they are simple to calculate and easy to understand at the operations level. Managers and operators can also examine these numbers to understand the reasons underlying productivity changes from one period to the next—better training of workers, lower absenteeism, lower labour turnover, better incentives, or improved methods. Management can then implement and sustain these factors in the future.

13-36 (25 min.) Balanced scorecard, ethics.

1. Yes, the Household Products Division (HPD) should include measures of employee satisfaction and customer satisfaction even if these measures are subjective. For a maker of kitchen dishwashers, employee and customer satisfaction are leading indicators of future financial performance. There is a cause-and-effect linkage between these measures and future financial performance. If HPD's strategy is correct and if the scorecard has been properly designed, employee and customer satisfaction information is very important in evaluating the implementation of HPD's strategy.

   HPD should use employee and customer satisfaction measures even though these measures are subjective. One of the pitfalls to avoid when implementing a balanced scorecard is not to use only objective measures in the scorecard. Of course, HPD should guard against inaccuracy and potential for manipulation. Patricia Conley appears to be aware of this. She has tried to understand the reasons for the poor scores and has been able to relate these scores to other objective evidence such as employee dissatisfaction with the new work rules and customer unhappiness with missed delivery dates.

2. Incorrect reporting of employee and customer satisfaction ratings to make divisions performance look good is unethical. In assessing the situation, a management accountant should consider the following:

   Accuracy is how close you are to the real-world value. Precision is reproductibility and is neither necessary nor sufficient with respect to accuracy.

   Clear reports using relevant and reliable information should be prepared. Preparing reports on the basis of incorrect employee and customer satisfaction ratings in order to make the division's performance look better than it is, is unethical.

   The management accountant has a responsibility to avoid actual or apparent conflicts of interest and advise all appropriate parties of any potential conflict. Conley may be tempted to report better employee and customer satisfaction ratings to please Emburey. The management accountant should communicate favourable as well as unfavourable information.

A management accountant should require that information be fairly and objectively communicated and that all relevant information should be disclosed.

Conley should indicate to Emburey that the employee and customer satisfaction ratings are, indeed, appropriate. If Emburey still insists on reporting better employee and customer satisfaction numbers, Conley should raise the matter with one of Emburey's superiors. If, after taking all these steps, there is continued pressure to overstate employee and customer satisfaction ratings, Conley should consider resigning from the company and not engage in unethical behaviour.

CHAPTER 14
COST ALLOCATION

14-2 The salary of a plant security guard would be a direct cost when the cost object is the security department or the plant. It would be an indirect cost when the cost object is a product.

14-4 Exhibit 14-2 lists four criteria used to guide cost allocation decisions:
1. Cause and effect.
2. Benefits received.
3. Fairness or equity.
4. Ability to bear.

Either the cause-and-effect criterion or the benefits received criterion is the dominant one when the purpose of the allocation is related to the economic decision purpose or the motivation purpose.

14-6 Cost-benefit considerations can affect costing choices in several ways:
(a) Classifying some immaterial costs as indirect when they could, at high cost, be traced to products, services or customers as direct costs.
(b) Using a small number of indirect cost pools when, at high cost, an increased number of indirect cost pools would provide more homogeneous cost pools.
(c) Using allocation bases that are readily available (or can be collected at low cost) when, at high cost, more appropriate cost allocation bases could be developed.

14-8 Examples of bases used to allocate corporate cost pools to operating divisions are:

Corporate Cost Pools	Possible Allocation Bases
Corporate executive dept.	Sales; assets employed; operating income
Treasury department	Sales; assets employed; estimated time or usage
Legal department	Estimated time or usage; sales; assets employed
Marketing department	Sales; number of sales personnel
Payroll department	Number of employees; payroll dollars
Human resources department	Number of employees; payroll dollars; number of new hires

14-10 Disagree. Allocating costs on "the basis of estimated long-run use by user department managers" means department managers can lower their cost allocations by deliberately underestimating their long-run use.

14-12 The *reciprocal method* is theoretically the most defensible method because it explicitly recognizes the mutual services rendered among all departments, irrespective of whether those departments are operating or support departments.

14-14 The basis for the cost allocation should be clearly defined within the government contract.

14-16 (15-20 min.) Single-rate versus dual-rate cost allocation methods.

1. The total costs in the single-cost pool are fixed ($1,100,000) and variable ($2,200,000) = $3,300,000. Ontario Company could use one of two allocation bases (budgeted usage or actual usage) given the information provided.
   - Allocation to Cambridge based on budgeted usage: (60/200) × $3,300,000 = $990,000
   - Allocation to Cambridge based on actual usage: (120/240) × $3,300,000 = $1,650,000

2. Using the dual-rate method (with separate fixed and variable cost pools), several combinations of the budgeted and actual usage allocation bases are possible:

   Fixed Cost Pool: Total costs of $1,100,000:
   - Allocation to Cambridge based on budgeted usage: (60/200) × $1,100,000 = $330,000
   - Allocation to Cambridge based on actual usage: (120/240) × $1,100,000 = $550,000

   Variable Cost Pool: Total costs of $2,200,000:
   - Allocation to Cambridge based on budgeted usage: (60/200) × $2,200,000 = $660,000
   - Allocation to Cambridge based on actual usage: (120/240) × $2,200,000 = $1,100,000

The combinations possible are:

Combination	Fixed Cost Pool	Variable Cost Pool	Allocation Function
I	Budgeted Usage	Budgeted Usage	= $330,000 + $660,000 = $990,000
II	Budgeted Usage	Actual Usage	= $330,000 + $1,100,000 = $1,430,000
III	Actual Usage	Budgeted Usage	= $550,000 + $660,000 = $1,210,000
IV	Actual Usage	Actual Usage	= $550,000 + $1,100,000 = $1,650,000

Combinations I and IV give the same cost allocations as in requirement 1. Combination II is a frequently used dual-rate method. The fixed costs are allocated using budgeted usage on the rationale that it better captures the cost of providing capacity. The variable costs are allocated using actual usage on a cause-and-effect rationale. Combination III is rarely encountered in practice.

14-18 (30 min.) Cost allocation to divisions.

1.

	Hotel	Restaurant	Casino	Rembrandt
Revenue	$16,625,000	$5,456,000	$12,540,000	$34,621,000
Direct costs	10,019,260	3,949,172	4,448,768	18,417,200
Segment margin	$ 6,605,740	$1,506,828	$ 8,091,232	16,203,800
Indirect costs				14,550,000
Income before taxes				$ 1,653,800
Segment margin %	39.73%	27.62%	64.52%	

2.

	Hotel	Restaurant	Casino	Rembrandt
Direct costs	$10,019,260	$3,949,172	$4,448,768	$18,417,200
Direct cost %	54.40%	21.44%	24.16%	100.00%
Square metres	80,000	16,000	64,000	160,000
Square metres %	50.00%	10.00%	40.00%	100.00%
# of employees	200	50	250	500
# of employees %	40.00%	10.00%	50.00%	100.00%

A: Cost allocation based on direct costs:

	Hotel	Restaurant	Casino	Rembrandt
Revenue	$16,625,000	$5,456,000	$12,540,000	$34,621,000
Direct costs	10,019,260	3,949,172	4,448,768	18,417,200
Segment margin	6,605,740	1,506,828	8,091,232	16,203,800
Allocated indirect costs	7,915,200	3,119,520	3,515,280	14,550,000
Segment pre-tax income	($ 1,309,460)	($1,612,692)	$ 4,575,952	$ 1,653,800
Segment pre-tax income %	–7.88%	–29.56%	36.49%	4.78%

B: Cost allocation based on floor space:

	Hotel	Restaurant	Casino	Rembrandt
Allocated indirect costs	$7,275,000	$1,455,000	$5,820,000	$14,550,000
Segment pre-tax income	($669,260)	$51,828	$2,271,232	$1,653,800
Segment pre-tax income %	–4.03%	0.95%	18.11%	4.78%

C: Cost allocation based on # of employees

	Hotel	Restaurant	Casino	Rembrandt
Allocated indirect costs	$5,820,000	$1,455,000	$7,275,000	$14,550,000
Segment pre-tax income	$785,740	$51,828	$816,232	$1,653,800
Segment pre-tax income %	4.73%	0.95%	6.51%	4.78%

3. The segment pre-tax income percentages show the dramatic effect of the choice of the cost allocation base on reported numbers:

Denominator	Hotel	Restaurant	Casino
Direct costs	–7.88%	–29.56%	36.49%
Floor space	–4.03	0.95	18.11
# of employees	4.73	0.95	6.51

The decision context should guide 1) whether costs should be allocated, and 2) the preferred cost allocation base. Decisions about, say, performance measurement may be made on a combination of financial and nonfinancial measures. It may well be that Rembrandt may prefer to exclude allocated costs from the financial measures to reduce areas of dispute.

Where cost allocation is required, the cause-and-effect and benefits-received criteria are recommended in Chapter 14. The $14,550,000 is a fixed overhead cost. This means that on a short-run basis, the cause-and-effect criterion is not appropriate. Rembrandt should look at how the $14,550,000 cost benefits the three divisions. This will help guide the choice of an allocation base.

4. The analysis in requirement 2 should not guide the decision on whether to shut down any of the divisions. Each division is not independent of the other two. A decision to shut down, say, the restaurant likely would negatively affect the attendance at the casino and possibly the hotel. Rembrandt should examine the future revenue and future cost implications of different resource investments in the three divisions. This is a future-oriented exercise, whereas the analysis in requirement 2 is an analysis of past costs.

14-20 (20 min.) Dual-rate cost allocation method, budgeted versus actual costs and quantities (continuation of 14-19).

1. Charges with Dual-Rate Method

Variable indirect cost rate = $1,500 per trip

Fixed indirect cost rate = $\dfrac{\$215,000 \text{ budgeted costs}}{250 \text{ budgeted trips}}$

= $860 per budgeted trip

Orange Juice Division
    Variable indirect costs, $1,500 × 200 $300,000
    Fixed indirect costs, $860 × 150   129,000
    $429,000

Grapefruit Division
    Variable indirect costs, $1,500 × 100 $150,000
    Fixed indirect costs, $860 × 100   86,000
    $236,000

2.

	Orange Juice Division	Grapefruit Juice Division
Single Rate I (budgeted rate × actual use)	$472,000	$236,000
Single Rate II (Actual rate × actual use)	440,000	220,000
Dual rate	429,000	236,000

If the dual-rate method used actual trips made as the allocation base, it would give the same answer as Single Rate I. The dual rate changes how the fixed indirect cost component is treated. By using budgeted trips made, the Orange

Juice Division is unaffected by changes from its own budgeted usage or that of other divisions.

14-22 (30 min.) Reciprocal cost allocation (continuation of 14-21).

1. The reciprocal allocation method explicitly includes the mutual services provided among all support departments. Interdepartmental relationships are fully incorporated into the support department cost allocations.

2.

$$AD = \$73,200 + 0.0833IS$$

$$IS = \$234,900 + 0.2308AD$$

$$AD = \$73,200 + [0.0833(\$234,900 + 0.2308AD)]$$

$$AD = \$73,200 + [\$19,567 + 0.019226AD]$$

$$0.980774AD = \$92,767$$

$$AD = \$92,767 \div 0.980774$$

$$\$94,586$$

$$IS = \$234,900 + (0.2308 \times \$94,586)$$

$$= \$256,730$$

Calculations with 5 decimals:

$$AD = \$73,200 + 0.08333\ IS$$

$$IS = \$234,900 + 0.23077\ AD$$

$$AD = \$73,200 + [0.08333\ (\$234,900 + 0.23077\ AD)]$$

$$AD = \$73,200\ [\$19,574 + 0.01923\ AD]$$

$$0.98077\ AD = \$92,774$$

$$AD = \$94,593$$

$$IS = \$234,900 + (0.23077 \times \$94,593)$$

$$IS = \$256,729$$

	Support Depts.		Operating Depts.		
		Info.			
	Admin.	**Systems**	**Corporate**	**Consumer**	**Total**
Costs Incurred	$73,200	$234,900	$998,770	$490,360	$1,797,230
Alloc. of Admin.					
(21/91, 42/91, 28/91)	(94,586)	21,828	43,655	29,103	
Alloc. of Info. Syst.					
(320/3,840,					
1,920/3,840,					
1,600/3,840)	21,394	(256,730)	128,365	106,971	
	$ 8*	$ (2)*	$1,170,790	$626,434	$1,797,230

*Rounding causes not to be exactly $0.

Alternative calculation with 5 decimals:

	Support Depts.		Operating Depts.		
		Info.			
	Admin.	**Systems**	**Corporate**	**Consumer**	**Total**
Costs Incurred	$73,200	$234,900	$998,770	$490,360	$1,797,230
Alloc. of Admin.					
(21/91, 42/91, 28/91)	(94,593)	21,829	43,658	29,106	
Alloc. of Info. Syst.					
(320/3,840,					
1,920/3,840,					
1,600/3,840)	21,394	(256,729)	128,365	106,970	
	$ 1*	$ 0*	$1,170,793	$626,436	$1,797,230

*Rounding causes not to be exactly $0.

3. The reciprocal method is more accurate than the direct and step-down methods when there are reciprocal relationships among support departments.

A summary of the alternatives is:

	Corporate Sales	Consumer Sales
Direct method	$1,170,817	$626,413
Step-down method		
(Admin. first)	1,169,896	627,334
Reciprocal method	1,170,790	626,434
(with 5 decimals)	1,170,793	626,436

The reciprocal method is the preferred method, although for September 2007 the numbers do not appear materially different across the alternatives.

14-24 (20-30 min.) **Allocation of common costs.**

1. The available criteria to guide cost allocations include:

    (a) Cause and effect. It is not possible to trace individual causes (either basic news <u>or</u> premium movies <u>or</u> premium sports) to individual effects (viewing by Sam or Sari or Tony). The $71 total package is a bundled product.

    (b) Benefits received. There are various ways of operationalizing the benefits received:

        (i) Monthly service charge for their prime interest—basic news for Sam ($33), premium movies for Sari ($26), and premium sports for Tony ($31). This measure captures the services available to be used by each person.

        (ii) Actual usage by each person. This would involve having a record of viewing by each person and then allocating the $71 on a % viewing time basis. This measure captures the services actually used by each person.

    (c) Ability to pay. This criteria requires the three people to agree upon their relative ability to pay. One measure here would be their respective salaries with the Toronto Fire Department.

    (d) Fairness or equity. This criteria is relatively nebulous. A straightforward approach would be to split the $71 equally among the three parties.

2. Three methods of allocating the $71 are:

	Sam	Sari	Tony
Stand-alone	$26.03	$20.51	$24.46
Incremental	12.00	26.00	33.00
Equal	23.67	23.67	23.67

(a) Stand-alone cost allocation method.

$$\text{Sam:} \quad \frac{\$33}{\$33 + \$26 + \$31} \times \$71 \quad = \quad 36.667\% \times \$71$$

$$= \quad \$26.03 \text{ (Rounded)}$$

$$\text{Sari:} \quad \frac{\$26}{\$33 + \$26 + \$31} \times \$71 \quad = \quad 28.889\% \times \$71$$

$$= \quad \$20.51 \text{ (Rounded)}$$

$$\text{Tony:} \quad \frac{\$31}{\$33 + \$26 + \$31} \times \$71 \quad = \quad 34.444\% \times \$71$$

$$= \quad \$24.46 \text{ (Rounded)}$$

(b) Incremental cost allocation method:

Assume Tony (the owner) is the primary person, Sari is first incremental party, and Sam the second incremental party.

Party	Cost Allocated	Cost Remaining to Be Allocated to Other Parties
Tony	$33	$38 ($71 − $33)
Sari	26	12 ($71 − $33 − $26)
Sam	12	0
Total	$71	

This method is sure to generate disputes over the ranking of the three parties. Notice that Sam pays only $12 despite his prime interest in the most expensive basic news package.

(c) Equal sharing of the $71 amount. Sam, Sari and Tony each pay $23.67.

Note: One student suggested the owner of the apartment (Tony) should pay the $71 and include the cable television service in the rental charge.

14-26 (30 min.) **Support department cost allocation, direct and step-down methods.**

			A/HR	IS	GOVT	CORP
1.	(a)	Direct Method				
		Costs	$620,000	$2,420,000		
		Alloc. of A/HR				
		(40/75, 35/75)	(620,000)		$330,667	$289,333
		Alloc. of I.S.				
		(30/90, 60/90)	_____	(2,420,000)	806,667	1,613,333
			$ 0	$ 0	$1,137,334	$1,902,666
	(b)	Step-Down (A/HR first)				
		Costs	$620,000	$2,420,000		
		Alloc. of A/HR				
		(0.25, 0.40, 0.35)	(620,000)	155,000	248,000	217,000
		Alloc. of I.S.				
		(30/90, 60/90)	_____	(2,575,000)	858,333	1,716,667
			$ 0	$ 0	$1,106,333	$1,933,667
	(c)	Step-Down (I.S. first)				
		Costs	$620,000	$2,420,000		
		Alloc. of I.S.				
		(0.10, 0.30, 0.60)	242,000	(2,420,000)	726,000	1,452,000
		Alloc. of A/HR				
		(40/75, 35/75)	(862,000)	_____	459,733	402,267
			$ 0	$ 0	$1,185,733	$1,854,267

2.

	GOVT	CORP
Direct method	$1,137,334	$1,902,666
Step-Down (A/HR first)	1,106,333	1,933,667
Step-Down (I.S. first)	1,185,733	1,854,267

The direct method ignores any services to other support departments. The step-down method partially recognizes support to other service departments. The information systems support group (with total budget of $2,420,000) provides 10% of its services to the A/HR group. The A/HR support group (with total budget of $620,000) provides 25% of its services to the information systems support group.

3. Three criteria that could determine the sequence in the step-down method are:

(a) Allocate service departments on a ranking of the % of their total services provided to other service departments.

    1.   Administrative/HR   25%
    2.   Information Systems   10%

(b) Allocate service departments on a ranking of the total dollar amount in the service departments.

    1.   Information Systems $2,420,000
    2.   Administrative/HR $ 620,000

(c) Allocate service departments on a ranking of the dollar amounts of service provided to other service departments

    1.   Information Systems
         $(0.10 \times \$2,420,000)$ = $242,000
    2.   Administrative/HR
         $(0.25 \times \$620,000)$ = $155,000

The choice Phoenix should make will depend on the terms of the government contract and the corporate contracts. Assume the government contract is cost plus and no terms specify the method of step-down allocation, and that Phoenix bids for corporate contracts in a highly competitive environment. Then Phoenix should choose the method that maximizes the costs charged to the government. This will increase revenue from government contracts. At the same time by reducing overhead charges on the competitive corporate contracts, Phoenix can sustain a profit at a lower bid than otherwise would be possible. In this case by allocating the IS costs first, Phoenix reduces total overhead that must be charged to corporate clients from $1,933,667 to $1,854,267. A word of caution, however, this question only provides information for a single quarter. If Phoenix' contracts extend over longer time periods and provide no flexibility to Phoenix to opportunely switch from one step-down method to another each quarter, then it would be unwise to base a decision on a single data point.

14-28 (30 min.) Support department cost allocation.

1. Using computer usage time as the allocation base for the Information Systems Department and square metres of floor space for the Facilities Department, the allocation of overhead from the support departments under the Direct and Step-Down Method, are presented below.

a) Direct Method

	Support Departments		Operating Departments		
	IS	Facilities	Programming	Consulting	Training
Budgeted overhead	$51,000	$ 26,000	$ 76,000	$ 111,000	$ 86,000
Proportion of service furnished:					
By IS:[1]			12/27	6/27	9/27
Allocation	(51,000)		$ 22,667	$ 11,333	$ 17,000
By Facilities:[2]			4/18	6/18	8/18
Allocation		($26,000)	$ 5,778	$ 8,667	$ 11,555
Totals	$ 0	$ 0	$104,445	$131,000	$114,555

[1]Allocated on the basis of 2,700 hours of computer usage.
[2]Allocated on the basis of 1,800 thousand square metres of floor space.

b) Step-Down Method

	Support Departments		Operating Departments		
	IS	Facilities	Programming	Consulting	Training
Budgeted overhead	$51,000	$ 26,000	$ 76,000	$ 111,000	$ 86,000
Proportion of service furnished:					
By IS:[1]		3/30	12/30	6/30	9/30
Allocation	(51,000)	$5,100	$ 20,400	$ 10,200	$ 15,300
By Facilities:[2]			4/18	6/18	8/18
Allocation		($31,100)	$ 6,911	$ 10,367	$ 13,822
Totals	$ 0	$ 0	$103,311	$131,567	$115,122

[1]Allocated on the basis of 3,000 hours of computer usage.
[2]Allocated on the basis of 1,800 thousand square metres of floor space.

2. The step method recognizes the services that Information Systems provides to the other support department (Facilities). In contrast, the direct method only recognizes services that support departments provide to operating departments.

    The step-down method is conceptually preferable to the direct method. Birch might consider using the reciprocal method. This method fully recognizes the reciprocal services provided between the Information Systems and Facilities departments.

14-30 (40-60 min.) Support department cost allocations; single-department cost pools; direct, step-down, and reciprocal methods.

All the following computations are in dollars.

1. Direct method:

	To X		To Y	
A	250/400 × $102,000 =	$63,750	150/400 × $102,000 =	$38,250
B	100/500 × $ 42,000 =	8,400	400/500 × $ 42,000 =	33,600
Total		$72,150		$71,850

2. Step-down method, allocating B first:

	A	B	X	Y
Costs to be allocated	$102,000	$42,000	—	—
Allocate B: (0.5, 0.1, 0.4)	21,000	(42,000)	$4,200	$16,800
Allocate A: (250/400, 150/400)	(123,000)	—	76,875	46,125
Total	$ 0	$ 0	$81,075	$62,925

Step-down method, allocating A first:

	A	B	X	Y
Costs to be allocated	$102,000	$42,000	—	—
Allocate A: (0.2, 0.5, 0.3)	(102,000)	20,400	$51,000	$30,600
Allocate B: (0.2, 0.8)	—	(62,400)	12,480	49,920
Total	$ 0	$ 0	$63,480	$80,520

Note that these methods produce significantly different results, so the choice of method may frequently make a difference in the budgeted department overhead rates.

3. Reciprocal method:

Stage 1: Let A = total costs of materials-handling department
B = total costs of power-generating department

(1) A = $102,000 + 0.5B
(2) B = $42,000 + 0.2A

Stage 2: Substituting in (1): A = $102,000 + 0.5($42,000 + 0.2A)
A = $102,000 + $21,000   + 0.1A
0.9A = $123,000
A = $136,667

301

Substituting in (2):
$$B = \$42,000 + 0.2(\$136,667)$$
$$B = \$69,333$$

Stage 3:

	A	B	X	Y
Original amounts	$102,000	$42,000	—	—
Allocation of A	(136,667)	27,333(20%)	$68,334(50%)	$41,000(30%)
Allocation of B	34,667(50%)	(69,333)	6,933(10%)	27,733(40%)
Totals accounted for	$ 0	$ 0	$75,267	$68,733

Comparison of methods:

Method of Allocation	X	Y
Direct method	$72,150	$71,850
Step-down: B first	81,075	62,925
Step-down: A first	63,480	80,520
Reciprocal method	75,267	68,773

Note that in this case the direct method produces answers that are the closest to the "correct" answers (that is, those from the reciprocal method), step-down allocating B first is next, and step-down allocating A first is least accurate.

2. At first glance, it appears that the total support cost will be $42 per unit of power plus the material handling costs. If so, Manes would be better off by purchasing from the power company. However, the decision should be influenced by the effects of the interdependencies and the fixed costs. Note that the power needs would be less (students miss this) if they were purchased from the outside:

	Outside Power Units Needed
X	100
Y	400
A (500 units minus 20% of 500 units, because there is no need to service the nonexistent power department)	400
Total units	900

Total costs, 900 × $42 = $37,800

In contrast, the total costs that would be saved by not producing the power inside would depend on the effects of the decision on various costs:

	Avoidable Costs of 1,000 Units of Power Produced Inside
Variable indirect labour and indirect material costs	$12,000
Supervision in power department	10,000
Materials handling, 20% of $72,000*	14,400
Probable minimum cost savings	$36,400
Possible additional savings:	
a. Can any supervision in materials handling be saved because of overseeing less volume? Minimum savings is probably zero; the maximum is probably 20% of $10,000 or $2,000.	?
b. Is any amortization a truly variable, wear-and-tear type of cost?	?
Total savings by not producing 1,000 units of power	$36,400 + ?

*Materials-handling costs are higher because the power department uses 20% of materials handling. Therefore, materials-handling costs will decrease by 20%.

In the short-run (at least until a capital investment in equipment is necessary) the data suggest continuing to produce internally because the costs eliminated would probably be less than the comparable purchase costs.

14-32 (15 min.) Cost allocation and motivation.

Because corporate policy encourages line managers to seek legal counsel on pertinent issues from the Legal Department, any step in the direction of reducing costs of legal department services would be consistent with the corporate policy.

Currently a user department is charged a standard fee of $400 per hour based on actual usage. It is possible that some managers may not be motivated to seek the legal counsel they need due to the high allocated cost of the service. It is also possible that those managers whose departments are currently experiencing budgetary cost overruns may be disinclined to make use of the service; it would save them from the Legal Department's cost allocation. However, it could potentially result in much costlier penalties for Environ later if the corporation inadvertently engaged in some activities that violated one or more laws.

It is quite likely that the line managers would seek legal counsel, whenever there were any pertinent legal issues, if the service were free. Making the service of the Legal Department free, however, might induce some managers to make excessive use of the service. To avoid any potential abuse, Environ may want to adjust the rate downward considerably, perhaps at a level lower than what it would cost if outside legal services were sought, but not eliminate it altogether. As long as the managers know that their respective departments would be charged for using the service, they would be disinclined to make use of it unnecessarily. However, they would be motivated to use it when necessary because it would be considered a "good value" if the standard hourly rate was low enough.

14-34 (20-30 min.) Cost allocation downward demand spiral.

1.

Total costs, six months ended June 30, 2007	$64,800,000
Fixed costs	16,700,000
Variable costs	$48,100,000

Fixed costs per month per square metre

$$= \frac{\$16,700,000 \div 6}{2,250,000} = \$7.42/6 = \$1.24$$

Variable costs per month per square metre

$$= \frac{\$48,100,000 \div 6}{2,250,000} = \$21.38/6 = \$3.56$$

2. Variable costs per month per square metre $\qquad = \qquad \$3.56$

Fixed costs per month per square metre

$$= \frac{\$36,500,000 \div 12}{2,500,000} \qquad = \qquad \underline{1.22}$$

Total costs per month per square metre $\qquad = \qquad \underline{\$4.78}$
Total costs per day per square metre (assuming 30 days) $\qquad = \qquad \underline{\$0.16}$

The cost per square metre of $0.16 per day is above the competitive rate of $0.14. Thus it is not surprising that many of his internal clients are seeking external bids.

3. Bubba should base his prices upon his total capacity of 5,000,000 square metres. This would result in costs as follows:

Variable costs per month per metre	=	$3.56
Fixed costs per month per metre		
($36,500,000 ÷ 12 ÷ 5,000,000 metres)	=	0.61
Total costs per month per metre	=	$4.17
Total costs per day per metre (assuming 30 days)	=	$0.14

Thus to generate a profit, Bubba needs to operate closer to capacity and seek ways to reduce costs.

4. The competitive rate is $0.14/m^2 per day. Based on a 30 day month the montly rate is $4.20/m^2. In the last 6 months the cost structure per month is:

Fixed	$1.24/m^2
Variable	$3.56/m^2
Total	$4.80/m^2

The gap between the competitive and actual monthly rate at full cost is $0.60/m^2 ($4.20/m^2 – $4.80/m^2). This must be a reduction to fixed costs to $0.64/m^2 ($1.24/m^2 – $0.60/m^2) in order to meet the competitive monthly rate. This requires a reduction of 51.6% ($0.64/$1.24). The capacity of Bubba must be reduced by 48.39% (1 – 0.516). The new breakeven capacity = 0.516 8 2,250,000 m^2 = 1,161,000m^2.

5. The budgeted allocated cost rate should be calculated on the basis of capacity available rather than capacity used. The fixed cost of operating Clean Shop should remain constant from one year to the next unless Clean Shop expanded its capacity or made a catastrophic error in estimating tax, insurance, lease or amortization expense that comprise fixed costs. These facts are in the data therefore you must assume there was no expansion and no unanticipated change to fixed cost components. Bubba appears to have arbitrarily doubled the fixed costs to achieve an allocated rate that will provide him a profit. His other choice is to bid for other jobs that would use his excess capacity and increase his revenue.

Bubba is not acting in Diversified's best interests by setting a rate per square metre that is above competitive market rates. In doing so he is overcharging the parent company. The situation for Bubba prior to Clean Shop being reassigned as a profit centre was that there was no incentive to find other clients to use the full capacity of Clean Shop. The internal price of the support service to Diversified was beyond the constraints set by the externally competitive market. This gave

Bubba the opportunity to charge whatever Diversified was willing to pay to cover the full costs of Clean Shop and provided no incentive to use the capacity efficiently.

14-36 (20 min.) Division managers' reactions to the allocation of central corporate costs to divisions (continuation of 14-35).

The effect of the changes proposed by Dusty Rhodes for divisional income is:

	Oil & Gas Upstream	Oil & Gas Downstream	Chemical Products	Copper Mining
Divisional income—single cost pool allocation scheme	$3,230	$(760.0)	$(240.0)	$(530.0)
Divisional income—four-cost pool allocation scheme	$2,354.4	$11.2	$(202.4)	$(463.2)

Given these changes, the reactions of the division managers are predictable. Rhodes should consider several general points when drafting his response:

- A controller is a staff function, while the division managers are line managers running multi-billion dollar enterprises.
- Cost allocation problems are ongoing issues in any organization, and ongoing refinements will likely occur continually in the future.
- Keep a clear distinction between evaluating the performance of a division and evaluating the performance of a division manager.

Oil & Gas Upstream: Observe that the proposed cost allocation scheme better captures cause-and-effect relationships than does the existing scheme. Note that the upstream division is highly capital intensive and that much of the debt was raised to acquire or develop those assets. Rhodes should also describe how Richfield Oil takes into account the Upstream's generation of a substantial positive cash flow in its performance evaluation of activities and managers.

Oil & Gas Downstream: Comment that you are glad that the proposed scheme was well received. However, stress that the changes are designed to capture cause-and-effect relationships. (You will be responding to the same manager in subsequent years and it is important that the motivations for the changes be understood. In subsequent years the same manager likely will argue the proposed changes are "unfair and inequitable.")

<u>Chemical Products:</u> Note that the manager's complaints are against cost allocation schemes in general and not against Rhodes' proposed changes. The appropriate response is to stress that the top management of Richfield Oil has decided to allocate central corporate costs (for reasons noted in requirement 1 of Problem 14-35). The manager should consider developing ways to improve the existing or proposed cost allocation schemes. Stress to the manager that top management distinguishes between the performance of a division and the performance of its manager. In evaluating the chemical products division, a better appreciation of the returns on Richfield Oil's investment can be obtained by considering the central corporate costs associated with the division. However, in evaluating managers, the ability to outperform competitors facing the same environment and to implement company-wide economy drives is highly valued (and hopefully rewarded by Richfield Oil).

<u>Copper Mining:</u> Agree with the manager that both the existing and the proposed schemes have imperfections. Specifically, admit that sometime in the future refinements in allocations of R&D may be made. One possible approach would be identification of R&D costs with projects done for each division; if no R&D is done for Copper Mining, no allocation of R&D cost would be made to Copper Mining. However, note that changes are being made gradually at Richfield Oil and that the current major issue is to get the proposed changes accepted. One point to stress is that the proposal recognizes the special problems of divisions with negative operating income (such as faced by the Copper Mining division). Rhodes proposes to allocate public affairs costs only to divisions with positive operating income.

<u>Note:</u> Richfield Oil may want to consider changes in its division compensation scheme if it makes changes in its cost allocation scheme. Major changes in one component of a management control system should not be made without considering changes in other components of the management control system.

14-38 (25 min.) Common costs.

1. Miller $= \dfrac{1,000 \times \$1.00}{(1,000 \times \$1.00) + (700 \times \$1.00)} \times (\$1,360)$

$= \dfrac{\$1,000}{\$1,000 + \$700} \times \$1,360 = \$800$

Jackson $= \dfrac{700 \times \$1.00}{(700 \times \$1.00) + (1,000 \times \$1.00)} \times (\$1,360)$

$= \dfrac{\$700}{\$700 + \$1,000} \times \$1,360 = \$560$

2.

Party	Costs Allocated	Costs Remaining to be Allocated
Miller (primary)	$1,000	$360 ($1,360 – $1,000)
Jackson (incremental)	$ 360	$ 0

If Jackson is the primary party, the allocation would be

Party	Costs Allocated	Costs Remaining to be Allocated
Jackson (primary)	$700	$660 ($1,360 – $700)
Miller (incremental)	$660	$ 0

3. Use the stand-alone cost-allocation method since it is fairer than the incremental one.

Using this approach, Miller is allocated $830 and Jackson is allocated $530 out of the total costs of $1,360. Miller and Jackson could also use the stand-alone cost allocation method to allocate the rent: Miller, $800; Jackson, $560. If they used the incremental cost-allocation method, Miller and Jackson would probably have disputes over who is the primary party because the primary party gets allocated all costs first.

14-40 (20 min.) Division cost allocation, R&D, ethics.

1. The overhead cost charged to each division for use of the Waterloo facility is:

$$
\begin{bmatrix} \text{Budgeted \% use} \\ \text{by division of} \\ \text{Waterloo facility} \end{bmatrix} \times \begin{bmatrix} \text{Budgeted overhead costs} \\ \text{at Waterloo facility} \end{bmatrix}
$$

If the ASD division understates its budgeted use of the Waterloo facility and all other divisions provide unbiased estimates of their budgeted use, the ASD division will have a lower budgeted % use factor for the Waterloo facility, and thus a lower overhead cost charge. If all divisions understate their budgeted use, those division(s) providing the greatest understatements will be those benefiting by their understatement.

2. Alternative approaches Waterloo might take include:

a. Charging a division a penalty rate when it uses a higher number of hours than it submitted as its budgeted amount.

b. Change the charge structure so that each hour of research scientist time used has a budgeted overhead charge component. (This approach only partially reduces the problem because the fixed overhead rate per hour must be determined.)

c. Use actual costs per hour rather than budgeted costs per hour as the charge to each using division.

3. Goodwin's first response should be to develop a well-constructed argument to present to Roy Masters for using the 30,000 number. Masters should be given at least one more chance to respond to Goodwin's concerns. Ideally, Goodwin should give Masters a short time period (say one week) to think about her concerns. This is especially the case if there is already documentation at ASD for the 30,000 number. Goodwin might note that if internal control people at WS are called in to consider any allegations by other divisions that ASD is deliberately understating budgeted usage, the 30,000 figure likely will be observable.

If Masters continues with his threats about dropping Goodwin from "the ASD team," she should contact the corporate controller at WS to seek guidance on how to handle the situation.

CHAPTER 15
COST ALLOCATION: JOINT PRODUCTS AND BYPRODUCTS

15-2 A *joint cost* is a cost of a single process that yields multiple products simultaneously.

15-4 A *product* is any output that has a positive sales value (or an output that enables an organization to avoid incurring costs). In some joint-cost settings, outputs can occur that do not have a positive sales value. The offshore processing of hydrocarbons yields water that is recycled back into the ocean while yielding oil and gas. The processing of mineral ore to yield gold and silver also yields dirt as an output, which is recycled back into the ground.

15-6 The joint production process yields individual products that are either sold this period or held as inventory to be sold in subsequent periods. Hence the joint costs need to be allocated between total production rather than just those sold this period.

15-8 Both methods use market selling-price data in allocating joint costs, but they differ in which sales-price data they use. The *sales value at splitoff method* allocates joint costs on the basis of each product's relative sales value at the splitoff point. The *estimated net realizable value method* allocates joint costs on the basis of the relative estimated net realizable value (expected final sales value in the ordinary course of business minus the expected separable costs of production and marketing).

15-10 The estimated NRV method can be simplified by assuming (a) a standard set of post-splitoff point processing steps and (b) a standard set of selling prices. The use of (a) and (b) achieves the same benefits that the use of standard costs does in costing systems.

15-12 No. Any method used to allocate joint costs to individual products that is applicable to the problem of joint product-cost allocation should not be used for management decisions regarding whether a product should be sold or processed further. When a product is an inherent result of a joint process, the decision to process further should not be influenced by either the size of the total joint costs or the portion of the joint costs assigned to particular products. Joint costs are irrelevant for these decisions. The only relevant items for these decisions are the incremental revenue and the incremental costs beyond the splitoff point.

15-14 Two methods to account for byproducts are:
a. Production method—recognizes byproducts in the financial statements at the time production is completed.
b. Sales method—delays recognition of byproducts until the time of sale.

15-16 (20-30 min.) Joint-cost allocation, insurance settlement.

1. (a) Sales value at splitoff method.

	Kilograms of Product	Wholesale Selling Price per Kilogram	Sales Value at Splitoff	Weighting: Sales Value at Splitoff	Joint Costs Allocated	Allocated Costs per Kilogram
Breasts	100	$1.32	$132.00	0.675	$ 67.50	0.6750
Wings	20	0.48	9.60	0.049	4.90	0.2450[1]
Thighs	40	0.84	33.60	0.172	17.20	0.4300[2]
Bones	80	0.24	19.20	0.098	9.80	0.1225[3]
Feathers	10	0.12	1.20	0.006	0.60	0.0600
	250		$195.60	1.000	$100.00	

Costs of Destroyed Product

Breasts: $0.6750 × 30 kg = $20.250
Wings: $0.2450 × 15 kg = 3.675
$23.925

[1] $4.90 ÷ 20 = $0.2450
[2] $17.20 ÷ 40 = $0.430
[3] $9.80 ÷ 80 = $0.1225

(b) Physical measures method

	Kilograms of Product	Weighting: Physical Measures	Joint Costs Allocated	Allocated Costs per Kilogram
Breasts	100	0.400	$ 40.00	$0.40
Wings	20	0.080	8.00	0.40[1]
Thighs	40	0.160	16.00	0.40[2]
Bones	80	0.320	32.00	0.40
Feathers	10	0.040	4.00	0.40
	250	1.000	$100.00	

Costs of Destroyed Product

Breast: $0.40 × 30 = $12
Wings: $0.40 × 15 = 6
$18

[1]$8.00 ÷ 20 = $0.40
[2]$16.00 ÷ 40 = $0.40

Note: Although not required, it is useful to highlight the individual product profitability figures:

Product	Sales Value	Sales Value at Splitoff Method		Physical Measures Method	
		Joint Costs Allocated	Gross Income	Joint Costs Allocated	Gross Income
Breasts	$132.00	$67.50	$64.50	$40.00	$92.00
Wings	9.60	4.90	4.70	8.00	1.60
Thighs	33.60	17.20	16.40	16.00	17.60
Bones	19.20	9.80	9.40	32.00	(12.80)
Feathers	1.20	0.60	0.60	4.00	(2.80)

2. The sales-value at splitoff method captures the benefits-received criterion of cost allocation. The costs of processing a chicken are allocated to products in proportion to the ability to contribute revenue. Chicken Little's decision to process chicken is heavily influenced by the revenues from breasts and thighs. The bones provide relatively few benefits to Chicken Little despite their high physical volume.

The physical measures method shows profits on breasts and thighs and losses on bones and feathers. Given that Chicken Little has to jointly process all the chicken products, it is counter-intuitive to single out individual products that are being processed simultaneously as making losses while the overall operations make a profit.

15-18 (20-30 min.) Net realizable value cost-allocation method, further process decision.

A diagram of the situation is in Solution Exhibit 15-18.

1.

	Quantity in Kilograms	Sales Price per Kilogram	Final Sales Value	Separable Processing Costs	Estimated Net Realizable Value at Splitoff	Weighting
Alco	20,000	$24.00	$ 480,000	$120,000	$360,000	360/672
Devo	60,000	7.20	432,000	240,000	192,000	192/672
Holo	100,000	1.20	120,000	0	120,000	120/672
Totals			$1,032,000	$360,000	$672,000	

Allocation of $504,000 joint costs:

Alco	360/672 × $504,000	=	$270,000
Devo	192/672 × $504,000	=	144,000
Holo	120/672 × $504,000	=	90,000
			$504,000

	Joint Costs Allocated	Separable Processing Costs	Total Costs	Units	Unit Cost
Alco	$270,000	$120,000	$390,000	20,000	$19.50
Devo	144,000	240,000	384,000	60,000	6.40
Holo	90,000	0	90,000	100,000	0.90
Totals	$504,000	$360,000	$864,000	180,000	

The ending inventory is:

Alco	1,000 × $19.50	=	$19,500
Devo	1,000 × $6.40	=	6,400
Holo	1,000 × $0.90	=	900
			$26,800

2.

	Unit Sales Price	Unit Cost	Gross Margin	Gross-Margin Percentage
Alco	$24.00	$19.50	$4.50	18.75%
Devo	7.20	6.40	0.80	11.11%
Holo	1.20	0.90	0.30	25.00%

3. Further processing of Devo yields incremental income of $48,000:

Incremental revenue of further processing Devo, ($7.20 – $2.40) × 60,000	$288,000
Incremental processing costs	240,000
Incremental operating income from further processing	$ 48,000

Tuscania should process Devo further. Note that joint costs are irrelevant to this decision; they remain the same, whichever alternative (sell at splitoff or process further) is selected.

SOLUTION EXHIBIT 15-18

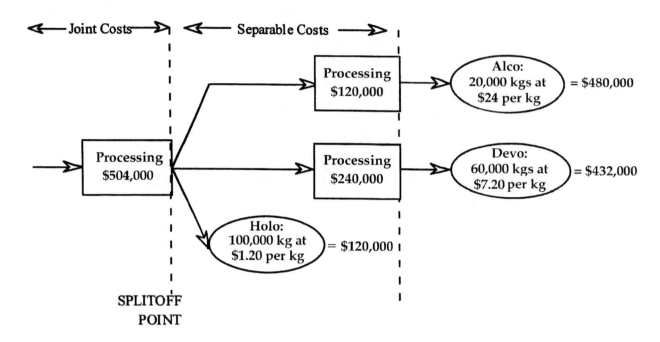

15-20 (10 min.) Estimated net realizable value method.

A diagram of the situation is in Solution Exhibit 15-20 (all numbers are in thousands).

	Cooking Oil	Soap Oil	Total
Expected final sales value of production, CO, 1,000 × $60; SO, 500 × $30	$60,000	$15,000	$75,000
Deduct expected separable costs to complete and sell	36,000	9,000	45,000
Estimated net realizable value at splitoff point	$24,000	$ 6,000	$30,000
Weighting	$\dfrac{\$24,000}{\$30,000}=0.8$	$\dfrac{\$6,000}{\$30,000}=0.2$	
Joint costs allocated, CO, 0.8 × $28,800; SO, 0.2 × $28,800	$23,040	$ 5,760	$28,800

SOLUTION EXHIBIT 15-20

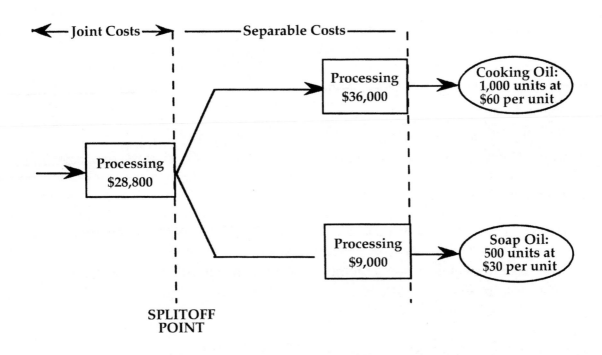

15-22 (20 min.) Joint-cost allocation, physical measures method (continuation of 15-21).

1.

	Crude Oil	NGL	Total
Expected final sales value of production	$3,240	$900	$4,140
Deduct expected separable costs	210	126	336
Estimated NRV at splitoff	$3,030	$774	$3,804
Weighting	0.7965	0.2035	1.000
Joint costs allocated (Weights × $2,160)	$1,720.44	$439.56	$2,160

	Crude Oil	NGL	Total
Sales	$3,240.00	$900.00	$4,140
Operating Costs			
Joint costs	1,720.44	439.56	2,160
Separable costs	210.00	126.00	336
Total operating costs	1,930.44	565.56	2,496
Operating margin	$1,309.56	$334.44	$1,644

2. The authorities' proposed method results in large profits on crude oil and large losses on gas:

	Crude Oil	NGL	Gas	Total
Sales	$3,240	$900	$0	$4,140
Operating Costs				
Joint costs	324	108	1,728	2,160
Separable costs	210	126	0	336
Total operating costs	534	234	1,728	2,496
Operating margin	$2,706	$666	$ (1,728)	$1,644

The main points to note are:

(a) Gas is not a salable product. It is simply a recycled output that adds no revenues. Indeed, costs are incurred to recycle the gas.

(b) The physical measure method has all the problems alluded to in the literature—e.g., it ignores the revenue-earning potential of products and it may not have a consistent denominator.

15-24 (40 min.) Process further or sell, byproduct.

1. The analysis shown below indicates that it would be more profitable for Newcastle Mining Company to continue to sell raw bulk coal without further processing. (This analysis ignores any value related to coal fines.)

Incremental sales revenues:

Sales revenue after further processing (9,500,000 tonnes × $43.20)	$410,400,000
Sales revenue from bulk raw coal (10,000,000 tonnes × $32.40)	324,000,000
Incremental sales revenue	86,400,000

Incremental costs:

Direct labour	720,000
Supervisory personnel	120,000
Heavy equipment costs ($30,000 × 12 months)	360,000
Sizing and cleaning (10,000,000 tonnes × $4.20)	42,000,000
Outbound rail freight (9,500,000 tonnes ÷ 60 tonnes) × $288 per car	45,600,000
Incremental costs	88,800,000
Incremental gain (loss)	$(2,400,000)

2. The analysis shown below indicates that the potential revenue from the coal fines byproduct would result in additional revenue, ranging between $5,250,000 and $9,000,000, depending on the market price of the fines.

a. Coal fines $\quad=\quad$ 75% of 5% of raw bulk tonnage
$\qquad\quad=\quad 0.75 \times (10,000,000 \times 0.05)$
$\qquad\quad=\quad$ 375,000 tonnes

Potential additional revenue:

	Market price	
	Minimum	**Maximum**
	$16.80 per tonne	$28.80 per tonne
Additional revenue	$6,300,000	$10,800,000

Since the incremental loss is $2.4 million, as calculated in requirement 1, including the coal fines in the analysis indicates that further processing provides a positive result and is, therefore, favourable.

b. Other factors that should be considered in evaluating a sell-or-process-further decision include:

- Stability of the current customer market and how it compares to the market for sized and cleaned coal.
- Storage space needed for the coal fines until they are sold and the handling costs of coal fines.
- Reliability of cost (e.g., rail freight rates) and revenue estimates, and the risk of depending on these estimates.
- Timing of the revenue stream from coal fines and impact on the need for liquidity.
- Possible environmental problems, i.e., dumping of waste and dust from unprocessed coal.

15-26 (35-45 min.) **Joint costs and byproducts.**

A diagram of the situation is in Solution Exhibit 15-26.

1. Computing byproduct deduction to joint costs:

Marketing price of X, 100,000 × $3.60	$360,000
Deduct: Gross margin, 10% of sales	36,000
Marketing costs, 25% of sales	90,000
Department 3 separable costs	60,000
Estimated net realizable value of X	$174,000
Joint costs	$960,000
Deduct byproduct contribution	174,000
Net joint costs to be allocated	$786,000

	Quantity	Unit Sales Price	Final Sales Value	Deduct Separable Processing Cost	Est. Net Realizable Value at Splitoff	Weighting	Allocation of $786,000 Joint Costs
L	50,000	$12.00	$ 600,000	$120,000	$ 480,000	40%	$314,400
W	300,000	2.40	720,000	—	720,000	60%	471,600
Totals			$1,320,000	$120,000	$1,200,000		$786,000

	Joint Costs Allocation	Add Separable Processing Costs	Total Costs	Units	Unit Cost
L	$314,400	$120,000	$434,400	50,000	$8.688
W	471,600	—	471,600	300,000	1.572
Totals	$786,000	$120,000	$906,000	350,000	

Unit cost for X: $3.60 − $0.36 − $0.90 = $2.34.
     or
$$\$1.74 + \$0.60^1 = \$2.34$$

---

[1] Department 3 costs = $60,000 producing 100,000 kg of X

2. If all three products are treated as joint products:

	Quantity	Unit Sales Price	Final Sales Value	Deduct Separable Processing Cost	Est. Net Realizable Value at Splitoff	Weighting	Allocation of $960,000 Joint Costs
L	50,000	$12.00	$ 600,000	$120,000	$ 480,000	48/150	$307,200
W	300,000	2.40	720,000	—	720,000	72/150	460,800
X	100,000	3.60	360,000	60,000	300,000	30/150	192,000
Totals			$1,680,000	$180,000	$1,500,000		$960,000

	Joint Costs Allocation	Add Separable Processing Costs	Total Costs	Units	Unit Cost
L	$307,200	$120,000	$427,200	50,000	$8.544
W	460,800	—	460,800	300,000	1.536
X	192,000	60,000	252,000	100,000	2.520
Totals	$960,000	$180,000	$1,140,000	450,000	

Call the attention of students to the differing unit "costs" between the two assumptions regarding the relative importance of Product X. The point is that costs of individual products depend heavily on which assumptions are made and which accounting methods and techniques are used.

SOLUTION EXHIBIT 15-26

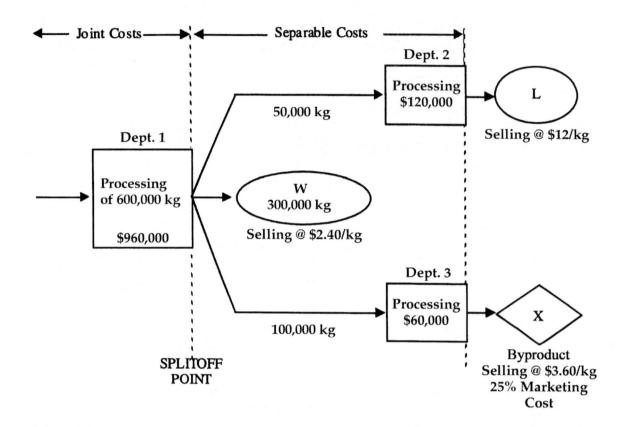

15-28 (30 min.) **Joint-cost allocation, process further or sell.**

A diagram of the situation is in Solution Exhibit 15-28.

1. a. Relative sales value method at splitoff.

	Monthly Unit Output	Selling Price per Unit	Relative Sales Value at Splitoff	% of Sales	Allocated Joint Costs
Studs (Building)	75,000	$9.60	$ 720,000	46.15%	$ 553,800
Decorative Pieces	5,000	72.00	360,000	23.08	276,960
Posts	20,000	24.00	480,000	30.77	369,240
Totals			$1,560,000	100.00%	$1,200,000

b. Physical–measure method at splitoff.

	Physical Unit Volume	% of Total Unit Volume	Allocated Joint Costs
Studs (Building)	75,000	75.00%	$ 900,000
Decorative Pieces	5,000	5.00	60,000
Posts	20,000	20.00	240,000
Totals	100,000	100.00%	$1,200,000

c. Estimated net realizable value method.

	Monthly Unit Output	Selling Price per Unit	Relative Sales Value at Splitoff	% of Sales	Allocated Joint Costs
Studs (Building)	75,000	$9.60	$ 720,000	44.44%	$ 533,280
Decorative Pieces	4,500ª	120.00	420,000ᵇ	25.93	311,160
Posts	20,000	24.00	480,000	29.63	355,560
Totals			$1,620,000	100.00%	$1,200,000

ª5,000 monthly units of output – 10% normal spoilage = 4,500 good units.
ᵇ4,500 good units × $120 = $540,000 – Further processing costs of $120,000 = $420,000

2. Presented below is an analysis for Sonimad Sawmill Inc. comparing the processing of decorative pieces further versus selling the rough-cut product immediately at splitoff.

	Units	Dollars
Monthly unit output	5,000	
Less: Normal further processing shrinkage	500	
Units available for sale	4,500	
Final sales value (4,500 units @ $120 per unit)		$540,000
Less: Sales value at splitoff (5,000 units @ $72 per unit)		360,000
Differential revenue		180,000
Less: Further processing costs		120,000
Additional contribution from further processing		$ 60,000

3. Assuming Sonimad Sawmill Inc. announces that in six months it will sell the rough-cut product at splitoff, due to increasing competitive pressure, at least three types of likely behaviour that will be demonstrated by the skilled labour in the planing and sizing process include the following.

- Poorer quality.
- Reduced motivation and morale.
- Job insecurity, leading to nonproductive employee time looking for jobs elsewhere.

Management actions that could improve this behaviour include the following.

- Improve communication by giving the workers a more comprehensive explanation as to the reason for the change in order to better understand the situation and bring out a plan for future operation of the rest of the plant.
- The company can offer incentive bonuses to maintain quality and production and align rewards with goals.
- The company could provide job relocation and internal job transfers.

SOLUTION EXHIBIT 15-28

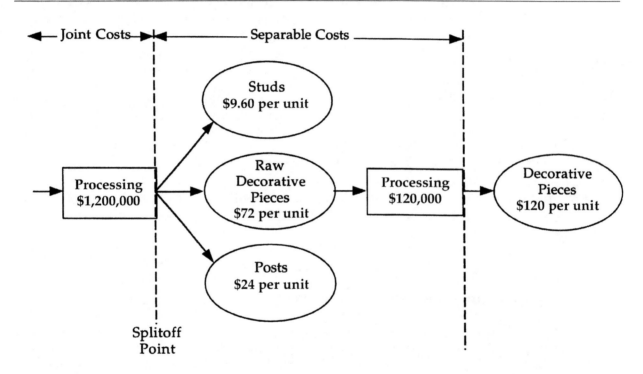

15-30 (40 min.) Alternative methods of joint-cost allocation, product-mix decisions.

A diagram of the situation is in Solution Exhibit 15-30.

1. Computation of joint-cost allocation proportions:

a.

	Sales Value at Splitoff	Proportions	Allocation of $120,000 Joint Costs
A	$ 60,000	60/240 = 0.25	$ 30,000
B	36,000	36/240 = 0.15	18,000
C	60,000	60/240 = 0.25	30,000
D	84,000	84/240 = 0.35	42,000
	$240,000	1.00	$120,000

b.

	Physical Measure	Proportions	Allocation of $120,000 Joint Costs
A	300,000 litres	300/500 = 0.60	$ 72,000
B	100,000 litres	100/500 = 0.20	24,000
C	50,000 litres	50/500 = 0.10	12,000
D	50,000 litres	50/500 = 0.10	12,000
	500,000 litres	1.00	$120,000

c.

	Final Sales Value	Separable Costs	Estimated Net Realizable Value	Proportions	Allocation of $120,000 Joint Costs
A	$360,000	$240,000	$120,000	120/240 = 0.50	$ 60,000
B	120,000	96,000	24,000	24/240 = 0.10	12,000
C	60,000	—	60,000	60/240 = 0.25	30,000
D	144,000	108,000	36,000	36/240 = 0.15	18,000
	$684,000	$444,000	$240,000	1.00	$120,000

Computation of gross-margin percentages:

a. Sales value at splitoff method:

	Super A	Super B	C	Super D	Total
Sales	$360,000	$120,000	$60,000	$144,000	$684,000
Joint costs	30,000	18,000	30,000	42,000	120,000
Separable costs	240,000	96,000	0	108,000	444,000
Total costs	270,000	114,000	30,000	150,000	564,000
Gross margin	$ 90,000	$ 6,000	$30,000	$ (6,000)	$120,000
Gross-margin percentage	25%	5%	50%	(4.17%)	17.54%

323

b.   Physical-measure method:

	Super A	Super B	C	Super D	Total
Sales	$360,000	$120,000	$60,000	$144,000	$684,000
Joint costs	72,000	24,000	12,000	12,000	120,000
Separable costs	240,000	96,000	0	108,000	444,000
Total costs	312,000	120,000	12,000	120,000	564,000
Gross margin	$ 48,000	$ 0	$48,000	$ 24,000	$120,000
Gross-margin percentage	13.33%	0%	80%	16.67%	17.54%

c.   Estimated net realizable value method:

	Super A	Super B	C	Super D	Total
Sales	$360,000	$120,000	$60,000	$144,000	$684,000
Joint costs	60,000	12,000	30,000	18,000	120,000
Separable costs	240,000	96,000	0	108,000	444,000
Total costs	300,000	108,000	30,000	126,000	564,000
Gross margin	$ 60,000	$ 12,000	$30,000	$ 18,000	$120,000
Gross-margin percentage	16.67%	10%	50%	12.5%	17.54%

Summary of gross-margin percentages:

Joint-Cost Allocation Method	Super A	Super B	C	Super D
Sales value at splitoff	25.00%	5%	50%	(4.17%)
Physical measure	13.33%	0%	80%	16.67%
Estimated net realizable value	16.67%	10%	50%	12.50%

2.   Further Processing of A into Super A:

Incremental revenue, $360,000 – $60,000	$300,000
Incremental costs	240,000
Incremental operating income from further processing	$ 60,000

Further Processing of B into Super B:

Incremental revenue, $120,000 – $36,000	$ 84,000
Incremental costs	96,000
Incremental operating income from further processing	$ (12,000)

Further Processing of D into Super D:

Incremental revenue, $144,000 – $84,000	$ 60,000
Incremental costs	108,000
Incremental operating income from further processing	$(48,000)

Operating income can be increased by $60,000 if both B and D are sold at their splitoff point.

SOLUTION EXHIBIT 15-30

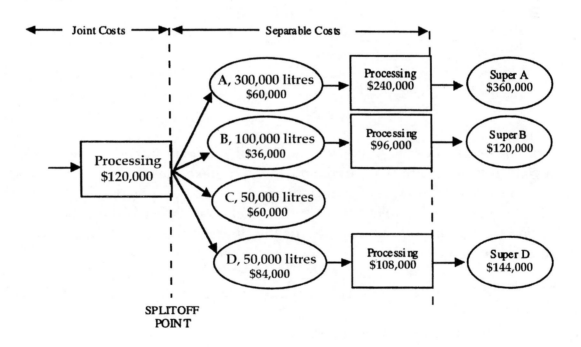

15-32 (25 min.) Joint-cost allocation, relevant costs (R. Capettini, adapted).

1. The "four-day progressive product trimming" ignores the fundamental point that the $360 cost to buy the pig is a joint cost. A pig is purchased as a whole. The butcher's challenge is to maximize the total revenues minus incremental costs (assumed zero) from the sale of all products.

    At each stage, the decision made ignores the general rule that product emphasis decisions should consider relevant revenues and relevant costs. Allocated joint costs are not relevant. For example, the Day 2 decision to drop bacon ignores the fact that the $360 joint cost has been paid to acquire the whole pig. The $172.80 of revenues are relevant inflows. This same position also holds for the Day 3 and Day 4 decisions.

2. The revenue amounts are the figures to use in the sales value at splitoff method:

Product	Revenue	Joint Costs Weighting	Allocated
Pork chops	$144.00	0.2899	$104.36
Ham	180.00	0.3623	130.43
Bacon	172.80	0.3478	125.21
	$496.80	1.0000	$360.00

3. No. The decision to sell or not sell individual products should consider relevant revenues and relevant costs. In the butcher's context, the relevant costs would be the additional time and other incidentals to take each pig part and make it a salable product. The relevant revenues would be the difference between the selling price at the consumer level for the pig parts and what the butcher may receive for the whole pig.

15-34 (30 min.) Estimated net realizable value method, byproducts.

A diagram of the situation is in Solution Exhibit 15-34.

a. For the month of November 2004, Princess Corporation's output was:
    - apple slices   89,100
    - applesauce   81,000
    - apple juice   67,500*
    - animal feed   27,000

These amounts were calculated as follows:

Product	Input	Proportion	Total Kilograms	Kilograms Lost	Net Kilograms
Slices	270,000 kg	0.33	89,100	—	89,100
Sauce	270,000	0.30	81,000	—	81,000
Juice	270,000	0.27	72,900	5,400	67,500*
Feed	270,000	0.10	27,000	—	27,000
		1.00	270,000	5,400	264,600

*Net kilograms: =   72,900 – (0.08 × net kilograms)
1.08 net kilograms =   72,900
Net kilograms   =   67,500

b. The estimated net realizable value for each of the three main products is calculated below:

Product	Net Kilograms	Price	Revenue	Separable Costs	Estimated Net Realizable Value
Slices	89,100	$0.96	$ 85,536	$13,536	$ 72,000
Sauce	81,000	0.66	53,460	10,260	43,200
Juice	67,500	0.48	32,400	3,600	28,800
			$171,396	$27,396	$144,000

c. and d.

The estimated net realizable value of the byproduct is deducted from the production costs prior to allocation to the joint products, as presented below:

Allocation of Cutting Department Costs to Joint Products and Byproducts

Net realizable value (NRV)
of byproduct

$= $ Byproduct revenue – Separable costs
$= $ $0.12 (270,000 \times 10\%) – $840
$= $ $3,240 – $840
$= $ $2,400

Costs to be allocated

$= $ Joint costs – NRV of byproduct
$= $ $72,000 – $2,400
$= $ $69,600

Product	Revenue	Separable Costs	Joint Costs	Gross Margin
Slices	$ 85,536	$13,536	$34,800[1]	$37,200
Sauce	53,460	10,260	20,880[2]	22,320
Juice	32,400	3,600	13,920[3]	14,880
	$171,396	$27,396	$69,600	$74,400

1) Slices 72K/144K × $69,600 = $34,800

2) Sauce 43.2K/144K × $69,600 = $20,880

3) Juice 28.8K/144K × $69,600 = $13,920

2. The gross-margin dollar information by main product is determined by the arbitrary allocation of joint production costs. As a result, these cost figures and the resulting gross-margin information are of little significance for planning and control purposes. The allocation is made only for purposes of inventory costing and income determination.

SOLUTION EXHIBIT 15-34

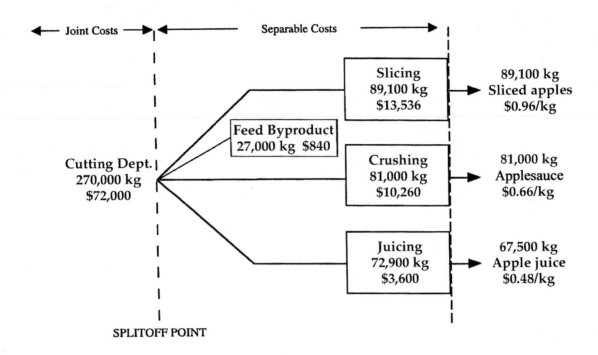

15-36 (20 min.) Byproduct, disposal costs, ethics.

1. The comparative analysis prepared by the cost accountant is flawed. In the process further alternative, he has erroneously included the $300,000 allocated joint costs. Allocated joint costs are irrelevant because they are not incremental costs of the alternative being considered. If the joint costs allocated are taken out, it becomes clear that financially it would be to the advantage of the company to process further the product as it would increase the operating income by $180,000 [$600,000 − ($360,000 + $60,000)]. Furthermore, the dumping alternative does not consider potential future costs that may arise from environmental liabilities.

2. It appears that there would be no legal ramifications if the company decided to dump the hazardous product into the Gulf. The country either may have no laws against such dumping, or even if they exist, they are not enforced in accordance with the government policy. A more important consideration, however, is the ethical implications. To knowingly dump a hazardous material into the Gulf would certainly result in water pollution. This is an unacceptable action from a societal standpoint. *It is important to remember that an act that does not violate any laws is not necessarily an ethical act.* Ethical considerations go beyond legal considerations. In different parts of the world, legal systems are imperfect and

not comprehensive. It is the responsibility of top management to take a broader, societal view when making decisions. In other words, a business should take its social responsibility seriously, by making it an integral part of the decision-making process. In the long run it is in the best interest of all stakeholders as well as the business itself.

CHAPTER 16
REVENUES, SALES VARIANCES, AND CUSTOMER-PROFITABILITY ANALYSIS

16-2 The *stand-alone revenue-allocation method* uses information about individual products in their separate markets when allocating bundled revenues to individual products. The *incremental revenue-allocation method* ranks the individual products in a bundle and then uses this ranking to allocate the bundled revenues to these individual products.

16-4 A dispute over the allocation of revenues of a bundled product could be resolved by (a) having an agreement that outlines the preferred method in the case of a dispute or (b) having a third party (such as the company president or an independent arbitrator) make a decision.

16-6 The total sales-mix variance for revenues arises from shifts in the revenues of individual products. The composite unit concept enables the effect of individual product changes to be summarized in a single intuitive number.

16-8 The sales-quantity variance can be decomposed into (a) a market-size variance (the actual total market-size change from that budgeted) and (b) a market-share variance (the actual market-share change from that budgeted). Both variances use the budgeted average selling price per unit, when the focus is on revenues.

16-10 Customer profitability analysis highlights to managers how individual customers differentially contribute to total profitability. It helps managers to see whether customers who contribute sizably to total profitability are receiving a comparable level of attention from the organization.

16-12 No. A customer profitability profile highlights differences in current period's profitability across customers. Dropping customers should be the last resort. An unprofitable customer in one period may be highly profitable in subsequent future periods. Moreover, costs assigned to individual customers need not be purely variable with respect to short-run elimination of sales to those customers. Thus, when customers are dropped, costs assigned to those customers may not disappear in the short run.

16-14 A process where the inputs are nonsubstitutable leaves workers no discretion as to the components to use. A process where the inputs are substitutable means there is discretion about the exact number and type of inputs or about the weighting of inputs where the number and type is mandated.

16-16 (30 min.) Revenue allocation, speaking fees.

1. The total revenues from the seminar are:
    $500 \times \$220 = \$110,000$.
    Revenues to be shared by speakers
    $0.30 \times \$110,000 = \$33,000$.

The stand-alone revenue allocation method could guide the allocations. Possible weights are individual speaking fees, number of speeches, and speaking fee revenues:

	Individual Speaking Fee (1)	Relative Speaking Fee % (2)=(1)÷17,600	# of Speeches (3)	Relative Number of Speeches (4)=(3)÷96	Speaking Fee Revenues (5)=(1)×(3)	Relative Speaking Fee Revenues (6)=(5)÷374,000
Linda Young	$11,000	0.625	6	0.0625	$ 66,000	0.1765
Vince Rock	4,400	0.250	50	0.5208	220,000	0.5882
Juan Malvido	2,200	0.125	40	0.4167	88,000	0.2353
	$17,600	1.000	96	1.0000	$374,000	1.0000

These three weightings give the following allocation of $33,000:

	Relative Speaking Fee Weights (1)	Allocation of $33,000 (2)	Relative Number of Speeches Weights (3)	Allocation of $33,000 (4)	Relative Speaking Fee Revenues Weights (5)	Allocation of $33,000 (6)
Linda Young	0.625	$20,625	0.0625	$ 2,063	0.1765	$ 5,824
Vince Rock	0.250	8,250	0.5208	17,187	0.5882	19,411
Juan Malvido	0.125	4,125	0.4167	13,750	0.2353	7,765
	1.000	$33,000	1.0000	$33,000	1.0000	$33,000

The incremental revenue-allocation method is not straightforward, as the sum of the individual speaking fees ($11,000 + $4,400 + $2,200 = $17,600) is less than the total $33,000 to be allocated.

2. Young could argue that she has the highest individual speaking fee and is high in demand. In contrast, the other two speakers have given numerous talks and likely will attract fewer people to the seminar. She could argue that Malvido should pay to be on the program, as he is marketing for the television network. The net of these arguments is that Young wants more than $11,000.

    Rock could argue that he is in huge demand as a speaker, as is evidenced by his 50 speeches at $4,400. People pay this amount because he is both entertaining and dynamic. He could also claim his Olympic gold medal brings an aura of accomplishment to the seminar. The net of these arguments is that Rock wants more than $11,000.

Malvido could argue that he is the "television personality" everyone wants to meet and hear. He could also argue he could give the seminar invaluable publicity by promoting it on his television show. The net of these arguments is that Malvido wants more than $11,000.

16-18 (10-15 min.) Revenue allocation, bundled products, additional complexities (continuation of 16-17).

Alternatives include:

(a) Use information about how each individual package is used to make the revenue allocations. Thus if one party uses only lodging and food, the $770 is allocated among those two groups. This would be the most accurate approach as it captures actual usage and non-usage of the facilities.

(b) Use the average non-usage information to compute an "adjusted unit selling price:"

Lodging: 704×1.00 = $ 704
Food: 176×0.95 =   167
Recreation: 330×0.90 =   297
                                       $1,168

These adjusted revenues can be used in either the stand-alone or incremental methods. For example, the stand-alone allocations are:

Lodging: $\dfrac{704}{\$1,168} \times \$770$ = $464

Food: $\dfrac{167}{\$1,168} \times \$770$ = $110

Recreation: $\dfrac{297}{\$1,168} \times \$770$ = $196

                                                  $770

16-20 (20 min.) 7-Up using variances to read the market.

1. 7-Up should have conducted a Level 1 to 4 variance analysis that is focused on the U.S. soft-drink market. If information is available, individual 7-Up products (7-Up and Diet 7-Up) could be included to compute a sales mix-variance. The sales-quantity variance could be divided into a market-share variance and a

market-size variance. 7-Up's market share has steadily declined from 3.2% to 2.4% over a 10-year period. This is a large decline.

7-Up could also conduct more detailed analyses, including:

1) Changes in the market share and the market size of the citrus-flavoured category.
2) Changes in its market share and market size share by demographic segment (0–11 years, 12–24 years, and so on).

2. The brand objectives are critical to consider when evaluating 7-Up's strategy. The trade magazine article has a negative tone. Much depends on whether 7-Up's management has attempted to make the brand investments required to compete in the soft drink market. If 7-Up's management has invested heavily in marketing, sales promotions, product extension, and so on, its decline in market share is a negative indicator. Suppose, however, 7-Up management has decided that they do not have the resources to compete with Coca-Cola or Pepsi-Cola. Their strategy is to budget for market declines, but extract higher profitability from the brand in the short run. This is a classic "milk-the-brand" strategy. Here, the issue is what is the optimal "milk-the-brand" strategy, which would consider the time period over which a market-share decline is predicted and the rate of decrease with alternative cutbacks in marketing outlays.

16-22 (30-40 min.) **Variance analysis of revenues, multiple countries**

1. All amounts are in thousands.

Budget for 2007

	Selling Price per Carton (1)	Units Sold (Cartons in 000s) (2)	Sales Mix (3)	Revenues (4) = (1) × (2)
Canada	$6.60	400,000	16%	$2,640,000
Mexico	4.40	600,000	24	2,640,000
U.S.	7.70	1,500,000	60	11,550,000
		2,500,000	100%	$16,830,000

Actual for 2007

	Selling Price per Carton (1)	Units Sold (Cartons in 000s) (2)	Sales Mix (3)	Revenues (4) = (1) × (2)
Canada	$6.82	480,000	16%	$3,273,600
Mexico	4.68	900,000	30	4,212,000
U.S.	7.48	1,620,000	54	12,117,600
		3,000,000	100%	$19,603,200

Solution Exhibit 16-22 summarizes the Level 1 to Level 3 variance analysis. Details of the underlying computations are presented below.

$$\text{Static-budget variance of revenue} = \text{Actual results} - \text{Static-budget amount}$$

Canada	=	$3,273,600 – $2,640,000	=	$ 633,600 F
Mexico	=	4,212,000 – 2,640,000	=	1,572,000 F
United States	=	12,117,600 – 11,550,000	=	567,600 F
Total				$2,773,200 F

$$\text{Flexible-budget variance of revenue} = \text{Actual results} - \text{Flexible-budget amount}$$

Canada	=	$3,273,600 – ($6.60 × 480,000)	=	$105,600 F
Mexico	=	4,212,000 – (4.40 × 900,000)	=	252,000 F
United States	=	12,117,600 – (7.70 × 1,620,000)	=	356,400 U
Total				$ 1,200 F

$$\text{Sales-volume variance of revenue} = \left(\begin{array}{c} \text{Actual sales} \\ \text{quantity} \\ \text{in units} \end{array} - \begin{array}{c} \text{Budgeted sales} \\ \text{quantity} \\ \text{in units} \end{array} \right) \times \begin{array}{c} \text{Budgeted} \\ \text{revenue} \\ \text{per unit} \end{array}$$

Canada	=	(480,000 – 400,000) × $6.60	=	$ 528,000 F
Mexico	=	(900,000 – 600,000) × $4.40	=	$1,320,000 F
United States	=	(1,620,000 – 1,500,000) × $7.70	=	$ 924,000 F
Total			=	$2,772,000 F

$$\begin{array}{ccc} \text{Sales-quantity} \\ \text{variance of} \\ \text{revenue} \end{array} = \left(\begin{array}{cc} \text{Actual units} & \text{Budgeted units} \\ \text{of all products} - \text{of all products} \\ \text{in units} & \text{sold} \end{array} \right) \begin{array}{cc} \text{Budgeted} & \text{Budgeted} \\ \times \text{ sales-mix } \times \text{ revenue} \\ \text{percentage} & \text{per unit} \end{array}$$

Canada	=	$(3,000,000 - 2,500,000) \times 0.16 \times \$6.60$	=	$\$ 528,000$ F
Mexico	=	$(3,000,000 - 2,500,000) \times 0.24 \times \$4.40$	=	$\$ 528,000$ F
United States	=	$(3,000,000 - 2,500,000) \times 0.60 \times \$7.70$	=	$\underline{\$2,310,000}$ F
Total				$\underline{\$3,366,000}$ F

$$\begin{array}{ccc} \text{Sales-mix} \\ \text{variance of} = \\ \text{revenue} \end{array} \begin{array}{c} \text{Actual units} \\ \text{of all} \\ \text{products sold} \end{array} \times \left(\begin{array}{cc} \text{Actual} & \text{Budgeted} \\ \text{sales-mix} - \text{sales-mix} \\ \text{percentage} & \text{percentage} \end{array} \right) \begin{array}{c} \text{Budgeted} \\ \times \text{ revenue} \\ \text{per unit} \end{array}$$

Canada	=	$3,000,000 \times (0.16 - 0.16) \times \$6.60$	=	$\$ \qquad 0$
Mexico	=	$3,000,000 \times (0.30 - 0.24) \times \$4.40$	=	$\$ 792,000$ F
United States	=	$3,000,000 \times (0.54 - 0.60) \times \$7.70$	=	$\underline{\$1,386,000}$ U
Total				$\underline{\$ \ 594,000}$ U

2. There is a sizable favourable static-budget variance (Level 1) of revenue of $2,773,200. The flexible-budget variance (Level 2) of $1,200 F shows that the net effect of the selling price changes is minimal (Canada increases $0.22 per carton, Mexico increases $0.28 per carton, and U.S. decreases $0.22 per carton).

   The Level 3 breakdown of the favourable sales-volume variance of $2,772,000 for revenues shows that the biggest contributor is the 500,000 unit increase in sales. There is a partially offsetting unfavourable sales-mix variance.

SOLUTION EXHIBIT 16-22
Revenue Analysis for Cola-King

Static-Budget Variance of Revenues

Canada	$ 633,600 F
Mexico	1,572,000 F
United States	567,600 F
Total	$2,773,200 F

Flexible-Budget Variance of Revenues

Canada	$105,600 F
Mexico	252,000 F
United States	356,400 U
Total	$ 1,200 F

Sales-Volume Variance of Revenues

Canada	$ 528,000 F
Mexico	1,320,000 F
United States	924,000 F
Total	$2,772,000 F

Sales-Mix Variance of Revenues

Canada	$ 0
Mexico	792,000 F
United States	1,386,000 U
Total	$ 594,000 U

Sales-Quantity Variance of Revenues

Canada	$ 528,000 F
Mexico	528,000 F
United States	2,310,000 F
Total	$3,366,000 F

16-24 (20-25 min.) Customer profitability, distribution.

1. The activity-based costing for each customer is:

		Maple Pharmacy	Oak Hill Pharmacy
1.	Order processing, $40 × 12; 10	$ 480	$ 400
2.	Line-item ordering, $3 × (12 × 10; 10 × 18)	360	540
3.	Store deliveries, $50 × 6; 10	300	500
4.	Carton deliveries, $1 × (6 × 24; 10 × 20)	144	200
5.	Shelf-stocking, $16 × (6 × 0; 10 × 0.5)	0	80
	Operating costs	$1,284	$1,720

The operating income of each customer is:

	Maple Pharmacy	Oak Hill Pharmacy
Revenues,		
$2,640 × 6; 1,980 × 10	$15,840	$19,800
Cost of goods sold,		
$2,310 × 6; $1,815 × 10	13,860	18,150
Gross margin	1,980	1,650
Operating costs	1,284	1,720
Operating income	$ 696	$ (70)

2.   Ways Figure Four could use this information include:

(a) Pay increased attention to the top 20% of the customers. This could entail asking them for ways you can improve service. Alternatively, you may want to highlight to your own personnel the importance of these customers, e.g., it could entail stressing to delivery people the importance of never missing delivery dates for these customers.

(b) Work out ways internally at Figure Four to reduce the rate per cost driver, e.g., reduce the cost per order by having better order placement linkages with customers. This cost reduction by Figure Four will improve the profitability of all customers.

(c) Work with customers so that their behaviour reduces the total "system-wide" costs. At a minimum, this approach could entail having customers make fewer orders and fewer line items. This latter point is controversial with students; the rationale is that a reduction in the number of line items (diversity of products) carried by Ma and Pa stores may reduce the diversity of products Figure Four carries.

16-26 (35 min.) Direct materials price, efficiency, mix, and yield variances.

1.   Solution Exhibit 16-26A presents the total price variance ($3,100F), the total efficiency variance ($2,760U) and the total flexible-budget variance ($340F).

Total direct materials price variance can also be computed as:

$$\text{Direct materials price variance for each input} = \left(\begin{array}{c} \text{Actual} \\ \text{Price} \end{array} - \begin{array}{c} \text{Budgeted} \\ \text{Price} \end{array} \right) \times \begin{array}{c} \text{Actual} \\ \text{Inputs} \end{array}$$

Tolman	=	($0.30 − $0.32) × 62,000	=	$1,240 F
Golden Delicious	=	($0.28 − $0.28) × 155,000	=	0
Ribston	=	($0.22 − $0.24) × 93,000	=	1,860 F

Total direct materials price variance $3,100 F

Total direct materials efficiency variance can also be computed as:

$$\begin{array}{c} \text{Direct materials} \\ \text{efficiency variance} \\ \text{for each input} \end{array} = \left(\begin{array}{cc} \text{Actual} & \text{Budgeted inputs allowed} \\ \text{Inputs} & \text{for actual outputs achieved} \end{array} \right) \times \begin{array}{c} \text{Budgeted} \\ \text{Prices} \end{array}$$

Tolman	=	(62,000 – 45,000) × $0.32	=	$5,440 U
Golden Delicious	=	(155,000 – 180,000) × $0.28	=	7,000 F
Ribston	=	(93,000 – 75,000) × $0.24	=	4,320 U
Total direct materials efficiency variance				$2,760 U

SOLUTION EXHIBIT 16-26A
Columnar Presentation of Direct Materials Price and Efficiency Variances for Greenwood Inc. for November 2007

	Actual Costs Incurred (Actual Inputs × Actual Prices) (1)	Actual Input × Budgeted Prices (2)	Flexible Budget (Budgeted Inputs Allowed for Actual Outputs Achieved × Budgeted Prices) (3)
Tolman	62,000 × $0.30 = $18,600	62,000 × $0.32 = $19,840	45,000 × $0.32 = $14,400
Golden Delicious	155,000 × $0.28 = 43,400	155,000 × $0.28 = 43,400	180,000 × $0.28 = 50,400
Ribston	93,000 × $0.22 = 20,460	93,000 × $0.24 = 22,320	75,000 × $0.24 = 18,000
	$82,460	$85,560	$82,800

$3,100 F → Total price variance

$2,760 U → Total efficiency variance

$340 F → Total flexible-budget variance

F = favourable effect on operating income; U = unfavourable effect on operating income

2. Solution Exhibit 16-26B presents the total direct materials yield and mix variances for Greenwood Inc. for November 2007.

The total direct materials yield variance can also be computed as the sum of the direct materials yield variances for each input:

$$
\begin{pmatrix} \text{Direct} \\ \text{materials} \\ \text{yield variance} \\ \text{for each} \\ \text{input} \end{pmatrix} = \left(\begin{array}{c} \text{Actual total} \\ \text{quantity of all} \\ \text{direct materials} \\ \text{inputs used} \end{array} - \begin{array}{c} \text{Budgeted total} \\ \text{quantity of all} \\ \text{direct materials} \\ \text{inputs allowed for} \\ \text{actual output} \\ \text{achieved} \end{array} \right) \times \begin{array}{c} \text{Budgeted} \\ \text{direct} \\ \text{materials} \\ \text{input mix} \\ \text{percentage} \end{array} \times \begin{array}{c} \text{Budgeted} \\ \text{price of} \\ \text{direct} \\ \text{materials} \\ \text{inputs} \end{array}
$$

Tolman	$= (310,000 - 300,000) \times 0.15 \times \$0.32 = 10,000 \times 0.15 \times \$0.32$	$= \$ 480$ U
Golden Delicious	$= (310,000 - 300,000) \times 0.60 \times \$0.28 = 10,000 \times 0.60 \times \$0.28$	$= 1,680$ U
Ribston	$= (310,000 - 300,000) \times 0.25 \times \$0.24 = 10,000 \times 0.25 \times \$0.24$	$= \underline{600}$ U
Total direct materials yield variance		$\underline{\underline{\$2,760}}$ U

The total direct materials mix variance can also be computed as the sum of the direct materials mix variances for each input:

$$
\begin{pmatrix} \text{Direct} \\ \text{materials} \\ \text{mix variance} \\ \text{for each} \\ \text{input} \end{pmatrix} = \left(\begin{array}{c} \text{Actual} \\ \text{direct materials} \\ \text{input mix} \\ \text{percentage} \end{array} - \begin{array}{c} \text{Budgeted} \\ \text{direct} \\ \text{materials} \\ \text{input mix} \\ \text{percentage} \end{array} \right) \times \begin{array}{c} \text{Actual total} \\ \text{quantity of} \\ \text{all direct} \\ \text{materials} \\ \text{inputs used} \end{array} \times \begin{array}{c} \text{Budgeted} \\ \text{price of} \\ \text{direct} \\ \text{materials} \\ \text{inputs} \end{array}
$$

Tolman	$= (0.20 - 0.15) \times 310,000 \times \$0.32 = 0.05 \times 310,000 \times \$0.32$	$= \$4,960$ U
Golden Delicious	$= (0.50 - 0.60) \times 310,000 \times \$0.28 = -0.10 \times 310,000 \times \$0.28$	$= 8,680$ F
Ribston	$= (0.30 - 0.25) \times 310,000 \times \$0.24 = 0.05 \times 310,000 \times \$0.24$	$= \underline{3,720}$ U
Total direct materials mix variance =		$\underline{\underline{\$ \quad 0}}$ U

3. Greenwood paid less for Tolman and Ribston apples and, so, had a favourable direct materials price variance of $3,100. It also had an unfavourable efficiency variance of $2,760. Greenwood would need to evaluate if these were unrelated events or if the lower price resulted from the purchase of apples of poorer quality that affected efficiency. The net effect in this case from a cost standpoint was favourable—the savings in price being greater than the loss in efficiency. Of course, if the applesauce is of poorer quality, Greenwood must also evaluate the potential effects on current and future revenues that have not been considered in the variances described in requirements 1 and 2.

The unfavourable efficiency variance is entirely attributable to an unfavourable yield. The actual mix does deviate from the budgeted mix but at the budgeted prices, the greater quantity of Tolman and Ribston apples used in the actual mix exactly offsets the fewer Golden Delicious apples used. Again, management should evaluate the reasons for the unfavourable yield variance. Is it due to poor quality Tolman and Ribston apples (recall from requirement 1 that these apples were acquired at a price lower than the standard price)? Is it due to the change in mix (recall that the mix used is different from the budgeted mix, even though the mix variance is $0)? Isolating the reasons can lead management to take the necessary corrective actions.

SOLUTION EXHIBIT 16-26B
Columnar Presentation of Direct Materials, Yield, and Mix Variances for Greenwood Inc. for November 2007

F = favourable effect on operating income; U = unfavourable effect on operating income

a 62,000 ÷ 310,000
b 155,000 ÷ 310,000
c 93,000 ÷ 310,000

d 45,000 ÷ 300,000
e 180,000 ÷ 300,000
f 75,000 ÷ 300,000

16-28 (60 min.) Variance analysis, sales-mix and sales-quantity variances.

1. Actual Contribution Margins

Product	Actual Selling Price	Actual Variable Costs per Unit	Actual Contribution Margin per Unit	Actual Sales Volume in Units	Actual Contribution Dollars	Actual Contribution Percent
PalmPro	$354	$178	$176	11,000	$ 1,936,000	15%
PalmCE	290	92	198	44,000	8,712,000	70%
PalmKid	107	73	34	55,000	1,870,000	15%
				110,000	$12,518,000	100%

The actual average contribution margin per unit is $113.80 ($12,518,000 ÷ 110,000 units).

Budgeted Contribution Margins

Product	Budgeted Selling Price	Budgeted Variable Costs per Unit	Budgeted Contribution Margin per Unit	Budgeted Sales Volume in Units	Budgeted Contribution Dollars	Budgeted Contribution Percent
PalmPro	$384	$182	$202	12,500	$ 2,525,000	19%
PalmCE	274	98	176	37,500	6,600,000	49%
PalmKid	154	65	89	50,000	4,450,000	32%
				100,000	$13,575,000	100%

The budgeted average contribution margin per unit is $135.75 ($13,575,000 ÷ 100,000 units).

2. Actual Sales Mix

Product	Actual Selling Price	Actual Variable Costs per Unit	Actual Contribution Margin per Unit	Actual Sales Volume in Units	Actual Sales Mix
PalmPro	$354	$178	$176	11,000	10.0%
PalmCE	290	92	198	44,000	40.0%
PalmKid	107	73	34	55,000	50.0%
				110,000	100.0%

Budgeted Sales Mix

Product	Budgeted Selling Price	Budgeted Variable Costs per Unit	Budgeted Contribution Margin per Unit	Budgeted Sales Volume in Units	Budgeted Sales Mix
PalmPro	$384	$182	$202	12,500	12.5%
PalmCE	274	98	176	37,500	37.5%
PalmKid	154	65	89	50,000	50.0%
				100,000	100.0%

3. Flexible-budget variance of contribution margin:

$$= \frac{\text{Actual}}{\text{Results}} - \frac{\text{Flexible-budget}}{\text{amount}}$$

PalmPro = ($176 × 11,000) – ($202 × 11,000)

= $1,936,000 – $2,222,000　　　　=　　$286,000 U

PalmCE = (198 × 44,000) – ($176 × 44,000)

= $8,712,000 – $7,744,000　　　　=　　968,000 F

PalmKid = ($34 × 55,000) – ($89 × 55,000)

= $1,870,000 – $4,895,000　　　　=　　3,025,000 U

Total flexible-budget variance　　　　　　=　　$2,343,000 U

Sales-volume variance of contribution margin:

$$= \left(\begin{array}{c} \text{Actual sales} \\ \text{quantity} \\ \text{in units} \end{array} - \begin{array}{c} \text{Budgeted sales} \\ \text{quantity} \\ \text{in units} \end{array} \right) \times \begin{array}{c} \text{Budgeted} \\ \text{contrib. margin} \\ \text{per unit} \end{array}$$

PalmPro = (11,000 – 12,500) × $202

= –1,500 × $202　　　　　　=　　$303,000 U

PalmCE = (44,000 – 37,500) × $176

= 6,500 × $176　　　　　　=　　1,144,000 F

PalmKid = (55,000 – 50,000) × $89

= 5,000 × $89　　　　　　=　　445,000 F

Total sales-volume variance　　　　=　　$1,286,000 F

Sales-mix variance of contribution-margin:

$$= \begin{pmatrix} \text{Actual units} \\ \text{of all} \\ \text{products sold} \end{pmatrix} \times \begin{pmatrix} \text{Actual} & \text{Budgeted} \\ \text{sales mix} & - & \text{sales mix} \\ \text{percentage} & \text{percentage} \end{pmatrix} \times \begin{pmatrix} \text{Budgeted} \\ \text{contrib. margin} \\ \text{per unit} \end{pmatrix}$$

PalmPro	=	$110,000 \times (0.10 - 0.125) \times \$202$		
	=	$110,000 \times -0.025 \times \$202$	=	$555,500 U
PalmCE	=	$110,000 \times (0.40 - 0.375) \times \$176$		
	=	$110,000 \times 0.025 \times \$176$	=	484,000 F
PalmKid	=	$110,000 \times (0.50 - 0.50) \times \$89$		
	=	$110,000 \times 0.00 \times \$89$	=	0 F
Total sales-mix variance			=	$ 71,500 U

Sales-quantity variance of contribution margin:

$$= \begin{pmatrix} \text{Actual units} & \text{Budgeted units} \\ \text{of all} & - & \text{of all} \\ \text{products sold} & \text{products sold} \end{pmatrix} \times \begin{pmatrix} \text{Budgeted} \\ \text{sales mix} \\ \text{percentage} \end{pmatrix} \times \begin{pmatrix} \text{Budgeted} \\ \text{contrib. margin} \\ \text{per unit} \end{pmatrix}$$

PalmPro	=	$(110,000 - 100,000) \times 0.125 \times \$202$		
	=	$10,000 \times 0.125 \times \$202$	=	$252,500 F
PalmCE	=	$(110,000 - 100,000) \times 0.375 \times \$176$		
	=	$10,000 \times 0.375 \times \$176$	=	660,000 F
PalmKid	=	$(110,000 - 100,000) \times 0.50 \times \$89$		
	=	$10,000 \times 0.50 \times \$89$	=	445,000 F
Total sales-quantity variance			=	$1,357,500 F

4. Static-Budget Variance

Static-Budget Variance

PalmPro	$ 589,000 U
PalmCE	2,112,000 F
PalmKid	2,580,000 U
Total	$1,057,000 U

Flexible-Budget Variance

PalmPro	$ 286,000 U
PalmCE	968,000 F
PalmKid	3,025,000 U
Total	$2,343,000 U

Sales-Volume Variance

PalmPro	$ 303,000 U
PalmCE	1,144,000 F
PalmKid	445,000 F
	$1,286,000 F

Sales-Mix Variance

PalmPro	$555,500 U
PalmCE	484,000 F
PalmKid	0
Total	$ 71,500 U

Sales-Quantity Variance

Palm Pro	$252,500 F
PalmCE	660,000 F
PalmKid	445,000 F
Total	$1,357,500 F

5. Some factors to consider are:
   - The difference in actual vs. budgeted contribution was $1,057,000. However, the contribution from the PalmCE exceeded budget by $2,112,000 while the contributions from the PalmPro and the PalmKid were lower than expected to an offsetting degree.
   - In percentage terms, the PalmCE accounted for 70% of total contribution vs. a planned 49% contribution. However, the PalmPro accounted for 15% vs. planned 19% and the PalmKid accounted for only 15% vs. a planned 32%.
   - In unit terms (rather than in contribution terms), the PalmKid accounted for 50% of the sales mix as planned. However, the PalmPro accounted for only 10% vs. a budgeted 12.5% and the PalmCE accounted for 40% vs. a planned 37.5%.
   - Variance analysis for the PalmPro shows an unfavourable sales-mix variance outweighing a favourable sales-quantity variance and producing an unfavourable sales-volume variance of $303,000. The drop in sales-mix share was far larger than the gain from an overall greater quantity sold.
   - The PalmCE gained both from an increase in share of the sales mix as well as from the increase in the overall number of units sold. These factors combined to a $1,144,000 favourable sales-volume variance.
   - The PalmKid maintained sales-mix share—as a result, the sales-mix variance is zero. However, PalmKid sales did gain from the overall increase in units sold.

- Overall, there was a favourable total sales-volume variance. However, the large drop in PalmKid's contribution margin per unit combined with a decrease in the number of PalmPro units sold vs. budget, led to the total contribution margin being much lower than budgeted.

Other factors could be discussed here—for example, it seems that the PalmKid did not achieve much success with a three digit price point—selling price was budgeted at $154 but dropped to $107. At the same time, variable costs increased. This could have been due to a marketing push aimed at announcing the lower price in some markets.

16-30 (40 min.) Variance analysis of contribution margin, multiple products.

1, 2, and 3.   Solution Exhibit 16-30 presents the sales-volume, sales-quantity, and sales-mix variances for each type of cookie and in total for Debbie's Delight Inc. in August 2007.

The sales-volume variances can also be computed as:

$$
\begin{array}{l}
\text{Sales-volume} \\
\text{variance of} \\
\text{contribution margin}
\end{array}
=
\left(
\begin{array}{cc}
\text{Actual sales} & \text{Budgeted sales} \\
\text{quantity in} - & \text{quantity in} \\
\text{kilograms} & \text{kilograms}
\end{array}
\right)
\times
\begin{array}{l}
\text{Budgeted} \\
\text{contribution} \\
\text{margin per} \\
\text{kilogram}
\end{array}
$$

The sales-volume variances are:

Chocolate chip	=	(57,600 – 45,000) × $2.10	=	$26,460 F
Oatmeal raisin	=	(18,000 – 25,000) × $2.40	=	16,800 U
Coconut	=	(9,600 – 10,000) × $2.70	=	1,080 U
White chocolate	=	(13,200 – 5,000) × $3.10	=	25,420 F
Macadamia nut	=	(21,600 – 15,000) × $3.20	=	21,120 F
All cookies				$55,120 F

The sales-quantity variance can be computed as:

$$
\begin{array}{l}
\text{Sales-quantity} \\
\text{variance of} \\
\text{contribution} \\
\text{margin}
\end{array}
=
\left(
\begin{array}{cc}
\text{Actual kilograms} & \text{Budgeted kilograms} \\
\text{of all cookies} - & \text{of all cookies} \\
\text{sold} & \text{sold}
\end{array}
\right)
\times
\begin{array}{l}
\text{Budgeted} \\
\text{sales-mix} \\
\text{percentage}
\end{array}
\times
\begin{array}{l}
\text{Budgeted} \\
\text{contribution} \\
\text{margin per} \\
\text{kilogram}
\end{array}
$$

The sales-quantity variances are:

Chocolate chip	=	(120,000 – 100,000) × 0.45 × $2.10	=	$18,900 F
Oatmeal raisin	=	(120,000 – 100,000) × 0.25 × $2.40	=	12,000 F
Coconut	=	(120,000 – 100,000) × 0.10 × $2.70	=	5,400 F
White chocolate	=	(120,000 – 100,000) × 0.05 × $3.10	=	3,100 F
Macadamia nut	=	(120,000 – 100,000) × 0.15 × $3.20	=	9,600 F
All cookies	=			$49,000 F

The sales-mix variance can also be computed as:

$$\begin{pmatrix} \text{Sales-mix} \\ \text{variance of} \\ \text{contribution} \\ \text{margin} \end{pmatrix} = \begin{pmatrix} \text{Actual sales-} \\ \text{mix percentage} \end{pmatrix} - \begin{pmatrix} \text{Budgeted sales-} \\ \text{mix percentage} \end{pmatrix} \times \begin{pmatrix} \text{Actual kilograms} \\ \text{of all cookies} \\ \text{sold} \end{pmatrix} \times \begin{pmatrix} \text{Budgeted} \\ \text{contribution} \\ \text{margin per} \\ \text{kilogram} \end{pmatrix}$$

The sales-mix variances are:

Chocolate chip	=	$(0.48 - 0.45) \times 120{,}000 \times \$2.10$	=	$ 7,560 F
Oatmeal raisin	=	$(0.15 - 0.25) \times 120{,}000 \times \$2.40$	=	28,800 U
Coconut	=	$(0.08 - 0.10) \times 120{,}000 \times \$2.70$	=	6,480 U
White chocolate	=	$(0.11 - 0.05) \times 120{,}000 \times \$3.10$	=	22,320 F
Macadamia nut	=	$(0.18 - 0.15) \times 120{,}000 \times \$3.20$	=	11,520 F
All cookies	=			$ 6,120 F

A summary of the variances is:

Sales-Volume Variance of C.M.

Chocolate chip	$26,460 F
Oatmeal raisin	16,800 U
Coconut	1,080 U
White chocolate	25,420 F
Macadamia nut	21,120 F
All cookies	$55,120 F

Sales-Mix Variance of C.M.

Chocolate chip	$7,560 F
Oatmeal raisin	28,800 U
Coconut	6,480 U
White chocolate	22,320 F
Macadamia nut	11,520 F
All cookies	$ 6,120 F

Sales-Quantity Variance of C.M.

Chocolate chip	$18,900 F
Oatmeal raisin	12,000 F
Coconut	5,400 F
White chocolate	3,100 F
Macadamia nut	9,600 F
All cookies	$49,000 F

4. Debbie's Delight shows a favourable sales-quantity variance because it sold more cookies in total than was budgeted. Together with the higher quantities, Debbie's also sold more of the high-contribution margin white chocolate and macadamia nut cookies relative to the budgeted mix—hence Debbie's also showed a favourable total sales-mix variance.

SOLUTION EXHIBIT 16-30
Columnar Presentation of Sales-Volume, Sales-Quantity and Sales-Mix Variances for Debbie's Delight Inc.

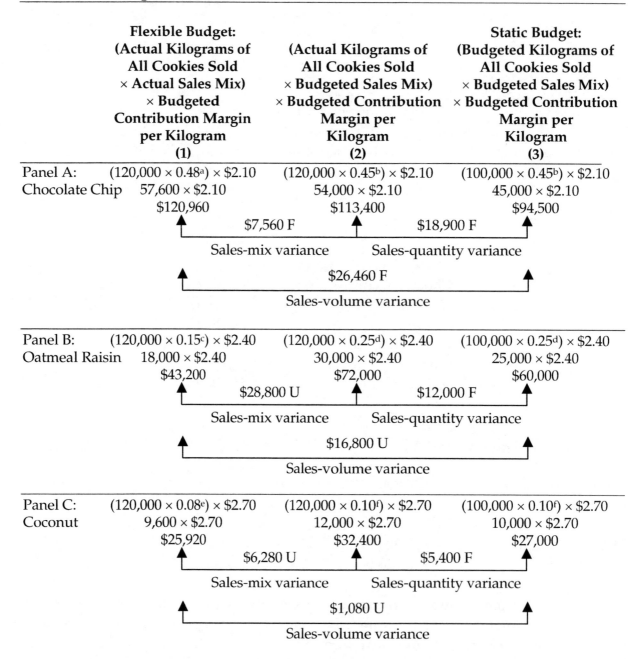

	Flexible Budget: (Actual Kilograms of All Cookies Sold × Actual Sales Mix) × Budgeted Contribution Margin per Kilogram (1)	(Actual Kilograms of All Cookies Sold × Budgeted Sales Mix) × Budgeted Contribution Margin per Kilogram (2)	Static Budget: (Budgeted Kilograms of All Cookies Sold × Budgeted Sales Mix) × Budgeted Contribution Margin per Kilogram (3)
Panel A: Chocolate Chip	$(120{,}000 \times 0.48^a) \times \$2.10$ $57{,}600 \times \$2.10$ $\$120{,}960$	$(120{,}000 \times 0.45^b) \times \$2.10$ $54{,}000 \times \$2.10$ $\$113{,}400$	$(100{,}000 \times 0.45^b) \times \$2.10$ $45{,}000 \times \$2.10$ $\$94{,}500$

$\qquad\qquad \$7{,}560\ \text{F} \qquad\qquad \$18{,}900\ \text{F}$

$\qquad\qquad$ Sales-mix variance $\qquad$ Sales-quantity variance

$\$26{,}460\ \text{F}$

Sales-volume variance

| Panel B:
Oatmeal Raisin | $(120{,}000 \times 0.15^c) \times \$2.40$
$18{,}000 \times \$2.40$
$\$43{,}200$ | $(120{,}000 \times 0.25^d) \times \$2.40$
$30{,}000 \times \$2.40$
$\$72{,}000$ | $(100{,}000 \times 0.25^d) \times \$2.40$
$25{,}000 \times \$2.40$
$\$60{,}000$ |

$\qquad\qquad \$28{,}800\ \text{U} \qquad\qquad \$12{,}000\ \text{F}$

$\qquad\qquad$ Sales-mix variance $\qquad$ Sales-quantity variance

$\$16{,}800\ \text{U}$

Sales-volume variance

| Panel C:
Coconut | $(120{,}000 \times 0.08^e) \times \$2.70$
$9{,}600 \times \$2.70$
$\$25{,}920$ | $(120{,}000 \times 0.10^f) \times \$2.70$
$12{,}000 \times \$2.70$
$\$32{,}400$ | $(100{,}000 \times 0.10^f) \times \$2.70$
$10{,}000 \times \$2.70$
$\$27{,}000$ |

$\qquad\qquad \$6{,}280\ \text{U} \qquad\qquad \$5{,}400\ \text{F}$

$\qquad\qquad$ Sales-mix variance $\qquad$ Sales-quantity variance

$\$1{,}080\ \text{U}$

Sales-volume variance

F = favourable effect on operating income; U = unfavourable effect on operating income.

Actual Sales Mix:				Budgeted Sales Mix:			
[a]Chocolate Chip	$= 57{,}600 \div 120{,}000$	$=$	48%	[b]Chocolate Chip	$= 45{,}000 \div 100{,}000$	$=$	45%
[c]Oatmeal Raisin	$= 18{,}000 \div 120{,}000$	$=$	15%	[d]Oatmeal Raisin	$= 25{,}000 \div 100{,}000$	$=$	25%
[e]Coconut	$= 9{,}600 \div 120{,}000$	$=$	8%	[f]Coconut	$= 10{,}000 \div 100{,}000$	$=$	10%

Columnar Presentation of Sales-Volume, Sales-Quantity, and Sales-Mix Variances for Debbie's Delight Inc.

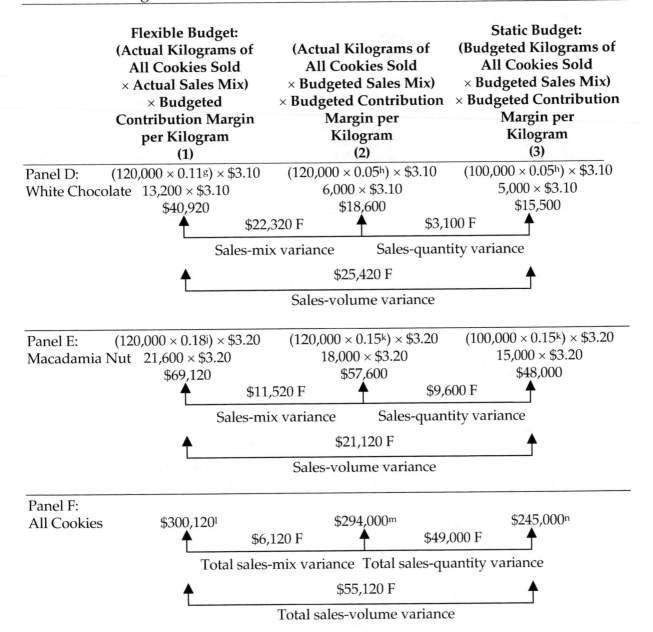

Flexible Budget: (Actual Kilograms of All Cookies Sold × Actual Sales Mix) × Budgeted Contribution Margin per Kilogram (1)	(Actual Kilograms of All Cookies Sold × Budgeted Sales Mix) × Budgeted Contribution Margin per Kilogram (2)	Static Budget: (Budgeted Kilograms of All Cookies Sold × Budgeted Sales Mix) × Budgeted Contribution Margin per Kilogram (3)

Panel D:
White Chocolate

$(120{,}000 \times 0.11^g) \times \$3.10$
$13{,}200 \times \$3.10$
$\$40{,}920$

$(120{,}000 \times 0.05^h) \times \$3.10$
$6{,}000 \times \$3.10$
$\$18{,}600$

$(100{,}000 \times 0.05^h) \times \$3.10$
$5{,}000 \times \$3.10$
$\$15{,}500$

$22,320 F — Sales-mix variance $3,100 F — Sales-quantity variance

$25,420 F — Sales-volume variance

Panel E:
Macadamia Nut

$(120{,}000 \times 0.18^j) \times \$3.20$
$21{,}600 \times \$3.20$
$\$69{,}120$

$(120{,}000 \times 0.15^k) \times \$3.20$
$18{,}000 \times \$3.20$
$\$57{,}600$

$(100{,}000 \times 0.15^k) \times \$3.20$
$15{,}000 \times \$3.20$
$\$48{,}000$

$11,520 F — Sales-mix variance $9,600 F — Sales-quantity variance

$21,120 F — Sales-volume variance

Panel F:
All Cookies

$\$300{,}120^l$ $\$294{,}000^m$ $\$245{,}000^n$

$6,120 F — Total sales-mix variance $49,000 F — Total sales-quantity variance

$55,120 F — Total sales-volume variance

F = favourable effect on operating income; U = unfavourable effect on operating income.

Actual Sales Mix:
gWhite Chocolate = 13,200 ÷ 120,000 = 11%
jMacadamia Nut = 21,600 ÷ 120,000 = 18%
l$120,960 + $43,200 + $25,920 + $40,920 + $69,120 = $300,120

Budgeted Sales Mix:
hWhite Chocolate = 5,000 ÷ 100,000 = 5%
kMacadamia Nut = 15,000 ÷ 100,000 = 15%
m $113,400 + $72,000 + $32,400 + $18,600 + $57,600 = $294,000

n $94,500 + $60,000 + $27,000 + $15,500 + $48,000 = $245,000

16-32 (50-60 min.) Revenue allocation, bundled products.

1. a. Stand-alone revenues in 2007:

Fraîche ($110 × 20,000)	$2,200,000
Désarmer ($88 × 37,500)	3,300,000
Innocence ($275 × 20,000)	5,500,000

The weights for Fraîche + Désarmer suite:

Fraîche: $\dfrac{\$2,200,000}{\$2,200,000 + \$3,300,000} \times \$165 = \$66$

Désarmer: $\dfrac{\$3,300,000}{\$2,200,000 + \$3,300,000} \times \$165 = \$99$

The weights for Fraîche + Innocence suite:

Fraîche: $\dfrac{\$2,200,000}{\$2,200,000 + \$5,500,000} \times \$308 = \$88$

Innocence: $\dfrac{\$5,500,000}{\$2,200,000 + \$5,500,000} \times \$308 = \$220$

b. Fraîche + Désarmer suite:

Product	Revenue Allocated	Revenue Remaining to be Allocated
Désarmer	$ 88	$77 ($165 – $88)
Fraîche	77	0
Total revenue allocated	$165	

Fraîche + Innocence suite:

Product	Revenue Allocated	Revenue Remaining to be Allocated
Innocence	$275	$33 ($308 – $275)
Fraîche	33	0
Total revenue allocated	$308	

2. Each product will be considered as a primary product and first incremental product. An average revenue is the final revenue allocation to the product. This approach is illustrated below.

Fraîche + Désarmer suite:

<u>Fraîche</u>

Allocation as the primary product	$ 110
Allocation as the incremental product ($165 – $88)	77
Total	$ 187
Allocation ($187 ÷ 2)	$93.50

<u>Désarmer</u>

Allocation as the primary product	$ 88
Allocation as the incremental product ($165 – $110)	55
Total	$ 143
Allocation ($143 + 2)	$71.50

According to this approach, Fraîche's revenue allocation is $93.50 and Désarmer's revenue allocation is $71.50 out of the total suite revenue of $165.

Fraîche + Innocence suite:

<u>Fraîche</u>

Allocation as the primary product	$ 110
Allocation as the incremental product ($308 – $275)	33
Total	$ 143
Allocation ($143 ÷ 2)	$71.50

<u>Innocence</u>

Allocation as the primary product	$ 275
Allocation as the incremental product ($308 – $110)	198
Total	$ 473
Allocation ($473 ÷ 2)	$236.50

Fraîche is allocated $71.50 revenue and Innocence is allocated $236.50 revenue out of the total suite revenue of $308.

An alternative approach is to take into account both the price and the units sold, that is, total revenues from each product when calculating the weights.

On a stand-alone basis, the price of Fraîche plus Désarmer is $110 + $88 = $198.

On a stand-alone basis the revenues are

Fraîche	$2,200,000
Désarmer	3,300,000
Total	$5,500,000

So Fraîche accounts for 40% ($2,200,000 ÷ $5,500,000) and Désarmer 60% ($3,300,000 ÷ 5,500,000) of total revenues from Fraîche and Désarmer.

Applying these percentages to the total stand-alone price of $198, we get revenue-weighted prices of $198 × 40% = $79.20 for Fraîche and $198 × 60% = $118.80 for Désarmer.

Using these revenue-weighted prices and considering each product as the primary product and then the incremental product:

Fraîche and Désarmer suite:
> Fraîche

Allocation as the primary product	$ 79.20
Allocation as the incremental product ($165 – $118.80)	46.20
Total	$125.40
Allocation ($125.40 ÷ 2)	$ 62.70

> Désarmer

Allocation as the primary product	$118.80
Allocation as the incremental product ($165 – $79.20)	85.80
Total	$204.60
Allocation ($204.60 ÷ 2)	$102.30

On a stand-alone basis, the price of Fraîche + Innocence is $110 + $275 = $385.
On a stand-alone basis, the revenues are

Fraîche	$2,200,000
Innocence	$5,500,000
Total	$7,700,000

So Fraîche accounts for 2/7 ($2,200,000 ÷ $7,700,000) and Innocence 5/7 ($5,500,000 ÷ $7,700,000) of total revenues from Fraîche and Innocence.

Applying these percentages to the total stand-alone price of $385, we get revenue-weighted prices of $385 × 2/7 = $110 for Fraîche and $385 × 5/7 = $275 for Innocence.

Using these revenue-weighted prices and considering each product as the primary product and then the incremental product:

Fraîche and Innocence suite:
> Fraîche

Allocation as the primary product	$ 110
Allocation as the incremental product ($308 – $275)	33
Total	$ 143
Allocation ($143 ÷ 2)	$71.50

> Innocence

Allocation as the primary product	$ 275
Allocation as the incremental product ($308 – $110)	$ 198
Total	$ 473
Allocation ($473 ÷ 2)	$236.50

A summary of the price allocations for the bundled products under different methods follows.

	Stand-alone Revenue Allocation (1)	Incremental With Fraîche Primary (2)	Incremental With Désarmer/ Innocence Primary (3)	Shapley Value Based on Price (4)	Shapley Value Based on Revenue-Weighted Price (5)
Fraîche	$ 66	$110	$ 77	$ 93.50	$ 62.70
Désarmer	99	55	88	71.50	102.30
Total	$165	$165	$165	$ 165.00	$ 165.00
Fraîche	$ 88	$110	$ 33	$ 71.50	$ 71.50
Innocence	220	198	275	236.50	236.50
Total	$308	$308	$308	$ 308.00	$ 308.00

Note that the Shapley value calculations based on price and revenue-weighted prices are the same for Fraîche and Innocence because the same number of units of each of these products is sold (20,000 units). In general, the Shapley value calculations based on revenue-weighted prices gives the most fair allocation of prices to each product in the bundle because it considers not only the prices of each product sold but also the units. Thus, if one of the products in the bundle sells very few units, it gets very few revenues allocated to it even if it sells for a high price. The table above also indicates that the stand-alone revenue allocation method closely approximates the Shapley value calculations based on revenue-weighted prices. Note that columns 2 and 4 in the above table allocate more revenues with Fraîche-Désarmer bundle to Fraîche because Fraîche sells for a higher price ($110 versus $88). But the allocations in these columns ignore the important fact that Fraîche sells far fewer units than Désarmer (20,000 versus 37,500).

16-34 (60 min.) Customer-profitability analysis.

1. Solution Exhibit 16-34 shows the customer-profitability analysis. Alternative rankings are:

    a.   Customer-level operating income
        1.   Brothers $501,464
        2.   April   455,609
        3.   Suitors   105,614

b. Gross margin/Net revenues
    1. Suitors, $304,800 ÷ $863,600   35.29%
    2. Brothers, $572,000 ÷ $1,830,400   31.25
    3. April, $501,600 ÷ $2,340,800   21.43

c. Customer-level operating income/Net revenues
    1. Brothers, $501,464 ÷ $1,830,400   27.40%
    2. April, $455,609 ÷ $2,340,800   19.46
    3. Suitors, $105,614 ÷ $863,600   12.23

A common-size breakdown of the revenues at list prices is:

	April	Brothers	Suitors
Revenues at list prices	100.00%	100.00%	100.00%
Discount	30.00	20.00	15.00
Sales returns	3.50	6.20	17.11
Cost of goods sold	52.25	50.74	43.93
Gross margin	14.25	23.06	23.96
Customer-level costs	1.31	2.84	15.66
Customer-level operating income	12.94%	20.22%	8.30%

The following conclusions relate to these percentages:

April—has high price discounting as its major differential to Brothers

Brothers—has lower price discounting than April and lower sales returns than Suitors

Suitors—has highest sales returns and highest customer-level costs

2. Key challenges facing Sims are:
    a. Reduce level of price discounting, especially by April,
    b. Reduce level of sales returns, especially by Suitors, and
    c. Reduce level of customer-level costs, especially by Suitors.

The ABC cost system highlights areas where the Suitors account is troublesome. It has a high number of orders, a high number of customer visits, a high number of rush deliveries, and a high number of sales returns. Sims needs to consider whether this high level of activity can be reduced without reducing customer revenues.

SOLUTION EXHIBIT 16-34
Customer-Profitability Analysis for Zoot's Suits

	April	Brothers	Suitors
Revenues at list prices			
44 × 400 × $200; 62 × 200 × $200;			
212 × 30 × $200	$3,520,000	$2,480,000	$1,272,000
Discount			
44 × 400 × $60[a]; 62 × 200 × $40[b];			
212 × 30 × $30[c]	1,056,000	496,000	190,800
Net revenues before returns	2,464,000	1,984,000	1,081,200
Sales returns			
880 × $140; 960 × $160; 1,280 × $170	123,200	153,600	217,600
Net revenues	2,340,800	1,830,400	863,600
Cost of goods sold			
16,720[d] × 110; 11,440[e] × 110;			
5,080[f] × 110	1,839,200	1,258,400	558,800
Gross margin	501,600	572,000	304,800
Customer-level costs			
Order processing			
44, 62, 212 × $269.50	11,858	16,709	57,134
Customer visits			
8, 12, 22 × $1,573	12,584	18,876	34,606
Delivery—regular			
41, 48, 166 × $330	13,530	15,840	54,780
Delivery—rushed			
3, 14, 46 × $935	2,805	13,090	43,010
Returns processing			
4, 6, 16 × $203.50	814	1,221	3,256
Return stocking fee			
880, 960, 1,280 × $5	4,400	4,800	6,400
Total customer-level costs	45,991	70,536	199,186
Customer-level operating income	$ 455,609	$ 501,464	$ 105,614

[a] $200 − $140 = $60
[b] $200 − $160 = $40
[c] $200 − $170 = $30
[d] (44 × 400) − 880 = 16,720
[e] (62 × 200) − 960 = 11,440
[f] (212 × 30) − 1,280 = 5,080

16-36 (40 min.) Customer loyalty clubs and profitability analysis.

1.

Gold Program

Revenues	
2,673 × 20 × ($200 × 0.90)	$ 9,622,800
2,673 × 30 × ($200 × 0.80)	12,830,400
2,673 × 10 × ($200 × 0.70)	3,742,200
Total revenues	26,195,400
Variable Costs	
Hotel variable costs, 2,673 × 60 × $65	10,424,700
Wine Costs	
2,673 × 50 × $5	668,250
2,673 × 10 × $20	534,600
Restaurant costs	
2,673 × 20 × $10	534,600
2,673 × 30 × $15	1,202,850
2,673 × 10 × $20	534,600
Total variable costs	13,899,600
Contribution margin	$12,295,800

Silver Program

Revenues	
9,174 × 20 × ($200 × 0.90)	$33,026,400
9,174 × 15 × ($200 × 0.80)	22,017,600
Total revenues	55,044,000
Variable Costs	
Hotel variable costs, 9,174 × 35 × $65	20,870,850
Wine costs, 9,174 × 35 × $5	1,605,450
Restaurant Costs	
9,174 × 20 × $10	1,834,800
9,174 × 15 × $15	2,064,150
Total variable costs	26,375,250
Contribution margin	$28,668,750

Bronze Program

Revenues, 88,330 × 10 × ($200 × 0.90)	$158,994,000
Variable costs	
Hotel variable costs, 88,330 × 10 × $65	57,414,500
Wine costs 88,330 × 10 × $5	4,416,500
Restaurant costs 88,330 × 10 × $10	8,833,000
Total variable costs	70,664,000
Contribution margin	$ 88,330,000

No Program

Revenues, 240,900 × 1 × $200	$48,180,000
Variable costs, 240,900 × 1 × $65	15,658,500
Contribution margin	$32,521,500

Loyalty Program	Total Revenues	Variable Costs	Contribution Margin	Contrib. Margin/ Total Revenues
Gold	$ 26,195,400	$ 13,899,600	$ 12,295,800	46.94%
Silver	55,044,000	26,375,250	28,668,750	52.08
Bronze	158,994,000	70,664,000	88,330,000	55.56
No program	48,180,000	15,658,500	32,521,500	67.50
Total	$288,413,400	$126,597,350	$161,816,050	

The no-program group of customers has the highest contribution margin per revenue dollar. However, it comprises only 16.71% ($48,180,000 ÷ $288,413,000) of total revenues. The gold program has the lowest contribution margin per revenue dollar. However, it is misleading to evaluate each program in isolation. A key aim of loyalty programs is to promote a high frequency of return business. The contribution margin to total revenue ratio of each program in isolation does not address this issue.

2.	Revenues	$288,413,400
	Variable costs	126,597,350
	Contribution margin	161,816,050
	Fixed costs	140,580,000
	Operating income	$ 21,236,050

3.	Number of room nights	
	Gold, 2,673 × 60	160,380
	Silver, 9,174 × 35	321,090
	Bronze, 88,330 × 10	883,330
	No program, 240,900 × 1	240,900
		1,605,670

Average room rate per night: $\dfrac{\$288,413,400}{1,605,670} = \$179.62$

Average variable cost per night: $\dfrac{\$126,597,350}{1,605,670} = \$78.84$

4. Sherriton Hotels has fixed costs of $140,580,000. A key challenge is to attract a high number of repeat business customers. Loyalty programs aim to have customers return to Sherriton multiple times. Their aim is increasing the revenues beyond what they would be without the program. It is to be expected that the higher the level of nights stayed, the greater the inducements necessary to keep attracting the customer to return. However, given the low level of variable costs to room rates, there is a considerable cushion available for Sherriton to offer high inducements for frequent stayers.

   Sherriton could adopt a net present value analysis of customers who are in the different loyalty clubs. It would be informative for Sherriton to have information on how much of each customer's total lodging industry expenditures it captures. It may well want to give higher levels of inducements to frequent stayers if the current program attracts only, say, 30% of each of its frequent customers' total business in cities where it has lodging properties available.

16-38 (15-20 min.) Customer profitability, responsibility for environmental cleanup, ethics.

1. Customer-profitability analysis examines how individual customers differ in their profitability. The revenues and costs of each customer can be estimated with varying degrees of accuracy. Revenues of IF typically would be known at the time of sale. Many costs also would be known, e.g., the cost of materials used to manufacture the fluids sold to each customer. A major area of uncertainty is future costs associated with obligations arising from the sale. There are several issues here:

   (a) Uncertainty as to the existence and extent of legal liability. Each customer has primary responsibility to dispose of its own toxic waste. Papandopolis needs to determine the extent of IF's liability. It would be necessary to seek legal guidance on this issue.

   (b) Uncertainty as to when the liability will occur. The further in the future, the lower the amount of the liability (assuming discounting for the time value of money occurs.)

   (c) Uncertainty as to the amount of the liability given that the liability exists and the date of the liability can be identified. Papandopolis faces major difficulties here—see the answer to requirement 2.

Many companies argue that uncertainties related to (a), (b), and (c) make the inclusion of "hard-dollar estimates meaningless." However, at a minimum, a contingent liability should be recognized and included in the internal customer-profitability reports.

2. Papandopolis' controller may believe that if estimates of future possible legal exposure are sufficiently uncertain they should not be recorded. His concern about "smoking guns" may have a very genuine basis—that is, if litigation arises, third parties may misrepresent Papandopolis' concerns to the detriment of IF. Any written comments that she makes may surface 5 or 10 years later and be interpreted as "widespread knowledge" within IF that they have responsibility for large amounts of environmental clean-up.

Given this background, Papandopolis still has the responsibility to prepare a report in an objective and competent way. Moreover, she has visited 10 customer sites and has details as to their toxic-waste-handling procedures. If Acme goes bankrupt and has no liability insurance, one of the "deep pockets" available to meet toxic-waste-handling costs is likely to be IF. At a minimum, she should report the likely bankruptcy and the existence of IF's contingent liability for toxic-waste clean-up in her report. Whether she quantifies this contingent liability is a more difficult question. Papandopolis has limited information available to make a meaningful quantification. She is not an employee of Acme Metal and has no information about Acme's liability insurance. Moreover, she does not know what other parties (such as other suppliers) are also jointly liable to pay Acme's clean-up costs.

The appropriate course appears to be to highlight the contingent liability but not to attempt to quantify it.

CHAPTER 17
PROCESS COSTING

17-2 Process-costing systems separate costs into cost categories according to the timing of when costs are introduced into the process. Often, only two cost classifications, direct materials and conversion costs, are necessary. Direct materials are frequently added at one point in time, often the start or the end of the process and all conversion costs are added at about the same time, but in a pattern different from direct materials costs.

17-4 The five key steps in process costing follow:
Step 1: Summarize the flow of physical units of output.
Step 2: Compute output in terms of equivalent units.
Step 3: Compute equivalent unit costs.
Step 4: Summarize total costs to account for.
Step 5: Assign these costs to units completed and to units in ending Work in Process.

17-6 Three inventory methods associated with process costing are:
- Weighted average.
- First-in, first-out (FIFO).
- Standard costing.

17-8 FIFO computations are distinctive because they assign the cost of the earliest equivalent units available (starting with equivalent units in beginning work in process inventory) to units completed and transferred out, and the cost of the most recent equivalent units worked on during the period to ending work in process inventory. In contrast, the weighted-average method costs units completed and transferred out and in ending work in process at the same average cost.

17-10 A major advantage of FIFO is that managers can judge the performance in the current period independently from the performance in the preceding period.

17-12 Yes. Standard-cost procedures are particularly applicable to process-costing systems where there are various combinations of materials and operations. Standard-cost procedures avoid the intricacies involved in detailed tracking with weighted-average or FIFO methods when there are frequent price variations over time.

17-14 No. Transferred-in costs or previous department costs are costs incurred in a previous department that have been charged to a subsequent department. These costs may be costs incurred in that previous department during this accounting period or a preceding accounting period.

17-16 (25 min.) Equivalent units: no beginning inventory.

1. Direct materials cost per unit ($740,000 ÷ 10,000) $ 74
    Conversion cost per unit ($780,000 ÷ 10,000)   78
    Assembly Department cost per unit $152

2. Solution Exhibit 17-16A calculates the equivalent units of direct materials and conversion costs in the Assembly Department of International Electronics in February 2007.

    Solution Exhibit 17-16B computes equivalent units costs
    Direct materials cost per unit $ 74.00
    Conversion cost per unit   82.11
    Assembly Department cost per unit $156.11

3. The difference in the Assembly Department cost per unit calculated in requirements 1 and 2 arises because the costs incurred in January and February are the same but fewer equivalent units of work are done in February than in January. In January, all 10,000 units introduced are fully completed resulting in 10,000 equivalent units of work done with respect to direct materials and conversion costs. In February, of the 10,000 units introduced, 10,000 equivalent units of work is done with respect to direct materials but only 9,500 equivalent units of work is done with respect to conversion costs. The Assembly Department cost per unit is therefore higher.

SOLUTION EXHIBIT 17-16A
Steps 1 and 2: Summarize Output in Physical Units and Compute Equivalent Units
Assembly Department of International Electronics for February 2007

| | (Step 1) | (Step 2) Equivalent Units | |
Flow of Production	Physical Units	Direct Materials	Conversion Costs
Completed and transferred out during current period	9,000	9,000	9,000
Add work in process, ending*	1,000		
1,000 × 100%; 1,000 × 50%		1,000	500
Total accounted for	10,000	10,000	9,500
Deduct work in process, beginning	0	0	0
Started during current period	10,000		
Work done in current period only		10,000	9,500

*Degree of completion in this department: direct materials, 100%; conversion costs, 50%.

SOLUTION EXHIBIT 17-16B
Step 3: Compute Equivalent Unit Costs
Assembly Department of International Electronics for February 2007

	Direct Materials	Conversion Costs
Costs added during February (given)	$740,000	$780,000
Divide by equivalent units of work done in February 2007 (from Soln. Exh 17-16A)	÷ 10,000	÷ 9,500
Cost per equivalent unit of work done in February 2007	$ 74	$ 82.11

17-18 (25 min.) No beginning inventory, materials introduced in middle of process.

1. Solution Exhibit 17-18A shows equivalent units of work done in the current period of Chemical P, 55,000; Chemical Q, 38,500; Conversion costs, 49,500.

2. (a) Solution Exhibit 17-18B calculates cost per equivalent unit of work done in the current period for chemical P, Chemical Q, and conversion costs.

   (b) Solution Exhibit 17-18C summarizes the total Mixing Department costs for July 2006, and assigns these costs to units completed (and transferred out) and to units in ending work in process.

SOLUTION EXHIBIT 17-18A
Steps 1 and 2: Summarize Output in Physical Units and Compute Equivalent Units
Mixing Department of Vaasa Chemicals for July 2006

| | (Step 1) | (Step 2) Equivalent Units | | |
| | Physical | Chemical | Chemical | Conversion |
Flow of Production	Units	P	Q	Costs
Completed and transferred out during current period	38,500	38,500	38,500	38,500
Add work in process, ending* 16,500 × 100%; 16,500 × 0%; 16,500 × 66 2/3%	16,500[†]			
	—	16,500	0	11,000
Total accounted for	55,000	55,000	38,500	49,500
Deduct work in process, beginning	0	0	0	0
Started during current period	55,000	—	—	—
Work done in current period only		55,000	38,500	49,500

*Degree of completion in this department: chemical P, 100%; chemical Q, 0%; conversion costs, 66 2/3%.

Note that chemical Q has not been included in the ending work in process, since the ending WIP is 66 2/3% complete and chemical Q is only added when the units are 75% or three-fourths complete.
[†]Ending work in process = Beginning work in process + Units started – Units completed
= 0 + 55,000 – 38,500 = 16,500 units

SOLUTION EXHIBIT 17-18B
Step 3: Compute Equivalent Unit Costs
Mixing Department of Vaasa Chemicals for July 2007

	Chemical P	Chemical Q	Conversion Costs
Costs added during July (given)	$275,000	$ 77,000	$148,500
Divide by equivalent units of work done in July 2007 (from Solution Exhibit 17-18A)	÷ 55,000	÷ 38,500	÷ 49,500
Cost per equivalent unit of work done in July 2007	$ 5	$ 2	$ 3

SOLUTION EXHIBIT 17-18C

Step 4: Summarize Total Costs to Account For and Assign These Costs to Units Completed, and Units in Ending Work in Process Mixing Department of Vaasa Chemicals for July 2007

	Chemical P			Chemical Q			Conversion Costs			Total Production Costs
	Equivalent Unit (4)	Cost per Equivalent Unit (2)	Total Costs (3)=(1)×(2)	Equivalent Unit (4)	Cost per Equivalent Unit (5)	Total Costs (6)=(4)×(5)	Equivalent Unit (7)	Cost per Equivalent Unit (8)	Total Costs (9)=(7)×(8)	(10)= (3)+(6)+(9)
Panel A: Total Costs to Account For Work done in July (from Solution Exhibit 17-18B)	55,000	$5	$275,000	38,500	$2	$77,000	49,500	$3	$148,500	$500,500
Panel B: Assignment of Costs										
Completed and transferred out: (38,500 × $5; $2; $3)	38,500[1]	$5	$192,500	38,500[1]	$2	$77,000	38,500[1]	$3	$115,500	$385,000
Work in process, ending (16,500 × $5; $0; $2; 11,000 × $3)	16,500[1]	$5	82,500	0[1]	$2	0	11,000[1]	$3	33,000	115,500
Accounted for	55,000		$275,000	38,500		$77,000	49,500		$148,500	$500,500

[1]From Solution Exhibit 17-18A.

Alternate Solution:
Problem 17-18: (25 min.) No beginning inventory, materials introduced in middle of process

1.

		Equivalent Units		
Physical Flow	Units	Chemical P	Chemical Q	Conversion
Beginning WIP	0			
Started into production	55,000			
Units to account for	55,000			
Transferred out	38,500	38,500	38,500	38,500
Ending WIP*	16,500	16,500 (100%)	0 (0%)	11,000 (66.7%)
Units accounted for	55,000			
Work done to date (1)		55,000	38,500	49,500

*Degree of completion in this department: chemical P, 100%; chemical Q, 0%; conversion costs, 66 2/3%.

Note that chemical P is added at the beginning of the process and chemical Q has not been included in the ending work in process, since the ending WIP is only 66 2/3% complete and chemical Q is only added when the units are 75% or three-fourths complete.

2.

Cost Per Unit Calculations

Beginning WIP	$ 0	$ 0	$ 0	$ 0
Costs added	500,500	275,000	77,000	148,500
Cost of work done to date (2)		$ 275,000	$ 77,000	$ 148,500
Costs to account for	$ 500,500			
Cost per equivalent unit (2/1)		$ 5.00	$ 2.00	$ 3.00

Assignment of costs

Transferred out**	$ 385,000	$ 192,500	$ 77,000	$ 115,500
Ending WIP**	115,500	82,500	0	33,000
Total costs accounted for	$ 500,500	$ 275,000	$ 77,000	$ 148,500

** Costs transferred out and in ending work-in-process inventory are equal to the appropriate equivalent unit amount for each component multiplied by the cost per equivalent unit for that component. For example: 38,500 × $5.00 = $192,500. Note that we add across the individual component costs to determine the total cost of goods transferred out and the balance in ending work-in-process.

17-20 (25 min.) FIFO method. See Solution Exhibit 17-20 below.

SOLUTION EXHIBIT 17-20

Step 4: Summarize Total Costs to Account For and Assign These Costs to Units Completed, and Units in Ending Work in Process Using the FIFO Method
Chatham Company for July 2007

	Direct Materials			Conversion Costs			Total Production Costs
	Equivalent Units	Cost per Equivalent Unit	Total Costs	Equivalent Units	Cost per Equivalent Unit	Total Costs	
	(1)	(2)	(3)=(1)×(2)	(4)	(5)	(6)=(4)×(5)	(7)=(3)+(6)
Panel A: Total Costs to Account For							
Work in process, beginning	22,000	$6.00	$132,000	15,400	$10.00	$154,000	$286,000
Work done in current period only	33,000	$7.00	231,000	30,800	$10.75	331,100	562,100
To account for	55,000		$363,000	46,200		$485,100	$848,100
Panel B: Assignment of Costs							
Completed and transferred out:							
Work in process, beginning	22,000	$6.00	$132,000	15,400	$10.00	$154,000	$286,000
Work done in current period to complete beginning work in process	0*	$7.00	0	6,600†	$10.75	70,950	70,950
Total from beginning inventory	22,000		132,000	22,000		224,950	356,950
Started and completed	15,400†	$7.00	107,800	15,400‡	$10.75	165,550	273,350
Total completed and transferred out	37,400		239,800	37,400		390,500	630,300
Work in process, ending	17,600	$7.00	123,200	8,800	$10.75	94,600	217,800
Accounted for	55,000		$363,000	46,200		$485,100	$848,100

*Beginning work in process is 100% complete as to direct materials so zero equivalent units of direct materials need to be added to complete beginning work in process.

†Beginning work in process is 70% complete, which equals 15,400 equivalent units of conversion costs. To complete the 22,000 physical units of beginning work in process, 6,600 (22,000 – 15,400) equivalent units of conversion costs need to be added.

‡37,400 total equivalent units completed and transferred out minus 22,000 equivalent units completed and transferred from beginning inventory equals 15,400 equivalent units.

Alternate Solution:
Problem 17-20: (25 min.) **FIFO method**

1.

Physical Flow	Units	Equivalent Units Materials	Conversion
Beginning WIP	22,000	22,000 (100%)	15,400 (70%)
Started into production	33,000		
Units to account for	55,000		
Beginning WIP	22,000		
To complete begin. WIP		0	6,600 (30%)
Started and completed	15,400	15,400	15,400
Transferred out	37,400		
Ending WIP	17,600	17,600 (100%)	8,800 (50%)
Units accounted for	55,000		
Work done this period (1)		33,000	30,800

Cost Per Unit Calculations

		Materials	Conversion
Beginning WIP	$ 286,000 (cost of work done before current period)		
Costs added this period (2)	562,100	$ 231,000	$ 331,100
Costs to account for	$ 848,100		
Cost per equivalent unit (2/1)		$ 7.00	$ 10.75

2.

Assignment of costs

Beginning WIP	$ 286,000		
To complete begin. WIP*	70,950	$ 0	$ 70,950
Started and completed*	273,350	107,800	165,550
Transferred out	$ 630,300		
Ending WIP*	217,800	123,200	94,600
Costs this period		$ 231,000	$ 331,100
Total costs accounted for	$ 848,100		

*Costs to complete beginning WIP, started and completed, and in ending work-in-process inventory are equal to the appropriate equivalent unit amount for each component multiplied by the cost per equivalent unit for that component. For example: 6,600 x $10.75 = $70,950. Note that we add across the individual component costs to determine the total cost of each line in the table.

17-22 (15 min.) Weighted-average method, equivalent units and unit costs.

Under the weighted-average method, equivalent units are calculated as the equivalent units of work done to date. Solution Exhibit 17-22 shows equivalent units of work done to date for the Satellite Assembly Division of Aerospatiale for direct materials and conversion costs.

SOLUTION EXHIBIT 17-22
Steps 1 and 2: Summarize Output in Physical Units and Compute Equivalent Units
Weighted-Average Method of Process Costing, Satellite Assembly Division
of Aerospatiale for May 2007

Flow of Production	(Step 1) Physical Units (given)	(Step 2) Equivalent Units	
		Direct Materials	Conversion Costs
Work in process beginning	8		
Started during current period	55		
To account for	63		
Completed and transferred out during current period	51	51.0	51.0
Work in process, ending*			
(12 × 60%; 12 × 30%)	12	7.2	3.6
Accounted for	63		
Work done to date		58.2	54.6

*Degree of completion in this department: direct materials, 60%; conversion costs, 30%.

Costs per equivalent unit:

$$DM = \frac{\$5,426,960 + \$35,420,000}{58.2} = \frac{\$40,846,960}{58.2}$$

$$= \$701,837.80 / \text{equivalent unit}$$

$$CV = \frac{\$1,001,440 + \$15,312,000}{54.6} = \frac{\$16,313,440}{54.6}$$

$$= \$298,780.95 / \text{equivalent unit}$$

17-24 (15 min.) FIFO method, equivalent units and unit costs.

1. Under the FIFO method, equivalent units are calculated as the equivalent units of work done in the current period only. Solution Exhibit 17-24 shows equivalent units of work done in May 2007 in the Assembly Department of Aerospatiale for direct materials and conversion costs.

SOLUTION EXHIBIT 17-24
Steps 1 and 2: Summarize Output in Physical Units and Compute Equivalent Units FIFO
Method of Process Costing, Satellite Assembly Division of Aerospatiale for May 2007

		(Step 2) Equivalent Units	
	(Step 1)		
	Physical	Direct	Conversion
Flow of Production	Units	Materials	Costs
Work in process, beginning (given)	8	(work done before current period)	
Started during current period (given)	55		
To account for	63		
(work done before current period)			
Completed and transferred out during current period:			
From beginning work in process§	8		
8 × (100% − 90%);			
8 × (100% − 40%)		0.8	4.8
Started and completed	43†		
43 × 100%, 43 × 100%		43.0	43.0
Work in process, ending* (given)	12		
12 × 60%; 12 × 30%		7.2	3.6
Accounted for	63		
Work done in current period only		51.0	51.4

§Degree of completion in this department: direct materials, 90%; conversion costs, 40%.
†51 physical units completed and transferred out minus 8 physical units completed and transferred out from beginning work-in-process inventory.
*Degree of completion in this department: direct materials, 60%; conversion costs, 30%.

2.
Direct material costs, added May	$35,420,000
Equivalent units	51
Cost per equivalent unit	$694,510
Conversion costs, May	$15,312,000
Equivalent units	51.4
Cost per equivalent units	$297,899

17-26 (25-30 min.) Standard-costing method, assigning costs.

1. The calculations of equivalent units for direct materials and conversion costs are identical to the calculations of equivalent units under the FIFO method. Solution Exhibit 17-24 shows the equivalent unit calculations under standard costing given by the equivalent units of work done in May 2007 in the Assembly Department.

2. Solution Exhibit 17-26 summarizes the total costs to account for, and assigns these costs to units completed and transferred out, and to units in ending work in process.

3. Solution Exhibit 17-26 shows the direct materials and conversion cost variances for

Direct materials	$280,000 F
Conversion costs	$108,000 F

SOLUTION EXHIBIT 17-26

Steps 3, 4, and 5: Compute Equivalent Unit Costs, Summarize Total Costs to Account For, and Assign Costs to Units Completed and to Units in Ending Work in Process

Use of Standard Costs in Process Costing, Satellite Assembly Division of Aerospatiale for May 2007.

		Total Production Costs	Direct Materials	Conversion Costs
(Step 3)	Standard cost per equivalent unit (given)		$ 700,000	$ 300,000
	Work in process, beginning (given)			
	Direct materials, 7.2* × $700,000; Conversion costs, 3.2* × $300,000	$6,000,000		
	Costs added in current period at standard costs Direct materials, 51 × $700,000; Conversion costs, 51.4 × $300,000	51,120,000	$35,700,000	$15,420,000
(Step 4)	Costs to account for	$57,120,000		
(Step 5)	Assignment of costs at standard costs:			
	Completed and transferred out (51 units):			
	Work in process, beginning (8 units)	$ 6,000,000		
	Direct materials added in current period	560,000	0.8* × $700,000	
	Conversion costs added in current period	1,440,000		4.8* × $300,000
	Total from beginning inventory	8,000,000		
	Started and completed (43 units)	43,000,000	43† × $700,000 + 43† × $300,000	
	Total costs of units transferred out	51,000,000		
	Work in process, ending (12 units)			
	Direct materials	5,040,000	7.2# × $700,000	
	Conversion costs	1,080,000		3.6# × $300,000
	Total work in process, ending	6,120,000		
	Total costs accounted for	$57,120,000		
Summary of variances for current performance:				
Costs added in current period at standard prices (see above)			$35,700,000	$15,420,000
Actual costs incurred (given)			35,420,000	15,312,000
Variance			$ 280,000 F	$ 108,000 F

*Equivalent units to complete beginning work in process from Solution Exhibit 17-24, Step 2.
†Equivalent units started and completed from Solution Exhibit 17-24, Step 2.
#Equivalent units in work in process, ending from Solution Exhibit 17-24, Step 2.

*Degree of completion: direct material 90%; conversion costs 40%
$$(8 \times 0.90 = 7.2) ; (8 \times 0.40 = 3.2)$$

17-28 (35-40 min.) **Transferred-in costs, FIFO method.**

1. The calculations for equivalent tonnes of solvent completed and ending work in process for each cost element are exactly as in requirement 1 of Exercise 17-27 shown in Solution Exhibit 17-27A.

2. Solution Exhibit 17-28A presents computations of equivalent unit costs under the FIFO method.

3. Solution Exhibit 17-28B presents a summary of total costs to account for and assigns these costs to tonnes completed and to tonnes in ending work in process using the FIFO method.

SOLUTION EXHIBIT 17-28A

Step 3: Compute Equivalent Unit Costs Under the FIFO Method Cooking Department of Hideo Chemicals for June 2007

	Transferred-in Costs	Direct Materials	Conversion Costs
Equivalent unit costs of beginning work in <u>process</u>			
Work in process, beginning (given)	$43,120	—	$19,800
Divide by equivalent units of beginning work in process (from Solution Exhibit 17-27A)	÷ 40	—	÷ 30
Cost per equivalent unit of beginning work in process	<u>$ 1,078</u>	—	<u>$ 660</u>
Equivalent unit costs of work done in current <u>period only</u>			
Costs added in current period (given)		$39,600	$54,697.50
Divide by equivalent units of work done in current period (from Solution Exhibit 17-27A)	÷ 80	÷ 90	÷ 75
Cost per equivalent unit of work done in current period only	<u>$ 1,177</u>	<u>$ 440</u>	<u>$ 729.30</u>

SOLUTION EXHIBIT 17-28B

Step 4: Summarize Total Costs to Account For and Assign These Costs to Units Completed, and Units in Ending Work in Process Using the FIFO Method Cooking Department of Hideo Chemicals June 2007

	Transferred-in Costs			Direct Materials			Conversion Costs			Total Production Costs
	Equivalent Unit (1)	Cost per Equivalent Unit (2)	Total Costs (3)=(1)×(2)	Equivalent Unit (4)	Cost per Equivalent Unit (5)	Total Costs (6)=(4)×(5)	Equivalent Unit (7)	Cost per Equivalent Unit (8)	Total Costs (9)=(7)×(8)	(10)=(3)+(6)+(9)
Panel A: Total Costs to Account for										
Work in process, beginning (from Solution Exhibit 17-28A)	40	$1,078	$43,120	0	—	$0	30	$660	$19,800	$62,920.00
Work done in current period only (from Solution Exhibit 17-28A)	80	$1,177	94,160	90	$440	39,600	75	$729.30	54,697.50	188,457.50
To account for	120		$137,280	90		$39,600	105		$74,497.50	$251,377.50
Panel B: Assignment of Costs										
Completed and transferred out: (90 physical tonnes)										
Work in process, beginning (40 physical tonnes)	40	$1,078	$43,120	0	—	$0	30	$660	$19,800	$62,920.00
Work done in current period to complete beginning work in process	0[*]		0	40[†]	$440	17,600	10[‡]	$729.30	7,293.00	24,893.00
Total from beginning inventory	40		43,120	40		17,600	40		27,093.00	87,813.00
Started and completed (50 physical tonnes)	50[¶]	$1,177	58,850	50[¶]	$440	22,000	50[¶]	$729.30	36,465.00	117,315.00
Total completed and transferred out (90 physical tonnes)	90[§]		101,970	90[§]		39,600	90[§]		63,558.00	205,128.00
Work in process, ending (30 physical tonnes)	30[§]	$1,177	35,310	0[§]	$440	0	15[§]	$729.30	10,939.50	46,249.50
Accounted for	120		$137,280	90		$39,600	105		$74,497.50	$251,377.50

[*]Beginning work in process is 100% complete as to transferred-in costs so zero equivalent tonnes of transferred-in costs need to be added to complete beginning work in process.

[†]Beginning work in process is 0% complete as to direct materials, which equals 0 equivalent tonnes of direct materials. To complete the 40 physical tonnes of beginning work in process, 40 equivalent tonnes of direct materials need to be added.

[‡]Beginning work in process is 75% complete as to conversion costs, which equals 30 equivalent tonnes of conversion costs. To complete the 40 physical tonnes of beginning work in process, 10 (40 − 30) equivalent tonnes of conversion costs need to be added.

[¶]90 total equivalent tonnes completed and transferred out (Solution Exhibit 17-28A) minus 40 equivalent tonnes completed and transferred from beginning inventory equals 50 equivalent tonnes.

[§]From Solution Exhibit 17-28A.

Alternate Solution:
Problem 17-28: (35 min.) **Transferred-in costs, FIFO method**

1.

Physical Flow	Physical Units	Equivalent Units		
		Transfer-in	Materials	Conversion
Beginning WIP	40	40 (100%)	0 (0%)	30 (75%)
Started into production	80			
Units to account for	120			
Beginning WIP	40			
To complete begin. WIP		0	40 (100%)	10 (25%)
Started and completed	50	50	50	50
Transferred out	90			
Ending WIP	30	30 (100%)	0 (0%)	15 (50%)
Units accounted for	120			
Work done this period (1)		80	90	75

2.

Cost Per Unit Calculations

Beginning WIP	$ 62,920.00*	(cost of work done before current period)		
Costs added this period(2)	188,457.50	$ 94,160	$ 39,600	$ 54,697.50
Costs to account for	$ 251,377.50			
Cost per equivalent unit (2/1)		$ 1,177	$ 440	$ 729.30

* $43,120 + 0 + $19,800 = $62,920

3.

Assignment of costs

Beginning WIP	$ 62,920.00	(cost of work done before current period)		
To complete begin. WIP**	24,893.00	$ 0	$ 17,600	$ 7,293.00
Started and completed**	117,315.00	58,850	22,000	36,465.00
Transferred out	$ 205,128.00			
Ending WIP**	46,249.50	35,310	0	10,939.50
Costs this period		$ 94,160	$ 39,600	$ 54,697.50
Costs accounted for	$ 251,377.50			

** Costs to complete beginning WIP, started and completed, and in ending work-in-process inventory are equal to the appropriate equivalent unit amount for each component multiplied by the cost per equivalent unit for that component. For example: 40 x $440 = $17,600. Note that we add across the individual component costs to determine the total cost of each line in the table.

17-30 (25 min.) Weighted-average method.

1. Solution Exhibit 17-30A shows equivalent units of work done in the current period of

Direct materials	85 equivalent units
Conversion costs	90.50 equivalent units

2. Solution Exhibit 17-30B calculates cost per equivalent unit of beginning work in process and of work done in the current period for direct materials and conversion costs.

3. Solution Exhibit 17-30C summarizes the total Assembly Department costs for October 2007, and assigns these costs to units completed (and transferred out) and to units in ending work in process using the weighted-average method.

SOLUTION EXHIBIT 17-30A
Steps 1 and 2: Summarize Output in Physical Units and Compute Equivalent Units
Assembly Department of Global Defence Inc. for October 2007

			(Step 2)
	(Step 1)		Equivalent Units
	Physical	Direct	Conversion
Flow of Production	Units	Materials	Costs
Completed and transferred out			
during current period	95	95	95
Add work in process, ending*	15		
15 x 100%†; 15 × 70%	___	15	10.5
Total accounted for	110	110	105.5
Deduct work in process, beginning§	25		
25 × 100%†; 25 × 60%		25	15.0
Started during current period	85	___	___
Work done in current period only		85	90.5

†Direct materials are 100% complete in work in process inventories since all direct materials are introduced at the beginning of the Assembly Process.

*Degree of completion in this department: direct materials, 100%; conversion costs, 70%.

§Degree of completion in this department: direct materials, 100%; conversion costs, 60%.

SOLUTION EXHIBIT 17-30B
Step 3: Compute Equivalent Unit Costs:
Assembly Department of Global Defence Inc. for October 2007

	Materials	Costs
Equivalent unit costs of beginning <u>work in process</u>		
Work in process, beginning (given)	$ 506,000	$132,000
Divide by equivalent units of beginning work in process (from Solution Exhibit 17-27A)	÷ 25	÷ 15
Cost per equivalent unit of beginning work in process	$ 20,240	$ 8,800
Equivalent unit costs of work done in <u>current period only</u>		
Costs added in current period (given)	$2,200,000	$1,028,500
Divide by equivalent units of work done in current period (from Solution Exhibit 17-30A)	÷ 85	÷ 90.5
Cost per equivalent unit of work done in current period only	$ 25,882.35	$ 11,364.64

SOLUTION EXHIBIT 17-30C

Step 4: Summarize Total Costs to Account For and Assign These Costs to
Units Completed, and Units in Ending Work in Process Using the Weighted-Average Method
Assembly Department of Global Defence Inc. for October 2007

	Direct Materials			Conversion Costs			Total Production Costs
	Equivalent Units (1)	Cost per Equivalent Unit (2)	Total Costs (3)=(1)×(2)	Equivalent Units (4)	Cost per Equivalent Unit (5)	Total Costs (6)=(4)×(5)	(7)=(3)+(6)
Panel A: Total costs to account for							
Work in process, beginning from Solution Exhibit 17-28B	25	$20,240	$506,000	15.0	$8,800	$132,000	$638,000
Work done in current period only (from Solution Exhibit 17-28B)	85	$25,882.35	2,200,000	90.5	$11,364.64	1,028,500	3,228,500
To account for	110	$24,600*	2,706,000	105.5	$11,000†	1,160,500	$3,866,500
Panel B: Assignment of costs							
Complete and transferred out: (90 physical units)	95‡	$24,600	$2,337,000	95.0‡	$11,000	$1,045,000	$3,382,000
Work in process, ending (10 physical units)	15‡	$24,600	369,000	10.5‡	$11,000	115,500	484,500
Accounted for	110		$2,706,000	105.5		$1,160,500	$3,866,500

*Weighted-average cost per equivalent unit of direct materials = Total direct materials costs divided by total equivalent units of direct materials
$2,706,000 ÷ 110 = $24,600

†Weighted-average cost per equivalent unit of conversion costs = Total conversion costs divided by total equivalent units of conversion costs $1,160,500
÷ 105.5 = $11,000

‡From Solution Exhibit 17-30A.

Alternate Solution:
Problem 17-30: (25 min.) Weighted-average method

1.

Physical Flow	Physical Units	Equivalent Units	
		Materials	Conversion
Beginning WIP	25	25 (100%)	15 (60%)
Started into production	85		
Units to account for	110		
Transferred out	95	95	95
Ending WIP	15	15 (100%)	10.50 (70%)
Units accounted for	110		
Work done to date (1)		110	105.50

2.

Cost Per Unit Calculations

Beginning WIP	$ 638,000	$ 506,000	$ 132,000
Costs added	3,228,500	2,200,000	1,028,500
Cost of work done to date (2)		$ 2,706,000	$ 1,160,500
Costs to account for	$ 3,866,500		
Weighted average cost per equivalent unit (2/1)*		$ 24,600	$ 11,000

* Cost per equivalent unit of beginning WIP was $506,000 / 25 = $20,240 for materials and $132,000 / 15 = $8,800 for conversion. Cost per equivalent unit of work done this period was $2,200,000 / (110 – 25) =$25,882 for materials and $1,028,500 / (105.5 – 15) = $11,365 for conversion.

3.

Assignment of costs

Transferred out**	$ 3,382,000	$ 2,337,000	$ 1,045,000
Ending WIP**	484,500	369,000	115,500
Costs accounted for	$ 3,866,500	$ 2,706,000	$ 1,160,500

** Costs transferred out and in ending work-in-process inventory are equal to the appropriate equivalent unit amount for each component multiplied by the cost per equivalent unit for that component. For example: 95 x $24,600 = $2,337,000. Note that we add across the individual component costs to determine the total cost of goods transferred out and the balance in ending work-in-process.

17-32 (20 min.) FIFO method (continuation of 17-30 and 17-31).

1. The equivalent units of work done in the Assembly Department in October 2007 for direct materials and conversion costs are the same as in Problem 17-30 and are shown in Solution Exhibit 17-30A.

2. The cost per equivalent unit of work done in the Assembly Department in October 2007 for direct materials and conversion costs are calculated in Problem 17-30 in Solution Exhibit 17-30B.

3. Solution Exhibit 17-32 summarizes the total Assembly Department costs for October 2007, and assigns these costs to units completed (and transferred out) and units in ending work in process under the FIFO method.

    The cost per equivalent unit of beginning inventory and of work done in the current period differ:

	Beginning Inventory	Work Done in Current Period
Direct materials	$20,240[a]	$25,882.35
Conversion costs	$8,800[b]	$11,364.64

[a]Cost per unit equals $506,000/25 = $20,240
[b]Cost per unit equals $132,000/15 = $8,800

The following table summarizes the costs assigned to units completed and those still in process under the weighted-average and FIFO process-costing methods for our example.

	Weighted Average (Solution Problem 17-30)	FIFO (Solution Problem 17-32)	Difference
Cost of units completed and transferred out	$3,382,000	$3,358,936	−$23,064
Work in process, ending	484,500	507,564	+$23,064
Total costs accounted for	$3,866,500	$3,866,500	

The FIFO ending inventory is higher than the weighted-average ending inventory by $23,064. This is because, FIFO assumes that all the lower-cost prior-period units in work in process are the first to be completed and transferred out while ending work in process consists of only the higher-cost current-period units. The weighted-average method, however, smoothes out cost per equivalent unit by assuming that more of the higher-cost units are completed and transferred out, while some of the lower-cost units in beginning work in process are placed in ending work in process. Hence, in this case, the weighted-average method results in a higher cost of units completed and transferred out and a lower ending work-in-process inventory than to FIFO.

SOLUTION EXHIBIT 17-32

Step 4: Summarize Total Costs to Account For and Assign These Costs to Units Completed, and Units in Ending Work in Process Using the FIFO Method

Testing Department of Global Defence Inc. for October 2007

	Direct Materials			Conversion Costs			Total Production Costs
	Equivalent Units	Cost per Equivalent Unit	Total Costs	Equivalent Units	Cost per Equivalent Unit	Total Costs	
	(1)	(2)	(3)=(1)×(2)	(4)	(5)	(6)=(4)×(5)	(7)=(3)+(6)
Panel A: Total costs to account for							
Work in process, beginning from Solution Exhibit 17-30B	25	$20,240.00	$506,000	15	$8,800	$132,000	$638,000
Work done in current period only (from Solution Exhibit 17-30B)	85		2,200,000	90.5		1,028,500	3,228,500
To account for	110	$25,882.35	$2,706,000	105.5	$11,364.64	$1,160,500	$3,866,500
Panel B: Assignment of costs							
Completed and transferred out (95 physical units):							
Work in process, beginning (25 physical units)	25	$20,240	$506,000	15.0	$8,800	$132,000	$638,000
Work done in current period to complete beginning work in process	0*	$25,882.35	0	10.0†	$11,364.64	113,646	113,646
Total from beginning inventory	25		506,000	25.0		245,646	751,646
Started and completed (70 physical units)	70‡	$25,882.35	1,811,765	70.0‡	$11,364.64	795,525	2,607,290
Total completed and transferred out (95 physical units)	95		2,317,765	95.0		1,041,171	3,358,936
Work in process, ending (15 physical units)	15§	$25,882.35	388,235	10.5§	$11,364.64	119,329	507,564
Accounted for	110		$2,706,000	105.5		$1,160,500	$3,866,500

*Beginning work in process is 100% complete as to direct materials so zero equivalent units of direct materials need to be added to complete beginning work in process.

†Beginning work in process is 60% complete as to conversion costs, which equals 15 equivalent units of conversion costs. To complete the 25 physical units of beginning work in process, 10 (25 – 15) equivalent units of conversion costs need to be added.

‡15 total equivalent units completed and transferred out (Solution Exhibit 17-30) minus 25 equivalent units completed and transferred from beginning inventory equals 70 equivalent units.

§From Solution Exhibit 17-30A.

Alternate Solution:
Problem 17-32: (25 min.) FIFO method

1.

Physical Flow	Physical Units	Equivalent Units	
		Materials	Conversion
Beginning WIP	25	25 (100%)	15 (60%)
Started into production	85		
Units to account for	110		
To complete begin. WIP	25	0	10 (40%)
Started and completed	70	70	70
Transferred out	95		
Ending WIP	15	15 (100%)	10.5 (70%)
Units accounted for	110		
Work done this period (1)		85	90.5

2.

Cost Per Unit Calculations

Beginning WIP*	$ 638,000	(cost of work done before current period)	
Costs added this period (2)	3,228,500	$ 2,200,000	$ 1,028,500
Costs to account for	$ 3,866,500		
FIFO cost per equivalent unit (2/1)		$ 25,882.35	$ 11,364.64

* $506,000 + $132,000 = $638,000

3.

Assignment of costs

Beginning WIP	$ 638,000		
To complete begin. WIP**	113,646	$ 0	$ 113,646
Started and completed**	2,607,290	1,811,765	795,525
Transferred out	$ 3,358,936		
Ending WIP**	507,564	388,235	119,329
Costs this period		$ 2,200,000	$ 1,028,500
Total costs accounted for	$ 3,866,500		

**Costs to complete beginning WIP, started and completed, and in ending work-in-process inventory are equal to the appropriate equivalent unit amount for each component multiplied by the cost per equivalent unit for that component. For example: 70 x $25,882.35 = $1,811,765. Note that we add across the individual component costs to determine the total cost of each line in the table.

17-34 (30 min.) Transferred-in costs, FIFO costing (continuation of 17-33).

1. As explained in Problem 17-33, requirement 1, transferred-in costs are 100% complete and direct materials are 0% complete in both beginning and ending work in process inventory.

2. The equivalent units of work done in October 2007 in the Testing Department for transferred-in costs, direct materials and conversion costs are exactly as in Solution Exhibit 17-33A.

3. Solution Exhibit 17-34A calculates the cost per equivalent unit of beginning work in process and of work done in October 2007 in the Testing Department for transferred-in costs, direct materials, and conversion costs.

4. Solution Exhibit 17-34B summarizes total Testing Department costs for October 2007, and assigns these costs to units completed and transferred out and to units in ending work in process using the FIFO method.

5. Journal entries:

    i.   Work in Process—Testing Department $3,358,936
              Work in Process—Assembly Department $3,358,936
         Cost of goods completed and transferred
         out during October from the Assembly Dept.
         to the Testing Dept.

    ii. Finished Goods $9,366,253
              Work in Process—Testing Department $9,366,253
         Cost of goods completed and transferred out
         during October from the Testing Department
         to Finished Goods inventory

SOLUTION EXHIBIT 17-34A

Step 3: Compute Equivalent Unit Costs Under the FIFO Method Testing Department of Global Defence Inc. for October 2007

	Transferred-in Costs	Direct Materials	Costs
Equivalent unit costs of beginning work in process			
Work in process, beginning (given)	$ 1,078,066	—	$364,980
Divide by equivalent units of beginning work in process (from Solution Exhibit 17-33A)	÷ 35	—	÷ 24.5
Cost per equivalent unit of beginning work in process	$30,801.885	—	$ 14,897.14
Equivalent unit costs of work done in current period only			
Costs added in current period (given)	$3,358,936	$3,885,000	$ 1,581,000
Divide by equivalent units of work done in current period (from Solution Exhibit 17-33A)	÷ 95	÷ 110	÷ 97.5
Cost per equivalent unit of work done in current period only	$35,357.22	$35,318.18	$16,215.38

SOLUTION EXHIBIT 17-34B

Step 4: Summarize Total Costs to Account For and Assign These Costs to Units Completed, and Units in Ending Work in Process Using the FIFO Method Testing Department of Global Defence Inc. for October 2007

	Transferred-in Costs			Direct Materials			Conversion Costs			Total Production Costs
	Equivalent Unit (4)	Cost per Equivalent Unit (2)	Total Costs (3)=(1)×(2)	Equivalent Unit (4)	Cost per Equivalent Unit (5)	Total Costs (6)=(4)×(5)	Equivalent Unit (7)	Cost per Equivalent Unit (8)	Total Costs (9)=(7)×(8)	(10)=(3)+(6)+(9)
Panel A: Total Costs to Account for										
Work in process, beginning (from Solution Exhibit 17-MA)	35	$30,801.885	$1,078,066	0	—	$0	24.5	$14,897.14	$364,980	$1,443,046
Work done in current period only (from Solution Exhibit 17-34A) To account for	95 / 130	$35,357.22	3,358,936 / $4,437,002	110 / 110	$35,318.18	3,885,000 / $3,885,000	97.5 / 122	$16,215.38	1,581,000 / $1,945,980	8,824,936 / $10,267,982
Panel B: Assignment of Costs										
Completed and transferred out: (110 physical units) Work in process, beginning (35 physical units)	35	$30,801.885	$1,078,066	0	—	$0	24.5	$14,897.14	$364,980	$1,443,046
Work done in current period to complete beginning work in process	0* / 35		0 / 1,078,066	35† / 35	$35,318.18	1,236,136 / 1,236,136	10.5‡ / 35.0	$16,215.38	170,261 / 535,241	1,406,397
Total from beginning inventory										2,849,443
Started and completed (75 physical units)	75¹¹	$35,357.22	2,651,792	75¹¹	$35,318.18	2,648,864	75.0¹¹	$16,215.38	1,216,154	6,516,810
Total completed and transferred out (110 physical units)	110§		3,729,858	110§		3,885,000	110.0§		1,751,395	9,366,253
Work in process, ending (20 physical tonnes) Accounted for	20§ / 130	$35,357.22	707,144 / $4,437,002	0§ / 110		0 / $3,885,000	12.0§ / 122.0	$16,215.38	194,585 / $1,945,980	901,729 / $10,267,982

*Beginning work in process is 100% complete as to transferred-in costs so zero equivalent tonnes of transferred-in costs need to be added to complete beginning work in process.

†Beginning work in process is 0% complete as to direct materials, which equals 0 equivalent tonnes of direct materials. To complete the 35 physical tonnes of beginning work in process, 35 equivalent tonnes of direct materials need to be added.

‡Beginning work in process is 70% complete as to conversion costs. To complete the 35 physical tonnes of beginning work in process, 10 (35 − 24.5) equivalent tonnes of conversion costs need to be added.

¹¹110 total equivalent tonnes completed and transferred out (Solution Exhibit 17-33) minus 35 equivalent tonnes completed and transferred from beginning inventory equals 75 equivalent tonnes.

§From Solution Exhibit 17-33A.

Alternate Solution:
Problem 17-34: (30 min.) Transferred-in costs, FIFO method
(continuation of 17-33)

1. As explained in Problem 17-33, requirement 1, transferred-in costs are 100% complete and direct materials are 0% complete in both beginning and ending work in process inventory.

2., 3., and 4.

		Equivalent Units		
	Physical	Transferred-in		
Physical Flow	Units	Costs	Materials	Conversion
Beginning WIP	35	35 (100%)	0 (0%)	24.5 (70%)
Started into production	95			
Units to account for	130			
To complete begin. WIP	35	0 (0%)	35 (100%)	10.5 (30%)
Started and completed	75	75	75	75
Transferred out	110			
Ending WIP	20	20 (100%)	0 (0%)	12 (60%)
Units accounted for	130			
Work done this period (1)		95	110	97.5

	Production	Transferred-in		
Cost Per Unit Calculations	Costs	Costs	Materials	Conversion
Beginning WIP	$ 1,443,046*	(cost of work done before current		
period)				
Costs added this period (2)	8,824,936	$ 3,358,936	$ 3,885,000	$ 1,581,000
Costs to account for	$ 10,267,982			
FIFO cost per equivalent unit (2/1)		$ 35,357.22	$ 35,318.18	$ 16,215.38

* $1,443,046 = $1,078,066 + $0 + $364,980

Assignment of costs				
Beginning WIP	$ 1,443,046	(cost of work done before current		
period)				
To complete begin. WIP	1,406,397**	$ 0	$ 1,236,136	$ 170,261
Started and completed	6,516,810**	2,651,792	2,648,864	1,216,154
Transferred out	$ 9,366,253			
Ending WIP	901,729**	707,144	0	194,585
Costs accounted for				
this period		$ 3,358,936	$ 3,885,000	$ 1,581,000
Total costs accounted for	$10,267,982			

**Costs to complete beginning WIP, started and completed, and ending work-in-process inventory are equal to the appropriate equivalent unit amount for each component multiplied by the cost per equivalent unit for that component. For example: 35 x $35,318.18 = $1,236,136. Note that we add across the individual component costs to determine the total cost of each line in the table.

5.   Journal entries:
   i.   Work in Process—Testing Department $3,358,936
            Work in Process—Assembly Department $3,358,936
            Cost of goods completed and transferred out
               during October from the Assembly Dept. to
               the Testing Dept.

   ii. Finished Goods $9,366,253
            Work in Process—Testing Department $9,366,253
            Cost of goods completed and transferred out
               during October from the Testing Department
               to Finished Goods inventory

17-36 (5-10 min.) Journal entries (continuation of 17-35).

1.   Work in Process—Forming Department $70,000
         Accounts Payable $70,000
      To record direct materials purchased and
      used in production during April

2.   Work in Process—Forming Department $42,500
         Various Accounts $42,500
      To record Forming Department conversion
      costs for April

3.   Work in Process—Finishing Department $102,926
         Work in Process—Forming Department $102,926
      To record cost of goods completed and
      transferred out in April from the Forming
      Department to the Finishing Department

Work in Process—Assembly Department

Beginning inventory, Apr. 1	$ 9,625	3. Transferred out to	
1. Direct materials	70,000	Work in Process-testing	$102,926
2. Conversion costs	42,500		
Ending inventory, Apr. 31	$19,199		

17-38 (30 min.) Transferred-in costs, weighted average (related to 17-35 through 17-37) (Chapter Appendix I).

1.   Solution Exhibit 17-38A computes the equivalent units of work done in April 2007 in the Finishing Department for transferred-in costs, direct materials, and conversion costs.

Solution Exhibit 17-38B calculates the cost per equivalent unit of beginning work in process and of work done in April 2007 in the Finishing Department for transferred-in costs, direct materials, and conversion costs.

Solution Exhibit 17-38C summarizes total Finishing Department costs for April 2007, and assigns these costs to units completed and transferred out and to units in ending work in process using the weighted-average method.

2.   Journal entries:

    i.   Work in Process—Finishing Department $102,926

            Work in Process—Forming Department $102,926

        Cost of goods completed and transferred

        out during April from the Forming

        Department to the Finishing Department

    ii.   Finished Goods $165,843

            Work in Process—Finishing Department $166,843

        Cost of goods completed and transferred

        out during April from the Finishing

        Department to Finished Goods inventory

SOLUTION EXHIBIT 17-38A
Steps 1 and 2: Summarize Output in Physical Units and Compute Equivalent Units
Finishing Department of Star Toys for April 2007

| | (Step 1) Physical Units | (Step 2) Equivalent Units | | |
Flow of Production		Transferred in Costs	Direct Materials	Conversion Costs
Completed and transferred out during current period	2,150	2,150	2,150	2,150
Add work in process, ending*	450			
(450 × 100%; 450 × 0%; 450 × 30%)		450	0	135
Total accounted for	2,600	2,600	2,150	2,285
Deduct work in process, beginning†	550			
(550 × 100%; 550 × 0%; 550 × 60%)		550	0	330
Transferred in during current period	2,050			
Work done in current period only		2,050	2,150	1,955

*Degree of completion in this department: transferred-in costs, 100%, direct materials, 0%; conversion costs, 30%.
†Degree of completion in this department: transferred-in costs, 100%; direct materials, 0%; conversion costs, 60%.

SOLUTION EXHIBIT 17-38B
Step 3: Compute Equivalent Unit Costs Under the Weighted-Average Method
Finishing
Department of Star Toys for April 2007

	Transferred-in Costs	Direct Materials	Conversion Costs
Equivalent unit costs of beginning work in process			
Work in process, beginning (given)	$ 17,750	—	$ 7,250
Divide by equivalent units of beginning work in process (from Solution Exhibit 17-38A)	÷ 550	—	÷ 330
Cost per equivalent unit of beginning work in process	$ 32.27	—	$21.969
Equivalent unit costs of work done in current period only			
Costs added in current period (given)	$102,926	$23,100	$38,400
Divide by equivalent units of work done in current period (from Solution Exhibit 17-38A)	÷ 2,050	÷ 2,150	÷ 1,955
Cost per equivalent unit of work done in current period only	$ 50.208	$10.744	$19.642

SOLUTION EXHIBIT 17-38C

Step 4: Summarize Total Costs to Account For and Assign These Costs to Units Completed, and Units in Ending Work in Process Using the Weighted-Average Method Finishing Department of Star Toys for April 2007

		Transferred-in Costs			Direct Materials			Conversion Costs			Total Production Costs
		Equivalent Unit (4)	Cost per Equivalent Unit (2)	Total Costs (3)=(1)×(2)	Equivalent Unit (4)	Cost per Equivalent Unit (5)	Total Costs (6)=(4)×(5)	Equivalent Unit (7)	Cost per Equivalent Unit (8)	Total Costs (9)=(7)×(8)	(10)= (3)+(6)+(9)
Panel A:	Total Costs to Account for:										
	Work in process, beginning (from Solution Exhibit 17-38B)	550	$32.27	$17,750	0	—	$0	330	$21.969	$7,250	$25,000
	Work done in current period only (from Solution Exhibit 17-38B)	2,050	$50.208	102,926	2,150	$10.744	23,100	1,955	$19.642	38,400	164,426
	To account for	2,600	$46.414*	$120,676	2,150	$10.744†	$23,100	2,285	$19.978‡	$45,650	$189,426
Panel B:	Assignment of Costs										
	Completed and transferred out: (2,150 physical units)	2,150**	$46.414	$99,790	2,150**	$10.744	$23,100	2,150**	$19.978	$42,953	$165,843
	Work in process, ending (450 physical units)	450**	$46.414	20,886	0**	—	0	135**	$19.978	2,697	23,583
	Accounted for	2,600		$120,676	2,150		$23,100	2,285		$45,650	$189,426

*Weighted-average cost per equivalent unit of transferred-in costs = Total transferred-in costs divided by total equivalent units of transferred-in costs
= $120,676 ÷ 2,600 = $46.414
†Weighted average costs per equivalent unit of direct materials = Total direct materials costs divided by total equivalent units of direct materials
= $23,100 ÷ 2,150 = $10.744
‡Weighted-average cost per equivalent unit of conversion costs = Total conversion costs divided by total equivalent units of conversion costs
= $45,650 ÷ 2,285 = $19.978
**From Exhibit 17-38A.

Alternate Solution:
Problem 17-38: (30 min.) **Transferred-in costs, weighted-average method (related to 17-35 to 17-37) (Chapter 17 Appendix I)**

1.

Physical Flow	Physical Units	Equivalent Units Transferred-in Costs	Materials	Conversion
Beginning WIP	550	550 (100%)	0 (0%)	330 (60%)
Started into production	2,050			
Units to account for	2,600			
Completed & Transferred out	2,150	2,150	2,150	2,150
Ending WIP	450	450 (100%)	0 (0%)	135 (30%)
Units accounted for	2,600			
Work done to date (1)		2,600	2,150	2,285

Cost Per Unit Calculations	Production Costs	Transferred-in Costs	Materials	Conversion
Beginning WIP	$ 25,000	$ 17,750	$ 0	$ 7,250
Costs added	164,426	102,926	23,100	38,400
Cost of work done to date (2)		$ 120,676	$ 23,100	$ 45,650
Costs to account for	$ 189,426			
Weighted average cost per equivalent unit (2/1)		$ 46.414	$ 10.744	$ 19.978

Assignment of costs

	Production Costs	Transferred-in Costs	Materials	Conversion
Transferred out*	$ 165,843	$ 99,790	$ 23,100	$ 42,953
Ending WIP*	23,583	20,886	0	2,697
Costs accounted for	$ 189,426	$ 120,676	$ 23,100	$ 45,650

*Costs transferred out and ending work-in-process inventory are equal to the appropriate equivalent unit amount for each component multiplied by the cost per equivalent unit for that component. For example: 2,150 x $46.414 = $99,790. Note that we add across the individual component costs to determine the total cost of goods transferred out and the balance in ending work-in-process.

2.   Journal entries:

    i.   Work in Process—Finishing Department $102,926

            Work in Process—Forming Department $102,926

          Cost of goods completed and transferred out

            during April from the Forming Department

            to the Finishing Department

    ii.   Finished Goods $165,843

            Work in Process—Finishing Department $165,843

          Cost of goods completed and transferred out

            during April from the Finishing Department

            to Finished Goods inventory

17-40 (45 min.) Transferred-in costs, weighted average and FIFO (Chapter Appendix I).

1.   Solution Exhibit 17-40A computes the equivalent units of work done in week 37 in the Drying and Packaging Department for transferred-in costs, direct materials, and conversion costs.

2.   Solution Exhibit 17-40B calculates the cost per equivalent unit of beginning work in process and of work done in week 37 in the Drying and Packaging Department for transferred-in costs direct materials, and conversion costs.

Solution Exhibit 17-40C summarizes total drying and packaging Department costs for week 37, and assigns these costs to units completed and transferred out and to units in ending work in process using the weighted-average method.

3.   Solution Exhibit 17-40D calculates the cost per equivalent unit of beginning work in process and of work done in week 37 in the Drying and Packaging Department for transferred-in costs, direct materials, and conversion costs.

Solution Exhibit 17-40E summarizes total Drying and Packaging Department costs for week 37, and assigns these costs to units completed and transferred out and to units in ending work in process using the FIFO method.

SOLUTION EXHIBIT 17-40A
Steps 1 and 2: Summarize Output in Physical Units and Compute Equivalent Units
Drying and Packaging Department of Frito-Lay Inc. for Week 37

| | (Step 1) | (Step 2) Equivalent Units | | |
| | Physical | Transferred- | Direct | Conversion |
Flow of Production	Units	in Costs	Materials	Costs
Completed and transferred out during current period	5,300	5,300	5,300	5,300
Add work in process, ending*	1,050			
(1,050 × 100%; 1,050 × 0%; 1,050 × 40%)		1,050	0	420
Total accounted for	6,350	6,350	5,300	5,720
Deduct work in process, beginning†	1,300			
(1,300 × 100%; 1,300 × 0%; 1,300 × 80%)		1,300	0	1,040
Transferred in during current period	5,050			
Work done in current period only		5,050	5,300	4,680

*Degree of completion in this department: transferred-in costs, 100%; direct materials, 0%; conversion costs, 40%.
†Degree of completion in this department: transferred-in costs, 100%; direct materials, 0%; conversion costs, 80%.

SOLUTION EXHIBIT 17-40B
Step 3: Compute Equivalent Unit Costs Under the Weighted-Average Method
Drying and Packaging Department of Frito-Lay Inc. for Week 37

	Transferred-in Costs	Direct Materials	Conversion Costs
Equivalent unit costs of beginning work in process			
Work in process, beginning (given)	$29,000	—	$ 9,060
Divide by equivalent units of beginning work in process (from Solution Exhibit 17-40A)	÷ 1,300	—	÷ 1,040
Cost per equivalent unit of beginning work in process	$22.308	—	$ 8.712
Equivalent unit costs of work done in current period only			
Costs added in current period (given)	$96,000	$25,200	$38,400
Divide by equivalent units of work done in current period (from Solution Exhibit 17-40A)	÷ 5,050	÷ 5,300	÷ 4,680
Cost per equivalent unit of work done in current period only	$ 19.01	$ 4.755	$ 8.205

SOLUTION EXHIBIT 17-40C

Step 4: Summarize Total Costs to Account For and Assign These Costs to Units Completed, and Units in Ending Work in Process Using the Weighted-Average Method Drying and Packaging Department of Frito-Lay for Week 37

	Transferred-in Costs			Direct Materials			Conversion Costs			Total Production Costs
	Equivalent Unit (1)	Cost per Equivalent Unit (2)	Total Costs (3)=(1)×(2)	Equivalent Unit (4)	Cost per Equivalent Unit (5)	Total Costs (6)=(4)×(5)	Equivalent Unit (7)	Cost per Equivalent Unit (8)	Total Costs (9)=(7)×(8)	(10)=(3)+(6)+(9)
Panel A: Total Costs to Account for Work in process, beginning (from Solution Exhibit 17-40B)	1,300	$23.308	$29,000	0	—	$0	1,040	$8.712	$9,060	$38,060
Work done in current period only (from Solution Exhibit 17-40B)	5,050	$19.01	96,000	5,300	$4.755	25,200	4,680	$8.205	38,400	159,600
To account for	6,350	$19.685*	$125,000	5,300	$4.755†	$25,200	5,720	$8.297‡	$47,460	$197,660
Panel B: Assignment of Costs Completed and transferred out: (5,300 physical units)	5,300**	$19.685	$104,331	5,300**	$4.755	$25,200	5,300**	$8.297	$43,975	$173,506
Work in process, ending (1,050 physical units)	1,050**	$19.685	20,669	0**	—	0	420**	$8.297	3,485	24,154
Accounted for	6,350		$125,000	5,300		$25,200	5,720		$47,460	$197,660

*Weighted-average cost per equivalent unit of transferred-in costs = Total transferred-in costs divided by total equivalent units of transferred-in costs = $125,000 ÷ 6,350 = $19.685.

†Weighted-average costs per equivalent unit of direct materials = Total direct materials costs divided by total equivalent units of direct materials = $25,200 ÷ 5,300 = $4.755.

‡Weighted-average cost per equivalent unit of conversion costs = Total conversion costs divided by total equivalent units of conversion costs = $47,460 ÷ 5,720 = $8.297.

**From Solution Exhibit 1740A.

SOLUTION EXHIBIT 17-40D
Step 3: Compute Equivalent Unit Costs Under the FIFO Method
Drying and Packaging Department of Frito-Lay Inc. for Week 37

	Transferred-in Costs	Direct Materials	Conversion Costs
Equivalent unit costs of beginning work in process			
Work in process, beginning (given)	$28,920	—	$ 9,060
Divide by equivalent units of beginning work in process (from Solution Exhibit 17-40A)	÷ 1,300	—	÷ 1,040
Cost per equivalent unit of beginning work in process	$22.246	—	$ 8.712
Equivalent unit costs of work done in current period only			
Costs added in current period (given)	$94,000	$25,200	$38,400
Divide by equivalent units of work done in current period (from Solution Exhibit 17-40A)	÷ 5,050	÷ 5,300	÷ 4,680
Cost per equivalent unit of work done in current period only	$18.614	$ 4.755	$ 8.205

SOLUTION EXHIBIT 17-40E

Step 4: Summarize Total Costs to Account For and Assign These Costs to Units Completed, and Units in Ending Work in Process Using the FIFO Method Drying and Packaging Department of Frito-Lay for Week 37

	Transferred-in Costs			Direct Materials			Conversion Costs			Total Production Costs
	Equivalent Unit (4)	Cost per Equivalent Unit (2)	Total Costs (3)=(1)×(2)	Equivalent Unit (4)	Cost per Equivalent Unit (5)	Total Costs (6)=(4)×(5)	Equivalent Unit (7)	Cost per Equivalent Unit (8)	Total Costs (9)=(7)×(8)	(10)= (3)+(6)+(9)
Panel A: Total Costs to Account for for Work in process, beginning (from Solution Exhibit 17-40D)		$22.246	$28,920		—	$0	1,040	$8.712	$9,060	$37,980
Work done in current period only (from Solution Exhibit 17-40D)	5,050	$18.614	94,000	5,300	$4.755	25,200	4,680	$8.205	38,400	157,600
To account for	6350		$122,920	5,300		$25,200	5,720		$47,460	$195,580
Panel B: Assignment of Costs Completed and transferred out: (5,300 physical units)		$22.246	$28,920		—	$0	1,040	$8.712	$9,060	$37,980
Work in process, beginning (1,300 physical units)	1,300			0						
Work done in current period to complete beginning work in process	0*	$18.614	0	1,300†	$4.755	6,180	260†	$8.205	2,133	8,313
Total from beginning inventory	1,300		28,920	1,300		6,180	1,300		11,193	46,293
Started and completed (4,000 physical units)	4,000¹¹	$18.614	74,456	4,000¹¹	$4.755	19,020	4,000¹¹	$8.205	32,820	126,296
Total completed and transferred out (5,250 physical units)	5,300§		103,376	5,300§		25,200	5,300§		44,013	172,589
Work in process, ending (1,000 physical units)	1,050§	$18.614	19,544	0§	$4.755	0	420§	$8.205	3,447	22,991
Accounted for	6,350		$122,920	5,300		$25,200	5,720		$47,460	$195,580

*Beginning work in process is 100% complete as to transferred-in costs so zero equivalent units of transferred-in costs need to be added to complete beginning work in process.

†Beginning work in process is 0% complete as to direct materials, which equals 0 equivalent units of direct materials. To complete the 1,300 physical units of beginning work in process, 1,300 equivalent units of direct materials need to be added.

‡Beginning work in process is 80% complete as to conversion costs, which equals 1,040 equivalent units of conversion costs. To complete the 1,300 physical units of beginning work in process, 260 (1,300 − 1,040) equivalent units of conversion costs need to be added.

¹¹5,300 total equivalent units completed and transferred out (Solution Exhibit 17-40A) minus 1,300 equivalent units completed and transferred from beginning inventory equals 4,000 equivalent units.

§From Solution Exhibit 17-40A.

Alternate Solution:
Problem 17-40: (45 min.) Transferred-in costs, weighted-average and FIFO (Chapter 17 Appendix I).

1. and 2. (Weighted Average)

Physical Flow	Physical Units	Equivalent Units (Weighted Average) Transferred-in Costs	Materials	Conversion
Beginning WIP	1,300	1,300 (100%)	0 (0%)	1,040 (80%)
Started into production	5,050			
Units to account for	6,350			
Completed & Transferred out	5,300	5,300	5,300	5,300
Ending WIP	1,050	1,050 (100%)	0 (0%)	420 (40%)
Units accounted for	6,350			
Work done to date (1)		6,350	5,300	5,720

Cost Per Unit Calculations	Production Costs	Transferred-in Costs	Materials	Conversion
Beginning WIP	$ 38,060	$ 29,000	$ 0	$ 9,060
Costs added	159,600	96,000	25,200	38,400
Cost of work done to date (2)		$ 125,000	$ 25,200	$ 47,460
Costs to account for	$ 197,660			
Cost per equivalent unit (2/1)		$ 19.685	$ 4.755	$ 8.297

Assignment of costs

	Production Costs	Transferred-in Costs	Materials	Conversion
Transferred out*	$ 173,506	$ 104,331	$ 25,200	$ 43,975
Ending WIP*	24,154	20,669	0	3,485
Costs accounted for	$ 197,660	$ 125,000	$ 25,200	$ 47,460

*Costs transferred out and ending work-in-process inventory are equal to the appropriate equivalent unit amount for each component multiplied by the cost per equivalent unit for that component. For example: 5,300 x $19.685 = $104,331. Note that we add across the individual component costs to determine the total cost of goods transferred out and the balance in ending work-in-process.

1. and 3. **(FIFO)**

<u>Equivalent Units **(FIFO)**</u>

Physical Flow	Physical Units	Transferred-in Costs	Materials	Conversion
Beginning WIP	1,300	1,300 (100%)	0 (0%)	1,040 (80%)
Started into production	5,050			
Units to account for	6,350			
To complete begin. WIP	1,300	0	1,300 (100%)	260 (20%)
Started and completed	4,000	4,000	4,000	4,000
Transferred out	5,300			
Ending WIP	1,050	1,050 (100%)	0 (0%)	420 (40%)
Units accounted for	6,350			
Work done this period (1)		5,050	5,300	4,680

Cost Per Unit Calculation	Production Costs	Transferred-in Costs	Materials	Conversion
Beginning WIP	$ 37,980*	(cost of work done before current period)		
Costs added this period (2)	157,600	$ 94,000	$ 25,200	$ 38,400
Costs to account for	$ 195,580			
Cost per equivalent unit (b/a)		$ 18.614	$ 4.755	$ 8.205

*($28,920 transferred-in costs + $9,060 conversion costs)

<u>Assignment of costs</u>

Beginning WIP	$ 37,980	(cost of work done before current period)		
To complete begin. WIP**	8,313	$ 0	$ 6,180	$ 2,133
Started and completed**	126,296	74,456	19,020	32,820
Transferred out	$ 172,589			
Ending WIP**	22,991	19,544	0	3,447
Costs accounted for this period		$ 94,000	$ 25,200	$ 38,400
Total costs accounted for	$ 195,580			

** Costs to complete beginning WIP, started and completed, and ending work-in-process inventory are equal to the appropriate equivalent unit amount for each component multiplied by the cost per equivalent unit for that component. For example: 4,000 x $18.614 = $74,456. Note that we add across the individual component costs to determine the total cost of each line in the table.

17-42 (15 min.) Operation Costing (Chapter Appendix II).

Costs of Work Order 815 and Work Order 831 are as follows:

	Work Order 815	Work Order 831
Number of units (pairs)	1,000	5,000
Direct materials costs	$30,000	$50,000
Conversion costs:		
Cutting (1,000; 5,000 × $11)	11,000	55,000
Sewing (1,000; 5,000 × $16)	16,000	80,000
Lining (1,000; 0 × $9)	9,000	—
Packing (1,000; 5,000 × $3)	3,000	15,000
Total costs	$69,000	$200,000
Total cost per unit	$\dfrac{\$69,000}{1,000}=\$69$	$\dfrac{\$200,000}{5,000}=\$40$

17-44 (20-25 min.) Equivalent unit computations, benchmarking, ethics.

1. The reported monthly cost per equivalent unit of either direct materials or conversion costs is lower when the plant manager overestimates the percentage of completion of ending work in process; the overestimate increases the denominator and thus decreases the cost per equivalent whole unit. By reporting a lower cost per equivalent unit, the plant manager increases the likelihood of being in the top three ranked plants for the benchmarking comparisons.

    A plant manager can manipulate the monthly estimate of percentage of completion by understating the number of steps yet to be undertaken before a suit becomes a finished good.

2. There are several options available:
   a. Major shows the letters to the line executive to whom the plant managers report in a hard-line way (say, the corporate manager of manufacturing). This approach is appropriate if the letters allege it is the plant managers who are manipulating the percentage of completion estimates.
   b. Major herself shows the letters to the plant managers. This approach runs the danger of the plant managers ignoring or reacting negatively to someone to whom they do not report in a line-mode questioning their behaviour. Much will depend here on how Major raises the issue. Unsigned letters need not have much credibility unless they contain specific details.
   c. Major discusses the letters with the appropriate plant controllers without including the plant manager in the discussion. While the plant controller has

responsibility for preparing the accounting reports from the plant, the plant controller in most cases reports hard-line to the plant manager. If this reporting relationship exists, Major may create a conflict of interest situation for the plant controller. Only if the plant controller reports hard-line to the corporate controller and dotted-line to the plant manager should Major show the letters to the plant controller without simultaneously showing them to the plant manager.

3. The plant controller's ethical responsibilities to Major and to Leisure Suits should be the same. These include:
   - The plant controller is expected to have the competence to make equivalent unit computations. This competence does not always extend to making estimates of the percentage of completion of a product. In Leisure Suits' case, however, the products are probably easy to understand and observe. Hence, a plant controller could obtain reasonably reliable evidence on percentage of completion at a specific plant.
   - The plant controller should not allow the possibility of the division being written-up favourably in the company newsletter to influence the way equivalent unit costs are computed.

4. Major could seek evidence on possible manipulations as follows:
   a. Have plant controllers report detailed breakdowns on the stages of production and then conduct end-of-month audits to verify the actual stages completed for ending work in process.
   b. Examine trends over time in ending work in process. Divisions that report low amounts of ending work in process relative to total production are not likely to be able to greatly affect equivalent cost amounts by manipulating percentage of completion estimates. Divisions that show sizable quantities of total production in ending work in process are more likely to be able to manipulate equivalent cost computations by manipulating percentage of completion estimates.

CHAPTER 18
SPOILAGE, REWORK, AND SCRAP

18-2 Spoilage—unacceptable units of production that are discarded or sold for net disposal proceeds.

Reworked units—unacceptable units of production that are subsequently reworked and sold as acceptable finished goods.

Scrap—residual material that has minimal (frequently zero) sales value compared with the sales value of the main or joint product(s).

18-4 Abnormal spoilage is spoilage that is not expected to arise under efficient operating conditions. Costs of abnormal spoilage are losses, measures of inefficiency that should be written off directly as losses for the accounting period.

18-6 Normal spoilage typically is expressed as a percentage of good units passing the inspection point. Given actual spoiled units, we infer abnormal spoilage as follows:

Abnormal spoilage = Actual spoilage – Normal spoilage

18-8 Yes. Normal spoilage rates should be computed from the good output or from the <u>normal</u> input, not the <u>total</u> input. Normal spoilage is a given percentage of a certain output base. This base should never include abnormal spoilage, which is included in total input. Abnormal spoilage does not vary in direct proportion to units produced, and to include it would cause the normal spoilage count to fluctuate irregularly but not vary in direct proportion to the output base.

18-10 No. If abnormal spoilage is detected at a different point in the production cycle than normal spoilage, then unit costs would differ. If, however normal and abnormal spoilage are detected at the same point in the production cycle, their unit costs would be the same.

18-12 No. Unless there are special reasons for charging rework to jobs that contained the bad units, the costs of extra materials, labour, and so on are usually charged to manufacturing overhead and allocated to all jobs.

18-14 A company is justified in inventorying scrap when its estimated net realizable value is significant and the time between storing it and selling or reusing it may be quite long.

18-16 (25 min.) Weighted-average method, spoilage

1. Solution Exhibit 18-16A calculates the equivalent units of work done for each cost element in September 2007.

2. Solution Exhibit 18-16B presents computations of the cost per equivalent unit of beginning inventory and of work done in the current period for each cost element under the weighted-average method.

3. Solution Exhibit 18-16C presents a summary of total costs to account for and assigns these costs to units completed, normal spoilage, abnormal spoilage, and to units in ending work in process using the weighted-average method.

SOLUTION EXHIBIT 18-16A
Steps 1 and 2: Summarize Output in Physical Units and Compute Equivalent Units
Superchip Company for September 2007

Flow of Production	(Step 1) Physical Units	(Step 2) Equivalent Units Direct Materials	Conversion Costs
Good units completed and transferred out during current period	1,400	1,400	1,400
Normal spoilage†	210		
210 × 100%; 210 × 100%		210	210
Abnormal spoilage‡	190		
190 × 100%; 190 × 100%		190	190
Work in process, ending§	300		
300 × 100%; 300 × 40%		300	120
Total accounted for	2,100	2,100	1,920
Deduct work in process, beginning*	400		
400 × 100%; 400 × 30%		400	120
Started during current period	1,700		
Work done in current period only		1,700	1,800

†Normal spoilage is 15% of good units transferred out: 15% × 1,400 = 210 units; Degree of completion of normal spoilage in this department: direct materials, 100%; conversion costs, 100%.
‡Abnormal spoilage = Actual spoilage – Normal spoilage = 400 – 210 = 190 units; Degree of completion of abnormal spoilage in this department: direct materials, 100%; conversion costs, 100%.
§Degree of completion in this department: direct materials, 100%; conversion costs, 40%.
*Degree of completion in this department: direct materials, 100%; conversion costs, 30%.
Actual spoilage = WIP Sept. 1 + Sept. STARTS – Sept. completed + and transferred out – WIP Sept. 30
= 400 + 1,700 – 1,400 – 300
= 400 units

SOLUTION EXHIBIT 18-16B
Step 3: Compute Equivalent Unit Costs:
Superchip Company for September 2007

	Direct Materials	Conversion Costs
Equivalent unit costs of beginning work in process		
Work in process, beginning (given)	$ 76,800	$12,240
Divide by equivalent units in beginning work in process (from Solution Exhibit 18-16A)	÷ 400	÷ 120
Cost per equivalent unit of beginning work in process	$ 192	$ 102
Equivalent unit costs of work done in current period only		
Costs added in current period (given)	$453,600	$184,320
Divide by equivalent units of work done in current period (from Solution Exhibit 18-16A)	÷ 1,700	÷ 1,800
Costs per equivalent unit of work done in current period only	$ 266.82	$ 102.40

SOLUTION EXHIBIT 18-16C

Step 4: Summarize Total Costs to Account For and Assign These Costs to Units Completed, Units Spoiled and Units in Ending Work in Process Using the Weighted-Average Method

Superchip for September 2007

	Direct Materials			Conversion Costs			Total Production Costs
	Equivalent Units (1)	Cost per Equivalent Unit (2)	Total Costs (3)=(1)×(2)	Equivalent Units (4)	Cost per Equivalent Unit (5)	Total Costs (6)=(4)×(5)	(7)=(3)+(6)
Panel A: Total Costs to Account For							
Work in process, beginning (from Solution Exhibit 18-16B)	400	$192	$76,800	120	$102	$12,240	$89,040
Work done in current period only (from Solution Exhibit 18-16B)	1,700	$266.82	453,600	1,800	$102.40	184,320	637,920
To account for	2,100	$252.571*	$530,400	1,920	$102.375†	$196,560	$726,960
Panel B: Assignment of costs							
Good units completed and transferred out (1,400 units):							
Costs before adding normal spoilage	1,400‡	$252.571	$353,600	1,400‡	$102.375	$143,325	$496,925
Normal spoilage (15% of good units)	210‡	$252.571	53,040	210‡	$102.375	21,499	74,539
(A) Total costs of good units transferred out			406,640			164,824	571,464
(B) Abnormal spoilage (actual spoilage 400 − normal spoilage 210)	190‡	$252.571	47,989	190‡	$102.375	19,451	67,440
(C) Work in process, ending	300‡	$252.571	75,771	120‡	$102.375	12,285	88,056
(A)+(B)+(C) Accounted for	2,100		$530,400	1,920		$196,560	$726,960

*Weighted-average cost per equivalent unit of direct materials — Total costs of direct materials divided by total equivalent units of direct materials = 530,400 ÷ 2,100 = $252.571

†Weighted-average cost per equivalent unit of conversion costs = Total conversion costs divided by total equivalent units of conversion Costs = $196,560 ÷ 1,920 = $102.375

‡From Solution Exhibit 18-16A.

Alternate Solution:
18-16 (25 min.) Weighted-average method, spoilage.

1, 2 and 3

	Physical	Equivalent units	
Physical Flow	Units	Materials	Conversion
Beginning WIP	400		
Started into production	1,700		
To account for	2,100		
Completed & transferred out	1,400	1,400	1,400
Normal spoilage (15%)*	210	210	210
Abnormal spoilage*	190	190	190
Ending WIP	300	300 (100%)	120 (40%)
Accounted for	2,100		
Work done to date (1)		2,100	1,920

* Normal spoilage is 15% of good units produced or 1,400 x 15% = 210. The number of units of abnormal spoilage is equal to 2,100 total units to account for – 1,400 good units – 210 normal spoilage – 300 in ending WIP = 190. Note that spoilage is identified at the end of the process and units are complete as to both materials and conversion costs.

COST RECONCILIATION

Beginning WIP	$ 89,040	$ 76,800	$ 12,240
Added this period	637,539	453,600	184,320
Costs to account for	$726,920		
Cost of work done to date (2)		$530,400	$196,560
Cost per equivalent unit (2)/(1)		$ 252.571	$ 102.375

Cost assignment			
Completed & transferred out**	$ 496,925	$ 353,600	$ 143,325
Normal spoilage**	74,539	53,040	21,499
Total cost of good units	571,464		
Abnormal spoilage**	67,440	47,989	19,451
Ending WIP**	88,056	75,771	12,285
Costs accounted for	$726,960	$530,400	$196,560

** Cost of goods completed and transferred out, normal spoilage, abnormal spoilage, and ending work-in-process inventory are equal to the appropriate equivalent unit amount for each component multiplied by the cost per equivalent unit for that component. For example: 1,400 x $102.375 =

$143,325. Note that we add across the individual component costs to determine the total cost of each line in the table.

18-18 (30 min.) **Standard costing method, spoilage.**

1. Solution Exhibit 18-16A shows the computation of the equivalent units of work done in September 2007 for direct materials (1,700 units) and conversion costs (1,800 units).

2. The direct materials cost per equivalent unit of beginning work in process and of work done in September 2007 is the standard cost of $246 given in the problem.

   The conversion cost per equivalent of beginning work in process and of work done in September 2007 is the standard cost of $96 given in the problem.

3. Solution Exhibit 18-18 summarizes the total costs to account for, and assigns these costs to units completed, normal spoilage, abnormal spoilage and ending work in process using the standard costing method.

SOLUTION EXHIBIT 18-18

Step 4: Summarize Total Costs to Account For and Assign These Costs to Units Completed, Units Spoiled and Units in Ending *Work in Process* Using Standard Costs
Superchip for September 2007

	Direct Materials			Conversion Costs			Total Production Costs
	Equivalent Units (Solution Exhibit 18-16A) (1)	Cost per Equivalent Unit (2)	Total Costs (3)=(1)×(2)	Equivalent Units (Solution Exhibit 18-16A) (4)	Cost per Equivalent Unit (5)	Total Costs (6)=(4)×(5)	(7)=(3)+(6)
Panel A: Total Costs to Account For							
Work in process, beginning	400	$246	$98,400	120	$96	$11,520	$109,920
Work done in current period only	1,700	$246	418,200	1,800	$96	172,800	591,000
To account for	2,100	$246	$516,600	1,920	$96	$184,320	$700,920
Panel B: Assignment of Costs							
Good units completed and transferred out (1,400 units):							
Costs before adding normal spoilage	1,400	$246	$344,400	1,400	$96	$134,400	$478,800
Normal spoilage (15% of good units)	210	$246	51,660	210	$96	20,160	71,820
(A) Total costs of good units transferred out			396,060			154,560	550,620
(B) Abnormal spoilage (400 – normal spoilage)	190	$246	46,740	190	$96	18,240	64,980
(C) Work in process, ending	300	$246	73,800	120	$96	11,520	85,320
(A)+(B)+(C) Accounted for	2,100		$516,600	1,920		$184,320	$700,920

Alternate Solution:
18-18 (30 min.) Standard costing method, spoilage.

Physical Flow	Physical Units	Equivalent units	
		Materials	Conversion
Beginning WIP	400	400 (100%)	120 (30%)
Started into production	1,700		
To account for	2,100		
		Current period only	
Completion of beginning WIP	400	0	280 (70%)
Started and completed	1,000	1,000	1,000
Normal spoilage*	210	210	210
Abnormal spoilage*	190	190	190
Ending WIP	300	300 (100%)	120 (40%)
Accounting for	2,100		
Work done in current period (1)		1,700	1,800

* Normal spoilage is 15% of good units produced or 1,400 x 15% = 210. The number of units of abnormal spoilage is equal to 2,100 total units to account for – 1,400 good units – 210 normal spoilage – 300 in ending WIP = 190. Note that spoilage is identified at the end of the process and units are complete as to both materials and conversion costs.

Cost per equivalent unit (given)		$ 246	$ 96

COST RECONCILIATION
Beginning WIP*	$ 109,920	$ 98,400	$ 11,520
Added this period*	591,000	$418,200	$172,800
	$700,920		
Costs to account for			

* At standard cost

Cost assignment			
Beginning WIP	$109,920		
Completion of beginning WIP**	26,880	0	26,880
Started and completed**	342,000	$ 246,400	$ 96,000
Normal spoilage**	71,820	51,660	20,160
Total cost of good units	550,620		
Abnormal spoilage**	64,980	46,740	18,240
Ending WIP**	85,320	73,800	11,520
Costs accounted for	$700,920	$418,200	$172,800

** Cost of goods completed and transferred out, normal spoilage, abnormal spoilage, and ending work-in-process inventory are equal to the appropriate equivalent unit amount for each component multiplied by the cost per equivalent unit for that component. For example: 1,400 x $246 = $344,400. Note that we add across the individual component costs to determine the total cost of each line in the table.

18-20 (5-10 min.) Normal and abnormal spoilage in units.

1. | | |
    |---|---:|
    | Total spoiled units | 14,400 |
    | Normal spoilage in units 5% × 158,400 | 7,920 |
    | Abnormal spoilage in units | 6,480 |

2. | | |
    |---|---:|
    | Abnormal spoilage, 6,480 × $12.00 | $ 77,760 |
    | Normal spoilage, 7,920 × $12.00 | 95,040 |
    | Potential savings, 14,400 × $12.00 | $172,800 |

Regardless of the targeted normal spoilage, abnormal spoilage is non-recurring and avoidable. The targeted normal spoilage rate is subject to change. Many companies have reduced their spoilage to almost zero, which would realize all potential savings. Of course, zero spoilage usually means higher-quality products, more customer satisfaction, more employee satisfaction, and various effects on nonmanufacturing (for example, purchasing) costs of direct materials.

18-22 (25 min.) FIFO method.

1. The calculation of the cost per equivalent unit of beginning work in process and of work done in the current period for direct materials and conversion costs is the same as in Solution Exhibit 18-21A, since this calculation does not depend on the specific weighted-average or FIFO cost-flow assumption.

2. Solution Exhibit 18-22 summarizes the total costs to account for, and assigns these costs to units completed, normal spoilage, abnormal spoilage and ending work in process using the FIFO method.

3. From Solution Exhibit 18-22, under the FIFO method,

$$\text{Cost of a good unit completed (and transferred out)} = \frac{\text{Total production costs of good units transferred out}}{\text{Number of good units completed}}$$

$$= \frac{508,740}{20,000} = \$25.437$$

Note that this cost is higher than the cost per equivalent unit of $22.98 (direct materials, $10.08 and conversion costs, $12.90). Why? Because the cost of good units completed and transferred out also includes the cost of normal spoilage of 15%.

SOLUTION EXHIBIT 18-22

Step 4: Summarize Total Costs to Account For, and Assign These Costs to, Units Completed, s
Units Spoiled and Units in Ending Work in Process Using the FIFO Method
Anderson Plastics for April 2007

	Direct Materials			Conversion Costs			Total Production Costs
	Equivalent Units	Cost per Equivalent Unit	Total Costs	Equivalent Units	Cost per Equivalent Unit	Total Costs	
	(1)	(2)	(3)=(1)×(2)	(4)	(5)	(6)=(4)×(5)	(7)=(3)+(6)
Panel A: Total Costs to Account For							
Work in process, beginning (from Solution Exhibit 18-21A)	15,000	$9.60	$144,000	14,000	$12.00	$168,000	$312,000
Work done in current period only (from Solution Exhibit 18-21A)	25,000		252,000	28,000		361,200	613,200
To account for	40,000		$396,000	42,000		$529,200	$925,200
Panel B: Assignment of Costs							
Good units completed and transferred out (20,000 physical units):							
Work in process, beginning	15,000	$9.60	$144,000	14,000	$12.00	$168,000	$312,000
Work done in current period to complete beginning work in process	0*	$10.08	0	1,000†	$12.90	12,900	12,900
Total from beginning inventory before normal spoilage	15,000		144,000	15,000		180,900	324,900
Started and completed before normal spoilage (5,000 units)	5,000‡	$10.08	50,400	5,000‡	$12.90	64,500	114,900
Normal spoilage (15% of good units = 3,000)	3,000	$10.08	30,240	3,000	$12.90	38,700	68,940
(A) Total costs of good units transferred out			224,640			284,100	508,740
spoilage	1,000	$10.08	10,080	1,000	$12.90	12,900	22,980
(C) Work in process, ending (20,000 units)	16,000	$10.08	161,280	18,000	$12.90	232,200	393,480
(A)+(B)+(C) Accounted for	40,000		$396,000	42,000		$529,200	$925,200

*Beginning work in process is 100% complete as to direct materials so zero equivalent units of direct materials need to be added to complete beginning work in process.

†Beginning work in process is 14/15 complete, as to conversion costs which equals 14,000 equivalent units of conversion costs. To complete the 15,000 physical units of beginning work in process, 1,000 (15,000 – 14,000) equivalent units of conversion costs need to be added.

‡20,000 total equivalent units completed and transferred out (given) minus 15,000 equivalent units completed and transferred out from beginning inventory equal to 5,000 equivalent units.

Alternate Solution:
18-22   (25 min.) FIFO method.

Physical Flow	Physical Units	Equivalent units	
		Materials	Conversion
Beginning WIP	15,000	15,000	14,000
Started into production	29,000*		
To account for	44,000		
		Current period only	
Completion of beginning WIP	15,000	0	1,000
Started and completed	5,000	5,000	5,000
Normal spoilage	3,000	3,000	3,000
Abnormal spoilage	1,000	1,000	1,000
Ending WIP	20,000	16,000	18,000
Accounted for	44,000		
Work done in current period (1)		25,000	28,000

*We know that there were 20,000 units completed and transferred out, 4,000 units spoiled, and 20,000 units in ending WIP for a total of 44,000 units to account for. Since we know that there were 15,000 units in beginning WIP, there must have been 29,000 units started into the process this period.

COST RECONCILIATION

Beginning WIP	$ 312,000**		
Added this period (2)	613,200	252,000	361,200
Costs to account for	$ 925,200		
Cost per equivalent unit this period (2)/(1)		$10.08	$12.90

** $144,000 + $168,000 = $312,000

Cost assignment

Beginning WIP	$ 312,000		
Completion of beginning WIP***12,900		0	12,900
Started and completed***	114,900	50,400	64,500
Normal spoilage***	68,940	30,240	38,700
Total cost of good units	508,740		
Abnormal spoilage***	22,980	10,080	12,900
Ending WIP***	393,480	161,280	232,200
Costs this period		$252,000	$361,200
Costs accounted for	$ 925,200		

*** Costs to complete beginning WIP, started and completed, normal spoilage, abnormal spoilage, and ending work-in-process inventory are equal to the appropriate number of equivalent units for each component multiplied by the cost per equivalent unit for that component. For example: 1,000 x $12.90 = $12,900. Note that we add across the individual component costs to determine the total cost of each line in the table.

3.   Cost of a good unit completed (and transferred out)

$$= \quad \frac{\text{Total cost of normal production}}{\text{Number of good units produced}} \quad = \quad \frac{\$508,740}{20,000} = \$25.437$$

Note that this cost is higher than the cost per equivalent unit of $22.98 (direct materials, $10.08 and conversion costs, $12.90). Why? Because the cost of good units completed and transferred out also includes the cost of normal spoilage of 15%.

18-24 (20 min.) Equivalent units, equivalent unit costs, spoilage.

1.   Solution Exhibit 18-24A calculates equivalent units of work done in the current period for direct materials and conversion costs.

2.   Solution Exhibit 18-24B calculates cost per equivalent unit of beginning work in process and of work done in the current period for direct materials and conversion costs.

SOLUTION EXHIBIT 18-24A

Step 1 and Step 2: Summarize Output in Physical Units and Compute Equivalent Units,

Grey Manufacturing Company for November 2007

Flow of Production	(Step 1) Physical Units	(Step 2) Equivalent Units Direct Materials	Conversion Costs
Good units completed and transferred out during November 2007	9,000	9,000	9,000
Normal spoilage[†]	100		
100 × 100%; 100 × 100%		100	100
Abnormal spoilage[‡]	50		
50 × 100%; 50 × 100%		50	50
Work in process, ending[§]	2,000		
2,000 × 100%; 2,000 × 30%	_____	2,000	600
Total accounted for	11,150	11,150	9,750
Deduct work in process, beginning[*]	1,000	1,000	500
1,000 × 100%; 1,000 × 50%			
Started during current period	10,150		
Work done in current period only		10,150	9,250

[†]Degree of completion of normal spoilage: direct materials, 100%; conversion costs, 100%.

[‡]Degree of completion of abnormal spoilage: direct materials, 100%; conversion costs, 100%.

[§]Degree of completion of ending work in process: direct materials, 100%; conversion costs, 30%.

[*]Degree of completion of beginning work in process: direct materials, 100%; conversion costs, 50%.

SOLUTION EXHIBIT 18-24B
Step 3: Compute Equivalent Unit Costs:
Grey Manufacturing Company Inc. for November 2007

	Direct Materials	Conversion Costs
<u>Equivalent unit costs of beginning work in process</u>		
Work in process, beginning (given)	$ 1,560	$ 1,500
Divide by equivalent units in beginning work in process (from Solution Exhibit 18-24A)	÷ 1,000	÷ 500
Cost per equivalent unit of beginning work in process	$ 1.56	$ 3.00
<u>Equivalent unit costs of work done in current period only</u>		
Costs added in current period (given)	$14,616	$33,300
Divide by equivalent units of work done in current period (from Solution Exhibit 18-24A)	÷ 10,150	÷ 9,250
Costs per equivalent unit of work done in current period only	$ 1.44	$ 3.60

18-26 (15 min.) FIFO method, spoilage, equivalent units (continuation of 18-25).

Solution Exhibit 18-26 calculates equivalent units of work done in the current period for direct materials and conversion costs and the costs per equivalent unit for direct materials and conversion costs.

SOLUTION EXHIBIT 18-26
Summarize Output in Physical Units and Compute Equivalent Units.
First-in, First-out (FIFO) Method of Process Costing with Spoilage
Grey Manufacturing Company for November 2007

		(Step 2)	
		Equivalent Units	
	(Step 1)	Direct	Conversion
	Physical		
Flow of Production	Units	Materials	Costs
Work in process, beginning (given)	1,000		
Started during current period (given)	10,150		
To account for	11,150		
Good units completed and transferred out during current period:			
From beginning work in process*	1,000	0	500
1,000 × (100% − 100%); 1,000 × (100% − 50%)			
Started and completed	8,000#	8,000	8,000
8,000 × 100%; 8,000 × 100%			
Normal spoilage**	100	100	100
100 × 100%; 100 × 100%			
Abnormal spoilage†	50	50	50
50 × 100%; 50 × 100%			
Work in process, ending‡	2,000	2,000	600
2,000 × 100%; 2,000 × 30%			
Accounted for			
Work done in current period only	11,150	10,150	9,250

*Degree of completion in this department: direct materials, 100%; conversion costs, 50%.

#9,000 physical units completed and transferred out minus 1,000 physical units completed and transferred out from beginning work-in-process inventory.

**Degree of completion of normal spoilage in this department: direct materials, 100%; conversion costs, 100%.

†Degree of completion of abnormal spoilage in this department: direct materials, 100%; conversion costs, 100%.

‡Degree of completion in this department: direct materials, 100%; conversion costs, 30%.

Cost of direct materials	$14,616
Equivalent units	÷10,150
Cost per equivalent unit	$1.44
Cost of conversion costs	$33,300
Equivalent units	÷ 9,250
Cost per equivalent unit	$3.60

18-28 (15 min.) Reworked units, costs of rework.

1. The two alternative approaches to accounting for the materials costs of reworked units are:

    (a) To charge the costs of rework to the current period as a separate expense item. This approach would highlight to White Goods the costs of the supplier problem.
    (b) To charge the costs of the rework to manufacturing overhead.

2. The $60 tumbler cost is the cost of the actual tumblers included in the washing machines. The $52.80 tumbler units from the new supplier units were never used in any washing machine and that supplier is now bankrupt. This would be included in the cost of rework.

3. The total costs of rework due to the defective tumbler units include:

    (a) The labour and other conversion costs spent on substituting the old tumbler units with the new ones.
    (b) The costs of any extra negotiations to obtain the replacement tumbler units.
    (c) Any higher price the existing supplier may have charged to do a rush order for the replacement tumbler units.

18-30 (30 min.) Weighted-average method, spoilage.

1. Solution Exhibit 18-30, Panel A, calculates the equivalent units of work done to date for each cost category in March 2007.

2.&3. Solution Exhibit 18-30, Panel B, calculates the cost per equivalent unit for each cost category, summarizes total costs to account for, and assigns these costs to units completed (including normal spoilage), to abnormal spoilage, and to units in ending work in process using the weighted-average method.

SOLUTION EXHIBIT 18-30
Weighted-Average Method of Process Costing with Spoilage Wang Manufacturing Company, March 2007

PANEL A: Steps 1 and 2—Summarize Output in Physical Units and Compute Eqvlt. Units

Flow of Production	(Step 1) Physical Units (given)	(Step 2) Equivalent Units	
		Direct Materials	Conversion Costs
Work in process, beginning	30,000		
Started during current period	50,000		
To account for	80,000		
Good units completed and transferred out during current period:	40,000	40,000	40,000
Normal spoilage*			
6,000 × 100%; 6,000 × 100%	6,000	6,000	6,000
Abnormal spoilage†			
2,000 × 100%; 2,000 × 100%	2,000	2,000	2,000
Work in process ending‡			
32,000 × 100%; 32,000 × 75%	32,000	32,000	24,000
Accounted for	80,000		
Work done to date		80,000	72,000

*Degree of completion of normal spoilage in this department: direct materials, 100%; conversion costs, 100%.
†Degree of completion of abnormal spoilage in this department: direct materials, 100%; conversion costs, 100%.
‡Degree of completion in this department: direct materials, 100%; conversion costs, 75%.

PANEL B: Steps 3, 4, and 5—Compute Equivalent Unit Costs, Summarize Total Costs to Account For, and Assign Costs to Units Completed, to Spoilage Units, and to Units in Ending Work in Process

		Total Production Costs	Direct Materials	Conversion Costs
(Step 3)	Work in process, beginning (given)	$504,000	$288,000	$216,000
	Costs added in current period (given)	1,203,840	504,000	699,840
	Costs incurred to date		$792,000	$915,840
	Divide by equiv. units of work to date		÷ 80,000	÷ 72,000
	Equivalent unit costs of work done to date		$ 9.90	$ 12,72
(Step 4)	Total costs to account for	$1,707,840		
(Step 5)	Assignment of costs			
	Good units completed and transferred out (40,000 units)			
	Costs before adding normal spoilage	$ 904,800	(40,000# × $9.90) + (40,000# × $12.72)	
	Normal spoilage (6,000 units)	135,720	(6,000# × $9.90) + (6,000# × $12.72)	
(A)	Total cost of good units completed and transferred out	1,040,520		
(B)	Abnormal spoilage (2,000 units)	45,240	(2,000# × $9.90) + (2,000# × $12.72)	
	Work in process, ending (32,000 units)			
	Direct materials	316,800	32,000# × $9.90	
	Conversion costs	305,280		24,000# × $12.72
(C)	Total work in process, ending	622,080		
(A)+(B)+(C)	Total costs accounted for	$1,707,840		

#Equivalent units of direct materials and conversion costs calculated in Step 2 in Panel A.

18-32 (30 min.) Standard-costing method, spoilage (Refer to the information in 18-30).

1. The equivalent units of work done in the current period for direct materials and conversion costs are calculated in Solution Exhibit 18-31, Panel A.

2. The cost per equivalent unit for direct materials and conversion costs equals the standard cost per unit given in the problem: $9.60 per equivalent unit for direct materials in both beginning inventory and work done in the current period, and $12.00 per equivalent unit for conversion costs in both beginning inventory and work done in the current period.

3. Solution Exhibit 18-32 summarizes the total costs to account for and assigns these costs to units completed and transferred out (including normal spoilage),to abnormal spoilage and to ending work in process using the standard costing method.

SOLUTION EXHIBIT 18-32
Standard Costing Method of Process Costing with Spoilage
Wang Manufacturing Company, March 2005

Compute Equivalent Unit Costs, Summarize Total Costs to Account For, and **Assign Costs to Units Completed, to Spoilage Units, and to Units in ending** Work in Process.

		Total Production Costs	Direct Materials	Conversion Costs
(Step 3)	Standard cost per equivalent unit (given)	$ 21.60	$ 9.60	$ 12.00
	Work in process, beginning*	$ 504,000		
	Costs added in current period at standard prices			
	Direct materials 50,000 × $9.60;			
	Conversion costs 54,000 × $12	1,128,000	$480,000	$648,000
(Step 4)	Costs to account for	$1,632,000		
(Step 5)	Assignment of costs at standard costs:			
	Goods units completed and transferred out (40,000 units)			
	Work in process, beginning (30,000 units)	$504,000		
	Direct materials added in			
	Current period	0	0§ × $9.60	
	Conversion costs added in			
	Current period	144,000		12,000§ × $12
	Total from beginning inventory before normal spoilage	648,000		
	Started and completed before normal spoilage (10,000 units)	216,000	(10,000§ × $9.60) + (10,000§ × $12)	
	Normal spoilage (6,000 units)	129,600	(6,000§ × $9.60) + (6,000§ × $12)	
(A)	Total cost of good units transferred out	993,600		
(B)	Abnormal spoilage (2,000 units)	43,200	(2,000§ × $9.60) + (2,000§ × $12)	
	Work in process, ending (32,000 units)			
	Direct materials	307,200	32,000§ × $9.60	
	Conversion costs	288,000		24,000§ × $12
(C)	Total work in process, ending	595,200		
(A)+(B)+(C)	Total costs accounted for	$1,632,000		

*Work in process, beginning has 30,000 equivalent units (30,000 physical units × 100%) of direct materials and 18,000 equivalent units (30,000 physical units × 60%) of conversion costs. Hence work in process, beginning inventory at standard cost equals ($9.60 × 30,000) + ($12.00 × 18,000) = $288,000 + $216,000 = $504,000.
§Equivalent units of direct materials and conversion costs calculated in Step 2 in Solution Exhibit 18-31 Panel A.

18-34 (25 min.) FIFO method, spoilage.

The equivalent units of work done in the Cleaning Department of the Alston Company in May for direct materials and conversion costs are the same as in problem 18-33 and are shown in Solution Exhibit 18-33A. The cost per equivalent unit of beginning inventory and of work done in the Cleaning Department in May for direct materials and conversion costs are calculated in problem 18-33 in Solution Exhibit 18-33B. Solution Exhibit 18-34 summarizes the total Cleaning Department costs for May, and assigns these costs to units completed (and transferred out), normal spoilage, abnormal spoilage, and units in ending work in process under the FIFO method.

SOLUTION EXHIBIT 18-34

Step 4: Summarize Total Costs to Account For, and Assign These Costs to Units Completed, Units Spoiled and Units in Ending Work in Process Using the FIFO Method Cleaning Department of Alston for May

	Direct Materials			Conversion Costs			Total Production Costs
	Equivalent Units (1)	Cost per Equivalent Unit (2)	Total Costs (3)=(1)×(2)	Equivalent Units (4)	Cost per Equivalent Unit (5)	Total Costs (6)=(4)×(5)	(7)=(3)+(6)
Panel A: Total Costs to Account For							
Work in process, beginning (from Solution Exhibit 18-33B)	1,000	$1.20	$1,200	800	$1.20	$960	$2,160
Work done in current period only (from Solution Exhibit 18-33B)	9,000	$1.20	10,800	8,000	$1.20	9,600	20,400
To account for	10,000		$12,000	8,800		$10,560	$22,560
Panel B: Assignment of Costs							
Good units completed and transferred out (7,400 physical units):							
Work in process, beginning (1,000 physical units)	1,000	$1.20	$1,200	800	$1.20	$960	$2,160
Work done in current period to complete beginning work in process	0*	$1.20	0	200†	$1.20	240	240
Total from beginning inventory before normal spoilage	1,000		1,200	1,000		1,200	2,400
Started and completed before normal spoilage (6,400 units)	6,400‡	$1.20	7,680	6,400‡	$1.20	7,680	15,360
Normal spoilage (740 units)	740§	$1.20	888	740§	$1.20	888	1,776
(A) Total costs of good units transferred out			9,768			9,768	19,536
(B) Abnormal spoilage (260 units)	260§	$1.20	312	260§	$1.20	312	624
(C) Work in process, ending (1,600 units)	1,600§	$1.20	1,920	400§	$1.20	480	2,400
(A)+(B)+(C) Accounted for	10,000		$12,000	8,800		$10,560	$22,560

*Beginning work in process is 100% complete as to direct materials so zero equivalent units of direct materials need to be added to complete beginning work in process.

†Beginning work in process is 80% complete as to conversion costs, which equals 800 equivalent units of conversion costs. To complete the 1,000 physical units of beginning work in process, 200 (1,000 − 800) equivalent units of conversion costs need to be added.

‡7,400 total equivalent units completed and transferred out (Solution Exhibit 18-33A) minus 1,000 equivalent units completed and transferred out from beginning inventory equal to 6,400 equivalent units.

§From Solution Exhibit 18-33A.

Alternate Solution:
18-34 (25 min.) FIFO method, spoilage.

Physical Flow	Physical Units	Equivalent units	
		Materials	Conversion
Beginning WIP	1,000	1,000 (100%)	800 (80%)
Started into production	9,000		
To account for	10,000		
		Current Period Only	
To complete beginning WIP	1,000	0 (0%)	200 (20%)
Started and completed	6,400	6,400	6,400
Normal spoilage	740	740	740
Abnormal spoilage	260	260	260
Ending WIP	1,600	1,600 (100%)	400 (25%)
Accounted for	10,000		
Work done in current period (1)		9,000	8,000

COST RECONCILIATION

Beginning WIP	$ 2,160*		
Added this period (2)	20,400	$10,800	$9,600
Costs to account for	$22,560		
Cost per equivalent unit this period (2)/(1)		$1.20	$1.20

* $1,200 in materials plus $960 in conversion costs

Cost assignment

Beginning WIP	$ 2,160		
To complete beginning WIP**	240	0	240
Started and completed**	15,360	7,680	7,680
Normal spoilage**	1,776	888	888
Total cost of good units	19,536		
Abnormal spoilage**	624	312	312
Ending WIP**	2,400	1,920	480
Costs in current period		10,800	9,600
Costs accounted for	$22,560		

** Costs to complete beginning WIP, started and completed, normal spoilage, abnormal spoilage, and ending work-in-process inventory are equal to the appropriate number of equivalent units for each component multiplied by the cost per equivalent unit for that component. For example: 200 x $1.20 = $240. Note that we add across the individual component costs to determine the total cost of each line in the table.

18-36 (25 min.) **FIFO method, Milling Department.**

The equivalent units of work done in the Milling Department in January for transferred-in costs, direct materials and conversion costs are the same as in problem 18-35 and are shown in Solution Exhibit 18-35A. The cost per equivalent unit of beginning inventory and of work done in the Milling Department in May for transferred-in costs, direct materials and conversion costs are calculated in problem 18-35 in Solution Exhibit 18-35B. Solution Exhibit 18-36 summarizes the total Milling Department costs for May, and assigns these costs to units completed (and transferred out), normal spoilage, abnormal spoilage, and units in ending work in process under the FIFO method.

SOLUTION EXHIBIT 18-36

Step 4: Summarize Total Costs to Account for, and Assign These Costs to Units Completed, Units Spoiled, and Units in Ending Work in Process Using the FIFO Method

Milling Department of Alston for May

	Transferred-in Costs			Direct Materials			Conversion Costs			Total Production Costs
	Equivalent Unit (1)	Cost per Equivalent Unit (2)	Total Costs (3)=(1)×(2)	Equivalent Unit (4)	Cost per Equivalent Unit (5)	Total Costs (6)=(4)×(5)	Equivalent Unit (7)	Cost per Equivalent Unit (8)	Total Costs (9)=(7)×(8)	(10)=(3)+(6)+(9)
Panel A: Total Costs to Account For:										
Work in process, beginning (from Solution Exhibit 18-35B)	3,000	$2.58	$7,740	—	—	—	2,400	$1.225	$2,940	$10,680
Work done in current period only (from Solution Exhibit, 18-35B)	7,400	$2.64	19,536	6,400	$0.12	$768	5,000	$1.188	5,940	26,244
To account for	10,400		$27,276	6,400		$768	7,400		$8,880	$36,924
Panel B: Assignment of Costs										
Good units completed and transferred out (6,000 physical units):										
Work in process, beginning (3,000 physical units)	3,000	$2.58	$7,740	—	—	—	2,400	$1.225	$2,940	$10,680
Work done in current period to complete beginning WIP	0#	$2.64	0	3,000*	$0.12	$360	600†	$1.188	713	1,073
Total from beginning inventory before normal spoilage	3,000		7,740	3,000		360	3,000		3,653	11,753
Started and completed before normal spoilage (3,000 units)	3,000‡	$2.64	7,920	3,000‡	$0.12	360	3,000‡	$1.188	3,564	11,844
Normal spoilage (300 units)	300§	$2.64	792	300§	$0.12	36	300§	$1.188	356	1,184
(A) Total costs of good units tfd out	6,300		16,452	6,300		756	6,300		7,573	24,781
(B) Abnormal spoilage (100 units)	100§	$2.64	264	100§	$0.12	12	100§	$1.188	119	395
(C) Work in process, ending (100 units)	4,000§	$2.64	10,560	0§	$0.12	0	1,000§	$1.188	1,188	11,748
(A)+(B)+(C) Accounted for	10,400		$27,276	6,400		$768	7,400		$8,880	$36,924

#Beginning work in process is 100% complete as to transferred-in costs so zero equivalent units of transferred-in costs need to be added to complete beginning work in process.

*Beginning work in process is 0% complete as to direct materials so 3,000 equivalent units of direct materials need to be added to complete the 3,000 physical units of beginning work in process.

†Beginning work in process is 80% complete as to conversion costs, which equals 2,400 equivalent units of conversion costs. To complete the 3,000 physical units of beginning work in process, 600 (3,000 – 2,400) equivalent units of conversion costs need to be added.

‡6,000 total equivalent units completed and transferred out (Solution Exhibit 18-35A) minus 3,000 equivalent units completed and transferred out from beginning inventory equal to 3,000 equivalent units.

§From Solution Exhibit 18-35A.

Alternate Solution:
18-36 (25 min.) FIFO method, Milling Department.

		Equivalent units		
	Physical	Transferred-in		
Physical Flow	Units	Costs	Materials	Conversion
Beginning WIP	3,000	3,000 (100%)	0 (0%)	2,400 (80%)
Started into production	7,400			
To account for	10,400			
To complete beginning WIP	3,000	0 (0%)	3,000 (100%)	600 (20%)
Started and completed	3,000	3,000	3,000	3,000
Normal spoilage	300	300	300	300
Abnormal spoilage	100	100	100	100
Ending WIP	4,000	4,000 (100%)	0 (0%)	1,000 (25%)
Accounted for	10,400			
Work done in current period (1)		7,400	6,400	5,000

COST RECONCILIATION

Beginning WIP	$ 10,680*			
Added this period (2)	26,244	19,536**	768	5,940
Costs to account for	$ 36,924			
Cost per equivalent unit this period (2)/(1)		$2.64	$0.12	$1.188

Cost assignment

Beginning WIP	$ 10,680			
To complete beginning WIP***	1,073	0	360	713
Started and completed***	11,844	7,920	360	3,564
Normal spoilage***	1,184	792	36	356
Total cost of good units	24,781			
Abnormal spoilage***	395	264	12	119
Ending WIP***	11,748	10,560	0	1,188
Costs this period		19,536	768	5,940
Total costs accounted for	$36,924			

* The beginning WIP consists of $7,740 in transferred in costs and $2,940 in conversion costs.

** The cost of goods transferred *into* the Milling department was calculated in Problem 18-34 as the cost of goods transferred *out* of the Cleaning department.

*** Costs to complete beginning WIP, started and completed, normal spoilage, abnormal spoilage, and ending work-in-process inventory are equal to the appropriate number of equivalent units for each component multiplied by the cost per equivalent unit for that component. For example: 3,000 x $0.12 = $360. Note that we add across the individual component costs to determine the total cost of each line in the table.

Note that materials are added in the Milling department at the end of the process. Therefore WIP does not include any new materials.

18-38 (30 min.) Job costing, rework.

1. Work in Process Control (SM-5 motors) ($660 × 80) $52,800
        Materials Control ($360 × 80) $28,800
        Wages Payable ($72 × 80)   5,760
        Manufacturing Overhead Allocated ($228 × 80)   18,240
    (Total costs assigned to 80 spoiled units of SM-5 Motors
    before considering rework costs.)

    Manufacturing Department Overhead Control (rework)
    ($216 × 50) $10,800
        Materials Control ($72 × 50) $3,600
        Wages Payable ($54 × 50)   2,700
        Manufacturing Overhead Allocated ($90 × 50)   4,500
    (Normal rework attributable specifically to the SM-5
    motor batches or jobs.)

    Loss from Abnormal Rework ($216 × 30) $6,480
        Materials Control ($72 × 30) $2,160
        Wages Payable ($54 × 30)   1,620
        Manufacturing Overhead Allocated ($90 × 30)   2,700
    (Cost of abnormal rework of 30 units.)

    Work in Process Control (SM-5 motors) $7,200
    Work in Process Control (RW-8 motors)   3,600
        Manufacturing Department Overhead Allocated (rework) $10,800
    (Allocating manufacturing department rework costs of normal
    work to SM-5 and RW-8 in the proportion 1,000:500 since
    each motor requires the same number of machine hours.)

2. Total rework costs for SM-5 motors in February 2007 are as follows:

Normal rework costs allocated to SM-5	$ 7,200
Abnormal rework costs for SM-5	6,480
Total rework costs	$13,680

We emphasize two points:

(i) Only $7,200 of the normal rework costs are allocated to SM-5 even though the normal rework costs of the 50 SM-5 motors reworked equal $10,800. The reason is that the normal rework costs are not specifically attributable to SM-5. For example, the machines happened to malfunction when SM-5 was being made but the rework was not caused by the specific requirements of SM-5. If it were, then all $10,800 would be charged to SM-5.

(ii) Abnormal rework costs of $6,480 are pegged to SM-5 in the management control system, even though for financial reporting purposes, the abnormal rework costs are written off to the income statement.

18-40 (15-20 min.) **Physical units, inspection at various stages of completion (Chapter Appendix).**

	Inspection at 15%	Inspection at 40%	Inspection at 100%
Work in process, beginning (23%)*	14,000	14,000	14,000
Started during March	120,000	120,000	120,000
To account for	134,000	134,000	134,000
Good units completed and transferred out	113,000[a]	113,000[a]	113,000[a]
Normal spoilage (8%)	8,800[b]	9,920[c]	9,040[d]
Abnormal spoilage			
(10,000 – normal spoilage)	1,200	80	960
Work in process, ending (69%)*	11,000	11,000	11,000
Accounted for	134,000	134,000	134,000

*Degree of completion for conversion costs of the forging process at the dates of the work in process inventories
[a] 14,000 beginning inventory +120,000 –10,000 spoiled – 11,000 ending inventory = 113,000 units
[b] $8\% \times (113,000 - 14,000 + 11,000) = 8\% \times 110,000 = 8,800$
[c] $8\% \times (113,000 + 11,000) = 8\% \times 124,000 = 9,920$
[d] $8\% \times (113,000) = 9,040$

18-42 (40 min.) **Job costing, spoilage, ethics.**

1. Analysis of the 5,000 units rejected by Richport Company for Job No. N1192-122 yields the following breakdown between normal and abnormal spoilage.

	Units
Normal spoilage*	3,000
Abnormal spoilage:	
Design defect	900
Other [5,000 – (3,000 + 900)]	1,100
Total units rejected	5,000

*Normal spoilage = 0.025 of normal input
When output equals 117,000 units,
Normal input = $117,000 \div (1 - 0.025)$
= 120,000 units
Normal spoilage = $120,000 \times 0.025$
= 3,000 units

2. The journal entries required to properly account for Job No. N1192-122 are presented below and use an average cost per unit of $68.40 ($8,344,800 ÷ 122,000).

Materials control (or A/R or cash)[1]	$34,440	
Abnormal loss[2]	129,000	
WIP control[3]		$162,000

Cash[4]   1,440
To account for 5,000 units rejected.

Finished good inventory[5] $8,182,800
  WIP control $8,182,800
To transfer 117,000 units to finished goods inventory.

[1]Units for sale 4,100 units sold at $8.40 each.

[2]Loss from abnormal spoilage:

2,000 units at $68.40	$136,800
Disposal cost	1,440
Cost recovery (1,100 × $8.40)	(9,240)
	$129,000

[3]WIP control:

900 defective units at $68.40	$ 61,560
1,100 other rejected units at $68.40	75,240
3,000 normal units at $8.40	25,200
	$162,000

[4]Additional cost to dispose of 900 units rejected because of design defect.

[5] Less	$8,344,800	Total manufacturing costs
	162,000	WIP control
	8,182,800	

3. a.   If all spoilage were considered normal, the journal entries to account for Job No. N1192-122 would be as follows:

Materials Control (or A/R or cash)	$34,440	
Finished Goods Inventory	8,311,800	
WIP Control		$8,344,800
Cash		1,440

To transfer 117,000 good units to finished goods inventory and to recognize the salvage value of 4,100 units of spoiled units (4,100 × $8.40 = $34,440) and the disposal cost of $1,440 of the other 900 spoiled units. All remaining WIP costs are treated as normal costs of production and charged to finished goods.

By considering all spoilage as normal, Richport will show no abnormal loss but instead will add $129,000 to the finished-goods inventory. Hence, showing all spoilage as normal will increase Richport's operating income by $129,000 in the short term since abnormal spoilage is expensed immediately to the income statement.

3b.   Incorrect reporting of spoilage as normal instead of abnormal with the goal of increasing operating income is unethical. In assessing the situation, the management accountant should consider the following:

•   Spoilage should be accounted for using relevant and reliable information. Accounting for spoilage incorrectly to make the company's operating performance look better than it is violates competence standards. It is unethical for Rutherford to suggest that Gonzales change abnormal spoilage to normal spoilage in order to make operating performance look good.

•   The management accountant has a responsibility to avoid actual or apparent conflicts of interest and advise all appropriate parties of any potential conflict. Rutherford's motivation for wanting Gonzales to revise the quality figures could well have been motivated by Rutherford's desire to please senior management. In this regard, both Rutherford's and Gonzales's behaviour (if Gonzales agrees to modify the spoilage classification) could be viewed as unethical.

• The management accountant should require that information be fairly and objectively communicated and that all relevant information should be disclosed. From a management accountant's standpoint, showing abnormal spoilage as normal spoilage to make operating performance look good would be unethical.

Gonzales should indicate to Rutherford that the classification of normal and abnormal spoilage established by Richport Company is, indeed, appropriate. If Rutherford still insists on modifying the spoilage classification for this job to report higher operating income figures, Gonzales should raise the matter with one of Rutherford's superiors. If, after taking all these steps, there is continued pressure to overstate operating income, Gonzales should consider resigning from the company, and not engage in unethical behaviour.

CHAPTER 19
COST MANAGEMENT: QUALITY, TIME, AND
THE THEORY OF CONSTRAINTS

19-2 Quality of design measures how closely the characteristics of products or services match the needs and wants of customers. Conformance quality measures whether the product has been made according to design, engineering and manufacturing specifications.

19-4 An internal failure cost differs from an external failure cost on the basis of when the nonconforming product is detected. An internal failure is detected *before a* product is shipped to a customer whereas an external failure is detected *after* a product is shipped to a customer.

19-6 No, companies should emphasize financial as well as nonfinancial measures of quality, such as yield and defect rates. Nonfinancial measures are not directly linked to bottom-line performance but they indicate and direct attention to the specific areas that need improvement. Tracking nonfinancial measures over time directly reveals whether these areas have, in fact, improved over time. Nonfinancial measures are easy to quantify and easy to understand.

19-8 Examples of nonfinancial measures of internal performance are:
1. The number of defects for each product line.
2. Process yield (rates of good output to total output at a particular process).
3. Manufacturing lead time (the time taken to convert direct materials into finished output).
4. Employee turnover (ratio of the number of employees who left the company in a year, say, to the total number of employees who worked for the company in that year).

19-10 No. There is a trade-off between customer-response time and on-time performance. Simply scheduling longer customer-response time makes achieving on-time performance easier. Companies should, however, attempt to reduce uncertainty of arrival of orders, manage bottlenecks, reduce setup and processing time and run smaller batches. This would have the effect of reducing both customer-response time and improving on-time performance.

19-12 No. Adding a product when capacity is constrained and the timing of customer orders is uncertain causes delays in delivering all existing products. If the revenue losses from delays in delivering existing products and the increase in carrying costs of the existing products exceeds the positive contribution earned by the product that was added, then it is not worthwhile to make and sell the new product, despite its positive contribution margin. The chapter describes the negative effects that one product can have on others when products share manufacturing facilities.

19-14 The four key steps in managing bottleneck resources are:

Step 1: Recognize that the bottleneck operation determines throughput contribution.

Step 2: Search for and find the bottleneck.

Step 3: Keep the bottleneck busy and subordinate all nonbottleneck operations to the bottleneck operation.

Step 4: Increase bottleneck efficiency and capacity.

19-16 (30 min.) **Costs of quality.**

1. The ratio of each COQ category to revenues for each period is as follows:

Semi-annual Costs of Quality Report Bergen, Inc.
(in thousands)

	(1)	6/30/2007 % of Rev. (2) = (1)÷4,944	(3)	12/31/2007 % of Rev. (4) = (3)÷5,448	(5)	6/30/2007 % of Rev. (6) = (5)÷5,580	(7)	12/31/2007 % of Rev. (8) = (7)÷5,412
Prevention costs								
Machine maintenance	$ 258		$ 258		$ 228		$ 192	
Training suppliers	6		54		24		18	
Design reviews	24		122		120		114	
	288	5.8%	434	8.0%	372	6.7%	324	6.0%
Appraisal costs								
Incoming inspection	54		64		43		26	
Final testing	192		192		168		113	
	246	5.0%	256	4.7%	211	3.8%	139	2.6%
Internal failure costs								
Rework	144		127		106		74	
Scrap	82		77		50		48	
	226	4.6%	204	3.7%	156	2.8%	122	2.2%
External failure costs								
Warranty repairs	83		37		30		28	
Customer returns	314		301		139		96	
	397	8.0%	338	6.2%	169	3.0%	124	2.3%
Total quality costs	$1,157	23.4%	$1,232	22.6%	$ 908	16.3%	$ 709	13.1%
Total production and revenues	$4,944		$5,448		$5,580		$5,412	

From an analysis of the Cost of Quality Report, it would appear that Bergen Inc.'s program has been successful since

- Total quality costs as a percentage of total revenues have declined from 23.4% to 13.1%.
- External failure costs, those costs signalling customer dissatisfaction have declined from 8% of total revenues to 2.3%. These declines in warranty repairs and customer returns should translate into increased revenues in the future.

- Internal failure costs have been reduced from 4.6% to 2.2% of revenues.
- Appraisal costs have decreased from 5.0% to 2.6%. Preventing defects from occurring in the first place is reducing the demand for final testing.
- Quality costs have shifted to the area of prevention where problems are solved before production starts. Maintenance, training, and design reviews have increased from 5.8% of total revenues to 6% and from 24.9% of total quality costs ($288 ÷ $1,157) to 45.7% ($324 ÷ $709). The $36,000 increase in these costs is more than offset by decreases in other quality costs.

Because of improved designs, quality training, and additional pre-production inspections, scrap and rework costs have declined. Production does not have to spend an inordinate amount of time with customer service since they are now making the product right the first time and warranty repairs and customer returns have decreased.

2. To measure the opportunity cost of not implementing the quality program, Bergen Inc. could assume that

- Sales and market share would continue to decline if the quality program had not been implemented and then calculate the loss in revenue and contribution margin.
- The company would have to compete on price rather than quality and calculate the impact of having to lower product prices.

Opportunity costs are not recorded in accounting systems because they represent the results of what might have happened if Bergen had not improved quality. Nevertheless, opportunity costs of poor quality can be significant. It is important for Bergen to take these costs into account when making decisions about quality.

19-18 (30-40 min.) Costs of quality analysis, nonfinancial quality measures.

1. and 2.

Sales, Costs of Quality and Costs of Quality as a Percentage of Sales for Olivia

Sales = $2,400 × 10,000 units = $24,000,000

Costs of Quality	Cost (1)	Percentage of Sales (2) = (1) ÷ $24,000,000
Prevention costs		
Design engineering ($90 × 6,000 hours)	$ 540,000	2.25%
Appraisal costs		
Testing and inspection ($48 × 1 hour × 10,000 units)	480,000	2.00%
Internal failure costs		
Rework ($600 × 5% × 10,000 units)	300,000	1.25%
External failure costs		
Repair ($720 × 4% × 10,000 units)	288,000	1.20%
Total costs of quality	$1,608,000	6.70%

Sales, Costs of Quality and Costs of Quality as a Percentage of Sales for Solta

Sales: $1,800 × 5,000 units = $9,000,000

Costs of Quality	Cost (1)	Percentage of Sales (2) = (1) ÷ $9,000,000
Prevention costs		
Design engineering ($90 × 1,000 hours)	$ 90,000	1.00%
Appraisal costs		
Testing and inspection ($48 × 0.5 × 5,000 units)	120,000	1.33%
Internal failure costs		
Rework ($480 × 10% × 5,000 units)	240,000	2.67%
External failure costs		
Repair ($540 × 8% × 5,000 units)	216,000	2.40%
Estimated forgone contribution margin on lost sales [($1,800 – $960) × 300]	252,000	2.80%
Total external failure costs	468,000	5.20%
Total costs of quality	$918,000	10.20%

Costs of quality as a percentage of sales are significantly different for Solta (10.20%) as compared with Olivia (6.70%). Ontario spends very little on prevention and appraisal activities for Solta, and incurs high costs of internal and external failures. Ontario follows a different strategy with respect to Olivia, spending a greater percentage of sales on prevention and appraisal activities. The result: fewer internal and external failure costs and lower overall costs of quality as a percentage of sales than with Solta.

3. Examples of nonfinancial quality measures that Ontario Industries could monitor as part of a total-quality-control effort are
   (a) Outgoing quality yield for each product.
   (b) Returned refrigerator percentage for each product.
   (c) On-time delivery.
   (d) Employee turnover.

19-20 (25 min.) Quality improvement, relevant costs, and relevant revenues.

1. Incremental costs over the next year of choosing the new lens — $60 × 20,000 copiers = $1,200,000.

2.

	Incremental Benefits over the Next Year of Choosing the New Lens
Costs of quality items	
Savings on rework costs	
$48 × 12,000 rework hours	$ 576,000
Savings in customer-support costs	
$24 × 800 customer-support hours	19,200
Savings in transportation costs for parts	
$216 × 200 fewer loads	43,200
Savings in warranty repair costs	
$54 × 8,000 repair hours	432,000
Opportunity costs	
Contribution margin from increased sales	720,000
Cost savings and additional contribution margin	$1,790,400

3. Since the expected benefits of $1,790,400 (requirement 2) exceed the costs of the new lens of $1,200,000 (requirement 1), Photon should introduce the new lens. Note that the opportunity cost benefits in the form of higher contribution margin from increased sales is an important component for justifying the investment in the new lens. The incremental costs of the new lens of $1,200,000 is greater than the incremental savings in rework and repair costs of $1,070,400. Investing in the new lens is beneficial provided it generates additional contribution margin of, at

least, \$129,600 (\$1,200,000 − \$1,070,400), that is, additional sales of at least \$129,600 ÷ \$7,200[1)] = 18 copiers.

1) 100 copies = \$720,000 contribution
   1 copies = \$7,200 contribution

19-22 (20 min.) Waiting time, banks.

1. If the branch expects to receive 42 customers each day and it takes 6 minutes to serve a customer, the average time that a customer will wait in line before being served is:

$$= \frac{\left(\begin{array}{c} \text{Average number} \\ \text{of customers} \end{array} \right) \times \left(\begin{array}{c} \text{Time taken to} \\ \text{serve a customer} \end{array} \right)^2}{2 \times \left\{ \begin{array}{c} \text{Available time} \\ \text{counter is open} \end{array} - \left[\left(\begin{array}{c} \text{Average number} \\ \text{of customers} \end{array} \right) \times \left(\begin{array}{c} \text{Time taken to} \\ \text{serve a customer} \end{array} \right) \right] \right\}}$$

$$= \frac{\left[42 \times (6)^2 \right]}{2 \times \left[300 - (42 \times 6) \right]} = \frac{(42 \times 36)}{2 \times (300 - 252)} = \frac{1,512}{2 \times 48} = \frac{1,512}{96} = 15.75 \text{ minutes}$$

2. If the branch expects to receive 50 customers each day and the time taken to serve a customer is 5 minutes, the average time that a customer will wait in line before being served is:

$$= \frac{\left[50 \times (5)^2 \right]}{2 \times \left[300 - (50 \times 5) \right]} = \frac{(50 \times 25)}{2 \times (300 - 250)} = \frac{50 \times 25}{2 \times 50} = \frac{1,250}{100} = 12.5 \text{ minutes}$$

3. If the branch expects to receive 50 customers each day and the time taken to serve a customer is 4.5 minutes, the average time that a customer will wait in line before being served is:

$$= \frac{\left[50 \times (4.5)^2 \right]}{2 \times \left[300 - (50 \times 4.5) \right]} = \frac{(50 \times 20.25)}{2 \times (300 - 225)} = \frac{50 \times 20.25}{2 \times 75} = \frac{1,012.5}{150} = 6.75 \text{ minutes}$$

19-24 (15 min.) Theory of constraints, throughput contribution, relevant costs.

1. Finishing is a bottleneck operation. Hence, producing 1,000 more units will generate additional throughput contribution and operating income.

Increase in throughput contribution (\$86.40 − \$38.40) × 1,000	\$48,000
Incremental costs of the jigs and tools	36,000
Net benefit of investing in jigs and tools	\$12,000

Mayfield should invest in the modern jigs and tools because the benefit of higher throughput contribution of $48,000 exceeds the cost of $36,000.

2. The Machining Department has excess capacity and is not a bottleneck operation. Increasing its capacity further will not increase throughput contribution. There is therefore no benefit from spending $6,000 to increase the Machining Department's capacity by 10,000 units. Mayfield should not implement the change to do setups faster.

19-26 (15 min.) Theory of constraints, throughput contribution, quality.

1. Cost of defective unit at machining operation which is not a bottleneck operation is the loss in direct materials (variable costs) of $38.40 per unit. Producing 2,000 units of defectives does not result in loss of throughput contribution. Despite the defective production machining can produce and transfer 80,000 units to finishing. Therefore cost of 2,000 defective units at the machining operation is $38.40 × 2,000 = $76,800.

2. A defective unit produced at the bottleneck finishing operation costs Mayfield materials costs plus the opportunity cost of lost throughput contribution. Bottleneck capacity not wasted in producing defective units could be used to generate additional sales and throughput contribution. Cost of 2,000 defective units at the finishing operation is

Loss of direct materials $38.40 × 2,000	$ 76,800
Forgone throughput contribution ($86.40 – $38.40) × 2,000	96,000
Total cost of 2,000 defective units	$172,800

Alternatively, the cost of 2,000 defective units at the finishing operation can be calculated as the lost revenue of $86.40 × 2,000 = $172,800. That is, the direct materials costs of $38.40 × 2,000 = $76,800 and all fixed operating costs in the machining and finishing operations are irrelevant since these costs would be incurred anyway whether a defective or good unit is produced. The cost of producing a defective unit is the revenue lost of $172,800.

19-28 (30 min.) Quality improvement, relevant costs, and relevant revenues.

1. By implementing the new method, Tan would incur additional direct materials costs on all the 200,000 units started at the moulding operation.
    Additional direct materials costs = $3.60 per lamp × 200,000 lamps $ 720,000

2. The relevant benefits of adding the new material are:

(a) Increased revenue from selling 30,000 more lamps
$48 per lamp × 30,000 lamps $1,440,000
(b) Additional variable costs incurred in the welding
department on the good lamps $3.00 × 30,000 lamps   (90,000)
Total benefits to Tan of adding new material to improve quality $1,350,000

Note that Tan Corporation continues to incur the same total variable costs of direct materials, direct manufacturing labour, setup labour, and materials handling labour and the same fixed costs of equipment, rent, and allocated overhead that it is currently incurring even when it improves quality. Since these costs do not differ among the alternatives of adding the new material or not adding the new material, they are excluded from the analysis. The relevant benefit of adding the new material is the extra revenue that Tan would get from producing 30,000 good lamps minus the additional variable welding costs it would incur on these lamps in the welding department.

An alternative approach to analyzing the problem is to focus on scrap costs and the benefits of reducing scrap.

The relevant benefits of adding the new material are:

(a) Cost savings from eliminating scrap:
Variable costs per lamp, $22.80[a] × 30,000 lamps $ 684,000
(b) Additional contribution margin from selling another
30,000 lamps because 30,000 lamps will no longer
be scrapped:
Unit contribution margin $22.20[b] × 30,000 lamps   666,000
Total benefits to Tan of adding new material to improve
quality $1,350,000

[a]Note that only the variable scrap costs of $22.80 per lamp (direct materials, $19.20 per lamp and direct manufacturing labour, setup labour, and materials handling labour, $3.60 per lamp) are relevant because improving quality will save these costs. Fixed scrap costs of equipment, rent, and allocated overhead are irrelevant because these costs will be incurred whether Tan Corporation adds or does not add the new material.

[b]Unit contribution margin

Selling price		$48.00
Variable costs:		
Direct materials costs per lamp	$19.20	
Moulding department variable manufacturing costs per lamp (direct manufacturing labour, setup labour, and materials handling labour)	3.60	
Welding department variable manufacturing costs per lamp	3.00	
Variable costs		25.80
Unit contribution margin		$22.20

436

3. On the basis of quantitative considerations alone, Tan should use the new material. Relevant benefits of $1,350,000 exceed the relevant costs of $720,000 by $630,000.

4. Other nonfinancial and qualitative factors that Tan should consider in making a decision include the effects of quality improvement on:

   (a) Gaining manufacturing expertise that could lead to further cost reductions in the future.
   (b) Enhanced reputation and increased customer goodwill which could lead to higher future revenues through greater unit sales and higher sales prices.
   (c) More worker empowerment and higher employee morale.

19-30 (30-40 min.) Compensation linked with profitability, on-time delivery, and external quality performance measures; balanced scorecard.

1.

	Jan.–March	April–June	July–Sept.	Oct.–Dec.
Detroit				
Add: Profitability				
2% of operating income	$19,200	$20,400	$16,800	$21,600
Add: On-time delivery				
$10,000 if above 98%	12,000	12,000	0	0
Deduct: Quality				
50% of cost of sales returns	(10,800)	(15,600)	(6,000)	(15,000)
Total: Bonus paid	$20,400	$16,800	$10,800	$ 6,600
Los Angeles				
Add: Profitability				
2% of operating income	$38,400	$36,000	$43,200	$45,600
Add: On-time delivery				
$10,000 if above 98%	0	0	0	12,000
Deduct: Quality				
50% of cost of sales returns	(21,000)	(20,400)	(16,800)	(13,200)
Total: Bonus paid	$17,400	$15,600	$26,400	$44,400

2. Operating income as a measure of profitability

    Operating income does capture revenue and cost-related factors. However, there is no recognition of investment differences between the two plants. Los Angeles sales are approximately double that of Detroit. This difference gives the Los Angeles plant manager the opportunity to earn a larger bonus due to investment size alone. An alternative approach would be to use return on investment (perhaps relative to the budgeted ROI).

    98% on-time benchmark as a measure of on-time delivery performance

    This measure does reflect the ability of Pacific-Dunlop to meet a benchmark for on-time delivery. Several concerns arise with this specific measure:
    (a) It is a yes-or-no cut-off. A 10% on-time performance earns no bonus, but neither does a 97.9% on-time performance. Moreover, no extra bonus is paid for performance above 98.0%. An alternative is to have the bonus be a percentage of the on-time delivery percentage.
    (b) It can be manipulated by management. The Pacific-Dunlop plant manager may quote conservative delivery dates to salespeople in an effort to "guarantee" that the 98% target is achieved.
    (c) It reflects performance only relative to scheduled delivery date. It does not consider how quickly Pacific-Dunlop can respond to customer orders.

    50% of cost of sales returns as a measure of quality

    This measure does incorporate one cost that arises with defective goods. However, there are several concerns with its use:

    (a) Not all sales returns are due to defective work by the plant manager. Some returns are due to tampering by the customer. Other returns arise from breakage during delivery and installation.
    (b) It does not systematically incorporate customer opinion about quality. Not all customers return defective goods.
    (c) It ignores important categories of the cost of defective goods. For example, dissatisfied customers may decline to make any subsequent purchases.

3. Most companies use both financial and nonfinancial measures to evaluate performance, sometimes presented in a single report called a *balanced scorecard*. Using multiple measures of performance enables top management to evaluate whether lower-level managers have improved one area at the expense of others. For example, did the on-time delivery performance of the Detroit plant manager decrease in the October-December period relative to the April-June period because the manager emphasized shipment of high-margin products to increase operating income?

4. If on-time delivery were dropped as a performance evaluation measure, managers will concentrate on increasing operating income and decreasing sales returns but will give less attention to on-time delivery. Consider the following situation. Suppose a manager must choose between (1) delivering a high-margin order that will add to operating income while delaying a number of other orders and adversely affecting on-time performance or (2) delaying the high-margin order and sacrificing some operating income to achieve better on-time performance. What action will the manager take? If on-time performance is excluded as a performance evaluation measure, the manager will almost certainly choose (1). Only if on-time performance is included in the manager's performance evaluation will the manager consider choosing option (2).

19-32 (20-30 min.) Waiting times, relevant revenues and relevant costs (continuation of 19-31).

1. The direct approach is to look at incremental revenues and incremental costs.

Average selling price per order for Y28, which has average operating throughput time of 420 hours	$ 9,600
Variable costs per order	6,000
Additional contribution per order from Y28	3,600
Multiply by expected number of orders	× 25
Increase in expected contribution from Y28	$90,000

Expected loss in revenues and increase in costs from introducing Y28

Product (1)	Expected Loss in Revenues from Increasing Average Manufacturing Lead Times for All Products (2)	Expected Increase in Carrying Costs from Increasing Average Manufacturing Lead Times for All Products (3)	Expected Loss in Revenues Plus Expected Increases in Costs of Introducing Y28 (4) = (2) + (3)
Z39	$30,000[a]	$ 7,650[b]	$37,650
Y28	—	2,625[c]	2,625
Total	$30,000	$10,275	$40,275

[a] 50 orders × ($32,400 − $31,800)
[b] (492 hours − 288 hours) × $0.75 × 50 orders
[c] (420 hours − 0) × $0.25 × 25

Increase in expected contribution from Y28 of $90,000 is greater than increase in expected costs of $40,275 by $49,725. Therefore, SRG should introduce Y28.

Alternative calculations of incremental revenues and incremental costs of introducing Y28.

	Alternative 1: Introduce Y28 (1)	Alternative 2: Do Not Introduce Y28 (2)	Relevant Revenues and Relevant Costs (3) = (1) – (2)
Expected revenues	$1,830,000[a]	$1,620,000[b]	$210,000
Expected variable costs	1,050,000[c]	900,000[d]	150,000
Expected carrying costs	21,075[e]	10,800[f]	10,275
Expected total variable and carrying costs	1,071,075	910,800	160,275
Expected revenues minus expected costs	$ 758,925	$ 709,200	$ 49,725

[a]$(50 \times \$31,800) + (25 \times \$9,600)$
[b]$50 \times \$32,400$
[c]$(50 \times \$18,000) + (25 \times \$6,000)$
[d]$50 \times \$18,000$
[e]$(50 \times \$0.75 \times 492) + (25 \times \$0.25 \times 420)$
[f]$50 \times \$0.75 \times 288$

2. Introducing Y28 results in an incremental cost of $40,275. To break even, we need to earn a total contribution of $40,275 over the 25 orders, or a contribution per order of $40,275 ÷ 25 = $1,611.

Variable costs per order of Y28	$6,000
Required contribution to break even	1,611
Selling price per dollar of Y28 to break even	$7,611

If Y28 sells above $7,611 per order, SRG should manufacture and sell Y28. If Y28 sells below $7,611 per order, SRG should not manufacture and sell Y28.

19-34 (20 min.) Theory of constraints, throughput contribution, relevant costs.

1. It will cost Columbia $60 per unit to reduce manufacturing time. But manufacturing is not a bottleneck operation, installation is. Therefore manufacturing more equipment will not increase sales and throughput

contribution. Columbia Industries should not implement the new manufacturing method.

2. Additional relevant costs of new direct materials, $2,400 × 320 units $768,000
    Increase in throughput contribution, $30,000 × 20 units $600,000

    The additional incremental costs exceed the benefits from higher throughput contribution by $168,000, so Columbia Industries should not implement the new design.

    Alternatively, compare throughput contribution under each alternative.

    Current throughput contribution is $30,000 × 300 $9,000,000
    With the modification, throughput contribution is $27,600 × 320 $8,832,000

    The current throughput contribution is greater than the throughput contribution resulting from the proposed change in direct materials. Hence, Columbia Industries should not implement the new design.

3. Increase in throughput contribution, $30,000 × 10 units $300,000
    Increase in relevant costs $60,000

    The additional throughput contribution exceeds incremental costs by $240,000 so Columbia Industries should implement the new installation technique.

4. Motivating installation workers to increase productivity is worthwhile because installation is a bottleneck operation and any increase in productivity at the bottleneck will increase throughput contribution. On the other hand, motivating workers in the manufacturing department to increase productivity is not as worthwhile. Manufacturing is not a bottleneck operation, so any increase in output will only result in extra inventory of equipment. However, if some of the excess labour in manufacturing is cross-trained to be able to perform installations, a benefit would be realized. A multiskilled and flexible workforce is always a plus to the bottom line. Columbia Industries should only encourage manufacturing to produce as much equipment as the installation department needs, not to produce as much as it can.

19-36 (25 min.) Quality improvement, Pareto charts, fishbone diagrams.

1. Examples of failures in accounts receivable management are:
    (a) Uncollectible amounts or bad debts.
    (b) Delays in receiving payments.

2. Prevention activities that could reduce failures in accounts receivable management include:
   (a) Credit checks on customers
   (b) Shipping the correct copier to the customer
   (c) Supporting installation of the copier and answering customer questions
   (d) Sending the correct invoice, in the correct amount and to the correct address promptly
   (e) Following up to see if the machine is functioning smoothly

3. A Pareto diagram for the problem of delays in receiving customer payments might look like the following:

SOLUTION EXHIBIT 19-36A
Pareto Diagram for Failures in Accounts Receivables at Murray Corporation

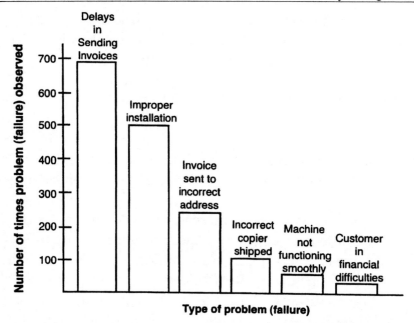

A cause-and-effect or fishbone diagram for the problem of delays in sending invoices may appear as follows:

SOLUTION EXHIBIT 19-36B
Cause-and-Effect Diagram for Problem of Delays in Sending Invoices
at Murray Corporation

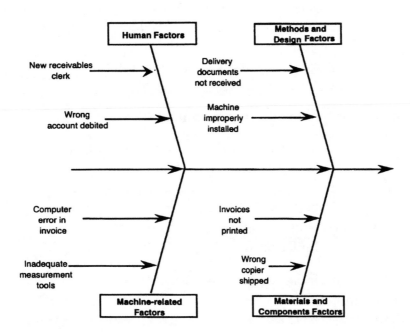

19-38 (45-50 min.) Quality improvement, relevant costs, and relevant revenues.

1. Consider the incremental revenues and incremental costs to Wellesley Corporation of purchasing grey cloth from outside suppliers.

Incremental revenues, $1,500 × (5,000 rolls × 0.90)		$6,750,000
Incremental costs:		
Cost of grey cloth, $1,080 × 5,000 rolls	$5,400,000	
Direct materials variable costs at printing operation, $120 × 5,000 rolls	600,000	
Incremental costs		6,000,000
Excess of incremental revenues over incremental costs		$ 750,000

Note that since the printing department has surplus capacity equal to 5,500 (15,000 – 9,500) rolls per month, purchasing grey cloth from outside entails zero opportunity costs. Yes, the Printing Department should buy the grey cloth from the outside supplier.

2. By producing a defective roll in the Printing Department, Wellesley Corporation is worse off by the entire amount of revenue forgone of $1,500 per roll. Note that

since the weaving operation is a constraint, any rolls received by the Printing Department that are scrapped result in lost revenue to the firm. All costs already incurred in manufacturing the roll (Weaving Department direct materials variable costs, $600, Weaving Department other operating costs, $342, Printing Department direct materials variable costs, $120, and Printing Department other operating costs, $54) are past costs and hence irrelevant.

An alternative approach to analyzing the problem is to focus on scrap costs and the benefits of reducing scrap.

The relevant costs of Printing Department scrap are:

(a)	Direct materials variable costs in the Weaving Department	$ 600
(b)	Direct materials variable costs in the Printing Department	120
(c)	Contribution margin forgone from not selling one roll, $1,500 – $600 – $120	780
	Amount by which Wellesley Corporation is worse off as a result of Printing Department scrap	$1,500

Note that only the variable scrap costs of $720 per roll (direct materials in the Weaving Department, $600 per roll, and direct materials in the Printing Department, $120 per roll) are relevant because improving quality will save these costs. Fixed scrap costs attributable to other operating costs are irrelevant because these costs will be incurred whether Wellesley Corporation reduces scrap in the Printing Department or not.

3. To determine how much Wellesley Corporation is worse off by producing a defective roll in the Weaving Department, consider the payoff to Wellesley from not having a defective roll produced in the Weaving Department. The good roll produced in the Weaving Department will be sent for further processing in the Printing Department. The relevant costs and benefits of printing and selling this roll follow:

Additional direct materials variable costs incurred in the Printing Department	$ (120)
Expected revenue from selling the finished product, 0.9 × $1,500 (since 10% of the Printing Department output will need to be scrapped and earn zero revenue)	1,350
Net expected benefit of producing a good roll in the Weaving Department	$1,230

By producing a defective roll in the Printing Department, Wellesley Corporation is worse off by $1,230 per roll. Note that since the weaving operation is a constraint, any rolls that are scrapped result in lost revenue to the firm. All costs already incurred in manufacturing the roll (Weaving Department direct materials variable costs, $600, Weaving Department other operating costs, $342) and future costs that will not change whether a roll is scrapped or not at the Weaving Department (for example, other operating costs in the Printing Department, $54) are irrelevant.

An alternative approach to analyzing the problem is to focus on scrap costs and the benefits of reducing scrap.

The relevant costs of Weaving Department scrap are:

(a)	Direct materials variable costs in the Weaving Department	$ 600
(b)	Expected unit contribution margin forgone from not selling	
	one roll, ($1,500 × 0.9) – $600 – $120	630
	Amount by which Wesley Corporation is worse off as a result	
	of Weaving Department scrap	$1,230

Note that only the variable scrap costs of $600 per roll (direct materials in the Weaving Department) are relevant because improving quality will save these costs. Fixed scrap costs attributable to other operating costs are irrelevant because these costs will be incurred whether Wellesley Corporation reduces scrap in the Weaving Department or not.

4. Wellesley Corporation should make the proposed modifications in the Printing Department because the incremental benefits exceed the incremental costs by $150,000 per month:

Incremental benefits of reducing scrap in the Printing	
Department by 4% (from 10% to 6%)	
4% × 9,500 rolls × $1,500 per roll (computed in requirement 2)	$570,000
Incremental costs of the modification	420,000
Excess of incremental benefits over incremental costs	$150,000

5. Wellesley Corporation should make the proposed improvements in the Weaving Department because the incremental benefits exceed the incremental costs by $36,000 per month:

Incremental benefits of reducing scrap in the Weaving Department	
by 2% (from 5% to 3%)	
2% × 10,000 rolls × $1,230 per roll (computed in requirement 3)	$246,000
Incremental costs of the improvements	210,000
Excess of incremental benefits over incremental costs	$ 36,000

6. Poor quality is often more costly at a bottleneck operation than it is at a nonbottleneck operation. The cost of poor quality at a nonbottleneck operation is largely the cost of materials wasted. No throughput contribution is forgone as a result of poor quality at a nonbottleneck operation. At a bottleneck operation, the cost of poor quality is the cost of materials wasted plus the opportunity cost of lost throughput contribution. At both the Weaving and the Printing Department, capacity not wasted in producing defective units could be used to generate additional sales and throughput contribution. Companies implementing quality programs should especially look at improving the quality of parts or products manufactured at the bottleneck operation.

CHAPTER 20
INVENTORY MANAGEMENT, JUST-IN-TIME,
AND BACKFLUSH COSTING

20-2 Five cost categories important in managing goods for sale in a retail organization are:
1. Purchasing costs.
2. Ordering costs.
3. Carrying costs.
4. Stockout costs.
5. Quality costs.

20-4 Costs included in the carrying costs of inventory are *incremental costs* for such items as insurance, rent, obsolescence, spoilage, and breakage plus the *opportunity cost* of capital (or required return on investment).

20-6 The steps in computing the costs of a prediction error when using the EOQ decision model are:

Step 1: Compute the monetary outcome from the best action that could have been taken, given the actual amount of the cost input.

Step 2: Compute the monetary outcome from the best action based on the incorrect amount of the predicted cost input.

Step 3: Compute the difference between the monetary outcomes from Steps 1 and 2.

20-8 Just-in-time (JIT) purchasing is the purchase of goods or materials such that a delivery immediately precedes demand or use. Benefits include lower inventory holdings (reduced warehouse space required and less money tied up in inventory) and less risk of inventory obsolescence and spoilage.

20-10 The sequence of activities involved in placing a purchase order can be facilitated by use of the Internet. For example, Cisco is streamlining the procurement process for its customers e.g., having online a complete price list, information about expected shipment dates, and a service order capability that is available 24 hours a day with e-mail or fax confirmation.

20-12 Obstacles to companies adopting a supply-chain approach include:
- Communication obstacles—the unwillingness of some parties to share information.
- Trust obstacles—includes the concern that all parties will not meet their agreed-upon commitments.
- Information system obstacles—includes problems due to the information systems of different parties not being technically compatible.

- Limited resources—includes problems due to the people and financial resources given to support a supply-chain initiative not being adequate.

20-14 Traditional normal and standard costing systems use sequential tracking, which is any product-costing method where recording of the journal entries occurs in the same order as actual purchases and progress in production.

    Backflush costing omits the recording of some or all of the journal entries relating to the cycle from purchase of direct materials to sale of finished goods. Where journal entries for one or more stages in the cycle are omitted, the journal entries for a subsequent stage use normal or standard costs to work backward to flush out the costs in the cycle for which journal entries were not made.

20-16 (20 min.) Economic order quantity for retailer.

1.   D = 12,000, P = \$270, C = \$12

$$\text{EOQ} \quad = \quad \sqrt{\frac{2\,DP}{C}} = \sqrt{\frac{2(12,000)\$270}{\$12}}$$

$$= \quad 734.85$$

$$= \quad 735 \text{ jerseys}$$

2.   Number of orders per year $\quad = \quad \dfrac{D}{\text{EOQ}} = \dfrac{12,000}{735}$

$$= \quad 16.33$$

$$= \quad 17 \text{ orders}$$

3.   Demand each working day $\quad = \quad \dfrac{D}{\text{Number of working days}}$

$$= \quad \dfrac{12,000}{365}$$

$$= \quad 32.88 = 33 \text{ jerseys per day}$$

Purchase lead time $\quad = \quad 7$ days

Reorder point $\quad = \quad 33 \times 7$

$$= \quad 231 \cong 231 \text{ jerseys}$$

20-18 (15 min.) **EOQ for a retailer.**

1. $D = 24,000, P = \$192, C = 20\% \times \$9.60 = \$1.92$

$$EOQ = \sqrt{\frac{2DP}{C}} = \sqrt{\frac{2(24,000)\$192}{\$1.92}} = 2,191\,\text{metres}$$

2. Number of orders per year: $\dfrac{D}{EOQ} = \dfrac{24,000}{2,191} = 10.95\ \text{orders} = 11\ \text{orders}$

3. Demand each working day $= \dfrac{D}{\text{Number of working days}}$

$$= \frac{24,000}{250}$$

$$= 96\ \text{metres per day}$$

$$= 480\ \text{metres per week}$$

Purchasing lead time = 2 weeks
Reorder point = $480 \times 2 = 960$ metres

20-20 (20 min.) **Sensitivity of EOQ to changes in relevant ordering and carrying costs.**

1. A straightforward approach to the requirement is to construct the following table for EOQ at relevant carrying and ordering costs. Annual demand is 12,000 units. The formula for the EOQ model is:

$$EOQ = \sqrt{\frac{2DP}{C}}$$

where D = demand in units for a specified period of time
P = relevant ordering costs per purchase order
C = relevant carrying costs of one unit in stock for the time period used for D (one year in this problem).

Relevant Carrying Costs Per Unit Per Year	Relevant Ordering Costs per Purchase Order	
	$360	$240
$12	$\sqrt{\dfrac{2 \times 12{,}000 \times \$360}{\$12}} = 849$	$\sqrt{\dfrac{2 \times 12{,}000 \times \$240}{\$12}} = 693$
18	$\sqrt{\dfrac{2 \times 12{,}000 \times \$360}{\$18}} = 693$	$\sqrt{\dfrac{2 \times 12{,}000 \times \$240}{\$18}} = 566$
24	$\sqrt{\dfrac{2 \times 12{,}000 \times \$360}{\$24}} = 600$	$\sqrt{\dfrac{2 \times 12{,}000 \times \$240}{\$24}} = 490$

2. For a given demand level, as relevant carrying costs increase, EOQ becomes smaller. For a given demand level, as relevant order costs increase, EOQ increases.

20-22 (20-30 min.) Purchase-order size for retailer, EOQ, just-in-time purchasing.

1. $EOQ = \sqrt{\dfrac{2DP}{C}}$

(a) D = 7,200; P = $36; C = $1.20

$$EOQ = \sqrt{\dfrac{2(7{,}200)\,(\$36)}{\$1.20}} = \sqrt{432{,}000} = 657.3 \text{ cases} \cong 658 \text{ cases}$$

(b) D = 7,200; P = $36; C = $1.80

$$EOQ = \sqrt{\dfrac{2(7{,}200)\,(\$36)}{\$1.80}} = \sqrt{288{,}000} = 536.7 \text{ cases} \cong 537 \text{ cases}$$

(c) D = 7,200; P = $6; C = $1.80

$$EOQ = \sqrt{\dfrac{2(7{,}200)\,(\$6)}{\$1.80}} = \sqrt{48{,}000} = 219.1 \text{ cases} \cong 220 \text{ cases}$$

2. A just-in-time purchasing policy involves the purchase of goods such that their delivery immediately precedes their demand. Given the purchase order sizes calculated in requirement 1, the number of purchase orders placed each month is (D ÷ EOQ):

(a) $\dfrac{D}{EOQ} = \dfrac{7,200}{658} = 11$ orders per month or $\cong 1$ every 2.7 days

(b) $\dfrac{D}{EOQ} = \dfrac{7,200}{537} = 14$ orders per month or $\cong 1$ every 2.15 days

(c) $\dfrac{D}{EOQ} = \dfrac{7,200}{220} = 33$ orders per month or $\cong 1.1$ every day

An increase in C and a decrease in P led to increases in the optimal frequency of orders. The 24-Hour Mart has increased the frequency of delivery from every third day (1a: P = \$36; C = \$1.20) to a delivery every day (1c: P = \$6; C = \$1.80). There is a reduction of 219 cases in the average inventory level: $(658 - 220) \div 2 = 219$.

20-24 (30 min.) Backflush costing and JIT production.

1.

(a)	Purchases of raw materials	Inventory: Raw and In-Process Control	\$3,304,800	
		Accounts Payable		\$3,304,800
(b)	Incur conversion costs	Conversion Costs Control	\$868,320	
		Various Accounts		\$868,320
(c)	Completion of finished goods	Finished Goods Control[a]	\$4,180,800	
		Inventory: Raw and In-Process Control[c]		\$3,280,320
		Conversion Costs Allocated[d]		900,480
(d)	Sale of finished goods	Cost of Goods Sold[b]	\$4,118,400	
		Finished Goods Control		\$4,118,400

[a] $26,800 \times (\$122.40 + \$33.60) = \$4,180,800$
[b] $26,400 \times (\$122.40 + \$33.60) = \$4,118,400$
[c] $26,800 \times \$122.40 = \$3,280,320$
[d] $26,800 \times \$33.60 = \$900,480$

2.

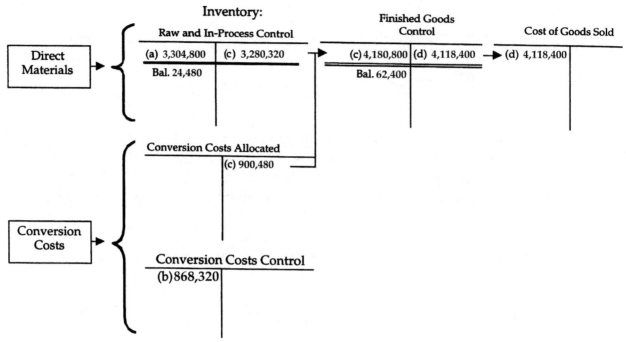

3.   Under an ideal JIT production system, there could be zero inventories at the end of each day. Entry (c) would be $4,118,400 finished goods production, not $4,180,800.

20-26 (20 min.)   **Backflush costing, two trigger points, production completion and sale (continuation of 20-24).**

(a)	Purchases of raw materials	No entry		
(b)	Incur conversion costs	Conversion Costs Control	$868,320	
		Various Accounts		$868,320
(c)	Completion of finished goods	Finished Goods Control	$4,180,800	
		Accounts Payable Control		$3,280,320
		Conversion Costs Allocated		900,480
(d)	Sale of finished goods	Cost of Goods Sold	$4,118,400	
		Finished Goods Control		$4,118,400
(e)	Underallocated or overallocated conversion costs	Conversion Costs Allocated	$900,480	
		Costs of Goods Sold		$ 32,160[1]
		Conversion Costs Control		868,320

[1] $900,480 − $868,320 = $32,160

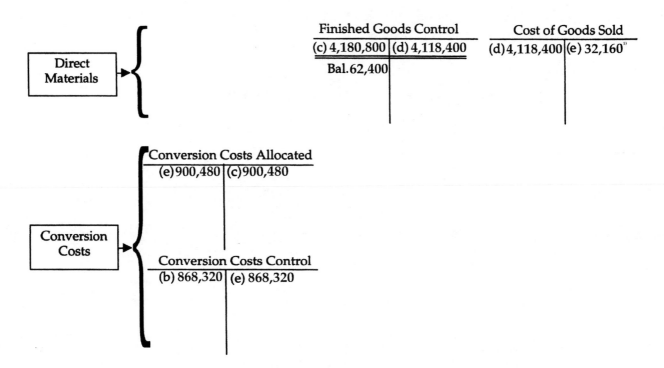

Finished Goods Control		Cost of Goods Sold	
(c) 4,180,800	(d) 4,118,400	(d) 4,118,400	(e) 32,160"
Bal. 62,400			

Conversion Costs Allocated	
(e) 900,480	(c) 900,480

Conversion Costs Control	
(b) 868,320	(e) 868,320

20-28 (30-45 min.) EOQ, uncertainty, safety stock, reorder point.

1. The Starr Company is searching for the safety stock level that will minimize the expected total of the costs of carrying additional inventory and the costs associated with insufficient inventories (stockout costs). The present reorder point, alternative safety stock levels, and probability of usage during lead time have to be computed before this level can be determined.

The present reorder point is calculated as follows:

$$\text{Average daily usage} = \frac{\text{Annual demand}}{\text{Number of working days}}$$

$$= \frac{30{,}000 \text{ units}}{300 \text{ days}} = 100 \text{ units per day}$$

$$\text{Reorder point} = \text{Average daily usage} \times \text{Lead time}$$
$$= (100 \text{ units per day}) \times 5 \text{ days} = 500 \text{ units}$$

Alternative safety stock levels would be the number of units needed to cover possible demand levels during lead time. These safety levels can be determined as follows:

Possible safety stock levels = Possible demand – Reorder point

The alternative safety stock levels are 0, 20, 40, and 60 units. The probability of demand during lead time is:

Demand During Lead Time	Number of Times Quantity Was Demanded	Probability
440	6	.03
460	12	.06
480	16	.08
500	130	.65
520	20	.10
540	10	.05
560	6	.03
	200	1.00

Safety Stock Level in Units (1)	Demand Realizations Resulting in Stockouts (2)	Stockout in Units[a] (3)=(2)− 500−(1)	Probability of Stockout (4)	Relevant Stockout Costs[b] (5)=(3)×$24	Number of Orders per Year[c] (6)	Expected Stockout Costs[d] (7)=(4)×(5) ×(6)	Relevant Carrying Costs[e] (8)=(1)× $12	Total Relevant Costs (9)=(7)+(8)
0	520	20	0.10	$480	10	$ 480		
	540	40	0.05	960	10	480		
	560	60	0.03	1,440	10	432		
						$1,392	$ 0	$1,392
20	540	20	0.05	480	10	$ 240		
	560	40	0.03	960	10	288		
						$ 528	$240	$ 768
40	560	20	0.03	480	10	$ 144	$480	$ 624
60	560	NIL	0.03	NIL	10	$ 0[f]	$720	$ 720

[a] Realized demand—inventory available during lead time (excluding safety stock), 500 units—safety stock.
[b] Stockout units × relevant stockout costs of $24 per motor.
[c] Annual demand 30,000 ÷ 3,000 EOQ = 10 orders per year.
[d] Probability of stockout x relevant stockout costs x number of orders per year.
[e] Safety stock x annual relevant carrying costs of $12 per motor (assumes that safety stock is on hand at all times and that there is no overstocking caused by decreases in expected usage).
[f] At a safety stock level of 60 motors, no stockouts will occur and hence expected stockout costs = $0.

Safety stock of 40 units would minimize Starr Company's total stockout and carrying costs.

2.   The new reorder point would be:

Present reorder point (demand during
     lead time: 100 × 5)   500 units
Safety stock   40 units
New reorder point   540 units

3.   The factors Starr Company should have considered when estimating the stockout costs include:

(a) Possible lost contribution margin on motors not sold.
(b) Costs associated with disruption or idle time.
(c) Forgone contribution margin on future sales from possible loss of customers and customer goodwill.
(d) Additional clerical costs involved in keeping records of back orders.
(e) How valid is the past empirical distribution of demand when predicting the future demand distribution.

20-30 (30 min.)   JIT purchasing, relevant benefits, relevant costs.

1.   Solution Exhibit 20-30 presents the $45,000 cash savings that would result if Margro Corporation adopted the just-in-time inventory system in 2007.

2.   Conditions that should exist in order for a company to install "just-in-time" inventory successfully include the following.

• Top management must be committed and provide the necessary leadership support in order to ensure a company-wide, coordinated effort.
• A detailed system for integrating the sequential operations of the manufacturing process needs to be developed and implemented. Direct materials must arrive when needed for each subassembly so that the production process functions smoothly.
• Accurate sales forecasts are needed for effective finished goods planning and production scheduling.
• Products should be designed to use standardized parts to reduce manufacturing time and reduce costs.
• Reliable vendors who can deliver quality direct materials on time with minimum lead time must be obtained.

SOLUTION EXHIBIT 20-30
Annual Relevant Costs of Current Purchasing Policy and JIT Purchasing Policy for Margro Corporation

	Incremental Costs Under Current Purchasing Policy	Incremental Costs Under JIT Purchasing Policy
Required return on investment		
20% per year × $720,000 of average inventory per year	$144,000	
20% per year × $0 inventory per year		$ 0
Annual insurance costs	16,800	0
Warehouse rent (revenue)	72,000	(16,200)[a]
Overtime costs		
No overtime	0	
Overtime premium		48,000
Stockout costs		
No stockouts		
$7.80[b] contribution margin per unit × 20,000 units	0	156,000
Total incremental costs	$232,800	$187,800
Difference in favour of JIT purchasing	$45,000	

[a]$(16,200) = Warehouse rental revenues, [(75% × 12,000) × $1.80].
[b]Calculation of unit contribution margin:

Selling price		
($12,960,000 ÷ 900,000 units)		$14.40
Variable costs per unit:		
Variable manufacturing costs per unit		
($4,860,000 ÷ 900,000 units)	$5.40	
Variable marketing and distribution costs per unit		
($1,080,000 ÷ 900,000 units)	1.20	
Total variable costs per unit		6.60
Contribution margin per unit		$7.80

Note that the incremental costs of $48,000 for overtime premiums to make the additional 15,000 units are less than the contribution margin from losing these sales equal to $117,000 ($7.80 × 15,000). Margro would rather incur overtime than lose 15,000 units of sales.

20-32 (20-25 min.) Backflush, two trigger points, materials purchase and sale (continuation of 20-31).

1.

(a)	Purchase of raw materials	Inventory Control Accounts Payable Control	$6,360,000	$6,360,000
(b)	Incur conversion costs	Conversion Costs Control Various Accounts	$3,696,000	$3,696,000
(c)	Completion of finished goods	No entry		
(d)	Sale of finished goods	Cost of Goods Sold Inventory Control Conversion Costs Allocated	$9,446,400	$5,990,400[1] 3,456,000[2]
(e)	Underallocated or or overallocated conversion costs	Conversion Costs Allocated Cost of Goods Sold Conversion Costs Control	$3,456,000[2] 240,000[3]	$3,696,000

[1] 192,000 units sold × $31.20 = $5,990,400
[2] 192,000 units converted × $18.00 = $3,456,000
[3] $3,696,000 actual conversion costs − $3,456,000 at standard = $240,000 cost of goods sold

2.

The $369,600 ending balance of Inventory Control consists of the $120,000 direct materials still on hand (same as shown in the solution to Problem 20-31) and the $31.20 × 8,000 = $249,600 direct materials embodied in the 8,000 units manufactured but not sold during June.

3.   Entry (e) in requirement 1 would be revised so that some conversion costs would be included in Inventory, 8,000 units × $18 conversion cost per unit = $144,000:

Conversion Costs Allocated	$3,456,000
Inventory Control	144,000
Cost of Goods Sold	96,000
Conversion Costs Control	3,696,000

If you assigned Problem 20-31, compare the answer here with the answer in the solution to Problem 20-31. Note that the underallocated conversion costs are $96,000 in both answers. Note especially that the monthly writeoffs of all conversion costs may not be acceptable for external reporting purposes if inventories are materially understated. This variation of backflush costing is suitable for production systems that have minimal finished goods inventories. It is less feasible otherwise.

20-34 (25 min.) Relevant benefits and relevant costs of JIT purchasing.

Solution Exhibit 20-34 presents the $869.40 cash savings that would result if Hardesty Medical Instruments adopted the Just-in-time inventory system in 2007.

SOLUTION EXHIBIT 20-34

Annual Relevant Costs of Current Purchasing Policy and JIT Purchasing Policy for Hardesty Medical Instruments

	Relevant Costs Under Current Purchasing Policy	Relevant Costs Under JIT Purchasing Policy
Purchasing costs		
$12.00 per unit × 20,000 units	$240,000.00	
$12.06 per unit × 20,000 units		$241,200.00
Ordering costs		
$6 per order × 20 orders per year	120.00	
$6 per order × 200 orders per year		1,200.00
Opportunity carrying costs, required return on investment		
20% per year × $12 cost per unit × 500[a] units of average inventory per year	1,200.00	
20% per year × $12.06 cost per unit × 50[b] units of average inventory per year		120.60
Other carrying costs		
$5.40 per unit per year × 500[a] units of average inventory per year	2,700.00	
$5.40 per unit per year × 50[b] units of average inventory per year		270.00
Stockout costs		
No stockouts	0	
$3.60 per unit × 100 units per year		360.00
Total annual relevant costs	$244,020.00	$243,150.60
Annual difference in favour of JIT purchasing	$869.40	

[a]Order quantity ÷ 2 = 1,000 ÷ 2 = 500
[b]Order quantity ÷ 2 = 100 ÷ 2 = 50

2. Hardesty may benefit from Morrison managing its inventories if there is high order variability caused by randomness in when consumers purchase surgical scalpels or by trade promotions that prompt retailers to stock for the future. By coordinating their activities and sharing information about retail sales and inventory held throughout the supply chain, Morrison can plan its manufacturing activities to ensure adequate supply of product while keeping inventory low. For this to succeed, Hardesty and Morrison must have compatible information systems, build trust, and communicate freely.

20-36 (25 min.) **Supplier evaluation and relevant costs of qualify and timely deliveries.**

Solution Exhibit 20-36 presents the $1,450 annual relevant costs difference in favour of purchasing from Quality Sports. Copeland should buy the footballs from Quality Sports.

SOLUTION EXHIBIT 20-36
Annual Relevant Costs of Purchasing from Big Red and Quality Sports

Relevant Item	Relevant Costs of Purchasing From	
	Big Red	**Quality Sports**
Purchasing costs		
$60 per unit × 12,000 units per year	$720,000	
$61.20 per unit × 12,000 units per year		$734,400
Inspection costs		
$0.02 per unit × 12,000 units	240	
No inspection necessary		0
Opportunity carrying costs, required return on investment,		
15% per year × $60 cost per unit × 100 units of		
average inventory per year;	900	
15% per year × $61.20 cost per unit × 100 units of		
average inventory per year		918
Other carrying costs (insurance, material handling,		
and so on)		
$4 per unit × 100 units of average inventory per year	400	
$4.50 per unit × 100 units of average inventory per year		450
Stockout costs		
$24 per unit × 350 units per year	8,400	
$12 per unit × 60 units per year		720
Customer returns costs		
$30 per unit × 300 units	9,000	
$30 per unit × 25 units		750
Total annual relevant costs	$738,940	$737,238
Annual difference in favour of Quality Sports		$1,702

20-38 (20 min.) Backflush, two trigger points, materials purchase and sale (continuation of 20-37).

1.

(a)	Purchases of raw materials	Inventory Control Accounts Payable Control	$660,000	$660,000
(b)	Incur conversion costs	Conversion Costs Control Various Accounts	$528,000	$528,000
(c)	Completion of finished goods	No entry		
(d)	Sale of finished goods	Cost of Goods Sold Inventory Control Conversion Costs Allocated	$1,080,000	$600,000[1] 480,000[2]
(e)	Underallocated or overallocated conversion costs	Conversion Costs Allocated Cost of Goods Sold Conversion Costs Control	$480,000 48,000[3]	$528,000

[1] 20,000 units finished goods × $30 = $600,000
[2] $1,080,000 − $600,000 = $480,000 conversion costs allocated or $24 × 20,000 = $480,000
[3] Conversion costs incurred − Conversion cost allocated = $48,000; $528,000 − $480,000 = $48,000

2.

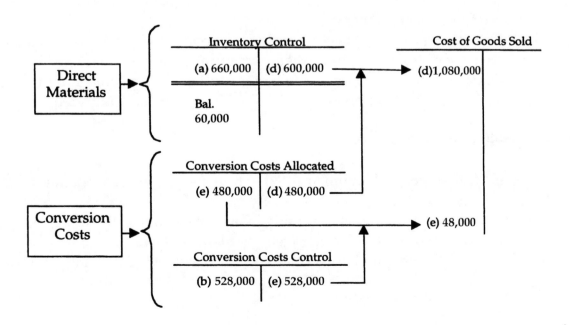

20-40 (20 min.) **Supply-chain analysis, company viewpoints.**

1. The major benefits to adopting a supply-chain approach include:

   a. Overall reduction in inventory levels across the supply chain:
      - "receiving better information has allowed us to forecast and reduce inventory levels ..."
      - "The inventory levels are lower ... by not overstocking the warehouses"

   b. Fewer stockouts at the retail level.

   c. Reduced manufacturing of items not subsequently demanded by retailers:
      - "You only produce what you need"
      - "We have less waste by not overstocking the warehouses"

   d. Lower manufacturing costs due to better production scheduling and fewer expedited orders:
      - "We can fine tune our production scheduling"

   These benefits can both increase revenues (fewer stockouts) and decrease costs (lower manufacturing costs, lower holding costs, and lower distribution costs).

2. Key obstacles to a manufacturer adopting a supply-chain approach are:

   a. Communication obstacles—includes the unwillingness of some parties to share information.
   b. Trust obstacles—includes the concern that all parties will not meet their agreed-upon commitments.
   c. Information system obstacles—includes problems due to the information systems of different parties not being technically compatible.
   d. Limited resources—includes problems due to the people and financial resources given to support a supply-chain initiative not being adequate.

20-42 (35-40 min.) **Backflushing.**

1. Glendale has successfully implemented JIT in its production operations and, hence, minimized work-in-process inventory. It still has a fair amount of raw material and finished goods inventory. Glendale should, therefore, adopt a backflush costing system with two trigger points, as follows:
   a. Direct materials purchases charged to Inventory: Raw and In-Process Control.

b. Finished goods recorded as Finished Goods Control. The backflush approach described closely approximates the costs computed using sequential tracking. There is no work in process so there is no need for a Work in Process inventory account.

Further, by maintaining a Raw and In-Process Inventory Control and Finished Goods Control account, Glendale can keep track of and control the inventories of direct materials and finished goods in its plant.

2. a. I would recommend that Glendale adopt a backflush costing system with trigger points at completion of finished goods and at the sale of finished goods. This would approximate the sequential tracking approach since the question assumes Glendale has no raw materials or work-in-process inventories. There is, therefore, no need for these inventory accounts.

b. A backflush costing system with two trigger points—when purchases of raw materials are made (debited to Inventory Control), and when Finished Goods are sold—would approximate sequential tracking, since the question assumes Glendale has no work-in-process or finished goods inventories.

c. A backflush costing system with a single trigger point when finished goods are sold would approximate sequential tracking, since the question assumes Glendale has no raw material, work-in-process or finished goods inventories.

   The principle here is that backflushing of costs should be triggered at the finished goods inventory stage if Glendale plans to hold finished goods inventory. If Glendale plans to hold no finished goods inventory, backflushing can be postponed until the finished goods are sold. In other words, the trigger points for backflushing relate to the points where inventory is being accumulated. As a result, backflushing matches the sequential tracking approach and also maintains a record for the monitoring and control of the inventory.

3. Some comments on the quotation follow:

a. The backflush system is a standard costing system, not an actual costing system.

b. If standard costing is used, an up-to-date realistic set of standard costs is always desirable—as long as the set meets the cost-benefit test as related to the task of updating.

c. The operating environments of "the present JIT era" have induced many companies toward more simplicity (back flush) and abandoning the typical standard costing system (sequential tracking).

d. Backflush is probably closer to being a periodic system than a perpetual system. However, a periodic system may be cost-effective, particularly where physical inventories are relatively low or stable.

e. The textbook points out that, to be attractive, backflush costing should generate the same financial measurements as sequential tracking—and at a lower accounting cost.

f. The choice of a product costing system is highly contextual. Its characteristics should be heavily affected by its costs, the preferences of operating managers, and the underlying operating processes. Sweeping generalizations about any cost accounting system or technique are unjustified.

CHAPTER 21
CAPITAL BUDGETING AND COST ANALYSIS

21-2 **The six stages in capital budgeting are:**
1. An *identification stage* to distinguish the types of capital expenditure projects that will accomplish organization objectives.
2. A *search stage* that explores several potential capital expenditure investment that will achieve organization objectives.
3. An *information-acquisition stage* to consider the predicted costs and consequences of alternative capital investments.
4. A *selection stage* to choose projects for implementation.
5. A *financing stage* to obtain project financing.
6. An *implementation and control* stage to put the projects in motion and monitor their performance.

21-4 No. Only quantitative outcomes are formally analyzed in capital-budgeting decisions. Many effects of capital-budgeting decisions, however, are difficult to quantify in financial terms. These nonfinancial or qualitative factors, for example, the number of accidents in a manufacturing plant, or employee morale, are important to consider in making capital-budgeting decisions.

21-6 The payback method measures the time it will take to recoup, in the form of net cash inflows, the total dollars invested in a project. The payback method is simple and easy to understand. It is a handy method when accuracy[1] in estimates of profitability is not crucial and when predicted cash flows in later years are highly uncertain. The main weakness of the payback method is its neglect of profitability and the time value of money.

[1] Accuracy is how close you are to the real-world value. Precision is reproducibility and is neither sufficient nor necessary with respect to accuracy.

21-8 No. The discounted cash-flow techniques implicitly consider amortization in rate of return computations; the compound interest tables automatically allow for recovery of investment. The net initial investment of an asset is usually regarded as a lump-sum outflow at time zero.

21-10 No. If managers are evaluated on the accrual accounting rate of return, they may not use the NPV method for capital-budgeting decisions. Instead, managers will choose investments that maximize the accrual accounting rate of return.

21-12 Four critical success factors that managers focus on when controlling job projects are (a) scope (b) quality (c) time schedule and (d) costs.

21-14 Exercises in compound interest.

The answers to these exercises are printed after the last problem, at the end of the chapter.

21-16 (30 min.) Comparison of approaches to capital budgeting.

1. Payback period = $132,000 ÷ $33,600   = 3.93 years

2. The table for the present value of annuities (Appendix A, Table 4) shows:
    10 periods at 12% = 5.650
    Net present value = $33,600(5.650) – $132,000
                       = $189,840 – $132,000 = $57,840

3. Internal rate of return:

    $132,000   =   Present value of annuity of $33,600 at X% for 10 years, or what factor (F) in the table of present values of an annuity (Appendix A, Table 4) will satisfy the following equation.

    $132,000   = $33,600F

    $$F = \frac{\$132,000}{\$33,600} = 3.929$$

On the ten-year line in the table for the present value of annuities (Appendix A, Table 4) find the column closest to 3.929; 3.929 is between a rate of return of 20% and 22%.

Interpolation can be used to determine the exact rate:

	Present Factors	Value
20%	4.192	4.192
IRR rate	—	3.929
22%	3.923	—
Difference	0.269	0.263

$$\text{Internal rate of return} = 20\% + \left[\frac{0.263}{0.269}\right](2\%)$$

$$= 20\% + (0.978)(2\%) = 21.96\%$$

4. Accrual accounting rate of return based on net initial investment:

Net initial investment	=	$132,000
Estimated useful life	=	10 years
Annual straight-line amortization	=	$132,000 ÷ 10 = $13,200

$$\text{Accrual accounting rate of return} = \frac{\$33,600-\$13,200}{\$132,000}$$

$$= \frac{\$20,400}{\$132,000} = 15.45\%$$

21-18 (20-30 min.) Net present value, internal rate of return, sensitivity analysis.

1. a. The table for the present value of annuities (Appendix A, Table 4) shows:

6 periods at 12% = 4.111

Net present value = $48,000 (4.111) – $144,000
= $197,328 – $144,000 = $53,328

b. Internal rate of return:

$144,000 = Present value of annuity of $48,000 at X% for 6 years, or what factor (F) in the table of present values of an annuity (Appendix A, Table 4) will satisfy the following equation.

$144,000 = $48,000F

$$F = \frac{\$144,000}{\$48,000} = 3.0$$

On the six-year line in the table for the present value of annuities (Appendix A, Table 4), find the column closest to 3.0; 3.0 is between a rate of return of 24% and 26%.

Interpolation is necessary:

	Present Factors	Value
24%	3.020	3.020
IRR rate	—	3.000
26%	2.885	—
Difference	0.135	0.020

$$\text{Internal rate of return} = 24\% + \left[\frac{0.020}{0.135}\right](2\%)$$

$$= 24\% + (0.148)(2\%) = 24.30\%$$

2. Let the minimum annual cash savings be $X.
Then we want

$$\$X\,(4.111) = \$144,000$$

$$X = \frac{\$144,000}{4.111} = \$35,028$$

Johnson Corporation would want annual cash savings of at least $35,028 for the net present value of the investment to equal zero. This amount of cash savings would justify the investment in financial terms.

3. When the manager is uncertain about future cash flows, the manager would want to do sensitivity analysis, a form of which is described in requirement 2. Calculating the minimum cash flows necessary to make the project desirable gives the manager a feel for whether the investment is worthwhile or not. If the manager were quite certain about the future cash-operating cost savings, the approaches in requirement 1 would be preferred.

21-20 (30 min.) **Payback and NPV methods, no income taxes.**

1. a. Payback measures the time taken to recoup, in the form of expected future cash flows, the net investment in a project. Payback emphasizes the early recovery of cash as a key aspect of project ranking. Some managers argue that this emphasis on early recovery of cash is appropriate if there is a high level of uncertainty about future cash flows. Projects with shorter paybacks give the organization more flexibility because funds for other projects become available sooner.

Strengths
- Easy to understand
- One way to capture uncertainty about expected cash flows in later years of a project (although sensitivity analysis is a more systematic way)

Weaknesses
- Fails to incorporate the time value of money
- Does not consider a project's cash flows after the payback period

b.

Project A

Outflow, $240,000
Inflow, $60,000 (Year 1) + $60,000 (Year 2) + $60,000 (Year 3) + $60,000 (Year 4)

Payback = 4 years

Project B

Outflow, $228,000
Inflow, $48,000 (Year 1) + $60,000 (Year 2) + $84,000 (Year 3) + $36,000 (Year 4)
_____
$90,000

$$\text{Payback} = 3 + \frac{\$36,000}{\$90,000} = 3.4 \text{ years}$$

Project C

Outflow, $300,000
Inflow, $90,000 (Year 1) + $90,000 (Year 2) + $72,000 (Year 3) + $48,000 (Year 4)
_____
$96,000

$$\text{Payback} = 3 + \frac{\$48,000}{\$96,000} = 3.5 \text{ years}$$

Project D

Outflow, $252,000
Inflow, $90,000(Year 1) + $90,000(Year 2) + $72,000(Year 3)

Payback = 3 years

2. Solution Exhibit 21-22 shows the following ranking:

		NPV
1.	Project C	$50,310
2.	Project B	$45,636
3.	Project D	$ 5,910
4.	Project A	$(12,600)

3. Using NPV, Project C is the preferred project despite its having the 2nd-longest payback. Project C has sizable cash inflows after the payback period. Nonfinancial qualitative factors should also be considered. For example, are there differential worker safety issues across the projects? Are there differences in the extent of learning that can benefit other projects? Are there differences in the customer relationships established with different projects that can benefit Cording Manufacturing in future projects?

SOLUTION EXHIBIT 21-20

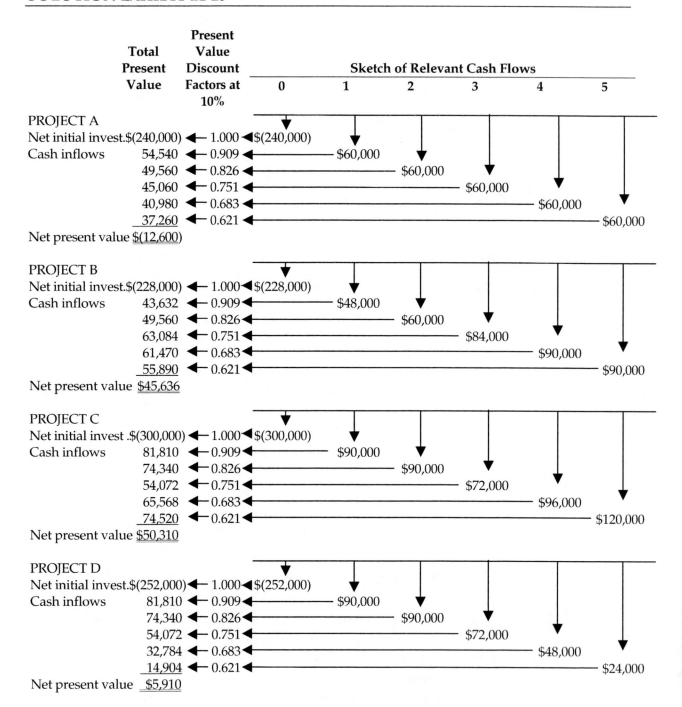

	Total Present Value	Present Value Discount Factors at 10%	Sketch of Relevant Cash Flows					
			0	1	2	3	4	5
PROJECT A								
Net initial invest.	$(240,000)	1.000	$(240,000)					
Cash inflows	54,540	0.909		$60,000				
	49,560	0.826			$60,000			
	45,060	0.751				$60,000		
	40,980	0.683					$60,000	
	37,260	0.621						$60,000
Net present value	$(12,600)							
PROJECT B								
Net initial invest.	$(228,000)	1.000	$(228,000)					
Cash inflows	43,632	0.909		$48,000				
	49,560	0.826			$60,000			
	63,084	0.751				$84,000		
	61,470	0.683					$90,000	
	55,890	0.621						$90,000
Net present value	$45,636							
PROJECT C								
Net initial invest.	$(300,000)	1.000	$(300,000)					
Cash inflows	81,810	0.909		$90,000				
	74,340	0.826			$90,000			
	54,072	0.751				$72,000		
	65,568	0.683					$96,000	
	74,520	0.621						$120,000
Net present value	$50,310							
PROJECT D								
Net initial invest.	$(252,000)	1.000	$(252,000)					
Cash inflows	81,810	0.909		$90,000				
	74,340	0.826			$90,000			
	54,072	0.751				$72,000		
	32,784	0.683					$48,000	
	14,904	0.621						$24,000
Net present value	$5,910							

21-22 (21-30 min.) **DCF, accrual accounting rate of return, working capital, evaluation of performance.**

1. a.

Present value of annuity of savings in cash operating
   costs ($30,000 per year for 8 years at 12%):
   $30,000 × 4.968 $149,040
Present value of $36,000 terminal disposal price of
   machine at 12% and at end of year 8: $36,000 × 0.404   14,544
Present value of $9,600 recovery of working capital at
   12% and at end of year 8: $9,600 × 0.404   3,878
Gross present value   167,462
Deduct net initial investment:
   Special-purpose machine, initial investment $132,000
   Additional working capital investment   9,600   141,600
Net present value $ 25,862

1   b. Use a trial and error approach. First, try a 16% discount rate:

$30,000 × 4.344	$130,320
($36,000 + $9,600) × 0.305	13,908
Gross present value	144,228
Deduce net initial investment	(141,600)
Net present value	$ 2,628

Second, try an 18% discount rate:

$30,000 × 4.078	$122,340
($36,000 + $9,600) × 0.266	12,130
Gross present value	134,470
Deduct net initial investment	(141,600)
Net present value	$ (7,130)

By interpolation:

Internal rate of return

$$= 16\% + \left(\frac{2,629}{2,629 + 7,130} \right)$$

$$= 16\% + (.269)\,(2\%) = 16.54\%$$

2. Accrual accounting rate of return based on net initial investment:

Net initial investment $= \$132,000 + \$9,600$
$\qquad\qquad\qquad\quad = \$141,600$

Annual amortization
$\qquad [\$141,600 - (\$36,000 + 9,600)] \div 8 \text{ years} = \$12,000$

$$\text{Accrual accounting rate of return} = \frac{\$30,000 - \$12,000}{\$141,600} = 12.71\%$$

3. If your decision is based on the DCF model, the purchase would be made because the net present value is positive, and the 16.54% internal rate of return exceeds the 12% required rate of return. However, you may believe that your performance may actually be measured using accrual accounting. This approach would show a 12.71% return on the initial investment, which is only slightly above the required 12% rate. Your reluctance to make a "buy" decision may be natural, unless you are assured of reasonable consistency between the decision model and the performance evaluation method.

21-24 (40 min.) NPV and customer profitability, no income taxes.

1.

Homebuilders	2007	2008	2009	2010	2011	2012
Revenues (5%)*	$54,000	$56,700	$59,535	$62,512	$65,637	$68,919
COGS (4%)*	26,400	27,456	28,554	29,696	30,884	32,120
Op. Costs (4%)*	12,000	12,480	12,979	13,498	14,038	14,600
Total costs	38,400	39,936	41,533	43,194	44,922	46,720
Cash flow from operations	$15,600	$16,764	$18,002	$19,318	$20,715	$22,199
Kitchen						
Revenues (15%)*	$390,000	$448,500	$515,775	$593,141	$682,112	$784,429
COGS (4%)*	216,000	224,640	233,626	242,971	252,689	262,797
Op. Costs (4%)*	90,000	93,600	97,344	101,238	105,287	109,499
Total costs	306,000	318,240	330,970	344,209	357,976	372,296
Cash flow from operations	$84,000	$130,260	$184,805	$248,932	$324,136	$412,133
Subdivision						
Revenues (8%)*	$1,032,000	$1,114,560	$1,203,725	$1,300,023	$1,404,025	$1,516,346
COGS (4%)*	660,000	686,400	713,856	742,410	772,107	802,991
Op. Costs (4%)*	282,000	293,280	305,011	317,212	329,900	343,096
Total costs	942,000	979,680	1,018,867	1,059,622	1,102,007	1,146,087
Cash flow from operations	$ 90,000	$134,880	$ 184,858	$ 240,401	$ 302,018	$ 370,259

*Annual increases given in question.

2.

Year	P.V. Factor for 10%	Homebuilders Cash Flow from Operations	Present Value	Kitchen Cash Flow from Operations	Present Value	Subdivision Cash Flow from Operations	Present Value
2008	0.909	$16,764	$15,238	$130,260	$118,406	$134,880	$122,606
2009	0.826	18,002	14,870	184,805	152,649	184,858	152,693
2010	0.751	19,318	14,508	248,932	186,948	240,401	180,541
2011	0.683	20,715	14,148	324,136	221,385	302,018	206,278
2012	0.621	22,199	13,786	412,133	255,935	370,259	229,931
			$72,550		$935,323		$892,049

Customer NPVs over next 5 years (2008 to 2012):

Homebuilders	$ 72,550
Kitchen Constructors	935,323
Subdivision Erectors	892,049

3.   Assume the 20% discount is given in 2008

	2007	2008	2009	2010	2011	2012
Revenues (5%)	$390,000	$312,000[a]	$327,600[b]	$343,980[b]	$361,179[b]	$379,238[b]
Total costs (4%)	306,000	318,240	330,970	344,208	357,976	372,296
Cash flow from operations	$ 84,000	$ (6,240)	$ (3,370)	$ (228)	$ 3,203	$ 6,942

[a]20% price discount
[b]5% annual increase

Net present value:

Year	PV Factor at 10%	Cash Flow from Operations	Present Value
2005	0.909	$(6,240)	$(5,672)
2006	0.826	(3,370)	(2,784)
2007	0.751	(228)	(171)
2008	0.683	3,203	2,188
2009	0.621	6,942	4,311
			$(2,128)

4.   The 20% discount and reduced subsequent annual revenue reduces the NPV from $892,049 to ($2,128). This is a drop of $894,177 in NPV.

The year ended is 2007; therefore, 2008 is the startup and the first 5% increase in revenue will occur in 2009 (after the 20% discount). In year 1 (2008), 100% of revenue will be obtained; in year 2 (2009) 105% of revenue, and so on.

Christen should consider whether the price discount demanded by Kitchen needs to be met in full to keep the account. The implication of meeting the full demand is that the account is minimally profitable at best. An equally serious concern is whether Christen's other two customers will demand comparable price discounts if Kitchen's full demands are met. The consequence would be very large reductions in the NPVs of all its customers.

Christen should also consider the reliability of the growth estimates used in computing the NPVs. Are the predicted differences in revenue growth rates based on reliable information? Many revenue growth estimates by salespeople turn out to be overestimates or occur over a longer time period than initially predicted.

21-26 (20-30 min.) Payback, net present value, relevant costs, sensitivity analysis.

All amounts are in thousands.

1. Old cash flow: Cash revenues, $144 – Cash costs, $149 $ (5.0)
   New cash flow: 10% of $96   9.6
   Expected increase in recurring operating cash flows
      for 10 years $14.6

2. Initial machine investment $77
   Deduct current disposal price of old equipment   (5)
   Net initial investment $72

   Payback period: $72 ÷ $14.6 = 4.93 years

3. NPV of cash inflows and outflows (in thousands):

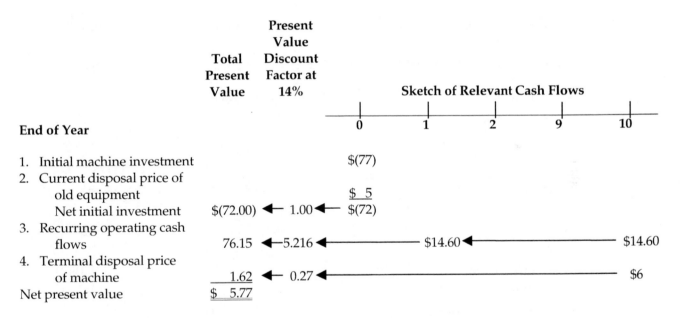

End of Year	Total Present Value	Present Value Discount Factor at 14%	Sketch of Relevant Cash Flows				
			0	1	2	9	10
1. Initial machine investment			$(77)				
2. Current disposal price of old equipment			$ 5				
Net initial investment	$(72.00) ← 1.00 ←		$(72)				
3. Recurring operating cash flows	76.15 ← 5.216 ←			$14.60 ←			$14.60
4. Terminal disposal price of machine	1.62 ← 0.27 ←						$6
Net present value	$ 5.77						

4. Let X = Annual gross vending machine receipts.

$$
\begin{aligned}
(.10X + \$5)(5.216) + \$1.62 &= \$72 \\
0.5216X + \$26.08 &= \$72 - \$1.62 \\
0.52\,X &= \$44.30 \\
16\,X &= \$44.30 \div 0.5216 \\
&= \$84.931 \text{ (or \$84,931)}
\end{aligned}
$$

Proof:		
$84,931 × 10%		$ 8,493.10
Add		5,000.00
Total		13,493.10
Multiply by		5.216
Total		70,380.00
Disposal price, $6,000 × 0.270		1,620.00
Total		72,000.00
Deduct investment		(72,000.00)
Difference		$ 0.00

Note: Both the book value and the amortization on the old equipment are irrelevant.

21-28 (30 min.) Special order, relevant costs, capital budgeting.

1. Relevant cash inflow from accepting the special order

	Relevant Cash Flows	
	Per Car (1)	**Total** (2)=(1) × 100,000
Incremental revenues (cash inflows)	$60.00	$6,000,000
Incremental costs (cash outflows)		
Neon paint	7.20	720,000
Boxes	3.60	360,000
Direct manufacturing labour	9.60	960,000
Total incremental costs	20.40	2,040,000
Net incremental benefit	$39.60	$3,960,000

Notes:
(a) The costs of plastic cars are irrelevant because these cars have already been purchased and so entail no incremental cash flow.
(b) Vat amortization is irrelevant because it is a past cost.
(c) Allocated plant manager's salary is irrelevant because it will not change whether or not the special order is accepted.
(d) Variable marketing costs are not deducted because they will not be incurred on the special order.

(e) Fixed marketing costs are irrelevant because they will not change whether or not the special order is accepted.

If it must offer the same $60 price to its other customers, Toys Inc. will lose cash flow of $10.80 × 130,000 = $1,404,000 per year for 4 years from its existing customers.

Note that whatever incremental costs Toys incurs on sales to its existing customers is irrelevant. These costs would continue to be incurred whether Toys prices the cars at $60 or $70.80. You can verify that Toys generates positive contribution margin at a price of $60 and so should continue to sell to its existing customers.

From Appendix A, the present value of a stream of $1,404,000 payments for 4 years discounted at 16% is $1,404,000 × 2.798 = $3,928,392.

The net relevant benefit of accepting the special order is $3,960,000 – $3,928,392 = $31,608. Therefore, Toys, Inc. should accept the special order.

2. Let the dollar discount from the current $70.80 price offered to existing customers be $X

Then $X (130,000) (2.798) = $3,960,000

$$X = \frac{\$3,960,000}{(130,000)(2.798)} = \$10.89$$

At a price of $59.91 ($70.80 – $10.89) per car to its existing customers, Toys would just be indifferent between accepting and rejecting Tiny Tot's special order.

21-30 (25 min.) Capital budgeting, computer-integrated manufacturing, sensitivity.

1. The net present value analysis of the CIM proposal follows. We consider the differences in cash flows if the machine is replaced. All values in millions.

		Relevant Cash Flows	Present Value Discount Factors at 14%	Total Present Value
1.	Initial investment in CIM today	$(54.0)	1.000	$(54.000)
2a.	Current disposal price of old production line	6.0	1.000	6.000
2b.	Current recovery of working capital ($7.2 – $2.4)	4.8	1.000	4.800
3.	Recurring operating cash savings $4.8[1] each year for 10 years	4.8	5.216	25.037
4a.	Higher terminal disposal price of machines ($16.8 – $0) in year 10	16.8	0.270	4.536
4b.	Reduced recovery of working capital ($2.40 – $7.2) in year 10	(4.8)	0.270	(1.296)
Net present value of CIM investment				$(14.923)

On the basis of this formal financial analysis, Dynamo should not invest in CIM—It has a negative net present value of $(14.923) million.

[1]Recurring operating cash flows are as follows:

Cost of maintaining software programs and CIM equipment	$(1.8)
Reduction in lease payments due to reduced floor-space requirements	1.2
Fewer product defects and reduced rework	5.4
Annual recurring operating cash flows	$ 4.8

2. Requirement 1 only looked at cost savings to justify the investment in CIM. Burns estimates additional cash revenues net of cash operating costs of $3.6 million a year as a result of higher quality and faster production resulting from CIM.

From Appendix A, the net present value of the $3.6 million annuity stream for 10 years discounted at 14% is $3.6 × 5.216 = $18.778. Taking these revenue benefits into account, the net present value of the CIM investment is $3.8546 ($18.778 – $14.923) million. On the basis of this financial analysis, Dynamo should invest in CIM.

3. Let the annual cash flow from additional revenues be $X. Then we want the present value of this cash flow stream to overcome the negative NPV of $(14.923) calculated in requirement 1. Hence,

$$X (5.216) = 14.923$$
$$X = \$2.861 \text{ million}$$

An annuity stream of $2.861 million for 10 years discounted at 14% gives an NPV of $2.861 × 5.216 = $14.923 (rounded).

4.

(000,000s)	Relevant Cash Flows	Present Value Discount Factors at 14%	Total Present Value
1. Initial investment in CIM today	$(54.0)	1.000	$(54.000)
2a. Current disposal price of old production line	6.0	1.000	6.000
2b. Current recovery of working capital ($7.2 – $2.4)	4.8	1.000	4.800
3a. Recurring operating cash savings $4.8 each year for 5 years	4.8	3.433	16.478
3b. Recurring cash flows from additional revenues of $3.6 each year for 5 years	3.6	3.433	12.359
4a. Higher terminal disposal price of machines ($24 – $4.8) in year 5	19.2	0.519	9.965
4b. Reduced recovery of working capital ($2.4 – $7.2) in year 5	(4.8)	0.519	(2.491)
Net present value of CIM investment			$(6.889)

The use of too short a time horizon such as 5 years biases against the adoption of CIM projects. Before finally deciding against CIM in this case, Bums should consider other factors including

(a) Sensitivity to different estimates of recurring cash savings or revenue gains.
(b) Accuracy of the costs of implementing and maintaining CIM.
(c) Benefits of greater flexibility that results from CIM and the opportunity to train workers for the manufacturing environment of the future.
(d) Potential obsolescence of the CIM equipment. Dynamo should consider how difficult the CIM equipment would be to modify if there is a major change in CIM technology.
(e) Alternative approaches to achieving the major benefits of CIM such as changes in process or implementation of just-in-time systems.
(f) Strategic factors. CIM may be the best approach to remain competitive against other low-cost producers in the future.

21-32 (50 min.) Relevant costs, capital budgeting.

1. Solution Exhibit 21-32 presents an analysis of cash inflows and outflows (in thousands) under the alternatives of (1) cease SPD operations and (2) buy a new machine.

      The Special Products Division should buy the new machine rather than cease operations because purchasing the new machine has a higher net present value ($194,592 versus $164,136).

^a Contribution margin from operations (in thousands):

Revenues		$1,440
Variable costs:		
Production	$924	
Marketing	156	
Total variable costs		1,080
Contribution margin	$360	

Note the following:

(a) The terminal disposal price of $4,800 for the old machine is irrelevant because the old machine will be disposed of under both alternatives—either if SPD ceases operations or if SPD buys a new machine.

(b) Machine amortization and patent amortization are noncash cost, and hence irrelevant for the NPV analysis.

(c) The allocated building costs of $24,000 are irrelevant for the analysis because the same building costs will be incurred in total under either alternative. The $36,000 additional cash flow that SPD will receive if it ceases operations and rents out the space is relevant in computing the NPV of the "cease operations" alternative, because this cash flow is only received if SPD shuts down operations.

(d) Machine fixed maintenance costs of $24,000 for the old broken down machine are irrelevant. Machine maintenance costs of $30,000 for the new machine are relevant.

2. In order to maximize compensation, the decision maker will favour the alternative that maximizes aggregate accounting income in 2005.

	Increase/(Decrease) in Plastics Unlimited's Total Operating Income in 2005 (in thousands)
Effect of ceasing operations on Plastics Unlimited's operating income	
Gain on sale of patent[b]	$132
Manager's salary in larger department	(72)
Rental income	36
Effect on Plastics Unlimited's operating income	$ 96
Effect of buying a new machine on Plastics Unlimited's operating income	
Contribution margin from operations	$360.00
Machine amortization ($384 − $60) ÷ 5 years	(64.80)
Patent amortization	(30.00)
SPD manager's salary	(66.00)
Assistant manager's salary in larger department	(78.00)
Machine maintenance	(30.00)
Other fixed costs	(18.00)
Effect on Plastics Unlimited's operating income	$ 73.20

[b]Proceeds from sale of patent	$282
Deduct book value of patent	150
Gain on sale of patent	$132

To maximize Plastics Unlimited's operating income in 2008, and hence bonus, the individual decision maker would prefer to cease SPD's operations even though buying a new machine has a higher NPV.

Note the following:
(a) The data relating to the disposal of the old machine are irrelevant since the old machine will be disposed of under both alternatives.
(b) Amortization on the new machine and patent amortization are relevant for the operating income computations. These costs will only be incurred if SPD continues operations and buys the new machine.
(c) The allocated building space costs of $24,000 are irrelevant because the same building costs will be incurred in total whether SPD ceases operations or SPD buys a new machine. The rental income of $36,000 by renting out building space if SPD ceases operations is relevant and is therefore included in the calculation of operating income under the "cease operations" alternative.

SOLUTION EXHIBIT 21-32
Net Present Value Analysis for Special Products Division
(in thousands)

End of Year	Total Present Value	Present Value of $1 Discounted at 16%	Sketch of Relevant Cash Flows					
			2007	2008	2009	2010	2011	2012
Cease Operations								
1. Sell patent	$282.00	1.000	$282					
2. Recurring operating cash flows								
a. Manager's salary in larger department	(235.728)	3.274		$(72)	$(72)	$(72)	$(72)	$(72)
b. Rental income from building space	117.864	3.274		$36	$36	$36	$36	$36
Net present value	$ 164.136							
Buy a New Machine								
1. Initial machine investment	$(384.00)	1.000	$(384.00)					
2. Recurring operating cash flows								
a. Contribution margin from operations	1,178.64	3.274		$360	$360	$360	$360	$360
b. Machine maintenance	(98.22)	3.274		$(30)	$(30)	$(30)	$(30)	$(30)
c. Other fixed costs	(58.932)	3.274		$(18)	$(18)	$(18)	$(18)	$(18)
d. Manager's salary in Special Products division	(216.084)	3.274		$(66)	$(66)	$(66)	$(66)	$(66)
e. Manager's salary in larger department	(255.372)	3.274		$(78)	$(78)	$(78)	$(78)	$(78)
3. Terminal disposal price of new machine	28.56	0.476						$60
Net present value	$ 194.592							

CHAPTER 22
CAPITAL BUDGETING: A CLOSER LOOK

22-2   Yes. To apply a consistent set of regulations and to provide for implementation of government initiatives, the federal government has implemented its own system of capital cost allowance (CCA). The Income Tax Act (ITA) does not permit a company to deduct amortization expense in determining taxable income but rather a company is allowed to deduct CCA. Therefore, the accounting amortization method will have no effect on taxes payable.

22-4   The total project approach calculates the present value of *all* cash outflows and inflows associated with each alternative. The incremental approach analyzes only the differences in those cash outflows and inflows that differ between alternatives.

22-6   No. Income taxes also affect the operating cash flows from an investment and the cash flows from current and terminal disposal of machines in the capital-budgeting decision. When a company has positive operating cash flows, income taxes reduce the cash flows available to the company from these sources.

22-8   The *real rate of return* is the rate of return required to cover only investment risk. This rate is made up of two elements: (a) a risk-free element and (b) a business-risk or equity element. The *nominal rate of return* is the rate of return required to cover investment risk and the anticipated decline, due to inflation, in general purchasing power of the cash that the investment generates. This rate is made up of two elements: (a) the real rate of return and (b) an inflation element.

   The *nominal rate of return* and the *real rate of return* are related as follows:

   a) Nominal rate (i) – Inflation rate (g) = Real rate (r) of Return
      The above is a good approximation especially when the term $r \times g$ is small.
      Real rates are the nominal rates adjusted for inflation.
      $$(1 + i) = (1 + r)(1 + g) = 1 + r + g + rg$$
      $$i = r + g + rg$$
   b) Nominal rate = $[(1 + \text{Real rate})(1 + \text{Inflation rate})] - 1$

22-10   The chapter outlines five approaches used to recognize risk in capital budgeting:
1.   Varying the required payback time.
2.   Adjusting the required rate of return.
3.   Adjusting the estimated future cash flows.
4.   Sensitivity ("what-if') analysis.
5.   Estimating the probability distribution of future cash inflows and outflows for each project.

22-12 No. Discounted cash-flow analysis applies to both profit-seeking and not-for-profit organizations. Not-for-profit organizations must also decide which long-term assets will accomplish various tasks at the least cost. Non-for-profit organizations incur an opportunity cost of funds.

22-14 NPV and IRR will not always rank projects identically. Different rankings occur when projects have unequal lives or unequal initial investments. The difference arises because the IRR method assumes a reinvestment rate equal to the indicated rate of return for the shortest-lived project. NPV assumes that funds can be reinvested at the required rate of return.

22-16 (15-20 min.) **Multiple choice.**

1. (a)

Before-tax annual cash flow	$12,000
Amortization ($36,000 ÷ 6)	(6,000)
Net income before tax	6,000
Income tax expense	2,400
Accounting income	$ 3,600

After-tax accrual accounting rate of return = $3,600 ÷ 36,000 = 10%

2. (b)

Year	CCA	Tax Shield (40%)	Operating Cash Flows	Total Cash Flows	Cumulative Cash Flows
1	$3,600	$1,440	$12,000	$13,440	$13,440
2	6,480	2,592	12,000	14,592	28,032
3	5,184	2,074	12,000	14,074	42,106

Payback period = 2 + (($36,000 − $28,032)/$14,074) = 2.6 years

3. (b)

	Relevant Cash Flows	Present-Value Discount Factors at 15%	Total Present Value
Initial investment	$(36,000)	1.000	$(36,000)
Recurring after-tax operating savings*	7,200	3.785	27,252
Tax shield from CCA**	7,692	1.000	7,692
Net present value			$ (1,056)

*$12,000 × (1 − 0.40) = $7,200
**($36,000 × 0.4) × (0.20/(0.20 + 0.15)) × (2 + 0.15)/2(1 + 0.15)) = $7,692

4. (b) Only one payment will be made which 5 years later must yield $36,000. Therefore, deduct the value of an annuity of four payments from the value of an annuity of five payments:

$$3.353 - 2.856 = 0.497$$

Note that $3.353 - 2.856 = 0.497$ is the present value of a cash outflow of $1 occurring at the end of period 5. Alternatively stated, $1 is the future value of $0.497 invested five years ago. Therefore, to have $36,000 now, we need to invest its present value 5 years ago discounted at 15% equal to:

$$\$36,000 \times 0.497 = \$17,892$$

or $\qquad (X)(1.15)^5 = \$36,000$

$$X = \$36,000 - (1.15)^5 = \$36,000 \div 0.49718 = \$17,898$$

Difference is rounding error

22-18 (40 min.) Total project versus differential approach, income taxes.

(a) Total Project Approach

Replace machine

	Relevant Cash Flows	Present-Value Discount Factors at 14%	Total Present Value
Initial new machine investment	$(75,600)	1.000	$ (75,600)
Disposal of old machine	34,800	1.000	34,800
Recurring after-tax cash operating costs*	(33,600)	2.322	(78,019)
Tax shield from CCA**	6,758	1.000	6,758
Net Present Value			$(112,061)

*$48,000 \times (1 - 0.3) = 33,600$
**$((\$75,600 - 34,800) \times 0.3) \times (0.2/(0.2 + 0.14)) \times ((2 + 0.14)/((2(1 + 0.14))) = \$6,758$

Keep machine

	Relevant Cash Flows	Present-Value Discount Factors at 14%	Total Present Value
Disposal of old machine at end of useful life	$7,200	0.675	$ 4,860
Recurring after-tax cash operating costs*	(50,400)	2.322	(117,029)
Tax shield from CCA**	(1,271)	0.675	(858)
Net Present Value			$(113,027)
Total Present Value			

*$72,000 \times (1 - 0.3) = 50,400$
**$((-\$7,200 \times 0.3) \times (0.2/(0.2 + 0.14)) = -\$1,271$

Net present value difference in favour of replacement	$ 966

(b) Total Project Approach

	Relevant Cash Flows	Present-Value Discount Factors at 14%	Total Present Value
Initial new machine investment	$(75,600)	1.000	$(75,600)
Disposal of old machine	34,800	1.000	34,800
Recurring after-tax cash operating costs*	16,800	2.322	39,010
Tax shield from CCA**	6,758	1.000	6,758
Difference in terminal value	(7,200)	0.675	(4,860)
Tax shield lost from terminal value	1,271	0.675	858
Net Present Value			$ 966

*($72,000 – $48,000) × (1 – 0.3) = $16,800

22-20 (40 min.) Project risk, required rate of return.

1.

Drilling equipment project

	Relevant Cash Flows	Present-Value Discount Factors at 12%	Total Present Value
1. Initial drilling equipment investment	$(1,200,000)	1.000	$(1,200,000)
2. Tax shield created by CCA*	230,212	1.000	230,212
3. Recurring cash-operating flows	$ 444,000		
Additional income taxes at 30%	(133,200)		
Recurring after-tax cash-operating flows each year for 5 years (excl. amort. effects)	$ 310,800	3.605	1,120,434
Net present value			$ 150,646

*($1,200,000 × 0.3) × (0.25/(0.25 + 0.12)) × ((2 + 0.12)/2(1 + 0.12)) = $230,212

Production equipment project

Initial production equipment investment	$(960,000)	1.000	$(960,000)
Tax shield created by CCA*	184,170	1.000	184,170
Recurring operating cash flows**	252,000	3.037	765,324
Net Present Value			$ (10,506)

*($960,000 × 0.3) × (0.25/(0.25 + 0.12)) × ((2 + 0.12)/2(1 + 0.12)) = $184,170
**$360,000 × (1 – 0.3) = $252,000

At a 12% discount rate for both projects, the drilling equipment project has the higher NPV and would be preferred.

2. We calculate the NPV of the high-risk drilling equipment project assuming a required rate of return of 18%.

	Relevant Cash Flows	Present-Value Discount Factors at 18%	Total Present Value
1. Initial drilling equipment investment	$(1,200,000)	1.000	$(1,200,000)
2. Tax shield created by CCA*	$193,339	1.000	193,339
3. Recurring cash-operating flows	$444,000		
Additional income taxes at 30%	(133,200)		
Recurring after-tax cash-operating flows each year for 5 years (excl. amort, effects)	$ 310,800	3.127	971,872
Net present value			$ (34,789)

*($1,200,000 × 0.3) × (0.25/(0.25 + 0.18)) × ((2+0.18)/2(1 + 0.18)) = $193,339

The lower-risk production equipment project for the refinery discounted at 12% has an NPV of $(10,506) (requirement 1) that is greater than the NPV of $(34,789) for the higher-risk drilling equipment project for oil exploration discounted at 18%.

3. Esso should favour the investment in the production equipment for the refinery because it has a less negative NPV. It should not invest in the drilling equipment because this project has a more negative NPV when discounted at the risk adjusted 18% required rate of return.

22-22 (25 min.) Inflation and not-for-profit institution, no tax aspects.

1. The university official calculated the following NPV using the 18.8% discount rate and real cash-operating savings.

Year	Relevant Cash-Operating Savings in Nominal Dollars as of 12-31-2007 (1)	Present-Value Discount Factors at 18.8% (2)	Present Value of Cash Flows (3) = (1) × (2)
2008	$1,200	0.842	$ 1,010
2009	1,200	0.709	851
2010	1,200	0.596	715
2011	1,200	0.502	602
2012	1,200	0.423	508
Present value of recurring cash-operating savings			3,686
Net initial investment			4,200
Net present value			$ (514)

Inflation effects are symmetric on cash inflows and outflows. On the one hand cash savings in inflated dollars tomorrow have lower purchasing power than cash savings in inflated dollars today. On the other hand, inflated costs today have a real value lower than uninflated costs of yesterday. Inflation helps those who owe money because they repay over time in dollars with lower purchasing power than the dollars they borrowed. Inflation hurts those who lend money, for the same reason.

Lenders factor inflation rate risk into their interest rates and for a borrower, interest expense is a cash outflow. In the same vein, labour contracts often include escalation rates to account for anticipated inflation. It is important for managers assessing the financial viability of a project to ensure they distinguish those cash outflows that already include inflation from those that do not in order to avoid "double" discounting.

Remember that the risk-free rate of return is a lending rate. In this case the Canadian government is the borrower and hence the risk-free rate it pays to lenders must include both time-value of money, a factor for anticipated domestic inflation, and a factor for anticipated foreign exchange rate risk—otherwise lenders would not loan their money. Therefore even the risk-free rate has been adjusted for inflation and the real rate of return is:

Real rate of return = Nominal rate of return – Rate of inflation

When companies set their required rates of return, unless they anticipate higher inflation rates and higher foreign exchange rate risk than those reflected in the risk-free rate, they should avoid increasing their required rate of return based on these two factors. Therefore in 2b, the real rate of return is:

Real rate of return = 18% − 10% = 8%

2. a. The real rate of return required by Eastern University can be computed using the following relationship:

$$(1 + \text{ real rate}) = \frac{1 + \text{ nominal rate}}{1 + \text{ inflation rate}} = \frac{1 + 0.188}{1 + 0.10} = \frac{1.188}{1.10} = 1.08$$

Real rate of return required = 0.08 or 8%

b. The net present value using real operating cash savings and real rates of return are as follows:

Year	Relevant Cash-Operating Savings in Real Dollars as of 12-31-2007 (1)	Present-Value Discount Factors at 8% (2)	Present Value of Cash Flows (3) = (1) × (2)
1	$1,200	0.926	$1,111
2	1,200	0.857	1,029
3	1,200	0.794	953
4	1,200	0.735	882
5	1,200	0.681	817
Present value of recurring cash-operating savings			4,792
Net initial investment			4,200
Net present value			$ 592

3. Requirements 1 and 2 when correctly done give the same NPV of $592. Consistency is key in capital budgeting. To be correct, requirement 1 should use nominal cash flows and nominal rates of return. Requirement 2 uses real cash flows and real rates of return. Both are valid approaches.

22-24 (20-30 min.) Comparison of projects with unequal lives.

1. <u>Internal rate of return</u>

<u>Project 1</u>

Let F = Present-value factor of $1 at X% received at the end of 1 year, Appendix A, Table 2.

$$\$12,000 \quad = \quad \text{PV of } \$14,400 \text{ at X\% to be received at the end of year 1}$$

$$F \quad = \quad \frac{\$12,000}{\$14,400} = 0.833$$

$$IRR \quad = \quad 20\%*$$

$$\frac{\$14,400}{(1+r)^1} = \$12,000$$

$$1 + r = \$14,400 \div \$12,000$$

$$1 + r = 1.20$$

$$r = 20\%$$

<u>Project 2</u>

Let F = Present-value factor of $1 at X% received at the end of year 4, Appendix A, Table 2.

$$\$12,000 \quad = \quad \text{PV of } \$21,000 \text{ at X\% to be received at the end of year 4}$$

$$F \quad = \quad \frac{\$12,000}{\$21,000} = 0.571$$

The internal rate of return can be calculated by interpolation:

		Present-Value Factors for $1 Received after 4 Years
14%	0.592	0.592
IRR rate	—	0.571
16%	0.552	—
Difference	0.040	0.021

$$\text{IRR rate: } 14\% + \left(\frac{0.021}{0.040}\right)(2\%) = 15.02\%*$$

$$*\frac{\$21,000}{(1+r)^4} = \$12,000$$

$$(1+r)^4 = \$21,000 \div \$12,000$$

$$(1+r) = \sqrt[4]{1.75}$$

$$1+r = 1.1502$$

$$r = 15.02\%$$

Project 1 is preferable to Project 2 using the IRR criterion.

2. <u>Net present value</u>

<u>Project 1</u>

Gross present value	=	PV of $14,400 at 10% to be received at the end of year 1
	=	$14,400 (0.909) = $13,090
Net present value	=	$13,090 – $12,000 = $1,090

<u>Project 2</u>

Gross present value	=	PV of $21,000 at 10% to be received at the end of year 4
	=	$21,000 (0.683) = $14,343
Net present value	=	$14,343 – $12,000 = $2,343

Project 2 is preferable to Project 1 using the net present-value criterion.

3. This problem contrasts the implied reinvestment rates of return under the internal rate of return and net present-value methods. Where the economic lives of mutually exclusive projects are unequal, this clash of reinvestment rates may give different conclusions under the two methods. This result occurs because the internal rate of return method assumes that the reinvestment rate is at least equal to the computed

rate of return on the project. The net present-value method assumes that the funds obtainable from competing projects can be reinvested at the rate of the company's required rate of return. Comparisons follow:

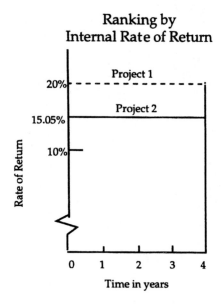

Ranking by Internal Rate of Return

Assumption: Project 1 funds can be reinvested at 20% over the life of the shorter-lived project.

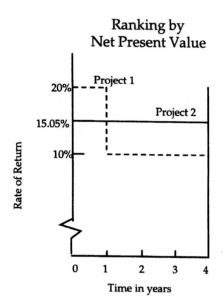

Ranking by Net Present Value

Assumption: Project 1 funds can be reinvested at 10%, the required rate of return.

22-26 (40 min.) Replacement of a machine, income taxes, sensitivity.

1.

	Relevant Cash Flows	Present-Value Discount Factors at 16%	Total Present Value
Initial machine investment	$(144,000)	1.000	$(144,000)
Proceeds from disposal of old machine	48,000	1.000	48,000
Tax shield created by CCA*	21,800	1.000	21,800
Recurring operating savings**	13,680	2.798	38,277
Proceeds from disposal of machine***	15,600	0.552	8,611
Lost tax shield because of disposal****	(3,805)	0.552	(2,100)
Net Present Value			$ (29,412)

*(($144,000 – $48,000) × 0.4) × (0.25/(0.25 + 0.16)) × ((2 + .16)/(2(1 + 0.16))) = $21,800
**$300,000 × ($0.24 – 0.168) × (1 – 0.4) + ($18,000 – $16,800)0.6 = $13,680
***$24,000 – $8,400 = $15,600
****(–$15,600 × 0.4) × (0.25/(0.25 + 0.16)) = –$3,805

WRL Company should retain the old equipment because the present value of the incremental cash flows is negative.

2. 0 = –$144,000 + $48,000 + $21,800 + 2.798atcs + $8,611 –$2,100
   atcs = $24,192
   $24,192 – $13,680 = $10,512

WRL would have to save $10,512 more after-tax dollars on an annual basis to earn a 16% rate of return.

3. The nonquantitative factors that are important to WRL Company's decision include the following:

   (a) The lower operating costs (variable and fixed) of the new machine would enable WRL to meet future competitive or inflationary pressures to a greater degree than the business could using the old machine.
   (b) If the increased efficiency of the new machine provides a labour or energy cost savings, then additional increases in these costs in the future would make the new machine more attractive.
   (c) Maintenance and servicing of both machines should be reviewed in terms of reliability of the manufacturer and the costs.
   (d) Potential technological advances in machinery over the next four years should be evaluated.
   (e) Space requirements for the new machine should be reviewed and compared with the space requirements of the present equipment to determine if more or less space is required.

22-28 (35 min.) Capital budgeting, inventory changes.

1. A schedule of relevant cash flows follows:

Sketch of Relevant Cash Flows

	Year 0	Year 1	Year 2	Year 3	Year 4
Acquire machines	$(131,040)				
Sales					
6,000 × $30.00		$180,000			
6,200 × $30.00			$186,000		
7,700 × $28.80				$221,760	
3,100 × $26.40					$81,840
Manufacturing Costs					
7,000 × $14.40		(100,800)			
6,500 × $15.60			(101,400)		
6,500 × $16.80				(109,200)	
3,000 × $18.00					(54,000)
Marketing, distribution & customer service costs					
6,000 × $3.60		(21,600)			
6,200 × $3.60			(22,320)		
7,700 × $3.60				(27,720)	
3,100 × $3.60					(11,160)
Disposal of machine					21,600
Taxes (see schedule)		(22,248)	(15,798)	(17,896)	(1,710)
Net cash flow					
after tax	($131,040)	$ 35,352	$ 46,482	$ 66,944	$36,570

	Year 1	Year 2	Year 3	Year 4
Sales	$180,000	$186,000	$221,760	$81,840
COGS*	86,400	95,520	127,800	55,680
Mkt., Dist. & Cust. serv.	21,600	22,320	27,720	11,160
CCA	16,380[1]	28,665[2]	21,499[3]	10,724[4]
Taxable income	$55,620	$39,495	$44,741	$ 4,276
Tax Rate	40%	40%	40%	40%
Taxes	$22,248	$15,798	$17,896	$ 1,710

*Using FIFO:
  Year 1: 6,000 × $14.40 = $86,400
  Year 2: (1,000 × $14.40) + (5,200 × $15.60) = $95,520

---

[1] $(1/2) \times 0.25 \times \$131,040 = \$16,380$
[2] $0.25 \times (\$131,040 - \$16,380) = \$28,665$
[3] $0.25 \times (\$131,040 - \$16,380 + \$28,665) = \$21,499$
[4] $0.25 \times (\$131,040 - \$16,380 + \$28,665 + \$21,499 - \$21,600) = \$10,724$

Year 3: (1,300 × $15.60) + (6,400 × $16.80) = $127,800
Year 4: (100 × $16.80) + (3,000 × $18) = $55,680

	Relevant Cash Flows	Present-Value Discount Factors at 16%	Total Present Value
Year 0	$(131,040)	1.000	$(131,040)
Year 1	35,352	0.862	30,476
Year 2	46,482	0.743	34,544
Year 3	66,944	0.641	42,888
Year 4	36,570	0.552	20,197
Remaining CCA tax shield*	8,579	0.476	4,084
Net Present Value			$ 1,149

*(($134,040 − $16,380 − $28,665 − $21,499 − $10,724 − $21,600) × 0.4) × (0.25/(0.25 + 0.16)) = $8,579

The NPV for adding a new line of running shoes is a positive $1,149.

Although the amounts arise in year 4, the income taxes are not filed until year 5.

22-30 (40 min.) **Mining, income taxes, inflation, sensitivity analysis.**

1. <u>Annual cash flow (Years 1-5)</u>

Revenue ($420 × 4,800[a])		$2,016,000
Cash-operating costs		
Variable costs ($120 × 4,800)	576,000	
Technicians ($132,000)	132,000	
Maintenance	60,000	
Total operating cash costs		768,000
Recurring cash-operating flows		1,248,000
Additional income taxes at 40%		499,200
Recurring after-tax operating cash flows		
each year for 5 years (excl. amort. effects)		$ 748,800

[a] 300 lb × 16 oz/lb = 4,800 oz

Year	CCA	Tax Shield	Operating Cash Flows	Total Cash Flows	Cumulative Cash Flows
1	$540,000	$216,000	$748,800	$ 964,800	$ 964,800
2	918,000	367,200	748,800	1,116,000	2,080,800
3	642,600	257,040	748,800	1,005,840	3,086,640
4	449,820	179,928	748,800	928,728	4,015,368

Payback period = 3 + (($3,600,000 – $3,086,640)/$928,728) = 3.55 years

2. The net present value of VanDyk Enterprises' proposed acquisition of the extraction equipment is $72,893, as shown in the following calculation:

	Relevant Cash Flows	Present-Value Discount Factors at 12%	Total Present Value
Initial equipment investment	$(3,600,000)	1.000	$(3,600,000)
Recurring cash-operating savings*	748,800	3.605	2,699,424
Tax shield created by CCA**	973,469	1.000	973,469
Net Present Value			$ 72,893

*$1,248,000 × (1 – 0.4) = $748,800
**(($3,600,000 × 0.4) × 0.3/(0.3 + 0.12)) × ((2 + 0.12) (2(1 + 0.12))) = $973,469

3. In order for VanDyk Enterprises' acquisition of the extraction equipment to break even from a net present-value perspective, the revenue per ounce of gold must be at least $412.98, calculated as follows.

$$0 = -\$3,600,000 + \$973,469 + 3.605os$$
$$os = \$728,580$$
$$\$728,580 = (\$4,800 × (rev - \$120) - \$132,000 - \$60,000) × (1 - 0.4)$$
$$rev = \$412.98$$

Therefore the minimum revenue per ounce is $412.98.

4. Under the assumptions given here, requirement 2 has already calculated NPV using nominal cash flows and nominal rates of return. It has already taken inflationary effects into consideration. Hence no new calculations are necessary. The after-tax net present value is $72,893 as calculated in requirement 2. Some students may question whether the assumptions specified in requirement 4 are appropriate since despite the 2% inflation per year, the revenues and cash-operating costs are assumed to be the same each year for the 5 years. There is no inconsistency here. Despite the 2% increase in general price levels, the specific revenues per ounce of gold and the specific cash-operating costs in this industry could well be the same either because of contractual reasons or because of the general economic conditions of supply and demand.

22-32 (40 min.) Ranking projects.

1. Project B

Let F = Present-value factor for an annuity of $1 for 10 years in Appendix A, Table 4

$$\$120,000 = \$24,000\ F$$
$$F = 5.000 \text{ for ten-year life}$$

The internal rate of return can be calculated by interpolation:

	Present-Value Factors for Annuity of $1 for 10 Years	
14%	5.216	5.216
IRR	—	5.000
16%	4.833	—
Difference	0.383	0.216

$$\text{IRR} = 14\% + \left(\frac{0.216}{0.383}\right)(2\%) = 15.1\%$$

Project C

$$\$240,000 = \$84,000\ F$$

Let F = Present-value factor for an annuity of $1 for 5 years in Appendix A, Table 4.
$$F = 2.857 \text{ for five-year life}$$

The internal rate of return can be calculated by interpolation:

	Present-Value Factors for Annuity of $1 for 5 Years	
22%	2.864	2.864
IRR	—	2.857
24%	2.745	—
Difference	0.119	0.007

$$\text{IRR} = 22\% + \left(\frac{0.007}{0.119}\right)(2\%) = 22.1\%$$

Project D

$240,000 = PV of a four-year annuity of $240,000 per year deferred five years

Trial and error:

	At 18%	At 20%	At 22%
$1 per year for 4 years	2.690	2.589	2.494
Multiply by $240,000, the total value of the annuity	$645,600	$621,360	$598,560
Multiply by the present value of $1 five years hence	0.437	0.402	0.370
PV of annuity in arrears	$282,127	$249,787	$221,467

$$\text{IRR} = 20\% + \left(\frac{249,787 - 240,000}{249,787 - 221,467}\right)(2\%)$$

$$= 20\% = \left(\frac{\$9,787}{\$28,320}\right)(2\%) = 20.69\% = 20.7\%$$

Ranking of Projects

Rank	Project	IRR	Initial Investment
1	C	22.1%	$240,000
2	D	20.7	240,000
3	B	15.1	120,000
4	A	14.0	120,000
5	E	12.6	240,000
6	F	12.0	60,000

2. Budget limit:

$600,000	$660,000	$780,000
C	C	C
D	D	D
B	B	B
	F	A
		F

3. Ranking by net present value, discounting at 16%:

Rank	Project	Net Present Value
1	D	$79,644
2	C	35,016
3	B	(4,008)
4	F	(4,061)
5	A	(15,804)
6	E	(43,156)

Because 16% is the implicit reinvestment rate, these rankings are different from the rankings made on the basis of internal rates of return in requirement 1.

Computations

Project D

PV of $240,000 per year for four years at 16% = $240,000 (2.798)	$ 671,520
It is in arrears five years, so PV = $671,520 (0.476)	319,644
Net initial investment	(240,000)
Net present value	$ 79,644

Project C

PV of $84,000 per year for five years at 16% = $84,000 (3.274)	$275,016
Net initial investment	(240,000)
Net present value	$ 35,016

Project B

PV of $24,000 per year for ten years at 16%= $24,000 (4.833)	$ 115,992
Net initial investment	(120,000)
Net present value	$ (4,008)

Project F

PV at 16%:	$27,600 × 0.862	$ 23,791
	24,000 × 0.743	17,832
	12,000 × 0.641	7,692
	12,000 × 0.552	6,624
	Total PV	55,939
Net initial investment		(60,000)
Net present value		$ (4,061)

Project A

PV of annuity of $24,000 for 15 years	= $24,000 × 5.575	$ 133,800
Deduct deferral of 2 years	= 24,000 × 1.605	(38,520)
PV of annuity in arrears		95,280
PV of $12,000 due in 2 years	= 12,000 × 0.743	8,916
Total PV		104,196
Net initial investment		(120,000)
Net present value		$ (15,804)

Project E

PV of annuity of $60,000 for 10 years	= $60,000 × 4.833	$289,980
Deduct deferral of 3 years	= 60,000 × 2.246	(134,760)
PV of annuity in arrears		155,220
PV of $36,000 due in 3 years	= 36,000 × 0.641	23,076
PV of $18,000 due in 2 years	= 18,000 × 0.743	13,374
PVof $6,000 due in 1 year	= 6,000 × 0.862	5,172
Total PV		196,842
Net initial investment		(240,000)
Net present value		$ (43,158)

4. Other influential factors include:

(a) The risk linked with a given proposal may prompt management to judge it more or less attractive than other proposals that promise a comparable internal rate of return.

(b) Future investment opportunities may affect the current relative attractiveness of alternative proposals. For example, if management expects that in five years hence the best available alternatives will bring less than 20%, Project D (which promises an internal rate of return of 20.7% for 9 years) may be preferable to Project C (which promises 22.1% for 5 years). However, if future opportunities are expected to bring equal or higher internal rates of return, a shorter-lived project may be more attractive, even though a longer-lived project may yield a higher rate of return. Thus, if a choice must be made now between E and F,

Project F (12.0% for 4 years) may be chosen instead of Project E (12.6%, but it locks in capital for 10 years and necessitates a much larger investment).

22-34 (40-50 min.) Ethics, discounted cash-flow analysis.

	Relevant Cash Flows	Present-Value Discount Factors at 12%	Total Present Value
Initial equipment investment	$(1,080,000)	1.000	$(1,080,000)
Initial working capital investment	(240,000)	1.000	(240,000)
Tax shield created by CCA*	248,629	1.000	248,629
Cash flow from canceling lease**	(23,040)	1.000	(23,040)
Additional working capital investment	(240,000)	0.797	(191,280)
Recurring rent cash flow forgone***	(34,560)	4.111	(142,076)
Recurring operating cash flows****			1,440,539
Market research and sales promotion cash flows*****	(230,400)	0.893	(205,747)
Recovery of working capital	480,000	0.507	243,360
Proceeds from disposal of equipment	360,000	0.507	182,520
Lost tax shield from disposal******	(87,568)	0.507	(44,397)
Net Present Value			$ 188,508

*($1,080,000 × 0.36) × (0.25/(0.25 + 0.12)) × ((2 + 0.12)/(2(1 + 0.12))) = –$248,629
**–$36,000 × (1 – 0.36) = –$23,040
***–$54,000 × (1 – 0.36) = –$34,560
****Recurring after-tax cash-operating flows

Year (1)	Cash-Operating Flows (2)	After-Tax Cash-Operating Flows (3) = 0.64 × (2)	Present-Value Discount Factors at 12%	Total Present Value
1	$480,000	$307,200	0.893	$ 274,330
2	480,000	307,200	0.797	244,838
3	720,000	460,800	0.712	328,090
4	720,000	460,800	0.636	293,069
5	720,000	460,800	0.567	261,274
6	120,000	76,800	0.507	38,938
				$1,440,539

*****–$360,000 × (1 – 0.36) =$–$230,400
******(–$360,000 × 0.36) × (0.25/(0.25 + 0.12)) =–$87,568

Dudley should launch the new household product because investing in the product has a positive net present value.

2.

	Relevant Cash Flows	Present-Value Discount Factors at 12%	Total Present Value
Initial equipment investment	$(1,380,000)	1.000	$(1,380,000)
Initial working capital investment	(240,000)	1.000	(240,000)
Tax shield created by CCA*	317,693	1.000	317,693
Cash flow from cancelling lease**	(23,040)	1.000	(23,040)
Additional working capital investment	(240,000)	0.797	(191,280)
Recurring rent cash flow forgone***	(34,560)	4.111	(142,076)
Recurring operating cash flows (see above)			1,440,539
Market research and sales promotion cash flows****	(230,400)	0.893	(205,747)
Recovery of working capital	480,000	0.507	243,360
Proceeds from disposal of equipment	360,000	0.507	182,520
Lost tax shield from disposal*****	(87,568)	0.507	(44,397)
Net Present Value			$ (42,428)

*($1,380,000 × 0.36) × (0.25/(0.25 + 0.12)) × ((2 + 0.12)/(2(1 + 0.12))) = $317,693
**–$36,000 × (1 – 0.36) = –$23,040
***–$54,000 × (1 – 0.36) = –$34,560
****–$360,000 × (1 – 0.36) = –$230,400
*****(–$360,000 × 0.36) × (0.25/(0.25 + 0.12)) = –$87,568

The overall NPV of the project would then be $(43,328). Griffey is unhappy with Chen's revised analysis because the NPV of the project is now negative, possibly leading to the project being rejected. He would like to resume production in the plant, and reemploy his friends who had been laid off earlier. There is also the possibility that Griffey may be hired as a consultant by the new plant management after he retires next year.

Considering the ethical issues, Andrew Chen should evaluate Eric Griffey's directives as follows:

- Chen should present complete and clear reports and recommendations after appropriate analyses of relevant and reliable information. Griffey does not wish the report to be complete or clear, and has provided some information which is not totally reliable.
- Chen should not disclose confidential information outside of the organization; but it also appears that Griffey wants to refrain from disclosing information to senior management that it should know about.

- In evaluating Griffey's directive as it affects Chen, Chen has an obligation to communicate unfavourable as well as favourable information and professional judgments or opinions.

The responsibility to communicate information fairly and objectively, as well as to disclose fully all relevant information that could reasonably be expected to influence an intended user's understanding of the reports and recommendations presented, is being hampered. Management will not have the full scope of information they should have when they are presented with the analysis.

Andrew Chen should take the following steps to resolve this situation:

- Chen should first investigate and see if Dudley Company has an established policy for resolution of ethical conflicts and follow those procedures.
- If this policy does not resolve the ethical conflict, the next step would be for Chen to discuss the situation with his supervisor, Griffey, and see if he can obtain resolution. One possible solution may be to present a "base case" and sensitivity analysis of the investment. Chen should make it clear to Griffey that he has a problem and is seeking guidance.
- If Chen cannot obtain a satisfactory resolution with Griffey, he could take the situation up to the next layer of management, and inform Griffey that he is doing this. If this is not satisfactory, Chen should progress to the next, and subsequent, higher levels of management until the issue is resolved (i.e., the president, Audit Committee, or Board of Directors).
- Chen may want to have a confidential discussion with an objective advisor to clarify relevant concepts and obtain an understanding of possible courses of action.
- If Chen cannot satisfactorily resolve the situation within the organization, he may resign from the company and submit an informative memo to an appropriate person in Dudley (i.e., the president, Audit Committee, or Board of Directors).

22-36 (40 min.) Equipment-replacement, income taxes, unequal project lives, ethics.

1. We use the total-project approach to calculate the net present value of the decision to replace forklifts with the AMMS based on the original estimates Rolland gave to Forrest. The NPV is $538,906 in favour of investing in the AMMS.

Investment in AMMS

	Relevant Cash Flows	Present-Value Discount Factors at 12%	Total Present Value
Initial AMMS investment	$(5,280,000)	1.000	$(5,280,000)
Initial working capital investment	(1,200,000)	1.000	(1,200,000)
Proceeds from disposal of forklift	120,000	1.000	120,000
Tax shield created by CCA*	1,395,306	1.000	1,396,306
Recurring operating cash flows**	864,000	5.650	4,881,600
Proceeds from disposal of AMMS	1,020,000	0.322	328,440
Tax shield loss because of disposal***	(291,429)	0.322	(93,840)
Recovery of working capital	1,200,000	0.322	386,400
Net Present Value			$ 538,906

*($5,280,000 − $120,000) × 0.4) × (0.3/(0.3 + 0.12)) × ((2 + 0.12)/(2(1 + 0.12))) = $1,395,306
**$1,440,000 × (1 − 0.4) = $864,000

Recurring cash operating flows equal:	
Increase in cash flow from higher sales revenue	$840,000
Reduction in annual manufacturing costs over current costs	480,000
Reduction in annual maintenance costs over current costs	360,000
Increased annual operating costs over current costs	(240,000)
Recurring cash operating flows	$1,440,000

***(−$1,020,000 × 0.4) × (0.3/(0.3 + 0.12)) = $−291,429

Keep Forklift Trucks

	Relevant Cash Flows	Present-Value Discount Factors at 12%	Total Present Value
1a. Lease payment on forklift truck in year 9	$(96,000)		
Deduct income tax savings at 40% of $96,000	38,400		
After-tax cost of lease payment in year 9	$(57,600)	0.361	$(20,794)
1b. Lease payment on forklift truck in year 10	$(96,000)		
Deduct income tax savings at 40% of $80,000	38,400		
After-tax cost of lease payment in year 10	$(57,600)	0.322	(18,547)
Net present value of all cash flows			$(39,341)
Net present value difference in favour of investment in AMMS ($538,906 − (−$39,341))			$578,247

2. The revised estimates of 8 years of useful life and $120,000 of estimated terminal disposal would result in a negative NPV of ($152,913).

Investment in AMMS

	Relevant Cash Flows	Present-Value Discount Factors at 12%	Total Present Value
Initial AMMS investment	$(5,280,000)	1.000	$(5,280,000)
Initial working capital investment	(1,200,000)	1.000	(1,200,000)
Proceeds from disposal of forklift	120,000	1.000	120,000
Tax shield created by CCA*	1,395,306	1.000	1,395,306
Recurring operating cash flows**	864,000	4.968	4,292,352
Proceeds from disposal of AMMS	120,000	0.404	48,480
Tax shield loss because of disposal***	(34,286)	0.404	(13,852)
Recover of working capital	1,200,000	0.404	484,800
Net Present Value			$ (152,914)

* ($5,280,000 – $120,000) × 0.4) × (0.3/(0.3 + 0.12)) × ((2 + 0.12)/(2(1 + 0.12))) = $1,395,306
** $1,440,000 × (1 – 0.4) = $864,000
***(–$120,000 × 0.4) × (0.3/(0.3 + 0.12)) = –$34,286.

3. Lealand Forrest should evaluate Bill Rolland's directives as follows:

- Forrest has a responsibility to present complete and clear reports and recommendations after appropriate analyses of relevant and reliable information. Rolland does not wish the report to be complete or clear.
- Forrest should not disclose confidential information outside of the organization; but it also appears that Rolland wants to refrain from disclosing information to the Board that it should know about.
- Rolland is engaging in activities that could prejudice him from carrying out his duties ethically.
- In evaluating Rolland's directive as it affects Forrest, Forrest has an obligation to communicate unfavourable as well as favourable information and professional judgments or opinions.
- The responsibility to communicate information fairly and objectively, as well as to disclose fully all relevant information that could reasonably be expected to influence an intended user's understanding of the reports and recommendations presented, is being hampered. The Board will not have the full scope of information that they should have when they are presented with the analysis.

4. Lealand Forrest should take the following steps to resolve this situation:

    - Forrest should first investigate and see if Instant Dinners, Inc. (IDI) has an established policy for resolution of ethical conflicts and follow those procedures.
    - If such a policy does not resolve the ethical conflict, the next step would be for Forrest to discuss the situation with his supervisor, Rolland, and see if he can obtain resolution. One possible solution may be to present a "base case" and sensitivity analysis of the investment. Forrest should make it clear to Rolland that he has a problem and is seeking guidance.
    - If Forrest cannot obtain a satisfactory resolution with Rolland, he could take the situation up to the next layer of management, and inform Rolland that he is taking this action. If this approach is not satisfactory, Forrest should progress to the next, and subsequent, higher levels of management until the issue is resolved (i.e., the president, Audit Committee, or Board of Directors).
    - Since Rolland has instructed him not to discuss the situation with anyone else at IDI, Forrest may want to have a confidential discussion with an objective advisor to clarify relevant concepts and obtain an understanding of possible courses of action.
    - If Forrest cannot satisfactorily resolve the situation within the organization, he may resign from the company and submit an informative memo to an appropriate person at IDI (i.e., the president, Audit Committee, or Board of Directors).

CHAPTER 23
MANAGEMENT CONTROL SYSTEMS, TRANSFER PRICING, AND MULTINATIONAL CONSIDERATIONS

23-2   To be effective, management control systems should be (a) closely aligned to an organization's strategies and goals, (b) designed to fit the organization's structure and the decision-making responsibility of individual managers, and (c) able to motivate managers and employees to put in effort to attain selected goals desired by top management.

23-4   The chapter cites five benefits of decentralization:
1.   Creates greater responsiveness to local needs.
2.   Leads to quicker decision making.
3.   Increases motivation of subunit managers.
4.   Aids management development and learning.
5.   Sharpens the focus of managers.

The chapter cites four costs of decentralization:
1.   Leads to suboptimal decision making.
2.   Results in duplication of activities.
3.   Decreases loyalty toward the organization as a whole.
4.   Increases costs of gathering information.

23-6   No. A transfer price is the price one subunit of an organization charges for a product or service supplied to another subunit of the same organization. The two segments can be cost centres, profit centres, or investment centres. For example, the allocation of service department costs to production departments that are set up as either cost centres or investment centres is an example of transfer pricing.

23-8   Transfer pricing systems should have the following properties. They should
1.   promote goal congruence,
2.   promote a sustained high level of management effort,
3.   promote a high level of subunit autonomy in decision making.
4.   contribute to subunit performance evaluation.

23-10 Transferring products or services at market prices generally leads to optimal decisions when (a) the intermediate market is perfectly competitive, (b) interdependencies of subunits are minimal, and (c) there are no additional costs or benefits to the corporation as a whole in using the market instead of transacting internally.

23-12 Reasons why a dual-pricing approach to transfer pricing is not widely used in practice include:

1. The manager of the division using a cost-based method does not have sufficient incentives to control costs.
2. This approach does not provide clear signals to division managers about the level of decentralization top management wants.
3. This approach tends to insulate managers from the frictions of the marketplace.

23-14 Yes. The general transfer-pricing guideline specifies that the minimum transfer price equals the additional *outlay costs* per unit incurred up to the point of transfer *plus* the *opportunity costs* per unit to the supplying division. When the supplying division has idle capacity, its opportunity costs are zero; when the supplying division has no idle capacity, its opportunity costs are positive. Hence the minimum transfer price will vary depending on whether the supplying division has idle capacity or not.

23-16 (25 min.) Decentralization, responsibility centres.

1. The manufacturing plants in the Manufacturing Division are cost centres. Senior management determines the manufacturing schedule based on the quantity of each type of lighting product specified by the sales and marketing division and detailed studies of the time and cost to manufacture each type of product. Manufacturing managers are accountable only for costs. They are evaluated based on achieving target output within budgeted costs.

2. a. If manufacturing and marketing managers were to directly negotiate the prices for manufacturing various products, Quinn should evaluate manufacturing plant managers as profit centres—revenues received from marketing minus the costs incurred to produce and sell output.

   b. Quinn Corporation would be better off decentralizing its marketing and manufacturing decisions and evaluating each division as a profit centre. Decentralization would encourage plant managers to increase total output to achieve the greatest profitability, and motivate plant managers to cut their costs to increase margins. Manufacturing managers would be motivated to design their operations according to the criteria that meet the marketing managers' approval, thereby improving cooperation between manufacturing and marketing.

Under Quinn's existing system, manufacturing managers had every incentive not to improve. Manufacturing managers' incentives were to get as high a cost target as possible so that they could produce output within budgeted costs. Any significant improvements could result in the target costs being lowered for the next year, increasing the possibility of not achieving budgeted costs. By the same line of reasoning, manufacturing managers would also try to limit their production so that production quotas would not be increased in the future. Decentralizing manufacturing and marketing decisions overcomes these problems.

23-18 (30 min.) Effect of alternative transfer-pricing methods on division operating income.

1.

	Internal Transfers at Market Prices Method A	Internal Transfers at 110% of Full Costs Method B
MINING DIVISION		
Revenues:		
$108, $79.20[1] × 400,000 units	$43,200,000	$31,680,000
Deduct:		
Division variable costs:		
$62.40[2] × 400,000 units	24,960,000	24,960,000
Division fixed costs:		
$9.60[3] × 400,000 units	3,840,000	3,840,000
Division operating income	$14,400,000	$ 2,880,000
METALS DIVISION		
Revenues:		
$180 × 400,000 units	$72,000,000	$72,000,000
Deduct:		
Transferred-in costs:		
$108, $79.20 × 400,000 units	43,200,000	31,680,000
Division variable costs:		
$43.20[4] × 400,000 units	17,280,000	17,280,000
Division fixed costs:		
$18[5] × 400,000 units	7,200,000	7,200,000
Division operating income	$ 4,320,000	$15,840,000

[1]$579.20 = $72 × 110%

[2]Variable cost per unit in Mining Division = Direct materials + Direct manufacturing labour + 75% of Manufacturing overhead = $14.40 + $19.20 + 75% × $38.40 = $62.40

[3]Fixed cost per unit = 25% of Manufacturing overhead = 25% × $38.40 = $9.60

[4]Variable cost per unit in Metals Division = Direct materials + Direct manufacturing labour + 40% of Manufacturing overhead = $7.20 + $24 + 40% × $30 = $43.20

[5]Fixed cost per unit in Metals Division = 60% of Manufacturing overhead = 60% × $30 = $18

2. Bonus paid to division managers at 1% of division operating income will be as follows:

	Method A Internal Transfers at Market Prices	Method B Internal Transfers at 110% of Full Costs
Mining Division manager's bonus (1% × $14,400,000; 1% × $2,880,000)	$144,000	$ 28,800
Metals Division manager's bonus (1% × $4,320,000; 1% × $15,840,000)	43,200	158,400

The Mining Division manager will prefer Method A (transfer at market prices) because this method gives $144,000 of bonus rather than $28,800 under Method B (transfers at 110% of full costs). The Metals Division manager will prefer Method B because this method gives $158,400 of bonus rather than $43,200 under Method A.

3. Brian Jones, the manager of the Mining Division, will appeal to the existence of a competitive market to price transfers at market prices. Using market prices for transfers in these conditions leads to goal congruence. Division managers acting in their own best interests make decisions that are also in the best interests of the company as a whole.

   Jones will further argue that setting transfer prices based on cost will cause Jones to pay no attention to controlling costs since all costs incurred will be recovered from the Metals Division at 110% of full costs.

23-20 (25 min.) General guideline, transfer price range.

1. If the Screen Division sells screens in the outside market, it will receive, for each screen, the market price of the screen minus variable marketing and distribution costs per screen = $132 − $4.80 = $127.20. The incremental cost of manufacturing each screen is $84. The Screen Division is operating at capacity. Hence, the opportunity cost per screen of selling the screen to the Assembly Division rather than in the outside market is the contribution margin the Screen Division would forgo if it transferred screens internally rather than sold them in the outside market.

Contribution margin per screen = $127.20 – $84 = $43.20.

Using the general guideline,

$$\text{Minimum transfer price per screen} = \text{Incremental costs per screen up to the point of transfer} + \text{Opportunity costs per screen to the selling division}$$

That is,

Minimum transfer price per screen = $84 + $43.20 = $127.20

2. If the two division managers were to negotiate a transfer price, the range of possible transfer prices is between $127.20 and $134.40 per screen. As calculated in requirement 1, the Screen Division will be willing to supply screens to the Assembly Division only if the transfer price equals or exceeds $127.20 per screen.

    If the Assembly Division were to purchase the screens in the outside market, it will incur a cost of $134.40, the cost of the screen equal to $132 plus variable purchasing costs of $2.40 per screen. Hence, the Assembly Division will be willing to buy screens from the Screen Division only if the price does not exceed $134.40 per screen. Within the price range of $127.20 to $134.40 per screen, each division will be willing to transact with the other. The exact transfer price between $127.20 and $134.40 will depend on the bargaining strengths of the two divisions.

23-22 (30 min.) Multinational transfer pricing, goal-congruence (continuation of 23-21).

1. After-tax operating income if Mornay Company sold all 1,000 units of Product 4A36 in Canada is

Revenues, $720 × 1,000 units	$720,000
Full manufacturing costs, $600 × 1,000 units	600,000
Operating income	120,000
Income taxes at 40%	48,000
After-tax operating income	$ 72,000

    From requirement 1, Mornay Company's after-tax operating income if it transfers 1,000 units of Product 4A36 to Austria at full manufacturing cost and sells the units in Austria is $134,400. Therefore Mornay should sell the 1,000 units in Austria.

2. Transferring Product 4A36 at the full manufacturing cost of the Canadian Division minimizes import duties and taxes (requirement 2), but creates zero operating income for the Canadian Division. Acting autonomously, the Canadian Division manager would maximize division operating income by selling Product

4A36 in the Canadian market which results in $72,000 in after-tax division operating income as calculated in requirement 1, rather than by transferring Product 4A36 to the Austrian division at full manufacturing cost.

3. The minimum transfer price at which the Canadian Division manager acting autonomously will agree to transfer Product 4A36 to the Austrian division is $720 per unit. Any transfer price less than $720 will leave the Canadian Division's performance worse than selling directly in the Canadian market. Since the Canadian Division can sell as many units of Product 4A36 in the Canadian market as it makes, there is an opportunity cost of transferring the product internally.

    This transfer price will result in Mornay Company as a whole paying more import duties and taxes than the answer to requirement 2 as calculated below:

CANADIAN DIVISION	
Revenues, $720 × 1,000 units	$720,000
Full manufacturing costs	600,000
Division operating income	120,000
Division income taxes at 40%	48,000
Division after-tax operating income	$ 72,000
AUSTRIAN DIVISION	
Revenues, $900 × 1,000 units	$900,000
Transferred in costs, $720 × 1,000 units	720,000
Import duties at 10% of transferred-in price,	
$72 × 1,000 units	72,000
Division operating income	108,000
Division income taxes at 44%	47,520
Division after-tax operating income	$ 60,480

Total import duties and income taxes at transfer prices of $600 and $720 per unit for 1,000 units of Product 4A36 follow:

		Transfer Price of $600 per Unit (Requirement 1 of Q23-21)	Transfer Price of $720 per Unit
(a)	Canadian income taxes	$ 0	$ 48,000
(b)	Austrian import duties	60,000	72,000
(c)	Austrian income taxes	105,600	47,520
		$165,600	$167,520

The minimum transfer price that the Canadian division manager acting autonomously would agree to results in Mornay Company paying $1,920 in additional import duties and income taxes.

A student who has done the calculations shown in requirement 2 of Problem 23-21 can calculate the additional taxes from a $720 transfer price more directly as follows:

Every $1 increase in the transfer price per unit over $600 results in additional import duty and taxes of $0.016 per unit

So a $120 increase ($720 – $600) per unit will result in additional import duty and taxes of $0.016 × 120 = $1.92

For 1,000 units transferred, this equals $1.92 × 1,000 = $1,920

23-24 (35 min.) Multinational transfer pricing, effect of alternative transfer-pricing methods, global income tax minimization.

1. This is a three-country, three-division transfer pricing problem with three alternative transfer-pricing methods. Summary data in Canadian dollars are:

<u>China Division</u>
   Variable costs: 1,200 Yuan ÷ 8 Yuan per $ = $150 per subunit
   Fixed costs: 2,160 Yuan ÷ 8 Yuan per $ = $270 per subunit

<u>South Korea Division</u>
   Variable costs: 288,000 Won ÷ 800 Won per $= $360 per unit
   Fixed costs: 384,000 Won ÷ 800 Won per $= $480 per unit

<u>Canadian Division</u>
   Variable costs: = $120 per unit
   Fixed costs: = $240 per unit

Market prices for private label sale alternatives:
   China Division: 4,320 Yuan ÷ 8 Yuan per $= $540 per subunit
   South Korea Division: 1,248,000 Won ÷ 800 Won per $ = $1,560 per unit

The transfer prices under each method are:
(a) Market price
     • China Division to South Korea Division   = $540 per subunit
     • South Korea Division to Canadian Division   = $1,560 per unit
(b) 200% of full costs
     • China Division to South Korea Division
          2.0 ($150 + $270) = $840 per subunit
     • South Korea Division to Canadian Division
          2.0 ($840 + $360 + $480) = $3,360 per unit

513

(c) 300% of variable costs
- China Division to South Korea Division
  3.0 ($150) = $450 per subunit
- South Korea Division to Canadian Division
  3.0 ($450 + $360) = $2,430 per unit

(In Canadian Dollars)	Method A Internal Transfers at Market Price	Method B Internal Transfers at 200% of Full Costs	Method C Internal Transfers at 300% of Variable
Costs			
1. **China Division**			
Division revenues per unit	$540	$840	$450
Deduct:			
Division variable costs per unit	150	150	150
Division fixed costs per unit	270	270	270
Division operating income per unit	120	420	30
Income tax at 40%	48	168	12
Division net income per unit	$ 72	$ 252	$ 18
2. **South Korea Division**			
Division revenues per unit	$1,560	$3,360	$2,430
Deduct:			
Transferred-in costs per unit	540	840	450
Division variable costs per unit	360	360	360
Division fixed costs per unit	480	480	480
Division operating income per unit	180	1,680	1,140
Income tax at 20%	36	336	228
Division net income per unit	$ 144	$1,344	$ 912
3. **Canadian Division**			
Division revenues per unit	$3,840	$3,840	$3,840
Deduct:			
Transferred-in costs per unit	1,560	3,360	2,430
Division variable costs per unit	120	120	120
Division fixed costs per unit	240	240	240
Division operating income per unit	1,920	120	1,050
Income tax at 30%	576	36	315
Division net income per unit	$1,344	$ 84	$ 735

2. Division net income:

	Method A Market Price	Method B 200% of Full Costs	Method C 300% of Variable Cost
China Division	$ 72	$ 252	$ 18
South Korea Division	144	1,344	912
Canadian Division	1,344	84	735
User Friendly Computer Inc.	$1,560	$1,680	$1,665

User Friendly will maximize its net income by using the 200% of full cost transfer-pricing method. This is because the 200% of full cost method sources most income in the country with the lowest income tax rate.

23-26 (5 min.)   Transfer-pricing problem (continuation of 23-25).

The company as a whole would benefit in this situation if C purchased from outside suppliers. The $18,000 disadvantage to the company as a whole by purchasing from the outside supplier would be more than offset by the $36,000 contribution margin of A's sale of 1,000 units to other customers.

Purchase costs from outside supplier, 1,000 units × $162		$162,000
Deduct variable cost savings, 1,000 units × $144		144,000
Net cost to company as a whole by buying from outside		$ 18,000
A's sales to other customers, 1,000 units × $186		$186,000
Deduct:		
Variable manufacturing costs, $144 × 1,000 units	$144,000	
Variable marketing costs, $6 × 1,000 units	6,000	
Variable costs		150,000
Contribution margin from selling A to other customers		$ 36,000

23-28 (30 min.)   Goal-congruence problems with cost-plus transfer-pricing methods, dual-price method (continuation of 23-27).

1. Two examples of goal congruence problems are:
   (a) Division managers using an outside supplier when Oceanic Products' operating income is maximized by buying from an internal division.
   (b) Division managers selling to an outside purchaser when it is better for Oceanic Products to further process internally.

2. <u>Transfers to buying divisions at market price</u>
Harvesting Division to Processing Division = $1.20 per kilogram of raw tuna
Processing Division to Marketing Division = $6.00 per kilogram of processed tuna

<u>Transfers out to selling divisions at 150% of full costs</u>
Harvesting Division to Processing Division
= 1.5 ($0.24 + $0.48) = $1.08 per kilogram of raw tuna
Processing Division to Marketing Division
= 1.5 [($1.20 × 2)* + $0.96 + $0.72] = $6.12 per kilogram
of processed tuna

*The transferred-in cost is $1.20 per kilogram of raw tuna. It takes two kilograms of raw tuna to produce one kilogram of tuna fillets.

<u>Tuna Harvesting Division</u>

Division revenues: $1.08 × 1,000	$ 1,080
Division variable costs: $0.24 × 1,000	240
Division fixed costs: $0.48 × 1,000	480
Division total costs	720
Division operating income	$ 360

<u>Tuna Processing Division</u>

Division revenues: $6.12 × 500	$3,060
Transferred-in costs: $1.20 × 1,000	1,200
Division variable costs: $0.96 × 500	480
Division fixed costs: $0.72 × 500	360
Division total costs	2,040
Division operating income	$1,020

<u>Tuna Marketing Division</u>

Division revenues: $14.40 × 300	$4,320
Transferred-in costs: $6.00 × 500	3,000
Division variable costs: $0.36 × 300	108
Division fixed costs: $0.84 × 300	252
Division total costs	3,360
Division operating income	$ 960

3.

	Division Income	Operating
Tuna Harvesting Division	$ 360	
Tuna Processing Division	1,020	
Tuna Marketing Division	960	
Oceanic Products	$2,340	

The overall company operating income from harvesting 1,000 kilograms of raw tuna and its further processing and marketing is $2,400 (see Problem 23-27, requirement 1).

A dual transfer-pricing method entails using different transfer prices for transfers into the buying division and transfers out of the supplying division. There is no reason why the sum of division operating incomes should equal the total company operating income.

4. Problems which may arise if Oceanic Products uses the dual-transfer pricing system include:
   (a) It may reduce the incentives of the supplying division to control costs since every $1.00 of cost of the supplying division is transferred out to the buying division at $1.50. It may also reduce the incentives of the supplying divisions to keep abreast of market conditions.
   (b) A dual transfer-pricing system does not provide clear signals to the individual divisions about the level of decentralization top management seeks.

23-30 (50-75 min.) Pricing in imperfect markets (continuation of 23-29).

An alternative presentation, which contains the same numerical answers, can be found at the end of this solution.

1. Potential contribution from external intermediate
   sale is $1,000 \times (\$234 - \$144)$ $90,000
   Contribution through keeping price at $240 is $800 \times \$96$.   76,800
   Forgone contribution by transferring 200 units $13,200

   Opportunity cost per unit to the supplying division by transferring internally:

   $$\frac{13,200}{200} = \$66$$

   Transfer price = $144 + $66 = $210

An alternative approach to obtaining the same answer is to recognize that the incremental or outlay cost is the same for all 1,000 units in question. Therefore the total revenue desired by A would be the same for selling outside or inside.

Let X equal the transfer price at which Division A is indifferent
between selling all units outside versus transferring 200 units inside

$$1,000\ (\$234) = 800\ (\$240) + 200X$$
$$X = \$210$$

The $210 price will lead to the correct decision. Division B will not buy from Division A because its total costs of $210 + $180 will exceed its prospective selling price of $360. Division A will then sell 1,000 units at $234 to the outside; Division A and the company will have a contribution margin of $90,000. Otherwise, if 800 units were sold at $240 and 200 units were transferred to Division B, the company would have a contribution of $76,800 plus $7,200 (200 units of final product × $36), or $84,000.

A comparison might be drawn regarding the computation of the appropriate transfer prices between the preceding problem and this problem:

$$\text{Minimum transfer price} = \begin{pmatrix} \text{Additional } \textit{incremental costs} \\ \text{per unit incurred up} \\ \text{to the point of transfer} \end{pmatrix} + \begin{pmatrix} \textit{Opportunity costs} \\ \text{per unit to the} \\ \text{supplying division} \end{pmatrix}$$

Perfect markets: $= \$144 + (\text{Selling price} - \text{Outlay costs per unit})$
$= \$144 + (\$240 - \$144) = \$240$

Imperfect markets: $= \$144 + \dfrac{\text{Marginal revenues} - \text{Outlay costs}}{\text{Number of units transferred}}$

$= \$144 + \dfrac{42,000^{a} - 28,800^{b}}{200} = \$210$

[a]Marginal revenues of Division A from selling 200 units outside rather than transferring to Division B
= ($234 × 1,000) – ($240 × 800) = $234,000 – $192,000 = $42,000.
[b]Incremental (outlay) costs incurred by Division A to produce 200 units
= $144 × 200 = $28,800.

Therefore, selling price ($234) and marginal revenues per unit ($210 = $42,000 ÷ 200) are not the same.

The following discussion is optional. These points should be explored only if there is sufficient class time:

Some students will erroneously say that the "new" market price of $234 is the appropriate transfer price. They will claim that the general guideline says that the transfer price should be $144 + ($234 – $144) = $234, the market price. This conclusion assumes a perfect market. But here there are imperfections in the intermediate market. That is, the market price is <u>not</u> a good approximation of alternative revenue. If a division's sales are heavy enough to reduce market prices, marginal revenue will be less than market price.

It is true that <u>either</u> $234 or $210 will lead to the correct decision by B in this case. But suppose that B's variable costs were $144 instead of $180. Then B would buy at a transfer price of $210 (but not at a price of $234, because then B would earn a negative contribution of $18 per unit [$360 − ($234 + $144)]. Note that if B's variable costs were $144, transfers would be desirable:

Division A contribution is:

800 × ($240 − $144) + 200 ($210 − $144)	=	$90,000

Division B contribution is:

200 × [$360 − ($210 + $144)]	=	1,200
Total contribution		$91,200

Or the same facts can be analyzed for the company as a whole:

Sales of intermediate product,

800 × ($240 − $144)	=	$76,800

Sales of final products,

200 × [360 − ($144 + $144)]	=	14,400
Total contribution		$91,200

If the transfer price were $234, B would not accept the transfer and would not earn any contribution. As shown above, Division A and the company as a whole will earn a total contribution of $90,000 instead of $91,200.

2. (a) Division A can sell 900 units at $234 to the outside market and 100 units to Division B, or 800 at $240 to the outside market and 200 units to Division B. Note that, under both alternatives, 100 units can be transferred to Division B at no opportunity cost to A.

Using the general guideline, the minimum transfer price of <u>the first 100 units</u> [901–1,000] is:

$$TP_1 = \$144 + 0 = \$144$$

If Division B needs 100 additional units, the opportunity cost to A is not zero, because Division A will then have to sell only 800 units to the outside market for a contribution of 800 × ($240 − $144) = $76,800 instead of 900 units for a contribution of 900 ($234 − $144) = $81,000. Each unit sold to B in addition to the first 100 units has an opportunity cost to A of ($81,000 − $76,800) ÷ 100 = $42.

Using the general guideline, the minimum transfer price of <u>the next 100 units</u> [801–900] is:

$$TP_2 = \$144 + \$42 = \$186$$

Alternatively, the computation could be:

Increase in contribution from 100 more units, $100 \times \$90$	$9,000	
Loss in contribution on 800 units, $800 \times (\$96 - \$90)$	<u>4,800</u>	
Net "marginal revenue"	<u>$4,200</u> $\div$ 100 units = $42	
(Minimum) transfer price applicable to first 100 units offered by A is $144 + $0	=	$144 per unit
(Minimum) transfer price applicable to next 100 units offered by A is $144 + ($4,200 ÷ 100)	=	$186 per unit
(Minimum) transfer price applicable to next 800 units	=	$234 per unit

(b) The manager of Division B will not want to purchase more than 100 units because the units at $186 would decrease his contribution ($186 + $180 > $360). Because the manager of B does not buy more than 100 units, the manager of A will have 900 units available for sale to the outside market. The manager of A will strive to maximize the contribution by selling them all at $234.

This solution maximizes the company's contribution:

$900 \times (\$234 - \$144)$	=	$81,000
$100 \times (\$360 - \$324)$	=	<u>3,600</u>
		<u>$84,600</u>

which compares favourably to:

$800 \times (\$240 - \$144)$	=	$76,800
$200 \times (\$360 - \$324)$	=	<u>7,200</u>
		<u>$84,000</u>

ALTERNATIVE PRESENTATION (by James Patell)

1. Company Viewpoint

    a: Sell 1.000 outside at $234   b: Sell 800 outside at $240, transfer 200

Price	$234		Transfer price	$240
Variable costs	144		Variable costs	144
Contribution	$ 90 × 1,000 = $90,000		Contribution	$ 96 × 800 = $76,800

Total contribution given up if transfer occurs*
= $90,000 − $76,800 = $13,200

On a per-unit basis, the relevant costs are:

$$\underset{\text{point of transfer}}{\text{Incremental costs to}} + \underset{\text{Division A of transfer}}{\text{Opportunity costs to}} = \text{Transfer price}$$

$$\$144 + \frac{13,200}{200} = \$210$$

By formula, costs are:

$$\begin{bmatrix} \text{Incremental costs} \\ \text{to point} \\ \text{of transfer} \end{bmatrix} + \begin{bmatrix} \text{Lost opportunity to} \\ \text{sell 200 at \$234, for} \\ \text{contribution of \$90} \end{bmatrix} - \begin{bmatrix} \text{Gain when 1st 800} \\ \text{sell at \$240} \\ \text{instead of \$234} \end{bmatrix}$$

$$= \quad \$144 + \frac{200 \times \$90}{200} - \frac{\left[(\$240 - \$234) \times 800 \right]}{200}$$

$$= \quad \$144 + \$90 - \$24 = \$210$$

*Contribution of $36 per unit by B is not given up if transfer occurs, so it is not relevant here.

2. (a) At most, Division A can sell only 900 units and can produce 1,000. Therefore, at least 100 units should be transferred, at a transfer price no less than $144. The question is whether or not a second 100 units should be transferred.

<u>Company Viewpoint</u>

a: <u>Sell 900 outside at $234 100</u>

Transfer price	$234	
Variable cost	144	
Contribution	$ 90	× 900 = $81,000

b: <u>Sell 800 outside at $240, transfer</u>

Transfer price	$240	
Variable cost	144	
Contribution	$ 96	× 800 = $76,800

Total contribution forgone if transfer of 100 units occurs
= $81,000 − $76,800 = $4,200 (or $42 per unit)

$$\begin{array}{c}\text{Incremental costs to}\\\text{point of transfer}\end{array} + \begin{array}{c}\text{Opportunity costs to}\\\text{Division A of transfer}\end{array} = \text{Transfer price}$$

$$\$144 \quad + \quad \$42 \quad = \quad \$186$$

(b) By formula:

$$\begin{bmatrix}\text{Incremental costs}\\\text{to point}\\\text{of transfer}\end{bmatrix} + \begin{bmatrix}\text{Lost opportunity to}\\\text{sell 100 at \$234, for}\\\text{contribution of \$90}\end{bmatrix} - \begin{bmatrix}\text{Gain when 1st 800}\\\text{sell at \$240}\\\text{instead of \$234}\end{bmatrix}$$

$$= \quad \$144 + \frac{100 \times \$90}{100} - \frac{\left[(\$240 - \$234) \times 800\right]}{100}$$

$$= \quad \$144 + \$90 - \$48 = \$186$$

Transfer Price Schedule (minimum acceptable transfer price)

Units	Transfer Price
0–100	$144
101–200	$186
201–1,000	$234

23-32 (30-40 min.) **Multinational transfer pricing and taxation.**

1. Anita Corporation and its subsidiaries' operating income if it manufactures the machine and sells it in Brazil or in Switzerland follows:

	If Sold in Brazil	If Sold in Switzerland
Revenue	$1,200,000	$1,140,000
Costs		
Manufacturing costs	600,000	600,000
Transportation and modification costs	240,000	300,000
Total costs	840,000	900,000
Operating income	$ 360,000	$ 240,000

Anita Corporation maximizes operating income by manufacturing the machine and selling it in Brazil.

2. Anita Corporation will not sell if the transfer price is less than $600,000—its outlay costs of manufacturing the machine.

   The Brazilian subsidiary, will not agree to a transfer price of more than $960,000. At a price of $960,000, the Brazilian subsidiary's incremental operating income from purchasing and selling the milling machine will be $0 ($1,200,000 – $240,000 – $960,000).

   The Swiss subsidiary will not agree to a transfer price of more than $840,000. At a price of $840,000, the Swiss subsidiary's incremental operating income from purchasing and selling the milling machine will be $0 ($1,140,000 – $300,000 – $840,000).

   Any transfer price between $840,000 and $960,000 will achieve the optimal actions determined in requirement 1. For prices in this range, Anita Corporation will be willing to sell, the Brazilian subsidiary willing to buy, and the Swiss subsidiary not interested in acquiring the machine.

   Where within the range of $840,000 to $960,000 the transfer price will be set depends on the bargaining powers of the Anita Corporation and the Brazilian subsidiary managers. Anita Corporation's main source of bargaining power comes from the threat of selling the machine to the Swiss subsidiary. If the transfer price is set at $840,000, then

Anita's operating income, $840,000 – $600,000	$240,000
Brazilian subsidiary's operating income, $1,200,000 – $840,000 – $240,000	$120,000
Overall operating income of Anita and subsidiaries	$360,000

Note that the general guideline could be used to derive the minimum transfer price.

$$\text{Minimum transfer price} = \left(\begin{array}{c}\text{Additional } \textit{incremental costs} \\ \text{per unit incurred up} \\ \text{to the point of transfer}\end{array}\right) + \left(\begin{array}{c}\textit{Opportunity costs} \\ \text{per unit to the} \\ \text{supplying division}\end{array}\right)$$

$$= \$600{,}000 + \$240{,}000 = \$840{,}000$$

Anita's opportunity cost of supplying the machine to the Brazilian subsidiary is the $240,000 in operating income it forgoes by not supplying the machine to the Swiss subsidiary. Note that competition between the Brazilian and Swiss subsidiaries means that the transfer price will be at least $840,000.

3. Consider the optimal transfer prices that can be set to minimize taxes (for Anita and its subsidiaries) (a) for transfers from Anita to the Brazilian subsidiary and (b) for transfers from Anita to the Swiss subsidiary.

   (a) Transfers from Anita to the Brazilian subsidiary should "allocate" as much of the operating income to Anita as possible, since the tax rate in Canada is lower than in Brazil for this transaction. Therefore, these transfers should be priced at the highest allowable transfer price of $840,000 to minimize overall company taxes.

      Taxes paid:

Anita, 0.40 ($840,000 – $600,000)	$ 96,000
Brazilian subsidiary, 0.60 ($1,200,000 – $840,000 – $240,000)	72,000
Total taxes paid by Anita Corporation and its subsidiaries on transfers to Brazil	$168,000

      After-tax operating income:

Anita, ($840,000 – $600,000) – $96,000	$144,000
Brazilian subsidiary ($1,200,000 – $840,000 – $240,000) – $72,000	48,000
Total after-tax operating income for Anita Corporation and its subsidiaries on transfers to Brazil	$192,000

   (b) Transfers from Anita to the Swiss subsidiary should "allocate" as little of the operating income to Anita as possible, since the tax rate in Canada is higher than in Switzerland for this transaction. Therefore, these transfers should be priced at the lowest allowable transfer price of $600,000 to minimize overall company taxes.

      Taxes paid:

Anita, 0.40 ($600,000 – $600,000)	$ 0
Swiss subsidiary, 0.15 ($1,140,000 – $600,000 – $300,000)	36,000
Total taxes paid by Anita Corporation and its subsidiaries on transfers to Switzerland	$36,000

After-tax operating income

Anita,($600,000 – $600,000) – $0 $ 0

Swiss subsidiary ($1,140,000 – $600,000 – $300,000) – $36,000   204,000

    Total net income for Anita Corporation and its subsidiaries

    on transfers to Switzerland $204,000

From the viewpoint of Anita Corporation and its subsidiaries together, overall after-tax operating income is maximized if the machine is transferred to the Swiss subsidiary (after-tax operating income of $204,000 versus after-tax operating income of $192,000 if the machine is transferred to the Brazilian subsidiary). Note that the corporation and its subsidiaries trade off the lower overall before-tax operating income achieved by transferring to the Swiss subsidiary with the lower taxes that result from such a transfer. Hence (a) the equipment should be manufactured by Anita and (b) it should be transferred to the Swiss subsidiary at a price of $600,000.

4. As in requirement 2, the Brazilian subsidiary would be willing to bid up the price to $960,000, while the Swiss subsidiary would only be willing to pay up to $840,000. Anita Corporation acting autonomously would like to maximize its own after-tax operating income by transferring the machine at as high a transfer price as possible. As in requirement 2, the price would end up being at least $840,000. Since the taxing authorities will not allow prices above $840,000, the transfer price will be $840,000. At this transfer price, the Swiss subsidiary makes zero operating income and will not be interested in the machine. Hence Anita Corporation will sell the machine to the Brazilian subsidiary at a price of $840,000.

The answer is not the same as in requirement 3 since, acting autonomously, the objective of each manager is to maximize after-tax operating income of his or her own company rather than after-tax operating income of Anita Corporation and its subsidiaries as a whole. Goal congruence is not achieved in this setting.

Can the company induce the managers to take the right actions without infringing on their autonomy? This outcome is probably not going to be easy.

One possibility might be to implement a dual pricing scheme in which the machine is transferred at cost ($600,000), but under which Anita Corporation is credited with after-tax operating income earned on the machine by the subsidiary it ships the machine to (in this example, $204,000 of net income earned by the Swiss subsidiary). A negative feature of this arrangement is that the $204,000 of after-tax operating income will be "double counted" and recognized on the books of both Anita Corporation and the Swiss subsidiary.

Another possibility might be to evaluate the managers on the basis of overall after-tax operating income of Anita Corporation and its subsidiaries. This approach will induce a more global perspective, but at the cost of inducing a larger noncontrollable element in each manager's performance measure.

23-34 (40-50 min.) **Utilization of capacity.**

1.

	Super-chip	Okay-chip
Selling price	$72.00	$14.40
Direct materials	2.40	1.20
Direct manufacturing labour	33.60	8.40
Contribution margin per unit	$36.00	$ 4.80
Contribution margin per hour		
($36 ÷ 2; $4.80 ÷ 0.5)	$18.00	$ 9.60

Because the contribution margin per hour is higher for Super-chip than for Okay-chip, CIC should produce and sell as many Super-chips as it can and use the remaining available capacity to produce Okay-chip.

The total demand for Super-chips is 15,000 units, which would take 30,000 hours (15,000 × 2 hours per unit). CIC should use its remaining capacity of 20,000 hours (50,000 – 30,000) to produce 40,000 Okay-chips (20,000 ÷ 0.5).

2.   Options for manufacturing process-control unit

	Using Circuit Board	Using Super-chip
Selling price	$158.40	$158.40
Direct materials	72.00	2.40
Direct manufacturing labour (Super-chip)	0	33.60
Direct manufacturing labour (Process-control unit)	60.00	72.00
Contribution margin per unit	$ 26.40	$ 50.40

Overall Company Viewpoint

Alternative 1:   No Transfer of Super-chips

Sell 15,000 Super-chips at contribution margin per unit of $36	$540,000
Transfer 0 Super-chips	0
Sell 40,000 Okay-chips at contribution margin per unit of $4.80	192,000
Sell 5,000 Control units at contribution margin per unit of $26.40	132,000
Total contribution margin	$864,000

Alternative 2:   Transfer 5,000 Super-chips to Process-Control Division. These Super-chips would require 10,000 hours to manufacture, leaving only 10,000 hours for the manufacture of 20,000 Okay-chips (10,000 ÷ 0.5)

Sell 15,000 Super-chips at contribution margin per unit of $36	$540,000
Transfer 5,000 Super-chips to Process-Control Division	0
Sell 20,000 Okay-chips at contribution margin per unit of $4.80	96,000
Sell 5,000 Control units at contribution margin per unit of $50.40	252,000
Total contribution margin	$888,000

CIC is better off transferring 5,000 Super-chips to the Process-Control Division.

3. For each Super-chip that is transferred, two hours of time (labour capacity) are given up in the Semiconductor Division, and, in those two hours, four Okay-chips could be produced, each contributing $4.80.

Minimum transfer price per Super-chip	=	Incremental cost per unit to the point of transfer	+	Opportunity cost per unit for the Semiconductor Division
	=	$36 + $19.20		
	=	$55.20 per unit		

If the selling price for the process-control unit were firm at $158.40, the Process-Control Division would accept any transfer price up to $60 ($72 price of circuit board – $12 incremental labour cost if Super-chip used).

However, consider what happens if the transfer price of Super-chip is set at, say, $58.80, and the price of the control unit drops to $129.60. From CIC's viewpoint:

	Using Circuit Board	Using Super-chip
Selling price	$129.60	$129.60
Direct materials	72.00	58.80
Direct manufacturing labour	60.00	72.00
Contribution margin per hour	$ –2.40	$ –1.20

Process-Control Division will not produce any control units. From the company's viewpoint, the contribution margin on the control unit if the Super-chip is used is:

Selling price	$129.60
Direct materials	2.40
Direct manufacturing labour (Super-chip)	33.60
Direct manufacturing labour (process-control unit)	72.00
Contribution margin per unit	$ 21.60

The contribution margin per unit from producing Super-chips for the process-control unit exceeds the contribution margin of $19.20 from producing 4 Okay-chips, each yielding a contribution margin of $4.80 per unit. Hence the Semiconductor Division should transfer 5,000 Super-chips as the following calculations show:

Alternative 1—No transfer (and, therefore, no sales of process-control units)

Sell 15,000 Super-chips at contribution margin per unit of $36	$540,000
Sell 40,000 Okay-chips at contribution margin per unit of $4.80	192,000
	$732,000

Alternative 2—Transfer 5,000 Super-chips.

Sell 15,000 Super-chips at contribution margin per unit of $36	$540,000
Sell 20,000 Okay-chips at contribution margin per unit of $4.80	96,000
Sell 5,000 control units at contribution margin per unit of $21.60	108,000
	$744,000

Therefore, if the price for the control unit is uncertain, the transfer price must be set at the minimum acceptable transfer price of $55.20.

4. For a transfer of any amount between 0 and 10,000 Super-chips (which require 2 hours each to produce), the opportunity cost is the production of Okay-chips (which require 1/2 hour each). In this range, the relevant costs are equal to the transfer price of $55.20 established in part 3.

   If more than 10,000 Super-chips are transferred, the opportunity cost becomes the sale of Super-chips on the outside market. Now the minimum transfer price per Super-chip becomes

$$\begin{array}{l}\text{Incremental cost} \\ \text{per Super-chip up to} + \\ \text{point of transfer}\end{array} \begin{array}{l}\text{Opportunity cost} \\ \text{per Super-chip to} \\ \text{the Semiconductor} \\ \text{Division}\end{array} = \$36 + (\$72 - \$36) = \$72, \text{ the market price.}$$

At this transfer price, it is cheaper for the Process-Control Division to buy the circuit board for $72, since $12 of additional direct manufacturing labour cost is saved.

The Semiconductor Division should at most transfer 10,000 Super-chips.

Internal Demand	Transfer Price
0–10,000	$55.20
10,000–25,000	72.00

3-36 (40-50 min.) Goal congruence, taxes, different market conditions.

1.

	New Engine	Existing Engine Used by Assembly
Sales price	$450	
Savings in purchase costs by making engines in-house		$480
Manufacturing costs:		
Direct materials	$120	$150
Direct manufacturing labour	48	60
Variable manufacturing overhead	30	30
Total costs of manufacturing	198	$240
Contribution margin from New Engine	$252	
Net savings in costs by making existing engine in-house		$240

If order for the new engine is accepted, Saskatchewan earns a contribution margin of $252 × 2,000 units. $504,000

In this case, Engine Division will only be in a position to supply 2,000 units to Assembly and Assembly will have to purchase 1,200 engines from outside. The incremental cost of buying engines from outside is $240 × 1,200.   288,000

Net benefit from accepting order $216,000

An alternative approach is to compare relevant costs of the accept order and reject order alternatives.

	Accept Order	Reject Order
1. Contribution margin from selling 2,000 units of new engine $252 × 2,000	$(504,000)	
2. Incremental cost of making and transferring 2,000 units of old engine $240 × 2,000, 3,200	480,000	$768,000
3. Incremental costs of purchasing 1,200 units from outside $480 × 1,200	576,000	
	$ 552,000	$768,000

Saskatchewan Corporation should
(a) make 2,000 units of the new engine in the Engine Division
(b) make 2,000 units of the existing engine for the Assembly Division and

(c) have the Assembly Division purchase 1,200 engines that it requires from the outside market.

2. The options facing the Engine Division manager are (a) to sell 2,000 units of the special order engine and make 2,000 units for the Assembly Division or (b) to make 3,200 units for the Assembly Division. The contribution margin per unit from accepting the special order is $252 per unit. Let the transfer price be $X. Then we want to find X such that

$$\$252 \times 2,000 + (\$X - \$240)\, 2,000 = (\$X - \$240)3,200$$
$$(\$X - \$240)(3,200 - 2,000) = \$504,000$$

$$\$X - \$240 = \frac{\$504,000}{1,200} = \$420$$
$$X = \$660$$

For transfer prices below $660, the Engine Division gets more by selling 2,000 units outside and transferring 2,000 units to Assembly Division. It will not transfer more than 2,000 units to Assembly even though the transfer price is greater than the variable costs of manufacturing the existing engine, $240 plus the contribution margin per unit from accepting the special order of $252 equal to $492 ($600, say). Why? Because by transferring an additional 1,200 units (say) it will have to give up $504,000 ($252 × 2,000) of contribution margin by not accepting the special order. The Engine Division manager would be willing to transfer the remaining 2,000 units for which it has capacity to the Assembly Division provided the transfer price covers the Engine Division's variable costs. So the range of transfer price that will induce the Engine Division manager to implement the optimal solution in requirement 1 is:

$$\$240 \le TP < \$660$$

The Assembly Division manager would be willing to buy from the Engine Division so long as the transfer price is less than or equal to the price at which the Assembly Division can buy the engines on the outside market.

$$TP \le \$480$$

It will not buy the engines from the Engine Division if TP > $480. The range of TP that will result in both managers favouring the optimal actions in requirement 1 are TPs that satisfy the respective constraints described above.

$$\$240 \le TP \le \$480 \text{ for the first 2,000 units}$$
$$\$480 < TP < \$660 \text{ for any additional units}$$

This transfer pricing scheme will induce both managers to transfer 2,000 units between the Engine and Assembly Divisions but no more.

3. a. The full manufacturing costs of the engines transferred to the Assembly Division are:

Direct materials	$150
Direct manufacturing labour	60
Variable manufacturing overheads	30
Fixed manufacturing overhead	

$$\left(\frac{\$624,000}{2} = \$312,000 \div 2,000 \text{ engines} \right)$$

since the engines transferred to the Assembly Division use up half the Engine Division's capacity	156
Total manufacturing cost	$396

b. A transfer price of $396 is in the optimal range identified in requirement 2 and so will achieve the optimal actions of selling 2,000 engines under the outside offer and transferring 2,000 engines to the Assembly Division as identified in requirement 1. (If we also want the Assembly Division manager to not ask for any additional engines beyond 2,000 units, the transfer price for any additional engines would have to be set such that $480 < TP < $660.) If the transfer price is set at $396, the Assembly Division manager will want more engines but the Engine Division manager will not have any incentive to transfer anything more than 2,000 units, preferring to supply 2,000 units for the special order.

c. One advantage of full cost transfer pricing is that it is useful for the firm's long-run pricing decisions.
   One disadvantage of full cost transfer pricing is that costs that are fixed for the corporation as a whole look like variable costs from the viewpoint of the Assembly Division manager. This is because by choosing not to have a unit transferred from the Engine Division, the Assembly Division manager would appear to save both the variable and fixed costs of the engine. This could lead to suboptimal decisions.

4. a. To minimize taxes, Saskatchewan should transfer the engines at the market price of $480. The Engine Division would pay no taxes on any income that it would report. By setting the transfer price as high as possible, the Assembly Division would minimize the income it would report and hence the taxes it would pay.

b. Yes, as in part 3b, the transfer price of $480 is also within the range identified in requirement 2 and so will achieve the outcome desired in requirement 1 (sell 2,000 engines under the outside offer and transfer 2,000 engines to the Assembly Division).

5. Recommend that Saskatchewan use a transfer price of $480 for transferring engines from the Engine Division to the Assembly Division. This transfer price minimizes tax payments for the Saskatchewan Corporation as a whole and also achieves goal congruence. That is, at a transfer price of $480 for all engines transferred from the Engine Division to the Assembly Division, both Divisions will be content with the following arrangement:

(a) The Engine Division will make 2,000 engines for outside customers and 2,000 engines for the Assembly Division.

(b) The Assembly Division will take 2,000 engines from the Engine Division and 1,200 engines from the outside market.

Of course the Assembly Division manager would like to negotiate a price lower than $480 (but greater than $240) for the 2,000 engines from the Engine Division, but this would increase Saskatchewan's tax payments.

At a transfer price of $480, it would still be alright to evaluate each division's performance on the basis of division operating income because the transfer price of $480 approximates the market prices for the engines transferred from the Engine Division to the Assembly Division. Market-based transfer prices give top management a reasonably good picture of the contributions of the individual divisions to overall companywide profitability.

CHAPTER 24
PERFORMANCE MEASUREMENT, COMPENSATION, AND MULTINATIONAL CONSIDERATIONS

24-2 The five steps in designing an accounting-based performance measure are:
1. Choosing the variable(s) that represent(s) top management's financial goal(s).
2. Choosing definitions of the items included in the variables in Step 1.
3. Choosing measures for the items included in the variables in Step 1.
4. Choosing a target against which to gauge performance.
5. Choosing the timing of feedback.

24-4 Yes. Residual income is not identical to ROI. ROI is a percentage with investment as the denominator of the computation. Residual income is an absolute amount in which investment is used to calculate an imputed interest charge.

24-6 Definitions of investment used in practice when computing ROI are:
1. Total assets available.
2. Total assets employed.
3. Working capital (current assets minus current liabilities) plus other assets.
4. Shareholders' equity.

24-8 Special problems arise when evaluating the performance of divisions in multinational companies because
(a) The economic, legal, political, social, and cultural environments differ significantly across countries.
(b) Governments in some countries may impose controls and limit selling prices of products.
(c) Availability of materials and skilled labour, as well as costs of materials, labour, and infrastructure may differ significantly across countries.
(d) Divisions operating in different countries keep score of their performance in different currencies.

24-10 Moral hazard describes contexts in which an employee is tempted to put in less effort (or report distorted information) because the employee's interests differ from the owner's and because the employee's effort cannot be accurately monitored and enforced.

24-12 Measures of performance that are superior (measures that change significantly with the manager's performance and not very much with changes in factors that are beyond the manager's control) are the key to designing strong incentive systems in organizations. When selecting performance measures the management accountant must choose those performance measures that change with changes in the actions taken by managers. For example, if a manager has no authority for making investments, then using an investment-based measure to evaluate the manager imposes risk on the manager and provides little information about the manager's performance. The management accountant might suggest evaluating the manager on the basis of costs, or costs and revenues, rather than ROI.

24-14 When employees have to perform multiple tasks as part of their jobs, incentive problems can arise when one task is easy to monitor and measure while the other task is more difficult to evaluate. Employers want employees to intelligently allocate time and effort among various tasks. If, however, employees are rewarded on the basis of the task that is more easily measured, they will tend to focus their efforts on that task and ignore the others.

24-16 (30 min.) Return on investment; comparisons of three companies.

1. The separate components highlight several features of return on investment not revealed by a single calculation:
   (a) The importance of investment turnover as a key to income is stressed.
   (b) The importance of revenues is explicitly recognized.
   (c) The important components are expressed as ratios or percentages instead of dollar figures. This form of expression often enhances comparability of different divisions, businesses, and time periods.
   (d) The breakdown stresses the possibility of trading off investment turnover for income as a percentage of revenues so as to increase the average ROI at a given level of output.

2. (Filled-in blanks are in bold face.)

	Companies in Same Industry		
	A	**B**	**C**
Revenue	$1,200,000	$ 600,000	**$12,000,000**
Income	$ 120,000	$ 60,000	$ **60,000**
Investment	$ 600,000	**$6,000,000**	$ 6,000,000
Income as a % of revenue	**10%**	10%	0.5%
Investment turnover	**2.0**	**0.1**	2.0
Return on investment	**20%**	1%	**1%**

Income and investment alone shed little light on comparative performances because of disparities in size between Company A and the other two companies. Thus, it is impossible to say whether B's low return on investment in comparison with A's is attributable to its larger investment or to its lower income. Furthermore the fact that Companies B and C have identical income and investment may suggest that the same conditions underlie the low ROI, but this conclusion is erroneous. B has higher margins but a lower investment turnover. C has very small margins (1/20th of B) but turns over investment 20 times faster.

I.M.A. Report No. 35 (p. 35) states:

"Introducing revenues to measure level of operations helps to disclose specific areas for more intensive investigation. Company B does as well as Company A in terms of income margin, for both companies earn 10% on revenues. But Company B has a much lower turnover of investment than does Company A. Whereas a dollar of investment in Company A supports two dollars in revenues each period, a dollar investment in Company B supports only ten cents in revenues each period. This suggests that the analyst should look carefully at Company B's investment. Is the company keeping an inventory larger than necessary for its revenue level? Are receivables being collected promptly? Or did Company A acquire its fixed assets at a price level that was much lower than that at which Company B purchased its plant?"

"On the other hand, C's investment turnover is as high as A's, but C's income as a percentage of revenue is much lower. Why? Are its operations inefficient, are its material costs too high, or does its location entail high transportation costs?"

"Analysis of ROI raises questions such as the foregoing. When answers are obtained, basic reasons for differences between rates of return may be discovered. For example, in Company B's case, it is apparent that the emphasis will have to be on increasing turnover by reducing investment or increasing revenues. Clearly, B cannot appreciably increase its ROI simply by increasing its income as a percent of revenue. In contrast, Company C's management should concentrate on increasing the percent of income on revenue."

24-18 (10-15 min.) **ROI and RI.**

$$\text{ROI} = \frac{\text{Operating income}}{\text{Investment}}$$

$$\text{Operating income} = \text{ROI} \times \text{Investment}$$

[No. of menhirs sold (Selling price − Var. cost per unit)] − Fixed costs = ROI × Investment

Let X = minimum selling price per unit to achieve a 20% ROI

1. $10,000 (X − \$360) − \$1,200,000 = 20\% (\$1,920,000)$
   $10,000X = \$384,000 + \$3,600,000 + \$1,200,000 = \$5,184,000$
   $X = \$518.40$

2. $10,000 (X − \$360) − \$1,200,000 = 15\% (\$1,920,000)$
   $10,000X = \$288,000 + \$3,600,000 + \$1,200,000 = \$5,088,000$
   $X = \$508.80$

24-20 (25 min.) **Financial and nonfinancial performance measures, goal congruence.**

1. Operating income is a good summary measure of short-term financial performance. By itself, however, it does not indicate whether operating income in the short run was earned by taking actions that would lead to long-run competitive advantage. For example, Summit's divisions might be able to increase short-run operating income by producing more product while ignoring quality or rework. Harrington, however, would like to see division managers increase operating income without sacrificing quality. The new performance measures take a balanced scorecard approach by evaluating and rewarding managers on the basis of direct measures (such as rework costs, on-time delivery performance, and sales returns). This motivates managers to take actions that Harrington believes will increase operating income now and in the future. The nonoperating income measures serve as surrogate measures of future profitability.

2. The semi-annual installments and total bonus for the Charter Division are calculated as follows:

Charter Division Bonus Calculation
For Year Ended December 31, 2007

January 1, 2007 to June 30, 2007

Profitability	(0.02) ($554,400)	$ 11,088
Rework	(0.02 × $554,400) − $13,800	(2,712)
On-time delivery	No bonus – under 96%	0
Sales returns	[(0.015 × $5,040,000) − $100,800] × 50%	(12,600)
Semi-annual installment		$ (4,224)
Semi-annual bonus awarded		$ 0

July 1, 2007 to December 31, 2007

Profitability	(0.02) ($528,000)	$10,560
Rework	(0.02 × $528,000) − $13,200	(2,640)
On-time delivery	96% to 98%	2,400
Sales returns	[(0.015 × $5,280,000) − $84,000] × 50%	(2,400)
Semi-annual installment		$ 7,920
Semi-annual bonus awarded		$ 7,920
Total bonus awarded for the year		$ 7,920

The semi-annual installments and total bonus for the Mesa Division are calculated as follows:

Mesa Division Bonus Calculation
For Year Ended December 31, 2007

January 1, 2007 to June 30, 2007

Profitability	(0.02) ($410,400)	$ 8,208
Rework	(0.02 × $410,400) − $7,200	0*
On-time delivery	Over 98%	6,000
Sales returns	[(0.015 × $3,420,000) − $53,700] × 50%	(1,200)
Semi-annual bonus installment		$13,008
Semi-annual bonus awarded		$13,008

July 1, 2007 to December 31, 2007

Profitability	(0.02) ($487,200)	$ 9,744
Rework	(0.02 × $487,200) − $9,600	0*
On-time delivery	No bonus—under 96%	0
Sales returns	[(0.015 × $3,480,000) − $51,000] which is greater than zero, yielding a bonus of	3,600
Semi-annual bonus installment		$13,344
Semi-annual bonus awarded		$13,344
Total bonus awarded for the year		$26,352

* 2% Operating income > rework costs: No reduction

3. The manager of the Charter Division is likely to be frustrated by the new plan as the division bonus is more than $24,500 less than the previous year. However the new performance measures have begun to have the desired effect—both on-time deliveries and sales returns improved in the second half of the year while rework costs were relatively even. If the division continues to improve at the same rate, the Charter bonus could approximate or exceed what it was under the old plan.

The manager of the Mesa Division should be as satisfied with the new plan as with the old plan as the bonus is almost equivalent. However, there is no sign of improvements in the performance measures instituted by Harrington in this division; as a matter of fact, on-time deliveries declined considerably in the second half of the year. Unless the manager institutes better controls, the bonus situation may not be as favourable in the future. This could motivate the manager to improve in the future but currently, at least, the manager has been able to maintain his bonus without showing improvements in the areas targeted by Harrington.

Ben Harrington's revised bonus plan for the Charter Division fostered the following improvements in the second half of the year despite an increase in sales
- increase of 1.9 percent in on-time deliveries.
- $600 reduction in rework costs.
- $16,800 reduction in sales returns.

However, operating income as a percent of sales has decreased (11 to 10 percent)

The Mesa Division's bonus has remained at the status quo as a result of the following effects
- increase of 2.0 percent in operating income as a percent of sales (12 to 14 percent).
- decrease of 3.6 percent in on-time deliveries.
- $2,400 increase in rework costs.
- $2,700 decrease in sales returns.

This would suggest that there needs to be some revisions to the bonus plan. Possible changes include:
- increasing the weights put on on-time deliveries, rework costs, and sales returns in the performance measures while decreasing the weight put on operating income.
- a reward structure for rework costs that are below 2 percent of operating income that would encourage managers to drive costs lower.
- reviewing the whole year in total. The bonus plan should carry forward the negative amounts for one six-month period into the next six-month period incorporating the entire year when calculating a bonus.
- developing benchmarks, and then giving rewards for improvements over prior periods and encouraging continuous improvement.

24-22 (25 min.) RI, EVA.

1.

	Truck Rental Division	Transportation Division
Total assets	$780,000	$1,140,000
Current liabilities	144,000	240,000
Investment		
(Total assets – current liabilities)	$636,000	$ 900,000
Required return		
(12% × Investment)	$ 76,320	$ 108,000
Operating income before tax	90,000	192,000
Residual income		
(Optg inc. before tax – Reqd. return)	$ 13,680	$ 84,000

2. After-tax cost of debt financing = $(1 - 0.4) \times 10\% = 6\%$

   After-tax cost of equity financing = 15%

   Weighted average cost of capital = $\dfrac{\$1,080,000 \times 6\% + 720,000 \times 15\%}{\$1,080,000 + 720,000} = 9.6\%$

Required return for EVA®		
9.6% × Investment		
(9.6% × $636,000; 9.6% × $900,000)	$61,056	$86,400
Operating income after tax		
0.6 × operating income before tax	54,000	115,200
EVA® (Optg inc. after tax – Reqd. return)	$(7,056)	$28,800

3. Both the residual income and the EVA® calculations indicate that the Transportation Division is performing better than the Truck Rental Division. The Transportation Division has a higher residual income ($84,000 versus $13,680) and a higher EVA® [$28,800 versus $(7,056)]. The negative EVA® for the Truck Rental Division indicates that on an after-tax basis the division is destroying value—the after-tax economic return from the Truck Rental Division's assets is less than the required return. If EVA® continues to be negative, Burlingame may have to consider shutting down the Truck Rental Division.

24-24 (20-30 min.) ROI, RI, measurement of assets (CMA, adapted).

The method for computing profitability preferred by each manager follows:

Manager of	Method Chosen
Bristol	Residual income based on net book value
Darden	Residual income based on gross book value
Gregory	ROI based on either gross or net book value

Supporting Calculations:

Return on Investment Calculations

Division	Operating Income Gross Book Value*	Operating Income Net Book Value*
Bristol	$113,640 ÷ $960,000 = 11.84% (3)	$113,640 ÷ $444,000 = 25.59% (3)
Darden	$110,040 ÷ $912,000 = 12.07% (2)	$110,040 ÷ $420,000 = 26.20% (2)
Gregory	$ 73,680 ÷ $600,000 = 12.28% (1)	$ 73,680 ÷ $264,000 = 27.91% (1)

Residual Income Calculations

Division	Operating Income – 10% Gross BV			Operating Income – 10% Net BV*		
Bristol	$113,640 – $96,000	=	$17,640 (2)	$113,640 – $44,400	=	$69,240 (1)
Darden	$110,040 – $91,200	=	$18,840 (1)	$110,040 – $42,000	=	$68,040 (2)
Gregory	$ 73,680 – $60,000	=	$13,680 (3)	$ 73,680 – $26,400	=	$47,280 (3)

*Net book value is gross book value minus accumulated amortization.

The biggest weakness of ROI is the tendency to reject projects that will lower historical ROI even though the prospective ROI exceeds the required ROI. RI achieves goal congruence because subunits will make investments as long as they earn a rate in excess of the required return for investments. The biggest weakness[1] of residual income is it favours larger divisions in ranking performance. The greater the amount of the investment (the size of the division), the more likely that larger divisions will be favoured assuming that income grows proportionately.

[1] One way to correct this weakness would be to measure the RI ÷ Net book value and/or RI ÷ Book value

24-26 (20 min.) Multinational performance measurement, ROI, RI.

1. (a) Dundas' ROI for 2005 $= \dfrac{\$918,000}{\$5,400,000} = 17\%$

    (b) Lyon Division's 2005 ROI in Euros $= \dfrac{648,000 \text{ Euros}}{3,600,000 \text{ Euros}} = 18\%$

    (c) We can't tell which division earned a better ROI because Lyon's return may have been helped by greater inflation in France and a weakening Euro.

2. To make RI comparable, we need to make the following conversions for the Lyon Division

    Operating assets at December 31, 2004 rate $= \dfrac{3,600,000 \text{ Euros}}{0.60 \text{ Euro per dollar}} = \$6,000,000$

    Convert operating income into dollars at the average exchange rate prevailing during 2005 when operating income was earned equal to

    $\dfrac{648,000 \text{ Euros}}{0.675 \text{ Euro per dollar}} = \$960,000$

    2005 RI for Lyon in dollars = $960,000 – 15% × $6,000,000 = $60,000

    2005 RI for Dundas = $918,000 – 15% × $5,400,000 = $108,000

    On a comparable basis, after adjusting for inflationary and currency differences, Dundas has the higher residual income.

3. Lyon's 2005 ROI calculated in dollar terms $= \dfrac{\$960,000}{\$6,000,000} = 16\%$

Both the ROI and the residual income calculations indicate that after removing the effects of any differences in inflation rates between the two countries, the Dundas Division has performed better than the Lyon Division in 2005 (ROI of 17% versus 16% and residual return of $108,000 versus $60,000).

Even after adjusting for inflation differences, the relative performance of the two divisions in 2005 is inadequate for making the decision about which manager to promote to the vice-president's position. The economic performance of the divisions must be distinguished from the performance of the managers of those divisions. For example, the poorer performance of the Lyon division in 2005 relative to that of the Dundas Division may be attributable to the more difficult business environment in Lyon. Recall that the economic, legal, political, social, and cultural environments differ significantly across countries as does the availability and costs of inputs such as materials and labour. Furthermore, promotion to the vice-president's position should not be based on the performance of the divisions in 2005 alone. The decision should consider the performance history of the two managers over the most recent few years.

24-28 (40-50 min.) **ROI performance measures based on historical cost and current cost.**

1. ROI using historical cost measures:

Calistoga : $\dfrac{\$156,000}{\$408,000}$ = 38.24%

Alpine Springs : $\dfrac{\$264,000}{\$1,380,000}$ = 19.13%

Rocky Mountains : $\dfrac{\$456,000}{\$1,944,000}$ = 23.46%

The Calistoga Division appears to be considerably more efficient than the Alpine Springs and Rocky Mountain Divisions.

2. The gross book values (i.e., the original costs of the plants) under historical cost are calculated as the useful life of each plant (12) × the annual amortization:

Calistoga : 12 × $ 84,000 = $1,008,000
Alpine Springs : 12 × $120,000 = $1,440,000
Rocky Mountains : 12 × $144,000 = $1,728,000

Step 1: Restate long-term assets from gross book value at historical cost to gross book value at current cost as of the end of 2007.

$$\text{Gross book value of long-term assets at historical cost} \times \frac{\text{Construction cost index in 2007}}{\text{Construction cost index in year of construction}}$$

Calistoga:	$1,008,000 \times (170 \div 100)$	=	$1,713,600
Alpine Springs:	$1,440,000 \times (170 \div 136)$	=	$1,800,000
Rocky Mountain:	$1,728,000 \times (170 \div 160)$	=	$1,836,000

Step 2: Derive net book value of long-term assets at current cost as of the end of 2007. (Assume estimated useful life of each plant is 12 years.)

$$\text{Gross book value of long-term assets at current cost at the end of 2007} \times \frac{\text{Estimated useful life remaining}}{\text{Estimated total useful life}}$$

Calistoga:	$1,713,600 \times (2 \div 12)$	=	$ 285,600
Alpine Springs:	$1,800,000 \times (9 \div 12)$	=	$1,350,000
Rocky Mountains:	$1,836,000 \times (11 \div 12)$	=	$1,683,000

Step 3: Compute current cost of total assets at the end of 2007. (Assume current assets of each plant is expressed in 2007 dollars.)

$$\text{Current assets at the end of 2007 (given)} + \text{Net book value of long-term assets at current cost at the end of 2007 (Step 2)}$$

Calistoga:	$240,000 + $ 285,600	=	$ 525,600
Alpine Springs:	$300,000 + $1,350,000	=	$1,650,000
Rocky Mountains:	$360,000 + $1,683,000	=	$2,043,000

Step 4: Compute current-cost amortization expense in 2007 dollars.

Gross book value of long-term assets at current cost at the end of 2007 (from Step 1) $\times (1 \div 12)$

Calistoga:	$1,713,600 \times (1 \div 12)$	=	$142,800
Alpine Springs:	$1,800,000 \times (1 \div 12)$	=	$150,000
Rocky Mountains:	$1,836,000 \times (1 \div 12)$	=	$153,000

Step 5: Compute 2007 operating income using 2007 current-cost amortization.

$$\text{Historical-cost operating income} - \left(\begin{array}{c} \text{Current-cost} \\ \text{amortization in} \\ \text{2007 dollars (Step 4)} \end{array} - \text{Historical-cost amortization} \right)$$

Calistoga:	$156,000 – ($142,800 – $ 84,000) =	$ 97,200
Alpine Springs:	$264,000 – ($150,000 – $120,000) =	$234,000
Rocky Mountains:	$456,000 – ($153,000 – $144,000) =	$447,000

Step 6: Compute ROI using current-cost estimates for long-term assets and amortization.

$$\frac{\text{Operating income for 2007 using 2007 current-cost amortization (Step 5)}}{\text{Current cost of total assets at the end of 2007 (Step 3)}}$$

Calistoga:	$ 97,200 ÷ $ 525,600 =	18.49%
Alpine Springs:	$234,000 ÷ $1,650,000 =	14.18%
Rocky Mountains:	$447,000 ÷ $2,043,000 =	21.88%

	ROI: Historical Cost	ROI: Current Cost
Calistoga	38.24%	18.49 %
Alpine Springs	19.13	14.18
Rocky Mountains	23.46	21.88

Use of current cost results in the Rocky Mountains Division appearing to be the most efficient. The Calistoga ROI is reduced substantially when the ten year old plant is restated for the 70% increase in construction costs over the 1997 to 2007 period.

3. Use of current costs increases the comparability of ROI measures across divisions operating plants built at different construction cost price levels. Use of current cost also will increase the willingness of managers, evaluated on the basis of ROI, to move from divisions with assets purchased many years ago to divisions with assets purchased in recent years.

24-30 (25 min.) ROI, RI, ROS management incentives.

1. If Mason Industries uses return on investment to measure the Jump-Start Division's (JSD's) performance, Grieco may be reluctant to invest in the new plant because, as shown below, return on investment for the plant of 19.2% is lower than JSD's current ROI of 24%.

Operating income for new plant	$ 576,000
New investment	$3,000,000
Return on investment for new plant	19.2%

Investing in the new plant would lower JSD's ROI and, hence, limit Grieco's bonus.

2. The residual income computation for the new plant is as follows:

$$\text{Residual income} = \text{Income} - (\text{Imputed interest} \times \text{Investment})$$

Investment	$3,000,000
Operating income	$ 576,000
Charge for funds	
(Investment, $3,000,000 × 15%)	450,000
Residual income	$ 126,000

Investing in the new plant would add $126,000 to JSD's residual income. Consequently, if Mason Industries could be persuaded to use residual income to measure performance, Grieco would be more willing to invest in the new plant.

3. $$\text{Return on sales (ROS)} = \frac{\text{Operating income}}{\text{Sales}} = \frac{\$576,000}{\$2,880,000} = 20\%$$

If Mason Industries uses ROS to determine Grieco's bonus, Grieco will be more willing to invest in the new plant because ROS for the new plant of 20% exceeds the current ROS of 19%.

The advantages of using ROS are (a) that it is simpler to calculate and (b) that it avoids the negative short-run effects of ROI measures that may induce Grieco to not make the investment in the new plant. Grieco may favour ROS because she believes that eventually increases in ROS will increase ROI and RI.

The main disadvantage of using ROS is that it ignores the amount of investment needed to earn a return. For example, ROS may be high but not high enough to justify the level of investment needed to earn the required return on an investment.

24-32 (30 min.) Relevant costs, performance evaluation, goal-congruence.

This problem illustrates the dysfunctional behaviour that could be motivated by arbitrary allocations of corporate overhead to profit-conscious divisional managers.

1. Without the $960,000 in sales from the low-margin product line in the Andorian Division, the second-quarter operating statements (in thousands) will be:

	Andorian	Orion	Tribble	Total
Net sales	$1,440	$1,440	$1,920	$4,800
Cost of sales	540	648	768	1,956
Divisional overhead	180	150	192	522
Divisional contribution	720	642	960	2,322
Corporate overhead	346	345	461	1,152
Operating income	$ 374	$ 297	$ 499	$ 1,170

2. The company is worse off as a result of dropping the low profitability line of products because it has lost $240,000 in gross margin from the dropped product line with no reduction in corporate overhead. Total operating income decreases $120,000 from $1,290,000 in the first quarter to $1,170,000 in the second quarter.

3. The Andorian Division manager's performance evaluation measure (divisional operating income) is lower ($374,000 in the second quarter versus $360,000 in the first quarter) as a result of dropping the low-profitability product line. The Andorian Division manager shows a $14,000 higher operating income because the $120,000 in lost contributions margin from the dropped product line is less than the $134,000 reduction in corporate overhead that is charged to the Andorian Division. Andorian Division sales are now only 30% of corporate sales rather than the previous 41.7% of sales (so 30% of total corporate overhead costs of $1,152,000 equal to $345,600 are allocated to the Andorian Division in the second quarter, whereas 41.7% of $1,152,000 equal to $480,000 are allocated to the Andorian Division in the first quarter).

4. The easiest solution is to not allocate fixed corporate overhead to divisions. Then, the problem of dysfunctional behaviour will not arise. But central management may want the division managers to "see" the cost of corporate operations so that they will understand that the corporation as a whole is not profitable unless the combined divisions' contribution margins exceed corporate overhead. In this case, an allocation basis should be chosen that is not manipulable or under the control of division managers. It must also have the property that the action taken

by one division does not affect the corporate overhead allocations that get made to the other divisions (as occurred in the second quarter for the company).

In general, a lump sum allocation based on, say, budgeted net income, or budgeted assets, rather than an allocation that varies proportionately with an actual measure of activity (such as sales or actual net income) will minimize dysfunctional behavior. The allocation should be such that managers treat it as a fixed, unavoidable charge, rather than a charge that will vary with the decisions they take. Of course, a potential disadvantage of this proposal is that managers may try to underbudget the amounts that serve as the cost allocation bases, so that their divisions get less of the corporate overhead charges.

24-34 (30-40 min.) ROI, RI, investment decisions.

1.

$\dfrac{\text{Revenues}}{\text{Total Assets}}$	$\times$	$\dfrac{\text{Operating Income}}{\text{Revenues}}$	$=$	$\dfrac{\text{Operating Income}}{\text{Total Assets}}$	
2007					
Newspapers		0.939		0.239	0.224
Television		2.133		0.025	0.053
Film Studios		0.635		0.121	0.077
2006*					
Newspapers		1.023		0.200	0.205
Television		2.222		0.022	0.049
Film Studios		0.640		0.137	0.088

*Not required.

The Newspaper Division has a high ROI because of its high income margin. The Television Division has a low ROI despite a high investment turnover because of its very low income margin. The Film Studios Division has a low ROI despite a reasonably high income margin because of its low investment turnover.

2. Although the proposed investment is small, relative to the total assets invested, it earns less than the 2007 return on investment (0.224) [or the 2006 return on investment (0.205)] (All dollar numbers in millions):

$$\text{2007 ROI (before proposal)} \quad = \quad \frac{\$1,320}{\$5,880} \quad = \quad 0.224$$

$$\text{Investment proposal ROI} \quad = \quad \frac{\$36}{\$240} \quad = \quad 0.150$$

$$\text{2007 ROI (with proposal)} \quad = \quad \frac{\$1,356}{\$6,120} \quad = \quad 0.222$$

Given the existing bonus plan, any proposal that reduces the ROI is unattractive.

3. Residual income for 2007 (before proposal, in millions):

Income	Operating Income		Imputed Interest Charge		Division Residual
Newspapers	$1,320	–	$705.60 (0.12 × $5,880)	=	$ 614.40
Television	$192	–	$432 (0.12 × $3,600)	=	$(240)
Film Studios	$240	–	$374.40 (0.12 × $3,120)	=	$(134.40)

4. Residual income for proposal (in millions):

Income	Operating Income		Imputed Interest Charge		Division Residual
	$36	–	$28.80 (0.12 × $240)	=	$7.2

Investing in the fast-speed printing press will increase the Newspaper Division's residual income. Hence, if Kearney is evaluated using a residual income measure, Kearney would be much more willing to adopt the printing press proposal.

24-36 (25 min.) Ethics, manager's performance evaluation.

1. a. Variable manufacturing cost per unit = $2.40

   Fixed manufacturing cost per unit = $10,800,000 ÷ 500,000 = $21.60

Revenues, $24 × 500,000	$12,000,000
Variable manufacturing costs, $2.40 × 500,000	1,200,000
Fixed manufacturing costs, $21.60 × 500,000	10,800,000
Fixed marketing costs	480,000
Total costs	12,480,000
Operating income	$ (480,000)

   b. Variable manufacturing cost per unit = $2.40

   Fixed manufacturing cost per unit = $10,800,000 ÷ 600,000 = $18

Revenues, $24 × 500,000	$12,000,000
Variable manufacturing costs, $2.40 × 500,000	1,200,000
Fixed manufacturing costs, $18 × 500,000	9,000,000
Fixed marketing costs	480,000
Total costs	10,680,000
Operating income	$ 1,320,000

2. Jones's behaviour is not ethical. Professional managers are expected to take actions that are in the best interests of their shareholders. Jones's action benefited himself at the cost of shareholders. Jones's actions are equivalent to "cooking the books," even though he achieved this by producing more inventory than was needed, rather than through fictitious accounting. Some students might argue that Jones's behaviour is not unethical—he simply took advantage of the faulty contract the board of directors had given him when he was hired.

3. Asking distributors to take more products than they need is also equivalent to "cooking the books." In effect, distributors are being coerced into taking more product. This is a particular problem if distributors will take less product in the following year or alternatively return the excess inventory next year. Some students might argue that Jones's behaviour is not unethical—it is up to the distributors to decide whether to take more inventory or not. So long as Jones is not forcing the product on the distributors, it is not unethical for Jones to push sales this year even if the excess product will sit in the distributors' inventory.